Visual Studio® .NET: The .NET Framework

Black Book

Julian Templeman

David Vitter

President and CEO
Roland Elgey

Publisher
Al Valvano

Associate Publisher
Katherine R. Hartlove

Acquisitions Editor
Jawahara Saidullah

Developmental Editor
Jessica Choi

Product Marketing Manager
Tracy Rooney

Project Editor
Jennifer Ashley

Technical Reviewer
Roberto Veiga

Production Coordinator
Peggy Cantrell

Cover Designer
Carla Schuder

CD-ROM Developer
Michelle McConnell

Visual Studio® .NET: The .NET Framework Black Book

Limits of Liability and Disclaimer of Warranty

The author and publisher of this book have used their best efforts in preparing the book and the programs contained in it. These efforts include the development, research, and testing of the theories and programs to determine their effectiveness. The author and publisher make no warranty of any kind, expressed or implied, with regard to these programs or the documentation contained in this book.

The author and publisher shall not be liable in the event of incidental or consequential damages in connection with, or arising out of, the furnishing, performance, or use of the programs, associated instructions, and/or claims of productivity gains.

Trademarks

Trademarked names appear throughout this book. Rather than list the names and entities that own the trademarks or insert a trademark symbol with each mention of the trademarked name, the publisher states that it is using the names for editorial purposes only and to the benefit of the trademark owner, with no intention of infringing upon that trademark.

The Coriolis Group, LLC
14455 N. Hayden Road
Suite 220
Scottsdale, Arizona 85260

(480) 483-0192
FAX (480) 483-0193
www.coriolis.com

Library of Congress Cataloging-in-Publication Data
Templeman, Julian
Visual Studio .NET: The .NET Framework black book / by Julian Templeman and David Vitter
p. cm.
Includes index.
ISBN 1-57610-995-X
1. Microsoft Visual studio. 2. Microsoft.net framework. 3. Web site development--Computer programs. 4. Application software--Development--Computer programs. I. Vitter, David. II. Title.
TK5105.8885.M57 T46 2001
005.2'76--dc21

2001047659

Printed in the United States of America
10 9 8 7 6 5 4 3 2 1

The Coriolis Group, LLC • 14455 North Hayden Road, Suite 220 • Scottsdale, Arizona 85260

A Note from Coriolis

Coriolis Technology Press was founded to create a very elite group of books: the ones you keep closest to your machine. In the real world, you have to choose the books you rely on every day *very* carefully, and we understand that.

To win a place for our books on that coveted shelf beside your PC, we guarantee several important qualities in every book we publish. These qualities are:

- *Technical accuracy*—It's no good if it doesn't work. Every Coriolis Technology Press book is reviewed by technical experts in the topic field, and is sent through several editing and proofreading passes in order to create the piece of work you now hold in your hands.
- *Innovative editorial design*—We've put years of research and refinement into the ways we present information in our books. Our books' editorial approach is uniquely designed to reflect the way people learn new technologies and search for solutions to technology problems.
- *Practical focus*—We put only pertinent information into our books and avoid any fluff. Every fact included between these two covers must serve the mission of the book as a whole.
- *Accessibility*—The information in a book is worthless unless you can find it quickly when you need it. We put a lot of effort into our indexes, and heavily cross-reference our chapters, to make it easy for you to move right to the information you need.

Here at The Coriolis Group we have been publishing and packaging books, technical journals, and training materials since 1989. We have put a lot of thought into our books; please write to us at **ctp@coriolis.com** and let us know what you think. We hope that you're happy with the book in your hands, and that in the future, when you reach for software development and networking information, you'll turn to one of our books first.

Coriolis Technology Press
The Coriolis Group
14455 N. Hayden Road, Suite 220
Scottsdale, Arizona
85260

Email: ctp@coriolis.com
Phone: (480) 483-0192
Toll free: (800) 410-0192

About the Authors

Julian Templeman has been involved with computers for nearly 30 years, beginning with punching Fortran onto cards when he was at college in London. He has worked as a developer in the fields of science and engineering, mainly in graphical application programming, and got into Windows programming way back in the days of Windows 3.0.

Julian has programmed in many languages, and for the past few years has majored in C++ and Java. He runs a consultancy and training company in London, and, when not consulting, running training courses, or running his company, he enjoys playing a variety of musical instruments.

David Vitter is a Technical Lead Developer with Computer Sciences Corporation (CSC) developing Web-based solutions for Department of Defense customers. Prior to joining CSC, David spent 10 years in the US Air Force where he served as both an ICBM Maintenance Technician and as an Electronic Intelligence Analyst.

David is a Microsoft Certified Professional (MCP) and a Microsoft Certified Solutions Developer (MCSD) with more than 7 years experience using Visual Basic and more than 20 years experience in writing Basic programs. When not writing code or books, David enjoys cheering for the University of Virginia lacrosse team or visiting one of Virginia's many beautiful points of interest with his family. His first book, *Designing Visual Basic. NET Applications*, was published in August of 2001 by the The Coriolis Group, Inc.

Acknowledgments

My thanks are due to all those who have helped bring this book into being. I must especially thank Kevin Weeks, who thought up this project and talked me into taking it on.

Special thanks also go to Jennifer Ashley, the Project Editor for the book, for putting up with my awful attitude to deadlines, and generally pushing things along with unfailing good humor. Thanks also to all those others at Coriolis who contributed to this project, including Jawahara Saidullah, acquisitions editor, Anne Marie Walker, copy-editor, Peggy Cantrell, Production Coordinator, and Carla Schuder, cover designer. Finally, I must thank David Vitter for being willing to contribute his excellent chapters on the Web, SOAP, Remoting, and ADO.NET.
—*Julian Templeman*

Contents at a Glance

Table of Contents

Immediate Solutions

Immediate Solutions

Chapter 5
The XML Namespaces 193

Immediate Solutions

Immediate Solutions

Introduction

Thanks for buying *Visual Studio .NET: The .NET Framework Black Book.*

.NET is the most exciting new technology released by Microsoft since the original release of Windows 3.0, and it will impact every Windows programmer, no matter what language you use. Whether you are a Visual Basic or C++ programmer or want to learn C#, you're need to get up to speed with the world of .NET and the many new paradigms and features it introduces.

This book is your guide to the .NET Framework, the library that underlies everything in .NET. You'll learn how to use the huge amount of functionality that Microsoft has provided in the Framework to write code for the new world of .NET.

Is This Book for You?

Visual Studio .NET: The .NET Framework Black Book was written with the intermediate or advanced user in mind. Among the topics that are covered are:

- How to use the .NET Framework to write applications for the .NET platform.
- An introduction to the exciting new features introduced by .NET, including Windows Forms, Web Forms, Web Services, ASP.NET, and ADO.NET.
- How to produce console and GUI programs.
- How to interoperate with existing Windows code and COM objects.

How to Use This Book

This book is designed so you can read the chapters in almost any order, without having to follow any particular sequence. Having said that, if you're new to the world of .NET, you'll want to read the first two chapters in order to give yourself the basic knowledge you'll need to understand the material in the rest of the book.

Chapters 1 through 3 set the stage, describing the world of .NET. Chapter 1, "Introduction to .NET," introduces you to the .NET platform: what it is and why it's there. It also introduces the key .NET technologies, explains the changes that have been made to C++ and VB, and introduces the new C# language.

The second chapter, "The .NET Programming Model," explains the structure that underlies all .NET code. Everything is truly object-oriented (OO) in .NET, so this chapter includes an introduction to OO programming for those who might not have done any before. It also explains the .NET programming constructs that are common to all .NET programming languages, such as properties, delegates, events, and exceptions.

Chapter 3, "The **System** Namespace," introduces the concept of namespaces as a way to organize code, and covers the most fundamental namespace, **System**. You'll learn about the basic types, objects, arrays, exceptions, and many more fundamental constructs.

The fourth chapter, "The **System.Collections** Namespace," provides a guide to the data structure (or "collection") classes provided by .NET and which can be used by any .NET language.

XML is very important in .NET, and Chapter 5, "The XML Namespaces," describes the rich support that the .NET Framework provides for XML programming. As well as details on parsing and writing XML, the chapter covers XPath and XSL, and C#'s XML-based documentation mechanism.

Chapter 6, "The I/O and Networking Namespaces," gives an introduction to .NET's I/O namespace, **System.IO**, covering console and file I/O. The chapter also looks at the **System.Net** namespace, and shows how to use sockets for interprocess communication.

Chapter 7, ".NET Security," looks at the topic of security and how .NET implements a system to allow safe use of components in a distributed environment.

Chapter 8, "The **System.Web** Namespace," covers the basics of working with the Web in the .NET world. Learn how to create ASP.NET Web interfaces, and how Microsoft's XML Web Services fit into the big picture of application development.

Chapter 9, "Windows Forms," is the first of three chapters that cover GUI programming issues. This chapter introduces the **System.Windows.Forms** namespace, which implements a Visual Basic-like GUI mechanism that all .NET programming languages can use.

Chapter 10, "Windows Forms and Controls," continues the investigation of Windows Forms, looking in detail at the components you can use to build form-based applications.

Chapter 11, "The Drawing Namespaces," deals with low-level graphics operations, such as how to draw on forms, display images, and handle printing.

Chapter 12, "Other Namespaces," covers a number of minor namespaces that don't merit a whole chapter to themselves. These include threading, diagnostics, Windows Services, text, and regular expression handling.

Chapter 13, ".NET Remoting," looks at .NET's built-in support for using components remotely as easily as if they were on the local machine.

Chapter 14, "SOAP and XML," gives an introduction to Simple Object Access Protocol (SOAP), a protocol that is becoming widely used in distributed applications, and shows how it can be used in .NET applications. The chapter also provides information on advanced XML topics, such as XML schemas and transformations.

Chapter 15, "ADO.NET," covers the new version of Active Data Objects: ADO.NET. Developers wanting to connect their .NET solutions to back-end data sources will absolutely want to become familiar with this new data access technology.

The final chapter, "Working with COM and the Win32 API," shows how .NET code can interoperate with the existing worlds of COM and plain Windows.

The *Black Book* Philosophy

Written by experienced professionals, Coriolis *Black Books* provide immediate solutions to global programming and administrative challenges, helping you complete specific tasks, especially critical ones that are not well documented in other books. The *Black Book*'s unique two-part chapter format—thorough technical overviews followed by practical immediate solutions—is structured to help you use your knowledge, solve problems, and quickly master complex technical issues to become an expert. By breaking down complex topics into easily manageable components, this format helps you quickly find what you're looking for, with the code you need to make it happen.

We welcome your feedback on this book, which you can pass on by emailing The Coriolis Group at **ctp@coriolis.com**. Errata, updates, and more are available at **www.coriolis.com**.

Chapter 1

Introduction to .NET

By Julian Templeman

What Is .NET?

.NET provides a new API, new functionality, and new tools for writing Windows and Web applications, components, and services in the Web age. Let's look at the pieces of this statement a little more closely.

Why do we need a new API? The Windows API, the library of functions used to write Windows applications, was originally written in C and has steadily grown over the years. It now consists of many thousands of routines and has several problems. First, it has grown very large and has no coherent internal organization, which can make it hard to use. During its growth, features were added piecemeal, so it doesn't always present a unified interface to developers, and it contains a lot of legacy functions and datatypes (and is just plain out-of-date). Second, a more major problem is that the Windows API was initially designed for use by C programmers. This means that it can be difficult to use in languages other than C, and it also doesn't fit in very well with modern object-oriented programming methods and languages.

.NET provides a new, object-oriented API as a set of classes that will be accessible from any programming language. This book describes this framework of classes and provides a reference to what is available and how you can use this framework to write Windows applications in the brave new world of .NET.

What about the new functionality of this API? Microsoft has made some radical decisions in the design of .NET and has incorporated many unique new features that will make writing applications—and especially distributed applications—much easier than ever before. An overview of the main technologies is presented under the section "Introduction to Key Technologies," and in the next chapter we'll investigate how they work together. A lot of the new technologies lurk under the surface and may not be highly visible to the casual user, but the infrastructure of Windows applications and the technologies on which they're built and with which they communicate are very different in the .NET world.

There's a whole new set of tools also being introduced with the next release of Visual Studio, which will be known as Visual Studio .NET. The Interactive Development Environment (IDE) is completely new, and Microsoft has radically overhauled Visual C++ and Visual Basic (VB) as well as introduced a whole new programming language in the form of C#. A new model for building distributed applications using the Web and XML means that a whole host of new tools and technologies are needed as well, and they're all integrated into Visual Studio .NET.

It's pretty evident that, as far as computers are concerned, the world is moving toward the Internet. Just pause and think for a minute about the number of ways you use the Internet:

- Sending and receiving email
- Using online newspapers, especially when away from home
- Buying books and other goods, and finding suppliers that may be on another continent
- Hotel reservations and other services
- Using online banking and stock trading
- Buying cars (especially relevant to those of us here in the UK!)
- Using dictionaries, encyclopedias, and other information services

Microsoft is convinced that the future of Windows lies in distributed applications, where the various components may not live on Windows machines connected by a company network. Over the years, Microsoft has introduced technologies aimed at building distributed systems, but each has had its shortcomings in one area or another. Let's briefly consider three of these technologies: Component Object Model (COM), Active Server Page (ASP), and VB.

For several years, COM has been Microsoft's model for programming components in a variety of languages, which can be built into distributed applications. COM has been very successful, but it has suffered from several problems. First, it is difficult to become an expert COM programmer, and building sophisticated COM applications is very hard indeed. You need a detailed knowledge of C++ and the internals of COM and Windows to be successful. Second, COM is a Microsoft-specific architecture and is only available on a limited number of platforms. Third, because of the proprietary binary protocols used to talk across networks, all you can easily talk to are other COM components. Although the idea behind COM is valid, its implementation is limiting the widespread development of distributed systems.

Microsoft introduced ASP as a way for Web servers to deliver customized content by executing scripting code embedded in the HTML of a Web page. ASP has been very popular, but it suffers from one shortcoming: It only supports scripting languages, such as VBScript and JScript. This has implications for efficiency—

because scripting languages are interpreted at runtime, and therefore are not as efficient as compiled languages—and also because you can't use other languages. If you have C++ code that you would like to use in an ASP page, you can't because C++ isn't a scripting language.

VB has enjoyed tremendous success as the major drag-and-drop Windows programming language, but it has well-known limitations. One of its major limitations has to be that it is tied to Windows, and so it isn't useful for writing systems that are distributed across a range of architectures. In addition, it has a narrow range of what it can do, only allows restricted access to the underlying operating system, and isn't object-oriented, which is a limitation when building large-scale systems. That said, many programmers have wished that its visual, drag-and-drop style was available with other Windows programming languages, such as Visual C++.

With the advent of .NET, Microsoft has introduced many new technologies that make writing component-based distributed systems easier, more flexible, and more powerful than ever before. It is now easier than it has ever been to write components in any programming language that can interoperate with components on other machines, which may not be Windows-based at all.

Enough preamble. Let's move on and take a look at what's new and improved in .NET.

Introduction to Key Technologies

.NET is bringing a host of new technologies and tools to the Windows platform. Each has its own name and terminology and many of them introduce new acronyms. In order to start swimming in the .NET world, you're going to have to get buzzword compliant with the names of these new technologies and tools. This section lists the major players, and briefly describes the part they play in the overall scheme.

Figure 1.1 shows how the major components of the .NET Framework sit on top of the operating system. High-level languages sit on top of a common intermediate language, which gives them access to the .NET system services. These services include high-level services such as ASP.NET and Windows Forms as well as lower-level access to the .NET class libraries on which everything is based.

Let's look at each of these components and try to build an overall picture of what .NET is.

IL and the Common Language Specification

You'll notice that the programming languages at the top of Figure 1.1. sit on top of two boxes labeled Common Language Specification (CLS) and Intermediate

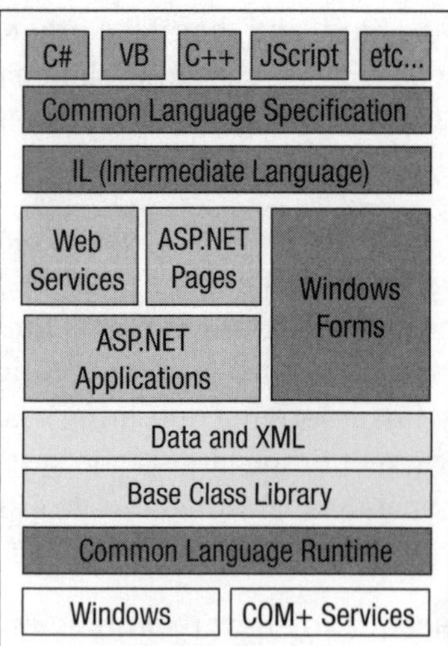

Figure 1.1 .NET architecture.

Language (IL). These two components, together with the box at the bottom of the figure, form part of the Common Language Runtime (CLR).

In .NET, Microsoft has taken a radical step in deciding that programming languages are no longer independent in the way that they are compiled or interpreted and build executable code. In traditional programming, each compiled language tends to produce its own unique form of intermediate binary code. Every language has its own data types, and may be object-oriented (OO) or not. Functions have their own particular parameter passing mechanisms, and differ in the order in which arguments are pushed onto the stack and whose responsibility it is to remove them. All these differences can make it very hard to use more than one language to build components and has resulted in the invention of several systems, such as Microsoft's COM, which provides a neutral middle layer. There are problems associated with such middle-layer software, such as the fact that they add complexity, and that they only tend to support a subset of functionality that all languages can agree on.

All languages that execute within the .NET Framework compile down to the same thing: a variety of bytecode known as Intermediate Language (or IL) rather than to a language-specific intermediate object code. This means that no matter if you compile a VB program, a Visual C++ program, or a C# program, you'll end up with the same form of intermediate code.

The idea of bytecodes isn't new, and those who have been in programming for a while may remember UCSD Pascal. A more recent example is Java, where source code is compiled into Java bytecode, which is then executed by the Java Virtual Machine.

NOTE: *IL isn't a traditional bytecode, but is more akin to the output from a compiler. There are, however, enough similarities to bytecode for the comparison to be useful in this discussion.*

IL is unusual among intermediate languages in that it has direct support for the constructs needed by OO programming languages, such as inheritance and polymorphism, along with other modern language features like exception handling. This means that it will be easy to port OO languages to work in .NET (subject to a few constraints, such as the use of single inheritance only). It will also make it possible to add OO support to languages that haven't had it before, as is the case with the .NET version of Visual Basic, known as Visual Basic .NET (or VB .NET).

This is a very important point, and one that is discussed in more detail in Chapter 2. In .NET, everything is OO because there is now a common underlying OO layer to all programming languages. This makes it very easy for OO languages to work together, but it does mean that an occasional language feature in some languages may have to be modified in order to make them work with the .NET model.

C++ programmers may be getting worried at this point because they know that Java-like bytecode-based languages aren't as efficient as traditional compiled ones. In .NET, C++ programmers have a choice of whether to compile and link code the traditional way (known as *unmanaged code*), or to join in with .NET and compile down to bytecode (called *managed code*). The choice is made per class, and you can mix and match managed and unmanaged classes within the same application.

It turns out that using an intermediate language has a lot of advantages, many of which are discussed in the rest of this chapter. One of these advantages is the fact that all compiled code ends up looking the same regardless of which source language it started out in. This means that it is easy to mix code written in different languages because they are now compatible at the bytecode level.

If languages are to be truly compatible in this way, they need to agree on a basic set of language features and data types, which all languages must support, as well as conventions for how they are used. The CLS provides this basic functionality, and it ensures that if a language follows its recommendations, it will be able to interoperate with others that do the same. The CLS has been made freely available to compiler developers, and many language designers and vendors have already said that they will provide support for IL in their compilers. Therefore, we can expect to see a wide variety of other languages—including COBOL, Fortran, Python, and Perl—joining the .NET family.

The Common Language Runtime

The CLR is the mechanism through which .NET code is executed. It is built upon a single, common language—IL—into which source languages are compiled and includes mechanisms for executing the compiled code. This includes code verification and just-in-time (JIT) compilation, garbage collection and enforcement of security policies, and the provision of profiling and debugging services.

The CLR provides a lot of added value to the programs it supports. Because it controls how a .NET program executes and sits between the program and the operating system, it can implement security, versioning support, automatic memory management through garbage collection, and provide transparent access to system services. These features are explained in more detail in the section "How Does the .NET Architecture Work?"

It is an important fact that IL code doesn't get executed itself, but is instead converted into platform native code before execution, a process known as JIT compilation. This compilation may happen at the time a program is installed or just before a piece of code runs, and it ensures that the code runs as efficiently as it can. The .NET Framework comes with several different JIT compilers, which are suited for different circumstances, such as whether you are primarily concerned with compilation speed or obtaining maximum optimization.

The Base Class Library

All programming languages and operating environments have libraries of functions available for use by programmers, for example, the C Runtime Library, the Windows API, the C++ Standard Template Library, and Microsoft's MFC and ATL libraries.

The problem with all these libraries is that they are either language-dependent or system-dependent (or both) and don't possess even the simplest of data types and operations in common. Anyone who has worked with COM is aware of the hassle involved in passing simple collections back and forth between C++ and VB, with all the attendant complications of SAFEARRAYs and IEnum interfaces.

.NET comes with its own class library, the Base Class Library, which provides all the functionality associated with traditional class libraries. It is special in two main ways:

- It is the class library for IL, and so can be used by any language that compiles down into IL.
- It is an OO class library, and so provides its functionality through a number of classes that are arranged into a hierarchy of namespaces.

High-level languages provide their own bindings onto the Base Class Libraries, and it is possible that not all features will be accessible from all the languages that may end up being ported to .NET. Although a fully OO Fortran or COBOL may be a possibility, don't hold your breath.

The Base Class Library contains a number of components:

- Definitions of basic types, such as Int32. These are mapped onto specific types by individual languages.
- Common collection classes, such as arrays, linked lists, hash tables, enumerations, queues, and stacks.
- Classes defining exceptions. All .NET languages can use exception handling because it is built into the Base Class Library, and it is now possible to throw an exception in, say, a C# method and catch it in VB.
- Classes for console, file, and stream I/O.
- Classes for network programming, including sockets.
- Database interface classes, including classes for working with ADO and SQL.
- Graphics classes, including 2D drawing, imaging, and printing.
- Classes for building graphical user interfaces (GUIs).
- Classes for object serialization.
- Classes to implement and handle security policies.
- Classes for building distributed, Web-based systems.
- Classes for working with XML.
- Other operating system features, such as threads and timers.

The Base Class Library is an OO, nonlanguage specific replacement for the old Windows API, which provides a wide range of services for writing modern applications that make heavy use of the Web, data exchange, and GUIs. Will it replace the existing Windows API? Microsoft has said nothing, but I wouldn't be at all surprised if it didn't.

The rest of this book explores this library, showing what it contains and how you can use it.

ASP.NET

ASP.NET is a new version of Microsoft's established ASP technology. It offers significant improvements over the original model.

An ASP is an HTML page that contains fragments of scripting language code in addition to HTML markup. When the page is accessed, the scripting code is executed, and the output from the code is sent to the client along with the rest of the

HTML on the page. This mixture of fixed HTML and scripting code means that Web pages can be customized, with the code generating custom HTML based on user input.

ASP has been extremely popular, and many Web servers now use it to generate custom content, but it does have its drawbacks. ASP.NET has been designed to address these drawbacks:

- In ASP, you're limited to using scripting languages, which in most cases means VBA or JScript. ASP.NET pages can now be written in any .NET language. So if you want to write ASP pages that use C++, C#, or even COBOL, you can.
- The scripting code in ASP pages is interpreted, which doesn't provide the best performance. Code in ASP.NET pages is compiled rather than interpreted, leading to great improvements in performance. In addition, code only needs to be compiled once.
- Code and HTML are intermixed in ASP pages, which makes pages hard to maintain as they get more complex. It is possible to separate the code and HTML using programming tricks, but it isn't supported in ASP itself. ASP.NET does support separation of the code from the HTML, maintaining the code in separate files. Because content and presentation is often developed by different people, separating the code aids the development of complex pages.
- If you want ASP pages to target multiple browsers or device types, you have to do it manually. ASP.NET has built-in support for multiple client types, using a range of server-side controls that automatically adjust their presentation depending on the capability of different clients. This means that it is possible to write ASP.NET pages that will display properly—and automatically—on traditional browsers as well as WAP phones and other small devices.

Perhaps the most radical development in ASP.NET is the introduction of Web Services. A Web Service is an application that can be found and accessed through a Web server, so that programmable functionality can be accessed over networks and the Internet using standard protocols. Figure 1.2 shows the architecture of a Web Service, where a client talks to a server using standard Web protocols—XML over HTTP for those clients that support it and standard HTTP **Get** and **Post** requests for all other clients. The server maintains a directory of Web Services that clients can query in order to find out exactly what methods are available and how they should be called.

Any method in a .NET object (written, of course, in any .NET language) can be marked very simply as a *Web method*. The compiler and CLR make all the necessary arrangements, registering the method so that it can be used through a Web server. The implications of this for Web application developments are tremendous because Web sites and other applications will be able to communicate at the

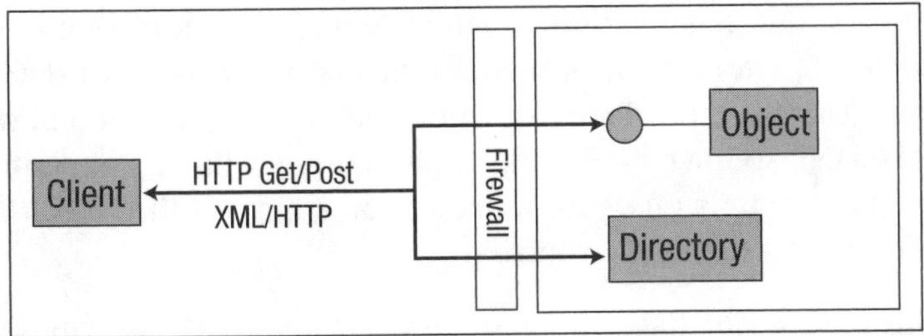

Figure 1.2 Web Services architecture.

method level, sending queries, invoking operations, and exchanging data. Communication takes place in XML, so that it is possible to link diverse systems using Web Services. In fact, because Web Services are simply a way of discovering and calling methods remotely using XML as the data transfer medium, it is quite possible that you will see Web Services being written on non-Microsoft platforms that have nothing whatsoever to do with .NET.

Along with Web Services, ASP.NET introduces a new version of ADO called ADO.NET, which makes it much easier to work with disconnected data and uses XML as its main means of data transfer. Working mainly with disconnected datasets means that ADO.NET is more scalable than ADO because the database connection is only required for a short time while the dataset is acquired. Working with XML as the data transfer mechanism rather than COM's binary protocol means that it's going to be easier to work through firewalls.

Windows Forms

For years, VB users have been used to being able to create GUIs by selecting controls from a palette, dragging and dropping controls onto forms, and then setting their properties and putting code behind the forms and controls. Windows Forms has taken this idea and has made it part of the .NET Framework, so that it is available for any .NET language to use.

The Windows Forms library contains a complete VB-like set of features that let you create forms, place controls onto them, set the properties of the controls, and set up interactions between controls and forms. You can create SDI and MDI applications and dialogs, and the set of controls supported is particularly full: Date/Time pickers, checked listboxes, and rich text edit controls.

XML

With all the hype that currently seems to surround the subject, you'd be forgiven for thinking that XML is the solution to every programming problem, and that every new product has to contain some form of XML-based functionality if it is to be taken at all seriously.

Although it is true that XML has become a bandwagon, in much the same way that OO did a couple of years ago, it is revolutionizing many areas of data retrieval and exchange. This isn't the place to go into a detailed explanation of what XML is and how it is used, so the next couple of paragraphs will only explain the basics. If you want more details on using XML, a good source is the *XML Black Book* (by Natanya Pitts, The Coriolis Group).

XML provides a way to describe data, in the same way that HTML describes presentation. When XML is saved to a stream or disk file, it uses the same tagging conventions as HTML

```
<library>
  <book topic="fantasy">
    <title>Why I Love Linux</title>
    <author>Bill Gates</author>
    <publisher>Microsoft Press</publisher>
  </book>
</library>
```

XML elements are enclosed between starting and ending tags, and they can be nested to any depth. The content of an XML element can be other XML elements, text, or a mixture of the two, and XML elements can also possess attributes, as shown in the preceding book element.

The big difference between XML and HTML is that in XML you define your own tags, and you (and your clients) decide on what they mean. This makes XML an ideal data exchange mechanism because it is possible to define complex data structures and send them as XML data streams. XML also provides two mechanisms—Document Type Definitions (DTDs) and Schemas—which can be used by recipients to validate XML data so they can check that, for example, the title element has to occur inside a book element, and that there can only be one title per book. There is also a standard method, known as XSL, to transform an XML document into other forms. This means that data can be stored or transmitted as XML and then turned into, say, HTML for display on a Web page.

Although XML is typically stored in its HTML-like serialized form, it needs to be parsed in order to be of use in programs. XML parsers are tools that can parse the XML tree and either build you a representation of the data in memory or use callbacks to tell you about each new element as it is parsed. Microsoft has an XML parser, MSXML, that is distributed with Internet Explorer and can be used from any application.

XML is used in many places in .NET. As an example, the C# language compiler can process special comments in code in order to produce documentation in XML format. This documentation can be turned into HTML using an XSL stylesheet or have many other transformations and operations applied to it.

Perhaps the most important use of XML is in the provision of Web Services. Earlier, you learned that a Web Service is a method that can be exposed by a Web site. Clients can obtain a list of the Services that a site exposes as well as details of arguments and return values and can then call the method at runtime, thus allowing applications to use Web-wide dynamic linking. Where does XML come into all this? The Web Service definitions are published in XML, and the method calls and returns are made using XML.

Using XML to make method calls is done using the Simple Object Access Protocol (SOAP). SOAP was invented by a consortium of companies, which includes DevelopMentor, Microsoft, and IBM, and provides a language- and system-independent way of making remote procedure calls using XML to define and pass method details. There are several advantages to the SOAP approach—it doesn't use proprietary binary protocols but simple streams of text, so it is possible to connect extremely different systems. And, because the method call is made using a text stream of XML sent over HTTP, it is much easier to make it work over the Internet, where traditional binary protocols can be difficult to use in the presence of firewalls.

C#

There's a lot of excitement about the new programming language that Microsoft has introduced with .NET. It's true to say that if C is the language of the Windows API and HTML is the language of Web pages, then C# is the language of .NET. Although C# is used in sample code, this book is not a C# programming text. If you are interested in learning more about the language, consult a good C# book.

C# is designed to be a modern, pure OO language that combines the best features of C++, Java, and VB, and is specially designed for writing .NET programs. The following code snippet is a fairly typical "Hello World" program to give you a flavor of what C# looks like:

```
using System;

public class Hello
{
  public static void Main(string[] args)
  {
    Console.WriteLine("Hello world!");
    Console.WriteLine("There were {0} arguments", args.Length);
  }
}
```

Those who already know some C++ or Java may be wondering what the differences are between those languages and C#. Table 1.1 summarizes some of the major similarities and differences.

How Does the .NET Architecture Work?

In this section, we look a little deeper into how the .NET architecture works. With .NET, Microsoft has created a whole new programming and runtime environment with a large number of completely new features and mechanisms. While it isn't necessary at this stage to understand how it all works in great detail, having a basic understanding of the architecture will help you to get started with .NET.

IL and Metadata

In the .NET world, compilers still produce EXE and DLL files, but the content of these files is different. As well as the IL that results from compiling the source code, executable files contain metadata.

Metadata is a word you'll hear a great deal when talking about .NET and how it works. Metadata is data that is used to describe classes and what they can do, separate from the code of the class itself. It's important to understand that metadata isn't part of the class in the same way that variables and methods are, but instead is used to describe classes.

Why do you need metadata? When you're dealing with components, there are properties that need to be discovered at runtime and don't really belong in the code. Take security as an example: Suppose an application contains a component that only certain users are allowed to access, and that the list of permitted users and groups can change over time. The runtime obviously needs to check the list of permitted users in order to validate requests—how is it going to do this? If the security data is provided in code, the runtime will need to create an object and query it, which is awkward. And if the list of permitted users changes, the developers will have to alter the code and rebuild the object.

The solution is to keep data like this separate from the object, so that it can be queried by system tools and other applications. Microsoft's existing component architecture, COM, uses two mechanisms to store metadata, and each is used to store different types of metadata. The first is the Windows Registry, which is used for identification and configuration data, and COM uses this to locate components and find out how they should be created. The second mechanism is the type library, which contains information about the internal structure of the component itself including descriptions of the methods, attributes, and events that the component supports.

Table 1.1 A comparison of the features of C++, Java, and C#.

ANSI C++	Java	C#
Has a full preprocessor	Has no preprocessor	Has a limited preprocessor, without macros
Compiles to native code	Compiles to bytecode with JIT compilation of programs on execution	Compiles to intermediate code with JIT compilation of methods on first use or on installation
Hybrid language	Pure OO language	Pure OO language
Supports multiple inheritance	Single inheritance only	Single inheritance only
No language support for interfaces	Language support for interfaces	Language support for interfaces
No single ultimate base class	All classes inherit from a single Object class	All classes inherit from a single Object class
Supports templates	No template support	No template support
Operator overloading	No operator overloading	Limited operator overloading
Conversion between bool and int types	No bool-to-int conversion	No bool-to-int conversion
No wrapper classes for built-in types	Wrapper classes for built-in types	Automatic "boxing" of built-in types, so they can easily be used as objects if required
Integer types used as case labels	Integer types used as case labels	Strings can also be used as case labels
Support for enums	No enums	Support for enums
C-style multidimensional array support	C-style multidimensional array support	Proper support for multidimensional arrays
Objects accessed directly, by pointer or by reference	All objects accessed by reference	Value versus reference types allows efficient pass-by-value semantics for some types
Pointers and references supported	Only references supported	References supported; pointers allowed in "unsafe" code blocks
Support for variable argument lists	No direct support for variable argument lists	No direct support for variable argument lists
No support for properties	Properties supported through coding conventions	Properties supported as first-class language feature
No support for events	Events supported through coding conventions	Events supported as first-class language feature
No delegate support	No delegate support	Support for delegates (class-based function pointer equivalent)

The trouble with these approaches is that both mechanisms use storage external to the component, and this raises the possibility of all sorts of problems. A component can get separated from its type library, or associated with one that belongs to another version, or its registry information can get overwritten or not written at all—the possibilities are (almost) endless. .NET components, on the other hand, are self-contained, with the metadata being held in the same file as the component itself. This makes them a lot more portable and a lot less susceptible to configuration errors.

The CLR uses metadata for many purposes including:

- Locating and loading classes
- Laying out objects in memory
- Finding out what methods and properties a class has
- Enforcing security
- Discovering a class's transactional behavior

Most of the metadata associated with a class is provided by the compilation process, but it is possible to create your own metadata items, called attributes, and attach them to your own classes. This topic is covered in Chapter 2.

JIT Compilation

JIT compilation is performed by just-in-time compilers, also known as JITters.

Why not compile source code straight down to native code? There are two reasons—portability and efficiency. Native code isn't portable, but IL is designed to be. If .NET gets ported to non-Windows platforms, it will be important that compiled modules can be run elsewhere. For efficiency, IL code is only JIT compiled as it is needed, and there may be parts of an application that are never used, so they will never take up machine resources by being compiled. It is important to note, though, that code is always JIT compiled before being run, so that IL code is never directly executed.

Each method in a .NET executable file has a stub attached to it by the class loader. When a method is first executed, the stub passes control to the JIT compiler, which converts the IL to native code and then modifies the stub so that subsequent invocations will cause direct execution of the native code. This means that methods are only JIT compiled when necessary; therefore, the more an application is run, the more of it tends to be converted to native code.

.NET code is JIT compiled in one of two ways. The normal way is for the code to be compiled as it is executed, as I outlined in the previous paragraph. It is, however, also possible for IL code to be JIT compiled when an application is installed.

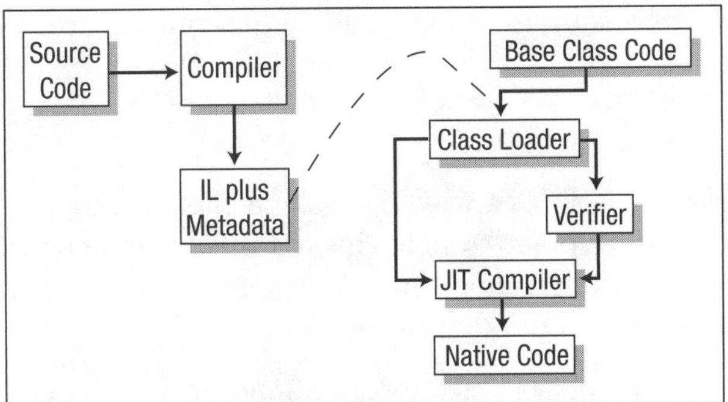

Figure 1.3 CLR compilation and loading.

The JIT compilation process, shown in Figure 1.3, is normally accompanied by verification, during which the IL is examined to check that it is type safe, and that objects are only performing legal operations. Note that not all code can be verified because some high-level languages that may compile down to IL use constructs that can't be checked, such as C pointers.

Managed Code and Garbage Collection

One of the problems with traditional C code is that programmers have to manually deallocate memory that they have dynamically allocated. This manual memory management has led to many problems. If a programmer forgets to deallocate memory, the program is subject to memory leaks, whereas if he or she deallocates memory more than once, the program may well crash.

The CLR implements dynamic memory management through the use of garbage collection. The programmer is responsible for allocating memory, but it is the CLR that clears up unused memory. Therefore, .NET programs never suffer from the problems traditionally associated with manual memory management. The system knows how many clients are referring to an object, and when that reference count drops to zero, the system knows that it is safe to delete the object.

Code that is run under the garbage collection system is known as *managed code*. All VB and C# code is managed, and C++ programmers have the option of compiling down to traditional object code or to .NET managed code. There are some restrictions when using C++ to write managed code, such as the limitation to single inheritance, but in many cases, the advantages to C++ programmers are tremendous.

Note that the garbage collector only reclaims unused objects when it needs to because it does not want to impact program performance unnecessarily. This means that it is not possible to tell exactly when an object will be reclaimed; if the program does not run short of resources, it may well be that objects are not reclaimed at all.

Namespaces

Namespaces are heavily used in .NET as a way to organize classes into a hierarchy. They are also used to stop developers from having to think up arcane naming conventions in order to ensure that the names they choose for their classes don't clash with those chosen by Microsoft or other developers.

The concept of a namespace is familiar to C++ programmers. They are used in a similar way in .NET, but have extra functionality. Java programmers will find that namespaces are similar to packages, but without the link to directory paths that packages impose.

Namespaces provide a way to group classes by providing an extra level of naming beyond the class name. For example, if you had several classes having to do with banking, you could wrap them in a namespace like this:

```
namespace Bank
{
  public class Account
  {
    ...
  }
  public class Teller
  {
    ...
  }
}
```

You can see that the definition of the Bank namespace wraps the definition of the **Account** and **Teller** classes.

What advantages does this give you? First, it gives you a way to organize your classes, so that related classes are bound together in a namespace. Second, it helps in large applications where different classes may be provided by different people, different teams, or even different organizations. Avoiding name clashes in large applications can be quite a headache, and in the past, developers have resorted to arcane naming conventions to ensure uniqueness for their class names.

This naming problem is greatly helped by the fact that namespaces can also be hierarchical, with namespace names being composed of several parts separated by dots. If you had a number of different namespaces having to do with financial matters, you could name them like this:

```
namespace Finance.Bank
{
  ...
}
namespace Finance.InsuranceCo
{
  ...
}
```

When building large applications or producing classes for others to use, multilevel namespace names can prove very useful in avoiding naming problems. All the classes provided by Microsoft as part of the base classes are part of the **System** namespace.

Assemblies

Windows uses EXEs and DLLs as its basic units, but .NET uses assemblies.

An assembly has been described as a "logical EXE or DLL" in that it consists of one or more physical EXEs and/or DLLs containing components, together with any other resources that are needed, such as HTML files, bitmaps, and sound files. An assembly contains a manifest that describes the contents of the assembly. Assemblies are thus self-describing and contain:

- Name and version information
- A list of what is in the assembly
- Dependency information in the form of references to other assemblies

There are two sorts of assembly—shared and private. A *shared* assembly is stored in the global assembly cache, where everyone has access to it. A *private* assembly, on the other hand, is used by a single application and is stored in the application's directory or somewhere else local to it. Assemblies are found by searching paths. For private assemblies, the path includes the application's directory and subdirectories. For shared assemblies, the path consists of the same directories plus the global assembly cache.

Assemblies are important because the assembly it belongs to is part of a type's identity. If assembly A contains a type T and assembly B also contains a type called T, then these are two different types as far as the CLR is concerned.

How do namespaces fit in with assemblies? The answer is that there's no firm connection. It may well be that all the classes belonging to a namespace—say Bank—may be built into an assembly called Bank.dll, but this isn't mandatory. In fact, all the standard **System** namespaces supplied by Microsoft reside in mscorlib.dll, the central .NET assembly.

A system of versioning is enforced on shared assemblies, with each assembly possessing a four part version number (known as a *compatibility version*) that looks like an IP address. A typical version number might be 1.3.6.9. The CLR uses the version number to determine whether the assemblies are compatible. There is a default policy for deciding compatibility, but if you do not like the policy, you can define your own. The default policy states that if the first two parts of the version are different, assemblies are viewed as incompatible. If the first two parts are the same but the third is different, they may be compatible, and if only the fourth part differs, they are most likely compatible.

Let's explore assemblies and IL by writing a simple "Hello World" application, compiling it, and then looking at the resulting executable. I'll write the example in C#, to give you a sample of what C# code looks like:

```
public class Hello {
  public static void Main() {
    System.Console.WriteLine("Hello World!");
  }
}
```

Assuming that you've entered the source code into a file called Hello.cs, you can compile it from the command line like this:

```
C:>csc Hello.cs
```

The result is an EXE file of about 3KB in size, which contains the IL code and a small loader that loads the CLR in order to run the JIT compiler.

You can see what is inside the file by using the IL disassembler utility, ILDASM, which comes as part of the .NET Framework SDK, and is located in the SDK's bin directory along with the other SDK tools. If you open the Visual Studio .NET Command Prompt you can run it by typing "ildasm" on the command line. Once loaded, use the File menu to open the EXE file; your screen should look like the display shown in Figure 1.4.

The tree in Figure 1.4 shows you that the file contains a manifest plus an assembly called Hello. The tree below Hello shows the class details next to the red triangle, and the fact that it has a default constructor (.ctor) and one method. Double-click on the Manifest line and a window opens that contains something very similar to the following listing:

```
.assembly extern mscorlib
{
  .originator = (03 68 91 16 D3 A4 AE 33 )
```

```
  .hash = (52 44 F8 C9 55 1F 54 3F 97 D7 AB AD E2 DF 1D E0
           F2 9D 4F BC )
  .ver 1:0:2204:21
}
.assembly Hello as "Hello"
{
  // -- The following custom attribute is added automatically...
  //  .custom instance void
[mscorlib]System.Diagnostics.DebuggableAttribute::.ctor(bool,
  //
bool) = ( 01 00 00 01 00 00 )
  .hash algorithm 0x00008004
  .ver 0:0:0:0
}
.module Hello.exe
// MVID: {2909C16C-A45A-4C39-B3E1-44EB8181F6D8}
```

Without discussing the code in detail, I'll pick out a few interesting points. The *.assembly* section halfway through the listing shows that the file contains an assembly called Hello, currently at version 0.0.0.0; the *.assembly extern* section at the top of the file makes reference to the assembly mscorlib, which is at version 1.0.2204.21. The *.module* entry shows that the Hello assembly only contains a single module, Hello.exe. Remember that an assembly can contain more than one module, although only one module contains the manifest.

The last line defines the Module Version ID (MVID), a unique identifier used to identify this version of the module. This identifier is in the form of a GUID (a Globally Unique Identifier), something that is thoroughly familiar to anyone who has done any COM programming.

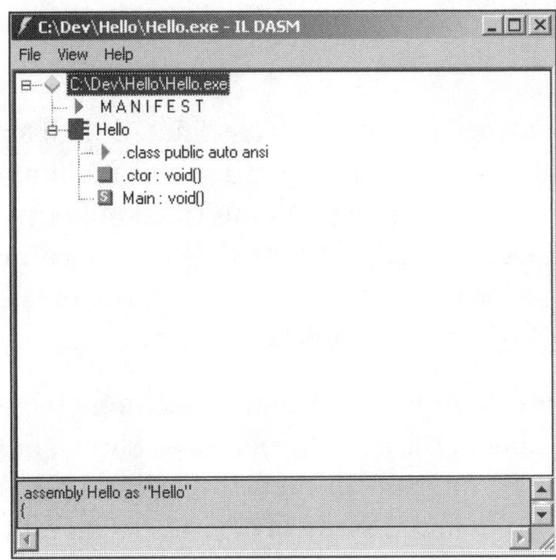

Figure 1.4 Running ILDASM.

Double-clicking on the **Main** method at the bottom of the tree in the ILDASM window displays the following:

```
.method public hidebysig static void Main() il managed
{
  .entrypoint
  // Code size       11 (0xb)
  .maxstack  8
  IL_0000:  ldstr      "Hello World!"
  IL_0005:  call       void [mscorlib]System.Console::WriteLine(class
     System.String)
  IL_000a:  ret
} // end of method Hello::Main
```

In the first line, you can see the signature of the method, and the fact that it is IL managed code. The body of the method consists of three IL instructions, one of which calls the **WriteLine()** method from the mscorlib assembly.

Application Domains

.NET has introduced the concept of an Application Domain, or AppDomain. These are like lightweight processes, meaning that you can have more than one inside a native operating system (i.e., Win32) process.

AppDomains provide a halfway house between threads and full processes. Processes are useful because they are completely isolated from one another; each has its own address space, and it isn't easy for one process to write to (and possibly corrupt) the address space of another. The problem with processes is that they are heavyweight—there's a lot of data associated with a running process, and creating them and then swapping between them in a multitasking system is expensive in time and resources. This is especially true under Windows, but less of a problem under Unix.

Threads are good because they don't have all the baggage associated with a process, and this makes them much more lightweight. Creating and maintaining threads is much less of a drain on system resources, and multitasking between them is much quicker. There's a problem, though, in that threads share many parts of their parent process, which leads to the many well-known problems concerned with unwanted (and unanticipated) interactions between threads.

An AppDomain, which may contain one or more assemblies, is completely isolated from any other AppDomains running in the same process, as shown in Figure 1.5, so there's no sharing of memory or data. In fact, the separation is so complete that another AppDomain running in the same process is treated in exactly the same way as one residing on another machine; the same .NET remoting mechanisms are used to communicate between them.

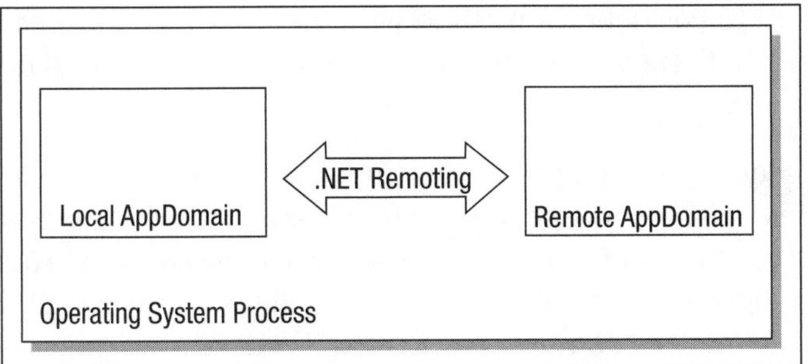

Figure 1.5 AppDomains.

How Does .NET Affect Visual C++?

With all the changes and new features that have been outlined thus far, you may well be wondering what is happening to Microsoft's traditional programming languages, VB and Visual C++. As you'll see shortly, VB has changed a lot, with a whole host of new features being added and some old ones being removed. Visual C++ hasn't changed quite as much, but it still has many interesting new features.

Visual C++

Microsoft has made several changes to its C++ compiler to make it as standard-compliant as possible. The documentation even includes a list of sections in the C++ standard where Visual C++ has compliance problems.

There are a number of new compiler and linker flags, many of which are concerned with managed code and attributes (such as the /IDLOUT linker option to control the output of IDL [Interface Definition Language] files). There are also a couple of new C++ language items that seem designed to mimic Java features. These include **__sealed**, which resembles Java's **final** construct in that you can't inherit from a sealed class, and you can't override a sealed member function.

The **__super** keyword lets you call a base class function in much the same way that **super** does in Java. C++ supports multiple inheritance, however; so this rather complicates things because more than one base class could define a function with the same signature. It turns out that normal function overloading rules apply, so there must only be one unique match provided by all the base classes.

Additionally, **__interface** behaves very much like Java's **interface** keyword. Earlier versions of Visual C++ had an **interface** keyword, but it was really only a **typedef** used as a marker to help identify COM interfaces. The new **__interface** is a real language feature, defining a classlike construct that can only contain public, pure virtual functions, which can only inherit from other interfaces. There's one other rather nice feature related to interfaces. If a class inherits from two interfaces and those interfaces define a method with the same signature, the derived class can override both members separately, using a notation based on the scope resolution operator.

Although Visual C++ code can be compiled down into traditional object code and linked into executables, it is now possible to write classes that are managed by the CLR. There are three types of managed classes: *garbage-collected classes*, *value classes*, and *managed interface classes*. Traditional C++ classes that don't interact with the CLR are called "unmanaged classes."

Garbage-collected classes are the most general-purpose of the three types. As the name suggests, deallocation is handled by the garbage collector, which means that you no longer have to worry about using "free." Because managed classes have to fit in with the OO model used by IL, there are restrictions on what you can do in managed classes. For example, such classes can only use single inheritance (although they can implement interfaces), they can only inherit from managed classes, they cannot have a copy constructor, and they cannot override the **new** and **delete** operators. You create a garbage-collected class in C++ by using the **__gc** keyword, and you can also use the **__nogc** keyword to declare an unmanaged type.

Value classes are intended to have short lifetimes and are usually allocated on the stack. Using the **__value** keyword on a class or **struct** declaration shows that it is a value class, and that garbage collection doesn't need to be used for its instances. A managed interface embodies the notion of a COM interface and is created by adding the **__gc** keyword to an interface definition. As well as classes, arrays and strings can be managed so that they are automatically deallocated when no longer needed. As a nice side effect, managed arrays are automatically given sensible default values on creation.

There's actually quite a lot more to managed classes than simply Java-like garbage collection. Because they use services provided by the .NET Framework, managed classes can be used by any other language that targets the COM+ runtime, which means that it is now very simple to share classes with VB or C# code. This raises the intriguing prospect that, because managed classes can inherit from one another and VB now has inheritance, a VB class can inherit from a managed C++ class!

Visual Basic

With the release of VB7 in VS .NET, Microsoft is finally proving that VB is more than a toy language, a criticism often leveled at it by C++ programmers because it hasn't had the sort of language constructs and syntax that other, more "grown up" languages possess. It's true that VB may have started out as such, but as time has passed, the way in which VB has been viewed has changed. It has gone from a limited but very simple way of writing Windows apps to a product capable of producing much more complex solutions. VB7 sees a fundamental change in the VB philosophy, with OO features being added to the language. The new VB inheritance follows a very Java-like model, as it has single inheritance, and all classes derive from an ultimate **Object** class.

Inheritance behavior is controlled by the **Inherits** keyword and the **NotInheritable** and **MustInherit** properties. **Inherits** lets a class specify its (one and only) base class, whereas the other two properties are VB's equivalent of Java's **final** and **abstract** class modifiers, which let you specify that a class cannot have descendents or that it must act as a base class. This means that you can now write code like this:

```
Class Vehicle
  ' stuff in here
End Class

Class Car Inherits Vehicle
  ' more stuff
End Class
```

Function overloading and polymorphism are handled in the base class by the **NotOverridable**, **Overridable**, and **MustOverride** modifiers, and by **Overrides** in the derived class, like so:

```
Class Vehicle
  MustOverride Sub Start()
  End Sub
End Class

Class Car
  Inherits Vehicle
  Overrides Sub Start()
    ' code in here
  End Sub
End Class
```

In this example, **MustOverride** provides an abstract method with no implementation, which must be overridden in derived classes. The **Car** class then uses the **Overrides** modifier to show that this is its version of **Start()**. Classes in VB now also have proper constructors and destructors via the **Sub New()** and **Sub Destruct()** procedures, which replace the old **Class_Initialize** and **Class_Terminate** event procedures. The following code fragment shows the constructor for the **Car** class calling its base class constructor:

```
Class Car Inherits Vehicle




  Overrides Sub Start()
     ' code in here
  End Sub
End Class
```

Along with single inheritance, VB has retained the interfaces that have been features for some time, and it has also gained shared members. These are what C++ and Java people know as *static members*—properties, procedures, and data members that are shared by all instances of a class.

Other language enhancements include namespaces, which work in a similar manner to their C++ counterparts but look like Java imports, and assemblies. In addition, error handling has been enhanced. Programmers who are used to the error-handling facilities provided by C++ and Java are often rather aghast at the rudimentary protection and unstructured coding provided by the **On Error** constructs. VB7 has also grown up in this area because it now supports proper exception handling using the **Try...Catch...Finally** syntax. This improvement appears to provide a nicer syntax wrapping around the existing error generation and handling mechanism because there doesn't seem to be any way to throw your own exceptions.

And then there's threading! VB7 now lets you write multithreaded code, using the **Thread** class. It isn't immediately apparent from the preliminary documentation how (or even whether) thread synchronization is going to be handled, but it is a welcome addition.

Here's C#

Where has C# come from? You can trace its origins back to two facts. It's no secret that Visual J++ met a rather untimely end, killed off by the bumpy relationship between Microsoft and Sun. Microsoft recognized that Visual J++ had two unique qualities: The first of which was that Java was a simpler language for OO programmers to use than C++, and the second was that it was very easy to write COM components in Visual J++.

C++ can be a very hard language to use well, so much so that it is overkill for a lot of Windows programming and component development tasks. Microsoft therefore sought to develop a proper OO language that had its roots in C++, but removed many of the features that make C++ difficult to use.

Writing fully-featured COM components in C++ using the ATL library is likewise not a simple task, but it was much simpler in Visual J++. This was partly due to the fact that the Java Virtual Machine could provide a lot of the functionality that C++ programmers had to provide for themselves, leaving the J++ programmers free to concentrate on what their code was supposed to do rather than on the mechanics/housekeeping of writing code.

The end result is C#, a language in the C family with specific features for component development. It extracts the best features from C++, Java, and even VB. C#'s basic syntax comes from C++ and includes operator overloading. C# doesn't currently support templates, but Microsoft says that it is looking into ways of providing a generic programming mechanism in a future release. The everything-declared-in-one-place class structure comes from Java, and C# also uses the Java-like idea of single inheritance and interfaces. It is important to note, though, that single inheritance isn't a feature of C# syntax that has been borrowed from Java, but is a reflection of the fact that the underlying CLR supports a single-inheritance model. From VB, C# has gained the **For Each** loop for iterating over collections as well as the idea of having properties and events built into the language.

The design goals of C# can be stated concisely as:

- Being based on a *simple extensible type system* where everything can be treated as an object
- Having first-class *support for writing components*
- Being designed to be *robust and durable* through the use of garbage collection, exceptions, type safety, and versioning
- Having a *high level of integration* into Visual Studio .NET with COM+, SOAP, and DLLs
- Being designed to *preserve existing investments* both in terms of existing knowledge of C++/Java and an investment in COM and Win32 through its ability to interoperate with COM components and code housed in DLLs

I've already talked about some of these design goals. Basically, C# is the high-level language for the .NET Framework and the base classes, and it provides the best fit between a high-level language and .NET.

And you've already seen the C# Hello World program:

```
using System;

// Here's a Hello World program in C#
class Hello
{
  public static int Main()
```

```
    {
      Console.WriteLine("Hello world!");

      return 0;
    }
}
```

Java programmers will probably feel thoroughly at home with this code, and C++ coders shouldn't be too alarmed. Let's just note a few important points about the code before moving on.

The first important fact, one that is familiar to Java programmers, is that because C# is a pure OO language, all data and method declarations have to be inside a class. In true C style, every program has to have exactly one **Main()** method where program execution starts. As with all other C family languages, I/O isn't a part of the language, but instead is provided in the runtime libraries. In this case, the **WriteLine()** method belongs to the **Console** class, which as you might expect writes a line of output to the console window. In order to use the **Console** class, you've got to let the compiler access the appropriate library. This is done with the **using** keyword, which is similar in concept to Java's **import** (and not at all like C's **#include**!).

If you're not using an IDE, such as Visual Studio .NET, you can type the code into a file with a .cs extension using your favorite editor, and then compile it from the command line:

```
C:> csc hello.cs
```

The output from this command is an EXE file, which you can run just like any other Windows executable.

What about COM?

By this time, experienced programmers may be wondering where COM fits in, or whether COM has a place at all in the brave new world of .NET. One thing that is definite is that COM isn't going to disappear, although it will be much less evident to the .NET programmer.

Microsoft introduced COM as a way for programmers to create distributed applications out of components that could be written in different languages and hosted on different operating systems. COM's interoperability was achieved by putting strong firewalls in between clients and objects in such a way that a client might well not know what language the component was written in or where it was located. This isolation is achieved through the use of interfaces, which require a

COM object to make callable methods available in a standard layout in memory and for methods to use a standard set of data types. Everything in the COM world—objects, interfaces, and lots of other things—is identified by a 128-bit identifier called a GUID. These GUIDs as well as other information about the COM object are stored in the Registry on a Windows machine.

COM+ is an extension of COM, introduced with Windows 2000, that extends the COM model to add features that are needed by enterprise applications, such as transaction management and increased security. Many of the features that were part of Microsoft Transaction Server (MTS) under Windows NT 4 are available as COM+ Services under Windows 2000.

.NET has taken a different approach to writing components, and therefore .NET components aren't the same as COM components. To give you a small idea of how different these components are, .NET components don't need to use the Registry and don't need type libraries because all information about a component is carried within the assembly in the form of metadata.

COM objects and .NET objects can work well with each other through a facility called COM Interop, which lets .NET objects access COM objects by providing a .NET wrapper class, and lets COM objects access .NET objects by providing all the requisite Registry entries and COM object creation mechanisms.

COM Interop is covered in detail in Chapter 16.

Chapter 2

The .NET Programming Model

By Julian Templeman

In Depth

Before examining the .NET base classes in any detail, the programming model used in the Common Language Runtime (CLR) and in particular the Intermediate Language (IL), which is rather unusual when compared to other bytecode systems, needs to be explained. Most other intermediate forms of code, such as Java bytecode, are very simple, and often bytecode instructions map straight onto processor or virtual machine instructions. This means that the bytecode tends to lose the structure of the high-level language that created it.

IL, on the other hand, is object-oriented (OO), which means that many features that have previously been exclusive to certain high-level languages are now available to any language that compiles down to IL. As mentioned earlier, Visual Basic 7 now has OO features, but the truth is that it really just reflects what is available in the underlying IL. The same is true of C# and managed C++. Thus, all the .NET languages use a common OO model provided by IL, and it is that model that this chapter investigates. You will see that many traditional OO language features—and several new ones—are provided by IL, and you will see how these features are expressed in the .NET languages, especially C# and Visual Basic (VB). You will also see that because high-level languages all have their own syntax and peculiarities (especially languages such as VB, which has a lot of history behind it), there are certain .NET OO features that are better expressed in some languages than in others. However, there may be some features that are not expressible in some languages at all.

OO Programming from 30,000 Feet

This section presents an introduction to object-oriented programming for those who may not have used an object-oriented programming language previously. This information is no substitute for a proper grounding in OO, but it should suffice to give you a basic understanding. If you are familiar with OO programming, you can quickly scan this section and continue on to the "Classes" section.

Object-oriented programming is not new. It originated in academic computer science studies in the 1960s. Despite its age, OO techniques and languages have only recently become more widely used. There are several reasons for this: First, early OO languages were very academic and were concerned with OO coding techniques, meaning that there really wasn't an emphasis on usability or runtime efficiency. Second, these languages only tended to run on large university mainframe machines, and so were not available to most programmers.

During the 1970s, several authors started to bring object orientation to a wider audience, arguing that it could solve many of the problems associated with large-scale program development. Several new OO languages, including C++, were developed toward the end of 1970s, and this, coupled with the increasing availability of powerful desktop hardware expanded the use of OO programming.

Nowadays, very few people would question the benefits of object-oriented programming (OOP) techniques. Almost every new language that is developed is object-oriented, and OO features are being added to many traditional languages.

Do you have to use an object-oriented programming language in order to do object-oriented programming? Perhaps surprisingly, the answer is no. Object-oriented programming is simply a technique that can be applied, with greater or lesser success, in almost any programming language. It is possible to write OO code in non-OO languages, and by the same token, it is possible to write non-OO (or very bad) code in OO languages. Using an OO language does not make you an OO programmer any more than buying a set of wrenches makes you a mechanic. An OO programming language simply makes it easier to express OO programming concepts in code.

What Is an Object?

It is very difficult to provide a concise definition of what an object is, and you would find considerable disagreement if you took a poll among programmers and computer scientists. Here's a simple but useful definition: An object is simply something you can put a name to, such as a car, a bank account, an array, or a button on a form. Some people define an object as representing something in the real world; that may be true, but when was the last time you saw an array or a linked list?

Object-oriented programming is a style of programming that represents a program as a system of objects. A banking program might consist of bank, account, and transaction objects; a model of a road transport system might consist of road, traffic signal, and vehicle objects, and so on. Objects such as cars and accounts are characterized by their behavior. You know that you can deposit money into an account, withdraw money from an account, and find out how much the account contains. You don't need to know how your bank account works in order to use it, but behind the scenes there has to be data that reflects the state of the account.

This data governs how the object responds to requests. Your bank account will allow you to withdraw money if you have sufficient credit; if credit is insufficient, your withdrawal request will be refused. The important point is that the object decides what to do based upon its state data, and this state data is managed by the object.

This mixture of state and behavior is what makes up an object. You'll notice in Figure 2.1 that clients interact with the behavior side of the object. This is intentional, as clients should not be able to directly modify the object's state. After all, the bank would really not be very happy if clients could directly alter the balance in their accounts.

When thinking about objects, you can divide them into three broad classifications, depending on whether state, behavior, or identity is the most important factor. If state is the most important classification, the object is known as a *value object*. Good examples of value objects are dates, times, strings, and currency objects. What's most important about these objects is the data they hold. If you have two date objects both holding October 27th, you can use either of them. Identity isn't important, but state is.

If behavior dominates state and identity, the object is known as a *service object*. Think of checking in at a major airport—you go to a check-in desk, and the clerk takes your ticket and checks you in. Does it matter which clerk? Not usually; any clerk can provide this service to you. A good example of a service object is one that checks a credit card number: All you do is pass the service object the number, and it tells you whether the number is valid or not. There is no state for it to remember; therefore any "card check" object will work as well as any other.

The third type of object is one where its identity is the most important factor. Consider the Account object previously described: state (such as the balance) is important, and behavior (depositing and withdrawing) is important as well, but identity (which account it is) is absolutely vital. Obviously, it is very important that your deposit go into your account. These objects are called *entity objects*, and often represent data that is retrieved from a database, which is identified by a key of some sort.

Why is this classification important? It can help you decide what needs to be provided in code, because certain operations only make sense for particular types

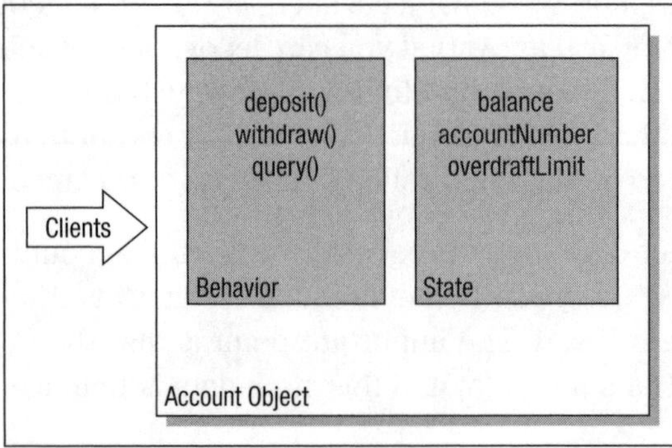

Figure 2.1 Structure of an object.

of object. Should you allow users to make exact copies (*clones*) of your objects? It's fine for value objects, because it doesn't matter which object you're talking to, so creating another one shouldn't be a problem. What about service objects? Cloning is concerned with duplicating state, and if your service object doesn't have any state, cloning it doesn't make much sense. You may as well create a new one. Entity objects are another matter altogether because you generally don't want to let people create identical copies. Having two objects representing the same bank account could be disastrous because both would have their own idea of what the balance should be.

Classes and Objects in Code

Let's start looking at some common OO concepts and see how they are expressed in code.

As mentioned earlier, an object is something that possesses behavior and state. In OO programming languages, the behavior is represented by functions (also known as *methods*) and the state by variables (also known as *fields*). A class is the definition of an object type, such as Account or Car, and it lists all the variables and functions that make up an object.

The following code shows how you would define a very simple **Account** class in Visual Basic 7:

```
Public Class Account
  Private balance As Double
  Private accountNo As Integer

  Public Function deposit(ByVal amount As Double) As Boolean
    balance = balance + amount
    Return True
  End Function

  Public Function withdraw(ByVal amount As Double) As Boolean
    If (balance-amount < 0) Then
      Return False
    End If
    balance = balance - amount
    Return True
  End Function

  Public Function query() As Double
    Return balance
  End Function
End Class
```

It is not necessary to understand much about Visual Basic in order to get a flavor of what is going on in this code. The first line starts the definition of a class called **Account**, and this definition continues until the closing **End Class**. Inside the Account definition, there are two variables that hold the state of the object: The first is a floating-point value that holds the balance, whereas the second is an integer that holds the account number. These are marked as Private, meaning that they cannot be accessed from outside the **Account** class.

These variables are followed by the code for the **deposit**, **withdraw**, and **query** functions, and they are marked Public so that they can be accessed from outside the class. You can see how these functions modify and maintain the balance. The **deposit** function adds the amount it is passed on to the balance; note that for simplicity the code does not check for invalid input data, although you could easily add that feature. The **withdraw** function checks that the account will not overdraw, and if all is okay, it adjusts the balance accordingly. The **query** function simply returns the current value of the balance. These three functions let clients interact with the account, but prevents them from directly manipulating the balance; the object can check the validity of actions proposed by the client.

Once you have defined the class, you can start to use it by creating objects. The sample code shows how you can create an **Account** object in VB and interact with it. Don't worry too much about the VB syntax; instead, concentrate on getting the overall idea of what's going on:

```
Dim myAccount As New Account
Dim yourAccount As New Account

myAccount.deposit(1000)          ' deposit 1000 in my account
yourAccount.deposit(100)         ' deposit 100 in your account

myAccount.withdraw(500)          ' withdraw 500 - OK
myAccount.query()                ' returns 500

yourAccount.withdraw(500)        ' fails!
```

In the first two lines, the compiler is told to create two **Account** objects called **myAccount** and **yourAccount**. Because the **Account** class has been defined, it knows what an **Account** is and how to create it.

In the third and fourth lines some money is deposited in each account—1,000 in one, and 100 in the other. Note how the calls are coded to these functions—each call starts with a reference to the object that should be used and is followed with the operation that it should perform. This is typical of the notation used by OO languages. Later in this section you'll see that C# does things in a similar manner.

In the fourth line, a withdrawal of 500 is made from **myAccount**, which succeeds because the account contains 1,000. A query is then made to the account to find out its balance, which returns the current value. The final line attempts to withdraw the same amount from the other account, but because that account only contains 100, the operation fails. In other words, I've tried the same operation—withdraw 500—on both accounts, and their response has been different because of their internal state.

When you look at the code in the **deposit**, **withdraw**, and **query** methods, you may wonder just how the method knows on which object's behalf it is acting. There's no mention in the code of whose balance is being adjusted or checked, and yet the correct accounts get credited and debited. The idea—approximately—is that a reference to the object is passed over to the method, and this is used to qualify all references to class members. So when **deposit()** is called for **myAccount**, it performs as if the following code has been executed:

```
Public Function deposit(myAccount, ByVal amount As Double) As Boolean
  myAccount.balance = myAccount.balance + amount
  Return True
End Function
```

You don't see this being done, but the method always knows which object has called it. Many OO languages let you access this reference to the calling object, which is called "Me" in Visual Basic and "this" in C# and C++.

To show you how the same principles apply across languages, look at the following code for the **Account** class in C#. You'll see later in this section that, allowing for minor syntax differences, the code structure is almost identical between the two languages:

```
public class Account {
  private double balance;
  private int accountNo;

  public boolean deposit(double amount) {
    balance = balance + amount;
    return true;
  }

  public boolean withdraw(double amount) {
    if (balance-amount < 0) return false;

    balance = balance - amount;
    return true;
  }
```

```
  public double query() {
    return balance;
  }
}
```

The code for using the class in C# is also very similar to how it is used in VB, differing only in the way in which the objects are initially created:

```
Account myAccount = new Account();
Account yourAccount = new Account();

myAccount.deposit(1000);              // deposit 1000 in my account
yourAccount.deposit(100);             // deposit 100 in your account

myAccount.withdraw(500);              // withdraw 500 - OK
myAccount.query();                    // returns 500

yourAccount.withdraw(500);            // fails!
```

Inheritance and Polymorphism

You've already learned two important principles of OO. *Encapsulation* binds together data and functions into a single construct, whereas *data hiding* restricts access to the variables that make up the state of your objects. Let's now look at *inheritance* and *polymorphism*, two other very important features that are supported by every true OO language.

In the real world, objects are classified as belonging to several different types at once. For example, a sports car is a car and also a vehicle, so you could say that a sports car has three types—sports car, car, and vehicle. The appropriate type is used depending upon the circumstances, so if asked to count all the cars in a car park, you would include the sports cars because they are cars. This ability to perform hierarchical classification comes naturally to humans, and it is very useful in programming.

Inheritance gives you the ability to express this "is a" relationship between classes in your code. Figure 2.2 shows a simple inheritance hierarchy, detailing how various types of vehicle are related.

In VB, you could set up these relationships in code like this:

```
Public Class Vehicle
  ' code for the Vehicle class
End Class

Public Class Car
  Inherits Vehicle
```

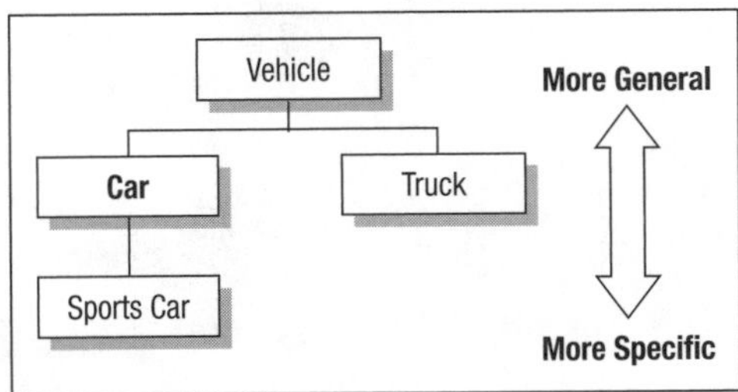

Figure 2.2 An inheritance hierarchy.

```
  ' code for the Car class
End Class

Public Class SportsCar
  Inherits Car
  ' code for SportsCar
End Class
```

You can see from the listing how the **Inherits** keyword is used to set up an inheritance relationship. Vehicle is known as a *base class* or *superclass*, and Car and SportsCar are *derived classes* or *subclasses*.

You can also see that inheritance is easy to do in code, but the art of writing good OO programs lies in determining which relationships you should set up—rather like in real life.

Why is this inheritance useful? Let's look at an example. If you ask someone to get you a vehicle, you are not being very specific, and so the person could bring you a car, a sports car, or a truck. If you ask for a car, then a car or a sports car will do, but a truck will not because it is not a type of car. The same thing happens in code; because a car is a vehicle, you can use a car object anywhere that a vehicle is specified. This turns out to be very powerful. You can write a program that originally has car and truck classes, and you can use these wherever vehicles are wanted. Later on someone can come along and add another kind of vehicle—say a bus—and because a bus is also a type of vehicle, you can use it wherever a vehicle is required. This means that you can add new functionality to the program without disturbing existing code, and this is of great benefit in complex modern programs.

As before, the same principles apply to other OO languages; the following is an example in C#:

```
class Vehicle {
  // code for the Vehicle class
}
```

```
class Car : Vehicle {
  // code for the Car class
}

class SportsCar : Car {
  // code for SportsCar
}
```

You've seen how inheritance works, but what about polymorphism? This is an important and very useful feature of true OO languages, whose name derives from the Greek for "many forms," and leverages the idea that you can consider an object to have several different types at once.

Suppose you are writing a drawing program and you have a class called **Shape**, from which all the shapes used in the program are derived. You know that each shape has to be able to draw itself, but only the individual child classes themselves will be able to say what needs to be done to produce the right output. So you end up with a series of classes, each of which implements a **Draw()** method that looks identical, but is implemented differently. The following is a bit of VB pseudocode that illustrates this idea:

```
Public Class Circle
  Inherits Shape
  Public Sub Draw()
    ' code for drawing circles
  End Sub
End Class

Public Class Square
  Inherits Shape
  Public Sub Draw()
    ' code for drawing squares
  End Sub
End Class
```

Why is this important or useful? You already know that you can consider Circles and Squares to be **Shapes**, and you know that all **Shapes** have a **Draw()** method. This means that you can be passed any **Shape** and call its **Draw()** method, and the **Shape** will do whatever is necessary to draw itself. The following method shows this in action:

```
Public Sub DrawShape(ByRef s As Shape)
  s.Draw()
End Sub
```

It doesn't matter what sort of shape you're passed, you can be sure that the correct **Draw()** method will be called. This has great implications for program maintainability and evolution because you can add new shapes to the hierarchy at any time, and they'll still work with your **DrawShape()** method.

In many OO languages, functions that work in this way are called *virtual functions*, and they're said to work by a process called *late binding*. The word *late* is used because you don't actually know until runtime which function is actually going to be executed. All the languages in .NET now support virtual functions, as you'll see.

A Small Digression into UML

When you start dealing with the design of OO programs, you will more than likely come across the Unified Modeling Language (UML). In a nutshell, UML gives you a notation for describing the structure and operation of object-oriented programs, and anyone who intends to use OO these days needs to know UML.

If you want to know more about UML, there are many good books available on the subject; one such book is *UML Distilled* (by Martin Fowler and Kendal Scott, Addison Wesley, 1999). To give you an idea of what UML looks like, Figure 2.3 shows the hierarchy diagram redrawn using the UML notation.

You can see how classes are represented by boxes, with the name of the class in the top section. The other two sections contain details of the classes' data and functions, and the arrows point from a class to its parent.

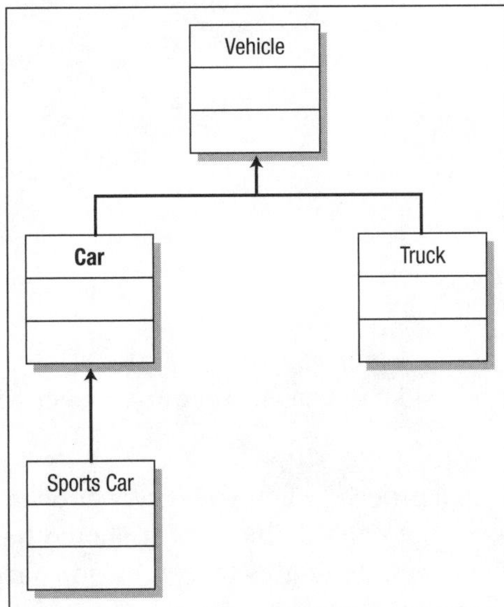

Figure 2.3 UML class diagram.

Interfaces

There is one other topic that needs to be discussed before leaving this brief overview of OO, and that is the idea of interfaces. They are used extensively within the .NET classes, and therefore, it is important that you understand what they are and how they are used.

Consider this rather simplistic definition: If a class represents something you can give a name to, then an interface represents some behavior that you can give a name to. For example, suppose you are writing software for a publishing company, such as The Coriolis Group. You will end up with a lot of classes representing items that you have to deal with such as books, catalogues, orders, and invoices. It turns out that all of these items will probably need to be printed. All of these types share the characteristic that they are "printable," even though they are not related by inheritance. An interface provides a way to indicate this behavior in code by specifying one or more functions that a class must implement. For example, a "printable" interface might specify a "print" function, which means that any class that wants to be considered printable has to implement the print function.

The following code shows how you can define and implement an interface in VB:

```
Interface Printable
  Sub print()
End Interface

Public Class Account
  Implements Printable

  Sub print() Implements Printable.print
    ' print the account
  End Sub

  Private balance As Double
  Private accountNo As Integer

  ' Rest of class definition omitted
End Class
```

The **Account** class is now "printable," so you can use an **Account** object wherever something printable is required.

Interfaces often originate during the design process when you discover behavior that needs to be implemented by classes, but can't define how it should be accomplished. It's a way of specifying "if you want to do this task, then you have to do it this way...."

Now that some of the major concepts involved in OO programming have been briefly discussed, let's move on to some .NET-specific material.

Classes

You now know that the idea of a class is central to OO programming, so let's look at how classes are implemented in the CLR. As previously mentioned, .NET is unusual in that the Intermediate Language (IL) directly supports OO constructs, whereas most bytecode systems are more akin to a traditional assembly language.

Because classes and other OO concepts are implemented in the CLR, there are certain OO features that all .NET languages can support. And, there are some OO features that languages will have to implement in a particular way in order to fit in with the .NET way of doing things.

Class Elements

.NET classes can consist of four elements:

- Methods
- Fields
- Properties
- Events

These elements are discussed throughout this section, but bear in mind that how these components are implemented (and even whether they're accessible at all) depends upon the language you're using.

Methods are the functions that provide the "workings" of the class. A method has a name, may take arguments, and has a return type. The return type is void if the method doesn't return anything, and this will map onto a VB Sub. Classes can contain constructor methods, which are executed when an object is being created and are used to initialize the new object, and a finalizer method, which can be used to tidy up after the object when it is being garbage collected.

Fields hold the data belonging to the object and are represented by value types or references to objects. It is good OO practice not to make object state data visible outside the object, so .NET objects can use *properties* to let clients interact with object state without having direct access to it.

The following code shows how a property looks in VB:

```
Property Color() As String
  Get
    Color = myColor
```

```
    End Get
    Set
      MyColor = Value
    End Set
  End Property
```


The property looks like a method whose body consists of a *get* and/or a *set* clause. The get clause returns the value of the property, whereas the set clause uses the special "Value" variable to retrieve the value passed in. The important thing is that, although you know that the property is implemented in code, to the client it looks like a field, so it can be used like this:

```
MyObject.Color = "red"
```

VB users will realize that this is very similar to what they've been used to in **Property Get** and **Property Set** constructs. But the point is that this is now available to every .NET language, so you can program properties in exactly the same way in C# and C++, and more importantly, you can use properties across languages.

Another important feature that distinguishes properties from fields is that even though a property is often used to manage the state of a class member variable, it doesn't have to be the case. This means that you can have a dynamic read-only property that, for example, gets its value from a database or some sort of online data feed.

Because .NET has been designed for writing GUI and Web code, and because *events* and event handling form a critical part of those types of applications, Microsoft decided to build an event-handling mechanism into the features supported by the CLR. If a class supports events, it is capable of notifying interested parties when something occurs. Other objects can find out what events a class publishes and can decide to subscribe to those they are interested in. An obvious example is a button on a form. The button may have one event, the "clicked" event, and the form can decide to subscribe to the event so that it gets told when the button has been clicked. Events form the basis of GUI programming, but are also useful in many other types of programs as well.

Class Characteristics

Table 2.1 shows the characteristics that .NET lets you apply to classes. Remember that how (or even whether) these are expressed in your own programming language will vary. Table 2.2 shows a number of characteristics that can apply to class members.

Table 2.1 Characteristics of .NET classes.

Characteristic	Description
Sealed	Marks a class that can't be used as the basis for inheritance.
Implements	Marks a class that implements one or more interfaces.
Abstract	Marks a class that contains one or more abstract methods. You can't create instances of abstract classes.
Inherits	Marks a class that inherits from another one.
Exported	Marks a class that is visible outside its assembly.

Table 2.2 Characteristics of .NET class members.

Characteristic	Description
Abstract	A method that has no implementation is abstract and makes its class abstract. Classes that inherit from an abstract class must implement the abstract method.
Private, Public, Family, Assembly, Family or Assembly	A *private* member is accessible only within the class in which it is defined. A *public* member is accessible to anyone. A member with *family* accessibility is accessible to the defining class and to all classes derived from it, whereas members with *assembly* accessibility are accessible to classes in the same assembly. *Family or assembly* accessibility gives access to classes that are either derived or in the same assembly.
Final	A final method cannot be overridden in a derived class.
Overrides	A method overrides one that it has inherited from a parent class.
Static	A member belongs to the class itself rather than to any instance of the class. This member is shared between all members of the class and can be accessed even if no class members exist.
Overloads	Used to mark methods that share the same name but differ in their argument lists.
Virtual	A virtual method is one that can be invoked by late binding. The type of the object used to make the call determines which method is called rather than the type of the reference through which the object is accessed.
Synchronized	Only one thread can access synchronized code at a time.

Reference and Value Types

In most programming languages, primitive types such as integers and characters are declared on the stack (rather than on the pile) and are copied when they are passed around. Objects, on the other hand, are usually created on the heap and are accessed via references. These references are passed around rather than the objects themselves.

The CLR divides its types into two categories:

- *Value types*—Are derived from **System.ValueType** and are passed around by value. They are stored as efficiently as primitive types are in other languages, but they are also objects and so methods can be called on them. Note that although you can derive new types from **System.ValueType**, you can't derive from the other value types provided in the **System** namespace.
- *Reference types*—As their name implies, are full classes whose objects are accessed via references. When you are creating new types, you need to think about how they will be used and whether objects will be more efficiently passed by value or by reference, and then define them as either value or reference types.

The system value types, such as **System.Int32**, provide exact equivalents to language primitive types. So an **Int32** is equivalent to an *int* in C# and an *Integer* in VB; you can use the underlying type if for some reason you don't want to use the language-specific equivalent.

Value types, such as **System.Int32**, pose a problem to the designers of OO languages. In order to have a nice, unified type system, it is desirable that everything be an object, but this isn't good for the language. It is clear that if every integer or character has to be created as an object, has methods called on it to do any operation (even adding two numbers), and has to be garbage collected, then basic operations, such as arithmetic, are going to be very inefficient. The other alternative is to make the basic types special, so that they are simply bytes holding data and not objects at all. If you do this, low-level operations are much more efficient, but you end up with a two-tier type system.

.NET has found a third way to treat types, which provides the advantages of both other approaches without the problems. In .NET, value types are only treated as objects when they need to be. So if you simply declare an integer, it is represented by a few bytes just as it would be in a non-OO language. If you add two integers, it will be done by using simple arithmetic, not by calling a class method. If you pass the integer to a method that needs an object, .NET will silently encase the integer in an object wrapper, which is a process called *boxing*.

When a value is boxed, an object is created that holds its type and value. For example, suppose you have a method in C# that takes an object reference, but you pass it an integer, like this:

```
int n = 3;
foo(n);
...
public void foo(object o) { ... }
```

What happens to the integer? You can see what happens if you look at the disassembly of the IL code:

```
.method public hidebysig static void Main(String[] args) cil managed
{
  .entrypoint
  // Code size       14 (0xe)
  .maxstack  1
  .locals ([0] int32 n)
  IL_0000:  ldc.i4.3
  IL_0001:  stloc.0
  IL_0002:  ldloc.0
  IL_0003:  box          [mscorlib]System.Int32
  IL_0008:  call         void Boxer.Class1::foo(class System.Object)
  IL_000d:  ret
} // end of method Class1::Main
```

The first highlighted line shows the declaration of an integer called *n*. The lines labeled IL_0002 and IL_0003 show *n* being boxed into a **System.Int32**, and the following line shows the call being made to **foo()**.

As you might expect, unboxing is the process of extracting the value type from the object and is usually done using a cast. If the **foo()** method was implemented like this:

```
public static void foo(object o)
{
  int n = (int)o;
  ...
}
```

You would expect the IL to contain something like the following, where you can clearly see the object being unboxed and stored into the integer:

```
.locals ([0] int32 n)
  IL_0000:  ldarg.0
  IL_0001:  unbox        [mscorlib]System.Int32
  IL_0006:  ldind.i4
  IL_0007:  stloc.0
```

Structs

As well as classes, .NET supports structs. The name comes from the C **struct** keyword that is used to define a structure or compound datatype. The following is a simple struct in VB that describes a point on a graph:

```
Public Structure Point
  Private myX As Integer
  Private myY As Integer

  Property X() As Integer
    Get
      X = myX
    End Get
    Set
      myX = value
    End Set
  End Property

  Property Y() As Integer
    Get
      Y = myY
    End Get
    Set
      myY = value
    End Set
  End Property

  Sub New(ByVal a As Integer, ByVal b As Integer)
    myX = a
    myY = b
  End Sub
End Structure
```

If we look at the same code in C#, we can see how similar the constructs are:

```
struct Point
{
  private int x,y;

  public int X
  {
    get { return x; }
    set { x = value; }
  }
  public int Y
  {
    get { return y; }
    set { y = value; }
  }
```

```
    public Point(int a, int b)
    {
      x = a; y = b;
    }
}
```


Structures are similar to classes in many ways, and they can contain fields, methods, properties, and events. But there's one major difference—structures are value types, whereas classes are reference types. This has several consequences:

- They are stored on the stack rather than on the heap.
- They are accessed directly, not through references, and so aren't garbage collected.
- They are passed by value when they're copied around.

These three differences mean that structs can be more efficient than classes for representing value types.

There are quite a few other differences between structures and classes. Let's look at three in particular. The first is that they don't take part in inheritance, which means that they can't inherit from other structures or classes, and they can't be used as a base class. They can, however, implement interfaces, and they do this in exactly the same way as a class does.

The second difference concerns constructors. You can implement constructors in structs, but they must have parameters. You'll get a compiler error if you try to give a struct a parameterless constructor, and you'll also get an error if you try to add a finalizer.

The third difference is that members of structs can't be initialized. This means that in C# you can't use:

```
struct Point
{
  private int x=0, y=0;     // error!
  ...
```

If you want to have your structs initialized, you need to provide a constructor to do it yourself.

Inheritance

.NET only allows classes to inherit from a single parent class, a process known as *single inheritance*. Some other OO languages, such as C++, allow classes to inherit from more than one parent class. However, it has been found that this *multiple inheritance* can cause problems in practice, so many OO languages have decided not to use it.

This use of single inheritance poses a slight problem to C++ programmers and means that when writing managed code in C++, you are restricted to one base class.

Often, multiple inheritance has been used to express multiple "is a" relationships rather than to inherit code from more than one parent class. When this is the case, you can use interfaces to model the relationships that multiple inheritance would provide as in traditional C++.

Interfaces

The topic of interfaces and their place in OO programming has already been touched upon. As you'll see, interfaces play a central role in the .NET architecture and can be used from all three of the initial .NET languages.

Let's look at the ICloneable interface as an example. The Object base class contains a **MemberwiseClone()** method that can be used to produce an exact copy of an object. The problem is that this produces a *shallow copy* of the object, which means that if the object contains references to other objects, then the references will be copied rather than the objects themselves, as shown in Figure 2.4. Only the top level of the object is copied, and this simple operation can be automatically carried out on any object, so it is provided as part of Object.

What if you want to copy the object, cloning all the objects to which it refers? This is called a *deep copy*, and because .NET has no idea of the structure of your objects, you have to implement it yourself. In other words, .NET knows what you have to do, but has no idea how to do it, so it defines the ICloneable interface with its single **Clone()** method. If you want to be able to make deep copies of your objects, you must implement ICloneable (and hence the **Clone()** method)

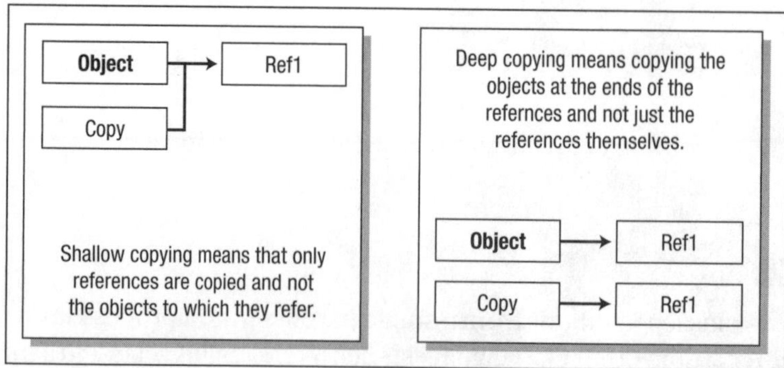

Figure 2.4 Shallow versus deep copying.

in your own classes. The following code snippet shows what the ICloneable interface looks like in VB:

```
Public Interface ICloneable
  Function Clone() As Object
End Interface
```

And here it is again in C#:

```
public interface ICloneable {
  object Clone();
}
```

By convention, interface names start with *I* so that it is easy to determine which names refer to interfaces and which to classes, but this is not a requirement. You can see that the interface specifies the signature of a single method, **Clone**, which takes no arguments and returns an object reference. Obviously, an interface definition needs to have with it some sort of description of the semantics of the interface so you know just what you have to do when you implement the interface.

Delegates

Delegates are objects supported by the .NET runtime, which performs roughly the same purpose as function pointers in C and C++.

So what does this mean for those who aren't C or C++ programmers? A delegate is an object that forwards a call to a particular method on a particular object. So a delegate that looks like this:

```
Delegate Function MyDelegate(ByVal X As Integer, ByVal Y As Integer) _
      As Double
```

would forward calls to a method that took two *ints* and returned a double. In other words, the signature of a delegate is the same as the signature of the method it is designed to call. In computer science terms, a delegate is an example of a *functor*, which is an object that wraps a method call, as shown in Figure 2.5.

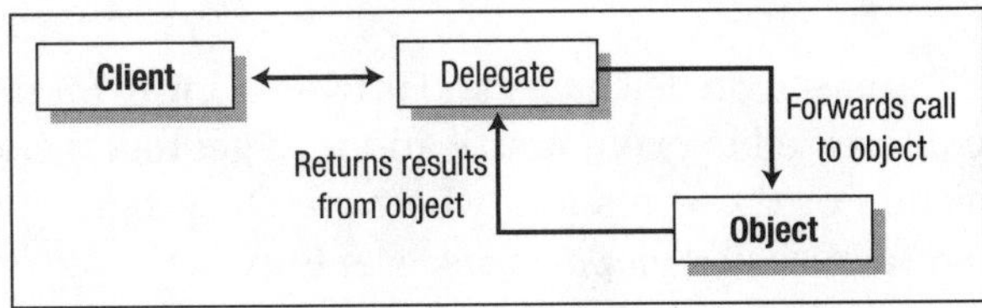

Figure 2.5 Delegates.

When you want to use a delegate, you create the delegate object and bind it to the method you want the delegate to call. Note that the inner workings of delegate objects are provided by .NET, and all you do is create the delegate and tell it where to forward calls. If you want to see how this works in code, take a look at the Immediate Solution "Creating and Using Delegates" later in the chapter.

Why are delegates useful? By creating and using a delegate object, you can call any method on an object that matches its signature without needing to know exactly which object—or even which type of object—you're talking to. This is very useful when working with callback mechanisms where you know which call needs to be made, but don't necessarily know in advance which object you're going to be using. This means that delegates are particularly suited to event handling and are heavily used for this purpose in .NET.

You may think that delegates and interfaces sound rather similar, and they are. The two main differences are that, first, you talk directly to the object implementing the interface, whereas the delegate is an intermediate between you and the object you're using. And second, a delegate maps onto a single method, whereas interfaces often define groups of related methods.

The standard **Delegate** class is used as a basis for delegates that can only invoke a single method. There is a second class, **MulticastDelegate**, which can be used to create delegates that can invoke more than one method. You'll see why these are useful in the next section, where events are discussed.

Events

Unlike many other development systems, .NET has been designed with Web and GUI applications particularly in mind, which means that certain features have been added to .NET to support their development. One of these features is the notion of events, something that is already familiar to VB programmers.

Most modern GUI applications use events as a notification mechanism; when a button on a form is pressed or the selection in a listbox changes, they generate (or "fire") events in order to tell the form what has happened. In practice, firing an event means calling a method in the object that wants to receive the event (see Figure 2.6).

The event mechanism in .NET is based on delegates and provides a way for event sources and objects that are interested in event notifications to get together and set up the callback mechanism. For those readers who have OO programming experience and who have come across *design patterns*, events are an application of the Observer pattern, which provides a standard way to set up notification links between an observed object and one or more observers.

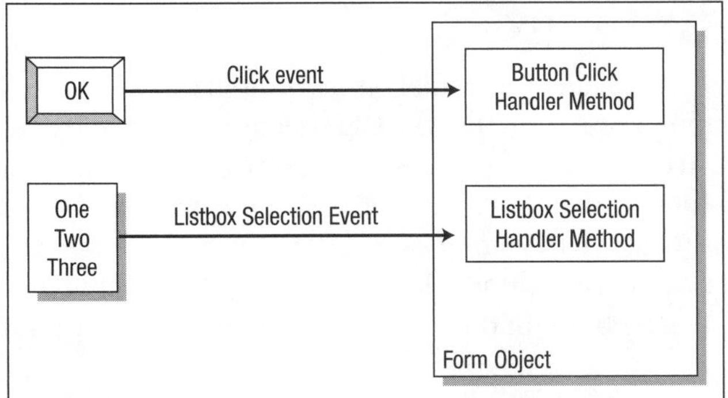

Figure 2.6 Event firing.

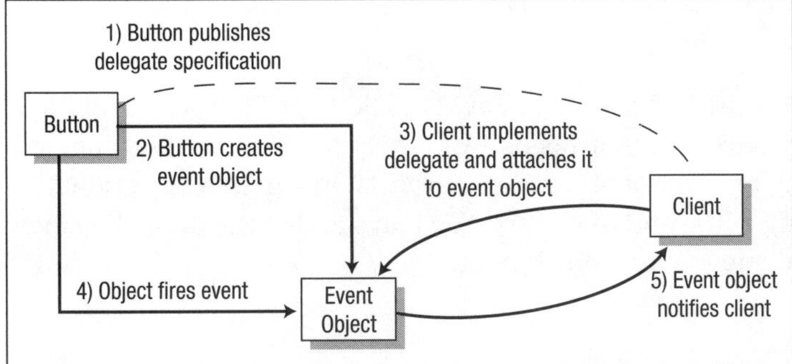

Figure 2.7 The .NET event mechanism.

You can see how the mechanism works in Figure 2.7. The object that is going to be the source of events creates a delegate and makes it public so that any other class can access it. It also creates an event object based on the delegate. Remember that a delegate is an object that calls a method on another object; the event knows about "firing," and the delegate provides the link back to the client objects that want to be notified.

A client can then obtain the delegate definition from the button object and implement a method with the appropriate signature for the delegate to call. It then passes a reference to its method over to the event object, which stores it in its list of clients. Events use a **MulticastDelegate**, which can call a list of methods; this enables one event object to notify more than one client.

When the button object wants to fire an event, it tells the event object, which calls each of the methods in its list. In this way, all clients get their notification methods called.

Metadata and Attributes

As discussed in Chapter 1, metadata is extremely important in the world of .NET, and it provides the essential information that the CLR needs in order to be able to load and execute code. You do not have control over much of the metadata that is stored in the executable files by the compiler, although there are a few standard items that you can choose to attach to your classes. However, the CLR will let you declare your own metadata items and attach them to classes; these home-brewed metadata items are called *attributes*, and they can be created and queried from all .NET languages.

A typical attribute used on a VB class might look like this:

```
<IsPlugin(" Foo Plugin", version=1.1)> Public Class Foo
...
```

The attribute, **IsPlugin**, is declared in angle brackets just before the class name, together with any parameters it needs. An attribute can have both named and positional parameters. Positional parameters must come first, with optional named parameters coming at the end of the list. You can see that the preceding example has one positional and one named attribute.

Exceptions

The CLR programming model supports error handling using exceptions, and this has two important consequences:

- All .NET languages now support exceptions.
- Exceptions can be used between languages.

Anyone who has programmed in Java or C++ will be familiar with the concept of exception handling. For those that are not, however, a brief explanation is provided in the following few paragraphs.

In many programming languages, errors are handled by returning an error code from a method or by setting some sort of flag. But it is difficult to ensure that the error is handled properly by the caller. This is especially true in C-type languages, where the return value of a method can be completely ignored. Exceptions solve many of the problems associated with traditional error-handling methods. The following brief list contains some of the most important problems solved by exceptions:

- An exception, once generated, cannot be ignored. It has to be handled somewhere in the calling code; otherwise the program will terminate.

- Exceptions do not have to be handled in the method where they originate, but can be caught anywhere above that method in the call stack. This makes them particularly suited to library code because the **library** method can generate an exception and leave it up to the client to handle it.
- Exceptions provide a way to signal errors where there is no alternative. As an example, consider constructors, which don't have a return value. This makes it hard to signal that an error has occurred in the course of constructing an object, but exceptions let you bypass this restriction.

Figure 2.8 summarizes what happens when an exception is generated, or "thrown." First, normal execution stops and the runtime takes over. The runtime looks in the routine where the exception occurred to see whether it contains a handler. If it does, the handler is executed and normal execution continues. If it doesn't, the runtime looks at the calling routine, the next routine up the call stack. It continues walking up the stack until it finds a routine that handles the exception; if it gets all the way back to the start of the client code without finding a suitable handler, the program will be terminated with an "unhandled exception" error.

The processing of exceptions has broadly the same syntax in VB, C#, and C++, with all three using the **Try**, **Catch** construct. The following is an example of how exceptions might be used within a VB program:

```
Imports System

Public Module modmain

Public Class Foo
  Public Sub Bar()
    Console.WriteLine("Foo:bar called")
  End Sub
```

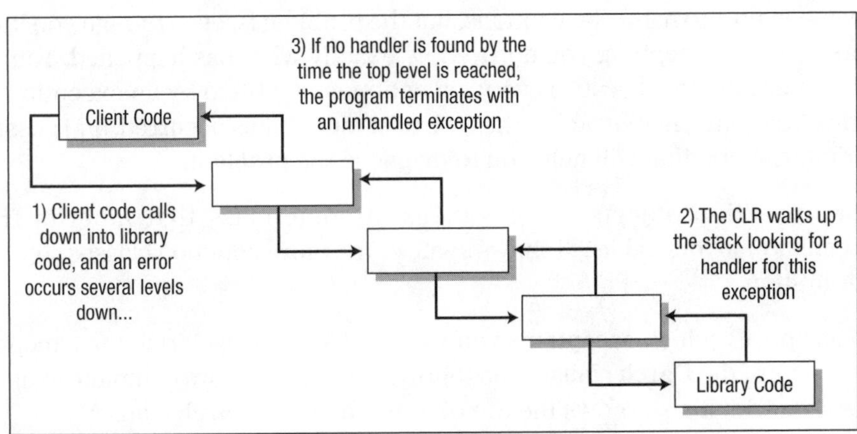

Figure 2.8 Exception handling.

```
End Class

Public Sub func(ByRef f As Foo)
  Try
    f.Bar()
  Catch
    Console.WriteLine("Exception!")
  End Try
End Sub

Sub Main()
  Dim f As Foo
  func(f)
End Sub

End Module
```

You declare a simple class called **Foo** that has one method, **Bar()**, and a function that takes a reference to a **Foo** object. Note what happens in **Main()**—you create a **Foo** reference but no object, and then pass this reference through to the function. As you would expect, you get a runtime error when you try to execute the **Bar()** method on this uninitialized reference; in this example, it is handled by using exceptions. If you try to execute this code, you'll see the "Exception!" message appear on the console.

You place code that may fail inside a **Try** block, and then specify one or more exception handlers using **Catch** statements, within which you do whatever is necessary to handle or report the error. When an exception occurs in a **Try** block, the runtime steps in and looks for a handler. If it finds one, the handler is executed and execution continues; if one is not found, the runtime checks the calling routine.

You've seen how to handle exceptions, but the problem is, even though you know there's been an exception, you don't know exactly what has happened. You can easily get around this because every exception is identified by an exception object that holds information about the type of error that has occurred, and possibly other information that will help you to diagnose the problem.

These exception objects are instances of some class that inherits from **System.Exception**. Table 2.3 shows some of the more common classes supplied by the system.

You can specify which exceptions you want to catch by declaring the exception type as part of the **Catch** clause. The following code is a more complete example that shows this; it also shows the use of more than one **Catch** clause:

Table 2.3 Commonly used .NET exception classes.

Exception Class	Description
SystemException	The base class for other user-handleable exceptions.
ArgumentException	An argument to a method was invalid.
ArgumentNullException	A null argument was passed to a method that doesn't accept it.
ArgumentOutOfRangeException	The value of an argument is out of range.
ArithmeticException	An arithmetic overflow or underflow occurred.
ArrayTypeMismatchException	An attempt was made to store the wrong type of object in an array.
BadImageFormatException	An image is in the wrong format.
DivideByZeroException	An attempt was made to divide by zero.
DllNotFoundException	A referenced DLL cannot be found.
FormatException	The format of an argument is wrong.
IndexOutOfRangeException	An array index is out of bounds.
InvalidCastException	An attempt was made to cast to an invalid class.
InvalidOperationException	A method was called at an invalid time.
MethodAccessException	An illegal attempt was made to access a private or protected method.
MissingMemberException	An invalid version of a DLL was accessed.
NotFiniteNumberException	An object does not represent a valid number.
NotSupportedException	A method has been called that is not implemented by a class.
NullReferenceException	An attempt has been made to use an unassigned reference.
OutOfMemoryException	There is not enough memory to continue execution.
PlatformNotSupportedException	Thrown when a particular feature is not supported on a platform.
StackOverflowException	A stack has overflowed.

```
Public Sub func(ByRef f As Foo)
  Try
    f.Bar()
  Catch ae As NullReferenceException
    Console.WriteLine("Caught NullReferenceException: {0}", ae)
  Catch ex As Exception
    Console.WriteLine("Caught Exception: {0}", ex)
  End Try
End Sub
```

The first **Catch** clause is intended to catch exceptions that are tagged with a **NullReferenceException**, whereas the second **Catch** will handle all others because all exceptions derive from the base **Exception** class. At runtime, the first **Catch** clause that matches the exception will be the one executed: In this case, there is a **NullReferenceException**, so the first of the two **Catch** blocks will be executed, and you will see something like the following on the console:

```
Caught NullReferenceException: System.NullReferenceException:
    Attempted to dereference a null object reference.
  at VBExcept.Module1.func(Module1$foo& f) in
    C:\dev\VBExcept\Module1.vb:line 12
```

Printing out the exception object prints out a message plus a stack trace that tells you exactly where the error occurred.

You can also add a **Finally** clause to a **Try** block. As a result, any code placed in the **Finally** clause will be executed before the method is exited regardless of whether an exception occurs or not:

```
Public Sub func(ByRef f As Foo)
  Try
    f.Bar()
  Catch ae As NullReferenceException
    Console.WriteLine("Caught NullReferenceException: {0}", ae)
    ' Exit here...
    Exit Sub
  Catch ex As Exception
    Console.WriteLine("Caught Exception: {0}", ex)
  Finally
    Console.WriteLine("Finally executing...")
  End Try
End Sub
```

The method is exited once the message has been printed out in the **Catch** clause, but the **Finally** clause will be executed before the exit takes place. **Finally** clauses are very useful when there is some action that has to be taken before a method exits, such as closing files or refreshing database tables. They save a lot of complex logic that might otherwise be needed.

Reflection and the Type Class

In .NET, it is possible to obtain information about assemblies once they have been loaded into memory, and in particular about the classes, interfaces, and value types that they include.

This information includes:

- A list of the classes contained in a module
- A list of the methods that a class defines

- Names and types of properties and fields
- Signatures of methods

As you might expect, this information comes from the metadata associated with the assembly and its classes; the process of obtaining it is called *reflection*.

Reflection is implemented by the **System.Reflection** namespace and the **System.Type** class. But because the whole idea of reflection is part and parcel of the .NET model that is being discussed, it will be covered in this section.

As well as simply letting you query metadata, reflection lets you dynamically create an object of a given type and call methods on it. It is the mechanism used by VB to implement late binding, as in the following code:

```
' Create a general object reference
Dim obj As Object
' Create an object of type Test
obj = New Test()

' Call one of its methods
obj.Foo
```

A generic Object reference has been used to refer to the object that was created, and as a result, the VB compiler doesn't know at compile time what type of object is being referred to, so it has no idea whether the call to **Foo()** is legal or not. At runtime, reflection is used to query the object on the other end of the reference to see whether it supports a **Foo()** method, and if so what arguments it requires.

If you run the code through the IL disassembler, ildasm.exe, you can see this late binding in operation in the following (slightly edited) listing:

```
IL_0000:  nop
IL_0001:  newobj   instance void Test::.ctor
IL_0006:  stloc.0
IL_0007:  ldloc.0
IL_0008:  ldnull
IL_0009:  ldstr    "Foo"
IL_000e:  ldc.i4.0
IL_000f:  newarr   [mscorlib]System.Object
IL_0014:  ldnull
IL_0015:  call     void [Microsoft.VisualBasic]
           Microsoft.VisualBasic.CompilerServices.LateBinding::LateCall
           (object, class [mscorlib]System.Type, ...)
IL_001a:  nop
IL_001b:  nop
IL_001c:  ret
```

You can see how the string containing the function name is loaded before a call is made to the **LateCall()** helper method, and that one of the parameters to this call is a **System.Type** object that describes the object being operated on.

The **System.Type** class is central to the practical use of reflection. You can obtain a **Type** object that represents a loaded type by reflection, and then use the **Type** object's methods, fields, and properties to find out everything you might need to know about that type and even create objects.

In VB, you can get the **Type** object representing a type using the **GetType** operator:

```
' Get the Type representing an Integer
Dim tf As Type = GetType(Integer)

' Get the Type representing an Integer array
Dim tf1 As Type = GetType(Integer())
```

Once you have a **Type** object, you can start to use it to find out about the type it represents. The **GetMembers()** methods return an array of **MemberInfo** objects describing each of the members; alternatively, you can call the more specific **GetMethods()**, **GetFields()**, or **GetProperties()** methods to get information about methods, properties, and fields, each of which returns an array of objects (**MethodInfo**, **FieldInfo**, or **PropertyInfo**).

Immediate Solutions

Creating Classes

If you want to create a class in VB, use the **Class** keyword:

```
Class Foo
...
End Class
```

Within the class definition you can add fields (data items), methods, properties, and events.

Overloading and Overriding Methods

The terms *overloading* and *overriding* are often used interchangeably, but they mean completely different things. If two or more methods within a class share the same name but have different arguments, they are said to be overloaded.

In VB, the **Overloads** keyword must be used to show overloaded methods:

```
Class Foo
  Public Overloads Sub Bar()
  End Sub

  Public Overloads Sub Bar(ByVal n As Integer)
  End Sub
End Class
```

The two **Bar()** methods have different arguments lists, so they are valid overloads.

In C# and C++, overloaded methods don't require any special keywords to be used, as long as the arguments lists of overloaded methods are different.

Overriding is related to inheritance and is discussed later in this chapter in the "Overriding Methods" section.

Implementing Fields and Methods That Belong to the Class

In .NET, you can define members that belong to a class as a whole rather than to any one object. As an example, consider a bank account class. Each **Account** object has a balance that is unique to the object; the **Account** class may also have an interest rate member, which sets the interest rate for Accounts. This value belongs to every Account rather than to any one **Account** object, so it makes sense that the interest rate variable belongs to the **Account** class itself. Members that work like this are called "static" in C# and C++ and "shared" in VB. Not only can you have static data, but you can also have static methods and properties.

The following shows how you could code some shared members in VB:

```
Public Class Account
  Private Shared InterestRate As Double
  ...
  Public Shared Function GetInterestRate() As Double
    GetInterestRate = InterestRate
  End Function
End Class
```

A single **InterestRate** member is shared by all **Account** objects as well as a **GetInterestRate()** method, which can be used to retrieve it. Because the function belongs to the class itself, you can use the class name to call it rather than an object name:

```
d = Account.GetInterestRate
```

You can read this as "ask the **Account** class for its interest rate." Note that because these members belong to the class as a whole, they are not called on behalf of an object, and so do not get passed a "this" or "Me" reference.

Creating Structs

In .NET, structs are similar to classes but are value types rather than reference types. Structs can contain all the same members as classes (methods, fields, properties, and events), but they are subject to certain restrictions, which were explained in the In Depth section.

You can create a struct in VB using the **Structure** keyword:

```
Public Structure Point
  Private myX As Integer
  Private myY As Integer

  Property X() As Integer
    Get
      X = myX
    End Get
    Set
      myX = Value
    End Set
  End Property

  ...

  ' A constructor to initialize a Point
  Sub new(ByVal anX As Integer, ByVal aY As Integer)
    myX = anX
    myY = aY
  End Sub
End Structure
```

In C#, structs are also declared using the **struct** keyword:

```
struct Point {
  int myX, myY;

  public int X {
    get {
      return myX;
    }
    set {
      myX = Value;
    }
  }

  ...

  // A constructor to initialize a Point
  public Point(int anX, int aY) {
    myX = anX;
    myY = aY;
  }
}
```

In Managed C++, things are done slightly differently; C++ uses the **__value** keyword. All C++ programmers know that just about the only difference between a class and a struct is the level of access to class members, so instances of classes and structs should behave the same. C++ programmers can use the **__value** keyword to declare C++ classes and structs to behave like .NET structs. Classes and structs declared using **__value** are value types and are subject to the same constraints.

```
__value struct Point {
  int myX, myY;
};
```

Object Construction and Destruction in VB

In VB the **Sub New()** and **Sub Destruct()** methods are used to provide object initialization and finalization. A **Sub New()** method will be called when an instance of your class is created, and you can overload this method to pass in parameters. Here's an example where **Car** objects will be created by passing in a string representing their make:

```
Class Car
  Public Sub New(ByRef make As String)
    ...
  End Sub
End Class

Sub Main()
  Dim c As New Car("Ford")
End Sub
```

A **Sub New()** has been declared that takes a string as its only parameter. When you create a **Car** object from the **Main()** method, you pass in the string that denotes the **Car's** make. You could overload the class to provide two constructors, the second of which takes a make and a model:

```
Class Car
  Public Sub New(ByRef make As String)
    ...
  End Sub

  Public Sub New(ByRef make As String, ByRef model As String)
    ...
  End Sub
End Class
```

```
Sub Main()
  Dim c As New Car("Ford")
  Dim c2 As New Car("Ford", "Orion")
End Sub
```

The compiler can tell which constructor needs to be used by the number of arguments that have been given.

It's important to realize that a constructor is always called when creating objects, so if you don't code any **Sub New()** methods in your class, the compiler will synthesize a do-nothing constructor for you.

You can also provide a **Sub Destruct()** method for your classes. This implements .NET finalization and is a method that will be called when your object is finally reclaimed by the garbage collector. The problem with **Destruct()** is that you can't tell when—or even whether—your object is going to get garbage collected, so you don't want to put any code into **Destruct()** that has to be called at any particular time, or that has to be called at all.

Note that because **Sub Destruct()** takes no arguments, it can't be overloaded.

How Do I Handle Cleanup in .NET Objects?

All .NET objects, regardless of the language they are written in, end up inheriting a method called **Finalize()** from the base **System.Object** class. This method is called when the garbage collector finally decides to reclaim your object; so you might be tempted to think that it's a useful way of tidying up and releasing the resources that your object has used.

The problem is that finalization in .NET is nondeterministic. In other words, you can't tell when it is going to occur, and because the garbage collector may not bother to collect any outstanding objects when the program terminates, finalization may not occur at all. This means that any clean-up operations that have to be done at a particular time—such as writing records back to a database—shouldn't be entrusted to finalization.

The recommended solution is to implement the IDisposable interface and provide a method called **Dispose()** that users have to call once they have finished with the object. When **Dispose()** is called, the object should clean itself up, and then mark itself as unavailable for further use. This may mean, in practice, setting a flag so that any subsequent method calls on the object will fail. Once the object has been cleaned up, it doesn't matter when, or even whether, it is finally garbage collected.

Using Inheritance

In VB, the **Inherits** keyword is used to set up an inheritance relationship between two classes:

```
Class Car
  Inherits Vehicle
  ...
End Class
```

The **Inherits** statement can only be used with classes and must be the first code (i.e., nonblank and noncomment) line of the class definition. The name of the parent class immediately follows **Inherits**, and in line with the .NET OO model, there can only be one parent class. Within a class, the parent class can be referred to by using the **MyBase** keyword.

If you set up a constructor for your class, the first line must be a call to the parent class constructor, **MyBase.New**:

```
Class Vehicle
  Public Sub New(ByRef make As String)
    ...
  End Sub
End Class

Class Car
  Inherits Vehicle

  Public Overloads Sub New(ByRef make As String)
    MyBase.New(make)
  End Sub
End Class
```

Overriding Methods

When a class is derived from another by inheritance, it inherits the methods that its parent has defined.

There are four possible actions that the derived class can take with a method that it inherits from a parent class:

- The derived class simply uses the method as inherited from the parent.

- The derived class overrides the method by providing its own version in order to customize its behavior. This version must have exactly the same signature as the method in the base class.
- The derived class is forced to override the method because the parent class has no default implementation.
- The derived class is forbidden to override the method.

VB uses specific keywords to handle the last three cases:

- A method marked as **Overridable** can be overridden by a derived class, but it isn't compulsory.
- A method marked as **NotOverridable** cannot be overridden by a derived class. This is the default state for methods that don't have any of these three keywords specified.
- If a method is marked **MustOverride**, it won't have any implementation in the parent class, and a deriving class must provide its own implementation. Classes that contain any **MustOverride** methods are abstract classes, which are discussed in the next section.

If a derived class wants to override a method, that method has to be marked as **Overridable** or **MustOverride** in the base class, and the derived class has to use the **Overrides** keyword:

```
Public MustInherit Class Shape
  Public MustOverride Sub Draw()
End Class

Public Class Square
  Inherits Shape
  Public Overrides Sub Draw()
    ' code for drawing circles
  End Sub
End Class
```

In C#, the method at the top of the inheritance hierarchy uses "virtual" to show that this is the start of a chain of virtual functions; all classes deriving from it have to use the **override** or **new** keywords if they define a method with the same signature:

```
public abstract class Shape {
  public virtual void Draw() {}
}
```

```
public class Square : Shape {
  public override void Draw() {
    // code for drawing circles
  }
}
```

The use of **override** shows that **Square**'s version of **Draw()** is intended to override **Shape**'s, so that if a **Square** is accessed through a **Shape** reference, the right version will be called. The alternative would be to use **new**, which tells the compiler that even though these two methods have exactly the same signature, **Square**'s method is not an override for the one in **Shape**. Note that you have to use either **override** or **new** if you provide a method in a derived class that has the same signature as one in its base class; otherwise the compiler will complain.

Creating Abstract Classes

An abstract class is one that cannot be directly instantiated, but can only be used as a base for inheritance. This doesn't mean, however, that an abstract class can't contain code. Many abstract classes contain common code, which is used by derived classes.

To declare an abstract class in VB, use the **MustInherit** keyword on the class definition:

```
Public MustInherit Class Shape
  ...
End Class
```

Now, you cannot create **Shape** objects, although you can derive from **Shape** and refer to derived objects using **Shape** references. Note that a **MustInherit** class doesn't have to contain any **MustOverride** methods, but they often will.

In C#, use the **abstract** keyword on the class definition:

```
public abstract class Shape {
  ...
}
```

To create a .NET abstract class in Managed C++, use the **__abstract** keyword. This prevents the class from being instantiated, but unlike a traditional C++ abstract class, you can provide implementations for all member functions:

```
__abstract __gc class MyBaseClass {
  // implementation...
};
```

Note that **__abstract** can also be applied to managed or nonmanaged classes and structs.

Creating Sealed Classes and Methods

A sealed class is the opposite of an abstract class in that a sealed class can't be used as a base class, whereas an abstract class has to be used as a base class in order to be useful.

Sealed classes are implemented in VB by using the **NotInheritable** modifier on the class definition:

```
Public NonInheritable Class MySealedClass
  ...
End Class
```

Sealed classes are implemented in Managed C++ by using the **__sealed** keyword:

```
__sealed __gc class MySealedClass {
  // implementation...
};
```

It should be obvious that **__abstract** and **__sealed** are mutually exclusive.

A sealed method cannot be overridden in a derived class. In VB, all public methods of a class are sealed by default, but you can use the **NotOverridable** keyword if you want to emphasize the fact that a method or property cannot be overridden.

In Managed C++, you use **__sealed** to seal a method, whereas in C#, the keyword is **sealed**.

Creating Properties

In VB, the .NET property replaces the old **Property Get** and **Property Set** constructs. Here's what a property might look like in VB:

```
Property Color() As String
  Get
```

```
    Color = myColor
  End Get
  Set
    MyColor = Value
  End Set
End Property
```

The **Get** and **Set** clauses hold code that is used to retrieve and set the value of the property. In this example, the value is being held in a class variable called **myColor**. Value is a special variable, which holds the value that has been passed in as part of the set operation. Its type is determined by the type of the property.

If you want to make the property read-only, use the **ReadOnly** qualifier, and omit the **Set** clause:

```
ReadOnly Property Color() As String
  Get
    Color = myColor
  End Get
End Property
```

The syntax is almost identical in C#:

```
public string Color {
  get {
    return myColor;
  }
  set {
    MyColor = Value;
  }
}
```

In this case, if you want to create a read-only or write-only property, you simply omit the **Get** or **Set** clause.

In Managed C++, you use two separate methods to implement a property by using the **__property** keyword to define a pair of methods that start with **get** and **set**:

```
__gc class test
{
        int prop;
public:
        __property int get_Prop() { return prop; }
        __property void set_Prop(int m) { prop=m; }
};
```

The compiler creates a virtual data member called "Prop" when it sees the **get_Prop()** and **set_Prop()** method declarations. Note that this name must be different from the name of the actual data member that the property represents, even if only in case. Once again, if you want to have a read-only or write-only property, omit the method you don't require.

Creating Interfaces

Interfaces in .NET can consist of virtual methods, properties, and events. In C#, interfaces can also contain indexers.

To create a simple interface in VB, use the **Interface** keyword:

```
Interface IAnimal
  Sub MakeNoise()
  ReadOnly Property Name() As String
End Interface
```

Note how the interface definition simply defines what the methods have to look like, but doesn't supply any implementation. By convention, names of interfaces in .NET always start with an *I*. The body of the interface contains the signatures of those methods that must be implemented in order to implement this interface. Note that you cannot put any modifiers on the method declaration, and that all methods are assumed to be public.

You can also see from this example that in version 7 VB has introduced a new way of specifying properties to replace the old **Property Get** and **Property Set** methods. Not only does this result in a cleaner syntax, but it also brings it more in line with C# and the other .NET languages. In order to show that **Name** can be queried but not set, the property specifies the **ReadOnly** modifier.

***NOTE:** Interfaces were always rather a kludge in previous versions of VB, relying on classes with stubbed-out methods. Visual Basic .NET provides for proper specification and implementation of interfaces.*

Interfaces can be specified in a very similar way in C#. Here's how the Animal interface would look in C#:

```
interface IAnimal {
  void MakeNoise();
  string Name { get; }
}
```

Implementing Interfaces

The way that you implement interfaces looks a lot like inheritance; however, you use the **Implements** keyword instead of **Inherits**:

```
Public Class Dog
    Implements IAnimal

    Sub MakeNoise() Implements IAnimal.MakeNoise
        Console.WriteLine("Woof!")
    End Sub

    ReadOnly Property Name() As String Implements IAnimal.Name
        Get
            Name = "dog"
        End Get
    End Property
End Class
```

There are two particular points to note in the preceding code. First, the **Implements** keyword tells VB that this class is going to implement the specified interface; once this is done, the compiler checks that you implement everything necessary. If you are implementing more than one interface, provide a list of interface names with the members separated by commas.

Second, you have to tell the compiler explicitly which methods in your class implement methods and properties in the interface by using the **Implements** keyword. For instance:

```
Sub MakeNoise() Implements Animal.MakeNoise
```

tells the compiler that this function, **MakeNoise()**, is the implementation of **MakeNoise** in the IAnimal interface. This has two immediate consequences. The first is that you can implement two interfaces that contain methods with the same name without any name resolution problems.

The second is that your method or property name doesn't have to be the same as the one it is implementing. You will probably want it to be the same (see the next section "Using an Object via an Interface" for reasons why this is so), but it doesn't have to be. So if you really want to, you can code **MakeNoise()** in the **Dog** class as follows:

```
Sub DogMakeNoise() Implements IAnimal.MakeNoise
```

Implementing interfaces in C# looks very much like inheritance. The class name is followed by a colon, and then a list of the interfaces to be implemented, which are comma-separated if there's more than one:

```
public class Dog : IAnimal {
  public void MakeNoise() {
    Console.WriteLine("Woof!");
  }

  public string Name {
    get { return "dog"; }
  }
}
```

Using an Object via an Interface

If you have an object that you know implements a given interface, it is easy to use it through that interface in VB:

```
' Create a dog and get it to bark...
Dim d1 As New Dog()
d1.MakeNoise()

' Think of the dog as an Animal
Dim a1 As IAnimal
a1 = d1
a1.MakeNoise()
```

When you create a **Dog** object, you can call its **MakeNoise()** method directly, as you would expect. In order to use the Dog via the IAnimal interface, you create an object reference of type IAnimal. This reference will let you refer to any object that has an IAnimal interface, be it a Dog, a Cat, or a Platypus.

The "a1 = d1" line effectively asks VB whether you can refer to d1 through an **IAnimal** reference. Because the **Dog** class implements the IAnimal interface, this is quite okay, and a reference is returned. If d1 wasn't something that implemented IAnimal (say, a Car), you would expect to get an error. Once you have an IAnimal reference, you can use the methods and properties that are defined on IAnimal.

***NOTE:** Users of previous versions of VB are used to using the **set** keyword when assigning references, but **set** is no longer necessary in Visual Basic .NET.*

As mentioned in the previous section, you don't have to name the implementing function the same name as it is in the interface. If you called the function **DogMakeNoise()** in the **Dog** class like this:

```
Sub DogMakeNoise() Implements IAnimal.MakeNoise
```

you would have to modify the calling code:

```
Dim d1 As New Dog()
d1.DogMakeNoise()

' Think of the dog as an Animal
Dim a1 As IAnimal
a1 = d1
a1.MakeNoise()
```

See the problem? When you are using the **Dog** object directly, you have to call **DogMakeNoise()**, but when you are accessing it through the IAnimal interface, you have to call **MakeNoise()**. Having to use two different names for the same method is confusing, so it is recommended that you implement interface members using the same names that they have in the interface.

Before leaving VB, let's consider one more question: What if you would like to check whether the **Dog** class implements the IAnimal interface before trying to use it? VB lets you use the **TypeOf** keyword within **If** statements to check the type of an object; you will find that it also works for interfaces:

```
' Check whether the object is a Dog
If TypeOf d1 Is Dog
  Console.WriteLine("Object is a Dog")
End If

' Now check whether it is an Animal
If TypeOf d1 Is IAnimal
  Console.WriteLine("Object implements IAnimal")
End If
```

The syntax for using objects via interfaces is similar in C#:

```
// Create a dog
Dog d = new Dog();
d.MakeNoise();

// Think of it as an animal
IAnimal a;
```

```
a = (IAnimal)d;
a.MakeNoise();
```

The important line is the one highlighted, where *d* is assigned to *a*. Because both are references to particular types, you ask the compiler whether you can make *a* refer to the same object that *d* refers to. This is only possible if the object implements IAnimal.

What if you are not sure whether the object does actually implement IAnimal or not? Use the "is" operator to check:

```
if (someObjectReference is IAnimal) {
  IAnimal ia = (IAnimal)someObjectReference;
  ia.MakeNoise();
}
else
  Console.WriteLine("This object isn't an animal...");
```

This operator looks at the object on the other end of the reference and returns true if it is of the appropriate type. If so, you can cast the reference to an **IAnimal** and use it.

The **as** operator provides an alternative way to do this test-and-cast operation:

```
IAnimal ia = someObjectReference as IAnimal;

if (ia != null)
  ia.MakeNoise();
else
  Console.WriteLine("This object isn't an animal...");
```

as does the test and cast, and returns null if the object isn't of the specified type.

Creating and Using Delegates

Delegates can be created and used in all .NET languages. In this first example, you'll learn how to create and use them in VB, then you'll move on to C#, and finally Managed C++.

As an example, let's use a simple class that can notify clients when something interesting happens. This is a simple model showing how delegates can be used in an "event" style of programming. Let's start with the **EventSource** class, which can be used to notify clients when something happens:

```
Imports System.Collections

Public Class EventSource
  Delegate Sub Notify(ByRef s As String)
  Dim al as New ArrayList()

  Public Sub AddMe(ByRef n As Notify)
    al.Add(n)
  End Sub

  Public Sub TellAll()
    Dim ie as IEnumerator
    ie = al.GetEnumerator

    While (ie.MoveNext)
      Dim n As Notify
      n = CType(ie.Current, Notify)
      n("Here you are")
    End While
  End Sub
End Class
```

The second line of the class declares a delegate called **Notify**, and you can see from its signature that it will take a string and not return anything. The **AddMe** method is called by clients who want to be notified, and they pass in a reference to a method that the delegate will call, which is stored in a dynamic array. This array is an **ArrayList** object, one of the standard container types provided by .NET in the **System.Collections** namespace.

When called, the **TellAll** method creates an enumerator to iterate over the items in the **ArrayList**. It then uses **MoveNext()** to walk through the list, accesses each item using the **Current()** method, and then invokes it with a string argument. **Current()** returns a reference of type **Object**, so the **CType** function is used to cast the **Object** reference returned by **ie.Current** into a **Notify** reference before you can use it.

Invoking the item will result in the delegate object calling back to the client and executing the appropriate method. The **EventSource** class has no idea what type of objects its clients are, only that they've passed it a delegate object to act as an intermediary. Note how invoking the delegate object looks like making a method call; whatever is in the brackets following the delegate name is used to invoke the one method that the delegate is bound to.

How would a client use this class? All the client needs to do is to define the callback function that the delegate is going to call. This obviously has to have the right signature, so in this case, it needs to take a string as its only argument and not return anything:

```
Public Class EventClient
  Public Sub CallbackFunction(ByRef s As String)
    Console.WriteLine(s)
  End Sub
End Class
```

How do we make these work together? Here's the code that does it:

```
Sub Main()
  ' declare client and source objects
  Dim es as New EventSource()
  Dim ec as New EventClient()

  ' set up a delegate to call its CallbackFunction method
  Dim en as EventSource.Notify
  en = New EventSource.Notify(AddressOf ec.CallbackFunction)

  ' tell the source about the delegate
  es.AddMe(en)

  ' use the delegate
  es.TellAll()
End Sub
```

Once you've created a client object, you can then create a delegate and pass it the address of the callback function using the **AddressOf** keyword. This means that when the delegate is invoked, it will call the **CallbackFunction** method on the "ec" object.

You now have a delegate object. But you have to pass it to the **EventSource**, so you call **AddMe()** to add the delegate to the list maintained by the source. Finally, you can call **TellAll()** on the source object, which causes it to call back to all the clients who have registered.

The C# code works in exactly the same way:

```
public class EventSource
{
  public delegate void Notify(String s);

  ArrayList al;
```

```
    public EventSource() {
      al = new ArrayList();
    }

    public void AddMe(Notify n)
    {
       al.Add(n);
    }

    public void TellAll()
    {
      IEnumerator ie = al.GetEnumerator();
      while (ie.MoveNext()) {
        Notify n = (Notify)ie.GetCurrent();
        n("Here you are!");
      }
    }
}
```

You can see how the C# code is indeed very similar to the VB code. It uses the same **ArrayList** collection to store the delegate references and the same **IEnumerator** to access them.

The **EventClient** class has no surprises at all; it simply declares the callback method that you will use with the delegate:

```
public class EventClient
{
  public void CallBackFunction(string s)
  {
    Console.WriteLine("String received was: " + s);
  }
}
```

After this has been done, the class can create a delegate object and use it:

```
public class EventClient
{
  public void CallBackFunction(string s)
  {
    Console.WriteLine("String received was: " + s);
  }

  public static int Main(string[] s)
  {
    EventClient ec = new EventClient();
```

```
    EventSource.Notify en = new EventSource.Notify(ec.CallBackFunction);

    EventSource e = new EventSource();
    e.AddMe(en);
    e.TellAll();

    return 0;
  }
}
```

The program starts by creating an **EventClient** object. The important part—as far as delegation goes—occurs in the second line, where you create a new **Notify** delegate and bind it to the **CallBackFunction** method on the **EventClient** object. This means that when this **Notify** object is executed, it will call back to a method on one specific object.

Delegates can also be used from Managed C++, as the following example shows:

```
#using <mscorlib.dll>
#include <tchar.h>
using namespace System;

__delegate void Notify(String* s);

public __gc class EventClient
{
public:
  void CallbackFunction(String* s)
  {
    Console::WriteLine(s);
  }
};

int _tmain()
{
  EventClient* pec = new EventClient;

  Notify* pn = new Notify(pec, &EventClient::CallbackFunction);

  pn->Invoke("Here you are...");

  return 0;
}
```

Managed C++ uses the **__delegate** keyword to create a delegate. This is the same basic example as before, so you pass in a pointer to a **System.String** object.

NOTE: *Remember that all managed types must be accessed via pointers when using them in Managed C++.*

EventClient is a managed class that implements the single callback function. In the main program, you create a delegate object, passing it the address of an **EventClient** object and a pointer to the method to be called. After you have set up the delegate, you can call its **Invoke()** method to cause the string to be passed to the **EventClient**'s callback function.

Creating and Using Events

Events are used to provide a standard asynchronous notification mechanism between objects. An event source class can publish details of one or more events that it will fire at appropriate times. Client objects can create callback methods, and then register them with the event object, which will then call them back when the source fires the event.

Events are very frequently used in GUI programs to implement communication between the components of the user interface, but in .NET they have much wider applicability. They are also based on delegates, and if you've read the previous section, you'll recognize a lot of what is discussed in this section.

VB programmers are used to using the existing VB **WithEvents** mechanism for handling events, and although VB still supports this, Microsoft has added a new event-handling mechanism that uses the .NET delegate method. As a result, using events is now very similar in VB and C#, but in VB you see less of the workings of the delegate and event objects. The following code shows the VB delegate example from the previous section converted to use events, with the significant lines highlighted:

```
Imports System

Module Module1
  Sub Main()
    Dim es As New EventSource()
    Dim ob As New EventClient(es)

    es.Notify("First call...")
  End Sub

  ' The Event source class
  Public Class EventSource
    Public Event MyEvent(ByVal msg As String)
```

```
    Public Sub Notify(ByVal msg As String)
      RaiseEvent MyEvent(msg)
    End Sub
  End Class

  ' The Event client class
  Public Class EventClient
    Private src As EventSource

    Public Sub New(ByRef es As EventSource)
      src = es
      AddHandler src.MyEvent, AddressOf Me.GotNotified
    End Sub

    Private Sub GotNotified(ByVal msg As String)
      Console.WriteLine("Message was '" + msg + "'")
    End Sub
  End Class
End Module
```

The class that will raise the event, **EventSource**, declares an **Event** object that passes a **String** to clients. For this demonstration, the event needs to fire somehow, so a **Notify()** method is added to fire the event when it is called. You can see that VB events are fired using the **RaiseEvent** keyword, passing it the name of the event you want to fire and any arguments needed by the event object.

The client class keeps a reference to an **EventSource** object as a member. Once it's been passed a reference, it uses the **AddHandler** keyword to attach its handler routine, **GotNotified**, to the event object. There's also a **RemoveHandler** method that allows an object to detach itself from an event when it no longer wishes to receive notifications.

Moving on, let's look at how you can use events in C#. One thing that will become apparent pretty quickly is that events in C# are more complicated than they are in VB. Here's how you can use the event:

```
public static int Main(string[] args) {
  // Create an event source
  EventSource es = new EventSource();

  // Create a client object to work with this source
  EventClient one = new EventClient(es);
  EventClient two = new EventClient(es);

  // Tell the source object to notify its clients
  es.Notify("Event Happened...");
```

```
  return 0;
}
```

You start by creating an object that acts as a source of events. This class exposes a delegate definition and an event object to clients. The second step is to create a pair of client objects and pass them references to the source. The clients will register their callback functions with the event and then wait to be called back. The third step is to tell the event source to notify its clients, and because you registered two clients, you should see two responses.

The **EventSource** class needs three components—a delegate definition, an event object definition, and the **Notify()** method:

```
public class EventSource {
  public delegate void MyEvent(object sender, EventInfo ei);
  public event MyEvent OnMyEvent;

  public void Notify(string msg) {
    if (OnMyEvent != null)
      OnMyEvent(this, new EventInfo(msg));
  }
}
```

In general, delegates can take any arguments you want them to, but in order to work with events, a delegate has to have an argument list of two items and return void. The first argument must be a reference to the object that originates the event, and the second one must be a reference to an object that holds some information about the event.

Every event can pass some information about itself to the client. This is done by defining a class that inherits from **System.EventArgs**, adding whatever fields, properties, and methods you need to support your event data, and then passing an object of this type along with the event. In this case, only a message string is passing across, so the class is very simple:

```
public class EventInfo : EventArgs {
  public readonly string msg;

  public EventInfo(string msg) {
    this.msg = msg;
  }
}
```

Notice how the string field has been made read-only. In C#, this gives you a way to declare a field whose value can be initialized once, but thereafter cannot be changed.

The second line of the **EventSource** class declares an event object called **OnMyEvent** and links it to the **MyEvent** delegate. This means that any client with a suitable method can link it in to the event's delegate, as you'll shortly see.

The final member of this class is the **Notify()** method. The **OnMyEvent** event object will be non-null if one or more clients have connected to it; if that's the case, you tell the event object to notify its clients using typical delegate execution syntax.

And here's the client class:

```
public class EventClient {
  EventSource src;
  EventSource.MyEvent evnt;

  public EventClient(EventSource src) {
    this.src = src;
    evnt = new EventSource.MyEvent(EventHasHappened);
    src.OnMyEvent += evnt;
  }

  public void EventHasHappened(object sender, EventInfo ei) {
    Console.WriteLine("Event string was '" + ei.msg + "'");
  }
}
```

At the start of the class, you declare an **EventSource** reference and a reference to the delegate that's declared in the **EventSource** class. The constructor is passed an **EventSource** reference, saves it, and then creates a delegate, attaching it to the **EventHasHappened** method. In the third line of the constructor, the **+=** syntax adds the delegate to the list maintained by the event object. The **+=** and **-=** operators are only available to multicast delegates and are used by clients to connect and disconnect themselves.

The second method in the class is **EventHasHappened()**, the notification method that matches the signature of **EventSource**'s delegate. A reference is passed from this method over to the event object, so that when the **EventSource** object fires the event, the **EventHasHappened()** method will be called.

And that's about it. If you type in and compile the code, you should see two strings printed out on the console as the callback methods of the two objects called.

The final example demonstrates how to detach an object from an event so that it no longer receives notifications. A simple way to do this is to add a **Dispose()** method to the class, which uses the **-=** operator to remove the reference from the list held by the event object.

```
public class EventClient : IDisposable {
  EventSource src;
  EventSource.MyEvent evnt;

  public EventClient(EventSource src) {
    this.src = src;
    evnt = new EventSource.MyEvent(EventHasHappened);
    src.OnMyEvent += evnt;
  }

  public void Dispose() {
    src.OnMyEvent -= evnt;
  }

  public void EventHasHappened(object sender, EventInfo ei) {
    Console.WriteLine("Event string was '" + ei.msg + "'");
  }
}
```


You could call it like this:

```
public static int Main(string[] args) {
  // Create an event source
  EventSource es = new EventSource();

  // Create a client object to work with this source
  EventClient one = new EventClient(es);
  EventClient two = new EventClient(es);

  // Tell the source object to notify its clients
  es.Notify("Event Happened...");

  // The first object disconnects itself
  one.Dispose();

  // Do the notification again...
  es.Notify("Second Event...");
  return 0;
}
```

If you run this code, you'll see that the second string is only printed once, because only one object is still registered. You may think of putting the detach code in a finalizer, but it's not a very good idea because your object will continue to receive events until it is finally garbage collected, and you know that that may not happen. The result is a lot of event calls being fired off to an object that isn't being used any more, which isn't very good for program efficiency.

Let's look at what happens in C++. In Visual Studio.NET, Microsoft has introduced a Unified Event Model, which lets C++ programmers use the same language constructs for coding event handling in plain C++, ATL, and Managed C++ code. All of these use the basic .NET event-handling mechanism, which means that all the work needed to attach clients to senders and maintain their state is done for you. The following example illustrates how this works, and as usual the important lines are highlighted:


```
#using <mscorlib.dll>
after #using <mscorlib.dll>
#include <tchar.h>
using namespace System;

[event_source(managed)]
public __gc class EventSource
{
public:
  __event void MyEvent(String* msg);

  void Notify(String* msg)
  {
    __raise MyEvent(msg);
  }
};

[event_receiver(managed)]
public __gc class EventClient : public IDisposable
{
  EventSource* pes;

public:
  EventClient(EventSource* pes)
  {
    this->pes = pes;
    __hook(&EventSource::MyEvent, pes, EventClient::GotNotified);
  }

  void GotNotified(String* msg)
  {
    Console::WriteLine("Message was '{0}'", msg);
  }

  void Dispose()
  {
    __unhook(&EventSource::MyEvent, pes, EventClient::GotNotified);
  }
};
```

```
int _tmain()
{
  // Create an event source and two clients
  EventSource* pes = new EventSource();
  EventClient* pecl = new EventClient(pes);
  EventClient* pec2 = new EventClient(pes);

  // Notify both clients
  pes->Notify("Hello!");

  // Unhook the second client
  pec2->Dispose();
  // Notify the one client left
  pes->Notify("Goodbye!");
  return 0;
}
```

A class that is going to be a source of events has to be marked with the **[event_source]** attribute and has to state whether it is going to use plain C++, COM, or Managed C++ events. In this case, managed code is used, so the attribute takes the "managed" argument. Within a class that is going to be a source of events, you can declare one or more events by using the **__event** keyword. In this example, a delegate is being set up for other objects to use. Another point to note in the **EventSource** class is the way in which you fire events; in C++, you use the **__raise** keyword, specifying the name of the event you want to raise and passing any arguments the event may need. You may have noticed that **__raise** is the exact equivalent of VB's **RaiseEvent** keyword.

A class that is going to use events is marked with the **[event_receiver]** attribute, which specifies that managed events will be used. A receiver class registers a handler using the **__hook** keyword and specifies the address of the event it wants to hook, the address of the event source object it wants to use, and the address of its own handler function. A class can deregister itself using the **__unhook** function, and you can see this being used in **EventClient::Dispose()**.

The **main()** method shows how all event producers and consumers can be used together. You can create an **EventSource** object and two **EventClient** objects, each of which registers itself with the source. When you tell the source to raise its event, each of the clients is notified. One of the clients then unhooks, and therefore only one client is notified the next time round.

How Do I Attach Attributes to My Classes and Members?

Most of the attributes used in .NET are invisible to you. They are produced by the compiler and included in the metadata in the executable file and then used by the CLR. There are, however, several standard attributes provided with .NET, most of which are involved with making .NET and COM work together. Table 2.4 summarizes the available attributes.

The following C# example shows the use of the conditional attribute:

```
public class Foo {
  [conditional(DEBUG)]
  void SomeMethod() {
    ...
  }
}
```

The attribute is specified in square brackets and placed immediately before the item it applies to. In this case, the conditional attribute applies to **SomeMethod()**, which will only be compiled into the class definition if the preprocessor symbol DEBUG has been defined. If you want to use more than one attribute, simply use a comma-delimited list.

All attribute names end with "Attribute" in order to minimize naming collisions, but you don't have to provide the full name if you don't want to. For example, an attribute called **AuthorAttribute** can be referred to either as **Author** or **AuthorAttribute**.

Table 2.4 Standard .NET attributes.

Attribute	Purpose
attributeusage	Applied to attributes themselves to determine which elements in a class an attribute can be applied to
conditional	Used to include a method in a class conditionally
obsolete	Indicates that a member is obsolete so that the compiler will give a warning or error if it is used
guid	Used to specify a GUID for a class or interface that is to be used with COM
in	Used to mark a parameter as an **[in]** parameter
out	Used to mark a parameter as an **[out]** parameter
returnshresult	Shows that a method returns a **COM HRESULT**
serializable	Marks a class or struct as being serializable
nonserialized	Marks a field or property as being transient

Attributes can take arguments, which may be *positional* or *named*. As their name implies, positional arguments are identified by their position in the argument list, whereas named arguments are identified using a "keyword=value" syntax. Here's an example:

```
[test("abc", 123, name="fred")]
```

This attribute has two positional arguments and one named argument. Named arguments must always appear at the end of the list and are used to specify optional items.

In VB, attributes are placed in angle brackets and appear immediately before the name of the item they apply to. A good example of this is using the **WebMethod** attribute to declare a class method that is exposed as part of a Web Service:

```
<WebMethod()> Public Function GetName() As String
 ' Code goes here...
End Function
```

In C++, attributes are specified in square brackets, as in C#. This style of attribute declaration will be familiar to anyone who has used COM attributes in IDL in the past:

```
[AnAttribute] __gc class Foo
{
  [conditional(DEBUG)]
  void SomeMethod() {
    ...
  }
};
```

How Can I Create Custom Attributes?

Custom attributes can be created in C++, C#, and also in VB. The important thing to realize about attributes is that they are represented by classes and so can have fields and members of their own.

Attributes can take parameters and these fall into two categories: Positional parameters are simply identified by their position in the argument list, whereas named parameters are identified by a keyword. Positional parameters, which must appear before any named parameters, are passed in constructors, whereas named parameters are implemented as properties.

Table 2.5 The AttributeTargets values that specify where custom attributes can be used.

Member	Description
All	The attribute can be applied to anything.
Assembly	The attribute can be applied to an assembly.
Class	The attribute can be applied to a class.
ClassMembers	The attribute can be applied to any class members, such as fields, methods, interfaces, properties, delegates, and events.
Constructor	The attribute can be applied to a class constructor.
Delegate	The attribute can be applied to a delegate.
Enum	The attribute can be applied to an enumeration.
Event	The attribute can be applied to an event.
Field	The attribute can be applied to a field.
Interface	The attribute can be applied to an interface.
Method	The attribute can be applied to a method.
Module	The attribute can be applied to a module.
Parameter	The attribute can be applied to a parameter.
Property	The attribute can be applied to a property.
ReturnValue	The attribute can be applied to a method return value.
Struct	The attribute can be applied to a value type.

A custom attribute in VB takes the form of a class that has to do two things: First, it must inherit from the **System.Attribute** class, and second, it has to use the **AttributeUsage** attribute to state where it can be used. The one argument for **AttributeUsage** is a member of the **AttributeTargets** class, as summarized in Table 2.5

The following sample code shows an attribute called **Author** that contains one positional and one named attribute, which can be attached to classes:

```
Imports System

<AttributeUsage(AttributeTargets.Class)> Public Class Author
  Inherits Attribute
  private authorName As String
  private lastModDate As String

  Public Sub New(ByVal name As String)
    authorName = name
  End Sub
```

```
  Public ReadOnly Property Name() As String
    Get
      Name = authorName
    End Get
  End Property

  Public Property ModDate() As String
    Get
      ModDate = lastModDate
    End Get
    Set
      lastModDate = value
    End Set
  End Property
End Class
```

Note how you can inherit from the **System.Attribute** class and use constructors and properties to model the attribute arguments. You could use this attribute on a VB class as follows:

```
<Author("Julian")> Public Class Fred
  ...
End Class
```

In C++, you use the "attribute" attribute to create a managed class or struct that represents a custom attribute. Note that this class doesn't have to inherit from **System.Attribute**:

```
[attribute(target)]
public __gc class Author
{
  ...
};
```

The class must be public if the attribute is going to be used in other assemblies. The *target* argument is a member of the **System.AttributeTargets** enumeration, which was shown previously in Table 2.5. In the attribute class, constructors are used to specify positional parameters, whereas data members and properties are used to implement named parameters. Here's the **Author** attribute written in C++:

```
[attribute(Class)]
public __gc class Author
{
  String *authorName;         // positional parameter
  String *lastModDate;        // named parameter
```

```
public:
  __property String* get_Name () { return authorName; }

  __property String* get_ModDate () { return lastModDate; }
  __property String* set_ModDate (String* date) { lastModDate = date; }

  Author(String* name) { authorName = name; }
};
```


You could attach the attribute to a class as follows:

```
[Author("Julian", Date="21/12/00")]
public __gc class Foo
{
};
```

You can see that because **Date** is a named parameter, it has to be specified by a keyword, and it has to be last in the list of arguments.

Attribute creation is similar in C#, with one or two differences:

```
[AttributeUsage(AttributeTargets.Class)]
public class Author : System.Attribute
{
  private string authorName;          // positional parameter
  private string lastModDate;         // named parameter

  public string Name {
    get { return authorName; }
  }

  public string ModDate {
    get { return lastModDate; }
    set { lastModDate = value; }
  }

  Author(string name) { authorName = name; }
};
```

The first difference is that your attribute class has to inherit from **System.Attribute**, whereas C++ doesn't require any inheritance. The second difference is the use of the **AttributeUsage** attribute to control where this attribute may be used. Apart from that, the code is structurally very similar, using constructors to implement positional parameters and properties to implement named ones.

How Do I Query Attributes?

Although most attributes are created by compilers and consumed by the CLR, there may be occasions when you need to know whether some item possesses a particular attribute and be able to look at its arguments.

In order to find out about attributes, you need to understand the **System.Type** class. **Type** is a class that represents type declarations for classes, interfaces, arrays, value types, and enumerations; it lets you find out a lot of details about the type and its properties. However, your only concern is how to use **Type** to get attribute information.

NOTE: *If you know C++, think RTTI and you'll be on the right track!*

Let's look at an example of how to retrieve attribute information in VB, and then analyze the code. Let's use the example of the **Author** attribute that was developed in the previous section:

```
<Author("Julian", Date="21/12/00")> Public Class Foo
  ...
End Class
```

You can find out whether the **Foo** class has an **Author** attribute by getting a **Type** object representing the class, and then querying it:

```
Imports System
...
' Create a Type reference
Dim tf as Type

' Create an object to query
Dim aa As New Foo()
' Get its type information
tf = aa.GetType

Dim obj, atts() As Object
atts = tf.GetCustomAttributes(True)

For Each obj In atts
  If (TypeOf obj Is Author) Then
    Console.WriteLine("Author attribute, name is {0}", _
              (CType(obj,Author)).Name)
  End If
Next
```

You create a **Foo** object, and then use the **GetType()** method that every .NET class inherits from its ultimate Object parent class to obtain a **Type** object representing the object's type information. Once you have this, you can call **GetCustomAttributes()** to get an array of Object references that refer to the custom attribute objects. This function takes a Boolean argument that tells it whether to walk up the inheritance tree looking for attributes; I've set it to **True**, but it really makes no difference in this case.

You can then walk over the array, checking the type of each reference to see if it is an **Author**. If it is, you can access the fields within the **Author** object by casting the reference appropriately.

Doing this in C# is pretty much the same:

```
using System;
...
Type tf = typeof(Foo);

object[] atts = tf.GetCustomAttributes(true);
foreach(object o in atts) {
  if(o.GetType().Equals(typeof(Author)))
    Console.WriteLine("Foo has an Author attribute");
}
```

The first thing you do is to use the **typeof** operator to get a **Type** object representing the class you want to query. Once you have that, you can use its **GetCustomAttributes()** method to get a list of references to the custom attributes this object supports. Because an array of plain object references is returned, you need to check the type of the objects to see whether one of them is an **Author**. Note the use of the **GetType()** method, which returns a **Type** object from an object reference, as opposed to the **typeof** operator, which returns a **Type** object from a class name. Once you have established that your class has an **Author** attribute, you can retrieve its arguments.

Finally, let's see how you can do this in Managed C++. As you might expect, it's a little more trouble than in C#, but still relatively straightforward:

```
#using <mscorlib.dll>;
using namespace System;
...
Foo* f = new Foo();
Type* pt = f->GetType();

Object* patts[] = pt->GetCustomAttributes(true);
```

```
for (int i=0; i<patts->Length; i++)
{
  Console::WriteLine("attribute {0} is {1}", __box(i),
      patts[i]->GetType()->get_Name());

  Type* pa = Type::GetType("Author");
  if (patts[i]->GetType()->Equals(pa))
    Console::WriteLine("Object has Author attribute");
}
```


The first task is to get the type of the managed class **Foo**, and then ask for the list of custom attributes. Checking these involves getting the **Type** object representing each attribute, and then comparing it with the **Type** object for the **Author** attribute class using the **Equals()** method. Note the use of **__box()** to turn the C++ int variable *i* into a **System.Int32**, which can be used with **Console::WriteLine()**.

How Do I Catch Exceptions?

Exceptions are caught using the **Try**, **Catch**, **Finally** construct; this works pretty much the same in all .NET languages. Here's an outline of the syntax:

```
Try
  ' Code that may fail goes here
Catch ex As SomeExceptionType
  ' Handle SomeExceptionType
Catch ex2 As SomeOtherExceptionType
  ' Handle SomeOtherExceptionType
Catch
  ' Handle any exception that gets here
Finally
  ' Code that's always executed
End Try
```

A **Try** block is placed around code that may give rise to an exception, and one or more **Catch** clauses are declared to handle exceptions. You can't have a **Try** without at least one **Catch** clause, and you can't have **Catch** clauses outside a **Try** block.

Exceptions are tagged with an exception object, and **Catch** clauses can be constructed to catch a particular class of exception, as in:

```
Catch ex As SomeExceptionType
```

All exception objects must be from classes that inherit from **System.Exception**. Once you've caught an exception, you can use its members to find out about the exception. The **StackTrace** property returns the stack trace (which tells you where the exception occurred) as a string; the **Message** property retrieves the message associated with the exception; the **Source** property returns a string indicating the name of the application or object that generated this exception; and **TargetSite** is a property that tells you which method threw the exception:

```
Try
  f.bar()
Catch ae As NullReferenceException
  Console.WriteLine("Exception stack trace was: {0}", ae.StackTrace);
  Console.WriteLine("Message was: {0}", ae.Message);
  Console.WriteLine("Source was: {0}", ae.Source);
  Console.WriteLine("TargetSite was: {0}", ae.TargetSite);
End Try
```

Because of the way that inheritance works, you can use **Exception** to catch any exception type, as it's the base class for all exceptions. If you use multiple **Catch** clauses, you need to be careful that one **Catch** does not hide another:

```
Try
  ' Code that may fail goes here
Catch ex As Exception
  ' Handle all exceptions...
Catch ex2 As SomeOtherExceptionType
  ' Nothing gets through to here...
End Try
```

Because all exceptions are **Exception** objects, all exception objects will be caught by the first clause and nothing will get through to the second. The C# compiler will warn you if you try to do this, but VB won't.

It is also quite possible to nest **Try/Catch** blocks inside one another, provided that you nest a complete **Try/End Try** construct, although this isn't done very often in practice because it can lead to code that is hard to read.

How Do I Generate Exceptions?

All .NET languages use the **Throw** statement to generate exceptions. The following VB code fragment shows a typical use of **Throw**; the same basic mechanism is used in C# and C++:

```
Public Sub someMethod(ByRef o As Object) {
  ' test for null reference
  If o = Nothing Then
    Throw New ArgumentException()
  End If
End Sub
```

The argument to the **Throw** statement must be a reference to an object whose class derives from **System.Exception**. This may be one of the standard system exception classes, as in this code, or one that you have derived yourself. Exception objects can take parameters to their constructors, which allows data to be passed to the exception handler.

It is valid to rethrow an exception from within a **Catch** clause, in which case it will be caught by an enclosing exception (if any) or passed up the call chain for handling at a higher level:

```
Try
  someFunc(obj)
Catch e As ArgumentException
  Console.WriteLine("Caught exception: {0}", e)
  throw
End Try
```

You can also throw a completely different exception type from within a **Catch** block if you need to.

How Do I Get a Type Object Representing a Type?

Instances of the **System.Type** class are used to represent types. When a **Type** object is created, the class code is queried by reflection, and the metadata is used to build a **Type** object that completely describes the makeup of the type, including all its fields, properties, and methods.

You can use the **Type** class to do some interesting and powerful things, but most often you'll be required to provide a **Type** object as a parameter to a function call. For example, the **System.Array** class lets you create arrays to hold objects of a given type, and it needs you to provide a **Type** object that describes what you want to hold in the array. In VB, you use the **GetType** operator to do this, as shown here:

```
Dim arr As Array = Array.CreateInstance(GetType(Integer), 10)
```

In this example, an array of integers is created with a length of 10 elements by specifying the type of the **Integer** class.

In C#, you use the **typeof** operator to get the same information:

```
Type t = typeof(Integer)
```


How Can I Find Out about a Type?

Once you have a **Type** object representing the type you want to investigate, you can use the methods of **Type** to retrieve the information you require:

```
' Get a Type object for a class
Dim t1 As Type = GetType(Test)

' Get the name
Console.WriteLine("Name of type is: {0}", t1.Name)
Console.WriteLine("Module is: {0}", t1.Module)

' Find out a few things...
Console.WriteLine("Is it a class: {0}", t1.IsClass)
Console.WriteLine("Is it a value type: {0}", t1.IsValueType)
```

For this **Test** class, the program displayed the following output:

```
Name of type is: Module1$Test
Module is: VBReflect.exe

Is it a class: True
Is it a value type: False
```

The first line shows that the **Test** class is part of the **Module1** module, and the second line tells you that the module lives in VBReflect.exe. **Type** contains over 30 query properties, some of which are quite esoteric. Table 2.6 lists a few of the most generally useful query properties.

In order to go get more information about a type, you have to use the **System.Reflection** namespace, as this defines many of the structures you'll need if you want to look at the methods, properties, and fields that make up a class.

Table 2.6 Query properties belonging to the System.Type class.

Query Property	Description
IsAbstract	Returns true if the type is abstract
IsArray	Returns true if the type is an array
IsClass	Returns true if the type is a class
IsInterface	Returns true if the type is an interface
IsPublic / IsNotPublic	Tells you whether the type is declared as public
IsSealed	Returns true if the type is sealed
IsSerializable	Returns true if the type is serializable
IsValueType	Returns true if the type is a value type

You can use the **System.Reflection** namespace in two ways. The first way is to fully qualify the names of all the classes you want to use from the namespace, as shown here:

```
Dim mi() As System.Reflection.MethodInfo
```

Although it is quite possible to work with fully qualified names, it gets a little tiring having to type them out. In addition, as you delve deeper into .NET, you will find that some of the namespace names get very long indeed, so this method is not very practical.

The second way to use **System.Reflection** namespace is to use an **Imports** statement in VB (or **using** in C#, or **#using** in C++). This tells the compiler that it can try to resolve type names by looking in the namespaces that you specify using the **Imports** statement, so that you no longer have to type fully qualified names:

```
Imports System.Reflection
...
dim mi() as MethodInfo
```

After you have done this, you are in a position to list the methods a class supports:

```
' Get a Type object for a class
Dim t1 As Type = GetType(Test)

' Get the MethodInfo objects
Dim mi() As MethodInfo = t1.GetMethods
Dim m As MethodInfo

For Each m In mi
  Console.WriteLine("Method: {0}", m)
Next
```

You first create an array of **MethodInfo** objects, and then call the **GetMethods** member of Type in order to fill it. Once you've done this, you can iterate over the array and print out the details of each method. The implementation of **ToString()** in **MethodInfo** returns the entire method signature; when you run the code, you get the following output:


```
Method: Int32 GetHashCode()
Method: Boolean Equals(System.Object)
Method: System.String ToString()
Method: Void Foo()
Method: System.Type GetType()
```

The listing contains all the methods exposed by the class, including those it has inherited from **Object**. You can extend this by adding information on whether the method is public and whether it is virtual:

```
For Each m In mi
  Console.WriteLine("Method: {0}, public: {1}, virtual: {2}", _
     m, m.IsPublic, m.IsVirtual)
Next
```

The amended output is as follows:

```
Method: Int32 GetHashCode(), public: True, virtual: True
Method: Boolean Equals(System.Object) , public: True, virtual: True
Method: System.String ToString(), public: True, virtual: True
Method: Void Foo(), public: True, virtual: False
Method: System.Type GetType(), public: True, virtual: False
```

Similar mechanisms let you find out about the fields and properties and about the parameters belonging to the methods.

How Can I Create Objects Dynamically?

Creating objects dynamically means deciding at runtime which class you want to instantiate. However, you may not have any idea until runtime which class you're going to use. For example, it may be that you need to load some sort of driver because a user has installed a new driver and has provided you with its class name. Dynamic creation lets you create and use objects even if all you have to go on is a string holding the class name.

If the class you want to use isn't already loaded, you need to load the assembly. This can easily be done using the **Load** method of the **Assembly** class. After the assembly is loaded, you can then use the **GetType()** method of the **Assembly** class to get an appropriate **Type** object representing the class you want to use. Here's an example:

```
' Load the assembly called MyAssembly
Dim ass As Assembly = Assembly.Load("MyAssembly")

' Get a Type object for the type we want to use
Dim tp As Type = ass.GetType("MyClass")
```

When you have the Type object representing the class you want to use, you can dynamically create an instance. You do this by using the **Activator** class, a member of **System.Reflection** that contains methods to create objects dynamically:

```
' Use the Activator to get an instance
Dim obj As Object = Activator.CreateInstance(tp)
```

Because **CreateInstance()** can be used with any type, it returns a plain **Object** reference.

The **InvokeMember()** function in the **Type** class lets you invoke a method by name on a dynamically created object; if you're at all familiar with COM and Automation, this is the equivalent of the **Invoke()** method on the IDispatch interface. In fact, **InvokeMember()** lets you do a good deal more, such as get and set property values as well, but let's stick to invoking a method to see how it's done. The function takes several parameters, as you can see from the following line of code:

```
tp.InvokeMember("Foo", _
     BindingFlags.Default Or BindingFlags.InvokeMethod _
     Nothing, obj, New Object(){})
```

The first parameter is the name of the function you want to execute, in this case "Foo". The second parameter tells **InvokeMember()** how you want it to work. There is a large **BindingFlags** enumeration that contains all the possible actions, and two have been chosen. The first, **BindingFlags.Default**, tells the function to use the language default rules for binding names, whereas the second tells it that you intend on invoking a method, as opposed to getting or setting a property. The third parameter is often **Nothing** (or **null** for C#) and can be used to specify an optional binder object that controls the name binding process. The fourth parameter provides a reference to the object on which the function is being invoked. The last parameter is an array containing references to any arguments needed by the function. In this case there aren't any, so an empty array is passed.

Chapter 3

The System Namespace

By Julian Templeman

In Depth

The **System** namespace is the most important namespace in the whole of .NET. It defines most of the basic entities supported by all the .NET languages plus a lot of commonly used functionality:

- Base classes for value and reference types
- Common basic types, such as integers, doubles, and Booleans
- Object and string classes
- Events and event handling
- Interfaces
- Attributes
- Exceptions
- Math functions

Basic Types

The **System** namespace contains definitions of the basic value types that are supported by a wide variety of .NET languages as shown in Table 3.1.

For ease of use, these types are mapped onto native types in each language, so that an **int** in C# is a synonym for a **System.Int32**. There's no reason why you shouldn't use the underlying **System** types rather than the language-specific mappings if you so desire.

All these derive from **System.ValueType**, and although you are free to derive your own types from **ValueType**, you can't derive types from the basic types themselves.

Basic Types and the CLS

The Common Language Specification (CLS) defines a range of types and language features (such as exception handling) that must be supported by a language if it is to work within the .NET world. As such, the CLS concerns compiler writers far more than it does developers, but there's one detail that needs to be noted about it.

Some of the types in Table 3.1—specifically the unsigned integer types—aren't CLS compliant. As a result, you won't be able to use them from every .NET language because languages aren't forced to support them. In particular, unsigned

Table 3.1 The .NET basic data types.

Structure	CLS Compliant?	Description
Boolean	Y	Can take the values **true** or **false**
Byte	Y	Represents an 8-bit unsigned integer
Char	Y	Represents a 16-bit Unicode character
Decimal	Y	Represents a decimal value with 28 significant digits
Double	Y	Represents an IEEE754 64-bit double-precision floating-point value. The range of values held in a **Double** is approximately +/- 1.8e308
Int16	Y	Represents a 16-bit signed integer
Int32	Y	Represents a 32-bit signed integer
Int64	Y	Represents a 64-bit signed integer
Single	Y	Represents an IEEE754 32-bit single-precision floating-point value. The range of values held in a **Single** is approximately +/- 3.4e38
UInt16	N	Represents an unsigned 16-bit integer
UInt32	N	Represents an unsigned 32-bit integer
UInt64	N	Represents an unsigned 64-bit integer
DateTime	N	Represents a date and time since 12:00 A.M. on January 1 A.D. 1
SByte	N	Signed 8-bit integer

integer types aren't supported by Visual Basic (I have no idea why; it is a decision that hasn't been popular with many VB programmers), so you may need to be careful if you want to use these types in components written in other .NET languages that may end up being used with VB.

Floating-Point Types

Doubles work to the IEEE 754 standard, which means that every floating-point operation has a defined result. One outcome of this is that you'll never get a floating-point divide by zero exception because the result of dividing by zero is defined as infinity. Floating-point classes have values to represent positive and negative infinity and Not-A-Number as well as methods to test for them. Here's an example using VB:

```
Dim d1,d2,d3 As Double

d1 = 1
d2 = 0
d3 = d1 / d2    ' divide by zero
```

```
If d3 = Double.PositiveInfinity Then
  Console.WriteLine("Division returned positive infinity")
ElseIf d3 = Double.NegativeInfinity Then
  Console.WriteLine("Division returned negative infinity")
ElseIf d3 = Double.NaN Then
  Console.WriteLine("Division returned not-a-number")
Else
  Console.WriteLine("Division returned something else!")
End If
```


Conversions

All the basic type classes support a **ToString()** method, and the **Convert** class is provided for general conversions between the built-in types. To give you an idea of the conversions that are available, Table 3.2 contains some of the conversions available from **Convert**.

Because all classes implement conversions and all the conversion methods return references to new objects, you can chain them together like this:

```
Dim p1 as System.Int32
p1 = 0
Dim s as String
s = Convert ToString(Convert.ToBoolean(p1))
Console.WriteLine("s is {0}", s)
```

The call to **ToBoolean()** converts the Int32 to a Boolean; I then call **ToString()** on the Boolean to convert it to a string. The result of this is that *s* holds the value **False**.

Table 3.2 A selection of the conversion methods provided by the Convert class.

Method	Description
ToBoolean(Short)	Converts a **Short** to a **Boolean**. Returns **True** if the value is non-zero, and **False** if it is zero.
ToBoolean(String)	Converts a **String** to a **Boolean**. Returns **True** if the **String** contains the text "True", otherwise it returns False.
ToDouble(Boolean)	Returns 1 if the value is True, and 0 if it is **False**.
ToDouble(String)	Returns a **Double** representing the **String**.
ToInt64(Int32)	Converts a 32-bit integer into a 64-bit integer.
ToDateTime(Long)	Tries to convert the **Long** into a **DateTime** object. Because **DateTime** holds its value as a large integer, this may be possible.
ToDateTime(String)	Tries to convert the **String** into a **DateTime** object.

Interfaces

If you examine the definitions of the basic value types, you'll find that they often implement one or more of a group of three interfaces: IComparable, IConvertible, and IFormattable. For example, the definition of the **Double** type is as follows:

```
Public Structure Double
  Implements IComparable, IFormattable, IConvertible
```

Interfaces (discussed in more detail in Chapter 4) are used to define behavior that can be implemented by a number of classes regardless of whether they are related by inheritance or not.

IComparable defines a single comparison function, **CompareTo()**. A class that implements this interface will provide an implementation of **CompareTo()** so that

```
myObject.CompareTo(someOtherObject)
```

returns zero if they are the same, less than zero if **myObject** is "less" than **someOtherObject** (in some class-dependent way), and greater than zero if **myObject** is "greater" than **someOtherObject**. Use of an interface in this way means that if a class implements IComparable, it is possible to sort a collection of those objects using **CompareTo()** without knowing anything else about the class.

IConvertible defines a number of conversion methods that classes can implement. Some of the conversions that **Convert** supports were shown previously: All of them—**ToString()**, **ToInt64()**, and so on—are in fact part of IConvertible. Once again, if a class supports IConvertible, client code knows which conversions it can apply. What if a class doesn't support a particular conversion, such as trying to convert a **Boolean** to a **DateTime**?

The **Convert** class implements every possible conversion between built-in types, but throws an **InvalidCastException** for those that make no sense. Some of the methods defined by IConvertible take an IFormatProvider argument, which can be used to provide a custom formatting object.

IFormattable provides a single **ToString()** method that is used to provide a formatted representation of the value as a **String**. It is used where a type needs more control over formatting than the general **Object.ToString()** method would provide. In this case we don't really need one, but I've included it to show you how it works. In VB, the **IFormattable.ToString()** function has the following signature:

```
Function ToString(ByVal fmt as String, _
    ByVal fp as IFormatProvider) As String
```

The first argument specifies the format to use; if it is **null** (**Nothing** in VB), then the default format for the type will be used. The second argument—which can also be **null**—can be used to specify a reference to an object that implements IFormatProvider. What is this and why might you want to use it? If you're writing any numeric class, the format is going to depend on the localization settings of the machine on which the code runs. In the United Kingdom, I'd write "10.75", whereas in France, someone would use a comma for the decimal separator; I'd write "10,000", whereas the French would write "10.000". The **IFormatProvider** object lets you retrieve a **NumberFormatInfo** object, which describes numerical formatting information including data on decimal and thousand separators and currency symbol placement.

The Object Class

The **Object** class is at the root of the type hierarchy. As a result, all classes in .NET are derived from **Object**. This inheritance is implicit; there is no need to explicitly declare that a class has **Object** as its superclass.

The fact that all classes inherit directly or indirectly from **Object** has certain consequences. First, there is only one class hierarchy in .NET; this stands in contrast to languages such as C++, where you can have as many separate class hierarchies as you like. Second, because all classes derive from **Object**, all objects can be passed around using **Object** references, which makes it quite easy to write generic classes, such as containers that can hold any kind of object.

Third, **Object** provides a base set of useful methods that all .NET classes inherit, as summarized in the Table 3.3.

I'll look at each of these in a little more detail and show you when (and how) derived classes might want to override the basic implementations provided by **Object**.

Table 3.3 Methods of the Object class.

Object Method	Description
Equals()	Tests whether two objects are the same
Finalize()	Called before an object is garbage collected, so that it can free up resources
GetHashCode()	Returns a hash code used to represent the object in hashtables and other data structures
GetType()	Returns a **Type** object that describes the object's type
MemberwiseClone()	Creates a shallow copy of the object
ReferenceEquals()	Shared (static) function that compares two references and returns **True** if they both refer to the same object
ToString()	Returns a string representing the object

Object Equality

The **Equals()** method is provided so you can test objects for equality, but that isn't always as simple as it may sound.

You may be wondering whether there's a difference between the **Equals()** method and the = operator in VB, or the == operator in C# and C++. There certainly is, and it's one that you need to understand in order to prevent problems in your code. Here's a summary of the operators and methods we've got to play with:

- **Equals()** tests for equality of content between objects.
- **Is** in VB, and == in C#, test for equality of reference.
- In VB, = tests for equality of value types, which aren't accessed via references.

This is illustrated in the following code fragment, where I am comparing two objects of a mythical **Person** class, which has an **Equals()** method implemented:

```
Dim person1 As New Person("Fred")
Dim person2 As New Person("Fred")

If person1 Is person2 Then
  Console.WriteLine("person references are equal")
Else
  Console.WriteLine("person references are not equal")
End If

If person1.Equals(person2) Then
  Console.WriteLine("person objects are equal")
Else
Console.WriteLine("person objects are not equal")
End If
```

I am creating two **Person** objects that have the same content, namely the string "Fred". When I use the **Is** operator to compare the two objects, the references are compared; because these are two different objects, the references to them are obviously different, and consequently the test fails. When I use **Equals()**, on the other hand, the code compares the content of the two objects and finds them to be equal.

The meaning of *equality* depends on the types of objects you are considering. For value types it is usually pretty easy—two value objects are the same if they contain the same value. So two **Doubles** that contain the value 12.3 can be considered equal. But what about something like a **Bank Account** class? Can two **Account** objects ever be "equal" given that they have unique account numbers? It may be that you decide that two **Accounts** are equal if their balances are equal, but it is by no means the only solution. For reference types, you may need to be careful in defining exactly what equality means if you decide to override **Equals()**.

NOTE: *If you override* ***Equals()****, the compiler will warn you about not overriding* ***GetHashCode()****. This is because when storing objects in collections the* ***Equals()*** *and* ***GetHashCode()*** *methods get used together—if you override one then you'll need to override the other if you intend to use your class in a hash table or similar collection.*

What happens if you decide not to override the **Equals()** method? Then your class will inherit the default implementation from **Object**, which does exactly the same thing as the **Is** (or **==**) operator—it compares references.

The following list summarizes the rules for value types and reference types:

- You can use **Is** or **==** with reference types (i.e., classes) to test for equality of references.
- You cannot use the **Is** and **==** operators with value types. By definition, value types are not accessed through references, so it doesn't make sense to try to compare them.
- You can override **Equals()** for reference types, so that you can define your own comparisons for your own classes. If you don't override it, the default **Equals()** checks for reference equality.
- Value types use the inherited **Equals()**, which tests for content equality, and they cannot override it.

The **ReferenceEquals()** method is used to test whether two references refer to the same object. In VB, you'd tend to use the **Is** operator rather than calling this method directly.

Finalization

The **Finalize()** method is called when an object is about to be reclaimed by the garbage collector. Its job is to let you reclaim any resources that may have been requested by the object. Java programmers can note that .NET's **Finalize()** is very similar in function to Java's **Finalize()**. C++ programmers should note that **Finalize()** is not equivalent to a destructor, for reasons that will become apparent very shortly.

Finalize() is called when the garbage collector finally decides to end an object's life. But the problem is that you don't know when that will be, or even if it will happen at all. The idea behind garbage collection is that it allows the system to minimize memory usage by recycling unused objects. If the amount of memory being used by the application is small and there is no danger of running out of resources, then there is no need for the garbage collector to run. In addition, there is little point in reclaiming resources when a program ends because it will happen anyway. So unless you tell it otherwise, the garbage collector will not call **Finalize()** for any objects at the end of a program.

This means that finalization is nondeterministic, so you really shouldn't put any code into **Finalize()** that has to run at a particular point in the program, or that has to run at all. See also my discussion in the Immediate Solution, "How Do I Handle Cleanup in .NET Objects," in Chapter 2.

GetHashCode()

The **GetHashCode()** method is used to generate a hash code for value types and classes that need one. Without getting too technical, a hash code is an integer that can be used to identify an object. They are used when storing objects in data structures, such as hash tables.

It is obvious what the hash code ought to be for some classes: For all my bank accounts, the account number is a unique integer value, so that will do very nicely. For other classes it isn't as obvious: What should the hash code of a string be?

GetHashCode() provides a way for class implementers to generate a suitable hash code for their classes, and it must be overridden for value types.

GetType()

GetType() is used to return a **Type** object that describes the class this object belongs to. This method cannot be overridden, and it is difficult to see why there would ever be a need to do so. See the section "Reflection and the **Type** Class" in Chapter 2 for details of this class and what it is used for.

Cloning and Copying

MemberwiseClone() can be called to produce a shallow copy of the object. Shallow copying only looks at the top level of an object. If an object contains references to other objects, the references will be copied. The shallow copy process is shown in Figure 3.1.

Note that the **MemberwiseClone()** method is protected; it can only be called from within the derived class. This means that you cannot use the following code:

```
Dim obj As New SomeObject()
obj.MemberwiseClone()
```

Why not? It may not be appropriate for your objects to be copied in this way, but if it is, you can choose to expose the function through a public method:

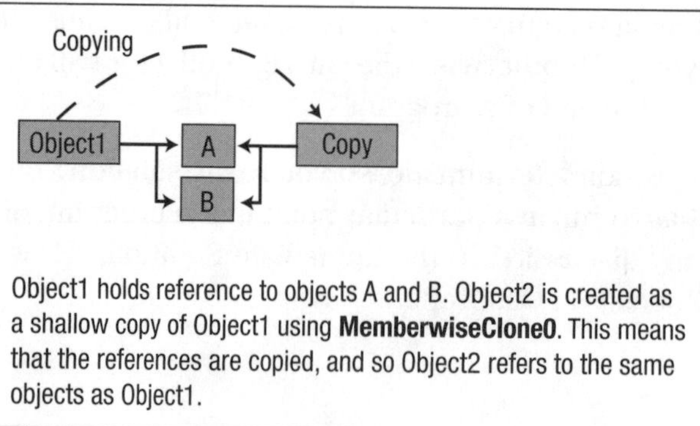

Copying
Object1
A
Copy
B
Object1 holds reference to objects A and B. Object2 is created as a shallow copy of Object1 using **MemberwiseClone0**. This means that the references are copied, and so Object2 refers to the same objects as Object1.

Figure 3.1 Shallow copying.


```
Public Function Copy() As Object
  Return MemberwiseClone()
End Function
```

Because the function is protected, you can choose whether to make it available for use or not.

What if you want to make a separate copy of the object and everything to which it refers, as shown in Figure 3.2? This is called a *deep copy*, and in order to instruct the Common Language Runtime (CLR) to use deep rather than shallow copying for a class, you have to implement the ICloneable interface. Details of how you do this in practice are given in the Immediate Solutions section in this chapter.

ToString()

By overriding **ToString()**, an object can return a string that represents it in some way. In the case of value types, it is normally pretty obvious what this method

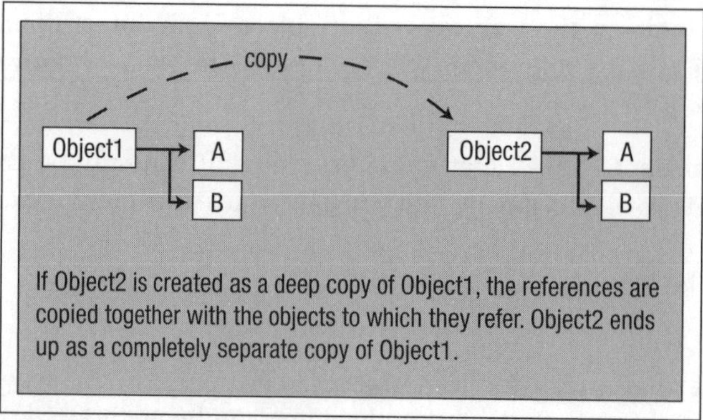

copy
Object1
A
B
Object2
A
B
If Object2 is created as a deep copy of Object1, the references are copied together with the objects to which they refer. Object2 ends up as a completely separate copy of Object1.

Figure 3.2 Deep copying.

should return: A **Double** returns a string containing the floating-point value it represents, a **Boolean** returns true or false, and so on.

Sometimes, it is not clear what reference types ought to return. What should an **Account** object or a **Car** object return? You'll find that in many cases overriding **ToString()** is essential in order to be able to use value types, but that its use with reference types may be mainly for diagnostic purposes.

Who uses **ToString()**? Although you can call **ToString()** on an object yourself, it will automatically be called in situations where you use an object where a **String** is wanted. For example, if you write:


```
Dim myObject As New SomeClass
...
Console.WriteLine(myObject)
```

WriteLine() doesn't know how to output **SomeClass** objects, so it checks to see whether the class implements **ToString()**. If it does, **WriteLine()** calls **ToString()** because it does know how to output a **String**. If the class doesn't implement **ToString()**, **WriteLine()** simply outputs the fully-qualified class name, which might look something like this:

```
TestProject.Module1$SomeClass
```

Which shows that **SomeClass** belongs to Module1 in the project called TestProject.

Arrays

Arrays in .NET are objects in their own right, objects that are responsible for holding a collection of other objects. This means that they have methods you can call and properties you can interact with, and as you would expect, they are mapped onto the native arrays supported by the .NET languages.

***NOTE**: For VB programmers, arrays are indexed from zero in .NET, which means you may have problems if you have relied in the past on using **Option Base** to set the array index base to one. See the Immediate Solutions section for details on how to deal with this situation.*

The **System.Array** class provides methods for creating, searching, manipulating, and sorting arrays, and it serves as the base for all arrays in the .NET world. It supports multidimensional arrays, although the syntax for using them is not very tidy.

In practice, you'll tend to use the native array types provided by the language you are coding in, but you can use the **System.Array** class if you want to. There are some members of **System.Array** that are very useful, and that aren't provided by most language array implementations.

Note that arrays are not thread safe. The array class does contain two properties relating to thread safety, but they don't do anything. The first one, **IsSynchronized()**, returns a Boolean value indicating whether access to the array is synchronized or not. By default, this simply returns False, although the method could be overridden by a derived class. The second property, **SyncRoot**, returns a reference to an object that can be used to synchronize access to an array.

If you want to implement thread-safe arrays, you can derive your own class from **System.Array** and override these properties.

Other Types

In this section, I'll discuss a few other useful utility classes that are defined within the **System** namespace.

String

System.String is used to represent character strings and is one of only two reference types that is provided for you along with the value types, the other being **Object**.

One thing you may find strange—but will be quite familiar if you've used Java—is that once you've stored something in a **String**, you can't change it. You can perform operations that retrieve a copy of part or all of the **String**, but you cannot change the underlying data. If you want to edit character strings, you need to use the **StringBuilder** class, which is discussed in Chapter 12.

You'll find some methods in the **String** class that appear to change the **String** object, but they always create a new object that contains the modified text.

DateTime and TimeSpan

DateTime is a value type that is used to store, examine, and manipulate dates and times. It stores its value in a property named **Ticks**, which holds the number of 100-nanosecond intervals since 12:00 A.M. on January 1, A.D. 1. This class uses the Gregorian calendar for interpreting and manipulating dates. See the discussion of the **Calendar** class in Chapter 12 for more details on how to create and manipulate calendars.

The **DateTime** class has a wide range of methods for manipulating, examining, and formatting dates and times. Details for using many of these methods are provided in the Immediate Solutions section.

The **TimeSpan** class is used to represent a period in time and can represent any number of days, hours, minutes, and seconds. The result of subtracting two **DateTime** objects is a **TimeSpan**; you can add a **TimeSpan** onto a **DateTime** to get a new **DateTime**.

TimeZone

The **TimeZone** class represents a time zone and can be used to query the time zone currently being used by the system.

The following sample code shows how **TimeZone** can be used; it demonstrates the main functions and properties of the class:

```
' Get the current time zone
Dim tz As TimeZone = TimeZone.CurrentTimeZone

Console.WriteLine("Timezone name is {0}", tz.StandardName)
Console.WriteLine("Daylight savings name is {0}", tz.DaylightName)
Console.WriteLine("Today is in daylight saving time: {0}",
tz.IsDaylightSavingTime(DateTime.Now))
```

Decimal

The **Decimal** class is useful in financial calculations because it can represent numbers to a high degree of accuracy (28 significant digits) and with no rounding errors. They are stored as 96-bit signed integers scaled by a variable power of 10. This power specifies the number of digits to the right of the decimal point and ranges from 0 to 28.

Decimal has a set of arithmetic and logical operators, and also a range of methods to let you perform arithmetic, such as **Add()**, **Subtract()**, **Multiply()** and **Divide()**, **Mod()**, **Floor()**, and **Round()**. It is recommended that **Decimal** be used to replace the older VB **Currency** type.

Enums

An *enum* is an enumerated type—a collection of related constants bound together as a type. A good example of an enumerated type would be the days of the week, which can take the values "Sunday" through "Monday", or the number of days in each month.

The System namespace contains the **System.Enum** value type, which is used as the basis for enumerations in higher-level languages and is seldom if ever used by application programmers.

The following is a simple example in VB:

```
Enum ErrorCodes
  BadFileName = 100
  NoPermission
  FileIsReadOnly
  SecurityError = 200
End Enum
```


An enum consists of one or more named members, each of which can optionally be assigned a numerical value. If you don't assign a value, the first one defaults to zero, and each succeeding member is incremented by one. You can mix assigned and unassigned members, as shown in the preceding example.

This enum can now be used to declare variables and be passed to and returned from functions.

Exceptions

The mechanics of exceptions and the way you use them was discussed in the "Exceptions" section in Chapter 2. You might want to refer to that section before reading on.

System.Exception is the base class for all exceptions. An object cannot be thrown or caught unless it inherits from **Exception**. The following listing shows all the exception classes that were documented in beta 2; you can see that there is a hierarchy of exception classes:

```
Exception
    ApplicationException
    SystemException
        MemberAccessException
            FieldAccessException
            MethodAccessException
            MissingMemberException
                MissingFieldException
                MissingMethodException
        AppDomainUnloadedException
        ArgumentException
            ArgumentNullException
            ArgumentOutOfRangeException
            DuplicateWaitObjectException
        ArithmeticException
            DivideByZeroException
            NotFiniteNumberException
            OverflowException
```

```
        ArrayTypeMismatchException
        BadImageFormatException
        CannotUnloadAppDomainException
        ContextMarshalException
        CoreException
            IndexOutOfRangeException
            NullReferenceException
            ExecutionEngineException
            StackOverflowException
        ExecutionEngineException
        FormatException
        IndexOutOfRangeException
        InvalidCastException
        InvalidOperationException
            ObjectDisposeException
        InvalidProgramException
        MulticastNotSupportedException
        NotImplementedException
        NotSupportedException
            PlatformNotSupportedException
        NullReferenceException
        OutOfMemoryException
        RankException
        ServicedComponentException
        TypeInitializationException
        StackOverflowException
        TypedInitializationException
        TypeLoadException
            DllNotFoundException
            EntryPointNotFoundException
        TypeUnloadedException
        UnauthorizedAccessException
        WeakReferenceException
    URIFormatException
```

System.Exception forms the base class for everything that can be thrown and caught. Under this parent class, there are two other main base classes from which all others are derived: **ApplicationException** and **SystemException**. Of these, the **ApplicationException** class can be used as a base for application-specific exceptions, whereas the **SystemException** class forms the base for exceptions that are thrown by the runtime.

Arranging exceptions in a hierarchy has advantages when using an object-oriented (OO) language because of the way that class hierarchies work. Because by inheritance an **OverflowException** is an **ArithmeticException**, an **ArithmeticException** is a **SystemException**, and a **SystemException** is an **Exception**, you can catch whole groups of exceptions by choosing the appropriate base class to use in your **Catch** clause. For example, the following VB code would catch all **ArithmeticExceptions** that arise:

```
Catch e as ArithmeticException
```

One useful facility offered by the **Exception** class is the ability to use one exception to wrap another. This is useful in situations that could give rise to a large number of different exceptions, but where you don't want to burden the client programmer with having to catch numerous different types. An example might be database access, where you could get exceptions due to security problems, network problems, errors in SQL, and any number of other reasons. In order to simplify things, the database code could catch all exceptions internally, wrap them in a (mythical) **DatabaseException** object, and rethrow them. The client programmer then only has to catch **DatabaseExceptions** and can if necessary use the **InnerException** property to see details of the original error.

The Console Class

The **Console** class has been used since the beginning of Chapter 1, so now would be a good time to examine it in more detail.

The **System.Console** class provides access to the standard input, standard output, and standard error streams. Standard input represents the stream from which input normally arrives; for a console application, this is the keyboard. Standard output represents the stream where output is normally sent, and for a console application, this is the console window. Standard error is a stream to which error messages can be written, and this defaults to the console window. Two separate output streams are provided because it is possible to redirect standard output to a file or another device, and you will probably want to see your error messages displayed on the screen rather than being sent along with your other output.

In this section, only console I/O is considered. The topic of I/O in general is covered more fully in Chapter 6.

One thing that sometimes puzzles people new to .NET is that it is possible to use the **Console** class in two ways, as shown in the following code:

```
Console.Writeline ("this is the first way")
Console.Out.Writeline ("this is the second way")
```

Out is a TextWriter, a shared member of the **Console** class, which writes to standard output, and the **Writeline** method belongs to **Out**. The **Console** class provides a shortcut by implementing **Writeline** as a shared method that delegates to the **Out** object, and thus saves you four characters every time you use an output statement. A similar shortcut is provided for **Console.In**, but if you want to write to standard error, you have to use the full form.

In comparison with some languages (such as Java), console I/O is very simple and there are few methods to master. The **Writeline()** and **Write()** methods output text with and without a trailing new line respectively; **Read()** gets the next character from the input stream, and **Readline()** obtains a complete line of text. Although it hasn't yet been used in this book, it is possible to produce formatted output; this topic is covered in the Immediate Solutions section at the end of this chapter.

The Math Class

The **System.Math** class is basically a placeholder for a number of constants and methods that are mathematical in nature and don't belong anywhere else.

The class includes definitions for Pi and E, as you would expect, and includes a number of methods that implement common math functions. These are implemented as static (or in VB terminology *shared*) members of the **Math** class because they don't belong to any one object. Remember that in .NET, every function has to be a part of a class. Table 3.4 shows some commonly used methods of the **Math** class.

Table 3.4 Commonly used methods of the Math class.

Method	Description
Abs()	Returns the absolute value of a number
Sin(), **Cos()**, **Tan()**	Standard trigonometric functions
Max(), **Min()**	Returns the maximum or minimum of two numbers
ACos(), **ASin()**, **ATan()**, **ATan2()**	Standard trigonometric arc functions
Ceil(), **Floor()**	Rounds up or down to the nearest integer
Cosh(), **Sinh()**, **Tanh()**	Standard trigonometric hyperbolic functions
Exp()	Returns e to the specified power
Log(), **Log10()**	Returns the natural and base-10 logarithm
Pow()	Raises a number to a specified power
Rint()	Returns the integer nearest to a given number
Round()	Returns the floating-point whole number nearest to a given number
Sign()	Returns the sign of a number
IEEERemainder()	Returns the remainder of x/y as defined by the IEEE 754 rules

This is a good place to introduce a couple of other math-related classes. First is the **Random** class, which as you would expect implements a random number generator. In fact, **Random** implements a pseudorandom number generator rather than generating truly random values. This means that the algorithm starts from an integer "seed" value and produces a new random value each time you ask it to. The "pseudo" comes from the fact that if the same seed is used, you'll get exactly the same set of random numbers produced. If this was a true random number generator, you would expect to get a completely random value each time, but it is very hard to write true random number generators, so you'll usually find the pseudo version implemented in software.

The Type Class

Instances of the **Type** class are used to hold the information that fully describes a type. This class and its uses are described more fully in Chapter 2 under "Reflection and the **Type** Class."

Miscellaneous Classes

The **OperatingSystem** class represents an operating system version. However, this isn't as useful as it might be because it doesn't tell you what system your code is running on; it only lets you construct an **OperatingSystem** object to represent a system version.

Immediate Solutions

How Do I Access Classes Defined in the **System** Namespace?

All the classes making up the **System** namespace and its subspaces are provided in a .NET assembly called mscorlib.dll. So, in order to use any of the **System** classes in code, you have to make sure that the **System** namespace has been imported into your code. How you do that depends on the language you're using.

In Visual Basic.NET you use the **Imports** statement to import names from a namespace, so that they're recognized by the compiler:

```
Imports System
```

The **Imports System** statement makes all type names defined in the namespace **System** available to the compiler. You'll have to do this if you are creating a VB project from scratch and building it from the command line. However, you won't need to do this if you are building a project using Visual Studio .NET because VB projects are automatically set up to import a number of common namespaces, including **System** and **System.Collections**.

As you might expect, **Imports** statements (of which there can be any number in a module) must occur before references to anything defined in the namespace.

In C#, you need to use the **using** keyword to import names from a namespace. The namespace name is given as an unquoted string, as shown here:

```
using System;
```

Managed C++ is rather different because instead of referring to the namespace, you have to refer to the assembly in which it is held. The **#using** directive is an extension provided with Managed C++ that directs the compiler to search a given assembly file for references. In normal C++ fashion, the file name is given in angle brackets if it is a **System** namespace:

```
#using <mscorlib.dll>;
using namespace System;
```

C++ namespaces are used to map onto .NET namespaces, so you need to use a standard C++ **using** directive to introduce the **System** namespace.

What's the Relationship between Language Types and Those Defined in **System**?

The **System** namespace defines a range of standard types, and these are mapped onto native types in .NET languages for convenience. For example, a **System.Double** is the same as a VB **Double** and a C# **double**, which makes it very easy to pass parameters between languages.

You can happily use the **System** type name in code, although it normally means more typing. Be aware that not all the .NET types are supported by all languages—only those that are defined in the CLS must be supported. The most noticeable consequence of this is that VB doesn't support unsigned types because unsigned integer types aren't part of the CLS.

How Do I Create a New Value Type?

Creating new value types isn't that difficult, although it can be a long-winded process if you want to implement a completely functional type. As an example, let's look at a simple value type implemented in VB, which formats negative numbers by placing parentheses around them the way you often see them in accounting and financial spreadsheets. It implements the three common interfaces: IComparable (so that you can easily write code to compare objects), IConvertible (to provide conversions between a **MyType** and other common value types), and IFormattable (so that it can be printed out in the correct format):

```
Public Structure MyType
  Implements IComparable, IConvertible, IFormattable

  Sub New(ByVal v As Double)
    d = v
  End Sub

  ' Here's the value contained in the type
  Dim d As Double
```

```
' IComparable implementation

Function CompareTo(ByVal o As Object) As Integer Implements _
          IComparable.CompareTo
  ' We're always greater than a null reference...
  If o Is Nothing Then
    Return +1
  End If

  ' Check we're not something we don't like...
  If TypeOf o Is MyType Then
    ' Create a temporary object
    Dim tmp As MyType
    tmp = o

    If d < tmp.d Then
      Return -1
    ElseIf d > tmp.d Then
      Return +1
    Else
      Return 0
    End If
  Else
    Throw New ArgumentException("Can't compare to this type!")
  End If
End Function

' IFormattable implementation

Overloads Function ToString(ByVal fmt As String, ByVal sop As _
          IFormatProvider) As String Implements IFormattable.ToString
  ' Format up negative numbers in parentheses, rather than
  'using a minus sign
  Dim tmp As Double
  tmp = Math.Abs(d)
  Dim s As String

  ' Turn the number into a string, and put parentheses round it if it is
  ' negative
  s = String.Concat(tmp.ToString(fmt, sop))
  If d < 0 Then
    s = String.Concat("(", s, ")")
  End If

  Return s
End Function
```

```
' IConvertible implementation
Function GetTypeCode() As TypeCode Implements IConvertible.GetTypeCode
  Return d.GetTypeCode()
End Function

Function ToBoolean(ByVal p As IFormatProvider) As Boolean _
          Implements IConvertible.ToBoolean
  Return Convert.ToBoolean(d, p)
End Function

Function ToByte(ByVal p As IFormatProvider) As Byte _
          Implements IConvertible.ToByte
  Return Convert.ToByte(d, p)
End Function

Function ToChar(ByVal p As IFormatProvider) As Char _
          Implements IConvertible.ToChar
  Return Convert.ToChar(d, p)
End Function

Function ToDateTime(ByVal p As IFormatProvider) As Date _
          Implements IConvertible.ToDateTime
  Return Convert.ToDateTime(d, p)
End Function

Function ToDecimal(ByVal p As IFormatProvider) As Decimal _
          Implements IConvertible.ToDecimal
  Return Convert.ToDecimal(d, p)
End Function

Function ToDouble(ByVal p As IFormatProvider) As Double _
          Implements IConvertible.ToDouble
  Return d
End Function

Function ToInt16(ByVal p As IFormatProvider) As Int16 _
          Implements IConvertible.ToInt16
  Return Convert.ToInt16(d, p)
End Function

Function ToInt32(ByVal p As IFormatProvider) As Int32 _
          Implements IConvertible.ToInt32
  Return Convert.ToInt32(d, p)
End Function

Function ToInt64(ByVal p As IFormatProvider) As Int64 _
          Implements IConvertible.ToInt64
```

```
    Return Convert.ToInt64(d, p)
  End Function

  ' SByte isn't supported by VB
  Function ToSByte(ByVal p As IFormatProvider) As SByte _
           Implements IConvertible.ToSByte
    Throw New InvalidCastException()
  End Function

  Function ToSingle(ByVal p As IFormatProvider) As Single _
           Implements IConvertible.ToSingle
    Return Convert.ToSingle(d, p)
  End Function

  Overloads Function ToString(ByVal p As IFormatProvider) As String _
           Implements IConvertible.ToString
    Return Convert.ToString(d, p)
  End Function

  ' Overload Object.ToString() as well…
  Overloads Function ToString() As String
    Return Convert.ToString(d)
  End Function

  Function ToType(ByVal convType As Type, ByVal p As IFormatProvider) _
           As Object Implements IConvertible.ToType
    Throw New InvalidCastException()
  End Function

  ' The unsigned types aren't supported by VB
  Function ToUInt16(ByVal p As IFormatProvider) As UInt16 _
           Implements IConvertible.ToUInt16
    Throw New InvalidCastException()
  End Function

  Function ToUInt32(ByVal p As IFormatProvider) As UInt32 _
           Implements IConvertible.ToUInt32
    Throw New InvalidCastException()
  End Function

  Function ToUInt64(ByVal p As IFormatProvider) As UInt64 _
           Implements IConvertible.ToUInt64
    Throw New InvalidCastException()
  End Function

End Structure
```

Let's look at some of the important parts of this code. Note that **MyType** is simply a wrapper around a **Double** value, which lets you use a lot of shortcuts in the implementation. The IConvertible interface requires that you implement no fewer than 17 methods, but because the value that is being converted is a double, you can make use of a lot of utility functions. The highlighted code for **GetTypeCode()** simply calls the appropriate member of the **Double** class to do the work, and most of the other functions call shared members of the **Convert** class to do the conversion. Note how the **SByte**, **UInt16**, **UInt32**, and **UInt64** types are handled: You have to implement the functions as part of the interface, but VB doesn't support these unsigned types, so you can arrange for the code to throw an **InvalidCastException** if they are ever called.

IComparable requires that you implement the **CompareTo()** method, which returns -1 if the value is less than that of the object passed as an argument, 0 if they have the same value, and +1 if the value is greater. There are a couple of things to remark on here, the first of which is the check for a **null** reference; if I get passed one of these, I return +1, because whatever my value, it is always greater than that of a **null** reference. Be careful when checking for the **null** reference, and make sure that you use "If o Is Nothing" rather than "If o = Nothing". If you use the latter, you'll get a recursive call to this function.

The second point to note is the way in which the code checks the type of the object it is being compared with. I have to do this because the argument only specifies a simple **Object** reference, and I'm not going to get very far comparing my object with (say) a **String**. I obviously could make the class more sophisticated by allowing comparison with **Doubles** as well, but I'm keeping it simple here.

In addition, IFormattable is used to format the object when a **String** representation is required. If you try printing out an object using **Console.WriteLine()** and that object isn't one of the classes **Console** knows about, the function needs to get a **String** representation of the object. It does this by checking whether your class implements IFormattable; if it does, it will call the **Format()** method to get the **String**. If it doesn't, you'll simply get the name of the class printed out, such as VBTest.Foo.

Once again, I can trade on the fact that my value is a **Double** object by calling the **Double** class's **ToString()** method to do all the hard work. All I have to do is to make sure that the value I pass to **Double.ToString()** is positive by using **Math.Abs()**. Once I've done that, if the value was negative, I'll use the **String.Concat()** method to add parentheses to the start and end of the string before returning it. Of course, if I wanted to, I could also look at the format string passed in, in order to support custom formats.

You can test the new type using test code like this:

```
Sub Main()
  ' Create a negative value
  Dim t As New MyType(-6.2)

  ' Printing it out causes Format() to be called
  Console.WriteLine("Value of t is {0}", t)

  ' Create a positive value
  Dim t1 As New MyType(5.5)

  ' Compare it to the last one... the answer should be 1, because 5.5 is
  ' definitely bigger than -6.2
  Dim n As Integer
  n = t1.CompareTo(t)

  ' Test against null references... once again, the answer should be 1
  n = t1.CompareTo(Nothing)
End Sub
```


How Do I Test Whether Two Objects Are the Same?

Determining whether two objects are the same depends on what is meant by "the same," and whether you're talking about value or reference objects.

Reference Types

Because reference types are accessed using references, there are two possible tests for equality:

- Are the two references the same? In other words, are they referring to the same object?
- Is the content of the two objects the same?

The first comparison is done using the = operator in VB—or the == operator in C# and C++—and it returns true if the two references are pointing at the same object.

The second comparison is done using the **Equals()** method, which all .NET classes inherit from **Object**. By default, this method does a reference comparison in the same way as =, and you should override it if you want to compare content.

The following code shows how you could implement **Equals()** in a mythical VB **Person** class, which has two **String** members **firstName** and **lastName**. Let's assume that two objects are equal if both first and last names are the same:

```
Public Overrides Function Equals(ByVal o As Object) As Boolean
  Dim b As Boolean

  If TypeOf o Is Person Then
    Dim tmp As Person
    tmp = o

    If (tmp.firstName.Equals(firstName) And _
            temp.lastName.Equals(lastName)) Then
      b = True
    Else
      b = False
    End If
  Else
    b = False
  End If

  Return b
End Function
```

The first thing to do is to check the type of object that is being compared. Because this function is inherited from **Object**, all that is passed in is a generic **Object** reference, which could point at anything. If the **TypeOf** operator indicates that it's not dealing with another **Person**, the code returns false because the object can't be equal to anything other than another **Person** object.

If you are dealing with another **Person**, the code checks the first and last names against those of the passed in object, and returns true if they both match.

Value Types

Value types are different because they are not accessed through references. In this case, the **Equals()** method tests for equality of value, and you can't use the **==** operator. In addition, you can't override **Equals()** for value types because it is fixed to check for value equality.

How Do I Implement Shallow and Deep Copying for a Class?

First, a brief recap: The **Object** class defines a **MemberwiseClone()** method that makes a shallow copy of an object. A shallow copy only looks at the top-level members of an object and copies them. This means that if an object contains references, then those references will get copied, and the original and copied objects will end up referring to the same data. In many—or even most—cases, this isn't what you want.

Here's an example of shallow copying in action. I'll start by defining a basic **Person** class, simply to use as data in what follows:

```
Public Class Person
  Private personName As String

  Property Name() As String
    Get
      Name = personName
    End Get
    Set
      personName = Value
    End Set
  End Property
End Class
```

Now I have **Person** objects that I can use as data and whose state I can modify. Let's use them in a class:

```
Public Class ShallowObject
  Public p As New Person()
End Class
```

The **ShallowObject** class simply has a reference to a **Person** object as a member, and (although it isn't recommended OO practice) I've declared it as **Public** to make the code more compact. If I want to allow shallow copying of objects of this class, I need to implement some sort of copying function that uses **MemberwiseClone()**:

```
Public Class ShallowObject
  Public p As New Person()

  Public Function Copy() As ShallowObject
    Return CType(MemberwiseClone(), ShallowObject)
  End Function
End Class
```

Note that because **MemberwiseClone()** returns an **Object** reference, I have to use **CType** to cast it to the right type before returning it. Now that I've added that function, I can demonstrate how shallow copying works:

```
' Create a new object and set its name to Fred
Dim object1 As New ShallowObject()
object1.p.Name = "Fred"

' Create a second reference and make it point to a copy of
' the first object
Dim object2 As ShallowObject
object2 = object1.Copy

Console.WriteLine("object2 name is {0}", object2.p.Name)
' Change the name in object1
object1.p.Name = "Bill"
Console.WriteLine("object2 name is now {0}", object2.p.Name)
```


If you run the preceding code, you'll get the following output:

```
object2 name is Fred
object2 name is now Bill
```

This shows that the **Person** reference in **object1** has been copied into **object2**. When I change the content of **object1** the change is immediately reflected in **object2**.

If I want to create **object2** as an independent copy of **object1**, I have to implement deep copying, which means making copies of all the objects to which my object holds a reference. Obviously, .NET cannot know what the structure of your objects is, so you have to do it all manually by implementing the ICloneable interface.

You do this by implementing the **Clone()** function, which copies the object and returns a reference to it. Obviously, just what copying your object entails will depend on your class; here's an example that copies an object containing a single string:

```
Module Module1
  Public Class Foo
    Implements ICloneable

    Private s As String

    Public Sub New()
      s = New String("hello")
    End Sub
```

```
    Public Function Clone() As Object Implements ICloneable.Clone
      Dim copy As New Foo()
      copy.s = New String(s)

      Return copy
    End Function
  End Class

  Sub Main()
    Dim obj1 As New Foo()

    Dim obj2 As Foo = CType(obj1.Clone, Foo)
  End Sub
End Module
```

You can see how **Clone()** is implemented: It makes a new **Foo** object, and then creates a new string as a copy of the existing one. In this way the two **Foo** objects have completely different string members, rather than sharing a reference.

How Do I Implement **ToString()** for a Class?

Here's an example of implementing **ToString()** for a class in VB, showing how a simple class can override **ToString()** to return a representation of its state:

```
Public Class Person
  Private firstName As String
  Private lastName As String

  Public Sub New(ByVal fn As String, ByVal ln As String)
    firstName = fn
    lastName = ln
  End Sub

  Public Overrides Function ToString() As String
    Return String.Concat(firstName, " ", lastName)
  End Function
End Class

Sub Main()
  Dim p As New Person("Bill", "Gates")

  Console.WriteLine("Person is {0}", p)
End Sub
```

The class contains two private strings holding the first and last names of the person. **ToString()** uses the **Concat()** shared function from the **String** class to build three **Strings** into a single output string. Note how I've had to use the **Overrides** keyword to show the compiler that this is an override for the inherited **ToString()** method.

Here's the same example in C#:


```
namespace CSToString
{
  using System;

  public class Class1
  {
    public static int Main(string[] args)
    {
      Person p = new Person("Scott", "McNeally");
      Console.WriteLine("p is {0}", p);

      return 0;
    }
  }

  public class Person
  {
    private String firstName;
    private String lastName;

    public Person(String fn, String ln)
    {
      firstName = fn; lastName = ln;
    }

    public override String ToString()
    {
      return firstName + " " + lastName;
    }
  }
}
```

If your class is part of a hierarchy, you may want to call the superclass **ToString()** method as part of your own **ToString()** implementation. In this way, you can build a string that completely describes your object. As an example, suppose you have a hierarchy of classes that deals with classification of biological organisms.

This classification occurs on five levels: From the top down, you have the kingdom (such as Animalia for animals and Plantae for plants), the phylum (Chordata for animals with backbones, Annelida for worms), the class (Mammalia for mammals), the genus or family (Canis for dogs, Felis for cats), and finally the species (such as Familiaris for domestic dogs). The last two classifications are used together when referring to species, so the full classification for a domestic dog is Canis Familiaris of the class Mammalia of the phylum Chordata of the kingdom Animalia.

You could model this structure using a hierarchy of classes; in order to print out a full classification, you can get each class to call the **ToString()** method of its superclass, like this:


```
Public Class Familiaris
  Inherits Canis
...

  Public Overrides Function ToString() As String
    Return String.Concat(MyBase.ToString(), ", Species: Familiaris")
  End Function
End Class
```

When this class is required to render itself as a string, it calls the superclass **ToString()** using the **MyBase** keyword, and uses the string it obtains to build its output. If each class does the same thing, you should end up with a full classification printed out as follows:

```
Kingdom: Animalia, Phylum: Chordata, Class: Mammalia,
         Family: Canis, Species: Familiaris
```

Dealing with Zero-Based Arrays in Visual Basic

In previous versions of VB, you could set the indexing of arrays to start from one rather than zero by using the **Option Base** statement. You could also set the upper and lower bound values explicitly when creating arrays.

In order to conform with the CLS, arrays in Visual Basic.NET are required to have a lower bound of zero. Any arrays that do not meet this requirement will give compilation errors, so preexisting code may need to be changed. The preferred course of action is to rewrite code so that it uses zero-based arrays, or to use the **System.Array** class, which lets you create and manipulate arrays with non-zero lower bounds.

How Do I Work with .NET Arrays?

The **System.Array** class forms the basis of all arrays in .NET languages. You will usually use the native array types provided by the high-level language you are programming in, but you can use the **System.Array** class itself if you wish. In this section, I'll show you the basics of representing arrays using **System.Array**.

Creating Arrays

Arrays are created using the **CreateInstance()** method, which takes type and dimension information:

```
' Create a 10 element array of integers
Dim arr1 As Array = Array.CreateInstance(GetType(Integer), 10)

' Create a 3D array of integers
Dim arr2 As Array = Array.CreateInstance(GetType(Integer), 2, 2, 2)
```

There is also an overload of **CreateInstance()** that takes lower bound information, if you want to create an array with non-zero lower bounds:

```
' Create a 2D array of integers with a non-zero lower bound
Dim arrDims() As Integer = { 2, 2 }
' Lower bounds are 2 and 3 respectively
Dim arrBnds() As Integer = { 2, 3 }

Dim arr2 As Array = Array.CreateInstance(GetType(Integer), arrDims, arrBnds)
```

As you can see, the overloaded function takes two arrays. The first specifies the lengths of each dimension (and implicitly defines the number of dimensions), whereas the second specifies the lower bounds for each dimension.

Finding Array Properties

Once you've created an array, the **Length** and **Rank** properties return the total number of elements and dimensions in the array, respectively.

```
Console.WriteLine("Ranks: arr1={0}, arr2={1}", arr1.Rank, arr2.Rank)
Console.WriteLine("Lengths: arr1={0}, arr2={1}", arr1.Length, arr2.Length)
```

For the arrays I've created, the result of executing this code is:

```
Ranks: arr1=1, arr2=3
Lengths: arr1=10, arr2=8
```

You can discover more information about the individual dimensions in an array using the **GetLength()**, **GetLowerBound()**, and **GetUpperBound()** functions:

```
For i = 0 To arr2.Rank-1
  Console.WriteLine("Size of dimension {0} is {1}, lb={2}, ub={3}" _
     i, arr2.GetLength(i), arr2.GetLowerBound(i), arr2.GetUpperBound(i))
Next
```

Each of these functions is passed the zero-based dimension index, and in this example, the values printed are as follows:

```
Size of dimension 0 is 2, lb=0, ub=1
Size of dimension 1 is 2, lb=0, ub=1
Size of dimension 2 is 2, lb=0, ub=1
```


The Boolean **IsReadOnly** property tells you whether an array is writeable or not, but it is always set to false. Derived array classes can override this property if they decide to implement read-only behavior.

Getting and Setting Values

You have to use the **GetValue()** and **SetValue()** functions in order to work with elements in arrays. **SetValue()** takes a reference to an object and the index or indices indicating the element to be set up. **GetValue()** takes an index or indices and returns an object reference. Because **GetValue()** returns a reference of type **Object**, you may have to cast this reference into the appropriate type before using it. Here's how you can set up and access the elements in a 2D array:

```
' Create a 2D array
Dim array2d As Array = Array.CreateInstance(GetType(Integer), 3, 3)

' Populate it
array2d.SetValue(10, 0, 0)
array2d.SetValue(11, 0, 1)
array2d.SetValue(12, 0, 2)
array2d.SetValue(100, 1, 0)
array2d.SetValue(110, 1, 1)
array2d.SetValue(120, 1, 2)
array2d.SetValue(200, 2, 0)
array2d.SetValue(210, 2, 1)
array2d.SetValue(220, 2, 2)

' Print out all the elements
For i = array2d.GetLowerBound(0) To array2d.GetUpperBound(0)
  For j = array2d.GetLowerBound(1) To array2d.GetUpperBound(1)
    Console.Write("{0} ", array2d.GetValue(i,j))
```

```
  Next
  Console.WriteLine()
Next
```

While I'm on the subject of printing out array elements, it is worth mentioning **GetEnumerator()** and the IEnumerator interface. This interface, discussed in more detail in Chapter 4, provides a way to iterate over all the elements in a collection using a simple set of methods that hide the way in which the collection actually stores its elements. I could use an enumerator to list the elements of an array like this:

```
' Import the Collections namespace, which is needed for enumerators
Imports System.Collections

' Create an enumerator
Dim en As IEnumerator = array2d.GetEnumerator

While en.MoveNext = True
  Console.WriteLine("{0} ", en.Current)
End While
```

IEnumerator only has three members; two of which are used in the preceding code. **MoveNext()** moves to the next element in the collection, returning false when it has moved past the end. It is initially positioned before the first element, so you need to call it once in order to move to the start. The **Current** property returns a reference to the current element in the collection, which is simply printed out. The **Reset()** method, not used here, can be used to reset the enumerator to its starting position.

Note that IEnumerator treats all collections as one-dimensional, so it isn't very useful with multidimensional arrays.

To round off this discussion of getting and setting values, the **Initialize()** method provides a way to initialize every element in an array by calling the default constructor for the element type. Be aware that this only works for arrays of value types, not for reference types.

NOTE: *C# programmers can only use this method for value types that have constructors, and value types that are native to C# do not have constructors.*

Array Operations

The **Array** class provides a number of methods for working with arrays. **Clear()** will empty the array, setting numeric values to zero and object references to **null** (or **Nothing** if you are programming in VB).

The **Copy()** method copies a section of one array into another array, performing any type casting as required. There are two overloads for this function, one of which uses the same starting index for both source and destination arrays, whereas the second lets you specify different indexes in the two arrays. This function can be useful because it also works with native language arrays as well as **System.Array** objects:

```
' Create a native integer array
Dim arrSrc() As Integer = { 10, 11, 12, 13, 14 }

' Create a System.Array and fill it
Dim arrDest As Array = Array.CreateInstance(GetType(Integer), 10)
For i = 0 To 9
  arrDest.SetValue(100 + i, i)
Next

' Copy part of the integer array over the System.Array
Array.Copy(arrSrc, 0, arrDest, 5, 3)
```


In this example, I've copied three elements from the source array, starting at element zero, into the destination array at position five. If I had copied arrays of different types where the conversion was safe—say integer to double—then the conversion would have been applied automatically.

The **CopyTo()** function performs the same function as **Copy()**, but it is an instance method where **Copy()** is shared. **Clone()** is an instance method that creates a shallow copy of an array. A shallow copy is one that only copies the top level of an object, so object references are duplicated.

Reverse(), as you might expect, reverses the order of all or part of a 1D array, whereas **Sort()** can perform a variety of sorting operations, again on 1D arrays. The simplest version of **Sort()** takes a reference to the array to be sorted, as shown here:

```
' Create a System.Array and fill it with random integers
Dim arrSrt As Array = Array.CreateInstance(GetType(Integer), 10)
Dim r As New Random(1000)

For i = 0 To 9
  arrSrt.SetValue(r.Next, i)
Next

' Create an enumerator
Dim en As IEnumerator = arrSrt.GetEnumerator
```

```
Console.WriteLine("Unsorted array:")
While en.MoveNext = True
  Console.WriteLine("{0} ", en.Current)
End While

' Sort the array and reset the enumerator
Array.Sort(arrSrt)
en.Reset
Console.WriteLine("Sorted array:")
While en.MoveNext = True
  Console.WriteLine("{0} ", en.Current)
End While
```

For this to work, the type being stored in the array must implement the IComparable interface. Other overloads of **Sort()** let you sort part of an array, sort a matching pair of key/value arrays, and let you specify an external "comparer" object that controls the sorting process.

IndexOf() and **LastIndexOf()** let you search an array for a particular value. As you might expect, they search for the first and last occurrences of a value, respectively. Overloads let you search the whole array, specify a starting index, or specify a range:

```
Dim ifind As Integer = 101
If Array.IndexOf(arrDest, ifind) = -1 Then
  Console.WriteLine("Value 101 doesn't occur in array")
Else
  Console.WriteLine("Value 101 occurs in array")
End If
```

You can see from the code that **IndexOf()** takes a reference to an object, but remember that you are dealing with value types, so the comparison is done on value. The test isn't whether object **ifind** occurs in the array, but whether the value 101 is present. In practice, you can substitute the value in the function call, like this:

```
If Array.IndexOf(arrDest, 101) = -1 Then ...
```

It will work because the integer value is *boxed* to produce an object that is used in the function call.

More efficient searching can be performed using the **BinarySearch()** method, which doesn't simply start at one end or the other when looking for a value. Instead, it divides the array into two pieces and determines in which of them the desired object is located. It then divides that piece in two and repeats the process, until it ends up with a piece containing just the object.

How Do I Work with Strings?

Let's look at how to work with the **String** data type.

Creating Strings

The **String** class is provided with a variety of constructors, although precisely what is available may vary from language to language. The **String** constructors supported by Visual Basic.NET are summarized in Table 3.5.

Here are some examples:

```
' Build a String from characters
Dim s1 As New String("Hello")

' Build a String from a single Char
Dim c As New Char()
c = "A"c                    ' Upper-case 'a'
Dim s2 As New String(c)
```

You can also create a **String** reference, and then attach the actual **String** object to it using an assignment:

```
' Create a String reference
Dim sref As String
' Point it at a string object
sref = "Hello"
```

Once you've built a **String**, you can find out how many characters it contains using the **Length** property, and extract a character from the **String** using **Chars**:

```
Dim abc As New String("Hello")
Console.WriteLine("Character 1 is {0}", abc.Chars(1))
```

The sample code prints *e* because indexing starts from zero.

Table 3.5 String class constructors supported by VB.

Constructors	Description
New(ByVal value() As Char)	Builds a **String** from an array of **Chars**
New(ByVal c As Char, ByVal count As Integer)	Builds a **String** from a single character repeated "count" times
New(value() As Char, start As Integer, length As Integer)	Builds a **String** from part of an array of **Chars**

Comparing Strings

The **Compare()**, **CompareOrdinal()**, **CompareTo()**, and **Equals()** methods are used to compare **Strings**. You met **Equals()** in the discussion of the **Object** class. It is implemented for **Strings** to return true if the content of both **Strings** is the same.

```
Dim s1 As New String("Hello")
Dim s2 As New String("Hello")

' Prints 'Equal' because the string content is the same
If (s1.Equals(s2)) Then
  Console.WriteLine("Equal")
Else
  Console.WriteLine("Not Equal")
End If
```

Compare() and **CompareOrdinal()** both work the same way in that they both take two **Strings** and return an **int** that tells you how they relate. The value returned will be zero if the two **Strings** are the same, a positive integer if the first is greater than the second, and a negative integer if the second is greater than the first. The difference between the two functions is that **Compare()** has several overloads that can be used to include language and culture information and case in the comparison, whereas **CompareOrdinal()** does not.

Here's a simple example using **Compare()**:

```
Dim s1 As New String("Hello")
Dim s2 As New String("Hello")

' Prints zero because the string content is the same
Console.WriteLine("Compare s1 and s2: {0}", String.Compare(s1,s2))
```

Note how **Compare()** is a static (shared) member of the **String** class, whereas **Equals()** is an instance member. **CompareTo()** is equivalent to **Compare()** and returns the same values, but is an instance member:

```
' Prints zero because the string content is the same
Console.WriteLine("Compare s1 and s2: {0}", s1.CompareTo(s2))
```

The static member **Concat()** is used to create a new **String** from one or more **Strings** or objects and has several overloads. If you pass one or more **Object** references to **Concat()**, the function will try to call the **ToString()** member of each class in order to obtain a **String** representation for the object:

```
Dim n1 As New Name("Fred")
Dim n2 As New Name("Smith")
Dim ss As String

' Calls the ToString() method on the two String objects
ss = String.Concat(n1, " ", n2)
```

Join() is similar to **Concat()** in that it concatenates **Strings**. But in this case, the function takes two arguments, an array of **Strings** to be joined and a separator **String** to use between them.

Copying and Modifying Strings

Copy() can be used to make a copy of an existing **String**. Remember that this is different from using = because the operator copies the reference without generating a new underlying **String** object.

The **Substring()** function is used to extract a substring; the two overloads take a starting index and optionally, a length:

```
Dim s1 As New String("Fred Smith")

' Print four characters starting at index 2 - prints 'ed S'
Console.WriteLine("{0}", s1.Substring(2,4))
```

The **Insert()**, **Remove()**, and **Replace()** functions can be used to modify a **String**. Remember that they will return a new **String** object containing the modified content because **Strings** cannot be changed. **Insert()** inserts a **String** at a given index, **Remove()** removes a number of characters, and **Replace()** replaces all occurrences of one character with another.

PadLeft() and **PadRight()** can be used to provide padding to the right or the left of a **String**. As you would expect, a new **String** object is constructed and returned. The opposite effect, that of removing white space, is provided by the **Trim()**, **TrimEnd()**, and **TrimStart()** functions.

ToUpper() and **ToLower()** return a new **String** containing an upper- or lowercase, as appropriate.

Split() creates an array of strings by splitting a single string using a user supplied array of separator characters to decide where to make the breaks:

```
' Here's a string that uses space and comma as separators
Dim sp As New String("one two,three,four five")
```

```
' Create an array of characters to represent the separators
Dim seps() As Char = {" "c, ","c}

' Split the string
Dim sarr() As String = sp.Split(seps)

' Print out the resulting array
Dim sa As String

For Each sa In sarr
  Console.WriteLine("token is {0}", sa)
Next sa
```


Searching Strings

IndexOf() and **LastIndexOf()** return the first or last occurrence of one or more characters or a string within the target string. There are numerous overloads to these functions in order to provide flexible searching capabilities:

```
Dim s1 As New String("Julian Templeman")

' Find the first occurrence of 'n'
Dim fpos As Integer = s1.IndexOf("n"c)
Console.WriteLine("First occurrence of 'n' is at {0}", fpos)
Console.WriteLine("Second occurrence of 'n' is at {0}", _
            s1.IndexOf("n"c, fpos+1))
```

The functions return a zero-based index, and -1 is returned if the character or string is not found.

The **IndexOfAny()** and **LastIndexOfAny()** methods let you search for the first or last occurrence of any character in an array.

StartsWith() and **EndsWith()** let you check whether a **String** starts or ends with a given string or characters.

Converting Strings

Although the **String** class implements the IConvertible interface, you should use the shared members of the **Convert** class to convert between **Strings** and other types. Using these methods, it is possible to convert a **String** to any other standard type. Here's an example:

```
Dim sbool As New String("True")
Dim b As Boolean = Convert.ToBoolean(sbool)
```

If the **String** has the value **True** or **False**, it will be converted to the appropriate Boolean value. If it doesn't contain one of these two values, you'll get an exception thrown. The **Boolean** class contains two properties, **TrueString** and **FalseString**, which can be used to identify strings that are valid.

How Do I Represent and Use Dates and Times?

Dates and times are represented by two classes: **System.DateTime** and **System.TimeSpan**. The **System.DateTime** class is used to represent dates and times, and it also contains many functions to let you examine, manipulate, and format date and time values. **System.TimeSpan** represents a period of time and can be used on its own or in conjunction with **DateTime**.

This section shows how you can use these classes to perform common operations on dates and times.

Creating **TimeSpan** Objects

TimeSpan objects represent periods of time, so you can construct them using day, hour, minute, second, and millisecond values. You can also construct them using a raw tick count, where a tick is 100 nanoseconds:

```
' Create a TimeSpan to represent one hour
Dim ts as New TimeSpan(1, 0, 0)
```

In addition, you can construct **TimeSpan** objects using a number of shared methods: **FromDays()**, **FromHours()**, **FromMinutes()**, **FromSeconds()**, **FromMilliseconds()**, and **FromTicks()** will construct a **TimeSpan** representing a period, whereas **Parse()** will attempt to construct a **TimeSpan** from a **String**:

```
' Create a TimeSpan to represent ten minutes
Dim ts1 as TimeSpan
ts1 = TimeSpan.FromMinutes(10)

' Create a TimeSpan from a String
Dim ts1 as TimeSpan
ts1 = TimeSpan.Parse("1:20:00")
```

Querying **TimeSpan** Objects

There are a number of class properties that will return part of a **TimeSpan** object: **Days**, **Hours**, **Minutes**, **Seconds**, **Milliseconds**, and **Ticks** will all return integers representing how many whole days (minutes, etc.) the object represents.

There is a matching set of properties for all but ticks—**TotalDays**, **TotalHours**, and so on—that return a **double** representing the exact values.

Manipulating **TimeSpan** Objects

A number of functions are available for working with **TimeSpan** objects, most of which don't require much in the way of explanation. The most common of these functions are summarized in Table 3.6.

Creating **DateTime** Objects

Like **TimeSpan**, the **DateTime** class has several overloaded constructors, enabling you to create **DateTime** objects and initialize them in a number of ways. The following code sample shows some of the most common constructions:

```
' Initialize to 28th February 2001
Dim dt as New DateTime(2001, 2, 28)

' Initialize to 28th February 2001, at 13:23:05
Dim dt as New DateTime(2001, 2, 28, 13, 23, 05)

' Initialize to 28th February 2001, at 13:23:05 and 47ms
Dim dt as New DateTime(2001, 2, 28, 13, 23, 05, 47)
```

Three other constructors mirror these, but take a **Calendar** as their final parameter, allowing you to choose to interpret dates according to a different calendar. Only two calendars are supplied with .NET (Gregorian and Julian), but it is possible to derive more from the **Calendar** superclass.

If you want to obtain a **DateTime** object that represents the current instant, **DateTime** has two shared properties that may be useful. The first, **Now**, returns a **DateTime** object initialized to the current date and time:

Table 3.6 Members of the TimeSpan class.

Function	Shared or Instance?	Description
Compare, **CompareTo**	S	Compares two **TimeSpans**, returning 0 if they are the same, 1 if the first is greater than the second, and -1 if it is less
Equals, **==**, **!=**	S	Checks two **TimeSpans** for equality
+, **-**, **Add**, **Subtract**	S	Adds or subtracts two **TimeSpans**
<, **<=**, **>**, **>=**	S	Tests two **TimeSpans**
Duration	I	Returns the duration of the current object
Negate	I	Returns a new **TimeSpan** that has a negated value

```
Dim dt as DateTime = DateTime.Now
```

If the exact time is important to you, note that the accuracy of the value compared to the current time depends on the operating system you are using: The timer resolution varies from approximately 55 milliseconds on Windows 95/98 to 10 milliseconds on Windows NT 3.51 and later.

The second property, **Today**, returns the current date with the time section set to zero.

There are three other ways to create a **DateTime**: from an operating system file time, from an OLE Automation Date, and from a **String**. If you obtain a file creation or modification date/time using the Windows API, it is held in a format that is incompatible with **DateTime** (it is actually the number of 100-nanosecond intervals since midnight on January 1, 1601, but you probably don't want to know that). The **FromFileTime()** function takes a file time and converts it to a **DateTime**. Note that you do not need to use **FromFileTime()** if you use the **System.IO.File** class because it returns its times as **DateTime** objects.

Automation, used a great deal with VB and C++ in the past, has a **Date** type that uses yet another representation, so the **FromOADate()** function is provided to do a conversion for you. The third way to create a **DateTime** takes a **String** containing a representation of a date (and optionally a time) in the format for the current locale and converts it.

Printing Dates and Times

ToString returns a string containing the date and time in ISO 8601 format, which looks like this:

```
26/02/2001 16:09
```

Querying **DateTime** Objects

DateTime supplies a number of properties and methods that provide query functions. These functions are summarized in Table 3.7.

The **IsLeapYear()** and **DaysInMonth()** functions are static members of **DateTime** and need to be passed a year, and a month and a year, respectively:

```
Console.WriteLine("2000 is a leap year: {0}", DateTime.IsLeapYear(2000))
```

Table 3.7 Query properties and methods provided by the DateTime class.

Member	Property or Method?	Shared or Instance?	Description
IsLeapYear	M	S	Returns true if a given year is a leap year
DaysInMonth	M	S	Returns the number of days in a month given a month and year
Year	P	I	Returns the year field of a **DateTime**
Month	P	I	Returns the month field of a **DateTime** in the range 1–12
Day	P	I	Returns the day field of a **DateTime** in the range 1–31
Hour	P	I	Returns the hour field of a **DateTime** in the range 0–23
Minute	P	I	Returns the minute field of a **DateTime** in the range 0–59
Second	P	I	Returns the second field of a **DateTime** in the range 0–59
Millisecond	P	I	Returns the millisecond field of a **DateTime**
DayOfWeek	P	I	Returns the day of the week in the range 0 (Sunday) to 6 (Saturday)
DayOfYear	P	I	Returns the day of the year in the range 1-366
TimeOfDay	P	I	Returns a **TimeSpan** object representing the time part
Ticks	P	I	Returns the 100-nanosecond tick count
Date	P	I	Returns a copy of a **DateTime** with the time section set to zero

Operations on **DateTime** Objects

The **DateTime** class contains a number of members that make it easy to operate on dates and times. Table 3.8 summarizes these functions.

Table 3.8 DateTime operations and operators.

Function	Shared or Instance?	Description
Compare	S	Compares two **DateTime** objects, returning 0 if they are the same, 1 if the first is greater than the second, and -1 if the first is less than the second
Equals, **==**, **!=**	S	Tests whether two **DateTime** objects are the same
+ operator, **Add**	S	Adds a **DateTime** and a **TimeSpan**
- operator	S	Subtracts a **TimeSpan** from a **DateTime** (giving a **DateTime**) or subtracts two **DateTimes** (giving a **TimeSpan**)
<, <=, >, >=	S	Compares two **DateTimes**, returning true or false as appropriate

Here's an example showing some of these methods in use:

```
' Initialize the Date to 28th February 2001, at 13:23:05
Dim dt as New DateTime(2001, 2, 28, 13, 23, 05)

' Create a TimeSpan representing 1 day, 1 hour and 22 minutes
Dim ts as TimeSpan = TimeSpan.Parse("1.01:22:00")

' Add the two
Dim dt2 As DateTime = dt1.Add(ts)
Console.WriteLine("dt2 is {0}", dt2)
```


How Do I Declare and Use Enumerations?

An enumeration is a collection of named constants; you create them in VB using the **Enum** keyword:

```
Enum ErrorCodes
  BadFileName = 100
  NoPermission
  FileIsReadOnly
  SecurityError = 200
End Enum
```

Each member of the enum is represented by a name and optionally a positive or negative integer value. The default value is zero for the first member and is incremented by one for each succeeding member.

Once you have an enum, you can use the type to create variables and pass parameters to functions:

```
Dim er As ErrorCodes
er = ErrorCodes.FileIsReadOnly
```

Values are specified using the *type.member* syntax. If you turn strict checking off in VB, you can use the underlying values, as shown next, but this isn't recommended:

```
' Sets er to NoPermission if strict checking is turned off
er = 101
```

In C#, enums are declared in a very similar way; you can choose which integer type you want to use to represent the constant values:

```
enum ErrorCodes : uint
{
  BadFileName = 100
  NoPermission
  FileIsReadOnly
  SecurityError = 200
}
```

In this example, I'm using an unsigned integer; the default is a signed integer.

How Do I Find Out What Exception Has Occurred and Where?

All exception objects have to be members of a class that inherits from **System.Exception**. This gives them a number of useful inherited properties, which are as shown in Table 3.9.

You can use these properties in VB code like this:

```
Catch ae As TestException
   Console.WriteLine("Exception message: {0}", ae.Message)
   Console.WriteLine(«Exception trace: {0}», ae.StackTrace)
   Console.WriteLine("Targetsite: {0}", ae.TargetSite.Name)
```

Table 3.9 Members of System.Exception that are inherited by all exception classes.

Property	Description
HelpLink	Gets or sets a reference to a URN or URL that identifies an entry in a help file.
HResult	Gets or sets the COM HRESULT assigned to an exception.
InnerException	Returns a reference to an inner exception object. If none exists, this property is set to **null**, or **Nothing** in the case of VB. (Read-only).
Message	Retrieves the string identifying the error. (Read-only).
Source	Gets or sets the name of the application or object that caused the error.
StackTrace	Retrieves the string holding stack trace information. (Read-only).
TargetSite	Retrieves a reference to the method that threw the object, in the form of a **MethodBase** object. You can use the **Name** property of the **MethodBase** to obtain the name of the method. (Read-only).

You would expect to see output like this:

```
Exception message: My exception has been thrown
Exception trace:   at VBTest.Tester.Thrower() in C:\test\Tester.vb:line 3
   at VBTest.Module1.Main() in C:\test\Module1.vb:line 6
TargetSite: Thrower
```

Note that all of these properties except **TargetSite** are marked as **Overridable**, so you can provide your own implementations to override or add to the inherited versions.

How Do I Use Inner Exceptions?

All exception classes have a constructor, inherited from **Exception**, that takes a reference to another exception object as well as a message string. Once constructed, you can use the **InnerException** property to obtain a reference to the original exception. Here's an example in VB where I define a new exception class, **TestException**, and then use it with an embedded exception:

```
' First module defines the test program
Module Module1
    Sub Main()
        Dim t As New Tester()
        Try
            t.Thrower()
        Catch ae As TestException
            Console.WriteLine("Exception caught: {0}", ae.Message)
            Console.WriteLine("Inner exception message: {0}",
ae.InnerException.Message)
        End Try
    End Sub
End Module

' Second module defines the test class and an exception class
Public Class Tester
    Public Sub Thrower()
        Throw New TestException("Testing...", _
             New ArithmeticException("Inner"))
    End Sub
End Class

Public Class TestException
    Inherits ApplicationException
```

```
    Public Sub new(ByVal s As String, ByRef e As Exception)
        ' Call superclass constructor
        MyBase.New(s, e)
    End Sub
End Class
```

As you can see, I'm simply defining a class called **Tester** whose only job is to throw an exception when its **Thrower()** method is called. The **TestException** class inherits from **ApplicationException** because this is an application generated exception rather than a system generated one. I want to use inner exceptions, so I have to define an override for the constructor that takes a message string and a reference to an inner exception object. Because there isn't a constructor that only takes an inner exception reference, I have to include the string as well. All I need to do in this constructor is to call the superclass constructor and pass it the parameters.

Once I've done this, I can throw a **TestException**, passing in a reference to a new **ArithmeticException**, which I want to use as its inner exception object. You can see that the **Catch** clause in the main function can print out the messages associated with both the outer and inner exceptions.

How do I know whether an inner exception exists? I simply test the **InnerException** property to see whether it contains a **null** reference:

```
Catch ae As TestException
   Console.WriteLine("Exception caught: {0}", ae.Message)
   if ae.InnerException <> Nothing Then
     Console.WriteLine("Inner exception message: {0}", _
                    ae.InnerException.Message)
   End If
End Try
```

You can use the same techniques in C# and Managed C++ with no significant differences.

How Are **Console.WriteLine()** and **Console.Out.WriteLine()** Different?

Console.WriteLine() and **Console.Out.WriteLine()** aren't really different. The **Console** class contains a shared member called **Out**, a **TextWriter** object that is responsible for actually doing the output. The **Writeline()** method actually belongs to the **TextWriter** class, so you really need to call **Console.Out.Writeline()** in order to save a little time and typing. However, the **Console** class implements a version of **Writeline** itself, which delegates to the **Out** object.

The same is true of **Console.Readline()** and **Console.In.Readline()**.

How Do I Produce Formatted Output?

Formatted output is produced by using a version of **Console.WriteLine()** that takes a string containing a format plus zero or more objects that are going to be inserted into the output string:

```
System.WriteLine(format, object1, ...)
```

Formats contain static text plus markers that show where items from the argument list are to be substituted and how they are to be formatted. In its simplest form, a marker is a number in curly brackets—the number showing which argument is to be substituted:

```
"Hello world!"            ' no argument
"The value is {0}"        ' use the first argument
"{0} plus {1} = {2}"      ' use the first three arguments
```

The more general form of a format marker looks like this:

```
{N[,M][:FormatString]}
```

N is the zero-based number of the argument to be substituted (as in the preceding example), and it can optionally be followed by an integer specifying a field width. If the field width value is negative, the value will be left justified within the field; if the field width value is positive, it will be right justified.

```
' Output the first argument
Console.WriteLine("{0}", n)

' Output the first argument, left justified
' in a field eight characters wide
Console.WriteLine("{0,-8}", n)
```

You can also include a formatting specification, which consists of a character and optionally, a precision specifier:

```
' Output the second argument as an integer,
' field width of 7, padded with zeros
Console.WriteLine("{0:D7}", n)

' Output in a field width of 15, in exponent notation with
' four decimal places
Console.WriteLine("d is >{0,15:E4}<", d)
```

If *d* is a **Double** with the value 14.337156, the statement will produce the following output:

```
d is >     1.4337E+001<
```

Table 3.10 shows the possible format characters. Note that they can be specified in either uppercase or lowercase.

Picture Formatting

If the standard formatting options don't meet your needs, you can use picture formatting, which uses format characters to build a picture of what the output should look like. Here's an example:

```
Dim d As Double = 14.337156
Console.WriteLine("d is {0:0000.00}", d)
```

Table 3.10 Formatting characters used with System.Write and System.WriteLine.

Format Character	Description	Notes
C	Locale specific currency format	
D	Integer format	If a precision specifier is given, for example {0:D5}, the output is padded with leading zeros.
E	Exponent (scientific) format	The precision specifier gives the number of decimal places, which is six by default.
F	Fixed-point format	The precision specifier gives the number of decimal places. Zero is an acceptable value.
G	General format	Uses whichever of E or F is most suitable.
N	Number format	Outputs a number with thousand separators, for example, 32,767.
P	Percent format	Represents a numeric value as a percentage.
R	Round-trip format	Guarantees that numbers converted into strings will have the same value when converted back into numbers.
X	Hexadecimal format	If a precision specifier is given, for example {0:X5}, the output is padded with leading zeros.

The output from this is:

```
d is 0014.34
```

The picture format consists of "0000.00", where a "0" denotes a placeholder for a digit or a zero if there isn't a digit available, and the "." outputs a decimal point.

There are a number of picture format characters, the most common of which are shown in Table 3.11.

The **ToString()** Method

Each .NET base data type (such as **Int32**, **Double**, and so on) has a **ToString()** method that can be used to format objects in order to present them to users in a particular style, like this:

```
' Create an integer and format it up as a currency
Dim amt As Integer = 5000
Dim s As String = amt.ToString("C")

Console.WriteLine("amount is {0}", s)
```

Assuming that you are in the United States, the output from this will be

```
amount is $5,000.00
```

Note that I haven't done anything to the underlying integer. I've only provided a string representation with a new format. You may wonder whether this is any different than:

```
Console.WriteLine("amount is {0:C}", amt)
```

The answer is that it produces exactly the same output. So when is **ToString()** useful? The answer lies in two of the other overloads of **ToString()**, both of which take an **IFormatProvider** object as a parameter.

Table 3.11 Picture format characters for use with System.Write and System.WriteLine.

Format Character	Description	Notes
0	Digit or zero placeholder	Outputs a zero if a digit isn't available
#	Digit placeholder	Only outputs significant digits
.	Decimal point	Displays a "."
,	Number group separator	Separates number groups, for example, 10,000
%	Percent sign	Displays the percent character used by the current culture

The IFormatProvider interface is implemented by several classes that generate culture-dependent formatting information. As a result, if you have an appropriate object available, it is quite possible to print out a sum of money as French Francs or Japanese Yen with all the correct formatting.

How Do I Generate Random Values?

The **System.Random** class implements a pseudorandom number generator, which means that it will always generate the same sequence of numbers if given the same integer "seed" value.

Here's an example of how to use **Random** to generate random integers:

```
Dim r As New Random(1200)
Dim i As Integer

For i = 1 To 10
  Console.WriteLine("Value is {0)", r.Next())
Next i
```

If you run this code, you'll find that your output is similar to this:

```
Value is 1367131677
Value is 1974968700
Value is 1188871133
Value is 1481071999
...
```

The fact that **Random** uses a pseudorandom generator means that you'll get exactly the same output each time you run the program unless you vary the seed in the constructor.

One common way of making the selection of values more random is to use the current time as a seed. This is a slightly involved procedure in VB because you need to do some rather messy conversion, as shown in the following code:

```
' Get the current time as a Long
Dim currentTime As Long = DateTime.Now.Ticks()

' Extract the bottom part as an integer
Dim seed as Integer = CInt(currentTime And &HFFFF)

' Use it to initialize the Random object
Dim r As New Random(seed)
```

DateTime.Now.Ticks() uses the **Now** property of **System.DateTime** to return an object representing the current time, and the **Ticks** property expresses that value as a 100-nanosecond tick count. This comes back, not surprisingly, as a **Long**, but you can't use that to initialize the **Random** object because the constructor requires an Integer. You can extract the bottom half of the **Long** using the **CInt** conversion, which uses the **And** (bitwise **AND**) operator to mask off the top half of the **Long** and return the rest as an integer.

NOTE: *This technique doesn't return the bottom four bytes exactly because VB always reserves the top bit for the sign, so you're actually returning the bottom 31 bits plus a sign bit.*

If you run this code several times, you should get a different series of random numbers generated each time. The code is pretty much the same in C#, as shown here:

```
' Get the current time as a Long
long currentTime = DateTime.Now.Ticks;

' Extract the bottom part as an integer
int seed = (int)(currentTime & 0xFFFF);

' Use it to initialize the Random object
Random r = new Random(seed);
```

The **Random** class also contains overloads to return integer values less than a maximum or falling within a range, like so:

```
' Only return values between 1000 and 2000
Console.WriteLine("Value is {0}", r.Next(1000,2000))
```

There is another method that will return a double value between 0.0 and 1.0 (**NextDouble**) and a method to fill a buffer with random bytes (**NextBytes**).

Chapter 4

The System.Collections Namespace

By Julian Templeman

In Depth

The **System.Collections** namespace, as its name implies, contains a selection of interfaces and classes that define various collections of objects, such as arrays, lists, and dictionaries. In this chapter, I'll explain each object collection, and in the Immediate Solutions section, I'll show you how they are used in practice.

The following code diagram shows the hierarchy of classes and structs defined in **System.Collections** as well as how they relate to each other:

```
System.Object
    ArrayList
    BitArray
    CaseInsensitiveComparer
    CaseInsensitiveHashCodeProvider
    CollectionBase
    Comparer
    DictionaryBase
    Hashtable
    NameObjectCollectionBase
        NameValueCollection
    Queue
    ReadOnlyCollectionBase
    SortedList
    Stack
    System.ValueType
        DictionaryEntry
```

The namespace also defines a number of interfaces, listed as follows:

```
ICollection
IComparer
IDictionary
IDictionaryEnumerator
IEnumerable
IEnumerator
IHashCodeProvider
IList
```

The **System.Collections.Specialized** namespace, as its name implies, contains various more specialized collections, as follows:

```
System.Object
    System.ValueType
        BitVector32
    HybridDictionary
    ListDictionary
    NameObjectCollectionBase
        NameValueCollection
    StringCollection
    StringDictionary
    StringEnumerator
```

The System.Collections Interfaces

Interfaces are very important in the **System.Collections** namespace because very few of the collection classes are related by inheritance, but many of them need to provide the same functionality. A good example of this is the ability to iterate over the members of a collection; moving from one element to another is the same no matter how the data is actually stored. Moving from one element of an array to the next is the same logical idea as moving from one element of a linked list to the next, but the way in which the collection navigates through its data is completely different.

The way that you provide the same behavior in otherwise unrelated classes is to use *interfaces*. If you haven't come across interfaces and how they are implemented and used, you may want to take a look at Chapter 3 before reading on.

The **System.Collections** namespace includes a number of interfaces that between them define all the common behavior required of collection classes; I'll explain each of these interfaces and what they do. When discussing the classes, I'll illustrate which interfaces they implement so that you can see the extra methods they are going to provide.

IEnumerable

If a collection implements the IEnumerable interface, it signals that it can provide an enumerator object that supports forward-only iteration over the collection. Because this behavior is very common, this interface is implemented by approximately 100 classes.

IEnumerable only has one member, the **GetEnumerator()** method, which takes no arguments and returns an enumerator object:

```
Function GetEnumerator() As IEnumerator
```

Note how the IEnumerable and IEnumerator interfaces work together. If a class implements IEnumerable, then this method will return a reference to an object that implements IEnumerator. You don't have to know exactly what type the returned object is, only that you can use it as an enumerator.

IEnumerator

IEnumerator is implemented by classes that support simple iteration over a collection. By simple, I mean that you can only move forward from element to element, although you can go back to the start at any time.

Enumerators are read-only because the object takes a snapshot of the collection when it is created. This means that it is perfectly possible to have more than one enumerator with access to the same collection. The underlying collection must not be changed while an enumerator is active because its snapshot would then be out of date. If this happens, the iterator will throw exceptions whenever you try to use it.

The IEnumerator interface has three members. The **MoveNext()** method advances the iterator to the next element in the collection. Note that the initial position of the iterator is *before* the first element in the collection, so you need to call **MoveNext()** once in order to advance to the first element.

The function returns a Boolean value, which will be true if the iterator successfully advanced to the next element, and false once it has passed the end. The **Reset()** method can be used to set the iterator back to its initial position, that is, before the first element in the collection.

The **Current** property returns a reference to the current object in the collection. This property will throw an invalid operation exception under two circumstances:

- If the enumerator is positioned before the start or after the end of the collection
- If the collection has been modified since the enumerator object was created

See the Immediate Solutions section for examples of enumerator usage.

ICollection

ICollection is a descendant of IEnumerable and defines size, enumerators, and synchronization methods for collections. Like IEnumerable, it is implemented by a very large number of classes, and because ICollection is based on IEnumerable, any class that implements ICollection has to implement IEnumerable as well.

ICollection adds the following functionality to the **GetEnumerator()** method defined by IEnumerable:

- **SyncRoot** and **IsSynchronized**—These properties allow classes to implement thread safe collections.
- **Count**—This property returns the number of items in the collection.

- **CopyTo()**—This method can be implemented to copy elements from a collection into a one-dimensional array.

IList

The IList interface, a descendent of ICollection, is implemented by classes that represent collections of objects that can be individually indexed, and it specifies all the properties and methods that must be supported by such classes. This means that it is implemented by array classes (such as **System.Array** and **System.Collections.ArrayList**) as well as other more specialized classes. Implementations of IList fall into three types: read-only, fixed-size, and variable-size.

The methods supported by IList are fairly self-explanatory:

- **Add()** and **Insert()** can be used to add items to the list. **Insert()** takes a zero-based index specifying where the item is to be inserted, whereas **Add()** appends the new item to the end.
- **Remove()** and **RemoveAt()** are used to remove items from the list. **RemoveAt()** takes an index specifying which item is to be removed, whereas **Remove()** takes an **Object** reference and removes that object. **Clear()** can be used to remove all entries.
- **IndexOf()** and **Contains()** are used to search the list. Both take an **Object** reference. **Contains()** returns a Boolean value, whereas **IndexOf()** returns a zero-based index.
- The **Item** property is used to get or set the value at the specified index.
- The **IsFixedSize** and **IsReadOnly** properties tell you whether the underlying collection is fixed size, and whether it can be modified.

IComparer

The IComparer interface implements a single method that compares two objects and returns a value indicating which one is greater:

```
Function Compare(ByVal x as Object, ByVal y As Object) As Integer
```

The function returns a negative value if x is less than y, zero if they are the same, and a positive value if x is greater than y.

Objects passed to compare must implement the **System.IComparable** interface; if they don't, the function will throw an **ArgumentException**. You'll find a discussion of the **System.IComparable** interface in Chapter 3.

The default implementation of this interface is provided by the **System.Collections.Comparer** class. This default implementation lets you easily create an object with which to perform comparisons.

This interface is often used with the **System.Array** class when using its **Sort()** and **BinarySearch()** methods. When using these methods, you can either use the default ICompare implementations of the objects themselves or provide your own comparison objects by implementing this interface.

IDictionary

A dictionary is a data structure consisting of a set of keyword/value pairs, where each value is identified by an associated key. Keys and values can be any type of object; keys have to be unique and non-null. IDictionary is implemented by over half a dozen classes including two members of **System.Collections**—**Hashtable** and **SortedList**—which are discussed under their own headers in the In Depth section.

The following list shows the properties and methods specified by IDictionary:

- **Add()** adds an entry with a specified key and value to the dictionary.
- The **Item** property retrieves the value corresponding to the specified key.
- The **Keys** and **Values** properties return collections containing all the keys and values respectively.
- **Contains()** determines whether a value with a specified key exists in the dictionary.
- **Clear()** removes all entries from dictionary, whereas **Remove()** removes the entry with a specified key.
- **GetEnumerator()** returns an IDictionaryEnumerator that you can use to walk through the dictionary.
- The **IsFixedSize** and **IsReadOnly** properties tell you whether the underlying collection is fixed size, and whether it can be modified.

IDictionaryEnumerator

The IDictionaryEnumerator interface is based on IEnumerator and provides extra methods to let you retrieve the key and/or value associated with an item.

You can use the standard enumerator methods, **MoveNext()** and **Reset()**. In addition, you can use the **Entry** property to retrieve the key and value of the current item or the **Key** and **Value** properties to retrieve them separately. Note that although the enumerator selects items in the dictionary one after another, this does not imply any ordering of the data.

The **Entry** property returns a **DictionaryEntry** object. **DictionaryEntry** is a value type that contains **Key** and **Value** public fields, each of which is an **Object** reference.

IHashCodeProvider

Objects are stored in a hash table using values known as "hash codes" as keys. The **Object** class provides the default **GetHashCode()** method, which generates a default hash code. But if this is not suitable, you can implement your own hash code-generating class by implementing this interface and coding the one **GetHashCode()** method.

ArrayList

An **ArrayList** is a dynamically growable (and shrinkable) array, unlike **System.Array** objects whose size is fixed at creation time. The following code shows the definition of the **ArrayList** class:

```
Public Class ArrayList
    Implements IList, ICollection, IEnumerable
```

By default, instances of this class are resizable and writable, but the class provides two shared methods that let you create read-only and fixed-size **ArrayLists**.

The capacity of an **ArrayList** is 16 elements by default, but this can be reset at any time using the **Capacity** property. If you exceed the capacity when adding elements, it will automatically be doubled. If your array is too large, you can reduce its capacity to match the actual number of elements stored by calling **TrimToSize()**.

The **Add()** method can be used to add an object to the end of the array, whereas **Insert()** will insert an object at a zero-based index. The **AddRange()** and **InsertRange()** methods will add or insert the elements of another collection, whereas **SetRange()** will copy the elements of a collection over a range of elements in the array. There are three ways to remove elements from an array: **Remove()** removes an object by reference, **RemoveAt()** removes an object by index, and **RemoveRange()** removes a range of elements.

ArrayList also provides the **Adapter()** method, which lets you wrap any other **IList** object in an **ArrayList**, so that you can use its **BinarySearch()**, **Sort()**, and **Reverse()** methods.

BitArray

It is very common to want to store a series of flags that simply have true or false (or on or off) values. You could use an array of Boolean values, but it isn't a very efficient way of representing quantities that really only need one bit to store them. You can also use the bitwise operators to switch the individual bits of integers on and off, but this can be tedious, and these bitwise operations are not supported by all languages.

The solution in .NET is the **BitArray**, a data structure that stores true and false values, and that implements several interfaces, as shown below:

```
Public Sealed Class BitArray
    Implements ICollection, IEnumerable, ICloneable
```

Precisely how it stores values does not matter, but you can be certain that it stores values as compactly as possible. You can simply access the bits in the array just as you would any other array elements.

Hashtable

A **Hashtable** represents a collection of associated keys and values organized in such a way that values can be efficiently retrieved:

```
Public Class Hashtable
    Implements IDictionary, ICollection, IEnumerable, ISerializable,
    IDeserializationCallback, ICloneable
```

A *hash key* (or hash code) is an integer value that can be rapidly calculated from a data item. A *hash table* contains a number of "buckets," each of which can hold the data associated with one hash key. An example of a hash table is shown in Figure 4.1.

For example, suppose that you had data consisting of a list of personal telephone numbers keyed by the person's name:

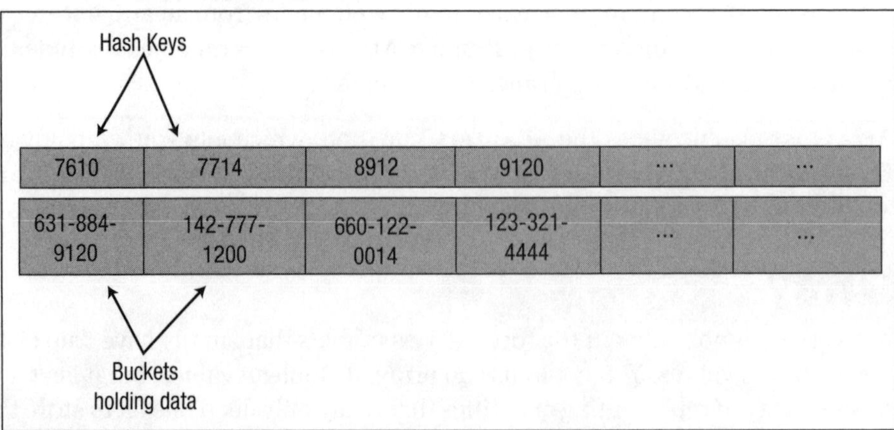

Figure 4.1 A hash table.

```
Ton Van Bergyk          631-884-9120
Dave Evans              142-777-2100
Leo Wijnkamp            660-122-0014
Dale Miller             123-321-4444
```

You can create a hash key based on each name. The hash key will determine which bucket of the **Hashtable** will hold the data. When you want to retrieve a phone number, you simply take the name and calculate its hash key, which will tell you where the data is located in the **Hashtable**. The algorithms for generating hash keys are designed to be very fast, so looking up entries in a **Hashtable** should be very quick. Note that the keys in a **Hashtable** have to be unique, although it is possible for more than one key to end up with the same hash key.

If two or more items have the same hash key, a bucket in the **Hashtable** will contain more than one value. In this case, once the bucket has been located, it will be necessary to compare the keys of every item in the bucket in order to find the one you want. This obviously slows down retrieval. Hashing algorithms are carefully designed to create a uniform distribution of values with as little chance of duplication as possible.

The ratio of entries to buckets is called the hash table's *load factor*, and smaller load factors will give faster retrieval at the cost of increased memory consumption. The load factor also determines how the size of the table is increased when all buckets have been filled.

The default load factor is 1.0, and other values can be specified when the **Hashtable** is created.

The **Object** class contains a method for generating hash keys, and this is inherited by every other .NET class. For many data structures, however, this default method will not create a good distribution of hash keys. Therefore, if you want to store your data in a hash table, it may be necessary to override **GetHashCode()** in order to implement your own hashing function.

Hashtables are thread safe, and the shared **Synchronized()** method can be used to obtain a thread-safe wrapper object.

NameValueCollection

NameValueCollection belongs to the **System.Collections.Specialized** namespace, and implements a collection class that stores key/value pairs of strings in a hash table, but also lets you access members by index as well as key. Unlike **Hashtable**, **NameValueCollection** uses strings as keys and will let you use a **null** reference (**Nothing** in VB) for a key. **NameValueCollection** inherits from **NameObjectCollectionBase**, extending it by allowing duplicate keys:

```
Public Class NameValueCollection
    Inherits NameObjectCollectionBase

Public MustInherit Class NameObjectCollectionBase
    Implements ICollection, IEnumerable
```

Queue

A Queue is an ordered list where items are added at one end and removed from the other, as shown in Figure 4.2. It is useful for processing items, such as messages, in the order in which they were received:

```
Public Class Queue
    Implements ICollection, IEnumerable, ICloneable
```


The **Queue** class supports three standard operations: **Enqueue()** adds an object to the tail of the Queue, **Dequeue()** removes an object from the head, and **Peek()** looks at the oldest object without removing it.

Queues are thread safe, and the shared **Synchronized()** method can be used to obtain a thread-safe wrapper object.

SortedList

A **SortedList** uses two arrays to store its data—one to hold keys and one to hold values, as shown in Figure 4.3. Therefore, an entry in the list consists of a key/value pair. Duplicate keys are not allowed, and a key cannot be a **null** reference (**Nothing** in VB), although values can be **null** references:

```
Public Class SortedList
    Implements IDictionary, ICollection, IEnumerable, ICloneable
```

As its name implies, the list maintains its entries in order, sorted on the keys, so adding an item to a **SortedList** is a relatively expensive process.

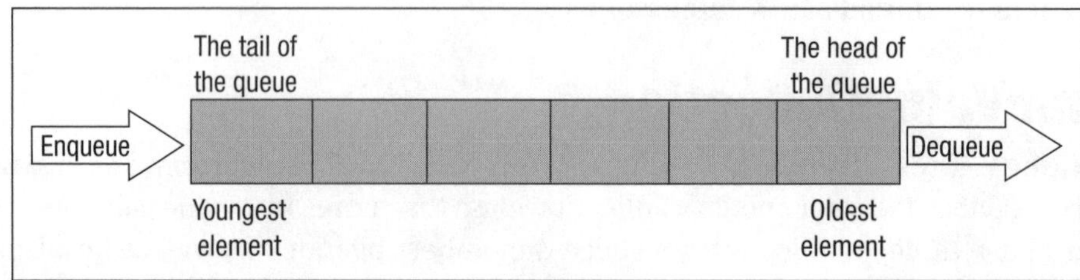

Figure 4.2 A Queue.

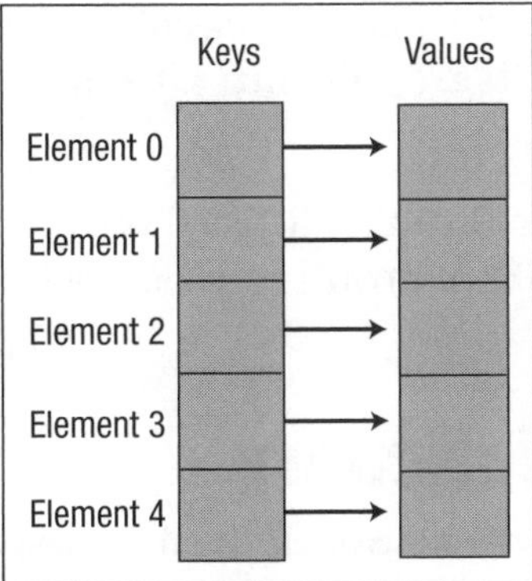

Figure 4.3 A SortedList.

A **SortedList** is similar to both a **Hashtable** and an **ArrayList** in that you can retrieve items by key and also by index. It is slower in operation than a **Hashtable** because it needs to find the index at which a new item is to be added in order to maintain the sorted order.

Static (shared) members of **SortedLists** are thread safe, and the shared **Synchronized()** method can be used to obtain a thread-safe wrapper object.

Stack

A stack is a simple ordered collection of objects in which items can only be added or removed from the top, as shown in Figure 4.4. In programming terminology, it is a LIFO (Last In, First Out) Queue. The usual real-world illustration of a stack is that of a pile of plates in a cafeteria. Another way to regard a stack is as a Queue where the **Enqueue()** and **Dequeue()** operations occur at the same end:

```
Public Class Stack
   Implements ICollection, IEnumerable, ICloneable
```

Stacks support three main operations: **Push()** adds a new item on the stack, **Pop()** removes the top item from the stack, and **Peek()** looks at the top item without removing it.

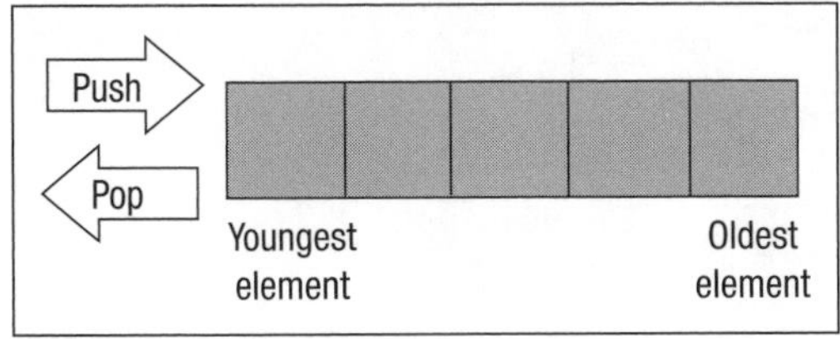

Figure 4.4 A stack.

Because stack implements ICollection, IEnumerable, and ICloneable, it has all the methods associated with those interfaces: **Clear()**, **Count()**, **Contains()**, **Clone()**, and **CopyTo()**.

Stacks support thread safety as well, and the **Synchronized()** method returns a thread safety wrapper around the stack. The **IsSynchronized** property can be used to test whether the stack is thread safe.

StringCollection and StringDictionary

StringCollection belongs to the **System.Collections.Specialized** namespace, and is a special purpose IList used for storing strings by index. It has methods for adding, inserting, and removing strings, removing a string by index, and copying part or all of the collection to an array. The strings within a string collection do not have to be unique:

```
Public Class StringCollection
    Implements IList, ICollection, IEnumerable
```

StringDictionary, also part of the **System.Collections.Specialized** namespace, is a dictionary that uses a **String** as a key.

Immediate Solutions

Which Collection Should I Use?

How do you decide which collection to use for a given programming task? The following points may help you decide:

- If you want a fixed-size array, use **System.Array**.
- If you want a dynamically sizable array, use **ArrayList**.
- If you want to store a list of elements and always retrieve the last one you added first, use a Stack.
- If you want to store elements and retrieve them using a key, use a **Hashtable**. If you also want to be able to access them by index, use a **SortedList**.
- If you want to store a list of elements and always retrieve them in the order in which you added them, use a Queue.
- If you want to store a series of true/false (or on/off) flags, use a **BitArray**.
- If you want to store a list of strings and refer to them by index, use a **StringCollection**.
- If you want to store a list of strings and refer to them by key or index, use a **NameValueCollection**.

Which Collections Are Thread Safe?

If you know what thread safety means, all you need to know is that **ArrayList**, **Queue**, **Hashtable**, **SortedList**, **HybridDictionary**, **ListDictionary**, and **StringDictionary** are thread safe.

If you don't, consider this brief explanation of thread safety. Nowadays, many programs are written using multiple threads of execution. A thread (looking at it very simply) is a function within a program that is executing at the same time as the rest of the code, and the operating system schedules them against one other in the same way that it schedules whole programs against one another. This is done by giving each thread (each function) a short time slice, and then suspending it in order to give another thread a chance to run. If it is done quickly and smoothly, it gives the illusion that functions are executing simultaneously. Intelligent use of scheduling by the operating system can result in much smoother program operation.

The problem, however, is that the scheduler can decide to suspend one thread while it is in the middle of an operation, which can cause real problems with shared data structures. Imagine that one thread has just started to retrieve item 5 from a collection when the scheduler decides to swap to another thread, and that this new thread promptly removes item 5. When control switches back to the original thread, the scheduler is not going to get the data item it was expecting. Errors due to shared data being accessed by multiple threads can be very hard to track down because of the unpredictability of the scheduler and when it decides to swap between threads.

A thread-safe class is one in which critical methods, such as insertion, removal, and retrieval of elements, are protected against being interrupted by another thread.

Consult Chapter 12 for more details on how to create and use threads and how to synchronize use of objects.

How Do I Iterate over a Collection?

If the collection implements the IEnumerable interface, you can use an enumerator object provided by the collection to iterate over the collection.

Collections that implement IEnumerable have a **GetEnumerator()** method that can be used to retrieve the enumerator object. This will be an object that supports the IEnumerator interface.

IEnumerator provides a simple way to iterate forward over a collection using three members:

- **MoveNext()**—A method that moves the enumerator to the next element. It returns true if the move was successful and false if the end of the collection has been reached. Note that it is initially positioned before the first element, so you need to call it once in order to position it at the first element.
- **Reset()**—A method that sets the enumerator back to its starting position before the first element.
- **Current**—A property that retrieves the current element as an **Object** reference.

Note that you cannot modify the contents of a collection through an iterator because iterators take a snapshot of the data.

The following code shows how to use an enumerator in VB:

```
' Create an array
Dim ar() As Integer = { 10, 11, 12, 13 }

' Create the elements an enumerator to work with it
Dim enm As IEnumerator = ar.GetEnumerator

' Use the enumerator to print each element
While enm.MoveNext = True
  Console.WriteLine(enm.Current)
End While
```

There are two things to note about this code: First, you ask the object for an enumerator, so each collection class is responsible for providing its own enumeration objects. Second, you access the object though IEnumerator, which isolates you from having to know exactly what type of object it is.

As you might expect, the code is very similar in C#, as shown below:

```
// Create an array
int[] ar = { 10, 11, 12, 13 };

// Create an enumerator to work with it
IEnumerator enm = ar.GetEnumerator();

// Use the enumerator to print each element
while (enm.MoveNext() == true)
  Console.WriteLine(enm.Current);
```

How Do I Use an ArrayList?

An **ArrayList** is a dynamically resizable array that can hold any kind of object and is a useful alternative to the fixed-size **System.Array**. Because **ArrayLists** are used quite heavily, I will discuss them in some detail.

Creating and Filling ArrayLists

An **ArrayList** can be created in four ways:

- As an empty array that has the default capacity of 16 elements
- As an empty array that has a specified initial capacity
- As an array containing elements copied from another collection
- As an array initialized with *n* copies of the same value

You can get or set the capacity of an **ArrayList** using the **Capacity** property, and the **Count** property will tell you how many elements an **ArrayList** currently contains.

The following example shows how to create and use **ArrayLists** in VB:

```
' Create ArrayList with default capacity
Dim al As New ArrayList()

' Add some values to the list
al.Add("zero")
al.Add("two")
al.Add("three")
al.Insert(1, "one")

' See what we have
Console.WriteLine("Capacity={0}, Count={1}, Item 1={2}", _
        al.Capacity, al.Count, al.Item(1))

' Create another initialized with ten elements, each
' containing the string "foo"
Dim al2 As ArrayList = ArrayList.Repeat("foo", 10)

Console.WriteLine("Capacity={0}, Count={1}, Item 1={2}", _
        al2.Capacity, al2.Count, al2.Item(1))
```

The **Add()** method adds a new object to the end of the list, whereas **Insert()** inserts an object at the given index. So the first **WriteLine()** statement gives the result:

```
Capacity=16, Count=4, Item 1=one
```

The second **ArrayList** is initialized with 10 copies of a string, but it is still created with the default capacity of 16 elements, so the second **WriteLine()** statement produces the following:

```
Capacity=16, Count=10, Item 1=foo
```

If you want to remove the unused elements from the second **ArrayList**, you can use **TrimToSize()**, which makes the capacity equal to the count:

```
al2.TrimToSize()
```

The **AddRange()** and **InsertRange()** methods let you insert the elements of a collection into an **ArrayList**, whereas **SetRange()** lets you copy the elements of a collection over a range of elements in an **ArrayList**. The following example shows **InsertRange()** at work. Notice that native language arrays count as collections:

```
' Create an integer array
Dim intArr() As Integer = {1, 2, 3}

al.InsertRange(2, intArr)
```

This code inserts the integer array at index 2, giving the sequence:

```
zero one 1 2 3 two three
```

Additionally, the **GetRange()** method can be used to copy a range of elements from one **ArrayList** to a new one:

```
' Create an ArrayList containing three elements from al2, starting
' at index 2
Dim al2 As ArrayList = al2.GetRange(2, 3)
```

Removing Items

The **Remove()** and **RemoveAt()** methods can be used to remove an item from an **ArrayList** by reference and index respectively. Suppose that you have an **ArrayList** that contains the following items:

```
one two foo three four bar
```

The following two statements can both be used to remove the third element in the list:

```
' Remove an element by reference
al.Remove("foo")

' Remove an element by zero-based index
al.RemoveAt(2)
```

If you supply an index that is out of range, you will get an **ArgumentOutOfRange** exception thrown, and if you try to remove an element that doesn't exist in the **ArrayList**, you will receive an **ArgumentException**. A **NotSupportedException** will be thrown if the **ArrayList** is read-only.

RemoveRange() can be used to remove a sequence of elements from the **ArrayList**:

```
' Remove two elements starting at index 3
al.RemoveRange(3, 2)
```

Operations on ArrayLists

Reverse() lets you reverse the order of all or part of an **ArrayList**, whereas **Sort()** will sort all or part of a list into ascending order:

```
' Create ArrayList with default capacity
Dim al As New ArrayList()

' Add five entries
al.Add("dingo")
al.Add("aardvark")
al.Add("cheetah")
al.Add("emu")
al.Add("bison")

' Sort the list
al.Sort()

' Now reverse the order of the three entries
' starting at index 1
al.Reverse(1, 3)
```

If you print out the list after the **Sort()** and **Reverse()** operations are complete, you get the following results:

```
After sort:    aardvark bison cheetah dingo emu
After reverse: aardvark dingo cheetah bison emu
```

The **Contains()** method determines whether the **ArrayList** contains a particular object, and **IndexOf()** and **LastIndexOf()** can be used to return the position at which an object lives in the list:

```
al.Contains("dingo")          ' returns true
al.Contains("elephant")       ' returns false
al.IndexOf("cheetah")         ' returns 2
al.IndexOf("lion")            ' returns -1 (not found)
```

By default, **IndexOf()** and **LastIndexOf()** start from the beginning and end of the list respectively, but there are overloads that let you set a starting index and a range to search.

BinarySearch() provides an efficient way to locate an object in a large **ArrayList** by using a binary search algorithm. Note that in order for this to work, the **ArrayList** has to be sorted because the algorithm assumes that all the values to one side of an element are less than—and all values on the other side are greater than—the current element. If the array isn't sorted, then this assumption probably won't be true, and you'll get the wrong answer. Here's an example:

```
' Binary search
Dim al4 As New ArrayList()
Dim i As Integer                ' loop index
Dim val As Integer              ' value to search for

' Initialize random number generator
Dim r As Random = New Random(999)

' Put a lot of random values into the list, and save number 500 to
' look for later
For i = 1 To 10000
  If i = 500 Then
    val = r.Next
    al4.Add(val)
  Else
    al4.Add(r.Next)
  End If
Next

' Sort the array
al4.Sort()

' Look for the value and print it out
Console.WriteLine("Found it at {0}", al4.BinarySearch(val))
```

Using Wrapper Methods

The **ArrayList** class provides several shared methods that let you create **ArrayList** objects of a particular type.

The **FixedSize()** method creates an **ArrayList** that cannot have members added or removed. **ReadOnly()** creates an **ArrayList** whose members cannot be modified; this obviously implies that the list is fixed size as well as read-only. **Synchronized()** creates an **ArrayList** that is thread safe. The **IsReadOnly** and **IsSynchronized** properties can be used to identify which lists are read-only and synchronized.

All three methods are used in the same way. You first create a standard **ArrayList**, and then use these methods to create a wrapper with the desired properties. Here's an example showing how you could create a read-only **ArrayList**:

```
' Create a read-only ArrayList... start by creating a normal one
Dim al5 As New ArrayList()
```

```
' Put some values into the list
For i = 1 To 10
  al5.Add(2 * i)
Next

' Create a read-only wrapper
Dim alRO As ArrayList = ArrayList.ReadOnly(al5)

' Look for the value and print it out
Console.WriteLine("alRO is read-only: {0}", alRO.IsReadOnly)
```


How Do I Store Values by Key?

If you have data that can be identified by a key, such as a list of names and phone numbers, you can use a **Hashtable** or **SortedList** to store them.

A **Hashtable** will be more efficient if you only want to search for and retrieve values by key. A **SortedList** maintains the data items in sorted key order and lets you retrieve them by key or index. **SortedLists** are not as efficient as **Hashtables** because of the need to maintain the sort order of the list when adding items, but they basically work the same way.

In the following code examples, I'll use a dataset consisting of names and (fictitious) phone numbers, like this:

```
Emmett Chapman          441-999-1010
Tony Levin              208-337-4880
Bob Culbertson          655-422-9023
Greg Howard             213-101-8032
```

A **Hashtable** can use two helper objects: an object that implements IComparer and an object that implements IHashCodeProvider. Because **Hashtable**s don't permit duplicate keys, the table needs to be able to decide whether two key objects are equal. It can normally do this using the key objects' **Equals()** method, but if you want to do something special—such as ignore case-sensitivity so that "smith" is equal to "SMITH"—you can implement an IComparer object and let the **Hashtable** use it. Similarly, the table will use the key objects' own **GetHashCode()** method unless you provide it a custom **IHashCodeProvider**, which it will use to calculate the hash key.

Creating and Filling Hashtables

The **Hashtable** class lets you create objects in a number of ways:

- As an empty **Hashtable** with a default or specified initial capacity
- By copying the entries from another IDictionary
- Specifying **IComparer** and **IHashCodeProvider** objects for both of the preceding ways

***NOTE**: If you don't know how **Hashtable**s work, before reading on, you may want to look at the discussion in the In Depth section to find out about load factors and how they influence the workings of a **Hashtable**.*

The **Hashtable** class has 10 possible constructors.

Here's an example showing how to create and fill a **Hashtable** in VB:

```
' Create a Hashtable
Dim ht As New Hashtable()

' Add some values to the table
ht.Add("Emmett Chapman", "441-999-1010")
ht.Add("Tony Levin", "208-337-4880")
ht.Add("Bob Culbertson", "655-422-9023")
ht.Add("Greg Howard", "213-101-8032")
```

In this case, I've used strings as keys, but you can use any type of object. Duplicate keys aren't allowed, so if you try to add one, you'll get an **ArgumentException**.

You can also use the **Item** property to set the value associated with a key. If the key exists, its value will be replaced; if it doesn't exist, a new one will be created, so you could rewrite the preceding code as:

```
' Add some values to the table using Item
ht.Item("Emmett Chapman") = "441-999-1010"
ht.Add("Tony Levin") = "208-337-4880"
ht.Add("Bob Culbertson") = "655-422-9023"
ht.Add("Greg Howard") = "213-101-8032"
```

In C#, **Item** is the indexer for the class, so you can use square-bracket notation if you prefer, so we could write the preceding code like this:

```
// Add some values to the table using Item
ht["Emmett Chapman"] = "441-999-1010";
ht["Tony Levin"] = "208-337-4880";
ht["Bob Culbertson"] = "655-422-9023";
ht["Greg Howard"] = "213-101-8032";
```

Finding Keys and Values

You can find out whether the table contains a particular key or value using the **ContainsKey()** and **ContainsValue()** methods. Because **Hashtables** are normally searched by key, you can also use **Contains()** as a synonym for **ContainsKey()**:

```
If ht.Contains("Greg Howard") = True Then
  Console.WriteLine("Table contains Greg Howard")
End If
```

If you want to know all the keys or all the values, the **Keys** and **Values** properties will return an ICollection:

```
' Get an enumerator on the Keys collection and print them out
Dim keyEnum As IEnumerator = ht.Keys.GetEnumerator
While keyEnum.MoveNext
  Console.WriteLine(keyEnum.Current)
End While
```

You can retrieve the value associated with a key using the **Item** property:

```
Console.WriteLine("Phone number for Tony Levin is {0}", _
          ht.Item("Tony Levin"))
```

Remember that in C# you can use square-bracket notation if you prefer:

```
Console.WriteLine("Phone number for Tony Levin is {0}", ht["Tony Levin"])
```

If you want to enumerate the entire table, the **GetEnumerator()** method will return an IDictionaryEnumerator, which you can query to find out keys and values:

```
' Get an enumerator on the entire table and print it out
Dim en As IDictionaryEnumerator = ht.GetEnumerator
While en.MoveNext
  Console.WriteLine("Key='{0}', Value='{1}'", en.Key, en.Value)
End While
```

Removing Entries

The **Remove()** method removes an entry by key, whereas **Clear()** removes all the entries:

```
' Remove an entry
ht.Remove("Tony Levin")
```

```
' Clear the table
ht.Clear()
```

Removing a nonexistent key simply does nothing.

Using Wrapper Methods

The **Synchronized()** shared member creates a **Hashtable** that is thread safe, and the **IsSynchronized** property can be used to identify which tables are synchronized.

You first create a standard **Hashtable** and then use these methods to create a wrapper with the desired properties. Here's an example showing how you can create a synchronized **Hashtable**:


```
' Create a synchronized Hashtable
Dim ht1 As New Hashtable()

' Put some values into the list
ht1.Add("First", "First Item")
ht1.Add("Second", "Second Item")
ht1.Add("Third", "Third Item")
ht1.Add("Fourth", "Fourth Item")

' Create a read-only wrapper
Dim htSync As Hashtable = Hashtable.Synchronized(ht1)

' Look for the value and print it out
Console.WriteLine("htSync is read-only: {0}", htSync.IsSynchronized)
```

Using SortedLists

A **SortedList** is one of the three classes in **System.Collections** that is designed for storing collections of key/value pairs, the others being **Hashtable** and **NameValueCollection**.

A **SortedList** maintains the data items in sorted key order and will let you retrieve them by key or by index. **SortedList**s are not as efficient as **Hashtable**s because they need to maintain the sort order of the list when adding items, but they basically work the same way. If you only want to retrieve your data by key, **Hashtable**s will be more efficient than **SortedList**s.

In order to be able to sort the entries, something has to be able to decide which relative order two items should occupy in the list. This can be done in two ways: First, the objects to be placed in the list can perform the comparison themselves. For this to work, the objects must implement the IComparable interface with its one **CompareTo()** member. All the value types, such as number and string classes, implement this interface, and it should be implemented by any other user-defined types whose values can be ordered.

The second way to sort entries involves the use of an external sorting object that implements the IComparer interface. This enables you to write a custom comparer object that implements the one **Compare()** method and can be used to decide the order in which objects should go into the list.

Creating and Filling SortedLists

A **SortedList** can easily be created and filled like this:

```
Dim sl As New SortedList()

' Add some items
sl.Add("two", 2)
sl.Add("three", 3)
sl.Add("one", 1)
sl.Item("zed") =  4

' See what we have
Console.WriteLine("Number of entries is {0}", sl.Count)
Console.WriteLine("Capacity is {0}", sl.Capacity)
```


There are several points to note about this code. Items can be added in two ways by using the **Add()** method or the **Item** property, which is read/write and can be used on either side of an equals sign. In this case, I've used integers as values, but you can use any object type.

***NOTE:** Keys have to be unique and cannot be **null** references (or **Nothing** in VB). You can use **null** references as values, however.*

The list is sorted as items are added, so that the actual order of the keys in the list is one-three-two-zed rather than the order in which they were added. This means that adding items to a **SortedList** is a time-consuming operation.

If you run this code, you'll find that the count of items in the list is four—which is reasonable—but that the capacity is 16 items, which may be surprising. The default capacity of a **SortedList** is 16 items, and it will double in size each time the limit is reached. So, if I add a 17th item, my list will grow to a capacity of 32; if I add a 33rd item, it will grow to 64; and so on. If there is too much spare capacity in a **SortedList**, you can use the **TrimToSize()** method to set the capacity to the actual number of elements.

Six constructors provide a number of ways in which you can construct **SortedLists**:

- Create an empty list with the default capacity of 16 items.
- Create an empty list with a specified capacity.
- Create a list from entries copied from another IDictionary object.
- Create an empty list with default capacity, and specify an IComparer object for sorting items as they are added.
- Create a list from entries copied from another IDictionary object, and specify a custom IComparer object.
- Create an empty list with a specified capacity, and specify a custom IComparer object.

Retrieving Elements

You can retrieve individual elements in the collection by key or by index, as shown in the following code:

```
' Get a value by key
Console.WriteLine("Value for key 'one' is {0}", sl.Item("one"))

' Get a value by index
Console.WriteLine("Value for index 1 is {0}", sl.GetByIndex(1))
```

Indexes are zero-based, and you have to remember that the keys were sorted when you added them to the list, so the index might not represent the key you think it ought to. In the preceding example, index 1 represents the key “three” because it is the second one in the list.

You can find the index for a given key or value by using the **IndexOfKey()** and **IndexOfValue()** methods:

```
' Get the index of a key
Console.WriteLine("Index of key 'zed' is {0}", sl.IndexOfKey("zed"))

' Get the index of a value
Console.WriteLine("Index of value '3' is {0}", sl.IndexOfValue(3))
```

These functions will return -1 if the key or value doesn't exist.

If you want to find out whether the list contains a particular key or value, you can use the **ContainsKey()** and **ContainsValue()** functions.

Modifying Elements

You can modify values by key or by index. As well as letting you add new keys, the **Item** property also lets you modify the value associated with an existing key:

```
' Store a new value with the 'zed' key
sl.Item("zed") = 50
```

If you want to modify a value by index, use the **SetByIndex()** method:

```
' Store a new value associated with key 1
sl.SetByIndex(1, 20)
```

Deleting Elements

The **Remove()** method removes a key/value pair by key, whereas **RemoveAt()** will do the same by index:

```
' Remove the 'zed' key and its associated value
sl.Remove("zed")

' Remove the key at index 1 and its associated value
sl.RemoveAt(1)
```

Trying to remove a nonexistent key doesn't do anything, but using an out-of-range index will produce an **ArgumentOutOfRangeException**. As you might expect, the **Clear()** method removes all items from the collection.

Using Thread-Safe SortedLists

The **Synchronized()** shared method creates a thread-safe wrapper class around a **SortedList**, so that it is protected from improper access by multiple threads. The **IsSynchronized** property tells you whether a given **SortedList** is synchronized or not:

```
Dim sl2 As New SortedList()

' Add some items
sl2.Add("A", "alpha")
sl2.Add("B", "bravo")
sl2.Add("C", "charlie")

' Create a thread-safe wrapper
Dim safeSL As SortedList = SortedList.Synchronized(sl2)

Console.WriteLine("safeSL is thread safe: {0}", safeSL.IsSynchronized)
```

How Do I Access Items in the Same Order They Were Received?

A Queue is a data structure that lets you recover items in the same order that they were added. It maintains items in the list, and you use the **Enqueue()** method to add items onto one end and the **Dequeue()** method to remove them from the other. Here's how you can set up and use a Queue in VB:

```
Dim qq As New Queue()

' Add some values to the queue
qq.Enqueue("first")
qq.Enqueue("second")
qq.Enqueue("third")
qq.Enqueue("fourth")
qq.Enqueue("fifth")

' See what we have
Console.WriteLine("Size is {0}, top element is {1}", qq.Count, qq.Peek)

' Remove the element from the head
qq.Dequeue()
```

I've created the Queue with its default capacity of 32 items, and the default growth factor of 2.0. If I exceed the current capacity, the Queue's capacity will be increased, and the new capacity will be the current value times the growth factor. So, as I add more and more items to this Queue, its capacity will grow from 32 to 64, to 128, to 256, and so on. It's quite obvious that the growth factor has to be at least 1.0, and the upper limit has been set to 10.0 to prevent Queues from growing too wildly.

Other constructors let you specify an initial capacity only or an initial capacity and a growth factor. You can also initialize a Queue with the contents of another collection.

You add elements using the **Enqueue()** method and can then look at the top element using **Peek()**. In this case, the element at the head of the Queue is "first" because it was the first one added. You can use the **Dequeue()** method to remove the element at the head of the Queue.

How Do I Use a Stack?

A Stack stores data so that the last object added is the first one to be retrieved; you can only add and remove objects from the top of Stack. The following example shows a simple use of a Stack in VB:

```
Dim s As New Stack()

' Add some values to the stack
s.Push(42)
s.Push(77)
s.Push(99)
s.Push(4)
s.Push(31)

' See what we have
Console.WriteLine("Size is {0}, top element is {1}", s.Count, s.Peek)

' Remove a value
s.Pop()

Console.WriteLine("Size is {0}, top element is {1}", s.Count, s.Peek)
```


I've created the Stack with its default capacity of 10 items. If I exceed the current capacity, its capacity will be doubled every time more is needed. Other constructors let you specify an initial capacity; you can also initialize a Stack with the contents of another collection.

Items are added to the Stack using the **Push()** method. You can add any object type to a stack; if you add primitive data types, they will be boxed before they are added. You can use the **Peek()** method to look at the top item on the Stack without removing it and the **Count** property to see how many items the Stack currently contains.

The **Pop()** method is used to remove the top item from the Stack, returning an **Object** reference. If you want to use this object, you'll have to cast it into the appropriate type, like this:

```
' Remove a value
Dim n As Integer = CType(s.Pop(), Integer)
```

The **Stack** class implements the ICollection, IEnumerable, and ICloneable interfaces, so it has all the methods associated with those interfaces, such as **Clear()**, **Count()**, **Contains()**, **Clone()**, and **CopyTo()**. The **ToArray()** method lets you copy the contents of the **Stack** to a standard language array or a **System.Array** object.

How Do I Store Flags in a **BitArray**?

A **BitArray** provides a compact way of storing a series of bits and lets you access them as if they are stored in an array. It provides you with compactness of storage without getting you involved in bit twiddling.

You can create a **BitArray** in several ways. The simplest way is to specify the number of bits you want to store in the array:

```
' Create a BitArray to hold five bits
Dim bt As New BitArray(5)
```

Elements in the array are initialized to false. There are several other constructors to let you initialize the array in different ways:

- By copying values from an array of Booleans
- By copying bits from an array of 32-bit integers
- By copying from another bit array
- By copying bits from an array of bytes
- By creating a sized array and initializing its elements to true

If you need to change the capacity of the array, you can use the **Length** property, which allows you to get and set the capacity. The **Count** property tells you how many bits are actually being used in the array.

Once you've created your array, you can access the bits using the **Item** property (or the **[]** indexer in C#):

```
' Set the second and fourth elements
bt.Item(1) = True
bt.Item(3) = True
```

Remember that as with all other index collections indexing starts from zero. As an alternative to **Item**, you can use the **Get()** and **Set()** methods:

```
' Equivalent to the previous code
bt.Set(1, True)
bt.Set(3, True)
```

If you want to change everything, the **SetAll()** method can be used to set the entire array to true or false.

The class implements a set of Boolean operations for working on **BitArrays**. The **And()**, **Or()**, and **Xor()** methods perform bitwise operations on two **BitArrays**, returning a new **BitArray** containing the result. The **Not()** method returns a **BitArray** containing the result of inverting all the bits in a **BitArray**.

As an example, let's use the five-element **BitArray** from the preceding code, where I've set bits 1 and 3 to true. You can use an enumerator to list the values:

```
Dim ie as IEnumerator = bt.GetEnumerator
While ie.MoveNext = True
  Console.Write("{0} ", ie.Current)
End While
Console.WriteLine()
```

You will get the following output:

```
False True False True False
```


You can now define a second **BitArray** and use the **And()** method to produce a third **BitArray**, which is the result of the logical **and** operation on the first two arrays:

```
' Create a BitArray to hold five bits
Dim bt1 As New BitArray(5)

' Set the second bit to true
bt1.Item(1) = True

Dim ie2 as IEnumerator = (bt.And(bt1)).GetEnumerator
```

Notice how I'm not saving the result of the **And()** operation, but simply getting an enumerator back from it. The **And()** method creates a **BitArray** with ones where both source arrays have ones, and zeros otherwise. Because only the second bit is set in both **bt** and **bt1**, printing out the array elements would look like this:

```
False True False False False
```

Storing Strings in a StringCollection

A **StringCollection** is a special purpose array for storing strings, and is part of the **System.Collections.Specialized** namespace. You can access the elements by index, and add, remove, and insert items. **StringCollections** are not synchronized.

The **StringCollection** class implements the ICollection, IEnumerable, and IList interfaces, so it has all the methods associated with those interfaces, such as **Clear()**, **Count()**, **Contains()**, and **CopyTo()**.

The following example shows how to use a **StringCollection** in VB:

```
' Import the Specialized namespace
Imports System.Collections.Specialized

Dim sc As New StringCollection()

' Add some values to the collection
sc.Add("Now is the time")
sc.Add("Now is the time")
sc.Add("For all good men")
sc.Add("To come to the party!")

' See what we have
Console.WriteLine("Size is {0}, first element is {1}", sc.Count, sc.Item(0))

' Remove the duplicate at index 1
sc.RemoveAt(1)

' The size is now three elements
Console.WriteLine("Size is {0}", sc.Count)
```


The **Add()** method is used to add strings to the end of the collection, and the **Item** property is used to locate an element by index. **RemoveAt()** is used to remove an element by index, and you can also use **Remove()** to remove an element by value.

Contains() can be used to determine whether the collection holds a particular string, and **IndexOf()** returns the zero-based index of the first occurrence of a string in the collection.

Using **StringCollections** in C# is very much the same as it is in VB, with the one exception that **Item** is used as the class indexer, so you can use the **[]** notation to access elements in the collection:

```
// See what we have (C# version)
Console.WriteLine("Size is {0}, first element is {1}", sc.Count, sc[0]);
```

Storing Strings by Key in a NameValueCollection

If you want to store a collection of strings and be able to retrieve them by key or index, a **NameValueCollection** is what you need, and you'll find it in the **System.Collections.Specialized** namespace.

Because **NameValueCollection** is based on **Hashtable**, it has the same variety of overloaded constructors that let you create objects in a number of ways:

- As an empty **NameValueCollection** with a default or specified initial capacity
- By copying the entries from another **NameValueCollection**
- By specifying IComparer and IHashCodeProvider objects for both of the preceding ways

The default comparer is the **CaseInsensitiveComparer**, which (as its name implies) ignores case when comparing strings. The default hash code provider is the **CaseInsensitiveHashCodeProvider**.

Here's a simple example showing how to create and use a **NameValueCollection** in VB:


```
' You need to import the namespace
Imports System.Collections.Specialized
...
Dim nv As New NameValueCollection()

' Add some values to the collection
nv.Add("one", "The first string in the collection")
nv.Add("two", "The second string")

Console.WriteLine("The collection has {0} key/value pairs", nv.Count())
```

NameValueCollection has two slightly unusual properties. The first is that you are allowed to add entries with duplicate keys, and when you retrieve by key, you get all the values back in a comma-separated list. The second is that you are allowed to use a **null** reference as a key, as shown here:

```
' Add an item with a null key
nv.Add(Nothing, "An item with a null key")
```

Remember that using a null key is different from using a zero-length string:

```
' Add an item with a zero-length string as a key
nv.Add("", "An item with a zero-length key")
```

Finding and Retrieving Entries

Entries can be retrieved by index or by key:

```
' Retrieve an entry by key
Console.WriteLine("Key 'one' has value '{0}'", nv.Item("one"))
```

```
' Retrieve an entry by index
Console.WriteLine("Entry 0 has value '{0}'", nv.Item(0))
```

New items are simply added onto the end of the collection, so the most recently added items will have the highest indices. The **Item()** method is used to select an entry by key or index and can be used on either side of the **=**, so you can add new entries like this:

```
' Add a value using Item()
nv.Item("three") = "Another string"
```

In C#, **Item()** is used as the indexer for the class, so you can refer to entries using array notation:

```
// Add a value
nv["three"] = "Another string"
```

The **GetKey()** method returns the key at a particular index, whereas the **AllKeys()** property returns an array of **String** objects containing all the keys in the collection.

```
' Retrieve a key by index
Console.WriteLine("Key 1 has value '{0}'", nv.GetKey(1))

' Write the list of keys
Dim keys() As String = nv.AllKeys()
Dim s As String

Console.WriteLine("Key list:")
For Each s In keys
  Console.WriteLine(s)
Next
```

In much the same way, you can use the **All** property to retrieve a collection of all the values in the collection.

Removing Items

There are two methods for removing entries from a collection. The **Remove()** method removes an entry by key, whereas **Clear()** removes all the entries:

```
' Remove an entry
nv.Remove("one")

' Clear the table
nv.Clear()
```

Removing a nonexistent key simply does nothing, whereas removing a duplicate key will remove all the values associated with that key.

NOTE: *There isn't a way to remove an entry by index, only by key.*

How Do I Implement Custom Sorting?

Several classes in **System.Collections** and **System.Collections.Specialized** (such as **SortedList**, **Hashtable**, and **NameValueCollection**) can use a "comparer" object in order to sort entries. By default, the objects themselves provide a sort order through their implementations of IComparable, but if you need to, it is possible to define a custom sorting mechanism.

This is done by providing a class that implements the IComparer interface. This interface has one member, **Compare( )**, which takes two **Object** references, returning -1 if the first is less than the second, 0 if they are the same, and 1 if the first is greater than the second.

The following example shows how this works by implementing a custom comparer object that sorts strings into reverse order. Here's the code for the custom comparer class:

```
' An example showing how to implement custom sorting for collections
Imports System.Collections

' A custom comparer class which implements IComparer, and which sorts
' strings in reverse order
Public Class JComparer
  Implements IComparer

  ' Note the use of the square brackets around the function name. This
  ' lets us use a VB keyword as a function name without the compiler
  ' objecting
  Function [Compare](ByVal first As Object, ByVal second As Object) _
              As Integer Implements IComparer.Compare

    ' we're only dealing with strings, so check the types...
    If Not (TypeOf first Is String And TypeOf second Is String) Then
      Throw New ArgumentException("Can't compare types that aren't strings")
    End If

    ' handle null references
    If first Is Nothing And second Is Nothing Then
      Return 0
```

```
    ElseIf first Is Nothing Then
      Return -1
    ElseIf Second Is Nothing Then
      Return 1
    End If

    ' now we can compare...
    Dim i As Integer = String.Compare(CType(first, String), _
              CType(Second, String))

    Return i * -1
  End Function
End Class
```

The class implements IComparer and therefore has to provide the one **Compare()** function. I run into an immediate problem here because **compare** is a keyword in VB. NET, so I can't use it as a function name. The solution is to enclose it in square brackets.

Compare() can be used to compare any object types, so I first check the types of both arguments to determine if they are both strings. The definition of IComparer states that I can throw an **ArgumentException** if I don't like the arguments I've been passed, so that's what I do if they are not both strings. My next task is to deal with **null** references. The rules states that a **null** reference is always "less than" an object, so I check the arguments for "nothingness" and return an appropriate value.

The final task is to perform the comparison, and here I cheat slightly. The **String** class itself already implements the **Compare()** function so I make it do the comparison for me, and because I want to sort into reverse order, I simply invert the value it gives me in return.

Once I've got the comparer class defined, I can use it to sort items as I add them to a **SortedList**:

```
Sub Main()
  ' Create a comparer object
  Dim cmp As New JComparer()

  ' Create a SortedList that uses this comparer
  Dim sl As New SortedList(cmp)

  ' Add items to the list...
  sl.Add("foo", "f")
  sl.Add("alice", "a")
  sl.Add("zebra", "z")
  sl.Add("codicil", "c")
  sl.Add("morph", "m")
```

```
    Console.WriteLine("Index 0 is {0}", sl.GetByIndex(0))
    Console.WriteLine("Index 4 is {0}", sl.GetByIndex(4))
End Sub
```

When the list is printed out, the items will appear in reverse order, with *zebra* first and *alice* last.

How Do I Create My Own Collections?

The **System.Collections** namespace provides you with three classes that can be used to create your own custom collection types. Two of these (**CollectionBase** and **ReadonlyCollectionBase**) are related, being read/write and read-only versions of a class that lets you store and manipulate a list of **Object** references. The third, **DictionaryBase**, lets you create custom **Hashtable**-like collections of keys and values.

You use all three of these classes in very much the same way, so I'll use **CollectionBase** as an example to show how to derive a custom collection. This class implements the IList, ICollection, and IEnumerable interfaces, which means that it provides a complete selection of the functionality needed by a custom collection including creating enumerators and adding, modifying, and removing entries. Creating your own custom collection class is simply a case of inheriting from this class, adding methods to handle your own data types.

You will first need a test class on which to base the collection, and this simple "Person" class will do nicely. I'm going to use it to create a custom **PersonCollection** class, which will only be able to hold and manipulate **Person** objects:

```
' Test Person class to store in our collection
   Public Class Person
       Private nameVal As String
       Private phoneVal As String

       Public Property Name() As String
           Get
               Name = nameVal
           End Get
           Set
               nameVal = Value
           End Set
       End Property
```

```
        Public Property Phone() As String
            Get
                Phone = phoneVal
            End Get
            Set
                phoneVal = Value
            End Set
        End Property
    End Class
```

The first step in defining a new collection class is to ensure that the right namespaces are imported. In this case, you need **System.Collections**:

```
' Import the necessary namespaces
Imports System.Collections
```


Here's the listing for the custom collection class itself:

```
' A custom collection of Person objects
Public Class PersonCollection
  Inherits CollectionBase

  ' Provide an Item property
  Default Public Property Item(ByVal index As Integer) As Person
    Get
      Item = CType(List.Item(index), Person)
    End Get
    Set
      List.Item(index) = Value
    End Set
  End Property

  ' Provide add and remove methods
  Public Function Add(ByVal p As Person) As Integer
    ' IList.Add returns the index at which the value was stored
    Return List.Add(p)
  End Function

  Public Sub Remove(ByVal p As Person)
    List.Remove(p)
  End Sub
End Class
```

There's not much to it, really. The class inherits from **CollectionBase**, and then implements three functions. The first is the **Item** property, which can be used to get and set items in the collection by value. Many of the classes in the **System.Collections** namespace provide an **Item** property, so it makes sense to provide one in this class. Note how it works with **Person** objects: That's what makes this a strongly typed class, you can only get and set **Person** objects. The data is held by the **CollectionBase** base class in a list, and you can use the inherited **List** property to interact with it.

Note also how **Item** is marked as "Default." The default property is one that can be directly invoked on an object without having to use the property name, so the following two lines of code mean the same:

```
myCollection.Item(0)
myCollection(0)
```


I've also added **Add()** and **Remove()** methods for completeness. Although it would obviously be easy to add any other functionality I might require, that's all I need to be able to demonstrate how useful this collection can be.

Here's a simple test program to demonstrate the use of the custom collection (the complete version of the code is included on the CD-ROM that accompanies this book):

```
Sub Main()
  ' Create and initialize a couple of Person objects
  Dim p1 As New Person()
  Dim p2 As New Person()

  p1.Name = "Fred"
  p1.Phone = "123-4567"

  p2.Name = "Bill"
  p2.Phone = "234-4321"

  ' Create a collection, and add the objects to it
  Dim coll As New PersonCollection()
  coll.Add(p1)
  coll.Add(p2)

  ' See how many items there are...
  Console.WriteLine("Number of items in the list: {0}", coll.Count)

  ' Enumerate the list...
  Dim p As Person
  For Each p In coll
    Console.WriteLine("Entry is {0}", p.Name)
  Next
```

```
  ' Get a value by index
  Console.WriteLine("Entry 1 is {0}", coll(1).Name)
End Sub
```

I start by creating and initializing a pair of **Person** objects and add them to a **PersonCollection** object. Once I've done that, I can see how many items there are in the list and enumerate over each item in the collection using **For Each**. If you've ever tried implementing a custom collection in VB6, I'm sure you'll agree that this is much simpler.

Chapter 5

The XML Namespaces

By Julian Templeman

In Depth

XML is very important in .NET because it provides a simple, structured way of storing and communicating data that is very useful in the distributed environment. By making XML the preferred way to communicate between the parts of distributed Web applications, Microsoft has ensured that the .NET architecture is open and expandable.

You'll get the most out of this chapter if you are somewhat familiar with XML. If you are unfamiliar with XML, the next section provides a brief introduction. However, you'll need to read more about the complex world of XML and XML technologies if you want to use it in the real world.

XML from 30,000 Feet

Before I get into the details of the .NET XML namespaces, I'll present a brief introduction to XML for those that haven't used it.

XML is becoming very complex and I cannot hope to turn you into an XML expert—or even cover everything you ought to know—in the course of a few pages. Therefore, I'll discuss the basics in enough detail so that you'll be able to understand how to parse, use, and create XML.

This section introduces you to the main features of XML and gives you enough information to get started. It does not cover details of the more advanced technologies—such as schemas and XSL. For more details, consult other XML texts, such as the *XML Black Book, 2nd Edition*, by Natanya Pitts (The Coriolis Group, Inc.).

What Is XML?

Nowadays, everyone is familiar with HTML and its use in creating Web pages; many people have a passing acquaintance at least with the angle brackets and tags used in creating HTML documents. Although HTML is very useful for its intended purpose—laying out Web pages—people are finding that it is limited in that it only describes the layout of data and not what the data represents. Consider the following HTML fragment:

```
<h1>Moby Dick</h1>
<h2>Herman Melville</h2>
```

The **<h1>** and **<h2>** tags denote first and second level headings, but there's nothing in the data that tells you what the data represents. From the content, you can probably guess that it describes a book, but there's nothing in the tags to tell you that. The fact is that HTML is simply used to pass formatting information to a browser, and anything that you can glean about the content is just extra information. In addition, the set of tags supported by HTML is fixed, so it's difficult to impart extra information in an HTML document without resorting to nonstandard extensions.

XML arose from the realization that the increasing sophistication of the Web demanded a richer way of marking up data than HTML could provide. There was a sophisticated general solution for markup in existence called Standard Generalized Markup Language (SGML), but it was far too complex for general use. SGML was invented in the 1970s, became an international standard in 1986, and has achieved some success in the defense and aerospace industries. But it is very large and complex, and mainly suited to markup of very large documents, such as Boeing 747 engineering documentation.

In 1996, a working party at W3C (the Web standards body) started work on a subset of SGML that would be suitable for Web use. The result in 1998 was XML 1.0, and it represented a version of SGML stripped of obscure, difficult, and redundant features. Since then, XML has been enthusiastically—sometimes too enthusiastically—adopted all over the IT world. In fact, it is now being used in a very wide variety of applications including:

- *Document markup*—Rather than storing textual material in HTML, Microsoft Word, or PDF formats, an increasing number of people are storing text as XML, and then using stylesheets to transform it into other formats as necessary. This means that you can store a manual as XML and use stylesheets to produce an HTML version for online viewing, another HTML version for viewing on a WAP device, or a PDF version for printing.
- *Data exchange*—XML can be used to exchange data between widely different applications and architectures because it is easily produced, easily transmitted, and easily parsed. XML's hierarchical nature means that it is easy to represent structured data, such as a database table. Several XML-based protocols have been developed that let Remote Procedure Calls (RPCs) work across languages and platforms, and through firewalls. Simple Object Access Protocol (SOAP) is particularly used in .NET, and we'll talk more about it in Chapter 14.
- *Data storage*—XML provides a simple, standardized means of storing data, and many applications are using XML so that their data can be easily exchanged with other applications.
- *Database operations*—Many databases, including Microsoft's Access and SQL Server, will now return the result of SQL queries as XML documents,

which makes it easy to work with the data in other applications. XML is also used with .NET to design database schemas.

Structure of an XML Document

Let's look at the HTML fragment rendered in XML:

```
<author>Herman Melville</author>
<title>Moby Dick</title>
```

Although the tags look the same, you can see an immediate difference—the tag names describe what the data is, not just how to display it. This means that it is easy to search XML to view, say, all the authors in a series of books. XML differs from HTML in that it is up to you to decide which tags to use and what they mean. This ability to customize the tags is what gives XML its extensibility and is the reason it is so widely used.

NOTE: *An XML element consists of the tags plus the content.*

Here's a more complete example of an XML document:

```
<?xml version="1.0"?>
<!-- My stocklist -->
<stocklist>
  <book>
    <author>Herman Melville</author>
    <title>Moby Dick</title>
    <publisher>White Whale Press</publisher>
    <category>fiction</category>
    <price>19.95</price>
    <stock>3</stock>
  </book>
  <book>
    <author>Bill Gates</author>
    <title>Linux Made Easy</title>
    <publisher>MS Press</publisher>
    <category>fiction</category>
    <price>40.00</price>
    <stock>5</stock>
  </book>
  <book>
    <author>Scott McNeally</author>
    <author>Bill Joy</author>
    <title>VB Programming</title>
    <publisher>Sun Publishing</publisher>
```

```
<category>fiction</category>
    <price>21.00</price>
    <stock>2</stock>
  </book>
</stocklist>
```

There are several important points that need to be discussed in this code. To start with, the first line (which must appear in all XML documents) identifies this as an XML document. Without it, many applications that can parse XML will refuse to go any further because they don't recognize a well-formed document.

This first line is called the *XML declaration* and is an example of a processing instruction (PI). PIs are enclosed in **<?** and **?>** markers and are intended as instructions to applications that use XML rather than being part of the data. This line is a special processing instruction intended for XML parsers, and it identifies what follows as an XML document. The second line is a comment and shows that comments in XML are the same as in HTML.

An XML document consists of a hierarchical set of tags, and there can only be one outermost tag--in this case **<stocklist>**—which is known as the root. Despite using a similar tag mechanism, XML differs from HTML in that all tags must be *well-formed*, meaning that all opening tags must have a matching end tag, and that tags must nest correctly. This means that common HTML practices, such as using **<p>** and **
** tags without end tags, won't work in XML, and you'll need to supply a closing tag.

If an element has no content, XML lets you merge the opening and closing tags, so that the following two lines of XML are equivalent:

```
<InStock></InStock>
<InStock />
```

Because tags must nest correctly, the following HTML is not well-formed:

```
<b><i>Bold and italic</b></i>
```

The bold and italic tags don't nest correctly, and although most browsers are able to use this line, it would be rejected by an XML parser.

Attributes

Similar to HTML, XML tags can contain attributes consisting of keyword/value pairs as in the following example:

```
<person firstName="fred" lastName="smith">
```

Entities and CDATA Sections

Certain characters have special meanings within XML documents. Therefore, you cannot arbitrarily scatter characters such as **<** throughout your XML data without causing confusion to programs reading it. XML has a mechanism that lets you get around this limitation by using *entities*.

NOTE: *Entities can be quite complex and are used for a lot more than the simple escape mechanism described here.*

An entity reference is a string of characters that come between a "&" and a ";" character, such as *<*. They are used in XML data as a general substitution mechanism. So, if you want to use the following string in an XML document:

```
The start of an XML tag is denoted by <
```

you would have to code it as

```
The start of an XML tag is denoted by &lt;
```

The parser will read the entity reference and substitute a **<** character, but will not treat it as the start of a tag.

If you have a lot of data containing **<** and **>** characters, it becomes awkward to keep using entities, which make the data far less readable. In that case, you may want to use a CDATA section, which effectively escapes a whole block of text:

```
<someData>
<! [CDATA [
Unparsed data such as <this> and <this> goes here...
]]>
</someData>
```

The syntax of CDATA sections, with their multiple square brackets, has been inherited from SGML.

XML Validation

You may be wondering how any order can be imposed if you can make up your own tags and make them mean whatever you like. For example, how do I know what is valid to put in the stocklist document and what isn't? Can I have more than one author? On the other hand, do I have to have an author at all?

The answer is that XML can be *validated* against other documents that describe the structure of a particular type of XML document. There are three types of these descriptive documents—Document Type Definitions (DTDs), schemas, and XDR Schemas:

- DTDs are an older mechanism inherited from SGML for describing the content of XML documents.
- Schemas are a newer XML mechanism.
- XDR Schemas are a Microsoft-specific mechanism.

All three of these mechanisms let you constrain the content of an XML document by specifying:

- What tags can appear in the document
- Whether they are optional
- Whether they can appear more than once
- The order in which they have to appear
- The way in which they have to be nested

Validation is supported in .NET through the **System.Xml.XmlValidatingReader** class.

Namespaces

You can run into problems when you try to use two XML documents together, because the creators of the two documents may have used the same tag names, but be using them for different purposes. Suppose you have one XML document that lists company employees and has **<address>** elements holding postal addresses, and another that lists employees' email addresses, also with an **<address>** tag, like this:

```
<!-- In the employee file -->
<address>1207 Pleinmont Blvd., Nowhere</address>

<!-- In the email file -->
<address>ed@trailingEdge.com</address>
```

If you want to merge the two sets of data, how are you going to distinguish between the two different addresses? You could write some code to edit the data and change the email address tags to **<emailAddress>**, but this is time-consuming and inefficient. Namespaces offer a way around this problem by providing an extra level of naming for elements.

NOTE: *The concept of using namespaces in this way will be familiar to C++ programmers; XML namespaces work in a similar way.*

Here's how you can fix the problem using namespaces:

```
<!-- In the employee file -->
<emp:address>1207 Pleinmont Blvd., Nowhere</emp:address>

<!-- In the email file -->
<email:address>ed@trailingEdge.com</email:address>
```

The parser (or any other application using this XML) can now tell which address is which by looking at the namespace prefix on the tag:

```
<!-- In the employee file -->
<emp:employees xmlns:emp="http://www.trailingEdge.com">
  ...
  <emp:address>1207 Pleinmont Blvd., Nowhere</emp:address>
  ...
</emp:employees>
```


A namespace is defined at the start of an element, and it applies to all nested elements. It is defined as an attribute starting with "xmlns:", which tells the parser that this is an XML namespace declaration. The value of the namespace attribute is normally a URL, and is simply there to provide a unique value to identify this namespace.

NOTE: *Many people get confused about namespaces and think that a namespace URL has to point somewhere ... it doesn't! The value doesn't even have to be a URL.*

When working with XML elements, it is usually possible to retrieve the element name with or without the namespace prefix and to find out what namespaces (if any) are in operation.

Processing XML

The XML examples I've shown thus far represent XML in its *serialized form*, as it is stored in a disk file or sent across the Web. In order to work with the data, a program has to read the XML and parse it. It would be possible for you to write your own code to do this, but it is such a common task that many parsers have been written that can convert to and from XML's serialized form. Parsing in the Windows world is very easy because Microsoft's XML parser, MSXML, is part of the Internet Explorer distribution and therefore is available on just about every Windows machine in the world. As you'll see in the Immediate Solutions, .NET uses MSXML for all its parsing needs.

There are two common ways of working with an XML document when using a parser. The first is to get the parser to read the entire document, parse it, and build a tree in memory. Once the tree has been built, you can traverse it at will and can also modify it, by adding, deleting, reordering, and changing elements. The second way is to read the document line by line, recognizing elements as they occur.

The W3C has produced a model of how an XML document is represented in memory, called the Document Object Model (DOM). There are bindings to many languages to let you work with a DOM representation of an XML document. In .NET, you can work with DOM representations of XML documents using the **System.Xml.XmlDocument** class.

The DOM is very flexible, but it suffers from one limitation in that the amount of memory needed to store the tree is directly proportional to the size of the XML document, which may be prohibitive for large documents. It may also be the case that you don't need to have the whole structure in memory at once and can make do with traversing the tree one element at a time from the top.

Many parsers implement ways to do simple, efficient, forward-only parsing of XML documents. One de facto standard that is widely used is Simple API for XML Parsing (SAX), where the parser reads the document element by element and uses callback functions that you provide, which tells you when something interesting has occurred, such as the start of an element, the end of an element, or the occurrence of a processing instruction. This is called a "push" model because it is event driven and the parser calls you when it is ready.

Microsoft has implemented a forward-only parsing mechanism that is a "pull" model, so you can ask the parser for the next element when you're ready and skip elements you're not interested in, which you cannot do with SAX. Microsoft supports this model through the **System.Xml.XmlTextReader** and **System.Xml.XmlTextWriter** classes.

XSL Transformations

The tags in an XML document describe the data, but do not provide information about how it should be presented when displayed in a browser. It turns out that this is just a small piece of a more general problem: XML is used to store and transport data, but it isn't very valuable unless it can be transformed into other useful forms, such as HTML for display by a browser, PDF for printing, or even as input for a database update operation.

It's always possible to write custom code to parse XML and transform it manually, but for many tasks this is unnecessary. The transformation can be accomplished by applying a stylesheet to the XML data in the same way that you would apply a stylesheet to a Word document in order to get a particular look and feel. In the HTML world, a good parallel would be CSS (Cascading Style Sheets), which lets you apply new styles to an HTML document. In fact, CSS can be used with XML, but XSL provides a better way.

The XML Stylesheet Language (XSL) provides a way to apply stylesheets to XML files, and it is used in many ways including:

- Converting XML to HTML for display in a browser
- Converting XML to different sets of HTML for display on different devices (WAP phones, browsers, Pocket PCs, and so on)
- Converting XML to other formats, such as PDF or RTF (rich text format)
- Transforming XML into other XML formats

The idea is very simple: You match sets of elements in the document (such as "all the authors" or "all books whose price is more than $30"), and then decide what to output. For example, consider the author of one of the books in the previous example:

```
<author>Herman Melville</author>
```

I may decide that I want to output this as a level 2 HTML heading, like this:

```
<h2>Herman Melville</h2>
```

I could do this in XSL using the following fragment of XSL code:

```
<!-- Match all authors -->
<xsl:template match="book/author">
  <h2><xsl:value-of select="." /></h2>
</xsl:template>
```

Note that XSL stylesheets are basically just XML documents and obey all the same rules. XSL "commands" are qualified with the **xsl:** namespace, so that it is unambiguous distinguishing between what is an XSL tag and what is part of the stylesheet data.

A "template" is used to match one or more elements in an XML document. In the preceding example, I'm assuming that I'm at the **<stocklist>** level, and I want to match **<author>** elements that are children of **<book>** elements, using the **/** to build hierarchies. Once a list of candidate elements has been prepared, the body of the template is processed: Any XSL commands are executed, and anything that isn't recognized is passed through to the output.

In the example, the **<h2>** isn't recognized as XSL, so it is passed through to the output. The next element is an XSL command; it selects the value of the current element, which in this case is "Herman Melville", and echoes that. The final **</h2>** tag isn't recognized and gets passed through, so the final output is

```
<h2>Herman Melville</h2>
```

One important point to note is that even though the HTML tags are simply being echoed to the output, they still need to be well-formed because they're going to be parsed as part of the XML stream. This means that if you want to output a **
** tag, you'll have to use **
** in order to make sure it is well-formed.

The "select" and "match" expressions in the XSL fragment are examples of **XPath** expressions. **XPath**, the XML Path language, is a notation for describing sets of nodes in an XML document and is similar to the idea of using regular expressions to match text in a text editor.

The System.Xml Namespace

Now that you have some idea of what XML is and how it is used, let's move on to see how Microsoft supports XML in .NET. Much of the XML functionality in .NET is provided in the **System.Xml** namespace, and classes in this namespace support many of the established XML standards:

- XML 1.0, including DTD support, via the **XmlTextReader** class
- XML namespaces, both stream level and DOM
- XML Schemas for schema mapping and serialization, and for validation using **XmlValidatingReader**
- **XPath** expressions via the **XPathNavigator** class
- XSLT via the **XslTransform** class
- DOM Level 2 via **XmlDocument**
- SOAP 1.1

In this chapter, I concentrate on the first six XML standards, covering reading, writing, validating, and transforming XML documents. SOAP and the use of XML for data transfer is covered in Chapter 14.

XmlTextReader

XmlTextReader is a reader class that, according to the documentation, provides "fast, noncached, forward-only stream access to XML data." Instead of loading the entire document into memory as is the case with DOM, **XmlTextReader** reads the XML one element (one "node") at a time. The properties of the **XmlTextReader** object reflect the properties of the current node, and once a node has been read, you cannot go back and read it again without starting from the beginning. This means that **XmlTextReader** is light on resources because there need only be one node in memory at a time.

I've already mentioned that **XmlTextReader** uses a "pull" model, which means it is up to you to access and get each new node as you want it. Other "one node at a time" forward-only parsing models tend to be event-driven and use callback functions, so the parser calls back into your code every time one of a standard set of events occurs. These include the start and end of elements and processing instruction definitions. This is fairly simple to set up because you only have to write a series of disconnected callback functions. But it makes it difficult to control when these functions get called and what you get told about; it can be very hard to keep track of state.

Table 5.1 and Table 5.2 show some of the important properties and methods of the **XmlTextReader** class.

Table 5.1 Important properties of the XmlTextReader class.

Property	Description
AttributeCount	Returns the number of attributes on the current node.
Depth	Indicates the depth of the current node in the element stack.
Encoding	Indicates the document's encoding attribute.
EOF	Returns true if the reader is at the end of the input stream.
HasValue	Returns true if the node has text.
IsEmptyElement	Returns true if the current node is empty (e.g., **<empty />**).
Item	Gets the value of an attribute.
LineNumber, **LinePosition**	Indicates the current line number and character position. Used mainly for error reporting.
LocalName	Indicates the name of the current node without the namespace prefix.
Name	Returns the name of the current node including the namespace prefix.
Namespaces	Gets or sets a value indicating whether namespaces are to be supported.
NodeType	Gets the type of the current node.
Prefix	Gets the namespace prefix associated with the current node.
ReadState	Gets the state of the input stream.
Value	Gets the text value of the node.
XmlLang	Gets the **xml:lang** scope for the current node.

Table 5.2 Important methods of the XmlTextReader class.

Method	Description
Close	Closes the input stream
GetAttribute	Gets the value of an attribute
MoveToAttribute	Moves to the specified attribute
MoveToElement	Moves to the element that contains the current attribute
MoveToFirstAttribute, **MoveToNextAttribute**	Moves to the first or last attribute
Read	Reads the next node from the stream
ReadAttributeValue	Returns the value(s) associated with an attribute
ReadBase64	Reads the text content of an element and does a Base64 decode on it
ReadBinHex	Reads the text content of an element and does a BinHex decode on it
ReadChars	Reads element text content into a char buffer
ReadInnerXML	Reads all the content of the current node including XML markup
ReadOuterXML	Reads all the content of the current node and all its children
ReadString	Reads element text content as a string

The class also has 13 constructors, allowing you to create **XmlTextReader** objects that get input from a number of sources including strings, files, and streams.

XmlTextReader is derived from the abstract **XmlReader** class, which provides basic reader functionality for three classes: **XmlTextReader**, **XmlValidatingReader**, and **XmlNodeReader**.

XmlValidatingReader

This class, **System.Xml.XmlValidatingReader**, is used to validate XML as it is being read. It can use all three of the commonly available validation types:

- Document Type Definitions (DTDs)
- W3C standard schemas
- Microsoft XDR Schemas

NOTE: *W3C has only recently standardized Schemas, and while waiting for the standard, Microsoft produced its own version, known as the XDR (XML Data Reduced) Schema. Now that the standard is available, the use of XDR should decrease, and you're encouraged to use the W3C standard model wherever possible.*

XmlValidatingReader has a property, **ValidationType**, that determines which type of validation is going to be used. See Table 5.14 in the Immediate Solution

"Parsing a Document with Validation" for details of the validation types that are supported.

When an **XmlValidatingReader** detects an error, it fires an event that contains information about the error that it found. You provide an event handler to catch and act on error events, and the Immediate Solution shows how to do this.

XmlTextWriter

If you want to write XML to a file or stream in serialized form, and you know exactly what you require, the **XmlTextWriter** class provides a fast, noncached, forward-only way to write XML. This class derives from the abstract **XmlWriter** base class, and you can provide your own specialized XML writer classes if necessary.

Using **XmlTextWriter**, you make a series of calls that result in output being produced, so you control what is output and when.

Table 5.3 and Table 5.4 list the important properties and methods of the **XmlTextWriter** class.

Table 5.3 Important properties of the XmlTextWriter class.

Property	Description
Formatting	Indicates how the output is formatted
Indentation	Gets or sets the indentation level
IndentChar	Gets or sets the character to be used for indentation
Namespaces	Gets or sets a value indicating whether to do namespace support
QuoteChar	Gets or sets the character to use to quote attribute values
WriteState	Gets the state of the stream

Table 5.4 Important methods of the XmlTextWriter class.

Method	Description
Close	Closes the output stream
Flush	Flushes the output stream
WriteBase64	Writes bytes encoded as Base64
WriteBinHex	Writes bytes encoded as BinHex
WriteCData	Writes a CDATA block containing the specified text
WriteChar, WriteChars	Writes one or more characters
WriteComment	Writes an XML comment

(continued)

Table 5.4 Important methods of the **XmlTextWriter** class *(continued)*.

Method	Description
WriteDocType	Writes a **DocType** declaration
WriteEndDocument	Closes any open elements or attributes and puts the writer back in the Start state
WriteEndElement	Closes an element
WriteFullEndElement	Closes an element, always writing a full end tag
WriteName	Writes a name
WriteProcessingInstruction	Writes a processing instruction
WriteQualifiedName	Writes a namespace-qualified name
WriteRaw	Writes raw markup
WriteStartAttribute, **WriteEndAttribute**	Starts and ends an attribute definition
WriteStartDocument	Writes an XML declaration
WriteStartElement	Writes a start tag
WriteString	Writes a **String** value
WriteWhiteSpace	Writes white space characters

XmlDocument

The **XmlDocument** class represents an entire XML document as a DOM tree and can be used to add, delete, and change nodes in the tree. DOM trees consist of nodes of different types, as shown in Figure 5.1.

Note how attributes and the text content of elements are nodes in their own right. The document itself is represented by a Document node (often known as the

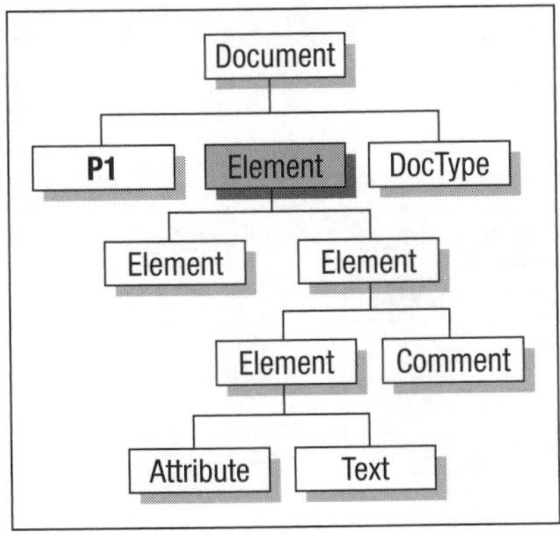

Figure 5.1 A DOM tree is a collection of nodes of different types.

Table 5.5 Node types in an XmlDocument DOM tree.

Class	Description
XmlAttribute	Represents an attribute on a node
XmlCDataSection	Represents a CDATA section
XmlComment	Represents a comment
XmlDeclaration	Represents an XML declaration
XmlDocumentType	Represents a **DOCTYPE** declaration
XmlElement	Represents an element
XmlEntityReference	Represents an entity reference
XmlProcessingInstruction	Represents a processing instruction
XmlText	Represents the text content of a node

document element), and beneath this is an Element node that represents the root of the XML document, shown shaded in gray in the figure. Table 5.5 lists the types of nodes that you may find in an **XmlDocument** DOM tree.

XmlNode

All the node types listed in the previous section are ultimately derived from the abstract **XmlNode** class, and it is this class that provides most of the functionality that you need when working with DOM trees.

Note that the **XmlDocument** class also inherits from **XmlNode**, so that it has all the methods and properties of a node. Because the **XmlNode** class is so important, I'll start by listing some of the properties and methods of the class in Tables 5.6 and 5.7.

Table 5.6 Important properties of the XmlNode class.

Property	Description
Attributes	Returns an **XmlAttributeCollection** object containing the attributes of this node.
ChildNodes	Returns an **XmlNodeList** that contains all the children of this node.
FirstChild	Returns the first child of this node, or **null** if there are no children.
HasChildNodes	Returns true if this node has children.
Item	Retrieves a specified child node.
LastChild	Returns the last child of this node.
Name, LocalName	Returns the name of the node with or without a namespace prefix.
NextSibling, PreviousSibling	Returns the node immediately following or preceding this node.

(continued)

Table 5.6 Important properties of the XmlNode class *(continued)*.

Property	Description
NodeType	Returns the type of the node.
OwnerDocument	Returns the **XmlDocument** to which this node belongs.
ParentNode	Returns the parent of this node. What this returns depends on the node type.
Value	Gets or sets the value of this node. What the value is depends on the node type.

Table 5.7 Important methods of the XmlNode class.

Method	Description
AppendChild, PrependChild	Adds a node to the end or beginning of the list of children for this node
Clone	Clones this node and all its children
CloneNode	Clones this node, choosing whether to include children
CreateNavigator	Creates an **XPathNavigator** to work with this node and its children
GetEnumerator	Gets an enumerator for a collection of nodes
InsertBefore, InsertAfter	Inserts a node before or after another node
Normalize	Normalizes the node by structuring the node and its children so that there are no adjacent text nodes
RemoveChild, RemoveAll	Removes one or all child nodes
ReplaceChild	Replaces one child node by another
SelectNodes, SelectSingleNode	Selects one or more nodes using an **XPath** expression
Supports	Tests whether the DOM implementation supports a feature
WriteContentTo	Writes the node content to an **XmlWriter**

Notice how many of these methods can be used to set up and modify hierarchies of nodes.

XmlElement

As mentioned previously, all the node types derive from **XmlNode**, but there is one that I'll explain in more detail because it is the one that you'll use most often: **XmlElement**, which represents an element within a DOM tree.

XmlElement differs from **XmlNode** in that it contains several new methods, including a number for getting, setting, and removing attributes, as shown in Table 5.8.

Table 5.8 Methods that XmlElement adds to those it inherits from XmlNode.

Method	Description
GetAttribute	Gets the value of a named attribute
GetAttributeNode	Gets an **XmlAttribute** object representing a named attribute
GetElementsByTagName	Gets a list of child elements matching a particular name
HasAttribute	Checks whether an element has an attribute
RemoveAttribute	Removes a named attribute from the element
RemoveAllAttributes	Removes all attributes from the element
RemoveAttributeAt	Removes an attribute by index
RemoveAttributeNode	Removes an attribute by reference to an **XmlAttribute** object
SetAttribute	Sets the value of a named attribute
SetAttributeNode	Sets the value of an attribute using an **XmlAttribute** object

XmlDocument Members

The **XmlDocument** class has a number of useful properties and methods, as summarized in Tables 5.9 and 5.10.

You can see that a number of methods create the various types of node that can exist within a DOM tree—processing instructions, comments, elements, and so on. Also a general **CreateNode()** element can be used to create any element type, as an alternative to using the individual methods.

Table 5.9 Important properties of the XmlDocument class.

Property	Description
DocumentElement	Returns the document element for this tree
DocumentType	Returns the **DOCTYPE** information for this document
IsReadOnly	True if the current node is read-only
Name, LocalName	Gets the name of the current node with or without a namespace prefix
NodeType	Gets the type of the current node as an **XmlNodeType**
OwnerDocument	Gets the **XmlDocument** that contains this node
PreserveWhiteSpace	Determines whether white space is preserved

Table 5.10 Important methods of the XmlDocument class.

Method	Description
CloneNode	Creates a duplicate of this node
CreateAttribute	Creates an **XmlAttribute** object to represent an attribute

(continued)

Table 5.10 Important methods of the XmlDocument class *(continued)*.

Method	Description
CreateCDataSection	Creates an **XmlCDataSection** object representing a CDATA section
CreateComment	Creates an **XmlComment** object representing a comment
CreateDocumentType	Creates an **XmlDocumentType** object representing a **DOCTYPE** declaration
CreateElement	Creates an **XmlElement**
CreateEntityReference	Creates an **XmlEntityReference** object representing an XML entity reference
CreateNode	Creates a node of a specific type
CreateProcessingInstruction	Creates an **XmlProcessingInstruction** object
CreateTextNode	Creates an **XmlText** object representing the content of an element
CreateXmlDeclaration	Creates an **XmlDeclaration** node representing an **XmlDeclaration**
GetElementByID	Gets the **XmlElement** with the specified ID
GetElementsByTagName	Retrieves a list of elements with a particular name
ImportNode	Imports a node from another document
Load	Loads XML from a file, stream or reader
LoadXml	Loads XML from a string
Save	Saves XML to a file, stream or writer

XSL and XPath

Support for XSL and XPath is provided by the **System.Xml.Xsl** and **System.Xml.XPath** namespaces.

The **XPath** namespace contains the XPath parser and evaluation engine, although the most useful member of the namespace is the **XPathNavigator** class (described in the next section), which provides a useful way to navigate through documents.

XSL transformations are provided by the **System.Xml.Xsl.XslTransform** class, a simple class that has only two methods: **Load()**, which is used to load the XSL stylesheet into the processor object, and **Transform()**, which is used to perform the transformation.

Documents are processed as follows:

1. Create an **XslTransform** object.
2. Use the **Load()** method to load the stylesheet into the object.
3. Load the XML data into an **XmlDocument**, and wrap this in an **XmlNavigator**.
4. Use the **Transform()** method to transform the XML.

XPathNavigator

System.Xml.XPath.XPathNavigator provides a way to read data from a data store using a cursor model.

NOTE: *Using a cursor means reading one item at a time from a table or document. You don't see the entire dataset, but only the one currently under the cursor.*

Datasets can be XML documents, or ADO DataSet objects. The "move" methods of the navigator give you random, read-only access to data, and the properties of the navigator reflect the properties of the current node in the dataset.

Table 5.11 Important properties of the XPathNavigator class.

Property	Description
HasAttributes	True if the current node has attributes
HasChildren	True if the current node has child nodes
IsEmptyElement	True if this node has no content
LocalName	Returns the name of the current node with no namespace prefix
Name	Returns the full name of the current node
NodeType	Gets the type of the current node.
Value	Gets or sets the value associated with the current node

Node types are specified in the **XPathNodeType** enumeration. For an **XmlDocument**, you will commonly encounter the node types listed in Table 5.12.

Table 5.12 Common node types defined in the XPathNodeType enumeration.

Node Type	Description
Attribute	An XML attribute, e.g., **name="fred"**.
Comment	An XML comment.
Element	An element node.
Namespace	A namespace node.
ProcessingInstruction	An XML Processing Instruction.
Root	The root of the node tree.
Text	The text content of an element. A **Text** node cannot have children.

The **XmlNavigator** class has nearly 30 methods, giving you a rich set of options for traversing a document. Table 5.13 summarizes the most important of these methods, and the Immediate Solutions section provides examples showing how to use them.

Table 5.13 Important methods of the XPathNavigator class.

Method	Description
Clone	Returns a new **XPathNavigator** pointing to the same node
ComparePosition	Compares the position of the current navigator with that of a second one
Compile	Compiles an XPath expression for future use
Evaluate	Evaluates an XPath expression and returns the **int**, **Boolean**, or **String** value
GetAttribute	Gets the value of the specified attribute on the current node
IsDescendant	True if the current navigator is a descendant of another
IsSamePosition	Compares the positions of two navigators
Matches	Determines whether the current node matches a given XPath expression
MoveTo	Moves to the same position as another navigator
MoveToAttribute	Moves to a particular attribute on the current node
MoveToFirst, MoveToNext, MoveToPrevious	Moves to the first, next, or previous sibling of the current node
MoveToFirstChild	Moves to the first child of the current node
MoveToId	Moves to the node with the given ID attribute
MoveToParent	Moves to the parent of this node
MoveToRoot	Moves to the root node
Select	Selects a new set of nodes using an XPath expression
SelectAncestors	Selects all ancestor nodes
SelectChildren	Selects all child nodes
SelectDescendants	Selects all descendant nodes

Immediate Solutions

The following solutions assume a basic knowledge of XML. If you haven't encountered XML previously, I recommend that you read the basic principles before continuing.

Which XML Class Should I Be Using?

There are a number of XML classes that you can use, depending on the tasks you need to perform:

- If you need simple, forward-only parsing of XML documents, use **XmlTextReader**.
- If you need simple, line-by-line writing of XML documents, use **XmlTextWriter**.
- If you want more complex parsing, consider using **XPathNavigator**.
- If you want to build or modify XML documents in memory, use **XmlDocument**.
- If you want to transform XML, use **XslTransform**.

Parsing an XML Document Using **XmlTextReader**

The **XmlTextReader** class provides a simple, forward-only way of parsing XML documents that is memory efficient and fast. It is similar in concept to the SAX model, but differs from it in that SAX uses a "push" model, whereas **XmlTextReader** uses a "pull" model. In practice, this means that when using an **XmlTextReader**, you access and get the next node when you are ready, whereas with SAX parsing, the parsing calls your code when it finds a node. Therefore, when using an **XmlTextReader**, you are more in control of what you read and when.

Let's start with a sample XML document, which I'll use throughout the Immediate Solutions:

```
<?xml version="1.0" encoding="utf-8" ?>

<dotnet_books>
  <book isbn="1861004877" topic="C#">
    <title>C# Programming with the Public Beta</title>
```

```
    <publisher>Wrox Press</publisher>
    <author>Burton Harvey</author>
    <author>Simon Robinson</author>
    <author>Julian Templeman</author>
    <author>Simon Watson</author>
    <price>34.99</price>
  </book>

  <book isbn="1861004915" topic="VB">
    <title>VB .NET Programming with the Public Beta</title>
    <publisher>Wrox Press</publisher>
    <author>Billy Hollis</author>
    <author>Rockford Lhotka</author>
    <price>34.99</price>
  </book>

  <book isbn="1893115860" topic="C#">
    <title>A Programmers' Introduction to C#</title>
    <publisher>APress</publisher>
    <author>Eric Gunnerson</author>
    <price>34.95</price>
  </book>

  <book isbn="073561377X" topic=".NET">
    <title>Introducing Microsoft .NET</title>
    <publisher>Microsoft Press</publisher>
    <author>David Platt</author>
    <price>29.99</price>
  </book>
</dotnet_books>
```


Creating a Reader

To parse the preceding document using an **XmlTextReader**, you first need to create a reader object, as shown in the following code:

```
' You need to import System.Xml to get access to classes
Imports System.Xml

Module Module1

  Sub Main()
    Dim xtr As XmlTextReader

    Try
      ' Construct a reader to read the file. You'll need to edit
      ' the file name to point to a suitable data source
```

```
      xtr = New XmlTextReader("\XmlFile1.xml")
    Catch e As Exception
      Console.WriteLine("Error creating reader: " + e.ToString)
    End Try

  End Sub
End Module
```

Visual Studio .NET imports many of the namespaces you need for a large number of applications, but if you want to use **System.Xml**, you'll have to import the namespace manually.

Although this code reads the XML document from a file, the **XmlTextReader** class has a number of other constructors that allow you to read data from other sources, such as:

- From a **TextReader** object
- From a **Stream** object
- From a URL

Reading Elements

Once the reader has been created to access the data source, you can then parse the XML. The following simple function parses the document and prints out the names of all the elements it finds:

```
Public Sub readXml(ByRef xr As XmlTextReader)
  ' Read() reads the next node in the stream, and will fail when the
  ' end is reached
  While xr.Read()
    ' If it is an element, print its name
    If xr.NodeType = XmlNodeType.Element Then
      Console.WriteLine("Element: " + xr.Name)
    End If
  End While
End Sub
```

The preceding function can be called from the **Main()** routine by passing a reference to the **XmlTextReader** object:

```
Try
  ' Construct a reader to read the file. You'll need to edit
  ' the file name to point to a suitable data source
  xtr = New XmlTextReader("\XmlFile1.xml")
```

```
  ' Parse the file
  readXml(xtr)
Catch e As Exception
  Console.WriteLine("Error creating reader: " + e.ToString)
End Try
```

Let's look at the **readXml()** function in more detail. The **XmlTextReader** "pull" model means that it is up to you to request the next node to be read from the file, which you do by calling the **Read()** function. Note that you do not get a reference returned to a node: the **XmlTextReader** object reads one node at a time, and the properties of the reader object reflect those of the current node. So to find out the type of the current node, you use the **NodeType** property and check it against the members of the **XmlNodeType** enumeration:

```
If xr.NodeType = XmlNodeType.Element Then ...
```

XmlNodeType.Element denotes an XML element, and you can access the name of the element through the **Name** property. If the element in the XML document is **<book>**, the **Name** property returns "book" without the angle brackets. Thus, if you run the program on an XML document, you would expect to see output similar to the following:

```
Element: dotnet_books
Element: book
Element: title
...
```

Note that this code only matches the start tag for an element. If you want to keep track of where you are in the document, you need to recognize the end tags as well. The following code shows how the **readXml()** function can be modified to print the start and end tags with indentation:

```
Public Sub readXml(ByRef xr As XmlTextReader)
  Dim level As Integer
  Dim istr As String
  level = 0

  ' Read() reads the next node in the stream, and will fail when the
  ' end is reached
  While xr.Read()
    ' If it is an element, print its name
```

```
    If xr.NodeType = XmlNodeType.Element Then
      istr = indent(level)
      Console.WriteLine(istr + "<" + xr.Name + ">")
      level = level + 1
    ElseIf xr.NodeType = XmlNodeType.EndElement Then
      level = level - 1
      istr = indent(level)
      Console.WriteLine(istr + "</" + xr.Name + ">")
    End If
  End While
End Sub

' Function to return a string representing the indentation level
Private Function indent(ByVal i As Integer) As String
  Dim s As String

  If i = 0 Then
    Return ""
  End If

  Dim n As Integer
  For n = 0 To i - 1
    s = s + " "
  Next
  Return s
End Function
```

You can see how the code now writes angle brackets around the node name and correctly labels the end tag. An integer variable maintains the current indent level, and the **indent()** function builds a string of blanks, which are used for indentation.

Working with Attributes

You can modify the part of **readXml()** that handles elements to read attributes like this:

```
While xr.Read()
  ' If it is an element, print its name
  If xr.NodeType = XmlNodeType.Element Then
    istr = indent(level)
    Console.WriteLine(istr + "<" + xr.Name + ">")
    level = level + 1

    ' Handle attributes
    If xr.AttributeCount > 0 Then
      Console.Write(istr)
```

```
        While xr.MoveToNextAttribute()
            Console.Write("   " + xr.Name + "=" + xr.Value)
        End While
        Console.WriteLine()
      End If
    ElseIf xr.NodeType = XmlNodeType.EndElement Then
      level = level - 1
      istr = indent(level)
      Console.WriteLine(istr + "</" + xr.Name + ">")
    End If
End While
```

The **AttributeCount** property tells you how many attributes the current element has. You can also use **MoveToNextAttribute()** to iterate over the collection of attributes, printing out the name and the value. Note that what is returned from **Name** and **Value** depends on the type of item the **XmlTextReader** is currently looking at.

Handling Namespaces

XmlTextReader can work with XML documents that use namespaces. If you are not sure what an XML namespace is, refer to the "Namespaces" section at the beginning of this chapter.

A namespace can be declared by attaching a namespace attribute to an element, like this:

```
<!-- Add namespace 'jt' -->
<jt:root xmlns:jt="http://www.foo.com">
```

The namespace is in scope within the element in which it is declared and can be attached to any element within that scope using the appropriate prefix (in this case, "jt:") before the element name. The name of an element is composed of a prefix and a **LocalName**, so that you can work with the whole name, or just the prefix or local name parts.

XmlTextReader uses the **NamespaceURI** property to return the URI of the current namespace. It will be an empty string if no namespace is in scope. The following code fragment shows how this can be used in code:

```
If xr.NamespaceURI.Length > 0 Then
  Console.WriteLine(istr + "  namespace=" + xr.NamespaceURI)
  Console.WriteLine(istr + "  name=" + xr.Name _
       + ", localname=" + xr.LocalName _
       + ", prefix=" + xr.Prefix)
End If
```

If you run this code against the sample **<jt:root>** element, you would see the following output:

```
namespace=http://www.foo.com
name=jt:root, localname=root, prefix=jt
```

Parsing a Document with Validation

XmlTextReader doesn't perform validation on XML as it reads it, and if you want to do validation you'll need to use the **XmlValidatingReader** class instead. The type of validation the parser performs depends on the setting of the **ValidationType** property, which can take one of the values from the **ValidationType** enumeration, as shown in Table 5.14.

The parser fires an event if it finds a validation error in the document as it is parsing. Note that the parser only stops if it encounters badly formed XML; it will not stop for well-formed XML that violates the rules of a DTD or schema.

In order to handle validation events, define an event-handler function similar to the following:

```
Public Sub ValHandler(ByVal sender As Object, _
      ByVal args As ValidationEventArgs)
  Console.WriteLine("Validation error: " + args.Message)
End Sub
```

NOTE: *If you are not familiar with how events work in .NET, consult Chapter 2.*

As with all event handlers, the function has two arguments, the first of which is a reference to the object that raised the event, and the second holds information about the error. In this example, you don't need to bother with the first argument because there is only one possible event source, and that is the parser. The

Table 5.14 Members of the ValidationType enumeration.

Member	Description
Auto	The reader validates according to the validation information found in the document.
DTD	The reader validates using a DTD.
None	The reader does no validation.
Schema	The reader validates using a W3C standard schema.
XDR	The reader validates using a Microsoft XDR Schema.

ValidationEventArgs class has two properties—**ErrorCode** and **Message**—and I use the latter to display the error message.

***NOTE:** You'll need to import the **System.Xml.Schema** namespace to get access to **ValidationEventArgs**.*

Before a handler can be called, it has to be registered with the event source, so I need to add a call to **AddHandler** before I start parsing:

```
Try
  ' Construct a reader to read the file
  Dim xtr As XmlTextReader
  xtr = New XmlTextReader("\XmlFile2.xml")
  ' Create a validating reader to read from the TextReader
  Dim xvr As New XmlValidatingReader(xtr)

  ' Tell the parser to validate against a DTD
  xtr.Validation = Validation.DTD
  ' Register the event handler with the parser
  AddHandler xtr.ValidationEventHandler, AddressOf ValHandler

  ' If all is OK, read the file
  readXml(xtr)
Catch e As Exception
  Console.WriteLine("Error creating reader: " + e.ToString)
End Try
```

The validating reader validates the input as it is read by an **XmlReader** object, so I first create an **XmlTextReader** and wrap it in an **XmlValidatingReader**. Before parsing, I set the validation type I want to use—in this case, an inline DTD—and set up the event handler.

To test this out, I created a simple XML file containing an inline DTD, shown in the shaded lines:

```
<?xml version="1.0" encoding="utf-8" ?>
<!DOCTYPE invoice [
<!ELEMENT invoice (customer, address)>
<!ELEMENT customer (#PCDATA)>
<!ELEMENT address (street, town)>
<!ELEMENT street (#PCDATA)>
<!ELEMENT town (#PCDATA)>
]>
<invoice>
  <customer>Acme, Inc</customer>
  <address>
```

```
    <street>2001, Acme Boulevard</street>
    <town>Anytown</town>
  </address>
</invoice>
```

The data that follows the DTD is correct, so it parses without error. If I change the data so that the **<town>** element is outside **<address>**, the data is no longer valid because the DTD states that **<address>** must consist of **<street>** and **<town>**:

```
<?xml version="1.0" encoding="utf-8" ?>
<!DOCTYPE invoice [
<!ELEMENT invoice (customer, address)>
<!ELEMENT customer (#PCDATA)>
<!ELEMENT address (street, town)>
<!ELEMENT street (#PCDATA)>
<!ELEMENT town (#PCDATA)>
]>
<invoice>
  <customer>Acme, Inc</customer>
  <address>
    <street>2001, Acme Boulevard</street>
  </address>
  <town>Anytown</town>
</invoice>
```

When I run the program again, I see the following output, including two validation errors:

```
<invoice>
 <customer>
 </customer>
 <address>
  <street>
  </street>
Validation error: Element 'address' has incomplete
    content. Expected
  'town'. An error occurred at file:///c:/dev/XmlFile2.xml(13,5)
 </address>
Validation error: Element 'invoice' has invalid content. Expected
  ''. An error occurred at file:///c:/dev/XmlFile2.xml(14,6)
 <town>
 </town>
</invoice>
```

These errors tell me that the content of **<address>** is incomplete (because **<town>** is missing), and that it doesn't expect to see **<town>** as part of **<invoice>**.

Related solution:	Found on page:
Creating and Using Events	78

Writing an XML Document Using **XmlTextWriter**

The **XmlTextWriter** class provides you with a toolkit for writing XML in its serialized form, complete with angle brackets, processing instructions, and all the other elements you see in XML documents. This class lets you concentrate on the logical structure of your XML, and frees you from having to worry about the formatting.

Here's a simple program showing how **XmlTextWriter** can be used to construct a simple XML document:

```
' Import the namespace so we can use all the XML stuff.
Imports System.Xml

Module Module1

    Sub Main()
        ' Create an XML writer to write to foo.xml, and use
        ' the default UTF-8 encoding
        Dim xtw As New XmlTextWriter("\foo.xml", _
            Nothing)

        ' Choose indented formatting (as opposed to none)
        xtw.Formatting = Formatting.Indented

        ' Write the XML declaration for a standalone document
        xtw.WriteStartDocument(True)

        xtw.WriteStartElement("books")
        WriteBook(xtw)
        xtw.WriteEndElement()  ' matches WriteStartElement

        xtw.Flush()
        xtw.Close()

    End Sub

    Public Sub WriteBook(ByRef xw As XmlTextWriter)
        xw.WriteStartElement("book")
        xw.WriteAttributeString("ISBN", "1-123-123456")
```

```
            xw.WriteStartElement("title")
              xw.WriteString("Moby Dick")
            xw.WriteEndElement()
          xw.WriteEndElement()
    End Sub

End Module
```

Here's the output that the program produces:

```
<?xml version="1.0" standalone="yes"?>
<books>
  <book ISBN="1-123-123456">
    <title>Moby Dick</title>
  </book>
</books>
```

XmlTextWriter isn't a very complex class, and this example shows all the essentials you need to know in order to use it. You first need to import the **System.Xml** namespace, so that the compiler can find the **XmlTextWriter** class.

An **XmlTextWriter** object can be constructed to output to one of three types of destinations. In this case, I'm specifying a file name, but you can also output to a **TextWriter** or a **Stream**.

***NOTE:** See Chapter 6 for details on **TextWriter**, **Stream**, and other classes in the **System.IO** namespace.*

As well as a file name, you need to specify a *character encoding*. Character encodings are ways of representing character sets, and there are several to choose from. If you have no reason to choose a particular encoding, put a **null** reference in this field, and you'll get the UTF-8 (UCS Transformation Format, 8-bit) encoding that XML uses by default.

***NOTE:** Encodings are part of the **System.Text** namespace, which is discussed in Chapter 12.*

The **Formatting** property of the **XmlTextWriter** has been set to **Indented** in order to produce XML output in typical indented form. The default indentation is two spaces, but you can use the **Indentation** property to set another value. You can even use the **IndentChar** property to choose a character other than a space to use for indentation.

The **WriteStartElement()** method writes a standard XML declaration as the first line of the file. Because all XML documents have to start with an XML declaration, this will usually be the first call you make when writing out an XML document.

You then need to write the start of the **<books>** element in, so put in a call to **WriteStartElement()** to put in the opening tag, passing the element name as the parameter. Because you are writing the XML document line by line, you have to remember to put in a call to **WriteEndElement()** in order to write the closing tag. The **XmlTextWriter** object can figure out which element to close, but you have to remember to make the call, as follows:

```
xtw.WriteStartElement("books")
' put content in here
xtw.WriteEndElement()  ' matches WriteStartElement
```

As an alternative to doing it this way, you can use the **XmlDocument** class to build a tree in memory representing an XML document, and then have the tree written out to disk, which takes care of all the formatting for you. See the Immediate Solution "Creating and Using DOM Trees Using **XmlDocument**" for more details.

I've used a function to write the **<book>** element within **<books>**, which takes the **XmlTextWriter** as its only argument. The **<book>** element is written in exactly the same way. This time I've added an attribute via a call to **WriteAttributeString()** and have provided some text content for the element using **WriteString()**. Note that attributes in XML are always strings.

Element content is always written out as a string, so if you want to use other data types you'll have to do the conversion to a string yourself. As an example, here's how you can write out a date that's been stored in a **System.DateTime** object:

```
' Set a DateTime to today's date
Dim dt As DateTime = DateTime.today

xtw.WriteStartElement("date")
xtw.WriteString(dt.ToShortDateString())
xtw.WriteEndElement()  ' matches WriteStartElement

The code produces XML output similar to this:
<date>06/07/2001</date>
```

One final note about the sample program is that you need to call **Flush()** and **Close()** in order to make sure that the XML is correctly written out to the file. If you don't do this, you may well find that some or all of the data is missing from the output file.

Adding Processing Instructions and Comments

The **XmlTextWriter** class contains methods that let you easily write processing instructions and comments into the output stream, as shown in the following code fragment:

```
xtw.WriteStartDocument(True)
xtw.WriteProcessingInstruction("proc", "an instruction")

xtw.WriteStartElement("books")
xtw.WriteComment("The book collection")
WriteBook(xtw)
xtw.WriteEndElement()
```

The result is as follows:

```
<?xml version="1.0" standalone="yes"?>
<?proc an instruction?>
<books>
  <!--The book collection-->
  <book ISBN="1-123-123456" Value="3.55">
    <title>Moby Dick</title>
    <date>2001-05-22</date>
  </book>
</books>
```


Handling Namespaces

You can include namespace information when you write an element start tag using **WriteStartElement()**. The following code fragment shows how to define a namespace for an element:

```
xw.WriteStartElement("jt", "book", "http://www.thingy.com")
```

This line of code associates the namespace prefix "jt" with the URI "http://www.thingy.com" and results in the following start tag being output:

```
<jt:book xmlns:jt="http://www.thingy.com">
```

You can see how the method has added the prefix to the element name and declared the namespace URI. Although the **XmlTextWriter** object automatically puts the prefix onto the closing tag when you write it, you need to include the namespace information on any nested elements; otherwise, they won't be correctly prefixed. For example, if you want to write the **<book>** element that declares the "jt" namespace prefix, and then nest **<title>** inside it, you'll have to code it like this:

```
xw.WriteStartElement("jt", "book", "http://www.thingy.com")
xw.WriteStartElement("jt", "title", "http://www.thingy.com")
...
xw.WriteEndElement()   ' for book
xw.WriteEndElement()   ' for title
```

Here's the result:

```
<jt:book xmlns:jt="http://www.thingy.com">
  <jt:title>
    ...
  </jt:title>
</jt:book>
```

Note how the namespace isn't added to the tag if it is already in scope, although you have to declare it in every call to **WriteStartElement()**.

Using XPathNavigator

The **XPathNavigator** class provides you with another way of reading XML documents. It is similar to the **XmlTextReader** class in that it uses a cursor model, so that an **XPathNavigator** object is always pointing to one node in a tree, and you read the properties of the current node. Essentially, **XPathNavigator** gives you another way of interacting with a DOM tree, which frees you from many of the housekeeping details.

Creating a Navigator

XPathNavigator is an abstract class, so you don't create **XPathNavigator** objects directly. Instead, the **XPathDocument**, **XmlDataDocument**, and **XmlDocument** classes provide methods to create navigator objects for you.

Here's how you can set up an **XPathNavigator** to work with an **XmlDocument**, using the same .NET books file that I introduced in the "Which XML Class Should I Be Using?" solution:

```
' Need to import System.Xml and System.Xml.XPath
Imports System.Xml
Imports System.Xml.XPath

Module Module1

  Sub Main()
    Try
      ' First create a document
      Dim doc As New XmlDocument()
      doc.Load("\XMLFile1.xml")

      ' Now create a navigator to work with it
      Dim nav As XPathNavigator = doc.CreateNavigator()
```

```
    Catch e As XmlException
      Console.WriteLine("Exception: " + e.ToString())
    End Try
  End Sub

End Module
```

The code creates an **XmlDocument**, loads it with an XML document from a file, and then creates an **XPathNavigator** to work with it. If anything goes wrong in the parsing process, an **XmlException** will get thrown, so it is a good idea to be prepared to catch them.

Moving around the Tree

Using an **XPathNavigator** is rather different from using an **XmlTextReader** because you aren't limited to reading forward through the tree. In fact, the **XmlNavigator** uses an **XmlDocument** to hold its data, so that you are free to traverse the tree as you wish. This means that you need to point the navigator at a node before you can start using it: A good place to start is with the document element at the top of the tree, which you can access as shown in the following code:

```
nav.MoveToRoot()
Console.WriteLine("name=" + nav.Name + ", type=" _
    + nav.NodeType.ToString() _
    + ", value=" + nav.Value)
```


The **MoveToRoot()** element method tells the navigator to position itself at the root element of the tree. You can access the name of the node using the **Name** property, the type of the node using the **NodeName** property, and the value of the node using **Value**. In the case of the node at the very top of the document, there is no name and the type is **Root**. The value of a node depends on what type of node it is, and for an element, it is the value of the element and all other child elements, so the value of the root is the concatenated text of all the nodes beneath it.

MoveToRoot() moves you to the very top of the tree, so you have to go down one level to get to the root element, like this:

```
nav.MoveToRoot()
Console.WriteLine("root name=" + nav.Name + ", type=" _
    + nav.NodeType.ToString() + ", value=" + nav.Value)

nav.MoveToFirstChild()
Console.WriteLine("first child: name=" + nav.Name + ", _
    type=" + nav.NodeType.ToString())
```

Run this code, and you'll find that the first child is **<dotnet_books>**.

If you want to print out the details of all four children of **<dotnet_books>**, here's how you would do it:

```
' Move to the root
nav.MoveToRoot()
Console.WriteLine("root name=" + nav.Name + ", type=" _
          + nav.NodeType.ToString() + ", value=" + nav.Value)

' Move to <dotnet_books>
nav.MoveToFirstChild()
Console.WriteLine("dotnet_books: name=" + nav.Name + ", _
                            type=" + nav.NodeType.ToString())

' Move to first book
nav.MoveToFirstChild()
Console.WriteLine("book: name=" + nav.Name + ", type=" _
                             + nav.NodeType.ToString())

' Iterate over the remaining book elements
While nav.MoveToNext()
  Console.WriteLine("next: name=" + nav.Name + ", type=" _
                             + nav.NodeType.ToString())
End While
```

The first **MoveToFirstChild()** moves to the first child element, which is the root **<dotnet_books>**. The second **MoveToFirstChild()** moves to the first child of **<dotnet_books>**, which is the first book. After printing out the details of the first book element, **MoveToNext()** moves to the next sibling element, and the **While** loop prints details of sibling elements until there are no more, when **MoveToNext()** returns false.

You have seen three **Move...()** methods in use in this section, and there are a number of others that can be used in the same way, such as:

- **MoveToFirst()**, which moves to the first sibling of the current node
- **MoveToPrevious()**, which moves to the previous sibling of the current node
- **MoveToParent()**, which moves to the parent of the current node

The **Clone()** method can be used to create another independent **XPathNavigator** working with the same document, and it will be set to point to the same position in the tree.

If you have two navigators open on the same document, **IsSamePosition()** returns true of they are positioned at the same place, and **MoveTo()** moves the first one to the same position as the second.

Navigating over Attributes

Attributes are held as nodes in the tree in the same way as elements, processing instructions and the other parts of an XML document.

Once you are positioned on an element, the **HasAttributes** property tells you whether there are any attributes. You can then use **MoveToFirstAttribute()** to position yourself at the first attribute, or **MoveToAttribute()** to move to a particular attribute by name. The following code shows how I iterate over the immediate children of **<dotnet_books>** and print out their attributes:

```
' Move to the root
nav.MoveToRoot()
Console.WriteLine("root name=" + nav.Name + ", type=" _
        + nav.NodeType.ToString() + ", value=" + nav.Value)

' move to <dotnet_books>
nav.MoveToFirstChild()
Console.WriteLine("dotnet_books: name=" + nav.Name + _
                       ", type=" + nav.NodeType.ToString())

' move to first book
nav.MoveToFirstChild()
Do
  Console.WriteLine("next: name=" + nav.Name + ", type=" _
                                 + nav.NodeType.ToString())
  ' do attributes
  If nav.MoveToFirstAttribute() Then
    ' there is at least one
    Console.WriteLine("  att: " + nav.Name + "=" + nav.Value)
    While nav.MoveToNextAttribute()
      Console.WriteLine("  att: " + nav.Name + "=" + nav.Value)
    End While
  End If
  ' go back from the attributes to the parent element
  nav.MoveToParent()
Loop While nav.MoveToNext()
```

After moving to the first book, I use a **Do** loop to print out the details of each book. The **While** clause at the end of the loop moves to the next book, and will terminate the loop when there are no more to process. Within the loop I use **MoveToFirstAttribute()** to start looking at the attributes, and **MoveToNextAttribute()** to iterate over the attribute list. Note the call to **MoveToParent()** at the bottom of the loop: Attributes are children of an element, so before I can process the next element, I have to move up a level to get back to the parent:

```
name=book, type=Element
    att: isbn=1861004877
    att: topic=C#
name=book, type=Element
    att: isbn=1861004915
    att: topic=VB
name=book, type=Element
    att: isbn=1893115860
    att: topic=C#
name=book, type=Element
    att: isbn=073561377X
    att: topic=.NET
```


Creating and Using DOM Trees Using **XmlDocument**

The **XmlDocument** class implements the W3C DOM model for working with XML documents in memory. In this Immediate Solution section, I'll use the same **<dotnet_books>** document that was featured in the "Parsing an XML Document Using **XmlTextReader**" solution: Take a look at that section to see a listing of the file.

Loading an Existing XML Document

The **XmlDocument** class will parse XML from several types of input sources:

- From strings, using **LoadXml()**
- From URLs, using **Load()**
- From streams, using **Load()**
- From TextReaders, using **Load()**
- From XmlReaders, using **Load()**

The following code shows how to load an XML document from a file into an **XmlDocument** object:

```
' Import System.Xml to get access to the XML classes
Imports System.Xml

Module Module1
```

```
  Sub Main()
    ' Create a new XmlDocument object
    Dim xd As New XmlDocument()

    Try
      ' Load a document from a file
      xd.Load("\XmlFile1.xml")
      Console.WriteLine("Document loaded OK")

    Catch e As XmlException
      Console.WriteLine("Exception caught: " + e.ToString)
    End Try
  End Sub

End Module
```

Before using **XmlDocument**, you need to import the **System.Xml** namespace. The **Load()** method causes the **XmlDocument** object to parse the file and build the tree. If the method encounters any problems during parsing, it will throw an **XmlException**, so it is wise to be prepared to catch these. If you get past the **Load()** call without getting an exception, then the XML was well-formed and has been parsed.

If you want to load XML from a string instead, use the **LoadXml()** method:

```
Dim myXml As String = _
        "<?xml version='1.0'?><root><a>bbb</a></root>"
xd.LoadXml(myXml)
```

In this code fragment, the **myXml** variable holds an entire XML document in a string, which is passed to the **XmlDocument** object for parsing by calling **LoadXml()**.

Navigation

The root of a DOM tree is called the *document element*, and you can obtain a reference to this node using the **DocumentElement** property. The following code shows how you acquire the document element once you've parsed the file:

```
' Now we've parsed the file, get the Document Element
Dim doc As XmlNode = xd.DocumentElement
```

The document element is of type **XmlNode**, as is everything in a DOM tree. If you receive a node reference and you want to find out what kind of node it is, the **NodeType** property will return one of the members of the **XmlNodeType** enumeration.

Once you have a node, the properties and methods of **XmlNode** enable you to find out information about the current node and navigate through the tree.

Working with Child Nodes

Because the nodes in an XML document are arranged in a tree, you need to process child nodes in order to move from level to level. The following code shows how to read all the nodes in a DOM tree and print it out in XML format:

```
' Import System.Xml and add a project reference to it
Imports System.Xml

Module Module1

  Sub Main()
    Dim xd As New XmlDocument()
    Try
      ' Create a new XmlDocument object
      xd.Load("\XmlFile1.xml")
    Catch e As XmlException
      Console.WriteLine("Exception caught: " + e.ToString)
    End Try

    ' Now we've parsed the file, get the Document Element
    Dim doc As XmlNode = xd.DocumentElement

    ' Process any child nodes
    If doc.HasChildNodes Then
      processChildren(doc, 0)
    End If
  End Sub

  Private Sub processChildren(ByRef xn As XmlNode, ByVal level As Integer)
    Dim istr As String

    istr = indent(level)
    Select Case xn.NodeType
      Case XmlNodeType.Comment
        ' output the comment
        Console.WriteLine(istr + "<!--" + xn.Value + "-->")
      Case XmlNodeType.ProcessingInstruction
        ' output the PI
        Console.WriteLine(istr + "<?" + xn.Name + " " + xn.Value + " ?>")
      Case XmlNodeType.Text
        ' output the text
        Console.WriteLine(istr + xn.Value)
```

```
        Case XmlNodeType.Element
          ' Get the child node list
          Dim ch As XmlNodeList = xn.ChildNodes
          Dim i As Integer

          ' Write the start tag
          Console.Write(istr + "<" + xn.Name)

          ' Process the attributes
          Dim atts As XmlAttributeCollection = xn.Attributes
          If Not atts Is Nothing Then
            Dim en As IEnumerator = atts.GetEnumerator
            While en.MoveNext = True
              Dim at As XmlNode = CType(en.Current, XmlNode)
              Console.Write(" " + at.Name + "=" + at.Value)
            End While
          End If
          Console.WriteLine(">")

          ' recursively process child nodes
          Dim ie As IEnumerator = ch.GetEnumerator
          While ie.MoveNext = True
            Dim nd As XmlNode = CType(ie.Current, XmlNode)
            processChildren(nd, level + 2)
          End While
          Console.WriteLine(istr + "</" + xn.Name + ">")
    End Select
  End Sub

  ' Function to return a string representing the indentation level
  Private Function indent(ByVal i As Integer) As String
    Dim s As String

    If i = 0 Then
      Return ""
    End If

    Dim n As Integer
    For n = 0 To i - 1
      s = s + " "
    Next
    Return s
  End Function
End Module
```

In this code, I start in **Main()** by using the **HasChildNodes** property to check whether there is anything to be done. **HasChildNodes** returns the number of children of the current node and will obviously return zero if there are none. If there are child nodes, **processChildren()** is called. This routine maintains an indentation level so that the output can be printed to look like properly indented XML. I first call the private **indent()** function to create a string that can be prepended to lines to maintain the indentation.

Once that has been done, a **Select Case** statement is used to match the node type. I am not checking for every possible node type, but I am processing the most common ones. Comments and processing instructions have their values printed out enclosed in suitable tags, whereas text is printed out as is. XML elements are more interesting because they can have both attributes and child elements of their own. Attributes are represented by a collection of name/value pairs called an **XmlAttributeCollection**, whereas child nodes are represented by a list called an **XmlNodeList**.

I use the **ChildNodes** property to get a list of the children as an **XmlNodeList**, and write the starting angle bracket **<** and the node name.

If there are any attributes for this node, I'll need to put them between the name and the closing angle bracket, so I get the attributes as an **XmlAttributeCollection**. If there aren't any attributes for this node, a **null** reference is returned. If there are attributes, the **GetEnumerator** property gets an enumerator to walk over the collection, and I can then use the **Name** and **Value** properties on each node to output the attribute. Once all the attributes have been output, I can write the closing angle bracket for the start tag.

Because all the children are **XmlNodes** as well, I can process them by making a recursive call to the **processChildren()** function, increasing the indent level for each nested call.

When you compile and run the program, you'll find that the output looks very similar to the input, differing only on minor points of formatting.

Creating and Modifying Nodes

It is possible to modify the nodes in a DOM tree, or even create a tree from scratch. Doing either of these tasks involves creating elements of the appropriate type and inserting them into the DOM tree. The following program shows how this can be done:

```
'Import the System.Xml namespace
Imports System.Xml
```

```
Module Module1

  Sub Main()
    Dim xd As New XmlDocument()

    ' Create an XML declaration and add it to the document
    Dim decl As XmlDeclaration = xd.CreateXmlDeclaration("1.0", "", "")
    xd.AppendChild(decl)

    ' Add a comment
    Dim cmt As XmlComment = xd.CreateComment("A comment")
    xd.InsertAfter(cmt, decl)

    ' Add an element
    Dim el As XmlElement = xd.CreateElement("root")
    xd.InsertAfter(el, cmt)

    ' Set an attribute using an XmlAttribute
    Dim att1 As XmlAttribute = xd.CreateAttribute("foo")
    att1.Value = "bar"
    el.SetAttributeNode(att1)

    ' Set a second attribute directly into the element
    el.SetAttribute("one", "two")

    ' Add some children
    Dim ch1 As XmlElement = xd.CreateElement("child1")
    Dim ch2 As XmlElement = xd.CreateElement("child2")
    el.AppendChild(ch1)
    el.AppendChild(ch2)

    ' Add some text
    Dim tx1 As XmlText = xd.CreateTextNode("content")
    ch1.AppendChild(tx1)

    ' Write the tree out...
    Dim writer As XmlTextWriter = New XmlTextWriter(Console.Out)
    writer.Formatting = Formatting.Indented
    xd.WriteTo(writer)
    writer.Flush()
    Console.WriteLine()
  End Sub

End Module
```

As with all the solutions in this chapter, the first task is to import the **System.Xml** namespace. Next, create a new **XmlDocument** object, which at this point is completely blank.

The first line in an XML file has to be an XML declaration, so I create an **XmlDeclaration** object. This has three parameters, one for the version, one for encoding, and one for standalone attributes: The first has to be "1.0" because it is the only version of XML currently supported. I've left the other two parameters blank because I don't require those attributes in this example. Once the object has been created, I add it as a child of the document. Remember that **XmlDocument** inherits from **XmlNode**, so all the operations you can perform on a node can be performed on a document.

In the next few lines, I create a comment and add it after the XML declaration. I then insert an element called **<root>** after the comment. Note that I'm using **InsertAfter()** because I want to add these elements on the same level as each other.

There are two ways to add attributes to an element. You can either create an **XmlAttribute** object, set its value, and then add it to the element, or you can use the **SetAttributeNode()** function to add the attribute information directly to an element. You can see examples of both approaches in use in the code sample.

Child elements can be linked into the tree by creating elements of the appropriate type and then using **AppendChild()** to add them as children of a node. In the example, I add two child nodes, and then add a text node to one of the children to add some content.

***NOTE:* AppendChild()** *adds a node to the end of the list of children for a node. You can also use* **PrependChild()** *to add a node to the start of the list of children.*

Finally, I write the DOM tree out to the console, so that I can see what has been built. A simple way to do this is to use the **WriteTo()** method, which is used to tell a node to pass its content to an **XmlWriter** for output. In this example, I create an **XmlTextWriter**, and then call **WriteTo()** on the document, treating the entire tree as a single node. After I've called **WriteTo()**, I need to call **Flush()** and **Close()** on the **XmlTextWriter** in order to make sure that all output is flush and appears on the screen. Here's the output that the program produces:

```
<?xml version="1.0"?>
<!--A comment-->
<root foo="bar" one="two">
  <child1>content</child1>
```

5. The XML Namespaces

```
  <child2/>
</root>
```

The **RemoveChild()** and **ReplaceChild()** functions can be used to remove an existing node from the tree and replace a node by another.

Using XPath

XPath provides you with a "language" for selecting sets of nodes within an XML document, such as "all the books with more than one author" or "the book with the highest price." If you are unfamiliar with **XPath**, I suggest you consult a good XML book, such as the *XML Black Book, 2nd Edition*, by Natanya Pitts (The Coriolis Group, Inc.).

You use the **XPathNavigator** class to work with **XPath** in .NET, using the **Select()** method. You call **Select()** with an **XPath** expression that defines the set of nodes you want to retrieve, and it returns you a collection of nodes that match the expression.

The following program returns the titles of the books in an XML document (see the solution "Parsing an XML Document using **XmlTextReader**" for a listing of the document):

```
Imports System.Xml
Imports System.Xml.XPath

Module Module1

  Sub Main()
    Try
      Dim doc As New XmlDocument()
      doc.Load("\XMLFile1.xml")

      ' create the navigator
      Dim nav As XPathNavigator = doc.CreateNavigator()

      nav.MoveToRoot()
      Console.WriteLine("At root")

      ' Select all the books
      Dim ni As XPathNodeIterator = nav.Select("//book/title")
      Console.WriteLine("Retrieved " + ni.Count.ToString() + " nodes")
```

```
      While ni.MoveNext
        Dim nav2 As XPathNavigator = ni.Current
        nav2.MoveToFirstChild()
        Console.WriteLine("title: " + nav2.Value)
      End While
    Catch e As Exception
      Console.WriteLine(e.ToString())
    End Try
  End Sub
End Module
```

I first create an **XmlDocument**, wrap it in an **XPathNavigator**, and point the navigator at the root element. The **Select()** method takes an **XPath** expression and evaluates it: In this case, the expression **//book/title** matches all **<title>** elements that are children of **<book>** elements that occur at any depth in the hierarchy (indicated by the *//*).

The **Select()** method returns a reference to an **XPathIterator** that you use to navigate over the collection of nodes that match the expression. The **Count** property tells you how many elements the collection contains, and in this case the value is 4. **XPathIterator** supports all the usual properties and methods you'd expect from an iterator, including **MoveNext()** and **Current**, although you use it in a slightly different way to other iterators. As you can see from the code, the **Current** property returns you another **XPathNavigator**, and this is because the XML node that you're referring to at this point—the current node—may well have child elements, attributes, and other XML structure. So **Current** returns you an **XPathNavigator** to help you navigate the structure of the current element. Note that before you can work with the title, you have to call **MoveToFirstChild()**.

If you run the program, you'll see output similar to this:

```
At root
Retrieved 4 nodes
title: C# Programming with the Public Beta
title: VB .NET Programming with the Public Beta
title: A Programmers' Introduction to C#
title: Introducing Microsoft .NET
```

Compiling **XPath** Expressions

The **Compile()** method lets you take an **XPath** expression and precompile it, so that it is more efficient when used in a **Select()**. The following code is equivalent to the simple **Select()** statement in the previous example:

```
Dim x As XPathExpression
x = nav.Compile("//book/title")
nav.Select(x)
```

I don't gain anything by compiling the expression when I'm only using it once, but if I was going to use the same **Select()** several times, I could save having to parse the expression every time.

Some **XPath** expressions don't evaluate to a set of nodes, but may return a string, numeric, or Boolean value. In this case, the **Evaluate()** method returns an object representing the result. Here's how you would count the number of book elements in the **<dotnet_books>** document:

```
' Move back to the root
nav.MoveToRoot()

' Count the number of books...
Dim num_books As Integer
num_books = CType(nav.Evaluate("count(//book)"), Integer)
Console.WriteLine("Number of books is " + num_books.ToString())
```

The **XPath** expression "count(//book)" tells the **XPath** processor to count the number of book child nodes, and the resulting expression is converted to an **Integer** and printed out.

Transforming XML Using XslTransform

Using XSL to transform XML isn't hard at all with .NET because the **System.Xml.Xsl.XslTransform** class gives you all the functionality you need with only two methods. The following example shows how to use an XSL stylesheet with an **XslTransform** object:

```
' Import the System.Xml namespaces
Imports System.Xml
Imports System.Xml.XPath
Imports System.Xml.Xsl

Module Module1

  Sub Main()
    Try
      ' Create the document and the navigator
      Dim doc As New XmlDocument()
      doc.Load("c:\dev\book\ch6-xml\vbxsl\XMLFile1.xml")

      ' create an XPathNavigator
      Dim nav As XPathNavigator = doc.CreateNavigator()
```

```
      nav.MoveToRoot()

      ' Create the XSL object
      Dim xt As New XslTransform()
      xt.Load("c:\dev\book\ch6-xml\vbxsl\style.xsl")

      ' Create a writer to write output to the console
      Dim writer As New XmlTextWriter(Console.Out)

      ' Do the transform
      xt.Transform(nav, Nothing, writer)
    Catch e As XmlException
      Console.WriteLine("XML Exception:" + e.ToString())
    Catch e As XsltException
      Console.WriteLine("XSLT Exception:" + e.ToString())
    End Try
  End Sub

End Module
```


The first step is to make sure that all the correct imports are included. In this program, I need three namespaces: **System.Xml**, **System.Xml.XPath** (for **XPathNavigator**), and **System.Xml.Xsl.**

An **XslTransform** object needs an **XPathNavigator** to represent the document, so I create the XML document object and use it to initialize a navigator, and then use **MoveToRoot()** to point the navigator at the root element of the document. Once the **XslTransform** object has been created, I call **Load()** to load the stylesheet: This way I can use the same XSL object to process many XML files without having to reload the stylesheet every time.

I also need an object to do the output. In this case, I've used an **XmlTextWriter**, which writes the resulting HTML to the console. Once everything is set up, a call to **Transform()** does the transformation, sending the output to the TextWriter. The **XmlDocument** and **XPathNavigator** classes may throw **XmlExceptions**, and the **XslTransform** may throw an **XsltException**, so it is wise to catch these.

Here's a sample XSL stylesheet that selects all the book titles from the **<dotnet_books>** document and formats them as HTML:

```
<?xml version="1.0" encoding="utf-8" ?>

<xsl:stylesheet
       xmlns:xsl="http://www.w3.org/1999/XSL/Transform" version="1.0">
```

```
  <xsl:template match="/dotnet_books">
    <html>
      <head><title>DotNet Books</title></head>
      <body>
        <ul>
        <xsl:for-each select="book">
          <li><xsl:value-of select="title"/></li>
        </xsl:for-each>
        </ul>
      </body>
    </html>
  </xsl:template>
</xsl:stylesheet>
```

If you run this program on the **<dotnet_books>** document, you should see output similar to the following (note that I've inserted new lines to make it readable):

```
<?xml version="1.0"?>
<html>
<head><title>DotNet Books</title></head>
<body>
  <ul>
    <li>C# Programming with the Public Beta</li>
    <li>VB .NET Programming with the Public Beta</li>
    <li>A Programmers' Introduction to C#</li>
    <li>Introducing Microsoft .NET</li>
  </ul>
</body>
</html>
```

Chapter 6

The I/O and Networking Namespaces

By Julian Templeman

In Depth

This chapter introduces you to three important .NET namespaces: **System.IO**, **System.Net**, and **System.Net.Sockets**.

System.IO is the namespace that contains all the classes needed for text and binary I/O as well as classes to represent files, directories, and streams. **System.Net** contains all the classes needed to write networking code including tasks such as working with IP addresses and URLs, and using sockets. There's a lot of very advanced material in **System.Net**, so in this chapter I'll provide an overview of what you can do with it and concentrate on using sockets, which are part of the **System.Net.Sockets** namespace.

Streams

Streams are objects that you use to perform I/O, such as reading text from a file or writing binary data to a piece of shared memory. The .NET Framework contains a number of **Stream** classes that cover almost any type of I/O you'll need to do, and in this section I'll describe each class, how they relate, and what they can do.

The Stream Class

The abstract **Stream** class contains a number of properties and operations that are needed by streams, and they're listed in Tables 6.1 and 6.2.

Asynchronous Operations

The **Stream** class supports *asynchronous* I/O operations through the **BeginRead()**, **EndRead()**, **BeginWrite()**, and **EndWrite()** methods.

As the name implies, *asynchronous* I/O means that when you issue a read or write request, the call returns immediately, and .NET does the operation asyn-

Table 6.1 Properties of the Stream class.

Property	Description
CanRead	True if the current stream supports reading
CanSeek	True if the current stream supports seeking
CanWrite	True if the current stream supports writing
Length	Returns the length of the stream in bytes
Position	Returns the current position for streams that support seeking

Table 6.2 Important methods of the Stream class.

Method	Description
BeginRead, **EndRead**	Begins or ends an asynchronous read operation
BeginWrite, **EndWrite**	Begins or ends an asynchronous write operation
Close	Closes the stream
Flush	Flushes the stream
Read	Reads a sequence of bytes from the stream
ReadByte	Reads one byte from the stream
Seek	Sets the position within the stream
SetLength	Sets the length of the stream
Write	Writes a sequence of bytes to the stream
WriteByte	Writes one byte to the stream

chronously so that your code can continue with other tasks. This is in contrast with the normal synchronous I/O where the read or write call blocks until the operation is completed.

Seeking

The idea of *seeking* within a file will be familiar to C programmers, but for those who are unfamiliar with seeking, I'll provide a brief explanation. Some streams let you position a *seek pointer* that governs where the next read or write operation will occur. The **CanSeek** property will be true for these streams, and you can use the **Seek()** method to set the position of the pointer. **Seek()** takes two arguments: a number of bytes representing the distance to move the seek pointer and a position relative to which the pointer will be moved. The positions are members of the **SeekOrigin** enumeration and can be one of the following:

- **SeekOrigin.Begin** (the beginning of the file)
- **SeekOrigin.Current** (the current position)
- **SeekOrigin.End** (the end of the file)

The following examples show you how seeking works:

```
'  Move to 200 bytes from the start of the stream
aStream.Seek(200, SeekOrigin.Begin)

'  Move to the end of the stream
aStream.Seek(0, SeekOrigin.End)

'  Move 20 bytes back from where we currently are
aStream.Seek(-20, SeekOrigin.Current)
```

FileStream

FileStream is a direct descendent of **Stream**. **FileStream** objects can read from and write to files, and can handle bytes, characters, strings, and other data types. It is also used to implement the standard input, standard output, and standard error streams that will be familiar to programmers in C and other C-type languages.

Note that **FileStream** isn't often used on its own as it is a little too low level. Because it only reads and writes bytes, you have to manually convert the strings, numbers, and objects into bytes in order to pass them through the **FileStream**. For this reason, **FileStream** is usually wrapped in other classes, such as **BinaryWriter** or **TextReader**, which deal in higher level constructs.

The **FileStream** class has no fewer than nine constructors, which allow you to construct **FileStreams** based upon combinations of:

- File name
- File handle, an integer representing the handle of the file
- Access mode, which is one of the members of the **FileMode** enumeration
- Read/write permission, which is one of the members of the **FileAccess** enumeration
- Sharing mode, which is one of the members of the **FileShare** enumeration
- Buffer size

Tables 6.3, 6.4, and 6.5 explain the access modes, access permissions, and sharing modes.

Table 6.3 File access modes defined in the FileMode enumeration.

Mode	Description
Append	If the file exists, it is opened and data added to the end. If the file doesn't exist, it is created.
Create	Specifies that a new file should be created. If one already exists, it is overwritten.
CreateNew	Specifies that a new file should be created. If one already exists, an **IOException** is thrown.
Open	Opens an existing file. An exception is thrown if the file doesn't exist.
OpenOrCreate	Opens an existing file or creates a new one if the file doesn't exist.
Truncate	Opens an existing file and overwrites it from the start of the data.

Table 6.4 File access permissions defined in the FileAccess enumeration.

Permission	Description
Read	Data can be read from the file.
Write	Data can be written to the file.
ReadWrite	Data can be read and written.

Table 6.5 File-sharing flags defined in the FileShare enumeration.

Flag	Description
None	This file cannot be opened again by any other process (including the current one) until it has been explicitly closed.
Read	This file can be opened for subsequent read access.
Write	This file can be opened for subsequent write access.
ReadWrite	This file can be opened for subsequent read and write access.

The following code fragment shows how to create a file that has shared read access:

```
' Create a FileStream to write to c:\temp\foo.txt
' Create the file if it doesn't already exist, and
' grant shared read access
Dim ds As New FileStream("c:\temp\foo.txt", FileMode.Create, _
      FileAccess.Read)
```

FileStreams can be created in synchronous or asynchronous mode and the class adds an **IsAsync** property to the five it inherits from **Stream**. It also adds the four methods listed in Table 6.6.

The **GetHandle()** method returns an identifier that can be used with native operating system functions (e.g., **ReadFile()** in Win32), but you need to use it carefully. If you use the file handle to make any changes to the underlying file and then try to use the **FileStream** on the same file, you risk corrupting the file's data.

Table 6.6 Methods that FileStream adds to those it inherits from the Stream class.

Method	Description
Finalize	Closes the **FileStream** and any associated disk files when the object is garbage collected
GetHandle	Returns the operating system file handle for the underlying file
Lock	Prevents access by other processes to all or part of the file
Unlock	Removes a previous lock

MemoryStream

MemoryStream is also a direct descendent of **Stream**. It uses memory to store the stream rather than a file, but its workings are very similar to **FileStream**. It holds data in memory as an array or unsigned bytes and can be used to replace the need for temporary files in applications.

Like **FileStream**, **MemoryStream** has a number of constructors. A **MemoryStream** tends to expand if you write at the end of the stream, but if you use one of the constructors that maps the stream onto an existing byte array, you obviously cannot extend it because arrays cannot be resized.

MemoryStream adds the **Capacity** property to the ones it inherits from **Stream**. The **Capacity** property tells you how many bytes are currently allocated for a stream. This is useful when you are using a stream based on a byte array, as **Capacity** will tell you the size of the array, whereas **Length** will tell you how many bytes are being used.

MemoryStream doesn't implement the asynchronous read/write methods because I/O to memory doesn't require that facility. However, it implements three extra methods:

- **GetBuffer()**—Returns a reference to the byte array underlying the stream
- **ToArray()**—Writes the entire content to a byte array
- **WriteTo()**—Writes the content of the stream to another **Stream**

Other Stream Classes

BufferedStream improves read and write performance by caching data in memory and reducing the number of calls that need to be made to the operating system. **BufferedStream** isn't used on its own, but instead is wrapped around certain other types of streams, in particular, the **BinaryWriter** and **BinaryReader** classes described as follows.

The **BinaryWriter** and **BinaryReader** classes are used to read and write primitive data types rather than raw bytes. In reality, these classes convert between primitive types and raw bytes, so they need to work with a basic **Stream** object—such as **FileStream** or **MemoryStream**—that handles the I/O of the bytes. The **BaseStream** property of both of these classes lets you get a reference to the underlying **Stream** object. Table 6.7 lists the methods of the **BinaryWriter** class.

The **Write()** method has no fewer than 18 overloads that handle writing .NET basic types, such as:

- The integer types (Int16, Int32, Int64, and their unsigned equivalents)
- Bytes and arrays of bytes

Table 6.7 The methods of the BinaryWriter class.

Method	Description
Close	Closes the **BinaryWriter** and releases any resources associated with it.
Flush	Causes any unwritten data that remains in the **BinaryWriter**'s buffers to be written.
Seek	Moves the seek pointer.
Write	Writes a value to the stream. See the following details of this method.
Write7BitEncodedInt	Writes a 32-bit integer in a compressed format.

- Single and double floating-point numbers
- **Char** and arrays of **Char**
- Strings

The **BinaryReader** has very nearly the same functionality, but the reading methods are not overloads of one function. For example, in **BinaryWriter**, you have **Write(Int16)** and **Write(Char)**, whereas in **BinaryReader**, you have **ReadInt16()** and **ReadChar()**. The reason is clear when you think about it: when writing, the writer object can deduce what it has to write from the type of the argument to **Write()**. When reading, faced with a stream of bytes, the reader does not know how it is supposed to put them together. You need to tell the reader how to put the stream of bytes together by calling a particular function. See the Immediate Solutions section for an example of using these classes to perform binary I/O.

And, finally, although it isn't part of the **System.IO** namespace, the **System.Net.Sockets.NetworkStream** class lets you perform stream-based I/O using network sockets.

Text I/O Using Readers and Writers

Thus far, I've discussed binary I/O, where data is represented as a series of bytes. I'll now go on to discuss the classes that are available for character I/O.

TextWriter Classes

TextWriter is an abstract base class that has a number of subclasses:

- **HtmlTextWriter** for writing HTML to browser clients
- **HttpWriter** for writing text to the HTTP response object in ASP.NET pages
- **IndentedTextWriter** for writing text with indentation control

- **StreamWriter** for writing characters to a stream
- **StringWriter** for writing characters to a string

NOTE: *For C programmers,* ***StreamWriter*** *is analogous to* ***printf()*** *or* ***fprintf()****, and* ***StringWriter*** *is analogous to* ***sprintf()****.*

TextWriter has three properties: **Encoding**, which returns the character encoding in which the output is written; **FormatProvider**, which gets a reference to the object that controls formatting for the text; and **NewLine**,which returns the line terminator string used on the current platform. This is "\r\n" (carriage return followed by line-feed) by default, but could also be "\r" or "\n".

The class has several methods, as shown in Table 6.8. The **Write()** method has 17 overloads that write .NET types (**Char**, **Boolean**, **Int32**, etc.) to the stream. There is a matching set of **WriteLine()** methods that do the same thing, but also append a newline character.

NOTE: *You may think that the name of the* ***WriteLine()*** *method seems familiar. It is because the* ***Console*** *class implements a* ***TextWriter*** *for its* ***Out*** *and* ***Error*** *members, so you've been using* ***TextWriter's Write()*** *and* ***WriteLine()*** *functions all along.*

The shared **Synchronized()** method provides thread safety for **TextWriters** by creating a thread-safe wrapper around a **TextWriter**, so that two threads trying to use the same **TextWriter** won't interfere with one another.

StreamWriter

StreamWriter is a subclass of **TextWriter** designed to write characters to a stream using a particular encoding method. The default encoding is UTF-8, which gives good results for Unicode characters on localized versions of the operating system. If you want to use another encoding method, you can use the ASCII and UTF-7 encodings provided in the **System.Text** namespace or create your own

Table 6.8 The methods of the TextWriter class.

Method	Description
Close	Closes the **TextWriter** and releases any resources associated with it.
Dispose	Releases the resources associated with the **TextWriter.**
Flush	Causes any unwritten data that remains in the **TextWriter**'s buffers to be written.
Synchronized	Creates a thread safe wrapper around the **TextWriter** object.
Write	Writes data to the stream.
WriteLine	Writes data to the stream followed by a newline sequence.

based on **System.Text.Encoding**. Details on creating your own encodings are outside the scope of this book.

When constructing a **StreamWriter**, you can specify a file name or an existing stream, and optionally an encoding. The following code fragment shows how to create a **StreamWriter** to write to a file:

```
' Create a FileStream to write bytes to the file
Dim ds As New FileStream("c:\temp\foo.txt", FileMode.Create)

' Create a StreamWriter to do the output, and connect
' it to the FileStream
Dim writer As New StreamWriter(ds)
```

The **FileStream** object is created to write to the foo.txt file, and it will create the file if it doesn't already exist or overwrite the file if it does. **FileStream** wants to output bytes, so I wrap it in an object that is going to take text data and output it as bytes. In other words, the **StreamWriter** converts characters to bytes and pipes them to the **FileStream**.

StreamWriter adds an **AutoFlush** property to **TextWriter**, which if true causes the object to flush its buffer every time it does a **Write()** operation. This ensures that the output is always up-to-date, but isn't as efficient as allowing the **StreamWriter** to buffer its output. The **BaseStream** property provides access to the underlying **Stream** object.

The **StreamWriter** class doesn't add any methods to those it inherits from **TextWriter**, but it does overload the **Write()** methods for writing characters and strings to the stream.

StringWriter

StringWriter is designed to write its output to a string. Because this string is being modified, the output is written to a **StringBuilder** rather than a **String** because **Strings** are immutable. It has a set of **Write()** methods as well as **GetStringBuilder()** and **ToString()** methods to help handle the buffer that is being built.

NOTE: *For C programmers,* ***StringWriter*** *provides some of the functionality of the* ***sprintf()*** *function from the C Standard Library.*

The following example shows how to create and use a **StringWriter**:

```
' Create a StringWriter
Dim sw As New StringWriter
Dim n As Integer = 42
```

```
' Write some text to the string
sw.Write("The value of n is {0}", n)
sw.Write("... and some more characters")

' Print out the content of the StringWriter
Console.WriteLine(sw.ToString())
```

TextReader Classes

As you might expect, there's also a **TextReader** class that has the subclasses **StreamReader** and **StringReader**. This class has fewer methods than **TextWriter**, although it works in the same way. The methods are summarized in Table 6.9.

StreamReader

The **StreamReader** class provides character-oriented input from streams, so it is this class that is used to read lines of text from files. **StreamReader** can use any character encoding you choose to give it, but will use UTF-8 by default, as this handles Unicode characters properly.

The class has 10 constructors that let you create **StreamReaders** in a number of ways, including:

- From a file name with or without a character encoding specified
- From a **Stream** reference with or without a character encoding specified

The class has two properties, **BaseStream**, which returns a reference to the **Stream** being wrapped by this object, and **CurrentEncoding**, which returns the current encoding being used by the reader.

StreamReader has several methods that read data. **ReadLine()** reads a single line, returning it as a string. **ReadToEnd()** reads the entire stream, returning it

Table 6.9 The methods of the TextReader class.

Method	Description
Close	Closes the **TextReader** and releases any resources associated with it
Peek	Looks at the next character without removing it from the input stream
Read	Reads characters into a character array
ReadBlock	Reads characters into a character array and blocks until the right number has been read or the end of the file has been reached
ReadLine	Reads a line of characters and returns it as a string
ReadToEnd	Reads to the end of the stream and returns the characters as a single string
Synchronized	Creates a thread safe wrapper around the **TextReader**

as a (possibly very large) string. There are also two **Read()** methods, the first of which returns the next character from the stream (or -1 if the end of the stream has been reached), and the second reads a specified number of characters into a character array. In addition, the **Peek()** method lets you look at the next character without removing it from the stream, so that it will be available to a subsequent **Read()** call. This is useful when you are parsing input character by character and won't know that you've reached the end of (say) a number until you find the next white space character.

StringReader

StringReader lets you read characters from a string, either one at a time, a number at a time, or a line at a time. It doesn't provide any formatting ability and is useful if you want to treat a string as if it was a text file.

Files and Directories

Files and directories are represented in .NET by six classes in the **System.IO** namespace:

- **FileSystemInfo**—Base class for **FileInfo** and **DirectoryInfo**
- **File**—Contains shared (static) methods used to manipulate files
- **FileInfo**—Used to represent a file and manipulate it
- **Directory**—Contains static methods to manipulate directories
- **DirectoryInfo**—Used to represent a directory and manipulate it
- **Path**—Used to manipulate path information

The FileSystemInfo Class

FileSystemInfo is the base class for the **FileInfo** and **DirectoryInfo** classes, which are used to manipulate files and directories. It provides a number of methods and properties that are common to both files and directories.

The fields and properties provided by **FileSystemInfo** are summarized in Tables 6.10 and 6.11. File attributes are represented by the **FileAttributes** enumeration, whose commonly used members are listed in Table 6.12. (See the Immediate Solutions section for an example of how to use the **FileAttributes** enumeration.) The **FileSystemInfo** class only has two methods, which are summarized in Table 6.13.

The File Class

All the methods in the **File** class are shared ("static" for C# and C++ programmers). This means that you don't create **File** objects, but simply call the shared methods.

Table 6.10 Fields of the FileSystemInfo class.

Field	Description
FullPath	The fully qualified path to the directory or file
OriginalPath	The original relative or absolute path specified by the user

Table 6.11 Properties of the FileSystemInfo class.

Property	Description
Attributes	Gets or sets the attributes of the object, using a **FileAttributes** object
CreationTime	Gets or sets the creation time of an object
Exists	True if the file or directory exists
Extension	Retrieves a file name extension
FullName	Retrieves the full name of the file or directory
LastAccessTime	Gets or sets the last access time of an object
LastReadTime	Gets or sets the last read time of an object
Name	Gets the name of the file or directory

Table 6.12 Commonly used members of the FileAttributes enumeration.

Member	Description
Archive	Indicates that a file's archive status is set
Compressed	Indicates that a file is compressed
Directory	Indicates that the object is a directory
Encrypted	Indicates that the object is encrypted
Hidden	Indicates that the file or directory is hidden
Normal	Indicates that the file has no other attributes set, and so must be used alone
Offline	Indicates that the file is offline; that is, the file's content is not immediately available
ReadOnly	Indicates that the file or directory is read-only
System	Denotes a system file
Temporary	Denotes a temporary file

Table 6.13 Methods of the FileSystemInfo class.

Method	Description
Delete	Deletes a file or directory
Refresh	Used to update the attribute information for an object

---

***NOTE:** Security checks are applied to all methods in the **File** class. If you want to perform a lot of operations on the same file, it is more efficient to create a **FileInfo** object to work with the file because a **FileInfo** object does not apply security to every call.*

Table 6.14 lists the methods provided by the **File** class. Most of these methods are self-explanatory: Refer to sections earlier in the chapter for details of the various **Stream** and **Writer** classes and how to use them. Remember that they are all shared methods, so you have to call them using the class name:

```
bOK = File.Exists("myfile.txt")
```

The FileInfo Class

FileInfo is used to represent a path to a file. Unlike the **File** class, all members are nonshared. Although some functionality is only offered by one class or the

Table 6.14 Methods of the File class.

Method	Description
AppendText	Opens a **StreamWriter** for appending text to a new or existing file
Copy	Copies an existing file to a new file
Create	Creates a new file
CreateText	Creates a new text file
Delete	Deletes a file
Exists	Returns true if a file exists
GetAttributes	Returns a **FileAttributes** structure representing a file's attributes
GetCreationTime	Gets a DateTime representing the file's creation time
GetLastAccessTime	Gets a DateTime representing the file's last access time
GetLastWriteTime	Gets a DateTime representing the file's last write time
Move	Moves a file to a new location
Open	Opens a file, returning a **FileStream**
OpenRead	Opens a file for read-only access, returning a **FileStream**
OpenText	Opens a text file for reading, returning a **StreamReader**
OpenWrite	Opens a file for writing, returning a **FileStream**
SetAttributes	Uses a **FileAttributes** structure to set the file attributes
SetCreationTime	Uses a DateTime to set the creation time attribute
SetLastAccessTime	Uses a DateTime to set the last access time attribute
SetLastWriteTime	Uses a DateTime to set the last write time attribute

other, in some cases, you have a choice of methods to use. **FileInfo** inherits methods and properties from its parent class, **FileSystemInfo**.

NOTE: *The path represented by a* ***FileInfo*** *doesn't have to exist.*

The properties and methods of the **FileInfo** class are listed in Tables 6.15 and 6.16.

The Directory Class

The **System.IO.Directory** class provides you with static methods to help you operate on directories and contains routines for creating, deleting, moving, copying, and enumerating directories. A **Directory** object represents a path that may name an existing directory or that can be used to create a new one.

Table 6.15 Properties of the FileInfo class.

Property	Description
Directory	Gets a **DirectoryInfo** representing the parent directory for this file
DirectoryName	Gets a string representing the full path to this file
Exists	True if the file exists
Length	Retrieves the length of the file in bytes
Name	Gets the name of the file

Table 6.16 Methods of the FileInfo class.

Method	Description
AppendText	Gets a **DirectoryInfo** representing the parent directory for this file
CopyTo	Copies the file to another location
Create	Creates a new file
CreateText	Creates a new text file
Delete	Deletes the file
MoveTo	Moves the file to a new location
Open	Opens a file, returning a **FileStream**
OpenRead	Opens a file for read-only access, returning a **FileStream**
OpenText	Opens a text file for reading, returning a **StreamReader**
OpenWrite	Opens a file for writing, returning a **FileStream**
ToString	Returns the fully qualified path as a string

Table 6.17 Shared methods in the Directory class.

Method	Description
CreateDirectory	Creates a new directory
Delete	Deletes a directory and possibly subdirectories and files
Exists	Returns true if a directory exists
GetCreationTime	Gets a DateTime representing the file's creation time
GetCurrentDirectory	Gets the current directory as a string
GetDirectories	Returns the names of the subdirectories of a given directory
GetDirectoryRoot	Gets the root of a directory path
GetFiles	Gets a list of the files in a given directory
GetFileSystemEntries	Gets a list of the files and directories in a given directory
GetLastAccessTime	Gets a DateTime representing the last access time
GetLastWriteTime	Gets a DateTime representing the last write time
GetLogicalDrives	Gets a list of the logical drives
GetParent	Gets the parent directory of a specified path
Move	Moves a directory to a new location
SetCreationTime	Uses a DateTime to set the creation time attribute
SetCurrentDirectory	Sets the current directory
SetLastAccessTime	Uses a DateTime to set the last access time attribute
SetLastWriteTime	Uses a DateTime to set the last write time attribute

Table 6.17 lists the shared methods provided by the **Directory** class. Note that you have to have the proper security settings (in particular, **FileIOPermission**) if you want to do anything that will affect the file system.

TIP: *See Chapter 7 for more details on security in .NET.*

The DirectoryInfo Class

The **System.IO.DirectoryInfo** class is used to represent directories. A **DirectoryInfo** object represents a path that may name an existing directory or that can be used to create a new one. **DirectoryInfo** inherits methods and properties from its parent class, **FileSystemInfo**. Tables 6.18 and 6.19 list the commonly used properties and methods of the **DirectoryInfo** class.

Table 6.18 Properties of the DirectoryInfo class

Property	Description
Exists	True if the directory exists.
Name	Gets the name of the directory.
Parent	Retrieves the parent of this directory as a string. Returns null if the directory is a root directory already.
Root	Retrieves the root portion of a path.

Table 6.19 Methods of the DirectoryInfo class.

Method	Description
Create	Creates a new directory
CreateSubdirectory	Creates one or more new subdirectories
Delete	Deletes the directory and optionally subdirectories and files
GetDirectories	Returns the names of the subdirectories of a given directory
GetFiles	Gets a list of the files in a given directory
GetFileSystemInfos	Gets a list of **FileSystemInfo** objects describing the contents of a given directory
MoveTo	Moves the file to a new location
ToString	Returns the fully qualified path as a string

The Path Class

The **System.IO.Path** class lets you process file and directory path names in a cross-platform manner. All methods in this class are shared, so you don't create **Path** objects in order to call them. Tables 6.20 and 6.21 list the fields and methods provided by this class.

Here are a few examples of how these functions can be used:

```
Path.IsPathRooted("c:\temp\foo.txt")         ' returns true
Path.GetExtension("c:\temp\foo.txt")         ' returns '.txt'
Path.GetPathRoot("c:\temp\foo.txt")          ' returns 'c:\'
Path.GetDirectoryName("c:\temp\foo.txt")     ' returns 'c:\temp'
```

NOTE: *When you use the **Path** class functions in Visual Basic, you'll have to qualify them with their full name because of a naming conflict, for example, **System.IO.Path.IsRooted**.*

Table 6.20 Fields of the Path class.

Field	Description
AltDirectorySeparatorChar	The platform-specific alternate directory separator character (which is slash '/' on Windows and the Mac, and backslash '\' on Unix)
DirectorySeparatorChar	The platform-specific directory separator character (which is backslash '\' on Windows, colon ':' on the Mac, and slash '/' on Unix)
InvalidPathChars	Returns an array of characters that can't be used in pathnames, such as '?', '*' and '>'
PathSeparator	The path separator character, which is semicolon ';' in Win32
VolumeSeparatorChar	The volume separator character, which is colon ':' for Win32 and the Mac, and slash '/' for Unix

Table 6.21 Methods of the Path class.

Method	Description
ChangeExtension	Changes the file extension
Combine	Combines two file paths
GetDirectoryName	Returns the directory path for a file
GetExtension	Returns the extension for a file
GetFileName	Returns the name plus extension for a file
GetFileNameWithoutExtension	Returns the name only for a file
GetFullPath	Returns a fully expanded path
GetPathRoot	Returns the root of a path
GetTempFileName	Returns a unique name for a temporary file
GetTempPath	Returns the path to the system's temp file folder
HasExtension	Returns true if the file has a given extension
IsPathRooted	Returns true if a path contains the root

FileSystemWatcher

FileSystemWatcher is an extremely useful class that lets you watch for changes to the files and subdirectories of a specified directory. The directory you're watching can be on the local machine, on a network drive, or on a remote machine.

NOTE: *You can't watch directories on remote machines that aren't running Windows 2000 or Windows NT. 4.0. In addition, you can't watch a remote Windows NT 4 machine from another Windows NT 4 machine. You also can't log events for DVD and CD sources because their timestamps can't change.*

You can create a **FileSystemWatcher** to watch a whole directory or a particular file type within the directory, and you can set up filters to narrow down the range of files that a watcher will report on.

As you might expect, **FileSystemWatcher** works by raising events when files or directories change, and client code needs to implement handlers for events of interest. Table 6.22 lists the events that can be raised by the **FileSystemWatcher** class.

The System.Net Namespace

The classes in the **System.Net** namespace provide a simple programming interface to many of the protocols found on networks and the Internet. Table 6.23 lists the major classes in the namespace.

Table 6.22 Events raised by the FileSystemWatcher class.

Event	Description
Changed	Raised when a file or directory is changed
Created	Raised when a file or directory is created
Deleted	Raised when a file or directory is deleted
Error	Raised when the internal buffer of the **FileSystemWatcher** overflows
Renamed	Raised when a file or directory is renamed

Table 6.23 Major classes in the System.Net namespace.

Class	Description
Cookie	Provides a set of methods and properties used to manage cookies
Dns	Provides simple domain name resolution functionality
EndPoint	An abstract class representing a network address
FileWebRequest	Interacts with URI's that begin 'file://' in order to access local files
FileWebResponse	Provides read-only access to a file system via 'file://' URIs
HttpWebRequest	Enables clients to send requests to HTTP servers
HttpWebResponse	Enables clients to receive responses from HTTP servers
IPAddress	Represents an IP address
IPEndPoint	Represents an IP endpoint (an IP address plus a port number)
IPHostEntry	Associates a DNS entry with an array of aliases and matching IP addresses
WebClient	Provides common methods for sending data to and receiving data from a URI
WebException	An exception thrown when using network access

IPAddress, IPEndPoint, and Dns Classes

IPAddress, **IPEndPoint**, and **Dns** classes are used to represent IP addresses and to perform DNS lookups.

Every machine on a TCP/IP network has an *IP address*, which can be expressed in one of several ways. The most basic is to use the *dotted quad* notation, which consists of four numeric values ranging from 0 to 255 separated by dots, for example, 255.1.64.9. These values aren't very easy for humans to remember, so there's usually an equivalent name, such as **www.foo.com**.

The **IPAddress** class represents an IP address. The easiest way to create one is to use the **Parse()** method, which takes a dotted quad address as a string:

```
Dim ip As IPAddress = IPAddress.Parse("217.49.2.77")
```

If you want to get the **IPAddress** object to tell you what dotted quad address it holds, use **ToString()**.

TCP/IP server processes listen on ports on server machines, so if you want to talk to a server, you'll need to specify the IP address of the machine and the port the server is listening on. This combination is called an *IP endpoint* and is represented by the **IPEndPoint** class. The constructors for **IPEndPoint** take a port number and an IP address, either as a string or as a reference to an **IPAddress** object.

Provided that you have access to a Domain Name server, the **Dns** class will let you perform DNS lookups and operate on the result. Here's how **Dns** is commonly used:

```
Dim ipa As IPHostEntry = Dns.GetHostByName("www.microsoft.com")
```

The static **GetHostByName()** function takes a hostname and returns the **IPHostEntry** initialized with the IP address and port number. The **GetHostByAddress()** method does the same thing; it takes a dotted IP address (such as 127.0.0.1) either as a string or an **IPAddress**. **GetHostName()** returns the DNS hostname of the local machine as a string, and **IpToString()** converts an IP address in the form of a long integer into a dotted quad address returned as a string.

The WebRequest and WebResponse Classes

Several of the classes in **System.Net** help you write software to talk to Web servers, and they're all based on the **WebRequest** and **WebResponse** superclasses.

The **FileWebRequest** and **FileWebResponse** classes are designed to let you work with URIs that represent local files, and as such, they start with **file://**.

Of more interest are the **HttpWebRequest** and **HttpWebResponse** classes, which allow you to interact with servers using HTTP. Creating an **HttpWebRequest** object allows you to send requests to a Web server using HTTP. In order to make this job easier, the class contains a number of properties that correspond to fields in the HTTP header sent to the server, a few of which are listed in Table 6.24.

The **GetResponse()** method makes a synchronous request to the server and returns an **HttpWebResponse** object containing the response. If you want to work asynchronously, you can use the **BeginGetResponse()** and **EndGetResponse()** methods.

The System.Net.Sockets Namespace

The classes and enumerations in the **System.Net.Sockets** namespace provide an implementation of the popular Windows Sockets (Winsock) interface for use with .NET languages.

What Are Sockets?

The original sockets were developed as part of the Unix operating system, and they have been widely used as a simple way to pass data between programs. They are widely used on the Internet and can be used between programs on a single machine as well.

Table 6.24 A selection of HTTP header properties of the HttpWebRequest class.

Property	Description
AllowAutoRedirect	True if the resource should automatically follow redirection requests from the server. The default is true.
ContentLength	Gets or sets the **ContentLength** header, which indicates how many bytes are to be sent to the server. The default is -1, meaning there is no request data.
ContentType	Gets or sets the **ContentType** header, which indicates the media type of the request.
IfModifiedSince	Gets or sets the date in the **IfModifiedSince** header, which is used to control when cached pages are updated.
KeepAlive	If true, tells the server that you want a persistent connection.
Timeout	Represents the time in milliseconds before the request times out.
UserAgent	Gets or sets the **UserAgent** header, which tells the server the type of client sending the request (e.g., Internet Explorer).

Sockets are similar to telephone communications between people working for different companies. If I'm going to contact you from my phone, I need to know your company phone number and your extension. In socket communication, the "phone number" is the IP address of the machine you want to talk to. You may know this as a dotted IP address of the form 123.123.1.65 or as a more humanly friendly representation of **foo.xyz.com**.

Just as everyone in an office has an extension on the same phone number, every program on a machine that wants to use sockets uses a unique *port number*. Port numbers range from zero upwards: Those in the range 0 to 1024 are reserved for official use and are used by programs such as Web servers and mail servers. You are free to use port numbers above 1024 for your own use.

A server process can reserve a port number and then sit on it waiting for incoming calls. A client process makes a call by opening a socket and specifying the IP address and port number it wants to connect to. If the address and port number are correct, the two processes will be connected.

How Do You Use Sockets?

Although the **System.Net.Sockets** namespace contains a **Socket** class that will do everything you want, Microsoft recommends that you use the two classes that it supplies to represent either end of a socket connection. **TcpClient** represents the client end, whereas **TcpListener** represents the server end.

At the client end, you create a **TcpClient**, passing it the IP address of the machine you want to connect to and the port that the server process is using.

NOTE: *If you are connecting to a server process on the local machine, the IP address to use is either "localhost" or "127.0.01".*

Alternatively, you can create an unconnected **TcpClient,** and then use the **Connect()** method to make the connection:

```
' Create a TcpClient
Dim tpc As New TcpClient()
' Connect to port 9999 on the local machine
tpc.Connect("localhost", 9999)
```

The **TcpClient** class has a number of useful methods and properties that can help manage the session. They are summarized in Table 6.25.

Table 6.25 Methods and properties of the TcpClient class.

Member	Description
Active	True if a connection has been made
Client	Gets or sets the underlying **Socket** object
Close()	Disposes of the TCP connection
Connect()	Connect to a TCP host
GetStream()	Gets the stream used for reading and writing through the socket
ReceiveBufferSize	Gets or sets the size of the receive buffer (default = 8192)
ReceiveTimeout	Gets or sets the receive timeout in milliseconds (default = 0)
SendBufferSize	Gets or sets the size of the receive buffer (default = 8192)
SendTimeout	Gets or sets the send timeout in milliseconds (default = 0)

When the connection has been established, the **GetStream()** method returns a reference to a **Stream** object, which is used to read and write through the socket:

```
Dim theStream As Stream = tpc.GetStream()
```

The **Stream's Read()** and **Write()** methods can be used to pass data through the socket, but because they use bytes, it is necessary to convert character data into bytes before sending. See the Immediate Solution "Using Sockets" for details on how to do this. As an alternative, you can use the **Send()** and **Receive()** methods that **TcpClient** inherits from **Socket**, which also work with byte arrays.

TcpListener implements a parallel set of functionality that helps implement the server side of a socket connection. The main methods and properties of the **TcpListener** class are summarized in Table 6.26.

Table 6.26 Methods and properties of the TcpListener class.

Member	Description
AcceptSocket()	Waits for a client to connect, returning a **Socket**
AcceptTcpClient()	Waits for a client to connect, returning a **TcpClient**
Active	True if a connection has been made
LocalEndpoint	Gets the active endpoint (IP address plus port number) for the listener socket
Pending()	Returns true if there are pending connection requests
Server	Gets the underlying **Socket** object
Start()	Start listening for network requests
Stop()	Stop listening for network requests

A **TcpListener** is created to listen on a particular socket, which obviously has to match the ones that clients will be calling in on:

```
' Create a TcpListener on port 1999
Dim tcl As New TcpListener(1999)
```

Once created, the **Start()** method starts the object listening for network connections. There are two ways in which a listener can connect to incoming clients. One way is to call **AcceptSocket()** or **AcceptTcpClient()**, both of which will block until a client connects. Alternatively, the server can periodically call the **TcpListener**'s **Pending()** method, which returns true if any clients are waiting to connect. If there are clients waiting, calls to **AcceptSocket()** or **AcceptTcpClient()** will connect immediately.

Calls to **AcceptSocket()** or **AcceptTcpClient()** return a **Socket** reference, so the server code can use the **Send()** and **Receive()** methods to pass data through the connection. Once the conversation is finished, the **Stop()** method stops the **TcpListener** from listening for network traffic.

Immediate Solutions

Using Binary I/O with Streams

The **BinaryReader** and **BinaryWriter** classes are used for binary I/O; this section shows how to use them with files.

NOTE: *If you want to read about text I/O rather than binary I/O, see the solution "Reading and Writing Text Files."*

The following sample program shows how to write data to a file in binary format, and then read it again:

```
' You need to import System.IO so that you can use file, reader and
' writer classes
Imports System.IO

Module Module1
  Sub Main()
    Try
      ' Create the FileStream to create a file
      ' Open it for read/write access
      Dim ds As New FileStream("\test.dat", _
             FileMode.Create, FileAccess.ReadWrite)

      ' Wrap it in a BinaryWriter
      Dim bw As New BinaryWriter(ds)

      ' Write some data to the stream
      bw.Write("A string")
      bw.Write(142)
      bw.Write(97.4)
      bw.Write(True)

      ' Open it for reading
      Dim br As New BinaryReader(ds)
      ' Move back to the start
      br.BaseStream.Seek(0, SeekOrigin.Begin)

      ' Read the data
      Console.WriteLine(br.ReadString())
```

```
      Console.WriteLine(br.ReadInt32())
      Console.WriteLine(br.ReadDouble())
      Console.WriteLine(br.ReadBoolean())

    Catch e As Exception
      Console.WriteLine("Exception:" + e.ToString())
    End Try
  End Sub
End Module
```

I start by importing the **System.IO** namespace, which contains all the I/O functionality. Note that you don't need to add a reference to the project because the classes themselves are in the default DLLs loaded for every project.

I then create a **FileStream** to operate on the file. The second parameter determines how the file will be opened; and in this case, it is set to **FileMode.Create**, which will create a new file or overwrite the file with the same name if it already exists. The third parameter controls the file access; in this example, because I'm going to read and write the file, I need to use **FileAccess.ReadWrite**.

It's good practice to put the creation of the **FileStream** in a **Try...Catch** block, as there are a lot of things that can go wrong when opening and writing to files. Rather than enclosing just this call in **Try...Catch**, I've placed the **Try** around the entire code so that I can handle any exception that occurs in one place. In a larger program, you would probably want to split your exception handling rather than use one **Try...Catch**.

FileStream reads and writes bytes, which is seldom very convenient, so a **FileStream** is normally wrapped in another class that handles the conversion to and from bytes. In this case, I'm using a **BinaryWriter**, which takes .NET primitive types and converts them into bytes. These bytes can then be passed to the **FileStream**.

BinaryWriter has a lot of overloaded **Write()** methods, one for each of the primitive types. In this example, you can see four in use, writing out a string, an integer, a floating-point value, and a Boolean.

If I wanted to terminate the program at this point, I could insert code similar to the following after the calls to **Write()**:

```
' Flush output and close the file
bw.Flush()
bw.Close()
```

These two calls would cause any unwritten data to be written to the stream, and the call to close would close the stream as well as the underlying file. I'm not going to close the file because I want to read the data I've just written. I can do this because I opened the stream in ReadWrite mode, so I create a **BinaryReader** to read from the **FileStream**.

Before I can use the **BinaryReader**, I have to move back to the beginning of the file. Whenever you are using a stream, the seek pointer marks the point at which the next read or write operation will occur. I've been writing to the stream, so the seek pointer is at the end of the file, ready to write the next item. If I want to read something earlier in the file, I need to reposition the seek pointer. You can see how this is done: The **BaseStream** property gets a reference to the **FileStream** inside the **BinaryReader**, and I then call the **Seek()** method to reposition the **FileStream**. **Seek()** takes two parameters—an offset in bytes and a position from which to calculate the offset. I've used **SeekOrigin.Begin**, which denotes the start of the file, so an offset of zero bytes puts me back to the beginning of the file. Other possible values are **SeekOrigin.End** (the end of the file) and **SeekOrigin.Current** (the current position). You can use negative offsets as well as positive offsets, so you can easily position yourself relative to the end of the stream. You also don't have to read from the start of the file, so if you know where to position yourself, you can start reading data at any arbitrary point in the file.

Once positioned, it is easy to read data from the file. As before, the **FileStream** only reads and writes bytes, so the **BinaryReader** converts them into .NET types. Unlike **BinaryWriter**, **BinaryReader** has a number of separate methods for reading, one for each basic type; you can see four of them used in the preceding example. You need to be sure that you use the correct methods. I wrote an integer out, so I need to use **ReadInt32()** to input it again. Likewise, 97.4 is a **Double**, so I need to use **ReadDouble()** to input it.

Reading and Writing Text Files

Working with text files is very easy using the **StreamWriter** and **StreamReader** classes. In this solution, I'll show you how to write text files, and then open them and read them.

Writing a File

I start by creating a normal VB Console application, which I've called VBTextWriter. Here's the listing of a simple program to write a text file:

```
' You need to add this Imports statement at the top
Imports System.IO

Module Module1
```

```
Sub Main()
  Try
  ' Create the FileStream
  Dim fs As New FileStream("\test.txt", FileMode.Create)

  ' Wrap it in a StreamWriter
  Dim wr As New StreamWriter(fs)

  ' Write some lines
  wr.WriteLine("line one")
  wr.WriteLine("line two")

  ' Flush and close the file
  wr.Flush()
  wr.Close()
  Catch e As Exception
    Console.WriteLine("Exception: " + e.ToString())
  End Try
End Sub
End Module
```

I first need to import the **System.IO** namespace into the project to save myself from having to qualify all the class names.

Once that's been done, I create a **FileStream** object. **FileStream** is a class that is used to create and perform I/O on disk files; it has several constructors. In the constructor used in this example, I pass it the file name and the access mode. There are several access modes you can use, and they are listed in Table 6.3. I'm using **Create** mode, which creates the file if it doesn't exist and overwrites it if it does.

The problem with using **FileStream** is that it reads and writes bytes, and I want to use character-based I/O. The solution is to wrap the **FileStream** in a **StreamWriter**, a class that accepts text as strings and characters, and converts it to bytes. The **StreamWriter** then passes these bytes to the **FileStream**, which writes them out to disk. You can see that the only argument to the **StreamWriter** constructor is the **FileStream** it is going to work with.

It's good practice to put the creation of the **FileStream** in a **Try...Catch** block, as there are a lot of things that can go wrong when opening and writing to files. The documentation for **FileStream** lists six different exceptions that can be thrown by the constructor:

- **ArgumentException**—The path was an empty string
- **ArgumentNullException**—The path was a **null** reference (**Nothing** in VB)

- **SecurityException**—You don't have permission to operate on this file
- **FileNotFoundException**—The file can't be found
- **IOException**—Some other I/O error has occurred, such as specifying an invalid drive letter
- **DirectoryNotFoundException**—The directory doesn't exist

Because of the number of things that can go wrong, it is a very good idea to trap these errors with a **Try** block. I've wrapped the entire code in a **Try** block and have caught the most general type of exception so that I can catch any type of error.

Related solution:	*Found on page:*
How Do I Catch Exceptions?	92
How Do I Generate Exceptions?	93

Once the file is open for writing, I can write something to it. You'll probably recognize the **WriteLine()** function because it is the one that is used by **Console**. The **Console** class uses a **StreamWriter**, but instead of writing its content to a file, it writes it to the screen. So, if you've done any .NET programming, you probably know how to use **StreamWriter**.

The two main methods used for output are **WriteLine()** and **Write()**. They are both pretty much the same, but **WriteLine()** adds a new line to the end of what it writes, whereas **Write()** doesn't. Both functions have numerous overloads for writing different types of output. The overloads for **WriteLine()** are shown in Table 6.27.

Table 6.27 Commonly used overloads of the WriteLine() method.

Overload	Description
WriteLine()	Writes a newline
WriteLine(Char)	Writes a single character
WriteLine(Char())	Writes an array of characters
WriteLine(Char(), Integer, Integer)	Writes part of an array of characters
WriteLine(String)	Writes a string
WriteLine(Boolean)	Writes a Boolean value as "true" or "false"
WriteLine(Decimal)	Writes a decimal value
WriteLine(Double)	Writes a double value
WriteLine(Integer)	Writes an integer
WriteLine(Long)	Writes a long integer

(continued)

Table 6.27 The overloads of the WriteLine() class *(continued)*.

Overload	Description
WriteLine(Object)	Calls **ToString()** on the object
WriteLine(Single)	Writes a single precision floating-point value
WriteLine(String, Object)	Writes a formatted string containing one object
WriteLine(String, Object, Object)	Writes a formatted string containing two objects
WriteLine(String, Object, Object, Object)	Writes a formatted string containing three objects
WriteLine(String, ParamArray Object())	Writes a formatted string containing a number of objects

Related solution:	*Found on page:*
How Do I Produce Formatted Output?	147

When I've finished with the file, I *flush* it and close it. Flushing it ensures that any data not yet written gets flushed from memory onto disk. **StreamWriter** has an **AutoFlush** property that you can set to true, in which case it will flush the output after each write operation. This ensures that you won't lose any data if your program crashes—because it will all be safely stored on disk—but it does slow down output.

Reading a File

Reading a text file is also a simple operation. The following sample program opens a text file and reads all the lines, copying each one to the console as it is read:

```
' You need to add this Imports statement at the top
Imports System.IO

Module Module1

Sub Main()
  Try
  ' Create the FileStream to open an existing file
  Dim fs As New FileStream("\test.txt", FileMode.Open)

  ' Wrap it in a StreamReader
  Dim rd As New StreamReader(fs)

  ' Read lines from the file and echo them
  Dim s As String

  s = rd.ReadLine()
  While Not s Is Nothing
    Console.WriteLine(s)
```

```
      s = rd.ReadLine()
    End While

    ' Close the file
    rd.Close()

    Catch e As Exception
      Console.WriteLine("Exception: " + e.ToString())
    End Try
  End Sub
  End Module
```

This program works in a way that is very similar to the file writing example in the previous section. This time the **FileStream** is created using **FileMode.Open**, which opens an existing file. The **FileStream** object is then used to initialize a **StreamReader**, which takes the bytes read by the **FileStream** and converts them into characters.

StreamReader has four ways of reading text from the file:

- **ReadLine()**—Reads up to the next end-of-line and returns a string
- **Read()**—Reads one or more characters, returning the result as a single character or a character array
- **ReadBlock()**—Reads a number of characters and returns them in a char array (inherited from **TextReader**)
- **ReadToEnd()**—Reads to the end of the stream, returning the result as one long string

In this example, I'm using **ReadLine()** to read each line from the file and print it out. Note how the *while* loop works: **ReadLine()** will return a **null** reference when it has run out of lines to read, so I read one line, and then enter the loop. If the file is empty, the loop will never be entered, and nothing will be printed; otherwise, each line will be printed and the next one read.

How Can I Work with Files and Directories on a Disk?

The **File** and **Directory** classes provide a high-level interface to disk filing systems and make it easy to browse, move, delete, and otherwise work with and organize the items on your disk.

In this solution, I'll show you how to write a simple file browser, which uses many of the features of the **File** and **Directory** classes, and which you can use as a basis for further experimentation.

Creating the Project

Start off by creating a normal VB Windows application, which in my case I've called VBDirList. Import the **System.IO** namespace into the project:

```
' You need to add this Imports statement
Imports System.IO
```

Next, add the UI components to the form, as shown in Figure 6.1. Table 6.28 lists all the components that appear on the form, together with their identifiers and the functions they perform in the program. Delete the value in the **Text** property of all the controls before going any further.

Getting the List of Drive Letters

The first serious coding task that needs to be done is to find all the logical drives on the machine and load their names into the ComboBox. The following function shows how to do this:

```
Private Sub Init_Drives()
  ' Fill a ComboBox with drive information
  Dim drives() As String
  drives = Directory.GetLogicalDrives()

  Dim ie As IEnumerator = drives.GetEnumerator
  While ie.MoveNext
    ComboBox1.Items.Add(ie.Current)
  End While

  ' Don't set a selection
  ComboBox1.SelectedIndex = -1;
End Sub
```

After declaring an array of strings, the first call is to **GetLogicalDrives()**, a shared (static) member of **Directory**. This function returns the name of each logical drive as a **String** in the form "C:\".

NOTE: *Physical drives are hardware, and on PCs, physical drives can be divided into more than one logical drive. On my main PC, the one hard disk is divided into the C: and D: logical drives.*

The easiest way to add each **String** to the ComboBox is to set up an enumerator and use the **MoveNext()** method and the **Current** property to access each string in turn.

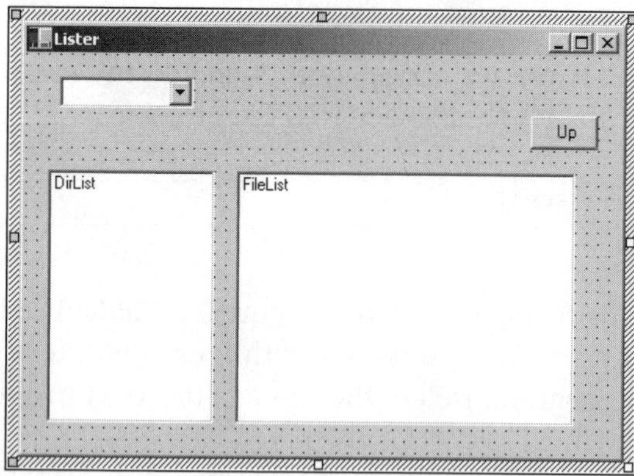

Figure 6.1 The user interface for the VBDirList project.

Table 6.28 The components of the VBDirList program user interface.

Type	Name	Description
ComboBox	**ComboBox1**	Holds the drive letters.
Label	**CurrentPathLabel**	Shows the currently selected path.
Button	**MoveToParentBtn**	Moves up a level in the directory tree. Does nothing if you are already at the root.
ListBox	**DirList**	Holds a listing of the current directory.
ListBox	**FileList**	Displays the properties of the item selected in the **DirList** control.

The final task is to set the selection in the ComboBox. I've chosen not to have an initial selection, but you could search the list of strings for "C" and choose that one.

Place a call to this function immediately before the end of the form's constructor:

```
Public Sub New()
  ...
  InitializeComponent

  Init_Drives()
End Sub
```

Handling a Change of Drive

Because the user is going to use the ComboBox to select a drive letter, you need to handle this selection process. The ComboBox raises a **SelectedIndexChanged** event when someone chooses an item, so you need to add a handler for this event to the **Form** class. In the Visual Studio Designer, you can do this by double-clicking on the **ComboBox** object:

```
Protected Sub ComboBox1_SelectedIndexChanged(ByVal sender _
        As System.Object, ByVal e As System.EventArgs) _
        Handles ComboBox1.SelectedIndexChanged
  ' Check we have a selection
  If ComboBox1.SelectedIndex <> -1 Then
    ' Get the selected item as a String
    Dim s As String = CType(ComboBox1.SelectedItem, String)
    ' Process it...
    Get_Content(s)
  End If
End Sub
```

The **If** statement checks whether there is a selected object in the ComboBox. If there isn't, the property will have the value of -1, and there's nothing more to do.

If there is a selection, it is retrieved as a string. I need to use the **CType** function because **SelectedItem** returns an **Object** reference, and VB won't let me assign an **Object** reference directly to a **String** reference.

Once I have the string, I pass it to the **Get_Content()** method, which fills the DirList control with the contents of the drive's root directory.

Processing a Directory

The **Get_Content()** function takes the full path to a directory, reads the contents of the directory, and puts the names of all the items into the DirList ListBox. It gets called on two occasions:

- When the user selects a new drive from the ComboBox
- When the user double-clicks on an entry in the DirList control and that entry is a directory

I first need to construct a **DirectoryInfo** object to represent the path that has been passed in, and because I'll want to use this later in other functions, I need to add a reference to the class:

```
Public Class Form1
    Inherits System.Windows.Forms.Form
  ' A Directory object that represents the current path
  Dim curDir As DirectoryInfo
  ...
End Class
```

Here's the listing for the **Get_Content()** function:

```
Private Sub Get_Content(ByRef dirPath As String)
  ' Create a DirectoryInfo object to represent the path
```

```
    Try
      curDir = New DirectoryInfo(dirPath)
    Catch e As Exception
      MessageBox.Show("Error getting content for '" _
         & dirPath & "'")
      Return
    End Try

    ' Display the current path in the Label
    CurrentPathLabel.Text = curDir.FullName

    ' Clear previous items from the ListBox
    DirList.Items.Clear()

    ' Get the directory content
    fse = curDir.GetFileSystemInfos()

    ' Add the names to the ListBox
    Dim ie As IEnumerator = fse.GetEnumerator
    While ie.MoveNext
      DirList.Items.Add(ie.Current)
    End While
End Sub
```


Although the code is straightforward, there are a couple of points to note about this routine. The first is that creating the **Directory** object is enclosed in a **Try** block. Although it is very unlikely that the path that is passed will be invalid, it is a good idea to code defensively and be sure that the code can handle that event.

The second point involves the **fse** variable. This variable holds the list of entries in the current directory and is an array of **FileSystemInfo** references. Because I want to refer to this list again in another routine, I've added it as a member of the class:

```
Public Class Form1
    Inherits System.Windows.Forms.Form
  ' A Directory object that represents the current path
  Dim curDir As Directory

  ' The contents of the current directory path
  Dim fse() As FileSystemInfo
  ...
End Class
```

Both the **FileInfo** and **DirectoryInfo** classes derive from **FileSystemInfo**, so an array of **FileSystemInfos** can hold references to both **FileInfo** and

DirectoryInfo objects, and that's just what I need to hold the mixture of items that are found in directory listings. Because **fse** is an array, I can use an enumerator to walk over it and add its contents to the DirList control. Note how I simply pass **ie.Current** to the **Add()** function: This will get a string representation of the **FileSystemInfo**, which is the full path.

Displaying Details of Files and Directories

When the user clicks on an entry in the DirList control, I want to be able to display some details about the file or directory in the other ListBox. Like ComboBoxes, ListBoxes raise a **SelectedIndexChanged** event when someone selects an entry, so I need a handler for that event. In the following code, I've added a representative selection of details on the selected item. You should find it fairly easy to amend the code to add the details you need:

```
Protected Sub DirList_SelectedIndexChanged(ByVal sender _
        As System.Object, ByVal e As System.EventArgs) _
        Handles DirList.SelectedIndexChanged
  ' Check we have a selection
  If DirList.SelectedIndex <> -1 Then

    ' Clear any existing details
    FileList.Items.Clear()

    ' Get the index of the selected item
    Dim idx As Integer = DirList.SelectedIndex

    ' Use the index to get the item from the FileSystemInfo array
    Dim entry As FileSystemInfo = CType(fse.GetValue(idx), FileSystemInfo)

    ' Now start displaying details - start with the type
    If CType(entry.Attributes() And _
          FileAttributes.Directory, Boolean) = True Then
      FileList.Items.Add("Type: Directory")
    Else
      FileList.Items.Add("Type: File")
    End If

    ' Display last access time. I'm using the default time
    ' format, but you can easily change it
    Dim latime As DateTime = entry.LastAccessTime()
    FileList.Items.Add("Last Access: " & latime.ToString())

    ' Process the attributes, building up a string
    Dim s As New String("Attributes: ")
```

```
        If CType(entry.Attributes() And _
                FileAttributes.Archive, Boolean) = True Then
          s = s & "Archive "
        End If

        If CType(entry.Attributes() And _
                FileAttributes.System, Boolean) = True Then
          s = s & "System "
        End If

        If CType(entry.Attributes() And _
                FileAttributes.ReadOnly, Boolean) = True Then
          s = s & "R/O "
        End If

        ' Add the attribute string to the list...
        FileList.Items.Add(s)
      End If
    End Sub
```

Let's look at what is going on in this code. After checking that there is a selection, I clear any existing information out of the ListBox. Next, I get the index of the selected item and use it to retrieve the **FileSystemInfo** for the selected item from the **fse** array. This is why I saved the **FileSystemInfo** array in **Get_Content()**, so that I could refer to it here.

GetValue() retrieves an entry from the array, but it gets returned as a generic **Object** reference, so I need to use **CType** to convert it to a **FileSystemInfo**.

I want to list some of the attributes associated with the class, which I do using the **Attributes()** method. This function returns an integer whose bits are set to represent the attributes associated with the item. I can tell whether the item has a particular attribute by using the **And** operator to perform a logical **AND** between the attributes' integer and the constant representing the attribute I want to test. If the result is true, I can then add that attribute to a string that I'm building. Note once again how I have to use **CType** to convert the result of the **And** to a Boolean so that I can use it in an **If** statement.

I start with **Directory** to determine whether the item is a file or a directory and add a suitable string to the ListBox.

***NOTE:** The methods and properties of **FileSystemInfo**, **FileInfo**, and **DirectoryInfo** are listed in Tables 6.10 through 6.19 in the In Depth section.*

Next, I use the **LastAccessTime()** method to obtain the date and time the item was last accessed as a **DateTime** object and add it to the ListBox. I'm using the default formatting provided by the **ToString()** function, but there are several other formatting options provided by **DateTime**.

Changing Directory

Users can navigate through the directory tree by clicking on directory entries in the DirList control. When this happens, I simply extract the path from the selected entry and call **Get_Content()** to load the new directory:

```
Protected Sub DirList_DoubleClick(ByVal sender _
        As System.Object, ByVal e As System.EventArgs) _
        Handles DirList.DoubleClick
  ' Check we have a selection
  If DirList.SelectedIndex <> -1 Then
    ' Get the index of the selected item
    Dim idx As Integer = DirList.SelectedIndex

    ' Use the index to get the item from the FileSystemInfo array
    Dim entry As FileSystemInfo = CType(fse.GetValue(idx), FileSystemInfo)

    ' Don't do anything if the item is a file
    If CType(entry.Attributes() And FileAttributes.Directory, _
            Boolean) = True Then
      FileList.Items.Clear()
      Get_Content(entry.FullName)
    End If
  End If
End Sub
```

There's nothing in this code that you haven't already seen: I get the index of the selected item and use it to get the **FileSystemInfo**. If the user has clicked on a directory (not a file), I clear the existing details and call **Get_Content()** with the full path of the directory.

Moving Up a Level

I've handled moving down the tree, but how is the user to navigate back up? I can think of two ways: The first would be to add a ".." entry to the top of the DirList control and handle that specially. The second, and the one I use in the following code, is to add a Back button. This is probably a better solution because it parallels the Back button found in the standard File Open and Save dialogs, so the idea will be familiar to users:

```
Protected Sub MoveToParentBtn_Click(ByVal sender _
                As System.Object, ByVal e As System.EventArgs) _
                Handles MoveToParentBtn.Click
  ' Get the parent of the current directory
  Dim parent As DirectoryInfo = curDir.Parent

  ' If the parent is null, we're at the top level
  If parent Is Nothing Then
    Beep()
    Return
  End If

  FileList.Items.Clear()

  Get_Content(parent.FullName)
End Sub
```

Once again, this is quite a simple function, and the only new element is the use of the **Parent** property to get the parent of the current directory. If you are already at the top level of a directory tree (e.g., at C:\), the **Parent** is set to **Nothing**. If that's the case, I issue a beep, and then return; otherwise, I call **Get_Content()** to display the content of the parent directory.

And that's it! Figure 6.2 shows the program in action.

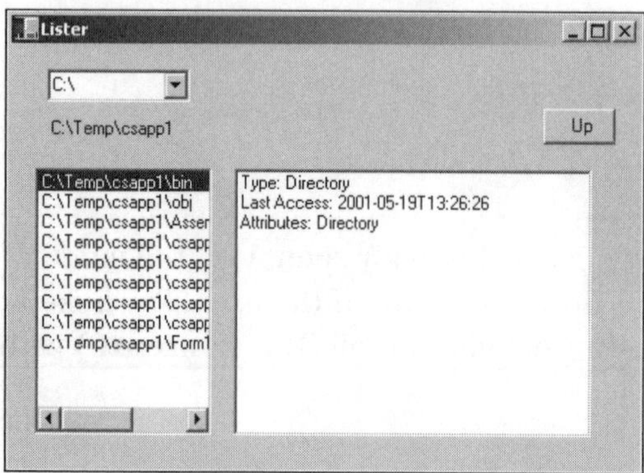

Figure 6.2 The VBDirList program in action.

6. The I/O and Networking Namespaces

How Can I Monitor Changes to Files and Directories?

The **System.IO.FileSystemWatcher** class is provided precisely for this task. You can set a **FileSystemWatcher** object to watch a given directory, and it raises events when things—such as creations, deletions, and changes—happen to the files and subdirectories within the nominated directory.

In this solution, I'll show you how to write an application that logs accesses to anything in a nominated directory.

Creating the Project

I start by creating a normal VB Windows application, which in this case I've called VBWatcher. Then, I import the **System.IO** package into the project:

```
' You need to import System.IO
Imports System.IO
```

Next, I add a **FileSystemWatcher** reference to the **Form** class:

```
Public Class Form1
    Inherits System.Window.Forms.Form

    ' The watcher object
    Private fs As FileSystemWatcher

    Public Sub New()
    ...
```

When the user tells the application to start logging, a **FileSystemWatcher** object is created and attached to the reference.

Creating the User Interface

You should add controls to the form so that you end up with a user interface similar to the one shown in Figure 6.3. The TextBox is used to enter the name of the directory to be watched, whereas the ListBox holds the logging messages. The two buttons are used to start the logging process and to clear the entries from the ListBox.

Using the Components tab on the toolbox, add a **FileSystemWatcher** component, which appears in the nonvisual components area at the bottom of the Designer window. Select this component in the designer, and change its name from the rather long **FileSystemWatcher1** to something more manageable, such as **fsw**. You can then set some of its properties in the Property Browser:

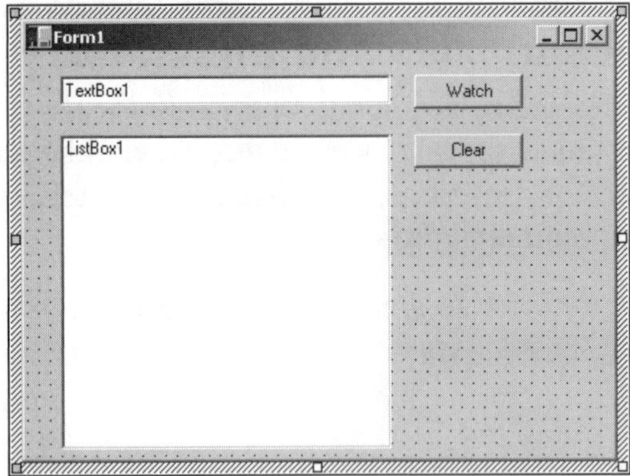

Figure 6.3 The user interface for the VBWatcher application.

- Set the value of the **Filter** property to ***.txt**, which will watch for changes to text files only. If you want to watch all files, leave this property blank.
- Set the value of the **NotifyFilter** property to **LastAccess**, which will filter the notifications coming from the file system and only let the "last access time" notifications through.
- Do not set the **Path** property because it is will be chosen by the user at runtime.
- Make sure that the **EnableRaisingEvents** property is set to true, so that events will be generated.

Add a handler for the Clear button by double-clicking on it; in the body of the function, clear the entries from the ListBox as follows:

```
Private Sub ClearButton_Click(ByVal sender As System.Object, _
      ByVal e As System.EventArgs) Handles ClearButton.Click
  ' Clear all text items from the ListBox
  ListBox1.Items.Clear()
End Sub
```

The handler for the Watch button is where the **FileSystemWatcher** object is created, has its parameters set, and is told to start logging. Here's the code:

```
Private Sub WatchButton_Click(ByVal sender As System.Object, _
      ByVal e As System.EventArgs) Handles WatchButton.Click
  ' Check that we have a path to watch
  If TextBox1.Text.Length = 0 Then
    MessageBox.Show("Please enter a directory path")
    Return
  End If
```

```
  ' Point the FileSystemWatcher object at the
  ' nominated directory
  fsw.Path = TextBox1.Text
End Sub
```

After checking that the user has entered a path into the TextBox, you need to use the **FileSystemWatcher's Path** property to tell it which directory to watch.

The **FileSystemWatcher** can log several different types of events:

- *Change events*—Occur when files or directories are changed in some way
- *Deletion events*—Occur when files or directories are deleted
- *Creation events*—Occur when files or directories are created
- *Renaming events*—Occur when files or directories are renamed
- *Error events*—Occur when the **FileSystemWatcher** has a problem, such as an internal buffer overflow

You can also choose which events you want to log from the following list:

- **Attributes**—Changes to the attributes of the file or directory
- **CreationTime**—The time the file or folder was created
- **DirectoryName**—The name of the directory
- **FileName**—The name of the file
- **LastAccess**—Changes to the time the file or directory was last opened
- **LastWrite**—Changes to the time the file or directory was last written
- **Security**—Changes to the security settings of the file or directory
- **Size**—Changes to the size of the file or directory

You choose the events you want by assigning a value to the **NotifyFilter** property of the **FileSystemWatcher** object, using members of the **NotifyFilters** enumeration. If you don't set the **NotifyFilter** property, the default is to log the **LastAccess** events. You can choose more than one event type by **OR**ing the values together using the **Or** operator.

You can provide further filtering by assigning a string, which describes the file or files you want to monitor, to the **Filter** property. This is a typical wild card file string, so "*.txt" will watch all text files.

I've already mentioned that the **FileSystemWatcher** object communicates by raising events, so you need to provide handler functions for the events you need to handle. I've chosen to monitor the **Changed** and **Deleted** events, so I've added two event handlers, as shown in the following code:

```
' Log Changed events to the ListBox
Private Sub fsw_Changed(ByVal sender As System.Object, _
        ByVal e As FileSystemEventArgs) _
        Handles fsw.Changed
  ListBox1.Items.Add(New String(_
             "File: " & e.FullPath & _
             " " & e.ChangeType.ToString()))
End Sub

' Log Deleted events to the ListBox
Private Sub fsw_Deleted(ByVal sender As System.Object, _
        ByVal e As FileSystemEventArgs) _
        Handles fsw.Deleted
  ListBox1.Items.Add(New String(_
        "File: " & e.FullPath & _
        " " & e.ChangeType.ToString()))
End Sub
```

***NOTE:** I'm using the **Handles** keyword as an alternative to the **AddHandler** method discussed in Chapter 2. **Handles** statically associates an event handler with an event, whereas **AddHandler** (and the matching **RemoveHandler** call) is dynamic and can be used to attach and remove handlers at runtime.*

Also note that the body of both functions is exactly the same, so I could have used the same handler function to log both events. When an event is fired, I get passed notification of the object that fired it—which isn't of any interest in this case—and a **FileSystemEventArgs** object that contains details of the event.

FileSystemEventArgs doesn't have many members; the ones you'll find most useful are:

- **FullPath**—Contains the full path to the file or directory that triggered the event
- **Name**—Only contains the name of the file or directory
- **ChangeType**—Tells you the type of change

ChangeType is useful if you're handling more than one event type in a single handler routine. In this case, it isn't very useful because it only tells me whether I have a **Deleted** or a **Changed** event, and I already know that!

If you build and run the application, you should see output similar to Figure 6.4.

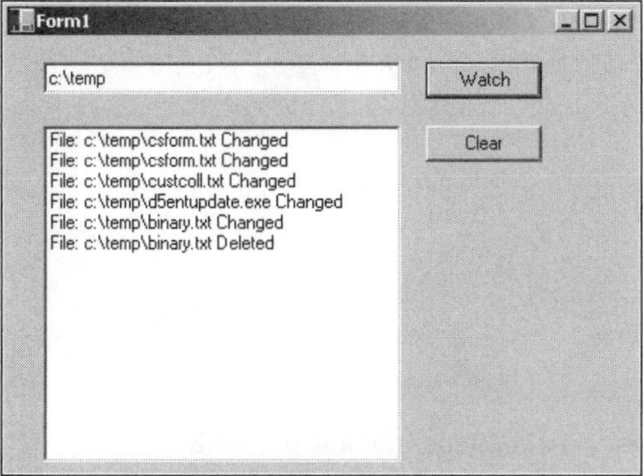

Figure 6.4 The VBWatcher application running.

Using Sockets

The sample program creates a pair of applications—a client and a server—that communicate using sockets. The client program invites the user to type a series of strings and sends them to the server program, which displays them on the console. This read-send-display behavior continues until the user enters a string that starts with a ".", and then both programs terminate.

The code assumes that both applications are running on the same machine. However, you should be able to run them on different machines without any trouble, providing that TCP/IP networking is installed correctly.

Writing a Socket Client

Here's the socket client code:

```
' Import the namespaces needed by the program
Imports System.Net.Sockets
Imports System.IO

Module Module1

  Sub Main()
    Try
      ' Create a TcpClient, passing a hostname and a port.
      ' You can also use IPAddress in here instead of a string
      Console.WriteLine("Connecting to 1999 on localhost")
      Dim myClient As New TcpClient("localhost", 1999)
```

```
        ' Get the stream for I/O, and set the send buffer size
        Dim myStream As Stream = myClient.GetStream()
        myClient.SendBufferSize = 256

        ' Invite the user to enter lines, and read the first one
        Console.WriteLine("Input lines:")
        Dim s As String = Console.ReadLine()

        While True
          ' Turn the string into a byte array
          Dim bbuff As Byte() = System.Text.Encoding.ASCII.GetBytes(s)

          ' Write it to the stream
          myStream.Write(bbuff, 0, bbuff.Length)

          ' Clear the array ready for the next read
          System.Array.Clear(bbuff, 0, bbuff.Length)

          ' If the string started with a '.', we're done
          If s.StartsWith(".") Then
            Goto done
          End If

          ' Get the next string from the user, and loop around
          s = Console.ReadLine()
        End While

      done: Console.WriteLine("Done")

      Catch e As Exception
        Console.WriteLine("Exception: " + e.ToString())
      End Try
    End Sub
End Module
```


I start by importing the two namespaces needed in the program: **System.Net.Sockets** for the socket classes and **System.IO** so that I can use streams. You don't need to add a reference to the project for either of these namespaces.

Setting Up the Socket

Although you can use the raw **Socket** class, Microsoft has provided the **TcpClient** and **TcpListener** subclasses to manage the client and server ends of socket connections and to do some of the housekeeping that you would otherwise need to handle yourself. Because I'm writing the client side in this program, I create a

TcpClient object, which is initialized with the hostname and the port I want to connect to.

***NOTE:** If you're going to run both programs on one machine, use "localhost" as the hostname, as in the example. If you're going to use another machine, you'll need to find out its IP address, and enter that as a string, for example, 154.14.65.123.*

I've decided to use port 1999 in this program. Port numbers are always positive integers. Values ranging from 0 through 1024 are reserved for "official" use by programs such as Web and mail servers. Port numbers above 1024 can be used by any application as long as the client knows which one it is.

The constructor for **TcpClient** can also use the **IPEndPoint** and **IPAddress** classes from the **System.Net** namespace to specify where you want to connect. An **IPAddress** object represents an IP address, and the **Parse()** method can be used to create an **IPAddress** object from a numeric address:

```
Dim ipa As IPAddress = IPAddress.Parse("198.162.1.5")
```

An **IPEndPoint** is a combination of an **IPAddress** and a port number:

```
Dim ipep As New IPEndPoint(ipa, 1999)
```

The **TcpClient** constructor will make the call; if it returns without throwing an exception, the connection has been established.

Getting the Stream

Once the connection has been made, I use **getStream()** to return a stream that I can use to communicate to the socket at the server end. The stream performs buffered I/O, and the default buffer size is 8192 bytes. Because I don't need a buffer that big, I can use the **SendBufferSize** property to adjust it to a smaller value, such as 256 bytes.

Writing Data to the Socket

By using **Console.ReadLine()**, getting a string from a user is simple. In order to write the string to the socket, I need to convert it to an array of bytes. The **System.Text** namespace (discussed in Chapter 12) contains a lot of useful utility functions; I use the **GetBytes()** method to take a string and convert it to an array of bytes.

Once it has been converted, the stream's **Write()** method takes the bytes and passes them to the server on the other end of the socket connection. The arguments to **Write()** specify the byte array, the starting position, and the number of bytes to write. In this case, because I specified a buffer size of 255, my byte array is always going to be 255 bytes long.

After writing the byte array through the socket, I clear the array using a call to **System.Array.Clear()**, which fills it with zeros. This is necessary because data stays in the array and is simply overwritten by the next lot of input: If the next string is shorter, there will be extra data on the end.

The code loops around, reading strings, converting them to bytes, and sending them until the user enters a string that starts with a single period. This is recognized as the "end of input" marker, so I jump out of the loop and the program exits.

Writing a Socket Server

Once you have completed the client code, you can focus on the server code:

```
' Import the namespace
Imports System.Net.Sockets

Module Module1

  Sub Main()
    Console.WriteLine("<Creating listener on 1999>")
    ' Create a listener on port 1999
    Dim myListener As New TcpListener(1999)

    ' Start listening for network traffic
    myListener.Start()

    ' Program blocks on Accept() until a client connects.
    Console.WriteLine("<Waiting for client...>")
    Dim mySocket As Socket = myListener.AcceptSocket()

    ' When this call returns, we've connected
    Console.WriteLine("<Client connected>")

    ' Get a line of text
    Dim bbuff(255) As Byte
    mySocket.Receive(bbuff, bbuff.Length, SocketFlags.None)
    Dim str As String = System.Text.Encoding.ASCII.GetString( _
            bbuff, 0, bbuff.Length).Trim( _
            Microsoft.VisualBasic.ChrW(0))

    ' A line consisting of just a '.' finishes things
    While Not str.StartsWith(".")
      ' Print the line
      Console.WriteLine(str)
```

```
      ' Get the next one
      mySocket.Receive(bbuff, bbuff.Length, SocketFlags.None)
      str = System.Text.Encoding.ASCII.GetString( _
            bbuff, 0, bbuff.Length).Trim( _
            Microsoft.VisualBasic.ChrW(0))
    End While

    ' Stop listening for network traffic
    Console.WriteLine("<Done>")
    myListener.Stop()
  End Sub
End Module
```

You should first import the **System.Net.Sockets** namespace, and create a **TcpListener**, which wraps the server end of a socket connection. **TcpListener**'s constructor only requires a port number on which to listen.

***NOTE:** Only one server program can use a port at a time; you'll get a **SocketException** if you try to create a second **TcpListener** to listen to the same socket.*

Once the **TcpListener** has been created, it starts listening for network traffic when I call its **Start()** method. Once started, I can call **AcceptSocket()** to wait for calls from clients. This function blocks until a client calls in, so servers don't have to poll or wait in a loop checking for clients to connect. When this method returns, I know that a connection has been established, so I can start the conversation.

***NOTE:** A real-life server application would use threads to handle multiple clients, creating a new thread to handle each call. See Chapter 12 for more details on threading.*

When the connection has been established, the program starts reading arrays of bytes from the socket and converting them to characters. As with the client program, a utility method from the **System.Text.Encoding** class is used for conversion, but this time there's an extra step involved. The whole buffer—all 255 characters—is sent over, and the unused portion is padded with nulls. A call to the **String** class's **Trim()** function can be used to eliminate these nulls, but you need to tell the function which Unicode character or characters to trim. In order to specify a null character, you can use the **Microsoft.VisualBasic.ChrW()** function to convert an integer value to a Unicode character.

The converted and trimmed line is printed out, and then the code loops around, reading and displaying lines until a line appears that starts with a ".". At this point, the **Stop()** call tells the socket to stop listening for network traffic, and the program terminates.

Chapter 7

.NET Security

By Julian Templeman

If you need an immediate solution to:	*See page:*

In Depth

.NET has its own security mechanism that provides a high degree of control over what code assemblies can and can't do, and which is especially useful in controlling which operations code from different sources (loaded as part of a distributed application) can perform.

This security mechanism is quite complex, and for many—if not most—applications, you won't need to concern yourself with the details or make any changes, as the .NET security mechanisms provide adequate default settings. This section discusses the security mechanism in some detail to give you a flavor of how it works and to give you a start if you do want to provide custom security settings.

The security namespaces consist of the following:

- **System.Security** provides the underlying structure for the .NET security system.
- The three **System.Security.Cryptography** namespaces provide cryptographic services, including secure encoding and decoding and message authentication.
- **System.Security.Permissions** defines permission classes that control access to resources and operations.
- **System.Security.Policy** contains classes that implement code groups, membership conditions, and evidence, which are used by the Common Language Runtime (CLR) security system to enforce security policy.
- **System.Security.Principal** defines classes that represent the security context under which code is running.

This chapter focuses on the **System.Security**, **System.Security.Permissions**, **System.Security.Policy**, and **System.Security.Principal** namespaces, because they are the ones you'll use most from day to day.

The .NET Security Model

Secure computing means that you usually need to know some essential information:

- Who originated a component
- Whether someone should be allowed to perform an operation
- What actions have been performed, and by whom

The third point is partially provided in Windows NT and 2000 by the audit features built into Windows, which allow administrators to trap accesses to the file system and write an audit trail to the Event log.

The current Windows model provides the first point using the system of Authenticode digital signatures. For example, suppose you access a Web page that needs to download an ActiveX control. You are asked whether you want to download the control and may be presented with a summary of the DLL's credentials in the form of a certificate. This certificate represents a digital signature that was issued to the originator of the DLL, who should be the only person with access to the signature. The DLL is check-summed to ensure that it has not been tampered with.

Therefore, when you are presented with a signed component, you can be sure that the component was originated by the source named in the certificate (provided, of course, that their signature information hasn't been stolen, and is being used to sign forged components). You can establish that a dynamic link library (DLL) has been created by DiskTrasher Industries Inc., but it doesn't let you control what it does after it has been downloaded and run.

.NET deals with the second point I listed above using a system of permissions, which it uses to decide what a particular piece of code is and isn't allowed to do at runtime. There are three kinds of permissions, all represented by classes:

- *Code access permissions*—Represent access to a protected resource or the ability to perform a protected operation
- *Identity permissions*—Indicate that code has a particular identity
- *Role-based security permissions*—Provide a way to discover whether the user (or the user's agent) is acting in a particular role, such as "developer" or "manager"

How Does .NET Security Work with Windows Security?

Many platforms have their own security mechanisms, although they vary widely in sophistication. The .NET mechanism is designed to work alongside the native platform mechanism, supplementing it where necessary.

For example, .NET's role-based security lets you check the identity of the current user based on the user ID and role that the user is currently adopting. When running on Windows NT or 2000, the user ID is mapped onto the Windows user ID, and the role is mapped onto the groups that the ID belongs to.

Code Access Permission

Code access permission is used to protect resources and operations from unauthorized access, such as accessing a file or accessing unmanaged code. Code access permissions form a fundamental part of the CLR's security mechanism. Programs use these classes to declare which permissions they want, and the CLR uses its security policy to decide which (if any) of them to grant.

All the code access permission classes derive from **System.Security.CodeAccessPermission** and are listed in Table 7.1.

The examples in the following sections and the Immediate Solutions show you how these classes are used in code.

Table 7.1 The code access permission classes.

Permission Class	Permission Represented
CodeAccessPermission	The base class for all the code access permission classes
DirectoryServicesPermission	Provides access to the **System.DirectoryServices** class
DnsPermission	Provides access to Domain Name Services (DNS)
EnvironmentPermission	Provides ability to read or write environment variables
EventLogPermission	Provides ability to access the Event log
FileDialogPermission	Provides access to files that have been selected by the user in a File Open dialog box
FileIOPermission	Controls read/write/append access to files and directory trees, including the entire file system
IsolatedStorageFilePermission	Controls access to private virtual file systems
IsolatedStoragePermission	Provides access to isolated storage; that is, storage associated with a specific user
MessageQueuePermission	Provides access to message queues through the Microsoft Messaging Service (MSMQ)
OleDbPermission	Provides access to databases using OLE DB
PerformanceCounterPermission	Provides access to performance counters
PrintingPermission	Provides access to printers
ReflectionPermission	Provides access to type information at runtime
RegistryPermission	Provides access to Registry keys or to the Registry as a whole
SecurityPermission	Provides ability to execute code, assert permissions, call into unmanaged code, and other rights
ServiceControllerPermission	Provides access to Windows services
SocketPermission	Provides ability to use socket services
SqlClientPermission	Provides access to SQL databases
UIPermission	Controls access to UI features, such as the clipboard and use of dialogs
WebPermission	Makes or accepts connections on a Web address

Identity Permission

The identity permission represents characteristics that identify code, such as the location from which it was loaded or the digital signature that was used to sign the assembly. This information is called *evidence* and is provided by the loader or a trusted host (such as IE or ASP.NET). The CLR uses the evidence to grant identity permissions to the code when it is loaded. The identity permission classes are listed in Table 7.2; they all derive from **CodeAccessPermission**.

Assemblies can be identified by their text name, version number, and culture information, but sometimes this is not adequate. Strong names provide a way to ensure that assemblies can be uniquely identified.

A *strong name* consists of the text name, version number, and culture information plus a public key and a digital signature. The strong name is generated from the assembly using a private key, and assemblies with the same strong name are expected to be identical. Using an encryption key to produce a strong name has several advantages:

- Names are unique because they use unique private keys for generation. It is therefore possible to determine who has created a particular assembly.
- No one can produce a new version of your assembly and pass it off as genuine because it will not have been signed with your private key.
- No one can tamper with the contents of an assembly because the signing process involves generating a check-sum for the assembly that will be checked at runtime.

Role-Based Security Permission

The role-based security permission is used to determine whether the user running the code has a particular identity or is a member of a particular role. There is one role-based security class, **PrincipalPermission**.

Table 7.2 The identity permission classes.

Permission Class	Permission Represented
CodeAccessPermission	The base class for all the identity permission classes.
PublisherIdentityPermission	The software publisher's digital signature.
SiteIdentityPermission	The site where the code originated.
StrongNameIdentityPermission	The strong name of the assembly.
URLIdentityPermission	The full URL where the code originated.
ZoneIdentityPermission	The security zone where the code originated.

Role-based security is used with programs in three ways:

- Imperative security checks
- Declarative security checks
- Accessing a **Principal** object directly

To use an imperative security check, you create a **PrincipalPermission** object representing a given user and role and call its **Demand()** method to check whether it matches the current user and role. If the user and role specified in the **PrincipalPermission** object doesn't match the current user and role, the demand fails and a **SecurityException** is thrown.

To use declarative security checks, you add attributes that declare which users and roles can execute a piece of code. If the user doesn't match the specification in the attributes, the call fails at runtime.

Alternatively, you can access the **Principal** object representing the current user directly and find out who it represents.

Security Policies

How does the CLR know whether an action—such as writing to a file—should be permitted or not? It looks at the security policy, which specifies the access rights that are to be granted to code based on where the code comes from, who has signed it, and other criteria. This policy can be customized on a machine-by-machine or user-by-user basis to provide complete custom security.

.NET implements an extensible security policy known as the Code Access Security (CAS) model. This takes the form of a hierarchy of code group entries, as shown in Figure 7.1.

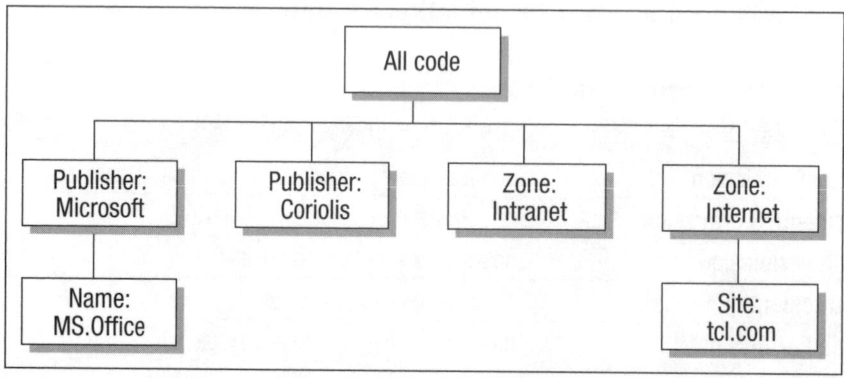

Figure 7.1 The hierarchy of code groups that determines Code Access Security.

Each box in the diagram represents a code group, which is a logical grouping of code that shares the same membership condition. For instance, the code group labeled "Zone: Intranet" would include all code that has its origins on the local intranet, whereas the group labeled "Publisher: Coriolis" would include all code that has been digitally signed by Coriolis.

The CLR uses identifying characteristics of assemblies (the evidence) to determine whether membership criteria have been met. Evidence includes where the code was loaded from, the site it came from, and who has digitally signed the code (if anyone). For instance, if the membership condition of the group is that software must originate from Coriolis, the CLR examines the evidence to ensure that the assembly has been signed using Coriolis's key.

Each code group represents one membership condition. The possible membership conditions are listed in Table 7.3.

The hierarchy of code groups gives you a way to refine the permissions granted to code. In Figure 7.1, code originating from the Internet will have the permissions associated with the code group on the far right of the diagram. If the code happens to come from site tcl.com, the permissions in the Site: tcl.com code group are added to those for Zone: Internet. This makes it possible to fine-tune the permissions granted, for example, to different sites on a corporate intranet. If code belongs to more than one code group, the permission sets of the groups are unioned together to produce the permission set that applies to the code.

Each code group has one membership condition plus an associated permission set. Permission sets contain at least one permission along with the name and description of the permission set. The permissions supported include all the types

Table 7.3 Membership conditions for code groups.

Membership Condition	Description
Application directory	The application's installation directory
Cryptographic hash	An MD5 or SHA1 cryptographic hash
Custom	A system- or application-defined condition
File	The rights to access a file
Net	The network where the code originates
Software publisher	The public key of a software publisher's Authenticode signature
Strong name	A .NET assembly strong name
URL	The URL where the code originates
Web site	The Web site where the code originates
Zone	The zone where the code originates

listed in Table 7.1, and developers can define their own custom permissions when necessary. See the Immediate Solutions section for details on how to set and use permission sets.

Three tiers of policy currently supported in .NET are enterprise, machine, and user levels. Enterprise-level policy applies to a group of machines and will be set by enterprise system administrators. Machine-level policy is typically set by the machine's administrator and applies to the entire machine. User-level policy represents the policy for an individual user and is typically modified by the users themselves. When using the policy tool, caspol.exe, users can specify which level of policy they want to examine or modify.

NOTE: *Users can only specify which level of policy they want to examine or modify if they have the correct permission. You won't be able to access the machine level if you are not an administrator.*

The intersection of the settings for these three policy sets governs the access that a code item actually receives. For example:

- Enterprise access grants full I/O access to file systems.
- Machine access only grants read-only access to the file system.
- A user grants read/write access to c:\temp.

The intersection of the rights means that code will have read-only access to c:\temp because the machine-level access overrides the read/write access granted at the user level.

Setting Security Policies

In .NET Beta 2 there is no GUI tool, and all policy manipulation is done using the caspol.exe command-line tool. Caspol can be used to edit enterprise-, machine-, and user-level policies using the appropriate switches. The tool is simply run from a command window by giving the command name followed by one or more options:

```
C:\> caspol -option1 -option2
```

A large number of flags can be used with caspol, and Table 7.4 lists some of the most commonly used options. Note that most of the options have one- or two-letter abbreviations, which are not shown in the table.

As an example, suppose I issue the following caspol command:

```
C:\> caspol -machine -listgroups
```

Table 7.4 Common options used with the caspol.exe security policy tool.

Option	Description
addgroup	Adds a new code group to the hierarchy, specifying the parent and permission set
addpset	Adds a new permission set to the policy
all	Indicates that the options following this apply to enterprise-, machine-, and user-level policies
chggroup	Changes a code group's membership condition, permission set, or flags
chgpset	Changes a permission set to use a new permission set definition
customall	Indicates that options following this apply to enterprise, machine, and custom user policies
enterprise	Indicates that the options following this apply to enterprise-level policies
execution on or **off**	Turns on or turns off the mechanism that checks for permission to run before executing code
help	Displays command syntax and options
list	Lists the code group hierarchy and permission sets
listdescription	Lists all code group descriptions
listgroups	Displays all code groups for the specified policy level
listpset	Displays permission sets for the specified policy level
machine	Indicates that the options following this apply to machine-level policies
polchgprompt	Enables or disables the prompt that is displayed whenever caspol is asked to do something that would cause policy changes
recover	Recovers policy from a backup file, which is made whenever a policy change is made
remgroup	Removes a code group by label or name
rempset	Removes a permission set by label or name
reset	Returns policy to its default state
resolvegroup	Shows the code groups that a specific assembly belongs to
resolveperm	Displays the permissions that would be granted to an assembly if it was run
security on or **off**	Turns code access security on or off
user	Indicates that the options following this apply to user-level policies

This instructs caspol to list all the code groups at the machine-policy level. I get the following output, which is slightly abbreviated so it doesn't take up too much space:

```
Microsoft (R) .NET Framework CasPol 1.0.2914.16
Copyright (c) Microsoft Corp 1999-2001. All rights reserved.
```

```
Security is ON
Execution checking is ON
Policy change prompt is ON

Level = Machine

Code Groups:

1. All code: Nothing
  1.1.  Zone - MyComputer: FullTrust
  1.2.  Zone - Intranet: LocalIntranet
    1.2.1.  All code: Same site Web.
    1.2.2.  All code: Same directory FileIO - Read, PathDiscovery
  1.3.  Zone - Internet: Internet
  1.4.  Zone - Untrusted: Nothing
  1.5.  Zone - Trusted: Internet
    1.5.1  All code: Same site Web
  1.6.  StrongName - 0024000... : FullTrust
  1.7.  StrongName - 00000... : FullTrust
```

The first three lines of output after the copyright message tell me that the security system is on, code will be checked before it is executed, and I'll be prompted if I make any changes to the policy.

What follows is the hierarchical list of code groups, each of which is identified by its name and a numerical identifier of the form "1.1". Thus, the first code group has the identifier "1" and the name "All code". Each of the names is followed by a colon and a description of the permissions for the group. For example, code group "1.1" is the MyComputer zone, representing locally loaded applications, which have full access rights.

At the bottom, groups 1.6. and 1.7 give full access rights to two particular assemblies that are specified by their strong names. The actual entries get quite long, so I've omitted most of the hex defining the strong name itself.

You can also list the descriptions of the code groups in order to get more information about what code they affect and the permissions they grant. You can do this by running caspol with the following command line:

```
C:\> caspol -machine -listdescription
```

Here's a sample from the output, showing the descriptions for a selection of the entries:

```
Microsoft (R) .NET Framework CasPol 1.0.2914.16
Copyright (c) Microsoft Corp 1999-2001. All rights reserved.
```

```
Security is ON
Execution checking is ON
Policy change prompt is ON

Level = Machine

Full Trust Assemblies:

1. All_Code: Code group grants no permissions and forms the root
   of the code group tree.
   1.1. My_Computer_Zone: Code group grants full trust to all code
   originating on the local computer.
...
   1.3. Internet_Zone: Code group grants code from the Internet
   zone the Internet permission set. This permission set grants
   Internet code the right to use isolated storage and limited
   UI access.
...
   1.6. Microsoft_Strong_Name: Code group grants full trust to code
   signed with the Microsoft strong name
   1.7. ECMA_Strong_Name: Code group grants full trust to code
   signed with the ECMA strong name
```

You can see that the descriptions make it simple to understand what the permissions stand for. You should always include descriptions if you add code groups to the policy set.

Use the following command line to see a listing of the permission sets:

```
C:\> caspol -machine -listpset
```

There is a lot of output from this command. Here are a couple of sample entries:

```
1. FullTrust (Allows full access to all resources) =
<PermissionSet class="System.Security.NamedPermissionSet"
         version="1"
         Unrestricted="true"
         Name="FullTrust"
         Description="Allows full access to all resources"/>

6. Internet (Default rights given to Internet applications) =
<PermissionSet class="System.Security.NamedPermissionSet"
         version="1"
         Name="Internet"
         Description="Default rights given to Internet applications">
```

```
<IPermission
   class="System.Security.Permissions.FileDialogPermission, mscorlib,
          Version=1.0.2411.0, Culture=neutral,
          PublicKeyToken=b77a5c561934e089"
   Version="1"
   Access="Open"/>
</PermissionSet>
...
<IPermission
   class="System.Security.Permissions.UIPermission, mscorlib,
          Version=1.0.2411.0, Culture=neutral,
          PublicKeyToken=b77a5c561934e089"
   Version="1"
   Window="SafeTopLevelWindows"
   Clipboard="OwnClipboard"/>
</PermissionSet>
```

This looks a lot like XML, and that's because it *is* XML. When you want to give permission-set information to caspol, you have to specify it as an XML document; so caspol reports it to you in the same format. Each **PermissionSet** element usually consists of one or more **IPermission** elements, each of which defines a specific permission.

NOTE: *There's one permission set that has no* ***IPermission*** *entries, and that's the one that grants no permissions whatsoever. Obviously you don't need more than one of these!*

Permissions in Code

Permissions are manipulated in code using permission objects from the **System.Security.Permissions** namespace and a few other useful objects from **System.Net**.

When a component wants to perform an operation—such as accessing the file system—the security system checks against the policy to see whether the operation is allowed. If this component is being used by another component, it is important to check whether it, in turn, is allowed to perform the operation, and so on, up the stack of callers.

In order to access the local file system, not only does the ultimate component doing the accessing have to have the correct **FileIOPermission**, but every caller in the chain has to have it as well. If anyone in the chain doesn't have the correct **FileIOPermission**, the request fails with a **SecurityException**.

It is easy to see why this is necessary. Components running on the local machine are highly trusted, and by default have a high level of access to the system. Likewise,

I'm granted a high level of access as the logged-in user, so I can make the component do pretty much as I like.

When a component is used by someone or something from outside the machine, that agent may or may not be allowed to access the local file system. It is important that the agent not be able to get in using the back door by getting the component to do for it what it wouldn't be able to do with its own security settings. This is shown in Figure 7.2.

Note that the .NET security mechanism sits on top of the one provided by the underlying operating system, but doesn't override it. This means that even if .NET decides that you can write to a file, the underlying security system may deny you access.

The CodeAccessPermission Class

System.Security.CodeAccessPermission forms the base for all the permission classes that are discussed in this chapter and contains several members that are inherited and used frequently by derived classes.

Table 7.5 lists the methods of the **CodeAccessPermission** class. Several of these members (namely **Assert()**, **Demand()** and **Deny()**) implement runtime checking of permissions and are discussed in the following sections.

Given two permission objects, **Intersect()** creates a new object that represents the permissions that both have in common. When **Union()** is invoked on a pair of permission objects, on the other hand, it creates a new object that contains the permissions from both other objects.

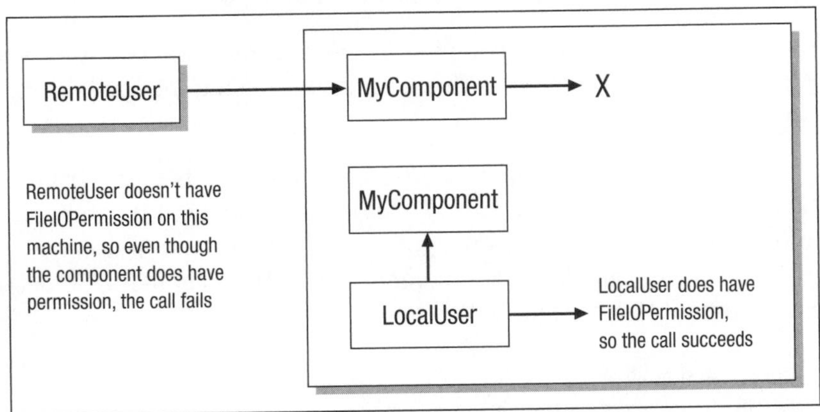
RemoteUser
MyComponent
X
RemoteUser doesn't have FileIOPermission on this machine, so even though the component does have permission, the call fails
MyComponent
LocalUser
LocalUser does have FileIOPermission, so the call succeeds

Figure 7.2 Security policy settings control what access users have to components.

Table 7.5 Methods of the CodeAccessPermission class.

Member	Description
Assert	Asserts that calling code can access the resource identified by the permission
Copy	Creates and returns a copy of the permission object
Demand	Determines at runtime whether all callers in the stack have been granted the permission
Deny	Denies access to callers higher in the stack
FromXml	Reconstructs a permission object from an XML encoding
Intersect	Creates a permission object that represents the intersection of two permission objects
IsSubsetOf	Determines whether one permission object is a subset of another
PermitOnly	Ensures that only resources specified in this permission can be called by callers higher in the stack
RevertAll	Causes all overrides to be revoked
RevertAssert	Causes any previous **Assert** for the current frame to be revoked
RevertDeny	Causes any previous **Deny** for the current frame to be revoked
RevertPermitOnly	Causes any previous **PermitOnly** for the current frame to be revoked
ToString	Returns a **String** representation of the permission object
ToXml	Writes a permission object as an XML encoding
Union	Creates a permission that is the union of two other permissions

IsSubsetOf() tells you about the relationship between two permission objects. If permission object A gives read/write access to all of the C: drive, whereas permission object B gives read/write access just to c:\temp, then B is a subset of A.

If code uses **PermitOnly()**, callers higher in the call stack will only be allowed access to the resources protected by this permission, even if they have access to other resources.

ToXml() and **FromXml()** let you serialize permission objects to and from XML. You'll find that the format produced by **ToXml()** is identical to the one that the policy editor, caspol.exe, produces for you when you list permission sets. For example, the following sample program creates a **FileIOPermission** object, and then dumps it out in XML format:

```
Imports System.Security
Imports System.Security.Permissions

Module Module1
```

```
    Sub Main()
        ' Create a FileIOPermission object to represent all access
        ' to c:\temp
        Dim fpa As New FileIOPermission(FileIOPermissionAccess.AllAccess, _
                    "c:\temp")

        ' ToXml() returns a SecurityElement
        Dim se As SecurityElement = fpa.ToXml()

        ' Dump out the SecurityElement
        Console.WriteLine(se.ToString())
    End Sub

End Module
```

The output from this program is:

```
<IPermission
   class="System.Security.Permissions.FileIOPermission, mscorlib,
          Version=1.0.2411.0, Culture=neutral,
          PublicKeyToken=b77a5c561934e089"
   Version="1"
   Read="c:\temp"
   Write="c:\temp"
   Append="c:\temp"
   PathDiscovery="c:\temp"/>
```

This small program can be very useful if you want to make up new permission sets to use with caspol, because the precise format of the XML needed for the various permissions is not always easy to find.

Demanding Permissions

Much of the time your components may not have much involement with permissions. If you use .NET classes to do I/O or other tasks, these .NET classes have all the security built in at a lower level, so there will be no need for you to deal with security in your code.

Suppose you do need to perform an action that is controlled by a permission, such as accessing a file. You will need to have your code tell the system what access you need. The system will then check against the security policy to see whether access can be granted. The following example shows how this works:

```
' I need "all access" to the file
Dim fpa As FileIOPermissionAccess = FileIOPermissionAccess.AllAccess
Dim fp As New FileIOPermission(fpa, filename)
```

```
' See if I can get it
Try
  fp.Demand()
Catch se As SecurityException
  ' No access, so report the error
  Console.WriteLine("I'm sorry, Dave, I can't do that")
End Try

' All is OK, so use the file.
```

I first construct a **FileIOPermissionAccess** variable that contains flags representing the access I want. In this case, I want all access, so I only need to specify one flag, but I could have used other flags listed in Table 7.6, **OR**ing them together as necessary.

Once I've set the flags I want, I construct a **FileIOPermission** object, passing in the flags and the file name, and then call its **Demand()** method to test whether I have permission. At this point, the CLR checks the security policy to determine whether the call should be allowed. As mentioned previously, it not only checks on behalf of this component, but also for every component up the call chain until it reaches the top. If it's a simple case of a client calling this component directly, there's only one extra level of checking, but there may be several levels involving remote users. If every component in the chain has the correct permissions, the call will succeed, but if any call doesn't, a **SecurityException** is thrown.

You can see how, using this declarative model, the component sets out what it needs to do, and then asks the runtime to check whether this is okay.

When do you need do these checks? They are expensive, so choose the times when you need to have a security checkpoint wisely. A good place may be at object construction time and also before critical operations. You may also need to check again if a reference to the object is passed around. If the check is only

Table 7.6 Members of the FileIOPermissionAccess enumeration.

Member	Description
AllAccess	Provides append, read, and write access to a file or directory
Append	Provides access to append to a file or directory
NoAccess	Provides no access to a file or directory
PathDiscovery	Provides access to information on the path itself, such as the directory structure revealed by the path
Read	Provides read access to a file or directory
Write	Provides write access to a file or directory

done at construction time, it may have been fine for the original caller, but a reference could then be passed to another caller who isn't trusted, and that caller would be able to use it!

Denying Permissions

What if you're using a component and you want to be sure that it isn't going to do anything it shouldn't? As an example, suppose I've been given a component that formats some data files and displays them, and I've installed it on my local machine. As far as I'm concerned, all the component should do is to read the files in order to display them, but you've seen that a component can request the permissions it wants at runtime. The problem is that because both client and component are local, they both have a high degree of trust, so in all likelihood if the component asks for write permission, it will be granted.

If I want to be sure that a component cannot misbehave, I can temporarily override the set of permissions in force in order to deny certain operations:

```
' Create an empty permission set
Dim p As New PermissionSet(PermissionState.None)

' Deny access to certain directory trees on the disk
p.AddPermission( _
        New FileIOPermission(FileIOPermissionAccess.AllAccess, _
        "c:\data"))
p.AddPermission( _
        New FileIOPermission(FileIOPermissionAccess.AllAccess, _
        "c:\personal"))

' Change the permissions
p.Deny()

' Do the operation
myObject.accessData()

' Remove the restriction
CodeAccessPermission.RevertDeny()
```

As its name implies, a **PermissionSet** object holds a set of permissions, and I use the **AddPermission()** method to create new permission objects and add them to the set.

Once I've built the set I need, I can call **Deny()** to change the set of active permissions, and succeeding operations will be checked against the modified permission set until I call **RevertDeny()** to revert to the original permission set.

Note that there's only one set of permissions in force at a time, so if I want to build two **PermissionSet** objects and call **Deny()** on each of them, the permissions I would get are those associated with the second call:

```
Dim p1 As New PermissionSet(PermissionState.None)
Dim p2 As New PermissionSet(PermissionState.None)

' Change the permissions
p1.Deny()
p2.Deny()

' The permissions defined in p2 are in force, overwriting the set
' provided in p1
```

If you only want to grant one or two specific access rights—such as the ability to read files in one directory—it is long-winded to create a permission set that denies access to all the other files, directories, and services you don't want touched.

In this case, you can use the **PermissionSet.PermitOnly()** and **CodeAccess Permission.RevertPermitOnly()** methods, which deny all permissions except those built into the permission set. The following code fragment shows how I could deny access to everything except two directories:

```
' Create an empty permission set
Dim p As New PermissionSet(PermissionState.None)

' Give access to two directory trees
p.AddPermission( _
      New FileIOPermission(FileIOPermissionAccess.AllAccess, _
      "c:\data"))
p.AddPermission( _
      New FileIOPermission(FileIOPermissionAccess.AllAccess, _
      "c:\personal"))

' Change the permissions
p.PermitOnly()

' Do the operation
myObject.accessData()

' Remove the restriction
CodeAccessPermission.RevertPermitOnly()
```

Asserting Permissions

As mentioned earlier, the security mechanism checks each call in the chain to decide whether an operation should be allowed or not. This is secure, but sometimes rather too restrictive.

Suppose that I have a component that wants to put a simple dialog up on the screen. In order to do this, everyone in the call chain has to have **UIPermission**, which may not be feasible because the component may be being called by some completely nonvisual component that hasn't asked for **UIPermission**. In this case, it is possible for the component that wants to display the dialog to "assert" one or more permissions, which effectively tells the runtime not to check any further. Asserting a permission means that the runtime won't walk up the call chain checking permissions unless there are other permissions to be checked that aren't included in the asserted set.

Using **Assert()** is very similar to using **Deny()**, as you can see from the following code:

```
' Create an empty permission set
Dim p As New PermissionSet(PermissionState.None)

' Add a UIPermission object asking for unrestricted access
' to the UI
p.AddPermission(New UIPermission(PermissionState.Unrestricted))

' Assert the permission
Try
  p.Assert()

  ' If the code got here, the Assert worked, so do the operation
  DisplayDialog()

  ' Remove the Assert
  CodeAccessPermission.RevertAssert()
Catch se As SecurityException
  Console.WriteLine("Assert failed")
End Try
```

Once again I create a **PermissionSet** object. This time I add a permission to it that requests unrestricted access to the UI. I may or may not be granted this access, so I call **Assert()** within a Try block, so that I can catch the **SecurityException** that will be generated if my call to **Assert()** fails.

Unlike the call to **Demand()**, which checks all the callers of this code, the call to **Assert()** tells the security system to grant access to me without checking anyone else. This can result in possible security loopholes, so **Assert()** should be used with care.

Immediate Solutions

Signing an Assembly with a Strong Name

A strong name consists of the text name, version and culture information for the assembly, a public key, and a digital signature. Although simple assembly names could be duplicated, the addition of the public key and digital signature make the name unique. See the section "Identity Permission" in the In Depth section for more discussion on strong names.

You need strong names in two particular cases:

- When you want to put an assembly in the Global Assembly Cache (GAC) so that everyone can use it
- When you want to give the assembly special permissions in the security policy

This solution shows you how to sign an assembly with a strong name. Start by generating a private/public key pair using the Strong Name tool, sn.exe, like this:

```
sn -k mykey.snk
```

Running **sn** with the **-k** flag generates a random key pair and stores it in the file mykey.snk. Once you have the key pair, there are two ways to use it to sign an assembly. I will describe each of these ways here.

Using Visual Studio .NET

Visual Studio .NET builds signed assemblies for you if you provide attributes to specify the key information. Visual Studio .NET projects contain a file that is used to specify attributes for the assembly. What this file is called depends on the language being used, but Visual Basic projects contain a file called AssemblyInfo.vb along with any other code files that the project may require.

Generate a key pair for the project using sn.exe, and then put it into the project directory along with the VB and SLN files. Then open the AssemblyInfo.vb file, and add the following line to the bottom:

```
<Assembly: AssemblyKeyFile("mykey.snk")>
```

The string "**mykey.snk**" must reflect the name of the key file you generated with sn.exe, and you can use relative paths if you want. Visual Studio checks for the presence of the file as soon as you've typed the line, so you'll soon find out if you've put it in the wrong place. Build the project, and your assembly will be signed with a strong name.

Using the Assembly Generation Tool

It is also possible to generate assemblies using the Assembly Generation tool, al.exe, which builds an assembly out of modules.

An assembly consists of one or more IL code modules plus a manifest, and a module is simply a compiled piece of IL code. Visual Studio always builds full assemblies for you, but if you want to use the command-line compilers, you can produce modules as compiler output, and then use al.exe to build the modules into assemblies. As well as creating a manifest, al.exe can also use a key pair to sign an assembly.

Here's an example using al.exe:

```
al /out:MyCode.dll MyCode.module /key:mykey.snk
```

The module **MyCode.module** is used to build the assembly MyCode.dll, and it is signed with the keys in the file mykey.snk.

NOTE: *See the .NET Framework SDK documentation for more details on building assemblies and using al.exe.*

Asking for Access to Resources

.NET components ask for the access they require to resources, such as files, by using permission objects. The CLR then checks the request against the security policy and either allows or denies the request.

The following example shows how a component would ask for access to a particular file:

```
Imports System.Security
Imports System.Security.Permissions

Module Module1

  Sub Main()
    ' Ask for all access to c:\temp
    Dim fpa As New FileIOPermission(FileIOPermissionAccess.AllAccess, _
        "c:\temp")
```

```
    Try
      fpa.Demand()
      Console.WriteLine("Access granted")
    Catch e As SecurityException
      Console.WriteLine("Access denied")
    End Try
  End Sub

End Module
```

The program starts by importing **System.Security**, which gives easier access to **SecurityException**, and **System.Security.Permissions**, which contains **FileIOPermission**.

I then construct a **FileIOPermission** object representing all access to c:\temp, and then test whether I can get that permission by using the **FileIOPermission** object's **Demand()** method. **Demand()** tells the security system to check whether this code—and any code that has called this code—has **AllAccess** permission to c:\temp. If all callers have access, the call succeeds; if any caller doesn't have access, the call fails and throws a **SecurityException**.

Using **Demand()** in this way means that you may get different results depending on where the code is loaded from. For example, if the code is run from the local machine, the default is to give all access to the local filing system. If, on the other hand, the code is loaded from a source on the Internet, it won't be given all access to the filing system unless the policy has been modified to let it do so.

Restricting a Component's Access to Files and Directories

It is very probable in the .NET world that components are going to call one another, and you may not be sure what the component you're using may try to do when you call a method. The .NET code access security mechanism lets you specify exactly what components can and cannot do by using permissions.

Here's an example: My program wants to use a class called **AccessIt**, which I know accesses the local disk. I'm not sure exactly what it is going to try to access, and I want to restrict the component so that it can only use the c:\temp directory.

The following program shows you how I can accomplish this restriction:

```
Imports System.Security
Imports System.Security.Permissions
Imports System.IO

Module Module1

  Sub Main()
    ' Create an empty permission set
    Dim p As New PermissionSet(PermissionState.None)

    ' Give access to one directory
    p.AddPermission(New FileIOPermission( _
       FileIOPermissionAccess.AllAccess, "c:\temp"))

    ' Change the permissions
    p.PermitOnly()

    ' Do the operation
    Dim a As New AccessIt()
    a.DoIt()

    ' Remove the restriction
    CodeAccessPermission.RevertPermitOnly()

  End Sub

  Class AccessIt
    Public Sub DoIt()
      ' Try to access some data...
      Try
        Dim sr As New StreamReader("c:\tcl\Directions1.htm")
        Console.WriteLine("File open OK")
      Catch e As Exception
        Console.WriteLine("File open failed: " + e.ToString())
      End Try
    End Sub
  End Class
End Module
```

The program starts by importing some namespaces—two for the security system and **System.IO** because I'm going to be using file I/O.

In order to restrict the permissions granted to components, I need to build a custom permission set that specifies the permissions I want to grant. The **System.Security.PermissionSet** class represents a set of permissions, and I create one that is initially set to "no access to anything" by specifying the **PermissionState.None** parameter.

I can now create one or more permission objects and add them to the **PermissionSet** using the **AddPermission()** function. Because I'm concerned with access to the file system, I create a **FileIOPermission** object that grants all access to the directory c:\temp.

Once I've set up the set of permissions I want to apply, I use the **PermissionSet**'s **PermitOnly()** to make the set active. This function won't allow any actions except those specified in the **PermissionSet**, hence the name: It permits only those actions named in the set. This set of permissions remains in force until I revoke them, by calling **RevertPermitOnly()**, at which time the set of permissions in force reverts to whatever it was originally.

The **AccessIt** class is very simple, consisting of one method, which tries to open a file in the c:\tcl directory. At the point **DoIt()** is called, the security permissions only permit operations on c:\temp, so attempting to open this file should fail.

When you run the code, you should find that it does indeed fail, and it shows you a security violation exception, as shown in Figure 7.3.

You can see that the exception was thrown in the **StreamReader** constructor in the **DoIt()** function, where it was trying to open the file. Further up the stack trace you can see a call to **Demand()**, where the I/O code is checking to see whether it has permission to open the file. Because of the permissions in force, it doesn't have permission, so the **SecurityException** is thrown.

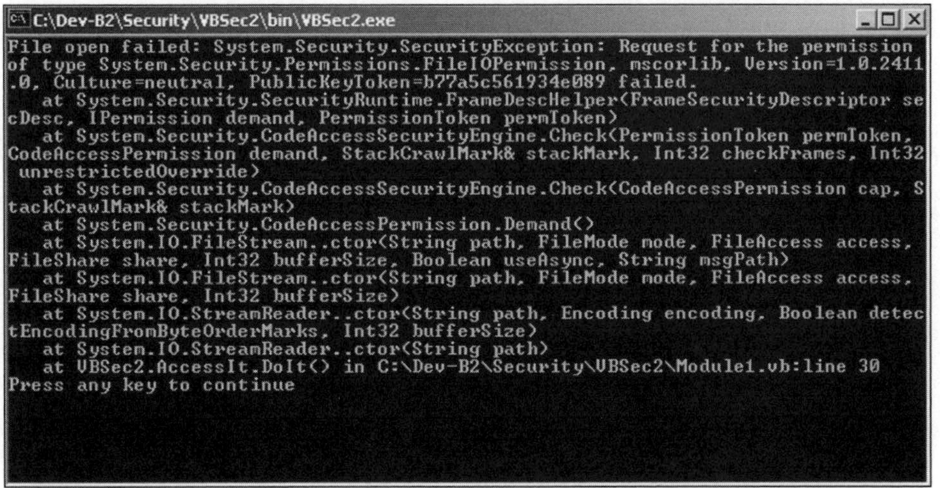

Figure 7.3 The **SecurityException** that results from trying to access a forbidden file.

You can see from this program how it is possible for client code—in this case, the **Main()** function—to control what components can access.

Ensuring That Only Specified Users Execute Code in a Method

There are three ways to ensure that only specified users execute code in a method: You can use an imperative security check, a declarative security check, or a **Principal** object directly.

Imperative Security Check

An imperative security check requires that you add code to your class to set up the security check. Here's a sample that shows you how this can be done:

```
' Needed for SecurityException
Imports System.Security
' Needed for PrincipalPermission
Imports System.Security.Permissions

Public Class Test
  Public Shared Sub SecureMethod()
    ' Create a permission object
    Dim pm As New PrincipalPermission("ZEPPO\Administrator", _
        "BUILTIN\Administrators")

    Try
      ' Demand the permission
      pm.Demand()
      Console.WriteLine("OK, you've got access")
    Catch se As SecurityException
      Console.WriteLine("Access denied")
    End Try
  End Sub
End Class
```

I want to make sure that code in the function **SecureMethod()** is only executed if the current user is Administrator on the Zeppo machine. The **System.Security.Permissions.PrincipalPermission** class represents a security permission and allows you to perform checks on users and roles. You can create a **PrincipalPermission** object to represent a particular user in a particular role; in this example, the user is “ZEPPO\Administrator” and the role is “BUILTIN\Administrators”.

***NOTE:** When using security functions, the names of security principals are specified in the Domain\UserID form.*

The first parameter given to the **PrincipalPermission** constructor is the ID of the user, and this maps onto a Windows NT or 2000 user ID. The second parameter is the name of the role that the user must be occupying. Although it is possible to have generic roles defined within .NET (and also to use roles defined for COM+ or MTS), most of the roles you use will map into Windows NT or 2000 groups. In order to use operating groups, you have to prefix the group name with "BUILTIN\", as in the preceding example.

The **Principal** permission object now represents the user, so I can then call **Demand()** on the object. This checks whether the current security principal matches the settings in the **Permission** object and throws a **System.Security.SecurityException** if they don't. This means that by enclosing the call to **Demand()** in a Try block, I can be sure that the rest of the code after the call to **Demand()** is only executed if the user has the right name and is in the correct role.

Declarative Security Check

Declarative security means adding attributes to code that tells the CLR which users are allowed to use a class or execute a method. The following C# example shows you how to use the **PrincipalPermission** attribute to control access in this way:

```
using System;
using System.Security;
using System.Security.Permissions;

namespace CSSec1
{
  class Class1
  {
    static void Main(string[] args)
    {
      Console.WriteLine("Trying...");
      // This call will fail
      Restricted r = new Restricted();

      // So will this one
      foo();
    }

    // Create a method with restricted access
    [PrincipalPermission(SecurityAction.Demand,
            Name="fred", Role="Administrators")]
```

```
    static void foo()
    {
      Console.WriteLine("In foo...");
    }
  }

  // Create a class with restricted access
  [PrincipalPermission(SecurityAction.Demand,
              Name="fred", Role="Administrators")]
  class Restricted {
    public void aMethod() {
    }
  }
}
```

***NOTE:** There appears to be a bug in Visual Basic in the .NET Beta 2 release related to using the **PrincipalPermission** attribute, so I've provided the example in C#, which works fine.*

The interesting parts of the code are highlighted. The static method **foo()** in **Class1** and the whole of class **Restricted** are marked with the **PrincipalPermission** attribute. This takes three arguments: The first is the action, which I've set to **SecurityAction.Demand**, meaning that the security settings will be checked at runtime. The next two parameters specify the user ID and role, which will be checked at runtime. The net result is that if the two calls in the **Main()** function are made by anyone other than fred, they will fail with a **SecurityException**.

Using a Principal Object

You can also check user identity by using the **WindowsIdentity** and **WindowsPrincipal** classes.

The following two lines of code show you how to see who the current user is:

```
Dim prin As WindowsIdentity = WindowsIdentity.GetCurrent()
Console.WriteLine("Current user is {0}", prin.Name)
```

The **WindowsIdentity** class represents a Windows user. The **GetCurrent()** shared method returns a **WindowsIdentity** object initialized with the details of the current user. Some other methods and properties of this class are listed in Table 7.7.

The **WindowsIdentity** class lets you check the name of the user, but doesn't provide any information about group membership, for which you'll need to use a **WindowsPrincipal** object.

Table 7.7 Useful methods and properties of the WindowsIdentity class.

Member	Description
AuthenticationType	Returns the type of authentication used, typically NTLM
GetAnonymous	Shared method that returns a **WindowsIdentity** object representing an anonymous user
GetCurrent	Shared method that returns a **WindowsIdentity** object representing the current user
Impersonate	Allows code to impersonate a user
IsAnonymous	**True** if the **WindowsIdentity** object represents an anonymous user
IsAuthenticated	**True** if the **WindowsIdentity** object represents an authenticated user
IsGuest	**True** if the **WindowsIdentity** object represents the guest account
IsSystem	**True** if the **WindowsIdentity** object represents the **System** account
Name	Returns the user's login name

NOTE: *A security principal represents the identity and role of a user. Windows principals in .NET represent Windows users and their roles (or their Windows NT and 2000 groups).*

You often want to create a **WindowsPrincipal** object to represent the current user, and you can do this using **WindowsIdentity.GetCurrent()**, as shown in the following code:

```
Dim prin As New WindowsPrincipal(WindowsIdentity.GetCurrent())
Console.WriteLine("Current user is {0}", prin.Identity.Name)
```

This class only has two members: an **Identity** property that returns a **WindowsIdentity** object representing the user, and an **IsInRole()** method that tells you whether the user belongs to a particular role:

```
If prin.IsInRole("BUILTIN\Administrators") Then
  Console.WriteLine("Administrator role")
End If
```

Chapter 8

The System.Web Namespace

By David Vitter

In Depth

The Web and the Internet play a crucial role in Microsoft's vision for the future of applications development. In fact, the role the Web plays in the .NET Framework is so important that it has its very own namespace! Housed within the **System.Web** namespace you will find all of the necessary ingredients to create an ASP.NET Web application or a .NET XML Web service.

In this chapter, you learn about .NET Web development using the **System.Web** namespace. You will see how easy it is to create an ASP.NET project using whichever .NET development language you prefer. I will also show you how ASP.NET applications work behind the scenes. In addition, you learn about XML Web services and how they can fit into a .NET application architecture. This exciting new area of Visual Studio development has received a great deal of attention in the media, and I am sure you are curious to learn all about it.

Introduction to ASP.NET

As you can probably tell by the name, Active Server Pages (ASP) are Web pages that are processed by a Web server. Static Web pages, which usually end with the .html extension, require no processing and can be sent in their natural form across the Internet to a user's browser. ASP pages are not static, and they need to be processed by a Web server before the resulting HTML page is sent to a user. For example, you might create an ASP page that displays today's weather report. That ASP page would contain the code necessary to query a weather-related database and then format the returned data into a Web page. ASP pages are said to be dynamic because the content and format can change depending on the inputs the page receives during processing.

ASP.NET represents the latest evolution of dynamic Web content development. Included within the realm of ASP.NET are Web Forms and Web controls. You will first learn about the dramatic changes made to ASP in ASP.NET, and then you will learn how Web Forms and Web controls work and interact. In addition, you will see how ASP.NET projects can be integrated with other projects that are created in .NET, including XML Web services and Windows applications.

From ASP to ASP.NET

Before the introduction of .NET, ASP pages were a great way to create dynamic Web content, but they had some serious drawbacks that developers had to deal with. ASP Web development projects all suffered from the following limitations:

- ASP pages could only use scripting languages, such as VBScript, which is a very limited subset of Visual Basic.
- Web pages were stored in raw text format and were interpreted at runtime by the Web server.
- Both the HTML formatting tags and the interpreted code were stored in the same source code file, making it difficult to reuse code segments in multiple Web pages.
- The basic set of HTML form controls was very limiting and creating fancy client-side displays, such as a sortable grid displaying a table of data, required a great deal of coding on the ASP developer's part.
- ASP development was not integrated into the main Visual Studio IDE (Integrated Development Environment). You had to use a text editing tool such as Window's Notepad, the Visual InterDev tool included with Visual Studio 6, or some other third-party tool such as Macromedia's Ultradev 4 to edit ASP pages.

ASP allowed developers with Visual Basic experience to develop quick-and-dirty Web pages to be hosted on a Microsoft Windows Web server. I use the term *dirty* because ASP pages often used crudely crafted code that was as un-object-oriented as any code could be. Due to its reliance on scripting languages, non-Visual Basic developers were basically locked out of ASP development projects, at least as far as the Web interfaces were concerned. Because of this exclusion, ASP Web page development was often considered a skill unto its own and not a talent often associated with high-end C++ developers.

ASP.NET seeks to remove all of these weaknesses and drawbacks by completely reincarnating itself as a respectable Web development technology. It addresses the weaknesses of its predecessor in the following ways:

- You can now create ASP.NET Web pages using any Visual Studio .NET development language including Visual Basic and C#.
- ASP.NET Web pages are compiled like Windows Forms, providing far better performance than ASP pages.
- The tags defining the Web pages interface and the programming source code are now stored in two different files, allowing developers to edit their code without affecting the interface designer's work. Multiple ASP.NET Web Forms can also reuse a single source code file.

- ASP.NET introduces server-side Web controls, which allow developers to create fancy and robust interfaces just as easily as you could create a Windows Form.
- You can design, code, and debug your ASP.NET Web pages in the same development environment as all of your other .NET projects.

ASP.NET levels the playing field for all developers. Everyone, from experienced ASP developers to experienced C++ developers, will all have to learn ASP.NET from scratch. The good news is that Microsoft has made it incredibly easy to learn how to create powerful Web pages using ASP.NET, and this wonderful application type is no longer restricted to a small subset of developers.

How Web Pages Work

If you are going to develop applications that use the Web as a communications medium, it is important to understand how the Web works. This information not only applies to ASP.NET Web pages, but also to XML Web services, which I will cover later in this chapter (see the "XML Web Services" section). In other words, if you are new to Web development, do not skip this section because you will be missing out on some very important background information.

I am certain you have used the Web before, probably for email and Web browsing. But what happens behind the scenes when you type a Uniform Resource Locator (URL) into your browser's Address box and click Go? The Web works by using a series of requests and responses. Simply stated, your Web browser sends out a request for the Web page matching the URL you typed in, and somewhere out in the world a Web server responds with that Web page. Take a look at Figure 8.1. In this figure, you see a step-by-step example of a user requesting a Web page from a remote Web server. The Web browser first sends a request to the Web server for the desired page. The server then responds to the browser with the HTML page.

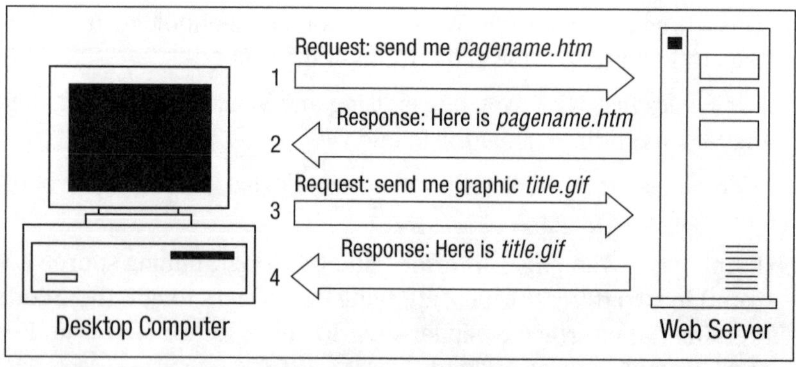

Figure 8.1 A Web browser requesting and receiving a Web page from a Web server.

When the browser processes the page, it may encounter one or more HTML tags that reference a graphic, so the browser sends a request for each required graphic, which the Web server responds back with.

The HTTP Protocol

These Web page requests and responses are transported back and forth across the globe using Hypertext Transfer Protocol (HTTP). HTTP is the language of the Web—it's how Web browsers talk to Web servers and how your applications will talk to XML Web services. Remember that Web-based communication is all about asking and receiving.

When you ask for some information, you must provide a couple of pieces of information to complete the transaction. The URL you request tells the Web server exactly what it is you desire, but within the HTTP request you can find many other tidbits of information. The requester's IP address is a critical piece of data without which the Web server would have no idea where to send the requested page. Also included inside the HTTP request is information on what type of browser the user is using and what file formats that browser will accept. This information is sort of like mailing someone a self-addressed return envelop and a little bit of information about your self to help the information provider tailor their response with.

Connectionless and Stateless Communications

There are two limitations you need to be aware of when communicating via the Web. The first is that the Web, by design, is *connectionless*. This means that your Web browser or application does not establish a hard, fixed link with a Web server. You simply send your request via HTTP, and then you wait for a response. I'll bet you have encountered a time-out message in your Web browser at one time or another. This means that your request was sent out, but a response did not come back in a reasonable amount of time. Because your browser does not establish a dedicated connection to a Web server, these request time outs are often the sole indicator that a server is down or that the URL provided was incorrect.

The other tricky aspect to Web development and communications is that the Web is a *stateless* medium. After a Web server provides you with the information you requested, it then forgets that it ever met you. Yes, that's kind of rude, but if your Web server had to keep tabs on everyone that ever visited it and what they asked for, your server would quickly come to a grinding halt due to overloaded resources. However, there are ways around this limitation. If your Web site needs to track a user's path through your site or remember some important information about that user, you have some options available to you. You can:

- Store information on the client's end in the form of a cookie
- Save this information to a database

- Write these bits of data to a text file on the Web server
- Store the user's data within his or her Web session

In the next section, I discuss each of these methods, along with their strengths and weaknesses.

Persisting Data

Most Web users are familiar with cookies. These are small files that are written to the user's hard drive to provide storage for some piece of information, such as the date of the user's last visit to a certain Web site. The Web server can request that the browser provide this cookie to help the server remember something about the user. Unfortunately, many users frown upon having information written to their hard drives unknowingly and therefore disable the use of cookies within their browsers. This places the burden of remembering bits of user-specific information squarely on the shoulders of the overloaded Web server.

***TIP:** Avoid using client-side cookies to persist data about your users—many users disable the use of cookies in their browser, which will cause your persistence plan to fail.*

On the Web server, the three most common ways to persist a piece of information from one Web page request to another are by saving the data to a database, writing it to a file, or storing it in the user's Web session. In terms of performance, reading and writing information from a database can be very costly and should be done as little as possible. Often your database will be stored on a separate server and making repeated calls to another server to persist user information would greatly slow down your Web site. Writing data to a text file on the server can offer some improvement over the database storage option, but you will still experience some slow downs with this method.

Despite their drawbacks, developers have been using cookies, databases, and the file system to persist data between requests since the birth of the Web. When working with Microsoft's Internet Information Server (IIS), developers have a fourth option available that offers a significant performance gain over the other three options: When a user requests a page from an IIS Web server, IIS creates what is called a *session* for that user. Each session created is unique to a single user. An IIS Web server has a time-out setting that decides how long the Web server will wait for a user to make another request before the server drops that session. By default, this time-out is set to 20 minutes.

For the Web developer, the session creates a temporary area for each visitor where you can store data. Say, for example, that the front page of your Web site asks a user to provide his age. When this page is submitted, you could store this information within that user's session and continue to reference this information while that session is active. A couple of page requests later, your code will be able to access the user's age, which was "remembered" by the session and provide some age-customized content back to your visitor.

In the Immediate Solutions section, you will learn how to read and write data to the IIS Web server's session. If you want to persist data to a database or the file system, you will do that just like you would any other database or file access routine in any normal application. Table 8.1 lists all of the persistent storage methods discussed previously along with their upsides and their downsides.

The GET and POST Form Methods

A simple request for a single Web page is easy to comprehend, but making requests for static HTML pages is fairly boring and does not represent the full power of Web applications. The Web is full of Search buttons and registration forms, all asking you to provide some information to be sent back to the Web server. These extra data elements are embedded into the HTTP request using either the **GET** or **POST** method. Most Web page requests use the **GET** method to send the request. If there is form data involved in a **GET** request, it is appended to the end of the URL to form one long URL. Special characters such as **?** and **&** are used to separate data elements in a **GET** request. If you submit a form that uses the **GET** method to send form data, you will see this data appended to the end of the URL in your Web browser's Address window.

If the Web page uses the **POST** method, you will not see the form data in the browser's Address window. Instead, these data elements are packaged inside the HTTP request message. The main difference between the **GET** and **POST** methods is how they package your form data. In the past, your server-side code had to know which request method was used so that it could properly extract these data elements. Luckily, with ASP.NET and XML Web services, the differences between **GET** and **POST** will be mostly transparent. If you do not want the form data to be visible in the URL Address text box, you should use **POST**. Otherwise, use the **GET** method.

Table 8.1 Data persistence options for Web developers.

Method	Pros	Cons
Cookie	Information storage occurs on client's machine, freeing up server resources.	Many users dislike cookies and disable these in the browser.
Database	A great way to associate data with a user's account.	Access times can be slow.
File System	A good choice to persist data close to the Web server.	Reading and writing to files can be slow.
IIS Session	Provides the fastest access to your data.	Excessive use of session storage can slow down your server.

Integrating ASP.NET into Your Applications

ASP.NET projects are not meant to be standalone applications. On the contrary, you should use an ASP.NET project as one of the building blocks that makes up a larger and more complex application. Sure, you could include all of your business logic and data access code within your ASP.NET project, but the result would be a tightly packaged unscalable application. For small Web applications, this is not such a bad thing, but if you are designing a large enterprise-level application, you need to understand how ASP.NET projects can fit in to an *n*-tier architecture.

Developing your application in tiers means that you separate the pieces of your application based on their functions. If a component contains business logic or performs calculations, it goes in the business tier. If it accesses data stores, a component is placed in the data tier. ASP.NET Web Forms are responsible for displaying information and accepting input from the users, similar to Windows Forms, so they belong in the presentation tier. If you use ASP.NET in this fashion, you can develop multi-interface applications that maximize code reuse. Imagine an application that features a Windows interface for employees working on the company network and a Web interface for customers accessing the application from outside the company. If you place all of your business logic on a tier separate from the presentation logic, both the Windows and Web interfaces can share the same back-end code. Figure 8.2 shows an example of an application that features these two different interface types.

To achieve this level of integration and code reuse, you will create a new project for your ASP.NET Web Forms, another project for your Windows Forms, and yet another class Library project that contains your business logic. The important thing to remember when separating presentation logic from business logic is to not place any code in your presentation tier projects that is not directly responsible

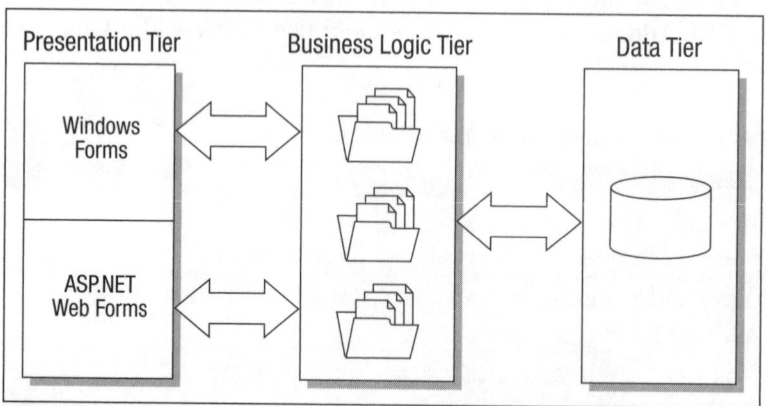

Figure 8.2 Integrating ASP.NET into your application designs.

for the display or collection of data. If a function performs any calculations or accesses any data stores, you will need to move it out of your presentation tier. This way you can reuse this piece of code in your other presentation tier projects.

You should no longer think of your applications as being either Windows applications or Web applications. In .NET, Web Forms represent one of many possible interfaces your application can have, and any .NET developer can easily create a Web Form for use with his application. Think of Web Forms as just another tool in your toolbox that you can use to make your project available via the Web.

TIP: *When thinking about Web interface development, use the term Web Forms, not ASP.NET. This will remind you that Web Forms are interchangeable with Windows Forms as the interface to your application.*

Web Forms

When accessing your ASP.NET Web applications, your users will be using Web Forms hosted within their browsers. In .NET, Web Forms are inherited from the **System.Web.UI.Page** namespace. Creating Web Forms in Visual Studio .NET is very similar to creating Windows Forms, so you should feel right at home working with Web Forms, especially if you are coming from a Visual Basic background. One of the major differences between Web Forms and Windows Forms is the fact that Web Forms are a platform-independent application interface. This means that users can access your Web Forms using any browser type hosted by any operating system running on any hardware platform. Windows Forms, on the other hand, are designed to only run on computers using the Windows operating system. The flexibility of Web Forms makes them an attractive choice when planning your application's front-end, and nowadays many customers are asking for Web-based applications that they can use in their mixed operating system environments. Let's take a look at how a Web Form works and how developers create these flexible Web-based interfaces.

How Web Forms Work

Web Forms live in the same realm as the HTML page. When you create an ASP.NET Web Form, you make it available for use by placing it within the directory structure of an IIS Web server. It's important to note that only an ASP.NET-aware Web server, such as IIS 5 running on Windows 2000, is capable of processing and serving ASP.NET applications. This is because, unlike HTML Web pages, an ASP.NET Web Form must be processed before the results can be sent to the requesting browser. You can think of your Web Forms as "HTML generators" because when processed, your Web Forms will produce HTML Web pages that are compatible with the requesting browser. None of the programming code that you will use to code your Web Forms will be sent to the user, so your coding secrets are safe with ASP.NET.

You can place controls on your Web Forms just as you can with Windows Forms except that you will have a different drawer full of controls to choose from with Web Forms. Web Forms and their associated Web controls can perform one nifty trick that their Windows counterparts cannot: They can adapt their output to be compatible with the user's browser type. As every Internet developer can attest to, some browsers are more powerful than others, and it seems that no two users can agree on which browser to use. Until ASP.NET, developers had to decide which browser types and versions they wanted to support, and then eliminate all features that the lowest supported browser could not use. This resulted in watered down Web-based applications that excluded advanced features in favor of maximizing browser compatibility.

Working in conjunction with the Web server, ASP.NET applications can detect what browser type and version a visitor is using, and then adapt the Web Form's output for that browser. For example, the Internet Explorer browser supports Dynamic HTML (DHTML), whereas most Netscape browsers do not, so an ASP.NET application can decide whether to send a version of itself that uses DHTML or an alternate version that does not. (You will learn more about Web controls and their abilities to adapt their outputs in the "Web Controls" section.) If you look at Figure 8.3, you will see how a Web server processes a request for an ASP.NET Web Form and how the Web Form detects and adapts itself to the user's browser.

Code Behind

One of the limitations of ASP was that your code (usually VBScript) was mixed in with your interface layout tags (HTML). This made it impossible to reuse your

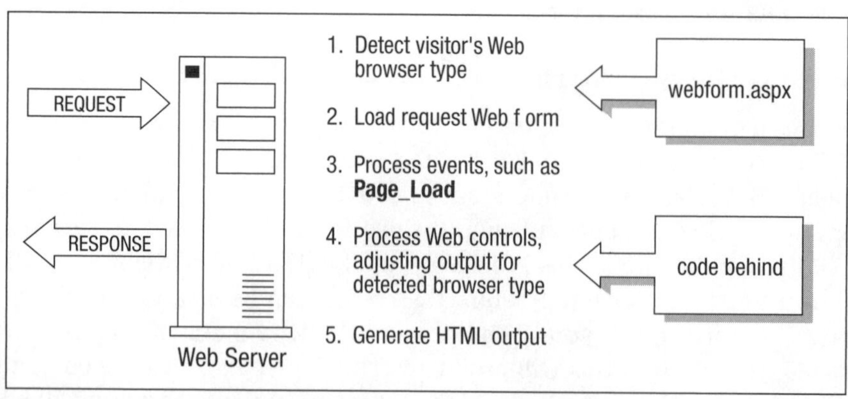

Figure 8.3 How ASP.NET Web Form requests are processed.

code among different pages unless you separated your code into standalone files and used **<Include>** tags to join your code to your ASP page. ASP.NET overcomes these problems by using a concept called *code behind*, which separates your interface designs from your source code, yet makes them appear as one solid file within Visual Studio .NET.

Each Web Form is made up of two files on the Web server: the main file containing the interface layout (ending in a .aspx extension) and the code behind file written in your programming language of choice. If you created an ASP.NET Web application using Visual Basic .NET and had a Web Form named EmployeeList, the main file would be named EmployeeList.aspx, and its associated code behind file would be named EmployeeList.aspx.vb. Within the Visual Studio .NET Solution Explorer window, you would only see the EmployeeList.aspx file, but if you selected this file and clicked on the View Code button at the top of the Solution Explorer, the .aspx.vb file would open to reveal the code behind this Web Form.

The ASPX file is the main piece of your Web Form, and this is the file that the URL references. Web visitors will not be able to directly view the code behind files. Each Web Form's ASPX file references its associated code behind files using a declaration statement. If you examine the raw HTML of a Web Form, which you can do by double-clicking on a Web Form in the Solution Explorer window and then clicking on the HTML button at the bottom of the Design view window, you will see a tag at the top of your HTML that looks something like this:

```
<%@ Page Language="vb" AutoEventWireup="false" Codebehind=_
    "EmployeeList.aspx.vb" Inherits="MyProject.EmployeeList"%>
```

This tag associates the code behind file containing your source code with your HTML interface file. There are many great advantages to separating your interface code from your source code, for example:

- It allows interface designers and coders to work on the same Web Form at once without overwriting each other's work.
- It gives developers the ability to reuse source code files among multiple Web Forms.
- You can quickly change a Web Form's code behind by simply changing the **CodeBehind** attribute of the Form's declaration line.

Visual Studio .NET realizes that not every developer is an interface designer, and not every Web designer knows how to write source code. In the next section, you will see some great examples of the source code that you will find in the code behind files.

ASP.NET Events

Like Windows Forms and their associated controls, ASP.NET Web Forms and Web controls have events that you can create code for to make your Forms reactive. There is one important difference between Windows Forms and Web Forms events. For a Windows Form, the code that is processed when an event fires is contained within that Form, whereas the code associated with a Web Form event is stored in the code behind file on the Web server. This means that when an event is fired in a Web Form running in the user's browser, the Form has to call back to the Web server to run its event.

This process of firing an event in the browser, calling back to the Web server to process the event and then returning the updated page to the browser, is called a *postback* because the Web Form posts its information back to the server. With Windows Forms, the event processes almost immediately without slowing down the user's interface, but because Web Forms must make a call across the Internet to the Web server, there can be a hefty price to pay for overusing these events. You can avoid using postback events by using client-side scripting, such as JavaScript, to handle events within the browser. This would require you to place your client-side scripting language within your ASPX Web Form layout code so that this code is sent to the browser along with the HTML. Of course, JavaScript is another skill set that you'll need to learn to accomplish this task, and you will have to perform some extensive testing of your scripts using multiple browsers because each browser type interprets client-side scripts differently.

The Page_Load Event

The most important page-level event you will work with is the **Page_Load**. This event fires on the Web server every time your Web Form processes a request. This event will not be fired within the user's browser, but the **Page_Load** code may execute in response to another event raised in the browser, such as a control's raised event. You will learn more about Web control events in the "Control Events" section, but for now picture a Web Form loaded in your browser with an empty text box and a button on its surface. The very first time your browser requests this page, the text box is empty. When you click on the button, you see that the browser contacts the Web server again, and in a few seconds, you see the same form again except this time when the page loads, the text box now says "Thank You" and the button now says "Clicked". Let's take a look at the code behind this form:

```
Public Class WebForm1

Private Sub Page_Load(ByVal sender As System.Object, ByVal e As System._
    EventArgs) Handles MyBase.Load
```

```
    If IsPostBack Then
        TextBox1.Text = "Thank You"
    End If
End Sub

Private Sub Button1_Click(ByVal sender As System.Object, ByVal e As _
      System.EventArgs) Handles Button1.Click
    Button1.Text = "Clicked"
End Sub

End Class
```

I could have easily made the changes to both the text box and the button within the button's **Click** event, but I chose to separate these two changes to both control's **Text** values to illustrate the **IsPostBack** feature. Notice that inside the **Page_Load** event I check to see if this page request is a postback. If it is a postback, that means that the user is already looking at this page, and the current request is in response to a page event, such as the button's **Click**. The first time the page loads, you see that the text box is empty because the **IsPostBack** is **False**, but clicking on the button causes a postback and its associated code to run. If you are coming from an ASP background, you will notice that you can now refer to the controls on your Web Forms as objects, which you were not able to do prior to ASP.NET. Buttons have properties such as **Text** and events such as **Click**, which you can now refer to in your code, just like you would in a Windows Form.

Postback also offers a second useful improvement over the older ASP way of doing things. Previously, your ASP page had to include a great deal of extra code if you wanted to preserve the control values whenever the page submitted itself to the Web server. If you failed to preserve these values, the new page that the user received would forget the user's settings and revert back to its original state. When Web Forms do a postback, the Web server automatically notes the current values of all of the pages' controls and preserves these values when it returns the next version of the page to the user. By preserving these settings, ASP.NET almost makes the postback process invisible to the developer. You know the postback process is occurring, but you do not have to do any additional coding because of it.

The Page_Unload Event

The Web Form's **Page_Unload** event is the ideal location to place your cleanup code to close any database or file connections used during the processing of a particular page. This event fires when the Web server is finished processing the Web Form and has completed sending the resulting Web page to the user's browser. In the Web application world, once a page has been rendered and sent out via

HTTP, the Web server will want to remove all local copies of that page in preparation for the next page request. Keep in mind that the Web Form's **Page_Unload** event fires when the Web server is done generating the page, not when the user closes that page in his browser.

TIP: *Use the **Page_Unload** event to clean up valuable resource connections created within your Web Forms' code.*

Integrating Web Forms into Application Designs

If you follow proper *n*-tier design principles and separate your business logic from your presentation logic, you will find that ASP.NET Web Forms can be easily substituted for Windows Forms in your application designs. Your physical application designs will have to include a Windows IIS Web server to serve out your Web Forms, but your application will gain the ability to be used on any operating system and platform. For applications that run on a Windows operating system and perform a large amount of client-side processing, you will probably want to use Windows Forms. But from here on out you should always consider using Web Forms as an interface alternative to Windows Forms. You can also choose to use both Web and Windows Forms in your application design. An online bookseller, for example, might use Windows Forms to allow its employees to edit the database of books while presenting the store's Internet visitors a Web-based interface to search and purchase from the same database.

Web Controls

You will be working with two types of controls on your Web Forms: Web controls and HTML controls. These two control types come from very different backgrounds, and as such, these controls are inherited from two different namespaces: **System.Web.UI.WebControls** and **System.Web.UI.HtmlControls**. When you are in design mode looking at one of your Web Forms, you will see two panels containing controls in the toolbar window: one panel named HTML, which lists your HTML controls, and another panel named Web Forms, which contains the Web controls. I will first discuss the HTML controls, which will be very familiar to anyone that has ever created a Web-based form. Next I will explore .NET's new Web controls, which promise to make interface designers' jobs easier and users' experiences more satisfying.

HTML Controls

All Web browsers support a small, common set of form controls. These include the button, text box, checkbox, and radio button (or the option button). Some browsers previously supported more robust controls, but if Web developers were required to support multiple browser types, they had to forgo these advanced controls and stick with the simple (and boring) controls. The following is an example of the HTML tags that would place a button on your Web page:

```
<Input Type="Button" Name="Button1" Value="Click Here">
```

Any events associated with this type of control are handled within the browser. You would need to add some client-side code to deal with this button's **Click** event. You can still add these older controls to your Web Forms using these HTML tags, but you would not be able to create server-side events for these controls. If you use the HTML controls from the Toolbox's HTML panel, your Web Forms will be using these same standard set of HTML tags to describe these controls, but you will not be able to handle events for these controls on the server. To create server-side event code for HTML controls, you need to convert these controls to their associated server-side versions.

Web Controls

HTML controls tell the browser to draw a control type that the browser is familiar with. If you only use HTML controls on your Web page, you will be limited to a very small set of basic controls. The trouble is, these are the only controls you can be sure all browsers know how to draw by name. Web controls, also known as server-side controls, are a special set of controls designed for use with ASP.NET Web Forms. When you look at the HTML in a Web Form, you will notice that the Web controls on the page use a different tagging format than the standard HTML controls. Here is what the Web control version of a TextBox would look like:

```
<asp:Button id=Button1 runat="server" Text="Click Here" Width="158px" _
   Height="30px"></asp:Button>
```

If you are familiar with HTML tagging, you might think that a browser is not going to understand that tag, and you would be correct. But the Web server will understand this tag, and this special **<asp>** tag will be converted to a more familiar **<Input>** tag displaying a button within the browser. The most important feature of this new control tag format is the **runat** attribute. By setting the **runat** equal to "server," the Web page is letting the Web server know that all events for this control will be handled via postback to the Web server.

Web Controls Generating HTML

Many of the standard set of HTML controls have Web control equivalents that you should favor in your Web Form designs. But the collection of Web controls included with Visual Studio .NET introduces some new controls to Web development. These Web controls use an incredibly cool trick to introduce advanced features to Web browsers that only support a limited set of basic controls. A single

Web control, when processed on the Web server, can generate a series of simple and basic HTML tags to direct the browser to draw a complex control.

If the Web control has an HTML tag equivalent, that tag is sent to the browser. If there is no HTML equivalent tag, the resulting control displayed in the browser will be made up of many separate HTML tags. For example, my favorite Web control is the DataGrid, which can help you display sets of data, such as those contained in an ADO.NET DataSet. Within the browser, the DataGrid will be drawn out using HTML tags such as the **<TABLE>** tag for the layout and the **<A HREF>** tag to make items within the DataGrid clickable. You will learn to use the DataGrid and see this powerful new control in the Immediate Solutions section of this chapter.

Validation Controls

Within the set of Visual Studio .NET Web controls is a collection of helpful items known as validation controls. You can drag-and-drop a validation control over to your Web Forms just like any other control, but these controls work a little differently than other Web controls. Instead of generating HTML tags to be sent to the user's browser, validation controls generate client-side script to be sent, and unless visitors look at the raw HTML source code for your page, the validation controls will be invisible to them.

Validation controls are designed to validate or check the values of other controls on a Web page without using a postback to perform these checks on the Web server. You could drop a RangeValidator control onto your Web Form, and then set its **ControlToValidate** property equal to **TextBox1**. Next, you could set the RangeValidator's **MaximumValue** and **MinimumValue** properties to represent a range of numbers to which you want to limit **TextBox1**. Whenever a user changes the value of **TextBox1** within the browser, the RangeValidator's code will check **TextBox1**'s value against its settings and provide an error message to the user if the value is outside the acceptable range. It's important to note that validation controls can only be used to validate other Web controls. Visual Studio .NET comes with the following validation controls in the Web Forms panel of the Toolbox:

- RequiredFieldValidator
- CompareValidator
- RangeValidator
- RegularExpressionValidator
- CustomValidator
- ValidationSummary

You will find an example of how to use and configure a validation control in the Immediate Solutions section.

Converting HTML Controls to Server Controls

When you are looking at a Web page in Visual Studio .NET's design mode, you will notice that the server-side Web controls have a little green arrow icon in the upper-left corner, whereas the HTML controls do not have this arrow. This feature allows you to quickly identify which controls are Web controls and which are not. In order to create server-side event code for an HTML control, you must first convert it to a Server control. You can do this by right-clicking on the HTML controls and selecting Run as Server Control. When you convert an HTML control to a Server control, Visual Studio simply adds a **runat** attribute to the HTML control's tag like so:

```
<Input Type="Button" Name="Button1" Value="Click Here" runat="Server">
```

The format of this control's tag still resembles an HTML control, but the **runat="Server"** property of this control lets the Web server know that the events for this control will be handled on the Web server.

TIP: *In most cases, Web controls are the best option when designing your Web Forms from scratch. You should only use HTML controls and HTML controls converted to Run as Server Controls when working with older Web pages you are migrating to .NET.*

Control Events

Your Web controls and HTML controls will have events associated with them, which you can create code for, just as you would controls on a Windows Form. When adding code to a Web Form control's event, remember that when this event fires it causes the Web page to communicate back to the Web server to process that code. For this reason, I recommend you use control events sparingly and only when absolutely necessary.

Every control will have a **Load** and **Unload** event. The **Load** event is triggered when the Web server is rendering the Web page and encounters the portion of the page where that control's tags will go. This is a good event in which to place any control initialization values. The **Unload** event will fire after the Web server has completed generating the HTML tags for the page and the page has been sent. You can use the **Unload** event to perform any special cleanup actions, such as closing files or database connections. Each control will have its own specific events. For example, the Button control has a **Click** event, and the TextBox control has a **TextChanged** event.

You can also create code within your HTML to handle control events on the client side. Typically, client-side code is written in JavaScript or JScript. Many controls will fire events that will not result in a postback to the Web server. For example, many Web developers use the **<IMG>** tag's **OnMouseOver** to change the graphic when a user's mouse point passes over the image. This is a really good trick to use to draw someone's attention to something, but it would not be appropriate for the Web page to contact the Web server every time the mouse point passes over a particular item.

AutoPostBack

The button is the traditional control used to submit form data to the Web server, and if you create server-side code for a button's **Click** event, clicking on a button will trigger the postback process. Other control types, such as TextBoxes and CheckBoxes, typically act as part of a large set of controls and should not immediately trigger the postback process. Even if you create some server-side code for one of these control's events, such as the TextBoxes **TextChanged** event, changing the text within a TextBox will not cause an immediate postback. Instead, the **TextChanged** event will be delayed until a postback is triggered by another control. If you want to ensure that a control's event is immediately processed and not delayed, you can override this delay by changing the control's **AutoPostBack** property to **True**. Controls with an **AutoPostBack** property are set to **False** by default to minimize the amount of back-and-forth communications happening between the Web server and the browser.

XML Web Services

One of the most talked about enhancements made in Visual Studio .NET is the introduction of XML Web services, and for good reason. The ability to create and make XML Web services available offers many attractive benefits to modern-day application development projects:

- Your applications can call XML Web services across the Internet. Now a "distributed" application can scatter its parts all over the world.
- XML Web services communicate using Simple Object Access Protocol (SOAP), an open source protocol that any application can use, which inherently makes your services available to any development language running on any operating system.
- Maximizing code reuse takes on a whole new meaning when dealing with XML Web services because you can reuse your code from applications located anywhere in the world and across multiple development environments.
- You can immediately start developing XML Web services today using your existing programming skills.

XML Web services have the potential to completely change the way you design and develop applications. The first important step to harnessing this new power is to understand how XML Web services work and how they overcome many of the limitations developers have fought for so long. Once you are comfortable with how XML Web services work, you can then begin to design your application architectures to take advantage of XML Web services.

Introduction to XML Web Services

Over the last few decades, application designs have been greatly affected by how far the application is able to communicate. Applications written to run on non-networked standalone computers are the simplest to comprehend. As businesses installed and improved upon their internal networks, application designs grew more and more complex and their individual components where scattered farther and farther apart, often across multiple machines. Now that almost every corporation's internal network is hooked into the Internet, your application's physical deployment diagram can potentially look like a map of the world!

XML Web services take the concept of remote procedure calls to the greatest extremes by allowing your applications to make calls to remote procedures that can be housed anywhere in the world. This also means that you can create your own XML Web services and host them on the Web for anyone to use. Many developers may read that definition and ask themselves, "Why would I want to do that?" I am sure that as you read on and see a few examples of XML Web services in action, you will immediately think of some terrific uses for this new project type.

The introduction of XML Web services to the Visual Studio environment also represents a radical new direction for Windows developers. XML Web services tightly embrace open source standards and can support application development for non-Microsoft platforms. You do not even have to use Visual Studio .NET to develop or use XML Web services. Applications communicate with XML Web services using SOAP. This is an open source protocol and is not proprietary or controlled by Microsoft. This means that you can host an XML Web service developed in Visual Studio .NET, and it will natively support request calls from any application that can communicate using SOAP, whether that application was written in Visual Studio .NET or Java. This also means that your applications can call upon any XML Web service available, no matter what language that XML Web service was written in. In just a bit I will discuss how XML Web services work, and you will see how elegantly simple they really are.

Code reuse is a big issue when designing an application. If designed properly, your application avoids duplicating pieces of code by placing commonly used routines and functions in shared classes so that the code can be reused throughout the application. What if you could reuse a function or a feature in multiple applications delivered to different clients? You could centrally host an XML Web service that makes a special feature available to multiple applications. You can even market this XML Web service to developers outside of your organization. There is already a large market for developing and selling third-party application components, such as controls for your Windows Form interfaces. The introduction of XML Web services to Visual Studio .NET is sure to result in a new services-based market. For a fee, your application will be able to call across the Web to someone else's XML Web service, which will provide a portion of your application's functionality, such as user authentication or file system storage. In the following discussion of some examples of services, you will begin to see the true potential of XML Web services.

XML Web Services Examples

XML Web services operate on the same principle as Web page requests. The client sends a request for a Web page or service to the hosting server, and that server returns your page or results to you. Just as with Web pages, interaction between clients and XML Web services is connectionless and stateless. If you are thinking about developing a XML Web service that will need to remember something about its users, you will have to include some sort of storage or caching scheme in your plans. Table 8.2 lists some examples of likely XML Web services you will encounter.

When looking at the examples in Table 8.2, you will see that there are many possible combinations for XML Web service inputs and outputs. In some cases, you can provide little or no data and still get back some usable information. For more personalized services, such as the online payment system or personal file storage, some means of securely identifying and authenticating a user is required to protect highly sensitive personal information. In all these examples, the client is

Table 8.2 XML Web services examples.

Service	Description
Weather	Provide this XML Web service with your zip code, and in return you will get a paragraph describing your local forecast.
Stock Prices	Send this XML Web service the name of a company and it will return that company's current stock value.
TV Programming	Give this service a time and a channel and receive a description of the television show airing at that time.
Online Payments	Provide this service with a username, password, dollar amount, and payee identification and this service could transfer funds from your online account to an online merchant.
File Storage	Accepts files as inputs for storage in a user's personalized file system. This same service can also field requests for documents the user has in storage.
Sales Tax	Provide a dollar amount and a state name, and this service can calculate and return the local sales tax.

asking to be provided some sort of service, whether it be providing information or storing a file.

In Figure 8.4, I have illustrated a fictional user's interaction with an online store. Many different XML Web services come in to play during this interaction. This fictional online store makes a call to an externally hosted XML Web service to calculate the shipping cost of the requested item. Next the online store contacts an XML Web service hosted at one of its suppliers to check on the desired product's availability status. Determining that this product is in stock, the online store uses the supplier's XML Web service to place the order for the product. The online store then contacts yet another XML Web service hosted by a different company to arrange the transfer of funds from the user's account to the store's account.

.NET My Services

You can accuse Microsoft of being a little slow to embrace the Internet in the beginning, but once it realized what a profound effect the Internet would have on computers and applications, Microsoft made developing for the Internet its number-one priority. With XML Web services, Microsoft has put the pedal to the metal in the race to become the world's leading XML Web services provider with a project called .NET My Services (originally codenamed Hailstorm). .NET My Services hopes to be *the* central point of user services for the Internet. Using Microsoft's Passport user authentication and identification technology, .NET My Services will provide user-specific data such as email inboxes, calendars, online wallets, and more.

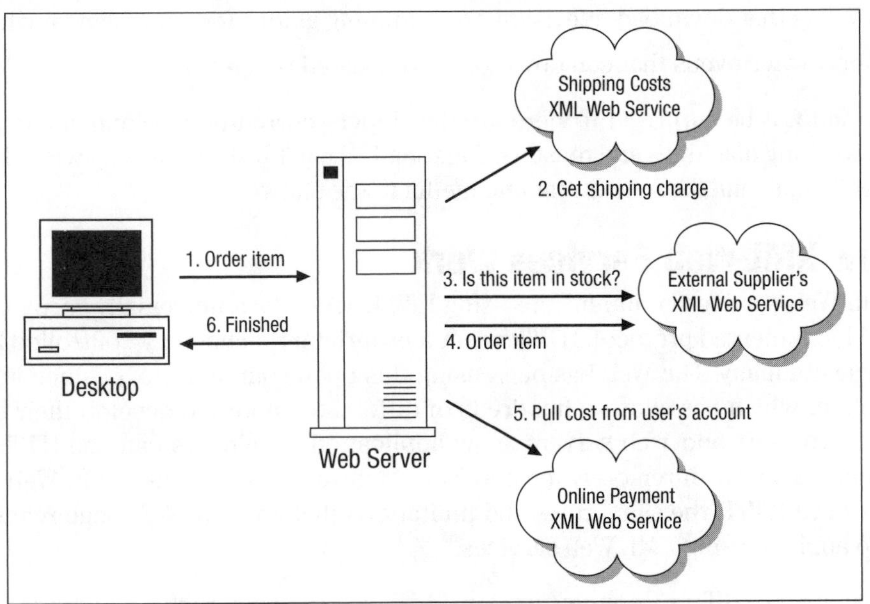

Figure 8.4 Examples of XML Web services used by an online retailer.

Imagine this scenario: You log on to your favorite online bookstore, and because both you and the bookseller are hooked into .NET My Services, you are immediately provided a tailored list of products you might be interested in. With a single click, you can complete a book order because the bookseller already has access to your address and online wallet. Of course, making shopping this easy and fast makes many users queasy, but this is only one possible future. For a less threatening example, picture logging in to a public kiosk at the mall to use the Internet, and you realize that your personalized favorite Web site list and favorite interface color scheme is automatically available on this machine. All this and more will be made possible through XML Web services.

Web-Enabled Devices

XML Web services will play a crucial role in the development of mobile and Web-enabled devices. If you look at a handheld digital phone, you can see that there is not a lot of room in that case for bulky hardware, such as RAM and hard drives. In order to make small devices useful and feature rich, developers must offload as much processing power as possible to servers housed on the Internet. XML Web services are the ideal way to provide this functionality because they communicate using open source protocols, which allow any developer working with any device to access them. Look around and I'll bet you can spot a couple of devices that could potentially be Web-enabled, for example:

- Alarm clocks that regularly compare their time to an accurate Web-based source
- TV sets that download television programming guides for on-screen viewing
- Microwave ovens that can download a requested recipe

I would not be surprised if there are developers currently developing software for washing machines and toasters. Personally, I can't wait for the day when I can check email and listen to streaming media in the shower.

How XML Web Services Work

XML Web services communicate using HTTP, which is a universally recognized and implemented protocol. HTTP is not a proprietary technology controlled by a single company. The Web has been using this open source protocol since its inception, which has allowed hundreds of different vendors to develop their own Web browsers and Web servers. Now application developers can use HTTP to communicate with remotely located XML Web services. Because XML Web services use HTTP, the same rules and limitations that apply to Web page requests also apply to using XML Web services.

What makes HTTP so wonderful? Consider a situation where the communication protocol is proprietary, such as when a COM object communicates with another

COM object using a Remote Procedure Call (RPC). If you were a Java developer, your Java code would not be able to talk to a COM object because Java does not utilize RPC in its communications. This same problem also prevents COM developers from calling Java objects. If your objects natively communicated using HTTP, anybody's code would be able to call upon them as long as they too use HTTP to make that call.

Figure 8.5 shows a TV channel viewing guide XML Web service hosted on a Web server. Because this XML Web service makes itself available to anyone on the Web and communicates using HTTP, many different application types written using many different development tools can all take advantage of this service. Web browsers, handheld devices, and applications developed using both Microsoft and non-Microsoft tools can all make requests of this service.

Changes in Design Paradigms

We are currently witnessing the sunrise period of the XML Web services era, and so far the day ahead looks fabulous. It's too early to tell how quickly developers will adopt XML Web services and make them a part of their application designs, but those changes are coming. Microsoft is not the only company that sees the

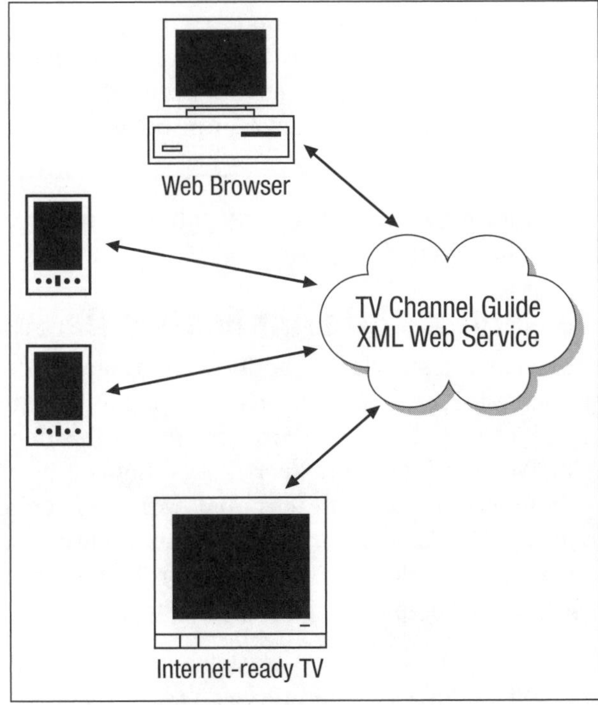

Figure 8.5 The TV viewing guide XML Web service.

beauty of service-based code. Sun, Hewlett Packard, and Oracle have all announced XML Web service development and support initiatives, signaling an industry-wide acceptance and enthusiasm for this new technology.

As a developer, how should you incorporate XML Web services into your future application designs? If you have experience developing distributed applications, you are already moving in the right direction. For the past couple of years, you have been breaking up your code into application tiers and components. You've created business logic components, data access components, and presentation components. If you understand *n*-tier development, adjusting your designs to allow for the inclusion of XML Web services is as simple as making a minor terminology change.

Traditionally, the presentation tier of your application contains the interface components, such as the Windows and Web Forms users interface with to use your program. XML Web services use the term *end-points* to refer to any device or application that makes use of a service. An example of a physical end-point would be a digital phone. Within that phone is some code that represents the logical end-point that communicates with remote services. If you think in terms of end-points, your Windows and Web Forms are logical end-points, and the computer terminal you access these forms with is the physical end-point. Take a look at Figure 8.6. In the first example, you see the standard *n*-tier architecture diagram using Windows Forms as the application's interface. In the second example, I rename the presentation tier as the end-points tier, which greatly broadens this realm to include nontraditional interfaces, such as digital phones and even refrigerators. I also add an XML Web service tier to the second diagram in between the end-points and business logic tier.

In the next section, I discuss integrating XML Web services into your application designs and explain why these belong in their own tier.

Integrating XML Web Services into Application Designs

You can create an XML Web service as a standalone application by simply creating an XML Web services project, adding all of the necessary code to that single project, and then posting it to a Web server. You will probably follow this method when you create your first XML Web service, just to keep things simple. But when it comes to designing and planning robust and professional XML Web services, placing all of your code into a single package severely limits your ability to scale or build upon that code. *N*-tier application design solves these problems for traditional applications, and these same principles can be applied to XML Web services as well.

Look at Figure 8.6 again. You will see that I made two changes to the standard tiers: I renamed the presentation tier the end-point tier, and then added a new tier in between the end-point and business tier named the XML Web services tier.

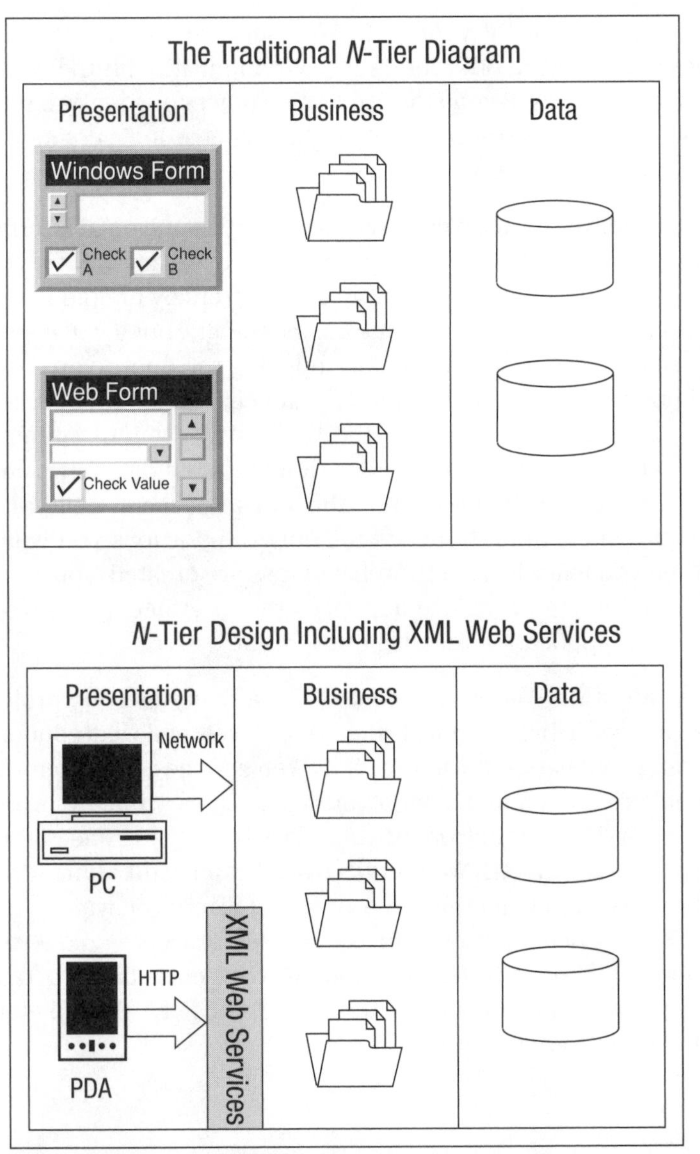

Figure 8.6 Working XML Web services into an *n*-tier architecture.

XML Web services do not belong in the end-point tier (formerly the presentation tier) because these services are not what users will directly interface with. Your user will use applications or devices that act as end-points, which connect to your Web Services. Although XML Web services could live in the business logic tier, I decided to create a new tier for two good reasons: code reuse and scalability. For the same reason that you separate business logic from your presentation logic, keeping your business logic out of your XML Web services tier allows you to reuse those business functions in other parts of your application. If the demand for your XML Web service grows beyond the processing power of your Web server, you will have the ability to offload some or all of the business logic components to another server with little or no effort.

Using this design method, your XML Web services will act as universal interfaces for your business logic tier, and they will not contain any business logic themselves. An *n*-tier design without XML Web services is extremely limited in terms of which end-points can communicate with the business logic, but if you insert an XML Web services tier into your design, you are opening the door to an endless list of possible end-points for your application. This tier can make your code available to any developer located anywhere in the world using any programming language. You can make portions of your application available on a function-by-function basis to the entire world. Of course, this does not mean that you are opening up your entire application to everyone, only the portions you want to make available. When you learn how XML Web services are created, you will see that the users of your service only have access to the interfaces you provide, whereas the rest of your application remains out of sight.

You can easily integrate XML Web services into your already existing projects. Take, for example, a class Library project you have developed that contains a series of functions and calculations. Without XML Web services, only your other .NET projects are able to communicate with your class Library functions, but if you add an XML Web services tier in front of your class Library, anyone is able to use your code. Simply create an XML Web services project and add a mirror set of functions to it that represent the functions in your class Library you want to make public. Each XML Web service function acts as a redirector to pass requests received via HTTP and SOAP back to the real code in your class Library. Take a look at the following simple function written in Visual Basic .NET that might represent one of your class Library functions:

```
Public Class CWeather

    Public Function LocalWeather(ByVal ZipCode As String) As String
        'Make database calls here to get a real weather forecast
        LocalWeather = "Sunny and 65 degrees all day long!"
    End Function

End Class
```

To make this function available via the Web, you would create an XML Web services project and add a reference to it for your class Library project, which I called

ClassLib_Chapt8. Next, you would create your redirector function inside your XML Web services project that would look like this:

```
Imports System.Web.Services

Public Class MyWeatherService
   Inherits System.Web.Services.WebService

    <WebMethod()> Public Function GetWeather(ByVal ZipCode As String) As _
      String
        Dim WeatherClass As New ClassLib_Chapt8.CWeather()
        GetWeather = WeatherClass.LocalWeather(ZipCode)
    End Function

End Class
```

In the preceding XML Web service code example, you will see that this class is inheriting from the **System.Web.Services.WebService** class. This XML Web service only makes one interface available via the Web, which is the **GetWeather** function. In an XML Web service project, you will be able to spot the publicly available interfaces by the **<WebMethod()>** tag in the function declaration line. Within this function, I simply **Dim** a reference to my **CWeather** class and then execute the matching method in that class, passing the result of this method back out as the results of the **GetWeather** Web method.

Making function calls through XML Web services will result in some slow downs, so if you have a project that is written in .NET that can access your class Library via a reference pointer, by all means use that route and avoid going through the XML Web service interfaces. XML Web services are meant to be used for remote procedure calls only, and by remote I mean calls originating from outside of your application's physical design.

Creating XML Web Services

The first time you create an XML Web service you might be surprised as to how easy it is and how familiar it feels. Coding an XML Web service is just like creating a class Library project, with one tiny difference. Any function you want to make externally visible through your service needs to have a **<WebMethod()>** attribute in its declaration line. Other than this small addition, your functions will look and act the same as you are used to. They will accept input parameters and provide output values, just like any other function. In fact, you can include functions in your XML Web service that do not use the **<Webmethod()>** attribute. These functions will be available to your XML Web services code like any other function, but they will not be visible to callers using your XML Web service. You will not be able to use the **<WebMethod()>** attribute in a normal class Library project, only in an XML Web service project.

The reason that you can only make functions available via the Web from an XML Web services project and not a class Library project has to do with how these projects are packaged for deployment. Class Library projects are either placed in the application's directory structure or in the computer's Global Assembly Cache (GAC), both of which are not directly accessible by the Web server. Class Libraries do not inherently know how to handle requests formatted with SOAP either. An XML Web services project is packaged in to a special file ending with an .asmx extension that is saved somewhere in the Web server's directory structure. The Web server is perfectly comfortable handling HTTP requests, and your ASMX XML Web service files understand SOAP messages. Later in Chapter 14, you will read about SOAP and learn why this extremely simple communications protocol is revolutionizing the way applications talk to one another.

Calling XML Web Services

You can call upon XML Web services from within your Windows application, Web application, and class Library projects. Formulating SOAP requests, communicating with remote Web servers using HTTP, and unpackaging the SOAP formatted results might sound like a daunting task, but if you are using Visual Studio .NET to create your projects, it's as simple as can be. All you need to do is to add a reference for a particular remote XML Web service to your project, and then use it like you would any other reference. You do not have to know about SOAP, XML, or HTTP to get the job done. Of course, understanding what's going on behind the scenes is always a good idea. The following steps are taken when your application makes a call to an XML Web service:

1. The developer adds a project reference to the XML Web service.
2. Visual Studio .NET contacts the hosting server to get a description of the service.
3. At runtime, your application makes a call to the XML Web service.
4. .NET creates a proxy class to represent the service, formats a message, and forwards your request to the XML Web service.
5. The proxy class receives a response from the service and unformats the message.
6. The proxy class provides the XML Web services' response to the calling code.

Now let's go over each step in detail to see what's going on. When you add a reference for an XML Web service to your .NET project, Visual Studio .NET learns all that it can about that XML Web service and stores that information within your project. During development, Visual Studio is not in constant contact with that

XML Service, so it needs to take a snapshot of the services' interfaces so that Visual Studio can provide you with *IntelliSense* feedback when you are coding your calls to this service. Visual Studio gathers this information through a process called *discovery*, which you will learn more about in the "Discovery" section later the chapter.

When your application makes a reference to a remote XML Web service, your application creates a proxy class, which is an empty local version of the remote service. To your code, this proxy class appears to be like any other referenced class, but there are some extra features at work inside this class. When your code makes a call to a proxy class, the proxy class must relay this request to the remote XML Web service where the real work takes place. To do this, the proxy class must format your code's request into a SOAP message and send it out via HTTP. When the response returns from the XML Web service in the form of a SOAP message, the proxy class decodes that message and returns to your code the response value using native Visual Studio data types. Because SOAP is an open source protocol, many of the supported data types do not directly match up with Visual Studio data types, so the proxy class often has to translate one data type to another to facilitate this transaction. Figure 8.7 shows this step-by-step process.

SOAP, GET, and POST

XML Web services communicate with their clients via messages sent using the HTTP protocol. As you learned earlier in the discussions on ASP.NET and form data, data is traditionally sent across the Internet using either the **GET** or **POST** method to format the data. These two methods have been around since the dawn

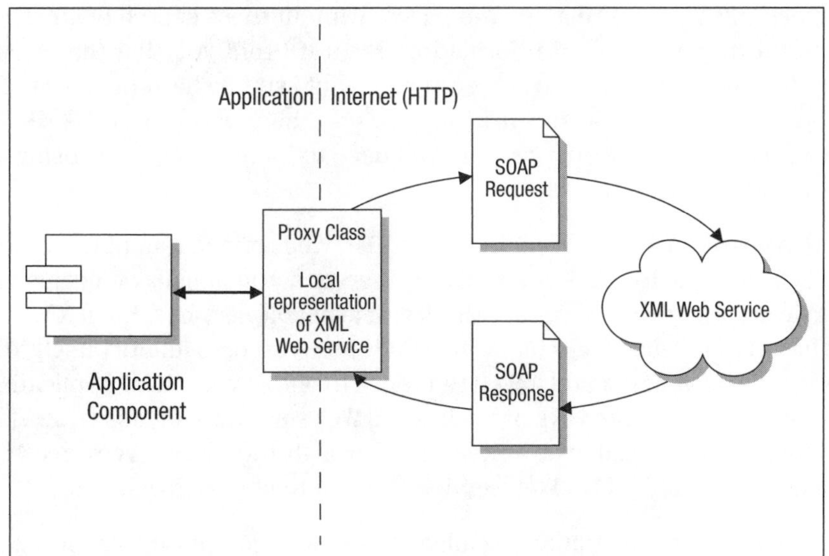

Figure 8.7 Using proxy classes to communicate with XML Web services.

of the Internet age, and although they do a decent job of passing form data to the Web server, they are not really robust enough to pass application data back and forth. SOAP, which uses XML to describe and send data elements, is a far better choice for exchanging application data via the Web. SOAP should be the communication protocol of choice when working with XML Web services. When you add a reference to an XML Web service to your .NET project, the proxy class discovers which protocols an XML Web service supports and formats your messages using the best possible supported protocol.

To support clients that do not use the SOAP protocol, Visual Studio .NET XML Web services are capable of communicating using all three protocols; SOAP, **GET**, and **POST**. By supporting **GET** and **POST**, even simple static HTML pages are capable of making calls to XML Web services, although the results of those requests will appear in the browser without the benefit of formatting. The following URL uses the **GET** method to access my Weather XML Web service:

```
http://mywebserver/Weather/Service1.asmx/GetWeather?ZipCode=22902
```

Using the **GET** method of appending your data values to the end of the URL, you could test your XML Web services by manually entering the URL and parameters into the Address window of any Web browser.

Discovery

Finding information on the Internet can be a challenge at best. Typically when you are looking for a piece of information, you turn to a Web-based search engine. By simply typing in a few keywords, the search engine provides you with a list of hyperlinks to some related Web pages. Without these search engines, you would be lost in a vast sea of information. Even if I told you that the piece of information you want is on Web server X, you would still be hard-pressed to find that needle in the haystack. But if I told you that there was a useful XML Web service on server X, you would have all you need to immediately start using that service in your applications.

How is this possible? Web servers that host XML Web services support a process called discovery, which enables these Web servers to automatically detect installed Web Services and provide visitors with a list of available services. Each XML Web service has a related discovery file, which ends in .vsdisco, to identify itself to the Web server. When you first add a Web reference to one of your .NET applications, you are asked to type in the URL of the hosting Web server. Using this URL, Visual Studio .NET contacts that Web server, and through the discovery process, receives a list of available XML Web services for you to choose from.

There is an industry-wide initiative called Universal Description, Discovery, and Integration (UDDI) that hopes to provide a central database where developers can look to find XML Web services located all over the globe. UDDI is an XML Web service that your applications can query and receive information from on other services. Many major companies, including Microsoft and IBM, support this initiative. You can learn more about UDDI and search its database by visiting its Web site at **www.uddi.org**.

XML Web Service Definition Language (WSDL)

Even when you know exactly where a service is located on the Web, if you do not know the details of what interfaces this service supports and their associated parameters, it is almost impossible to figure out how to use it. In order to create a proxy class that exactly duplicates a service locally in the Visual Studio environment, you need as much detail on these interfaces as possible. Luckily, XML Web services have a way to describe themselves in detail—WSDL.

A WSDL document describes a service's supported interfaces and parameters to a perspective client. Visual Studio .NET uses this information to generate a proxy class for the XML Web service, but non-Visual Studio development languages can also use the WSDL description to gain an understanding of the service. A WSDL document also describes which protocols a service supports and which can include SOAP, **GET**, and **POST**. For each supported protocol, there is a separate section describing the service's interfaces and parameters customized for that protocol.

The XML in XML Web Services

Although it is SOAP that makes it possible for anyone to communicate with your Web Service, within those SOAP messages you will find another open source technology that makes the information your service provides universally understandable: XML. If a Web Service developed in .NET responded with .NET-specific data types, only .NET applications would be able to use it. By formatting the Web Services output using XML, any application is able to interpret your services' results. The following is the XML output of the Weather service, which is wrapped in a SOAP message during transmission:

```
<?xml version="1.0" encoding="utf-8"?>
<string xmlns="http://mywebserver">Its 65 and sunny outside!</string>
```

The requesting application receives the services response formatted with XML. In .NET, the proxy class interprets this data and forwards the message using a **String** data type to the calling code. The data types used in the XML message often have to be converted to data types native to your development environment before you can use them. Take a look at the following WebMethod, which calculates a discount percentage based on the users age:

```
<WebMethod()> Public Function CalcDiscount(ByVal Age As Integer) As Single
    CalcDiscount = Age * 0.005
End Function
```

This function uses the .NET-specific **Single** data type. But take a look at the XML response this WebMethod provides:

```
<?xml version="1.0" encoding="utf-8"?>
<float xmlns="http://tempuri.org/">0.375</float>
```

The **Short** becomes a **<float>** data type in XML. If a .NET proxy class receives this message, it can choose to convert this value back to a **Short** data type, whereas non-.NET development languages that do not use **Short** data types will understand what a float data type is and handle this data accordingly.

XML Web Service Availability Issues

When designing applications that make use of XML Web services, you need to develop a backup plan in case the XML Web services become unavailable. Occasionally, Web servers do fail, whether due to administrative error or malicious hacker attacks. To prevent an XML Web service's unavailability from causing your own application troubles, your code should have a way of dealing with unexpected results or request timeouts. You could cache XML Web service results locally to give yourself some data to fall back on in case later requests fail. You could also create a workaround that hides this missing data.

If you create a Web application that provides a page full of sports scores reported from multiple XML Web services, you could place a message in the spot where a score would normally be letting users know that this data is currently not available. The last thing you want to happen is for your application to crash due to an unavailable XML Web service, so anticipate problems during the design phase and ask yourself, "What should the application do if the XML Web service fails?"

The design phase is also a great time to assess the type of connection your application will have with the enlisted XML Web service and what effects this connection will have on performance. An application running on a home computer with a 56K dial-up connection to the Internet will experience far slower XML Web service response times than an application running on a corporate network with a dedicated T1 line to the Internet. If you come to the conclusion that using a remote XML Web service would result in acceptable response times, you may want to try to host a local copy of this service on your network for a big performance boost. Over the next few years, as broadband access makes its way into houses and offices around the world, the issue of XML Web services performance will fade away, but for now this is a big issue you should address during your application's design phase.

Immediate Solutions

Creating a Web Form

Although Web Forms can be created using any of the Visual Studio .NET development languages, you can only add Web Forms to two of the .NET project types: the ASP.NET Web Application and the ASP.NET XML Web Service. This restriction to Web Form usage is due to the fact that a Web server is required to process these pages, and non-Web project types do not interface with the Web server. You will not be able to add Web Forms to projects such as the class Library and Windows application projects.

The following steps explain how to create an ASP.NET Web Applications project, which includes a Web Form by default:

1. Open Visual Studio .NET, and select File|New Project.
2. In the Project Types window on the left, highlight the Visual Basic Projects folder.
3. Highlight the ASP.NET Web Application icon in the right side of the Templates window.
4. In the Name TextBox below these two windows, enter a name for your Web application project, such as MyFirstWebApp.
5. Ensure that the machine name listed in the Location TextBox is a valid .NET Web server (if you are using a Web server on your local machine, this TextBox should read: "http://localhost").
6. Click OK at the bottom of the New Project window.

When you create a new Web application project, Visual Studio .NET contacts the Web server you entered in Step 5 and coordinates with the Web server to set up a new subdirectory in which to house your project. If the machine named in Step 5 does not have a Web server installed or is using a Web server that is not .NET aware, the project creation will fail.

Once Visual Studio .NET is finished creating the project's directory and starting files, you will be able to see all of the files associated with your Web application project in Visual Studio's Solution Explorer window. The MyFirstWebApp project starts out with the six files listed in Table 8.3 already created for you.

Table 8.3 ASP.NET Web Application default files.

File Name	Description
AssemblyInfo.vb	Contains metadata for your entire project including the Assembly version number.
Global.asax	Contains code for application-level events such as **Application_BeginRequest**.
MyFirstWebApp.vsdisco	Used by the Web server to discover information about XML Web services.
Styles.css	Web page style sheet containing definitions of display tags (font styles, sizes, etc.).
Web.config	Configuration file for Web server options such as authentication and globalization.
WebForm1.aspx	The initial Web Form for your project.

If you want to add a new Web Form to either an open Web application or XML Web service project, all you need to do is to right-click the project's name in the Solution Explorer window, and then select Add|Add Web Form.

Adding Web Controls to a Web Form

You can design ASP.NET Web Form interfaces in the same way that you create Windows interfaces. When you have a Web Form open in design mode, the Toolbox window will feature two panels full of controls that you can use. The HTML panel contains the basic set of HTML controls, and the Web Forms panel contains all of your server-side Web controls. You can add one of these controls to your Web Form by either dragging one from your Toolbox to your form or by selecting a control in the Toolbox and then clicking and dragging your mouse pointer on the form's surface to draw this control on the form.

Web Form Layout Mode

Before you begin adding controls to your Web Form, you need to decide which layout style you will use to place these controls. Each Web Form has a **pageLayout** property that can either be set to **FlowLayout** or **GridLayout**. **FlowLayout** is the traditional way that Web pages are coded and designed. Web browsers read HTML from top to bottom, and then draw the page items in the order they appear in the HTML starting at the top of the browser window. If you are designing a Web Form that has its **pageLayout** property set to **FlowLayout** and you drag a control to the center of this form, you will see that control relocate itself to the upper-left corner of the page.

GridLayout mode uses an advanced browser ability called *absolute positioning* to assign coordinates to page items. When you draw a control on the surface of your Web Form, the corresponding coordinates are recorded inside that control's tag. When your Web Form is in **GridLayout** mode, you will see tiny dots on the surface of your Web Form to aid you in your layout chores. **GridLayout** is selected by default to make Web Form design as easy as possible; you will want to use **GridLayout** for most of your Web Form designs.

Working with Controls and Web Form Layout Modes

The following example shows you how to set the Web Form's layout mode and add various control types to the form's surface. The example also examines a control's properties and appearance:

1. Create a new ASP.NET Web Application project. The project starts with WebForm1 loaded in design mode.
2. Click once on the surface of the Web Form, and then locate the **pageLayout** property in the Properties window. By default this is set to **GridLayout**, and you see tiny dots on the surface of the Web Form.
3. In the Toolbox window, you see a panel named HTML and another named Web Forms. Click the HTML panel to expose its contents.
4. Click and hold the left mouse button on the Text Field control in the HTML panel and drag it over to the center of your Web Form. Notice that this control stays where you place it in the center of the page.
5. Select the Web Forms panel in the Toolbox window. Click and hold your left mouse button on the Button control and drag it over to the surface of your form, placing it directly below the Text Field control. Again, you see that this control stays where you place it.
6. Click once on the surface of your Web Form to deselect the button you placed.
7. In the Property window, change the Web Form's **pageLayout** property to **FlowLayout**. Because the two controls already on the surface of this form were placed in **GridLayout** mode, their tags include coordinates that allow them to stay in place even in **FlowLayout** mode.
8. Again, left-click and hold on the Button control in the Web Forms Toolbox panel and drag this control to the center of the form. When you let go of this control, it relocates itself to the upper-left corner of the Web Form. When the page's layout mode is set to **FlowLayout**, any controls you place on the form's surface will not be assigned coordinates and will instead start stacking at the top of the page.
9. Click once on the Button control added in Step 8. In the Properties window you see all of the display properties for this button. Change the button's **Text** property to say Click Me.

10. Notice that the two Button controls added from the Web Forms panel both have tiny green arrows in their upper-left corners, whereas the TextBox control you added from the HTML panel does not. The little green arrow indicates which controls are server-side Web controls.

Creating Code to Handle Web Control Events

You can add code to the Web Form's code to handle events raised by Web controls hosted in the browser. Web control event code is executed on the Web server. HTML controls do not support server-side event processing, only client-side events using a client-side scripting language such as JavaScript. In the following example, I create a Web Form with a Button on it and add some code to this Button's **Click** event to add a special message to the form when the button is clicked:

1. Create a new ASP.NET Web Application project using Visual Basic as your development language. When the project opens, you see **WebForm1** open in design mode.
2. From the Web Forms panel in the Toolbox, drag a Button control over to the center of your Web Form.
3. Next, drag a Label control and place it below the Button control.
4. Double-click the Button control you placed on your Web Form. The code behind the file opens and your cursor is located within the **Button1_Click** event subroutine. You also see a subroutine named **Page_Load** within this class named **WebForm1**.
5. Enter the following code within the **Button1_Click** subroutine:

```
Label1.Text = TimeOfDay
```

6. Save your Web application by selecting File|Save All.
7. To see this Web Form in action, click the F5 key to run your Web application. A browser window opens and displays the Web Form you created. You will see a Button that reads "Button", and some text below it that reads "Label".
8. Click the button. This triggers the Button's **Click** event within the browser, which in turn causes the Web Form to submit itself back to the Web server. When the Web server is contacted by your Web Form, it sees that the Button's **Click** event caused this postback. It then processes the code in the **Click** event and returns an updated version of the Web page to you. The Label control on the Web Form should now display the current time of day. If you

keep clicking on the Button, the displayed time will be updated. Note that the time displayed is coming from the Web server because this is where the server-side code was processed.

Each Web control has its own associated events, such as the Button's **Click** event and the TextBoxes **TextChanged** event. You can find out which events a control supports by adding that control to your form, and then switching over to the Web Forms code view. At the top left of the code view is a drop-down menu containing a list of all the items in your Web Form. Select your control's name from this list and the drop-down menu to the right will list all of this control's programmable events.

Detecting Postbacks in the **Page_Load** Event

A postback is when a Web page in the user's browser calls back to a copy of itself on the Web server to perform some server-side processing. If you create server-side code for a Button's **Click** event, a postback will occur whenever a user clicks on that Button in the browser. Why would you want to deal with initial page requests differently than you would a postback page request? Every time your Web Form is requested, the **Page_Load** event is fired. If your Web Form requires a lot of initialization processing, such as a database query to request a table of information that is then used to initialize a DataGrid on the Web Form, you will probably not want to continually requery your database and redraw the DataGrid during a postback.

You do not need to redraw or reinitialize the controls on your Web Form during a postback because ASP.NET preserves these controls for you. An unmodified DataGrid, for example, is returned to the browser after a postback with the exact same data displayed. If a user enters some text into a TextBox and then clicks on a button that causes a postback, the text the user entered will still be there when the same page is returned to the user.

When initializing a Web Form, the smart thing to do is to first determine whether the request is a postback within the Web Form's **Page_Load** event; if it is a postback, bypass all of the Web Form's initialization code. The following ASP.NET Web Application example shows you how to detect whether or not a request is a postback by checking the **IsPostBack** value within the Web Form's **Page_Load** event. It also shows how controls on a Web Form preserve their current state during the postback process:

1. Create a new ASP.NET Web Application named PostBackTest.
2. From the Toolbox's Web Forms panel, add a Button control to the center of **WebForm1**, add a TextBox control below this Button, and then add a Label control above this Button.

3. Double-click on the Button and add the following line of code to the **Button1_Click** event:

```
Label1.Text = TimeOfDay
```

4. Add the following code to **WebForm1**'s **Page_Load** event:

```
Private Sub Page_Load(ByVal sender As System.Object, ByVal e As System._
        EventArgs) Handles MyBase.Load
    If IsPostBack Then
        Button1.Text = "POSTBACK"
    Else
        Button1.Text = "INITIAL REQUEST"
    End If
End Sub
```

5. Save your project by selecting File|Save All, and then run your Web Form by pressing the F5 key.
6. When your Web Form first loads in your Web browser, the Button will read "INITIAL REQUEST". This occurs because at the time the Web server was processing the page, the value of **IsPostBack** was **False**.
7. Type your name into the TextBox below the Button.
8. Click the Button and the Web page will submit itself back to the Web server. This time the value of **IsPostBack** will be **True**, which causes the **Text** property of the Button to change. Because the Button control's **Click** event triggered the postback, the code in this **Click** event will also be run, changing the value of the Label control. Note that the page's **Page_Load** event executes before the Button's **Click** event.
9. When the Web page returns to the browser after its postback, the Button will read "POSTBACK", and the Label above it will display the current time of day.
10. Notice that the name you entered into the TextBox in Step 7 is still there. Prior to ASP.NET, Web developers had to create extra code in their page to preserve a control's current values during a postback, but ASP.NET automatically does this for you.

Working with Delayed Web Control Events

Although the Button's **Click** event always triggers an immediate postback to the Web server to process its associated code, other Web controls may have events that, by default, do not trigger a postback when they fire. These events will fire, but their associated server-side code will not be processed until another event explicitly causes a postback. By storing these events and delaying their processing, you can avoid unnecessary calls back to the Web server, which could possibly slow down your Web application and annoy your users.

Web controls that allow you to delay processing their events have an **AutoPostBack** property. By default, this property is set to **False**, which means that when an event fires within this control, a postback is not automatically triggered. You can force these controls to cause a postback by setting their **AutoPostBack** properties to **True**. Let's take a look at a Web Form that uses delayed event processing. In this example, the Web Form is a simple calculator that figures out an item's price with sales tax. To make this a little more interesting, the Web Form features a CheckBox to give customers a 10 percent discount, but this discount only applies if the item's price is greater than $100:

1. Create a new ASP.NET Web Application named DelayedEvents using Visual Basic as your programming language of choice.
2. From the Web Forms panel of the Toolbox window, drag a TextBox control over to the Web Form's upper-left corner. Below this, place a CheckBox control and set its **Text** property to "10% Discount". Above the TextBox, add a Label control and make this control's **Text** value blank (no text). Then, add a Button control below the CheckBox and set its **Text** property to "Calculate Price". When your Web Form design is complete, it should look something like mine in Figure 8.8.
3. Click the CheckBox control and note that its **AutoPostBack** property is set to **False** by default. This control has a **CheckedChanged** event that fires when the box is checked or unchecked. Because **AutoPostBack** is

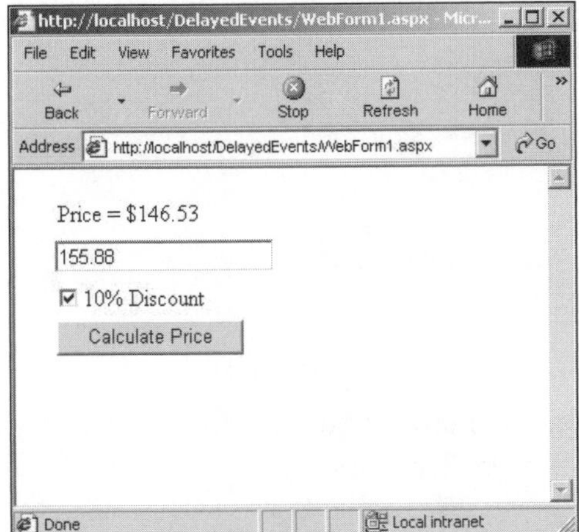

Figure 8.8 The price calculator Web Form.

set to **False**, checking or unchecking this box will not cause an immediate postback, but it will raise the control's event.

4. Double-click the CheckBox control and the code view will open with your cursor inside the **CheckBox1_CheckedChanged** event. Place the following code inside this event:

```
Private Sub CheckBox1_CheckedChanged(ByVal sender As System.Object, _
          ByVal e As System.EventArgs) _
          Handles CheckBox1.CheckedChanged
    Dim StartPrice As Double
    StartPrice = CDbl(TextBox1.Text)
    If CheckBox1.Checked = True And StartPrice < 100 Then
        Label1.Text = "ERROR! Price under $100!"
        CheckBox1.Checked = False
    End If
End Sub
```

5. At the top of the code view window, click the left drop-down menu and select the **Button1** item. In the right drop-down menu, click the **Click** event. This adds a **Button1_Click** event to your code and places your cursor inside this event. Add the following code to the **Click** event:

```
Private Sub Button1_Click(ByVal sender As System.Object, ByVal e As _
      System.EventArgs) Handles Button1.Click
    Dim FinalPrice As Double
    Dim StartPrice As Double
    StartPrice = CDbl(TextBox1.Text)
    If CheckBox1.Checked = True Then
        'Calculate price WITH 10% discount
        FinalPrice = (StartPrice - (StartPrice * 0.1)) + _
             (StartPrice * 0.04)
    Else
        'Calculate price WITHOUT discount
        FinalPrice = StartPrice + (StartPrice * 0.04)
    End If
    Label1.Text = "Price = " & Format(FinalPrice, "$#,##0.00")
End Sub
```

6. Select File|Save All to save your project. Press F5 to run your project.
7. When your Web Form finishes loading in the browser, type "45.95" into the TextBox control, and then click Button. The Label at the top reports that the item's price is $47.79.
8. Click the CheckBox to check that control, and then click the Button control. When the Web page finishes processing, the price will still be

$47.79 and the CheckBox will be unchecked. When you checked its box, the **CheckedChange** event fired but did not process immediately. When you clicked Button, the Button's **Click** event fired, but back at the Web server, the CheckBoxes **CheckedChange** event was processed before the Button's **Click** event, and this event determined that the item price was under $100, did not qualify for the discount, and therefore unchecked the CheckBox control. When the Button's **Click** event was processed next, the value of **CheckBox1.Checked** was **False**, so the discount was not applied. Notice that you never saw the "ERROR" message in the Label control because the Button's **Click** event replaced this message with the "Price" message before the page completed processing.

9. Change the item's price in the TextBox to 145.95 and click Button. The item's price is reported to be $151.79.
10. Check the CheckBox to enable the discount, and then click Button. Because the price is more than $100, the CheckBoxes **CheckedChanged** event does not uncheck this box, and the Button's **Click** event includes the discount in its calculation.
11. Close your browser window, which should take Visual Studio .NET out of Debug mode and place you back in the code view window.
12. At the top of the code view window, click the WebForm1.aspx tab to look at the Web Form in design mode.
13. Click the CheckBox control, and then change its **AutoPostBack** property to **True**.
14. Save your project, and then run it by pressing F5.
15. When the Web Form loads in your browser, enter the value 55.88 in the TextBox.
16. Click the CheckBox to check it. The **CheckedChanged** event then fires and triggers an immediate postback. Because the value of **TextBox1** is less than $100, the CheckBox unchecks itself and places an error message in **Label1**.
17. Change the value of **TextBox1** to 155.88, and then try to check the CheckBox. Again this event triggers a postback to the Web server, but this time the box stays checked because the value of **TextBox1** is more than $100. With a local Web server, you will not have to wait long for the postback to process this event, but if your browser does not have a fast connection to the Web server, waiting for a postback can severely affect your application's performance.

When working with delayed event processing, you need to take these delays into account when processing the event. For instance, if I check the discount CheckBox, and then realize that my price is less than $100 and uncheck the

CheckBox, this should not result in an error on the Web server. In the calculator example, I avoid raising an error in this situation by checking the CheckBox's value as well as the TextBox's value in the **CheckedChanged** event. If a delayed event raises an error that affects the event that caused the postback (the Button's **Click** event in this example), try to work around this problem and avoid sending a blank result back to the user. Users will become frustrated if they ask for a calculation and they receive an error message after a long pause. Instead, try to fix these problems for the user, and hopefully you will avoid additional postback requests.

Using the DataGrid Web Control

Visual Studio .NET comes with a Web control version of the DataGrid control, which you may be familiar with from Windows Form development projects. This control has the ability to display tables of data to the user and provide view-management features such as the ability to sort columns. This control represents an amazing breakthrough in Web development because before there were server-side Web controls, developers had to create pages and pages of server-side code to draw out database tables and make them easily manageable and updateable. With the DataGrid Web control, a developer can display a table of data within the user's browser with only a few lines of code.

To show you how you can use the DataGrid control on your Web Forms, I am going to create a Web page that displays a table of data from a sample database. All you have to provide the DataGrid is a data source for it to display, and all of the hard work of drawing tables and formatting HTML text is handled by the control. You can also give your DataGrid some advanced functions with only a few mouse clicks. These advanced features include the ability to sort columns and page through tables of data a few records at a time. Try the following example to see how easy it is to use the DataGrid Web control on your Web Forms:

1. Create an ASP.NET Web Application named DataGrid under the Visual Basic Project folder.
2. From the Web Forms panel of the Toolbox window, select the DataGrid controls, and then drag it over to the surface of your Web Form. After you drop this control, resize its edges so that it fills most of the visible portion of the Web Form in the design view.
3. Click the DataGrid and look at the Properties window. Under the AlternatingItemStyle header you will find a **BackColor** property. Set this property to be the lightest shade of blue (when you click this property's value column, a color-picker window opens and displays a palette of colors to choose from). Note that every other row in the DataGrid control is the

color you selected. This feature makes it a little bit easier to read rows and rows of data.

4. In the Properties window under the Behavior section, you will find the **AllowSorting** property. By default this is set to **False**, but let's change this to **True**.
5. In the Properties window under the Paging section, change the **AllowPaging** property to **True**, and then set the **PageSize** property to 5. This property limits the number of rows of data returned to the user to five. The first time the user requests this Web Form, the first five rows of data returned by the query will be displayed. The user will be able to then ask for the next five rows of data if he or she wants to see more.

TIP: *If your DataGrid control is dealing with large tables of data, using the **AllowPaging** and **PageSize** properties is an excellent choice because these properties limit the amount of data that is rendered and transmitted across the Web, resulting in fast page response times.*

NOTE: *At this time, I am not going to explain the intricacies of .NET data access because you will find plenty of details in Chapter 15. Step 7 uses the Server Explorer window to locate a database table for display in the DataGrid. If you do not have any data connections defined in the Server Explorer window, refer to Chapter 15 to find out how to add data connections.*

---

6. From the Server Explorer window, expand one of your database connections, and then below that connection expand the Tables tree. Left-click and hold on one of these tables, drag it over to the surface of your Web Form, and drop it. You will see an **OleDbConnection1** and an **OleDbDataAdapter1** component added below your Web Form.
7. From the Toolbox window, click the Data panel. Drag a DataSet component over to your Web Form and drop it. A window named Add Dataset will pop up asking you if you are adding a typed or untyped dataset. Select the Untyped option and click OK. You should then see a DataSet1 component below your Web Form.
8. Double-click the surface of your Web Form, and the code behind opens. Place your mouse cursor inside the **Page_Load** event and add the following code to it:

```
Private Sub Page_Load(ByVal sender As System.Object, ByVal e As System._
        EventArgs) Handles MyBase.Load
    If IsPostBack Then
        'Do NOT reload the DataSet, Postback preserves the data
    Else
        OleDbDataAdapter1.Fill(DataSet1)
```

```
            DataGrid1.DataSource = DataSet1
            DataGrid1.DataBind()
        End If
    End Sub
```

9. Notice that in the **Page_Load** event, I do not contact the database and initialize the DataGrid during a postback, only during the initial page request. Save your project by selecting File|Save All.
10. Run your Web Form by pressing F5. When the browser finishes loading your page, you should see the table of data you selected in Step 7 displayed on the Web Form. Figure 8.9 shows an example of a Web browser using the DataGrid control to display a table of data. The column names at the top of this table of data will be hyperlinks that you can click to sort a column. Earlier, you set the **PageSize** to 5, so if your select table of data returns more than five rows, you will only see the first five rows and a left and right arrow at the bottom of those rows. These arrows allow you to ask for the next or previous five records in the table.
11. Right-click the surface of the browser window, and select View Source. This is the raw HTML that the Web server provided to the browser. You will see a lot of HTML tags, most of which were generated by the DataGrid control. The DataGrid control also generated a JavaScript function to

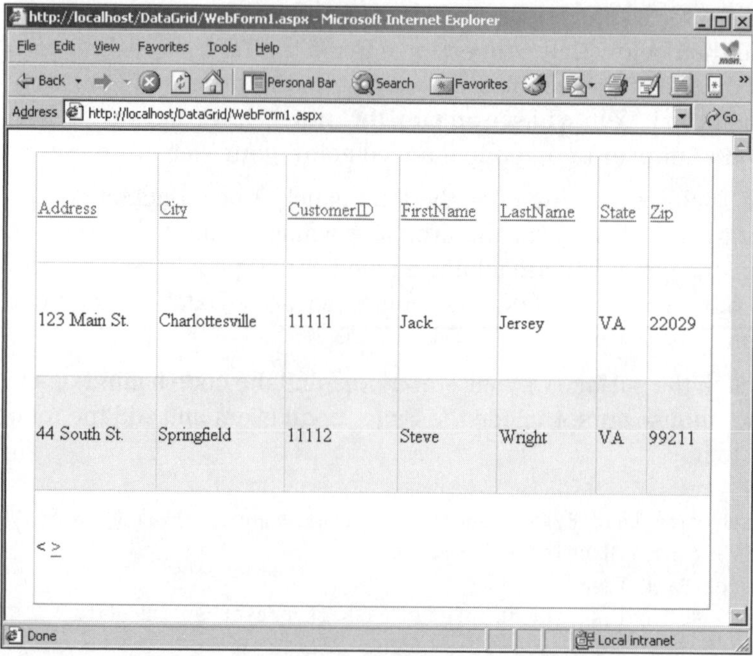

Figure 8.9 A DataGrid control shown in the Web browser.

handle the postback function on the client-side. If you can imagine trying to create this raw HTML page manually, you will understand why server-side Web controls are so powerful and how they will save you hours, if not days, of development time.

Working with the Validation Web Controls

There will be times when you will want to check the value of control on a Web Form without triggering a postback to the Web server. To accomplish this task, you need to execute some code on the client-side within the browser window. Prior to ASP.NET, your Web development team would have needed a developer skilled in JavaScript coding to create this code, but currently, with the help of a powerful set of validation Web controls, you can create this client-side code with a few simple mouse clicks.

The following exercise shows you how to use three of the available validation controls. Setting up these controls is as simple as placing a control on your Web Form and editing a few of its properties. When you observe these controls in action within the browser, you will see that these controls generate JavaScript code to perform their magic on the client-side:

1. Create an ASP.NET Web Application using Visual Basic, and name it WebValidation.
2. From the Web Forms panel of the Toolbox window, select the TextBox control and drag it over to the upper-left corner of your Web Form. Add two more TextBox controls directly below it for a total of three TextBox controls.
3. Drag a RegularExpressionValidator control over to the center of the Web Form. Set its **ControlToValidate** property to **TextBox1**. Next, edit its **ValidationExpression** property, and select the U.S. Social Security Number from the list of possible expressions. Set the **ErrorMessage** property to "TextBox1 must be a valid Social Security Number". Drag this control up, and place it to the right of **TextBox1**.
4. Drag a RangeValidator control over to the center of your Web Form. Set the RangeValidator control's **ControlToValidate** property to **TextBox2**. Next, set its **Type** property to **Integer**, set the **MaximumValue** property to 10, and set the **MinimumValue** property to 1. Finally, set the **ErrorMessage** property to "Must be a number between 1 and 10". Drag this control over to the right of **TextBox2**.

5. Drag a CompareValidator over to the center of your Web Form. Set its **ControlToValidate** property to **TextBox3** and its **ControlToCompare** property to **TextBox2**. Set the **Type** property to **Integer**. Verify that the **Operator** property is set to **Equal**, its default value. Finally, set the **ErrorMessage** property to "2 and 3 are NOT equal". When you are done setting this control, drag it over to the right of **TextBox3**.
6. Select File|Save All to save your project, and then press F5 to run your Web Form. When the Web Form finishes loading, you will see three TextBox controls on it, but you will not see any of your validation controls.
7. In **TextBox1**, type in your name, and then press the Tab key. The RegularExpressionValidator error message turns on, letting you know that you did not enter a valid Social Security Number.
8. Enter the value 99 in **TextBox2** and press the Tab key. The RangeValidator error message lights up telling you that you did not enter a number between 1 and 10.
9. In **TextBox3**, enter the number 6 and press the Tab key. The CompareValidator's error message lets you know that the values of **TextBox2** and **TextBox3** are not equal.
10. Tab back to **TextBox1** and enter a valid Social Security Number (###-##-####). Tab to the next field and the error message disappears.
11. In **TextBox2**, enter the number 6 and press the Tab key. The remaining two error messages disappear.

If you look at the raw HTML behind the Web page displayed in the browser, you will see all of the JavaScript code that was generated for you by these validation controls. Not only do these controls save you time by creating source code for you, they also greatly reduce the need to post a Web Form back to the server to validate and check these control values. The more you minimize the back and forth communications between the Web browser and the server, the better your application will perform, and the happier your users will be.

Caching Data in the Web Server's Session

Because of the connectionless nature of Web communications, every request received by the Web server is treated as a request from a brand new user. This makes it difficult to know where users have been and what information has already been provided to them. Take an e-commerce Web site with a shopping cart feature for instance. Without some way to persist which items a visitor has placed into his shopping cart as the user navigates from one page to another, the shopping cart will always remain empty. In order to remember which items a user selected as he travels from page to page, the Web site needs to save this information using a client-side cookie, a database, a text file on the server, or a user's session on the Web server.

A user's Web server session is a special area in memory that is directly tied to an individual visitor to the Web site. If the Web server currently has 10 visitors, there will be 10 sessions being stored in memory. Each Web session has a timeout period. If a visitor does not return to the Web server and request another Web page within the designated timeout period, the session and all of its data is destroyed by the Web server to make room for new sessions. By default, the session's timeout length is 20 minutes, although Web server administrators can increase or decrease this value as needed.

For Web site developers, the Web server's session provides a powerful tool to persist data associated with a particular user. Imagine that you are developing an online bookstore, and you want to store the name of the book a user is ordering while you present him with a Web page asking for his mailing address and credit card information. The following example shows a Button's **Click** event that would write this data to the user's session:

```
Session("BookName") = strBookName
```

As long as the user stays active on this Web site, the session will remain active and will remember the name of the book the user selected. To access this information in the Web server's session, all you need to do is assign to it to a variable like so:

```
StrBookToOrder = Session("BookName")
```

A developer could also opt to store the book's title in a client-side cookie, but if the user has cookies disabled in his browser, this plan would fail. You could also use a database in which to create a permanent or temporary user account, and then add books to that account to persist the data. Unfortunately, database calls come at a high price in terms of application performance, so this may not be the best choice for a visitor that may or may not actually purchase all of the books he is looking at. Storing data in the Web server's session is the fastest and most efficient way to persist this data. Access to data stored within a session is almost instantaneous because the session is directly connected to the Web server that is responsible for processing your Web Form. If the user abandons his shopping spree and logs off, the Web server will delete the session data after the timeout period expires. This feature eliminates the problem of cleaning up unneeded cookies or data stored in a database.

Testing and Debugging Web Forms

Not only can you design your Web Forms in the powerful Visual Studio .NET environment, but you can also use the same debugging features that you use to test other Visual Studio .NET applications. When you run your Web Form, Visual Studio .NET connects to the hosting Web server and allows you to debug your server-side code just like Windows application code. This means that when the Web server is processing a part of your Web Form, you have the ability to use Visual Studio's debugging windows and breakpoints. You will not be able to use Visual Studio's debugging facilities to track down problems that occur within the browser, such as problems with client-side JavaScript code.

Breakpoints and Debugging Tools

In the following exercise, I use many of the familiar Visual Studio .NET debugging features to test and debug a simple Web Form. I place some breakpoints in the code, and then view the form's current values using the Locals window. You can also step through your code or jump to a different line of execution:

1. Create a new ASP.NET Web Application using Visual Basic as your development language.
2. Add a Button and a Label control to **WebForm1**'s surface from the Web Forms panel of the Toolbox.
3. Double-click the Button to access its **Click** event, and add the following code:

```
Private Sub Button1_Click(ByVal sender As System.Object, ByVal e As_
      System.EventArgs) Handles Button1.Click
   Dim AverageScore As Double
   Dim ScoreA, ScoreB, ScoreC, ScoreD As Double
   ScoreA = 87.5
   ScoreB = 90.2
   ScoreC = 97.4
   ScoreD = 78
   AverageScore = (ScoreA + ScoreB + ScoreC + ScoreD) / 4
   Label1.Text = "Average Score = " & CStr(AverageScore)
End Sub
```

4. In the code window, locate the **Page_Load** event, and add the following line of code to it:

```
Label1.Text = "Click on the button"
```

5. Save your project by selecting File|Save All.
6. Add a breakpoint on the line of code added to the **Page_Load** event in Step 4 by left-clicking once on the gray bar to the left of this line of code.

7. Add another breakpoint in the Button's **Click** event where the **ScoreA** variable is set to 87.5.
8. Press F5 to run your Web Form. The browser will open while the Web server is processing your page. When the server encounters the breakpoint within your **Page_Load** event, your application will enter break mode, and the current line of code will be highlighted in yellow. In break mode, you can step through your code by pressing F8, or you can tell the page to continue processing normally by pressing F5.
9. Press F5 to continue processing the page. The browser will finish loading your page, and you will see the message "Click on the button" below the Button.
10. Click the Button on the form. This action causes the Web Form to postback to the server to process the **Click** event. Again, you will enter break mode, and again the line with the breakpoint in the **Page_Load** event will be highlighted. Press F5 to continue processing the page. Processing will pause again when the breakpoint in the **Click** event is encountered.
11. Press F8 to step forward one line of code to the **ScoreB** variable initialization line.
12. Open the Locals debugging window by selecting Debug|Windows|Locals. In this window, you will see all of the variables currently in scope and their current values. **ScoreB**, **ScoreC**, and **ScoreD** will all have a value of zero because their lines have not yet been processed. **ScoreA** will have a value of 87.5, and this value will be in red because it was just changed in the previous line of code. Press F8 once to see the **ScoreB** value change and turn red.
13. If you expand the tree named Me in the Locals window, you will be able to view the values of the items on your Web Form, such as the **Button1** and **Label1** control.
14. In the Locals window, click the current value for **ScoreA**, change it to 33.1, and then right-click on the line that computes the **AverageScore**. Select Set Next Statement.
15. Press F8 once. Processing skips over the **ScoreB**, **ScoreC**, and **ScoreD** initialization lines, processes the **AverageScore** computation, and then stops on the line that sets the **Label1**'s **Text** value. Hover your mouse pointer over any of the **AverageScore** variable names in the code, and you should see its current value. Press F5 to finish processing the page.

You have the ability to set watches on variables within your Web Form or set conditional breakpoints within your code. The ability to interactively debug your Web Forms is a major improvement over the last version of ASP, where most developers resorted to writing debugging messages to the browser window to trap errant code or page failures.

Web Forms **Trace** Property

If you are looking at a Web Form in design mode, you will see a property named **Trace** in the Properties window. By default, this property is set to **False**, but if you set it to **True**, your Web Form will provide a wealth of debugging and testing information for you to see in the browser. You will be able to see what request format was used to call your Web Form and how long different phases of your Web Form's processing took to execute. All of the header information that came with the request will be visible as well as the current values of the Web server variables. This Trace information can provide you with some valuable insight into what information your Web Form is processing and what kind of performance you are getting out of your Web Form. Figure 8.10 shows an example of a Web Form's browser output with its **Trace** property set to **True**.

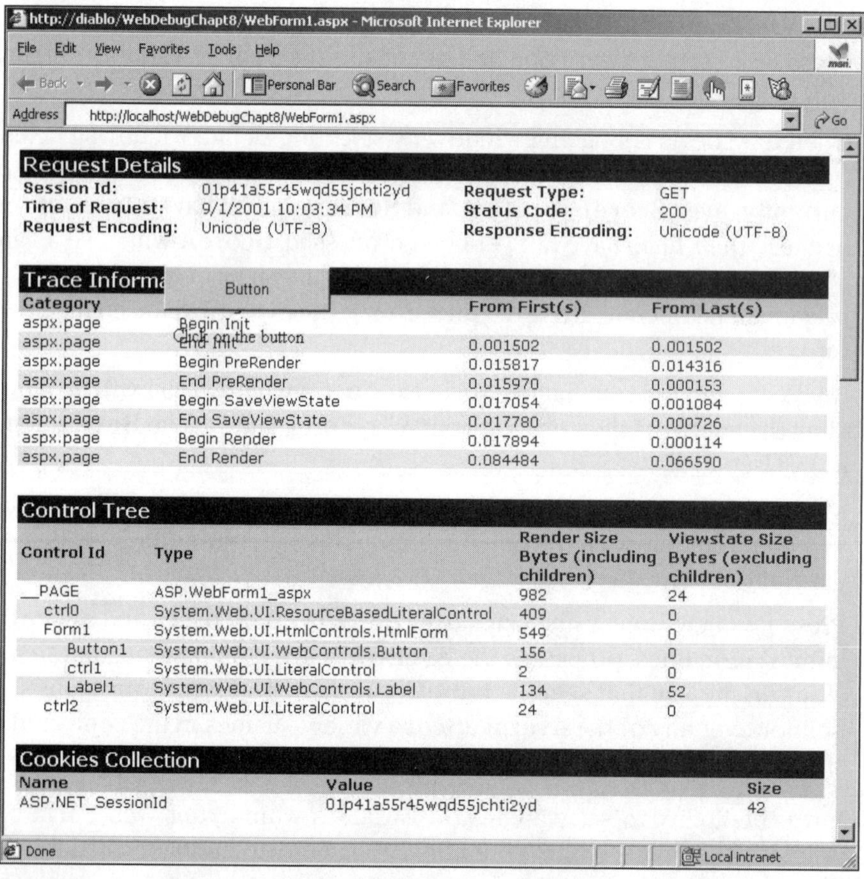

Figure 8.10 Web Form's output with **Trace** turned on.

Creating an XML Web Service

XML Web services play a very important role in the .NET vision of the future, and any developer working with Visual Studio .NET should be familiar with how XML Web services work and how to create them. Among the many exciting features of XML Web services is the fact that they are incredibly easy to create, as you are about to discover. You can use any .NET programming language to create your XML Web service, but in my example, I will use Visual Basic, which just about any developer should be able to understand.

The BookService

To illustrate how easy it is to create an XML Web service, I am going to create one that exposes a simple object named **Book** to the world. With the obvious exception of the **<WebMethod()>** tag added to every property and function, this object will look exactly like a Book object created in a class Library project. This is because XML Web services are not about changing the way you program, only the communication methods you use to make your properties and methods accessible to the outside world. Remember, because XML Web services make themselves available via HTTP and the Web, you need to host these services on a Web server such as Microsoft's IIS. Try the following example, which steps you through creating and running your first XML Web service:

1. Create a new ASP.NET Web Service project named BookService using Visual Basic as the development language. Visual Studio .NET will communicate with your selected Web server to set up a project directory on that server.
2. When the project finishes loading, the main XML Web service file, Service1.asmx in the Solution Explorer window, will open in design view. Click once on the XML Web services surface. In the Properties window, change the **Name** property from **Service1** to **Book**. Your class is now named **Book**.
3. Right-click the surface of the design view, and select View Code to access the source code for your service. Notice the **Inherits** line directly below the class declaration line, which shows that your XML Web service class is inherited from the **System.Web.Services.WebService** class.
4. In your **Book** class, add the following three functions:

```
<WebService(Namespace:="http://microsoft.com/webservices/")> _
       Public Class Book
    Inherits System.Web.Services.WebService

    <WebMethod()> Public Function BookName() As String
        BookName = "Visual Studio .NET Black Book"
    End Function
```

```
    <WebMethod()> Public Function BuyBooks(ByVal Quantity As Integer) _
          As Double
        Dim TotalCost As Double
        TotalCost = 49.99 * CDbl(Quantity)
        TotalCost = TotalCost + CalcTax(TotalCost)
        'Add shipping and handling to TotalCost
        TotalCost = TotalCost + 5.99
        BuyBooks = Format(TotalCost, "###,##0.00")
    End Function

    Public Function CalcTax(ByVal TotalCost As Double) As Double
        'Internal function to calculate the total tax
        CalcTax = TotalCost * 0.04
    End Function

End Class
```

5. Notice that only two of the functions you are creating have **<WebMethod()>** tags. You should also note that the **BuyBooks** function requires an input parameter to do its job.
6. Save your project by selecting File|Save All.
7. XML Web services do not directly define user interfaces like Web Forms do. XML Web services are designed to support other applications, and like class Library projects, are not meant to stand alone. Luckily, in order to support the discovery process where developers locate and learn about XL Web services, a .NET XML Web service will create some Web-based interfaces for you to examine and test your services without creating an external test application. Simply press F5 to run your XML Web service project.
8. Your Web browser will open, and you will see the URL path to your XML Web service in the Address box. At the top of this page, you will see the name of the class, **Book**, and below it the two functions made public with the **<WebMethod()>** tag, **BookName** and **BuyBooks**. You will also see a hyperlink near the top of the page, which shows you the Service Description, or WSDL information. Take a look at Figure 8.11 to see what this page looks like.
9. Click the **BuyBooks** hyperlink. The next Web page you see describes the **BuyBooks** function of the BookService XML Web service. The bottom half of the page shows potential developers how the SOAP, **GET**, and **POST** requests and responses will be formatted when using this interface. This information is helpful if you are not using Visual Studio .NET to access XML Web services. The top half of this Web page allows you to test your **BuyBooks** function by providing you with a TextBox where you can enter

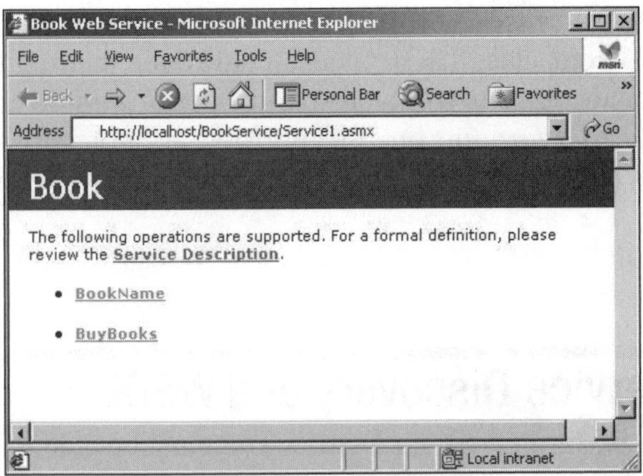

Figure 8.11 The BookService discovery page.

the required **Quantity** parameter. Enter the number **2** into this TextBox, and click Invoke.

10. A new browser window opens, and you see an XML message displayed. This is the response from the XML Web service based on your input parameter. When provided a **Quantity** parameter of 2, the **BuyBooks** function calculated the total price of this transaction to be 109.97, which includes sales tax and shipping and handling. Even though you cannot see the **CalcTax** function as one of the XML Web services interfaces, this function is available to the **BuyBooks** function.

Migrating Class Libraries to XML Web Services

Because XML Web services communicate differently than a class Library, you will not be able to add XML Web services or the **<WebMethod()>** tag to an existing class Library project. If you want to migrate an existing class Library project to an XML Web service, there are only a few simple steps you need to perform:

1. Create a new ASP.NET Web Service project using the same development language you used to create the class Library.
2. Copy the code from your class Library project and paste it into your XML Web service source code file ending in .asmx.
3. Add the **<WebMethod()>** tag to the beginning of every property and method declaration line that you want to make available via the Web.

If you do not add the **<WebMethod()>** tag to a property or method, that code will not be directly accessible via the XML Web services interface, but your code inside the XML Web service will still be able to enlist these nonpublic functions. Because XML Web services often have a wider audience than a class Library, you will probably want to limit the interfaces to your service more than you would a class Library. For example, if your class Library has an **AddUser** method that allows callers to add new user accounts to a database, you may not want to make this same method available to everyone on the Internet. By not adding a **<WebMethod()>** tag to this method, you prevent direct access to it via HTTP calls.

Exploring XML Web Service Discovery and WSDL

In order to use an XML Web service in your application, you must be able to:

- Locate the XML Web service's host
- Discover which services that host provides
- Select and understand a service's interfaces and parameters

To start, you have to know where on the Internet to locate this service. You may find this out through an XML Web service lookup service, such as **www.uddi.org**, or through a service's vendor that provides you with the URL to its Web server. Next, you need to find out which services that Web server is making available to you. Many times this information will be provided to you along with the URL to the server, but sometimes you may only know the server's name and not the full path to its hosted services.

XML Web Service Discovery

To find out which services are being hosted, you can simply query that server's discovery file. In an ASP.NET project, you will see a file in your Solution Explorer ending in .vsdisco. As you add XML Web services to your project, this file is automatically updated with the necessary descriptive data. To query a locally installed Web server that is hosting a project named BookService, you could open a browser window and type in the following URL:

```
http://localhost/BookService/BookService.vsdisco
```

In response to this request, the Web server will return a file of XML describing the XML Web services housed within this project. If there were two services in the BookService project, BookInfo and Customers, the discovery file might look like this:

```
<?xml version="1.0" encoding="utf-8" ?>
<discovery xmlns="http://schemas.xmlsoap.org/disco/">
  <contractRef ref="http://localhost/BookService/BookInfo.asmx?wsdl" _
      docRef="http://localhost/BookService/BookInfo.asmx" _
```

```
      xmlns="http://schemas.xmlsoap.org/disco/scl/" />
  <contractRef ref="http://localhost/BookService/Customers.asmx?wsdl" _
      docRef="http://localhost/BookService/Customers.asmx" _
      xmlns="http://schemas.xmlsoap. org/disco/scl/" />
</discovery>
```

This XML file tells you that there are two XML Web services hosted, BookInfo and Customers. You are also provided with a URL to query each of these services to discover more information about their interfaces and parameters. This information is provided in a service's WSDL.

The WSDL

Once you know where the actual XML Web service file is located (in .NET, these files end in .asmx), you can query that file to obtain its WSDL information. You can obtain this data using any Web browser by entering the URL path to the XML Web service followed by ?wsdl. The following is an example of a WSDL query:

```
http://localhost/BookService/BookInfo.asmx?wsdl
```

The XML Web service would respond back with another XML file describing itself. Take a look at the following example of a WSDL file:

```
<?xml version="1.0" encoding="utf-8"?>
<definitions xmlns:s="http://www.w3.org/2001/XMLSchema"_
   xmlns:http="http://schemas.xmlsoap.org/wsdl/http/" _
   xmlns:mime="http://schemas.xmlsoap.org/wsdl/mime/" _
   xmlns:tm="http://microsoft.com/wsdl/mime/textMatching/" _
   xmlns:soap="http://schemas.xmlsoap.org/wsdl/soap/" _
   xmlns:soapenc="http://schemas.xmlsoap.org/soap/encoding/" _
   xmlns:s0="http://microsoft.com/webservices/" _
   targetNamespace="http://microsoft.com/webservices/" _
   xmlns="http://schemas.xmlsoap.org/wsdl/">
  <types>
    <s:schema attributeFormDefault="qualified" _
      elementFormDefault="qualified" _
      targetNamespace="http://microsoft.com/webservices/">
      <s:element name="BuyBooks">
        <s:complexType>
          <s:sequence>
            <s:element minOccurs="1" maxOccurs="1" name="Quantity" type=_
              "s:int" />
          </s:sequence>
        </s:complexType>
      </s:element>
      <s:element name="BuyBooksResponse">
```

```
            <s:complexType>
              <s:sequence>
                <s:element minOccurs="1" maxOccurs="1" name="BuyBooksResult" _
                  type="s:double" />
              </s:sequence>
            </s:complexType>
          </s:element>
          <s:element name="string" nillable="true" type="s:string" />
          <s:element name="double" type="s:double" />
        </s:schema>
      </types>
      <message name="BuyBooksSoapIn">
        <part name="parameters" element="s0:BuyBooks" />
      </message>
      <message name="BuyBooksSoapOut">
        <part name="parameters" element="s0:BuyBooksResponse" />
      </message>
      <portType name="BookSoap">
        <operation name="BuyBooks">
          <input message="s0:BuyBooksSoapIn" />
          <output message="s0:BuyBooksSoapOut" />
        </operation>
      </portType>
      <binding name="BookSoap" type="s0:BookSoap">
        <soap:binding transport="http://schemas.xmlsoap.org/soap/http" style=_
            "document" />
        <operation name="BuyBooks">
          <soap:operation soapAction="http://microsoft.com/webservices/_
              BuyBooks" style="document" />
          <input>
            <soap:body use="literal" />
          </input>
          <output>
            <soap:body use="literal" />
          </output>
        </operation>
      </binding>
      <service name="Book">
        <port name="BookSoap" binding="s0:BookSoap">
          <soap:address location="http://localhost/BookService/Service1.asmx" _
            />
        </port>
      </service>
    </definitions>
```

This is an abbreviated example of a WSDL file provided by the BookService XML Web service you created earlier. To condense this file, I removed the **GET** and **POST <message>**, **<portType>**, and **<binding>** information tags. The tags provide similar information to the SOAP sections except in a format that clients using **GET** or **POST** requests would adhere to. A WSDL provides a great deal of redundant information in order to make a service available to the widest possible audience.

If this is your first exposure to an XML message, you might feel a bit overwhelmed, so let's start at the top of this file and examine the information that is being provided.The very first tag lets you know which version of XML tagging is being used. Following this section is the **<definitions>** tag, which provides URL links to resources on the Web that define the tags used within the message. The next section of the message starts with the **<type>** tag and describes the remaining messages schema and major elements. Notice that the **BuyBooks** element has a subelement named **Quantity** that is of type **int**. This directly matches up with the **BuyBooks** function's **Integer** parameter named **Quantity**. The **BuyBooksResponse** element also has a subelement, **BuyBooksResult,** which is of type **dbl**. This is the **Double** data type that the **BuyBooks** function replies with.

The remainder of the WSDL message describes the SOAP messaging format for both the request and the XML Web service's response. With this information, developers or the tool they are using should be able to format a valid SOAP message to send a request to an XML Web service. They will also have all the information necessary to decode the XML Web services response message in SOAP format. If you are worried about how you are going to work this into your application, don't be! The Visual Studio .NET development environment will handle the discovery and WSDL processing steps for you, and you will never have to look at these XML files if you do not want to. You won't even have to format your requests using SOAP because this will all be made transparent to you.

Accessing an XML Web Service from an Application

It's an XML Web service's lot in life to be a supporting actor and not the main act. XML Web services can be used by both Web and Windows applications. Knowing how to use an XML Web service from your applications will not only give you a better idea of how XML Web services work, but also how Visual Studio .NET simplifies your dealings with these services and handles all of the communication and message formatting complexity for you.

To see how simple it is to use an XML Web service in your applications, try the following example. The project you will create uses the BookService XML Web service created in the "Creating an XML Web service" solution, so if you have not already created this service, do so now. The BookService must be hosted on an available Web server that the Windows application you are about to create can access:

1. Under Visual Basic Projects, create a new Windows application named BookOrders.
2. From the Windows Forms panel of the Toolbox window, drag a TextBox control over to the upper-left corner of the Windows Form. Below this, add a Button control, and below the Button add a Label control. Set both the TextBox and Label control's **Text** properties to be blank.
3. To add a reference to the BookService, in the Solution Explorer window, right-click the BookOrders project name, and select Add Web Reference. A window named Add Web Reference opens. This window looks like a Web browser because it has an Address box at the top and some of the familiar browser buttons next to it like Refresh and Back. There are two panes below the Address box. The right pane, named Available references, will be blank at the moment, whereas the left pane will feature links to the Microsoft UDDI site to help you search for XML Web services on the Internet.
4. In the Address TextBox, type the URL pointing to the actual XML Web service, BookService. If this service is hosted on your local machine, the URL should look like this:

```
http://localhost/BookService/Service1.asmx
```

5. After you type the XML Web service's URL, press Enter. Visual Studio .NET will contact this XML Web service, and in the left pane, you will see a Web page listing the functions associated with this service. The right pane will provide links to the WSDL information and documentation for the located service. Click the Add Reference button at the bottom of this window. You will see a Web References folder underneath your BookOrders project in the Solution Explorer window. If you expand this folder, you will see there is a reference to the Web server that is hosting the BookService.
6. On the Windows form, double-click the Button control to access its **Click** event code. Add the following code to the **Click** event:

```
Private Sub Button1_Click(ByVal sender As System.Object, ByVal e As _
      System.EventArgs) Handles Button1.Click
    If Not (IsNumeric(TextBox1.Text)) Then
        MsgBox("ERROR! Please enter an integer")
        Exit Sub
    End If
    Dim GetCost As New localhost.Book()
    Dim BookCount As Integer
```

```
        Dim FinalPrice As Double
        BookCount = CInt(TextBox1.Text)
        FinalPrice = GetCost.BuyBooks(BookCount)
        Label1.Text = "Cost = " & Format(FinalPrice, "$###,##0.00")
    End Sub
```

7. Because your application already holds a reference to the Web server, using this service is just like using any other class reference. In the **Click** event, I **Dim** a variable named **GetCost** to be a new instance of **localhost.Book()**, which is the name of the Web server hosting the service followed by the class name within the XML Web service. A single application can hold multiple references to XML Web services hosted on multiple Web servers.
8. Save your project and run it by pressing F5. When the Windows Form is loaded, enter the number **4** in the TextBox, and then click Button. After a brief pause, your Windows Form will display the results of the price calculation, which will be $213.95 for four books.

As you can see, making calls to XML Web services is so simple that you might forget you are even using an XML Web service hosted on a remote machine. When creating this sample application, you never once had to look at any XML tags or SOAP messages. Visual Studio .NET did all of this for you. If you wanted to access an XML Web service from an ASP.NET Web Application, you would follow the exact same steps to reference that service, and then use it in your code.

Testing and Debugging XML Web Services

XML Web services are not intended to run alone, so you need a way to test your services that lets you simulate making requests from remote clients. Visual Studio .NET developers have a great many debugging tools at their disposal, and you will be relieved to hear that you can use your favorite debugging tools while developing XML Web services as well.

Debuging a Standalone XML Web Service in Visual Studio .NET

If you create an XML Web service in .NET and then run it using the F5 key, the XML Web service generates a special Web page for display in the browser. This dynamically generated page is necessary because an XML Web service was designed to respond to a specific request, which is not provided when you run the XML Web service in this way. But the Web pages generated by Visual Studio .NET allow the developer to test his XML Web service from within a Web browser. The first Web page that is generated lists the interfaces exposed by your XML Web service. If you click on one of these interfaces, you will get another dynamically generated page that you can use for testing your service.

On the testing Web page, you will get a TextBox for each input parameter that your interface accepts and a Button that reads "Invoke," which submits the values you enter into the TextBoxes as parameters to your XML Web service. Developers can use this Web-based testing platform to try out different pieces of test data to validate their service's output as well as its response to unexpected inputs.

***TIP:** As with any function you design, you should thoroughly test your code using unexpected input data that includes data type mismatches (for example, enter a **String** data type when an **Integer** is expected).*

Breakpoints and Debugging Tools

One of the benefits of testing your XML Web service from within the Visual Studio .NET environment is that it allows you to add breakpoints to your code and use the IDE's advanced debugging features. Whenever a breakpoint is encountered in your XML Web service's code, the processing of your service will pause and Visual Studio .NET will become visible with the current line of code highlighted in yellow. In break mode, you can use debugging tools such as the Locals window and variables watches to track and check your code's progress. If you read the "Testing and Debugging Web Forms" solution, you will see an example of how Visual Studio .NET can help you debug your Web-based applications.

Using Remote XML Web Services

If you are testing and debugging an application that uses a remotely hosted XML Web service, you will not be able to directly troubleshoot the XML Web service itself, only the results that the service sends back to your application. This limitation is similar to a situation where your development team is provided with a component for your application, but not the source code. This can be considered *black box* testing because you cannot actually see inside the code, and you are limited to only testing the values that go into or come out of this component.

If you are using an XML Web service you did not develop that is hosted by a third party, you should spend a great deal of time testing that service's interfaces to ensure that what you get back is what you expected. I highly recommend you perform validation checks on every value passed to your code from an XML Web service, and surround your XML Web service calls with exception-handling routines to handle those unexpected uh-ohs.

Chapter 9

Windows Forms

By Julian Templeman

In Depth

This chapter discusses the new GUI architecture that is shared by all .NET programming languages, Windows Forms. This architecture was previously known as WinForms, but Microsoft ran into problems with the name and had to change it.

Windows Forms provide you with a set of classes for writing form-based Windows applications. These forms are very similar in appearance and operation to the way forms have been built and used in Visual Basic for some years, but Windows Forms can be used by any .NET language, and so bring the ease of VB style drag-and-drop UI programming to other .NET languages.

The Windows Forms namespace, **System.Windows.Forms**, is very complex, containing more than 200 classes and interfaces. Because an entire book could be devoted to just this topic, I'll only provide an overview of how Windows Forms work and what you can do with them. Even then, I'll have to split the discussion over two chapters, with this chapter concentrating on the basic form mechanism, and Chapter 10 discussing controls and how you use them with forms.

Forms and Controls

Many of the classes in the namespace represent familiar Windows GUI elements, such as buttons, listboxes, menus, and common dialogs, but two of them stand out from the rest.

The **Form** class represents a window or dialog box and is the base for all windows. The **Control** class is the base class for "components with visual representation," so it forms the base for everything you see on the screen and interact with.

Figure 9.1 shows the overall class hierarchy in the **System.Windows.Forms** namespace and how **Form** and **Control** fit in.

Table 9.1 describes what each class does and what functionality it provides to the hierarchy. I'll describe some of these classes used in more detail in this chapter.

Anatomy of a Windows Forms Application

Now let's take a look at what a Windows Forms application actually looks like using a hand-written application written in Visual Basic. It's rather unlikely that you'll write many Windows Forms applications by hand because you lose the

Table 9.1 The major classes in the System.Windows.Forms namespace.

Class	Description
Object	The base class for all other classes
MarshalByRefObject	The base class for all objects that need to communicate with one another
Component	Provides a base implementation of the IComponent interface
Control	The base class for "components with visual representation," which provides message and user input handling
ScrollableControl	Provides a base class for controls that need to have scrolling functionality
ContainerControl	Represents a control that can act as a container for other controls handling focus management
UserControl	Represents an empty control that can be used in the Form Designer to create other controls
Form	Provides a base class from which custom forms can be derived

advantages of the Forms Designer and the visual layout tools. But hand-written code is very useful when you're trying to understand how things work, and you can be sure that the wizards and designers aren't doing sneaky things behind the scenes.

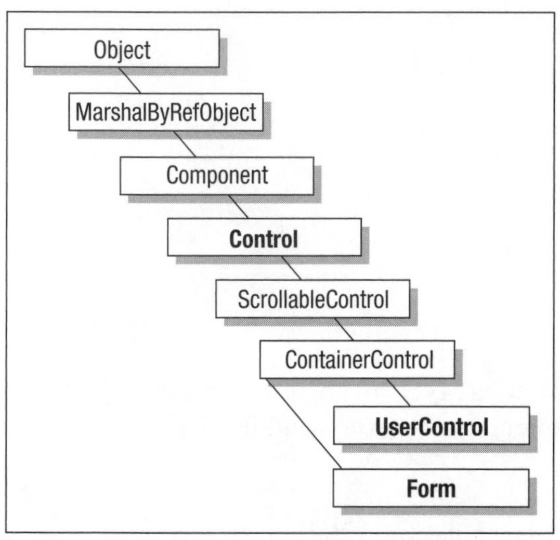

Figure 9.1 **Relationships between the major classes in the System.Windows.Forms namespace.**

Creating a Skeleton Application

Here, then, is some code that simply creates a form and displays it on the screen:

```
Imports Microsoft.VisualBasic
Imports System
Imports System.Collections
Imports System.Data
Imports System.Diagnostics
Imports System.ComponentModel
Imports System.Drawing
Imports System.Windows.Forms

Module MyMod

Public Class MyForm
  Inherits System.Windows.Forms.Form

  Public Sub New()
    MyBase.New
  End Sub

  Overrides Public Sub Dispose()
    MyBase.Dispose
  End Sub
End Class

Public Sub Main()
  Dim form1 As New MyForm()
  form1.Show()
End Sub

End Module
```

You can type this into a file, save it as MyForm.vb, and then compile it with the command-line VB compiler by opening a console window and typing the following command line:

```
vbc /t:winexe /main:MyForm /r:System.Data.dll /r:System.Drawing.dll _
  /r:System.Windows.Forms.dll /r: System.dll MyForm.vb
```

Remember that you need to type the entire command line on one line. Figure 9.2 shows what the compilation process should look like:

```
Select Visual Studio.NET Command Prompt

C:\Dev-B2\Ch10\ByHand>dir
 Volume in drive C has no label.
 Volume Serial Number is 8855-06B8

 Directory of C:\Dev-B2\Ch10\ByHand

13/07/2001  08:26       <DIR>          .
13/07/2001  08:26       <DIR>          ..
13/07/2001  08:12                  119 build.bat
13/07/2001  08:26                3,584 frm1.exe
13/07/2001  08:26                  607 frm1.vb
               3 File(s)          4,310 bytes
               2 Dir(s)   7,431,185,408 bytes free

C:\Dev-B2\Ch10\ByHand>build

C:\Dev-B2\Ch10\ByHand>vbc /t:winexe /main:MyForm /r:System.data.dll /r:System.dr
awing.dll /r:System.windows.forms.dll /r:System.dll frm1.vb
Microsoft (R) Visual Basic.NET Compiler version 7.00.9254
for Microsoft (R) .NET CLR version 1.00.2914.16
Copyright (C) Microsoft Corp 2001. All rights reserved.

C:\Dev-B2\Ch10\ByHand>_
```

Figure 9.2 Compiling a Visual Basic application from the command line.

Figure 9.3 The most basic of Windows Forms applications.

When you run the application, you won't see anything spectacular; all you'll see is a blank form that you can close using the system menu or the close button, as shown in Figure 9.3.

Let's take a look at how the code and compilation process works.

Understanding the Application Code and the Command Line

The code begins with a host of "imports" statements because Windows Forms applications can use a lot of .NET classes from many namespaces. Although the basic application doesn't need all of these namespaces at this time, I've put them in so I won't have to remember to add them later on. Here's what each namespace is for:

- **Microsoft.VisualBasic**—Contains (obviously) basic classes and interfaces needed by VB.

- **System**—Contains definitions of many .NET basics, including the built-in types and the **String** and **Object** classes.
- **System.Collections**—Contains the common collection classes (discussed in Chapter 4).
- **System.Data**—Contains the ADO.NET classes.
- **System.Diagnostics**—Contains classes that let you trace the execution of your code and debug the application.
- **System.ComponentModel**—Provides classes used to implement components.
- **System.Drawing**—Contains the GDI+ classes that will be needed if you want to do any drawing.
- **System.Windows.Forms**—Contains all the Windows Forms functionality, so you'll definitely need this one.

The second part of the code defines a new form class, which inherits from the **System.Windows.Forms.Form** base and provides **Sub New()** and overridden **Sub Dispose()** functions. At present, these two functions are used in order to call the base class function, but I'll add more code to these functions as we go through the rest of the In Depth section.

The command line looks quite complex, so let's consider it piece by piece. The first option, **/t:winexe**, tells the compiler that I'm building a Windows executable as opposed to a console application or a DLL. The second option, **/main:MyForm**, tells the compiler where to start executing the program, and in the case of a form-based application like this, I give it the name of the main form class. The following four options, all starting with **/r:**, tell the compiler which DLLs it needs to reference. I need to do this because the compiler needs to check the use of namespaces, classes, interfaces, and other programming constructs at runtime; the four DLLs I've listed contain all the namespaces I mentioned in the **Imports** statements. The final parameter is, of course, the name of the file I'm compiling.

The Form Class

Now that you've seen how to create a basic form, let's take a look at the **Windows.Forms.Form** class. I'm only going to provide you with an overview of **Form** because it is a very large and complex class that contains more than 250 methods, properties, and events. This isn't too surprising when you consider that a form represents a window on the screen, and windows have a great deal of functionality that needs to be encapsulated in this class.

Forms can be used to display several kinds of windows, such as:

- *Ordinary Single Document Interface (SDI) forms*—Each window stands on its own.
- *Multiple Document Interface (MDI) forms*—One form contains zero or more child forms.
- *Dialog boxes*—Forms optimized to contain controls.

Creating forms is very simple, as the **Form** class only has one constructor that takes no arguments:

```
Dim form1 As New MyForm()
```

Form Properties

Forms have a number of properties. Table 9.2 shows the property values that a form has when it has just been created.

These default values fit with what we saw in the simple form created earlier, and you can change any of these properties in order to affect the appearance and operation of the form.

Table 9.2 The initial properties of a Form object.

Property	Value	Description
AutoScale	true	The window and its controls will scale to the font being used (and rescale if the font is changed).
BorderStyle	FormBorderStyle.Sizable	The window border is resizable.
ControlBox	true	The window displays a control box in the top-left corner.
MaximizeBox	true	The window displays a maximize box in the top-right corner.
MinimizeBox	true	The window displays a minimize box in the top-right corner.
ShowInTaskBar	true	This window will have an entry in the task bar.
StartPosition	FormStartPosition.WindowsDefaultLocation	Windows will choose the default location for the window.
WindowState	FormWindowState.Normal	The window will be displayed normally (as opposed to maximized or minimized).

The **Form** class has approximately 100 properties, many of them inherited from **Control** and other classes higher in the hierarchy. Table 9.3 lists some of the most useful properties of the **Form** class. Several of these properties are discussed in more detail throughout the rest of the chapter.

The **Form** class also has a large number of methods; some of the most common are listed in Table 9.4.

Table 9.3 A selection of commonly used Form class properties.

Property	Description
AcceptButton	Gets or sets the button that performs an action equivalent to the user pressing the Enter key
Anchor	Determines which, if any, of the sides of the object are anchored to the container's edges
AutoScale	Determines whether the form and its controls autoscales to suit the font being used
AutoScroll	Determines whether the form supports autoscrolling
BackColor	Gets or sets the background color of the form. **ForeColor** represents the foreground color
Bottom	Gets the bottom of this control. There are matching **Top**, **Left**, and **Right** properties
Bounds	Gets or sets the bounding rectangle of this control
CancelButton	Gets or sets the button that performs an action equivalent to the user pressing the Esc key
ClientRectangle	Gets the rectangle that represents the client area of the form
ClientSize	Gets or sets the client area of the form
ContainsFocus	Tells you whether this form (or a child control) currently has the focus
ContextMenu	Gets or sets the context menu associated with this control
ControlBox	Determines whether this form displays a control box in the top-left corner
Controls	The collection of child controls
DesktopLocation	Gets or sets the location of the form on the Windows desktop
Dock	Controls the docking of the control in its container
Enabled	Determines whether the control is enabled
Focused	Read-only property telling you whether the control has the focus
Font	Represents the font used in this form
Height	The height of the form
Icon	Gets or sets the icon associated with the form
IsMDIChild	Tells you whether a form is an MDI child window
IsMDIContainer	Tells you whether a form contains MDI child windows

(continued)

Table 9.3 A selection of commonly used Form class properties *(continued)*.

Property	Description
MaximizeBox	Determines whether this form displays a maximize box in the top-left corner
MDIChildren	For an MDI container, returns an array of forms representing the MDI children
MDIParent	For an MDI child, holds a reference to its container
Menu	Gets or sets the main menu for the form
MinimizeBox	Determines whether this form displays a minimize box in the top-left corner
OwnedForms	Returns an array of owned forms
Owner	Gets or sets the owner for this form
Parent	Gets the parent of this form
Size	Gets or sets the size of this form
Text	Gets or sets the text associated with the form (i.e., the window title)
TopLevel	Determines whether this is a top-level window
TopMost	Determines whether a window is displayed as the topmost window in your application
Visible	Determines whether a form is visible or not
Width	Gets or sets the width of this form
WindowState	Determines how a window is to be displayed—normal, minimized, or maximized

Table 9.4 A selection of commonly used Form class methods.

Method	Description
Activate	Activates a form and gives it the focus
BringToFront	Brings a form to the front of the Z-order
Close	Closes the form
DoDragDrop	Begins a drag-drop operation
Hide	Hides the form by setting its **visible** property to false
Invalidate	Causes a paint message to be sent to the form in order to cause it to redraw itself
LayoutMDI	Lays out the MDI child windows in an MDI container
PointToClient	Converts from screen coordinates to client coordinates
PointToScreen	Converts from client coordinates to screen coordinates
Refresh	Forces the repaint of this form and any children
Scale	Scales this form and any children
Show	Shows the form by setting its **visible** property to true
ShowDialog	Displays this form as a modal dialog
Update	Forces the control to repaint any invalid areas

Table 9.5 Events associated with the Form class.

Event	Description
Activated	Occurs when the form is activated. The **Deactivate** event occurs when the form has lost focus
Click	Occurs when the form is clicked
Closing	Occurs when the form is closing. The **Closed** event occurs when the form is closed
DoubleClick	Occurs when the form is double-clicked
GotFocus	Occurs when the form gets the focus. The **LostFocus** event occurs when the control loses the focus
Invalidated	Occurs when the form receives a paint message
KeyPress	Occurs when a key is pressed while the form has the focus. **KeyUp** and **KeyDown** events will also be generated
Load	Occurs before the form is displayed for the first time
MDIChildActivate	Occurs when an MDI child window is activated
MouseDown	Occurs when a mouse button is pressed over the form. **MouseUp** and **MouseMove** events are also sent when necessary
MouseEnter	Occurs when the mouse enters the form. The **MouseLeave** event occurs when the mouse leaves the form
Move	Occurs when the form is moved
Paint	Occurs when the form needs to repaint itself
Resize	Occurs when the form is resized

And finally, Table 9.5 shows some of the most common events associated with the **Form** class.

Form Relationships

Several times in this chapter I've used terms that imply that relationships exist between windows, such as *parent* and *child*, *owner* and *owned*. If you're not familiar with the way windows can be related, I provide a brief account in this section. Consider the simple About box shown in Figure 9.4.

This simple window contains a number of controls that are themselves windows, such as the close button at the top right and the OK button at the bottom. The form is the parent and the controls are children of the form. This leads to some important consequences:

- A child window always displays on top of its parent. The window isn't much use if the OK button gets behind the form.
- A child window always moves and gets minimized and maximized with its parent.

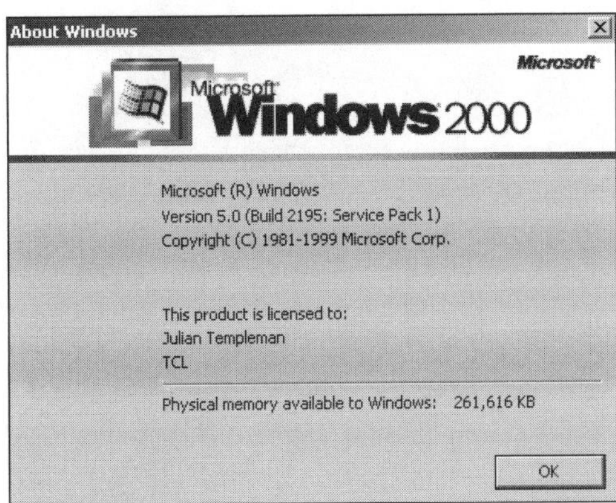

Figure 9.4 An About box showing a form and child controls.

- A child window is clipped by its parent window, so it can't display outside its parent window's bounding rectangle.
- A child window's lifetime is bound to that of its parent, so that when the About box is destroyed, its child controls are also destroyed.

The relationship between owner and owned windows is slightly different than that between parent and child. Owned windows display on top of their owners and will still be maximized, minimized, and destroyed along with them, but they can display outside the border of their parent and won't move when the parent is moved. The About box is a good example of an owned window.

Windows that don't have a parent are called *top-level* windows, and they're usually used for the main window in an application.

The last term I'll define is *topmost*. A topmost window is one that floats above all others in the application regardless of whether it has the focus or not. Windows will usually move to the front of the stack of windows when they get the focus and may move in front of whichever window had the focus previously. A topmost window may lose the focus, but will still display on top of all others. A good example of a topmost window is the Find And Replace window you can display in Microsoft Word.

TIP: *Be careful when giving more than one window in your application topmost status at the same time. They can interact with unexpected results.*

Using MDI Forms

There are several styles of Windows applications commonly in use. The simplest is the SDI style where all information is displayed in a single window; Notepad is a good example of an SDI application.

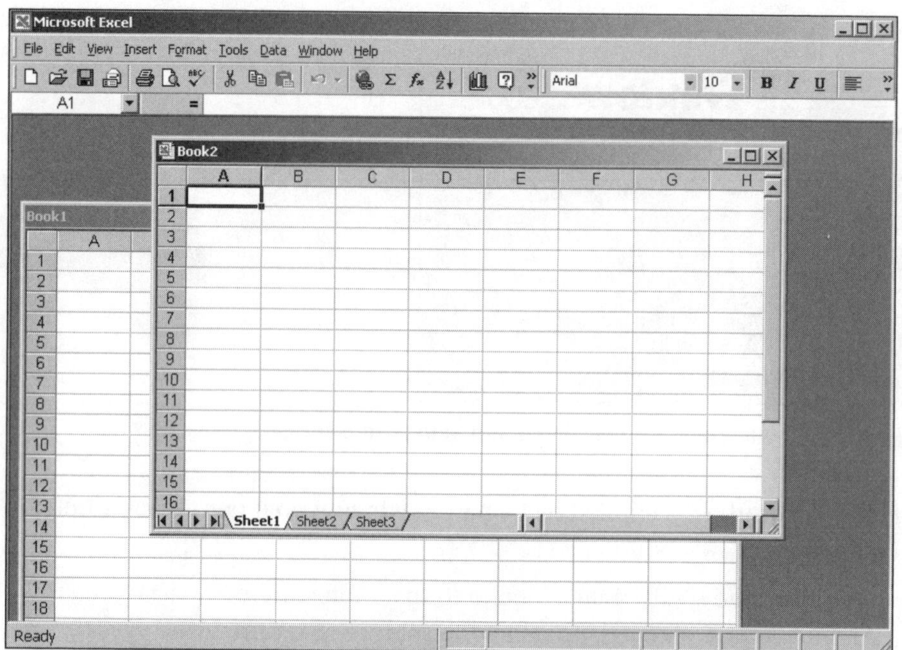

Figure 9.5 The Excel MDI user interface showing the frame and two child windows.

A second style is the MDI style, where a parent frame window can hold zero or more child windows. The Excel user interface, shown in Figure 9.5, is a good example.

The figure shows the parent frame window (known as the *container*), holding menu and toolbars and two child windows. You can see that these are children because they display inside the parent and are clipped where they might try to display outside the parent's bounding rectangle. Programming MDI forms is a little more work than using SDI, but Windows Forms makes it pretty painless.

In order to create an MDI application, you simply set the **IsMDIContainer** property of the frame window to true, and then create another window and set its **MDIParent** property to refer to the parent window reference. Here's an example in VB:

```
Imports Microsoft.VisualBasic
Imports System
Imports System.Collections
Imports System.Data
Imports System.Diagnostics
Imports System.ComponentModel
Imports System.Drawing
Imports System.Windows.Forms
```

```
Module MyMod

' Sample MDI application

Public Class MyMDIForm
  Inherits System.Windows.Forms.Form

  Public Sub New()
    MyBase.New

    ' Set us to be an MDI container
    IsMDIContainer = true

    Dim child1 As New MyMDIChild()
    child1.MDIParent = Me
    child1.Show()
  End Sub

  Overrides Public Sub Dispose()
    MyBase.Dispose
  End Sub

End Class

Public Class MyMDIChild
  Inherits System.Windows.Forms.Form

  Public Sub New()
    MyBase.New

  End Sub

  Overrides Public Sub Dispose()
    MyBase.Dispose
  End Sub
End Class

Public Sub Main()
  Dim form1 As New MyMDIForm()
  form1.Show()
End Sub

End Module
```

I've simply created a second **Form** class to act as the MDI child window. The highlighted lines show how I set the main form to be an MDI container, and then add a child window. If I had more than one child window, I could use the **MDIChildren** property to get an array of **Form** references for each child, and I can use the **ActiveMDIChild** property to get a reference to the active MDI child window. If you compile and run the code, you should see an application similar to the one shown in Figure 9.6.

You can see how the child window is clipped to the area of the container, and in this case, .NET automatically provides scrollbars to let you see the part of the child window that's hidden.

Just for completeness, let me mention that there's a third style of application that is becoming more common, which is the "multiple top-level window" style. When you're running Internet Explorer, you can open as many Explorer windows as you like, and they all display separately, but there's only one application running behind all the windows. You can also close the windows in any order, and the application won't quit until the last window is closed. This style of application doesn't get any special support in Windows Forms.

Using Dialogs

Windows applications use two kinds of dialogs—*modal* and *modeless*. Modal dialogs, such as About boxes and File Open dialogs, prevent users from interacting with an application until they've finished with the dialog. Modeless dialogs, such as Word's Find dialog, exist alongside the main form, and you can switch back and forth between the form and the dialog.

In many ways, modeless dialogs are simply another form displayed by your application, and there is no special support for them in Windows Forms. If you want to display a window as a modal dialog, use the **Form** class **ShowDialog()** method, which ensures that the form behaves as a modal dialog and prohibits interaction with an application until it is dismissed.

Figure 9.6 An MDI application in Visual Basic.

ShowDialog() returns a **DialogResult** value, which tells you which button on the dialog was clicked to dismiss it. **DialogResult** is an enumeration, and its members are shown in Table 9.6.

User interface design guidelines state that a dialog has to have buttons that let the user choose how to dismiss the dialog. There should always be an OK button, and if the user wants to dismiss the dialog without making any changes, there should be a Cancel button as well. These two buttons are rather special in that pressing the Enter key is taken as the equivalent of clicking the OK button, whereas pressing the Esc key is taken as the equivalent of clicking the Cancel button. You can indicate which buttons on the form represent the OK and Cancel buttons by assigning button references using the **AcceptButton** and **CancelButton** properties of the form.

You set the value to be returned from a dialog by assigning a suitable value to the form's **DialogResult** property, like this:

```
' Report that the user pressed the 'Yes' button
Me.DialogResult = DialogResult.Yes
```

Assigning a value to the **DialogResult** property normally closes the dialog box and returns control to the form called **ShowDialog()**. If for some reason you want to prevent the property from closing the dialog, use the **DialogResult.None** value, and the dialog will remain open.

You can also assign a value to the **DialogResult** property of a **Button** object, in which case, clicking the button dismisses the dialog and returns the value to the parent form.

Table 9.6 Members of the DialogResult enumeration.

Member	Description
Abort	Returned when the Abort button is clicked.
Cancel	Returned when the Cancel button is clicked.
Ignore	Returned when the Ignore button is clicked.
No	Returned when the No button is clicked.
None	Nothing has been returned, which means that the modal dialog is still running.
OK	Returned when the OK button is clicked.
Retry	Returned when the Retry button is clicked.
Yes	Returned when the Yes button is clicked.

Handling Events

The .NET event mechanism is used by forms and controls to communicate with one another, and an event is simply a notification sent by a form or a control to let the world know that something has happened. Examples of events include clicking a button and selecting an item in a listbox.

The "event sender" originates the event, and there may be one or more "event receivers" that are interested in knowing what has happened. A receiver that wants to accept notifications registers a handler function with the sender, and at the appropriate time, the sender calls the handler function. The mechanism used to make this work involves delegates, which were discussed in Chapter 2 in the "Delegates" section. If you are unfamiliar with delegates, you may want to review the material in Chapter 2 before reading on.

The way in which you use events in code is different in VB than it is in C#. In VB, a lot of the mechanism is hidden from you, whereas in C#, you can still see it and have to be prepared to work with it. For this reason, I'll discuss events in VB first, and then cover C#.

In VB, all event-handler functions follow the same pattern:

```
Protected Sub Control_EventName (ByVal sender As Object, _
          ByVal e As System.EventArgs) Handles Control.EventName
  ' Handler code here
End Sub
```

The function name (**Control_EventName**) consists of the name of the form or control to which this handler applies plus the name of the event you want to handle. So if you want to handle the **Click** event for a button called OKButton, you would code a handler called **OKButton_Click**, and if you want to handle the user changing the selection in a listbox called Listbox1, the handler would be called **Listbox1_SelectedIndexChanged**. You can find out which events are supported by a control by consulting the .NET Framework documentation.

The arguments to the handler function are largely superfluous in VB. They provide information about which object was the source of the event and about what the event actually was, but in VB, Visual Studio adds a custom handler function for each event you want to handle on an object. This means that when the user, for instance, clicks on Button1, you'll end up in the **Button1_Click()** handler, so there's no need to check the "sender" argument to determine that it was Button1 that was the source of the event. It must have been Button1 or else you wouldn't be here in the handler function. C# and C++ give you a lot more flexibility (or unnecessary complexity, depending on your viewpoint), and these arguments are often needed.

Handlers are easy to add even if you are manually editing code. Provided you use the right naming convention, VB links the event handler to the control automatically.

Things are not quite as simple in C#, where you actually see the delegate mechanism in use. Adding a handler in C# involves code like this:

```
this.OKButton = new Button();
...
OKButton.Text = "OK";
OKButton.Click += new System.EventHandler(this.OKButton_Click);
...
protected void OKButton_Click(object sender, System.EventArgs e)
{
  // Handler code here
}
```

There is a very similar handler function, which takes the same two arguments as in the VB version, but in C# you have to link the event handler to the object manually. As the highlighted line of code shows, this means creating a new **EventHandler** object and initializing it with the name of the handler function. Remember that the function of a delegate is to call a function when it itself is called, effectively "passing on" the function call to the function it is managing. In this case, the **EventHandler** object is going to call the **OKButton_Click()** function. Note that it would be quite possible to have a general button click handler and associate that with **OKButton**, **CancelButton**, and all manner of other buttons. In that case, you would need to use the "sender" argument to find out which button was the source of the event, and you may need to use the second argument to find out just what happened.

What does the **+=** operator do, though? A **Button** object—along with many other control and form types—can associate a list of **EventHandler** delegate objects with its events, and the **+=** operator adds an entry to that list. When the event is fired, the **Button** object uses the delegates in the list to call all the handler functions that have been registered via delegates.

This mechanism has two useful consequences. First, it is possible to associate more than one handler with an event, and they'll be called in the order they were added when the event fires. Second, it is possible to use -= to remove a handler from an event, so you can choose when you want to handle events.

NOTE: *You can call your event handler functions anything you like in C#, but Microsoft recommends using the naming convention that I've followed in this section.*

The Application Class

The **System.Windows.Forms.Application** class represents the application itself and provides several properties and methods that can be useful. This class is sealed, so you cannot derive any other classes from it, and all its methods and properties are shared (or static in C# and C++), so you use them without creating an instance of the class.

Table 9.7 lists some of the more useful properties exposed by the **Windows.Forms. Application** class.

There are a number of shared methods in the **Application** class, some of which are rather esoteric. Some of the most useful shared methods are listed in Table 9.8.

The **AddMessageFilter()** function is used when you want to view Windows messages before they are processed by the framework, usually to prevent them from being processed or monitoring application behavior. You can remove a filter with **RemoveMessageFilter()**. The **Exit()** method is used to shut down the application.

Table 9.7 Properties of the Windows.Forms.Application class.

Property	Description
CommonAppDataPath	Returns a path for the application data that is common to all users
CommonAppDataRegistry	Returns a Registry key for the application data that is common to all users, which was set up during installation
CompanyName	Gets the company name associated with the application
CurrentCulture	Gets or sets the locale information for the current thread
ExecutablePath	Gets the path to the executable that started this application
ProductName	Gets the product name associated with the application
ProductVersion	Gets the product version associated with the application as a string in the form of "123.2.1.2"
StartupPath	Gets the path to the executable that started the application

Table 9.8 Common shared methods in the Windows.Forms.Application class.

Method	Description
AddMessageFilter	Adds a filter for Windows messages
Exit	Terminates the application
RemoveMessageFilter	Removes a previously installed filter
Run	Begins a standard message loop on the current thread

Visual Inheritance

You might be used to the idea of inheritance in object-oriented (OO) programming languages, but .NET has taken inheritance one step further in Windows Forms.

Inheritance lets you create a new class based on an existing one, so that the new class inherits the properties, events, and methods of the parent (or "base") class, and can then build on them. If you want to read more about inheritance, see the section "OO Programming from 30,000 Feet" in Chapter 2.

You can see inheritance in action whenever you create a new form, as in the following code fragment:

```
Public Class MyMDIForm
  Inherits System.Windows.Forms.Form
```

The **Inherits** keyword shows that the **MyMDIForm** class inherits from **System.Windows.Forms.Form**.

So what does *visual inheritance* mean, and how does it take inheritance further? It's easier to demonstrate than explain in words, so I'll start by creating a project that has a main form. This will be a standard form called Form1 that inherits from **System.Windows.Forms.Form** as in the previous example. Now, I'll add a picture box to the form in order to add a logo to the top-right corner, as shown in Figure 9.7.

I then add a second form to the project, and by default, this will also inherit from System.Windows.Forms.Form. But what if I change the code so that my new form inherits from my main form, like this:

```
Public Class NewForm
  Inherits MyProject.Form1
```

The design view for the form—shown in Figure 9.8—shows that the new form has inherited the picture box from its parent form, which is just what *visual inheritance* means. Deriving a new form from one that contains controls results in

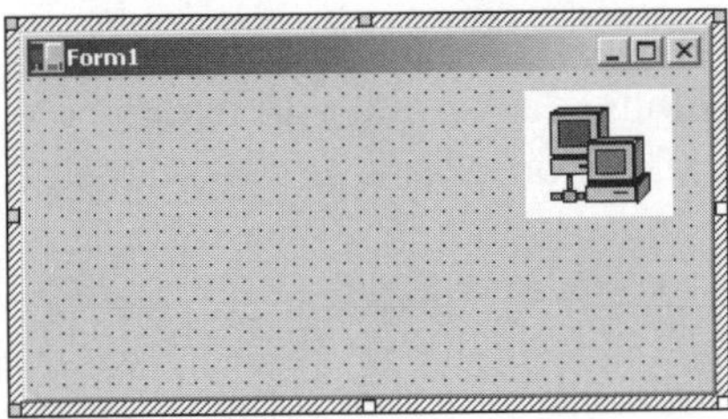

Figure 9.7 The main form showing a logo in the top-right corner.

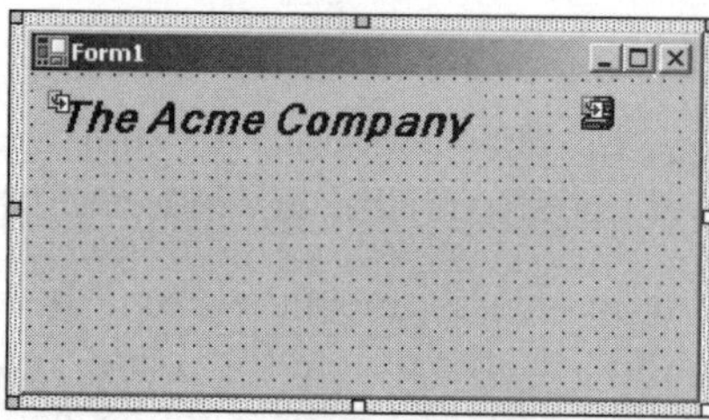

Figure 9.8 A form that inherits from the main form showing the inherited logo in the top-right corner.

all the controls (and their behavior) being inherited from the parent form. This is very neat and makes it simple to establish a look and feel for a set of dialogs or forms, together with common behavior for inherited controls.

Visual Studio provides tools to help manage inherited forms. See the Immediate Solutions section "How Can I Create a Form Based on One I've Already Defined?" for details on how to manage visual inheritance within the Visual Studio environment.

Common Dialogs

Windows possesses a selection of common dialogs that let you perform common tasks, such as opening and closing files and choosing fonts and colors. You're advised to use these dialogs rather than inventing your own for several reasons:

- Writing a good file open dialog or color selector is surprisingly difficult. Why reinvent what has already been done quite adequately?
- These dialogs provide a standard way of performing their tasks, and using them will give your application a recognizable and familiar GUI.
- These dialogs are future-proof because their screen appearance is provided by the version of the operating system your code is running on. If you run your applications on Windows 2000, you'll get the Windows 2000 version of the dialogs. If the Windows UI changes when Windows XP becomes available, your code will display the Whistler version of the dialogs with no effort on your part.

You'll find the seven common dialogs in the Toolbox. Table 9.9 also lists them and provides a description of each. Although I'll only discuss how to use the file dialogs, you can extend the technique quite easily in order to use the others.

Table 9.9 The .NET common dialogs.

Class	Description
OpenFileDialog	Lets the user choose a file to open
SaveFileDialog	Lets the user choose a directory and file name for saving a file
FontDialog	Lets the user choose a font
ColorDialog	Lets the user choose a color
PrintDialog	Displays a print dialog, letting the user choose the printer and which portion of the document to print
PrintPreviewDialog	Displays a dialog that displays print preview of a print job
PageSetupDialog	Displays a dialog that lets users choose page settings, including margins and paper orientation

Immediate Solutions

How Do I Create a Windows Forms Application?

To create a Windows Forms application, start a new project in Visual Studio, and select the Windows Application project type, as shown in Figure 9.9

Once the project has been created, you'll be presented with a form in Visual Studio, shown in Figure 9.10, which looks remarkably similar to the ones you've been using in VB for years.

Now let's take a look at the code that was actually generated when I created the basic application. Here's the code that I copied from the code editor in Beta 2—be aware that it may change in future releases:

```
Public Class Form1
    Inherits System.Windows.Forms.Form

#Region " Windows Form Designer generated code "

    Public Sub New()
        MyBase.New()

        'This call is required by the Windows Form Designer.
        InitializeComponent()

        'Add any initialization after the InitializeComponent() call

    End Sub

    'Form overrides dispose to clean up the component list.
    Protected Overloads Overrides Sub Dispose(ByVal disposing _
                As Boolean)
        If disposing Then
            If Not (components Is Nothing) Then
                components.Dispose()
            End If
        End If
        MyBase.Dispose(disposing)
    End Sub
```

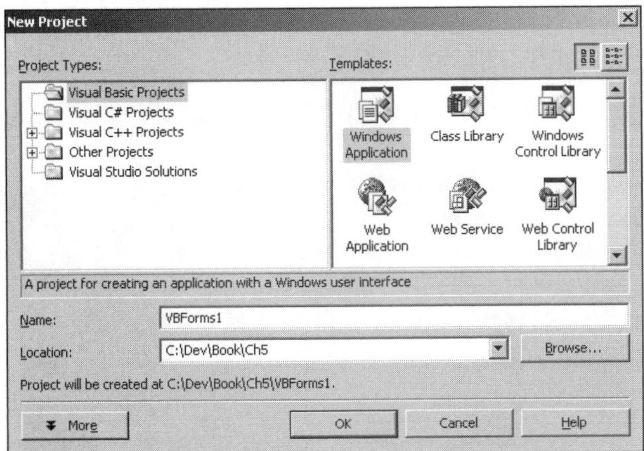

Figure 9.9 Creating a Windows Forms application in Visual Basic.

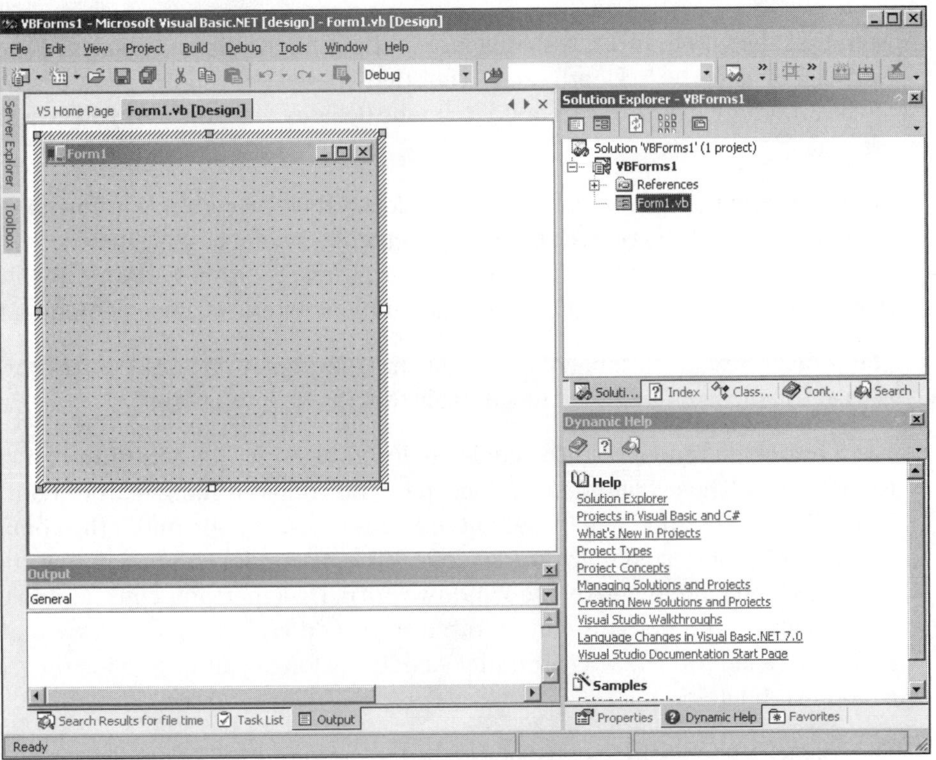

Figure 9.10 Starting a Windows Forms application in Visual Studio.

```
    'Required by the Windows Form Designer
    Private components As System.ComponentModel.Container

    'NOTE: The following procedure is required by the Windows
    'Form Designer
    'It can be modified using the Windows Form Designer.
    'Do not modify it using the code editor.
    <System.Diagnostics.DebuggerStepThrough()> Private _
          Sub InitializeComponent()
        components = New System.ComponentModel.Container()
        Me.Text = "Form1"
    End Sub

#End Region

End Class
```

Note that the whole form is simply a class that inherits from **System.Window. Forms.Form**. In the In Depth section entitled "Visual Inheritance," you learn how to use inheritance of forms to build upon the designs of forms that you've already created.

The program imports three namespaces: obviously there's **System.Windows.Forms**, but you also need **System.Drawing** (which gives you access to the GDI+ drawing functionality, which I describe in Chapter 11) and **System.ComponentModel** (which contains a number of classes that implement and license components).

The code declares a variable of type **System.ComponentModel.Container** that is used to hold references to the controls that this form contains.

You'll notice that most of the code is enclosed between the **#Region** and **#End Region** lines. These commands are used by the code-outlining feature built into Visual Studio .NET and will by default hide this block of code under the comment "Windows Form Designer generated code." The reason for this is that this code is generated and maintained by the Windows Form Designer, and you shouldn't edit it manually. If you do, you may reformat it or add code in such a way that the Designer cannot find its way around the code any longer, and you'll lose access to a lot of useful help.

The constructor code then calls the **InitializeComponent()** function that is used to set up the form. The first line actually creates the container variable to hold the form components, and the final line sets the text for the window title bar.

The final function in the code is **Dispose()**, which is used to dispose of any components the form may contain.

Just for comparison, the following code is produced if you create the same basic Windows Forms project in C#:

```
using System;
using System.Drawing;
using System.Collections;
using System.ComponentModel;
using System.Windows.Forms;
using System.Data;

namespace CSBasic
{
   /// <summary>
   /// Summary description for Form1.
   /// </summary>
   public class Form1 : System.Windows.Forms.Form
   {
      /// <summary>
      /// Required designer variable.
      /// </summary>
      private System.ComponentModel.Container components = null;

      public Form1()
      {
         //
         // Required for Windows Form Designer support
         //
         InitializeComponent();

         //
         // TODO: Add any constructor code after InitializeComponent call
         //
      }

      /// <summary>
      /// Clean up any resources being used.
      /// </summary>
      protected override void Dispose( bool disposing )
      {
         if( disposing )
         {
            if (components != null)
            {
               components.Dispose();
            }
         }
```

```
            base.Dispose( disposing );
        }

        #region Windows Form Designer generated code
        /// <summary>
        /// Required method for Designer support - do not modify
        /// the contents of this method with the code editor.
        /// </summary>
        private void InitializeComponent()
        {
            this.components = new System.ComponentModel.Container();
            this.Size = new System.Drawing.Size(300,300);
            this.Text = "Form1";
        }
        #endregion

        /// <summary>
        /// The main entry point for the application.
        /// </summary>
        [STAThread]
        static void Main()
        {
            Application.Run(new Form1());
        }
    }
}
```

You can see that the structure is almost identical. The main differences are the addition of a **Main()** function to start the program and the use of **System.Drawing.Size** to set the size of the form.

How Can I Create a New Form and Display It?

To add a new form to a project, right-click on the project name in the Solution Explorer window to display the context menu. Select Add, and then select Add Windows Form from the context menu, as shown in Figure 9.11.

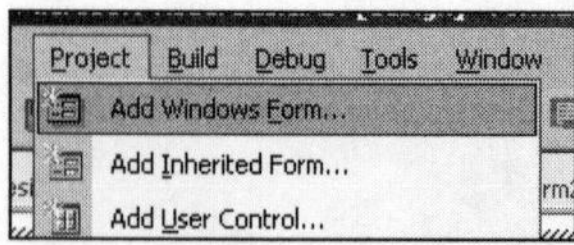

Figure 9.11 Use the Add Windows Form menu item to create a new form.

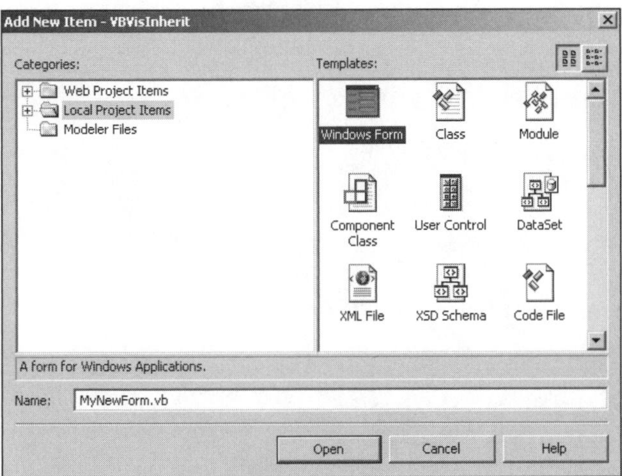

Figure 9.12 The Add New Item dialog lets you create a new form and add it to a project.

The Add New Item dialog, shown in Figure 9.12, is displayed. Make sure that Windows Form is selected in the Templates window, and then type in a name for your new form. When you click the Open button, a new class is added to your project, and the design window is opened for the new form.

Creating a form object and displaying it is simple:

```
' Create another form and display it
Dim newForm As New Form2()
newForm.Show()
```

The first line creates the form object, and the second line displays it on the screen.

Creating MDI Forms

The main window of a MDI application acts as a frame that contains zero or more child windows.

To create an MDI application, start by creating a standard Windows application. If you are using Visual Studio, use the Property Browser to set the form's **IsMDIContainer** property to true; if you are not using Visual Studio, set the property in code, as shown earlier in the section "Using MDI Forms" in the In Depth section. Once you've done this, the main form will display as a frame. You can then create other forms and get them to display as child windows by setting their **MDIParent** property to refer to the frame window:

```
' The MDI Frame window class
Public Class MyMDIForm
  Inherits System.Windows.Forms.Form

  Public Sub New()
    MyBase.New

    Form1 = Me

    ' This call is required by the Win Form Designer
    InitializeComponent

    ' Create another form as an MDI child
    Dim child1 As New MyMDIChild()
    child1.MDIParent = Me
    child1.Show()
  End Sub
  ...
End Class
```

Creating and Using Dialogs

A dialog in .NET is simply another form, which you may choose to display in a particular manner.

There are two kinds of dialogs:

- *Modal dialogs*, such as About boxes and File Open dialogs, prevent you from interacting with an application until you've closed them.
- *Modeless dialogs*, such as Word's Find And Replace dialog, let you interact with the application as well as the dialog.

Modeless dialogs don't need much at all in the way of special support because they can be displayed as simply another form. Modal dialogs, on the other hand, need some way of preventing the user from interacting with the rest of the application. This is done by using the form's **ShowDialog()** method.

Setting Up a Dialog

In order to create a modal dialog, start by creating a new form, as detailed in the solution "How Can I Create a New Form and Display It?" GUI design guidelines state that dialogs should always have a button that the user clicks to dismiss it, and that this button is usually labeled OK or something similar. If the dialog lets users make changes to data, which they may want to cancel, then the dialog should display a second button, typically labeled Cancel. It is also very common in dialogs for the Enter key to have the same effect as clicking OK and for the Esc key to have the same effect as clicking the Cancel button. You can let .NET know which buttons to associate with the Enter and Esc keys by using the form's **AcceptButton()** and **CancelButton()** functions.

Dialogs are usually created by other forms, so how do you let the parent form know which button was pressed in order to dismiss the dialog? Dialog forms have a **DialogResult** property, so you can set this property in order to pass a value back, like this:

```
' Set the dialog return value
Me.DialogResult = DialogResult.OK
```

The values you can use are laid out in the **DialogResult** enumeration, and they're listed in Table 9.6. The **DialogResult** property not only sets a value that can later be retrieved, but it also sends the dialog away. This means that **DialogResult** is typically used in the handler for the OK and Cancel buttons, like this:

```
Protected Sub OKButton_Click(ByVal sender As Object, _
            ByVal e As System.EventArgs)
  ' Set the return value and close the dialog
  Me.DialogResult = DialogResult.OK
End Sub
```

An alternative way of doing this is to assign the value to the **DialogResult** property of the buttons themselves. When a button with a **DialogResult** is clicked, it causes the dialog to close and sends the result back to the parent form.

Using the Dialog

In order to display a dialog as a modal dialog, create a form object, and call its **ShowDialog()** method, like this:

```
' Create a form and display it as a dialog
Dim dlg As New MyDialog()
dlg.ShowDialog()
```

If you're interested in knowing which button was clicked to dismiss the dialog, check the **DialogResult** property:

```
' Create a form and display it as a dialog
Dim dlg As New MyDialog()
Dim result As DialogResult
```

```
result = dlg.ShowDialog()

If result = DialogResult.OK Then
  ' OK button pressed
End If
```

Displaying MessageBoxes

Everyone knows what a MessageBox is—a small dialog designed to display a text message to the user along with an icon to indicate whether the message is informative, is a warning, or is an error. Figure 9.13 shows a typical MessageBox.

MessageBoxes are represented by the **MessageBox** class. You don't create instances of MessageBox yourself, but instead use the shared (static) **Show()** method. Like dialogs, a **Show()** returns a **DialogResult** value telling you which button was clicked to dismiss the dialog.

There are 12 overrides of **Show()**. The most basic simply takes a text string for the message and displays a MessageBox with no title or icon and a single OK button. The others let you create MessageBoxes based on combinations of

- message
- title
- button type(s)
- icon type

The button and icon types are represented by members of the **MessageBoxButtons** and **MessageBoxIcon** enumerations, and the most commonly used values are shown in Tables 9.10 and 9.11.

Here's an example showing how to display a MessageBox in VB:

```
MessageBox.Show(""Message", "Title", _
       MessageBoxButtons.OK, MessageBox.IconHand)
```

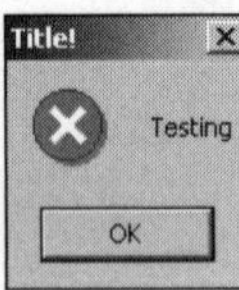

Figure 9.13 A typical MessageBox with text, a title, and an icon.

Table 9.10 Members of the MessageBoxButtons enumeration.

Member	Description
AbortRetryIgnore	Specifies that the MessageBox contains Abort, Retry, and Ignore buttons
OK	Specifies that the MessageBox contains an OK button
OKCancel	Specifies that the MessageBox contains OK and Cancel buttons
RetryCancel	Specifies that the MessageBox contains Retry and Cancel buttons
YesNo	Specifies that the MessageBox contains Yes and No buttons
YesNoCancel	Specifies that the MessageBox contains Yes, No, and Cancel buttons

Table 9.11 Members of the MessageBoxIcon enumeration.

Member	Description
Asterisk, **Information**	Specifies that the MessageBox contains an asterisk icon
Error, **Hand**, **Stop**	Specifies that the MessageBox contains a hand icon
Exclamation, **Warning**	Specifies that the MessageBox contains an exclamation point ('!') icon
Question	Specifies that the MessageBox contains a question mark icon

How Do I Work with Menus on Forms?

You can add a menu to a form by choosing the MainMenu control from the Toolbox and dragging it onto the form. The visual menu designer lets you create the menu items directly on the form. In Figure 9.14, I've created an example of a top-level File menu with a single Exit menu item. The pane at the bottom of the designer window holds a small icon entitled MainMenu1, and you'll see an entry in this pane for controls, such as menus and timers.

You add more menu items by entering text into the Type Here boxes. The one on the menu bar creates a new top-level menu, whereas entering text into the box below Exit adds an item to the File menu, and the one to the right of Exit adds a submenu. Figure 9.15 shows a more complete menu with submenus.

TIP: *Putting an & character before one of the characters in the menu text string will provide the quick access character for that menu item, and the character will appear underlined when you run the application.*

TIP: *You can insert a separator bar by right-clicking on a menu item and selecting Insert Separator from the context menu.*

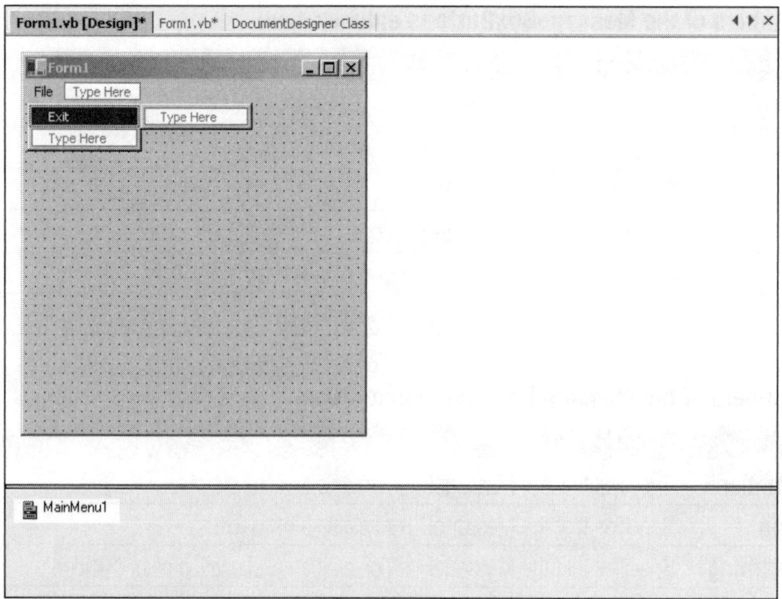

Figure 9.14 Creating a menu in a Windows Forms application.

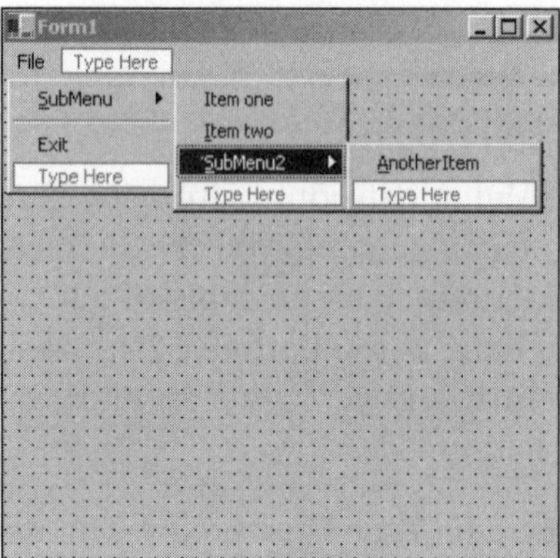

Figure 9.15 A more complete menu on a Windows Form.

You can delete menu items by right-clicking on the item and selecting Delete from the context menu. Inserting new items means right-clicking on the item below where you want the new item, and then choosing Insert New from the context menu. Moving items around is done by using Cut or Copy and Paste from the context menu.

Handling Menu Events

To add a handler for a menu item, simply double-click on the menu item in the Designer. You'll be taken to the code window where you will be presented with a skeleton handler function, which looks like this:

```
Private Sub MenuItem2_Click(ByVal sender As System.Object, _
                  ByVal e As System.EventArgs)
   ' Handle the menu item here...
End Sub
```

In VB, the arguments to this function are seldom used, but if you're handling a menu in C# or C++, you may well need to use them in order to find out which item originated the event and what event it was. VB handles this internally, and you can be sure that if you end up in the **MenuItem2_Click()** function, then it was **MenuItem2** that sent you a **Click** event.

Working with Menus in Code

It is very simple to work with **Menus** and **MenuItems** in code. You can make use of the properties of the **Menu** and **MenuItem** classes to add, remove, and change menu items at runtime.

TIP: *Although it is possible to modify menus at runtime, user interface creation guidelines recommend that dynamic modification of menus be kept to a minimum because of the risk of creating confusing and hard-to-work-with menu hierarchies.*

There are several tasks you may want to accomplish when working with menus:

- Adding and removing menu items
- Enabling and disabling items
- Adding and removing checks
- Changing menu text
- Adding and displaying shortcuts

Adding and removing menu items is accomplished using the **MenuItems** property of a **Menu** or **MenuItem**:

```
' Add an item
item = New MenuItem("one")
main.MenuItems.Add(item)
```

The **MenuItems** property is a .NET collection that holds all the **MenuItems** belonging to a **Menu** or **MenuItem**, so it has all the usual properties and methods belonging to collections, including **Add()**, **Remove()**, and **Clear()** methods and the ability to use enumerators. If you want to add more than one item at a time to a menu, put them into an array and use the **AddRange()** method.

It is recommended that programs display a consistent menu hierarchy, and that options currently unavailable are disabled, which can be done using the **Enabled** property:

```
' Disable this item
printItem.Enabled = False
```

If you want to display a checkmark next to a menu item, use the **Checked** property:

```
' Check this item
optionItem.Checked = True
```

The **Index** property represents the zero-based position of this item within its parent, and you can assign a different value in order to move the item within the list. However, this should be avoided to prevent user confusion.

The **Text** property represents the text of the **MenuItem**, and once again, you can change it in order to modify the appearance of the item.

Shortcuts are key combinations, which frequently use Ctrl, Shift, or Alt combined with other keys, which enable users to activate frequently used menu items without navigating through a menu hierarchy. The **Shortcut** and **ShowShortcut** properties let you assign and display shortcuts:

```
' Add a shortcut to this item
printItem.Shortcut = Shortcut.CtrlP
printItem.ShowShortcut = True
```

The **Windows.Forms.Shortcut** enumeration defines a number of values corresponding to useful key combinations.

TIP: *Try to use the commonly accepted shortcuts in your applications, such as Ctrl+P for File | Print, Ctrl+N for File | New, Ctrl+S for File | Save, and so on. Assigning such shortcuts to other menu items or using other shortcuts for common menu items will lead to a confusing and unintuitive user interface.*

How Do I Associate a Context Menu with a Form?

A context menu is a menu that pops up when you click the right mouse button over a form or control. They are very popular, appearing in many applications, and very easy to add to a project. Start by selecting the ContextMenu control from the Toolbox, and draw a context menu on the form or control that is going

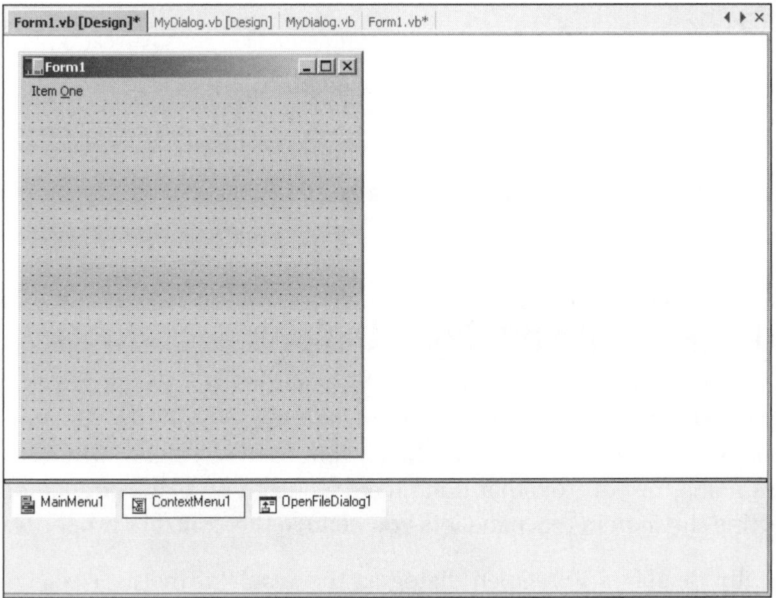

Figure 9.16 Adding a context menu to a form.

to host the menu. Notice in Figure 9.16 how a ContextMenu1 icon has been added to the pane at the bottom of the Designer window: There's only one menu editor, which displays at the top of the form, so you use the icons to decide which menu you want to edit.

You can add menu items to the form in exactly the same way as you do for a main menu, which I described in the previous solution. Note that all the items you want to display in the pop-up menu need to be defined as top-level menu items, as shown in Figure 9.17.

Before this menu will pop up, you need to let the form or control know that it has a context menu. You do this by setting the **ContextMenu** property of the form or control to refer to the **ContextMenu** item. Once you've done this, build and run the application. You'll find that you can pop up the menu using the right-mouse button, as shown in Figure 9.18.

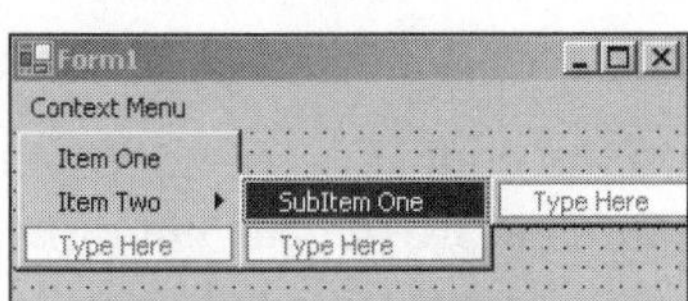

Figure 9.17 Creating context menu items.

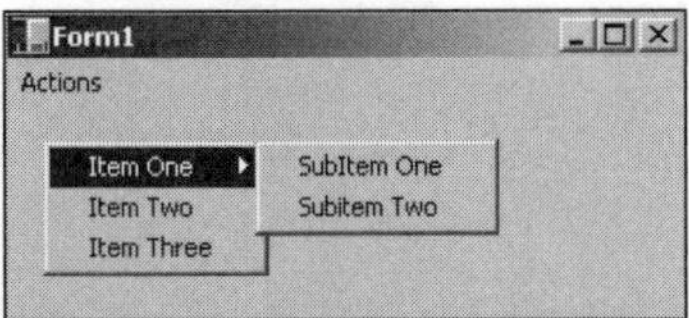

Figure 9.18 Displaying the context menu for a form.

Displaying File Open and Close Dialogs

To use a File Open dialog, select the OpenFileDialog in the Toolbox, and draw one on the form that is the parent of this dialog. You'll see an icon for OpenFileDialog1 appear in the pane at the bottom of the Designer window. This pane shows icons for controls that don't have a design time appearance on the form. Selecting the icon in this pane lets you change the control's properties.

You'll typically display a File Open dialog as the result of the user selecting a menu item. The following code shows how you can do this:

```
Protected Sub FileOpen_Click(ByVal sender As Object, _
            ByVal e As System.EventArgs)
  ' Set up the dialog
  OpenFileDialog1.InitialDirectory = "d:\"
  OpenFileDialog1.Filter = "txt files (*.txt)|*.txt|All files (*.*)|*.*"
  OpenFileDialog1.FilterIndex = 1
  OpenFileDialog1.RestoreDirectory = True

  ' Show the dialog and handle the result
  If OpenFileDialog1.ShowDialog() = DialogResult.OK Then
    MessageBox.Show("File chosen was " & OpenFileDialog1.FileName)
  End If
End Sub
```

The Designer will already have created the **OpenFileDialog1** object for you, but before you show the dialog, you need to set its properties to provide a useful starting point for the user. The class has a number of properties, which are summarized in Table 9.12.

Using this table, it is easy to see what I'm doing in the code. I've set up the dialog to point to the root of the D: drive initially, and then restore the current directory when finished. File dialogs can contain filters that will cause the dialog to display only those files that match a pattern. In this example, the filter string specifies two filters and contains a description of the filter, such as "text files (*.txt)" followed

Table 9.12 Useful properties of the OpenFileDialog class.

Property	Description
AddExtension	Determines whether an extension is automatically added to the file name if the user doesn't provide one.
CheckFileExists	Determines whether a warning is displayed if the user tries to open a file that doesn't exist.
CheckPathExists	Determines whether a warning is displayed if the user tries to specify a path that doesn't exist.
DefaultExt	Provides a default extension.
FileName	When the dialog has been closed, holds the name chosen by the user.
FileNames	When the dialog has been closed, holds an array of all the names selected by the user. This only works if **MultiSelect** has been set to true.
Filter	Holds the current filter string, which appears in the Save As File Type box on the dialog.
FilterIndex	Indicates which filter is being used.
InitialDirectory	Indicates the initial directory to be displayed by the dialog.
MultiSelect	Indicates whether multiple selection is supported.
ReadOnlyChecked	Indicates whether the read-only checkbox is selected.
RestoreDirectory	Indicates whether the current directory is to be restored when the dialog exits.
ShowReadOnly	Indicates whether the dialog shows a read-only checkbox.
ValidateNames	Indicates whether the dialog only accepts valid Win32 file names.

by the filter pattern itself. The components of the filter string are separated by vertical bars. The **FilterIndex** property is set to one, so the first filter is displayed by default.

Once the dialog has been set up correctly, I show the dialog, which displays something very similar to Figure 9.19.

When the user dismisses the dialog, I check which button was clicked by looking at the result returned from **ShowDialog()**. If the OK button was clicked, I display the **FileName** property in a MessageBox.

The File Save dialog has many of the same properties, and using it is very similar to using the File Open dialog.

***NOTE:** It is frequently asked whether there is a way to use a File Open dialog to implement a directory selector, so that you can navigate around and select a directory rather than a file. Unfortunately, there isn't an easy way because the File Open dialog wants you to select a file before returning and won't accept a directory.*

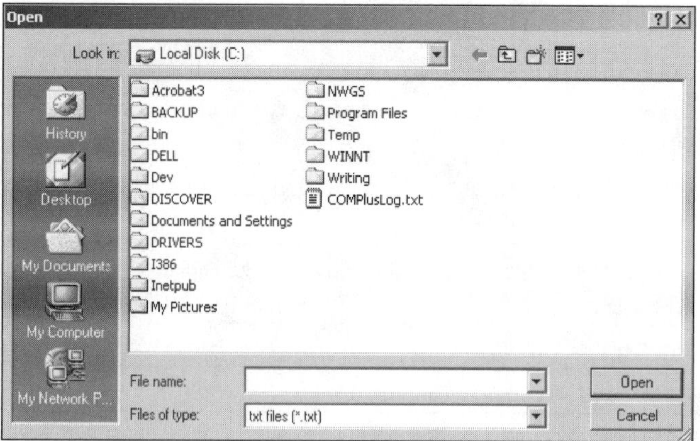

Figure 9.19 A File Open common dialog.

How Can I Create a Form Based on One I've Already Defined?

.NET's new visual inheritance feature lets you create a form or dialog, and then use it as a base for creating new ones. All the new forms will contain the same controls as the base form, together with all their functionality.

Here's an example of how to make visual inheritance work. Start by creating a standard Windows application, and then add some controls to the main form, as shown in Figure 9.20. I've set the background of the form to white, just to make it look a little different.

You need to build the project before visual inheritance can be demonstrated, so press Ctrl+Shift+B or choose the Build | Build menu item.

Next, choose Add Inherited Form from the Project menu. The Add New Item dialog appears, as shown in Figure 9.21.

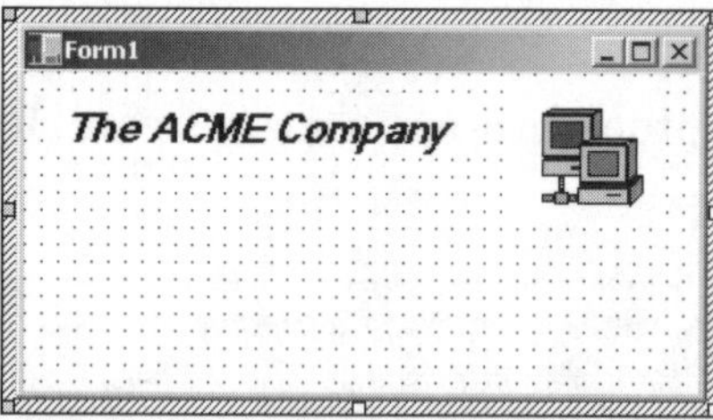

Figure 9.20 A form that is used to demonstrate visual inheritance.

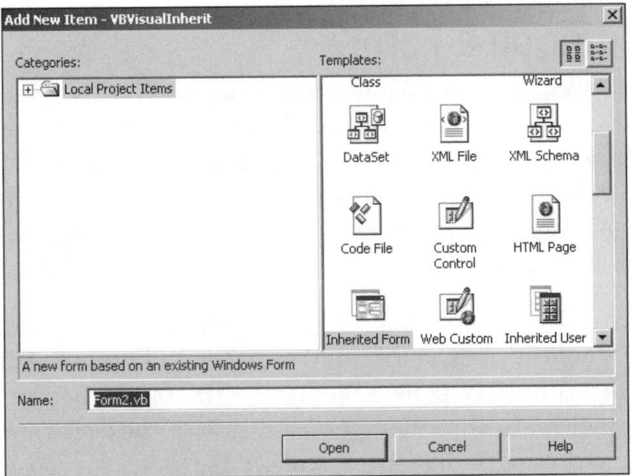

Figure 9.21 The Add New Item dialog.

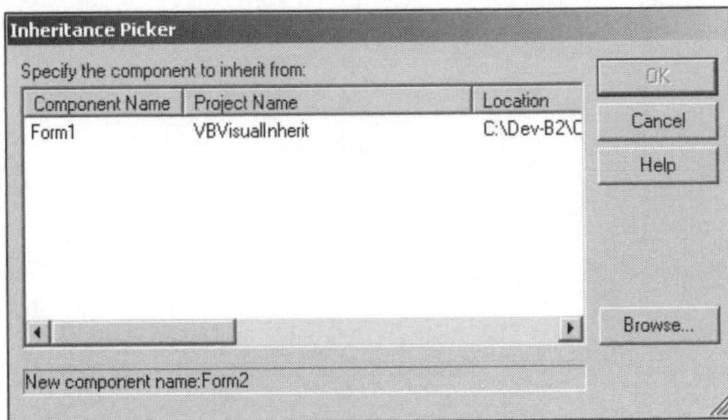

Figure 9.22 Choosing a form to inherit using the Inheritance Picker dialog.

Make sure that Inherited Form is selected in the Templates pane, choose a name for your new form, and click Open. The Inheritance Picker dialog opens, as shown in Figure 9.22, and displays a list of all the forms in your dialog from which you can derive your new form.

Choose the form, click OK, and a new form class is added to your project. When you look at the design view, you'll see that the new form has inherited all the controls from its parent, and that the controls are marked with a small arrow, very much like the one used to mark a file shortcut, to give you a clue that they are inherited.

And of course, you can have as many levels of inheritance as you like—deriving Form3 from Form2, which in turn is derived from Form1—adding new controls and functionality at each level.

How Do I Use a Splitter on a Form?

Splitters have become very popular with Windows programmers in the past few years, and you'll find that more and more programs incorporate them. Newcomers to Windows Explorer soon discover that by dragging the central divider between the tree and list panes, they can alter how the screen real estate is shared between the two panes. In early implementations, this was done by careful custom programming, but in .NET there is a control to help.

Here's how you can use a splitter to produce a Windows Explorer-like interface. Start by placing a TreeView control on the form, and set its **Dock** property so that it fills the left-hand side of the form. Now place a Splitter control onto the form, and you should find that it attaches itself to the right-hand side of the TreeView. Finally, place a ListView control onto the TreeView, and set its **Dock** property to fill the rest of the form. You end up with an application containing a ListView on the right, a TreeView on the left, and a splitter in the middle, as shown in Figure 9.23.

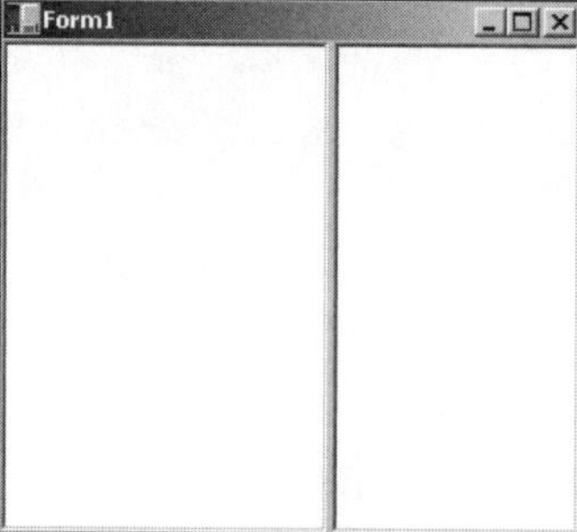

Figure 9.23 A form containing a Splitter control.

Chapter 10

Windows Forms and Controls

By Julian Templeman

If you need an immediate solution to:	*See page:*

In Depth

Chapter 9 discussed forms and how they are used. This chapter focuses on the controls that live on those forms.

.NET has a rich set of controls that let you build complex and sophisticated user interfaces, so there's a lot to cover in this chapter. I'll start by describing the **Control** base class before going on to examine individual controls in detail.

Forms and Controls

You've seen how the **Form** class represents a window and forms the base class for all other windows. The **Control** class is the base class for "components with visual representation"; it forms the base for everything you see on the screen and interact with.

You can create your own control classes by deriving from one of the control classes. You don't normally derive directly from **Control** itself, but from **UserControl** or one of the built-in controls. As you can see in Figure 10.1, **UserControl** adds functionality—such as scrolling—to **Control**, and it provides a blank control to which you can add your own user interface (UI) and functionality.

Figure 10.1 shows the overall class hierarchy in the **System.Windows.Forms** namespace and how the **Control** classes fit in.

If you want to know what each of the classes does and what functionality it provides to the hierarchy, refer to Table 9.1 in Chapter 9.

The Control Class

Controls are actually two-part entities in .NET. When you create a control, such as a button in a .NET program, you start by creating an object in memory. This object then creates the actual button on the screen, so that the .NET object is managing a Windows button for you. It's possible to have a .NET control object without it creating a Windows control, and it is also possible for the Windows control to be destroyed before the .NET object.

If you look in the methods of the **Control** class, you'll see the **CreateControl()** method that is used to force creation of the underlying Windows control. You don't very often call this yourself because a form will call it automatically for all its child controls at runtime.

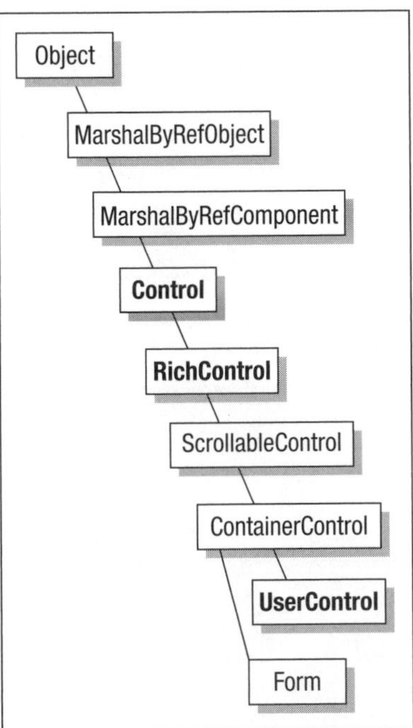

Figure 10.1 How the **Control** classes fit into the **System.Windows.Forms** namespace.

Control is a very complex class and possesses a lot of properties, methods, and events. I'll list some of the main ones in this section, so that you can get a feel for just what controls can do. Table 10.1 lists the class's main properties.

You'll notice that several properties mention *handles* or *window handles*. Previously, I explained how a control is composed of a .NET object plus a Windows control object. Every window belonging to an application—and that includes buttons, listboxes, and scrollbars—has a unique identifier called a *window handle*. If you're going to use some part of the underlying Windows API that isn't wrapped in .NET yet, you may need to refer to the handle. Because the handle belongs to the underlying Windows control, your control object won't have a handle until the screen control has been created.

One of the most useful of these properties is **Controls**. Many controls—such as GroupBoxes and Panels—can have others as children, and **Controls** is a collection that holds references to all the child controls. Because it is a standard collection, it has **Add()**, **Remove()**, and **Clear()** methods that can be used to change the content, and you can obtain an enumerator to walk over the collection.

TIP: *For details on how to use enumerators with collections, see Chapter 4.*

Table 10.1 The main properties of the Control class.

Property	Description
Anchor, **Dock**	Controls the positioning of controls relative to form borders.
BackColor, **ForeColor**	Gets and sets the background and foreground colors of the control.
BackgroundImage	Represents the background image associated with the control.
Bottom, **Top**, **Left**, **Right**	Coordinates in pixels the bottom, top, left, and right of the control.
Width, **Height**	The width and height of the control in pixels.
Bounds	The bounding rectangle within which this control fits.
CanFocus, **CanSelect**	Read-only properties that indicate whether the control can receive the focus and can be selected.
CausesValidation	Indicates whether entering this control causes validation of controls that require validation.
ContainsFocus	Read-only property showing whether this control (or one of its children) has the focus.
Controls	The collection of children of this control.
ContextMenu	Represents the context menu associated with this control. The menu will be shown when the user right-clicks on the control.
Cursor	Represents the cursor that will be displayed when the mouse is over this control.
Created	Read-only property indicating whether the underlying screen control has been created.
Disposing, **Disposed**	Read-only property indicating whether the underlying screen control is in the process of or has been destroyed.
Enabled	Indicates whether the control is enabled.
Focused	Read-only property indicating whether the control has the focus.
Font	Gets and sets the font associated with the control.
Handle	Read-only property representing the underlying window handle. Use the Boolean **IsHandleCreated** to determine whether a control has an associated handle.
Location, **Size**	Represents the location and size of the control.
ModifierKeys, **MouseButtons**, **MousePosition**	Retrieves the current state of the modifier keys (Ctrl, Alt, and Shift), the mouse buttons, and the current mouse position.
Parent	The parent of this control.
TabIndex	An integer representing the tab index of this control.
TabStop	A Boolean property indicating whether the user can give the focus to this control using the Tab key.
Text	The text associated with this control. Exactly what this text represents (if anything) varies with the control type.
Visible	Indicates whether the control is visible.

The **Control** class has just over 100 methods, many of which are somewhat esoteric. Table 10.2 lists some of the most commonly used methods.

Table 10.2 Commonly used methods of the Control class.

Method	Description
BringToFront, **SendToBack**	Sends the control to the front or back of the Z-order. (The "Z-order" is a computer graphics term denoting the front-to-back ordering of overlapping windows on the screen.).
Contains	Verifies whether the control has a particular child.
CreateControl	Forces creation of the underlying Windows control, including the creation of the window handle and any children.
DoDragDrop	Begins a drag-drop operation.
FindForm	Retrieves the form hosting this control. It may not be the same as the parent.
Focus	Attempts to set the focus to this control.
FromChildHandle, **FromHandle.**	Returns the control associated with a particular handle.
GetChildAtPoint	Retrieves the child control at a particular set of coordinates.
GetNextControl	Retrieves the next child control in the tab order.
GetStyle, **SetStyle**	Gets and sets the control's style.
Hide, **Show**	Hides or shows the control by toggling the **Visible** property.
Invalidate	Cause a paint message to be sent to the control.
OnClick	Raises the **Click** event.
OnGotFocus	Raises the **GotFocus** event.
OnKeyDown, **OnKeyPress**, **OnKeyUp**	Handles keyboard messages.
OnMouseDown, **OnMouseUp**, **OnMouseMove**	Handles mouse messages.
OnPaint	Handles a paint request.
OnResize	Called when the control is resized.
ResetBackColor, **ResetForeColor**, **ResetFont**, **ResetCursor**	Sets the properties to those of the control's parent
Scale	Scales the control and any child controls.
Update	Forces the control to repaint any invalid areas.

Control Styles

The style of a **Control** can be acquired and set using the **GetStyle()** and **SetStyle()** methods, which both use the **Windows.Forms.ControlStyles** enumeration, as shown in Table 10.3.

NOTE: *These styles are .NET control styles, not the Win32 control styles of the underlying Windows control.*

Painting and Invalidation

It is often necessary to tell a control—or, indeed, any window—that it needs to repaint itself. This may happen for a number of reasons: The content of the control may have been updated, or the application may have been minimized or obscured by another window.

Table 10.3 The Windows.Forms.ControlStyles enumeration.

Member	Description
AllPaintingInWmPaint	**WM_ERASEBKGND** is ignored, and both **OnPaintBackground** and **OnPaint** are called directly from **WM_PAINT**. This can reduce flicker.
CacheText	Controls cache a copy of their text, rather than getting it from the underlying control each time.
ContainerControl	Indicates whether the control is a container-like control.
DoubleBuffer	Performs double-buffered drawing to reduce flicker.
EnableNotifyMessage	If true, **OnNotifyMessage()** is called for each message sent to the control.
FixedHeight, FixedWidth	The control has a fixed height and/or width.
Opaque	A **PaintBackground** event will not be called, and **Invalidate()** won't invalidate the background of the control.
ResizeRedraw	The control is redrawn when it is resized.
Selectable	The control is selectable.
StandardClick	Windows Forms calls **OnClick** when the control is clicked. The control can also call **OnClick** directly if desired.
StandardDoubleClick	Windows Forms calls **OnDoubleClick** when the control is double-clicked. The control can also call **OnDoubleClick** directly if desired.
SupportsTransparentBackColor	This control can use a transparent background.
UserPaint	The control paints itself, and **WM_PAINT** and **WM_ERASEBKGND** messages aren't passed on to the underlying Windows control.
UserMouse	The control does its own mouse processing.
ResizeRedraw	The control is completely redrawn when it is resized.

If you need to cause a control to repaint itself, call its **Invalidate()** method. This causes a paint message to be sent to the control, which will be processed in due course. In the case of controls with complex content, it is also possible to pass **Invalidate()** a rectangle indicating the region that needs updating.

Calling **Invalidate()** doesn't force the control to repaint itself there and then, but simply queues a request for future processing. If you want to force an immediate repaint, call the control's **Update()** method. **Refresh()** is similar to **Update()** in that it forces an immediate repaint of the control and its children.

Working with Controls

A large number of controls are provided by .NET for you to use on forms, and almost all of them are available via the Visual Studio.NET Toolbox. Figure 10.2 shows what this Toolbox looks like.

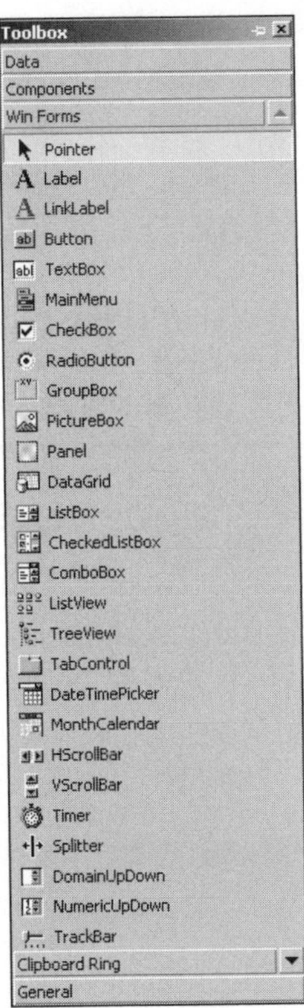

Figure 10.2 The Visual Studio .NET Toolbox.

Labels and LinkLabels

Labels are among the simplest of controls and are used to represent simple decoration—usually text—on forms. The **Text** property governs what displays on a Label, and the **UseMnemonic** property determines whether **&** characters are to be interpreted as keyboard shortcut mnemonic markers.

Labels can also be used to display images, and the **Image** property can be set to point to an object of type **System.Drawing.Bitmap**. See Chapter 11 for more details on image handling in .NET.

The label can be text or an image, and the navigation is handled in the label's **LinkClick()** handler. You can use a LinkLabel to navigate to a Web site or to another form in the application. Various properties are available to set the colors of active, disabled, and visited links.

***NOTE:** The LinkLabel itself doesn't have any navigation functionality. Its purpose is to display text or an image that behaves in the same way as a link does in a browser.*

Buttons

Everyone is familiar with buttons in graphical user interface (GUI) applications: controls whose only purpose in life is to be clicked. Some may toggle between the on and off positions, such as checkboxes and radio buttons, whereas normal buttons have a momentary press-and-release action. .NET contains support for these three types of button, all of which inherit from the abstract class **ButtonBase**.

ButtonBase has several useful properties that are shared by all button classes, as shown in Table 10.4.

The **FlatStyle** property can be used to create buttons that behave like those on the Internet Explorer toolbar, which are normally flat and only pop up with a 3D border when the mouse moves over them.

Table 10.4 Properties of the ButtonBase class.

Property	Description
FlatStyle	Governs whether the button will display flat or raised
Image	Represents the image that is displayed on a button
ImageAlign	Represents the alignment of the image on the button
IsDefault	Determines whether a button is the default button for a form
Text	Represents the text on the button
TextAlign	Represents the alignment of the text on the button

A button displays as a rectangular control that fires a **Click** event when the user clicks on it; the **Click** event can also be fired if the user presses the Enter key when the button has the focus. It returns to its unselected state when the **Click** event has been fired.

Buttons are often used to control dialogs, and you can associate a value with the button object's **DialogResult** property, which is returned when the dialog is closed:

```
' Associate the OK value with the button
Button1.DialogResult  = System.WinForms.DialogResult.OK
```

Associating a **DialogResult** with a button has two consequences. First, it sets the value that is returned to the parent form when the dialog is closed. Second, it causes the dialog to be closed when the button is pressed.

NOTE: *See Chapter 9 for more details on working with dialogs.*

CheckBoxes and RadioButtons

CheckBoxes and RadioButtons are similar in that they allow the user to choose from a list of alternatives. The difference between them is that CheckBoxes allow the user to choose a number of items, whereas only one of a group of RadioButtons can be chosen. Figure 10.3 shows both CheckBoxes and RadioButtons being used on a form. Table 10.5 lists the properties that **CheckBox** adds to **ButtonBase**.

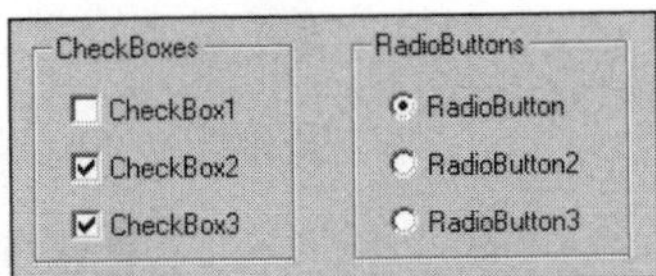

Figure 10.3 CheckBoxes and RadioButtons on a form.

Table 10.5 Properties of the CheckBox class.

Property	Description
Appearance	Determines whether the CheckBox appears as normal or as a latchable button.
AutoCheck	Determines whether the CheckBox automatically responds to user clicks. If false, you need to code the **Click** event handler to set the state of the CheckBox.
CheckAlign	Specifies the alignment of the text.
Checked	A Boolean property representing the state of the CheckBox.
CheckState	Represents the state of the CheckBox (Checked, Unchecked, or Indeterminate).
ThreeState	True if the CheckBox can display three states.

Figure 10.4 A CheckBox with its Appearance property set to Button.

The **Appearance** property determines whether the CheckBox appears as a traditional checkbox (as in Figure 10.3) or as a latchable button, shown in Figure 10.4.

A three-state CheckBox is one that can cycle through three states—Checked, Unchecked, and Indeterminate—the latter being shown by a grayed-out box, as in Figure 10.5.

CheckBoxes support two events over and above buttons: **OnCheckedChanged**, which is fired when the checked state of the control changes, and **OnCheckedStateChanged**, which is used for three-state CheckBoxes.

RadioButtons are very similar to CheckBoxes. The major differences are their appearance (round button instead of square checkbox) and the only-one-selected behavior. Like CheckBoxes, RadioButtons can be displayed as latchable buttons.

Grouping RadioButtons

The **GroupBox** control is used to create groups of RadioButtons that behave in the traditional way, so that only one of the group can be selected. GroupBoxes can be used with any controls, but they only have this special effect with RadioButtons.

The GroupBox has a **Controls** property, and you can use the **Add()** method to add a control to the group.

ListBoxes

This section discusses the **ListBox** control and its subclasses—**CheckedListBox** and **ComboBox**.

A ListBox displays a list of items, usually strings, in a scrolling window. If more items are added to the list than can be displayed at once, a scrollbar is added automatically. The user can select an item using the mouse or the keyboard. Table 10.6 lists some of the most commonly used properties of the **ListBox** class.

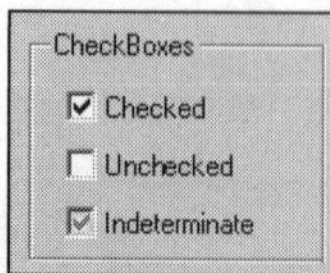

Figure 10.5 Three-state CheckBoxes on a form.

Table 10.6 Properties of the ListBox class.

Property	Description
BackgroundImage	Defines an image to be used as the background for the listbox
BorderStyle	Represents the border style for the listbox
DrawMode	Determines whether all items in the control are drawn by the system or by the program
HorizontalExtent	Indicates the width in pixels by which a listbox can be scrolled horizontally
HorizontalScrollbar	Determines whether the listbox displays a scrollbar for items that are too wide
IntegralHeight	Indicates that the listbox should avoid showing partial items
ItemHeight	Returns the height of an item in an owner-draw listbox
Items	The collection of items in the listbox
MultiColumn	Indicates whether this listbox is multicolumn
PreferredHeight	The total height of all the items in the listbox
ScrollAlwaysVisible	Determines whether the scrollbars are always visible
SelectedIndex	Represents the index of the currently selected item
SelectedIndices	A collection representing the currently selected items. If there are none, the result is an empty collection
SelectedItem	The value of the currently selected item or null if there isn't one
SelectedItems	A collection of the selected items or an empty collection if there are none selected
SelectionMode	Represents the current selection mode of the listbox
Sorted	A Boolean property indicating whether the items in the listbox are to be sorted or not
TopIndex	The index of the item at the top of the listbox

I'll briefly mention a few of the more noteworthy of these properties. The **BorderStyle** property controls how the border is drawn around the control; its value must be one from the **System.Windows.Forms.BorderStyle** enumeration and can be one of None, FixedSingle, or Fixed3D, with the default being Fixed3D.

DrawMode takes one of the values from the **Windows.Forms.DrawMode** enumeration, which indicates whether the items in the control are drawn by the system (Normal) or are drawn by the program (OwnerDrawFixed for fixed height items, OwnerDrawVariable for variable height items).

NOTE: *An owner-draw control is one where the programmer writes code to draw part or all of the control at runtime. This is an advanced GUI programming topic and outside the scope of this book.*

The **Items** property represents the list of items being displayed by the control as a **ListBox.ObjectCollection**. This class is a standard .NET collection, implementing the ICollection and IEnumerable interfaces, so it is very simple to work with the **Items** property if you know how collections work. If you need more information about collections, see Chapter 4, which provides details on working with collection classes.

The selection mechanism will be familiar to anyone who has worked with Windows listboxes in the past. ListBox controls can be set to allow single or multiple selection, which is controlled via the **SelectionMode** property. This property takes one of the values from the **System.Windows.Forms.SelectionMode** enumeration, namely:

- **None** (nothing can be selected)
- **One** (one item can be selected at a time)
- **MultiSimple** (more than one item can be selected at a time)
- **MultiExtended** (more than one item can be selected, and keyboard combinations, such as Ctrl and Shift, can be used in selection)

If a ListBox supports single selection, you can use the **SelectedIndex** property to get or set the index of the currently selected item. This index is zero-based, and when retrieving the index, a value of -1 indicates that nothing is selected. You can get a reference to the currently selected object using the **SelectedItem** property, which will be **Nothing** (**null** in C#) if nothing is selected.

Multiple selection controls use the **SelectedIndices** and **SelectedItems** properties, which return collections representing the selection. If nothing is selected, empty collections are returned.

Table 10.7 shows some the most commonly used methods of the **ListBox** class.

The **BeginUpdate()** and **EndUpdate()** methods are worth mentioning in a little more detail. The preferred way to add items to a ListBox is to create an array of items, and then use them to set the **All** property of **ListBox.Items**, like this:

```
' Create an array of Strings
Dim listItems As String() = { "One", "Two", "Three" }

' Add them all to the ListBox
ListBox1.Items.All = listItems
```

Sometimes you don't know what you're going to need in advance, so you can use the **Items.Add()** method to add items individually. The problem with this is that the ListBox will want to repaint itself every time you add an item, which can

Table 10.7 Methods of the ListBox class.

Method	Description
BeginUpdate	Prevents the control from repainting when adding items one by one
EndUpdate	Tells the control it can update
FindString	Finds the first item in the listbox that starts with the given string. The match isn't case-sensitive
FindStringExact	Finds the first item in the listbox that matches the given string. The match isn't case-sensitive
GetSelected	Tells you whether the item at the given index is selected or not
IndexFromPoint	Returns the index of the item at the given point
SetSelected	Sets an item as selected or deselected
Sort	Sorts the items in the list box alphabetically

make for annoying flickering. The **BeginUpdate()** and **EndUpdate()** methods can be used to switch repainting off before adding items, and then back on again afterwards, thus making for efficient IU updating:

```
' Turn updating off
ListBox1.BeginUpdate()

' Add items...
ListBox1.Items.Add(New String("One"))
ListBox1.Items.Add(New String("Two"))
ListBox1.Items.Add(New String("Three"))

' Turn updating back on
ListBox1.EndUpdate()
```

The **ListBox** class has many events, most of which are inherited from its parent **Control** class. The one that is specific to this class that you'll use often is **SelectedIndexChanged**, which is fired whenever the user selects another item in the ListBox.

CheckedListBoxes

A CheckedListBox is a ListBox in which each item has a checkbox in front of it.

CheckedListBox doesn't add much to its **ListBox** parent class. One significant addition is the **CheckOnClick** property, which determines whether selecting the item and the checkbox is done with one click or whether you have to check the box and select the item using two mouse clicks. The **ThreeDCheckBoxes** property determines whether checkboxes appear flat or in 3D.

The **GetItemChecked()** method returns true if a particular item is checked, and **GetItemCheckState()** tells you the check state of an item, which may be checked, unchecked, or indeterminate.

SetItemChecked() and **SetItemCheckState()** lets you manipulate the state of checkboxes on items.

ComboBoxes

A ComboBox is a combination of a listbox and an edit control, designed to save space in that the list is only displayed when you want to select an item. The **Style** property determines how the ComboBox looks and behaves. Figures 10.6 through 10.8 show the three styles.

A Simple ComboBox always has the list portion visible, and the text in the edit control is editable. The text in the edit control is also editable in a DropDown ComboBox, but the list only drops down when the user clicks on the button. In a DropDownList ComboBox the text is not editable, and the list appears when the button is pressed.

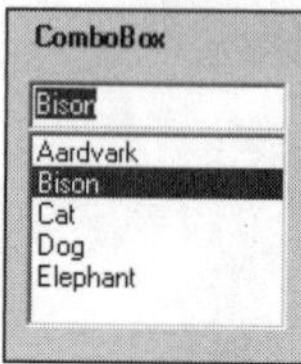

Figure 10.6 A ComboBox with Simple style.

Figure 10.7 A ComboBox with DropDown style showing the list hidden and text selected in the edit control.

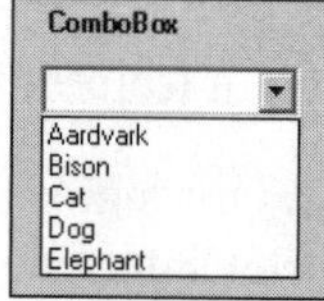

Figure 10.8 A ComboBox with DropDownList style showing the list displayed.

***NOTE:** ComboBoxes with Simple style are not often used nowadays, and it is recommended that if you always want to display the list, use a plain ListBox instead.*

You can retrieve the text displayed in the edit control using the **Text** property and get the index and value of the currently selected item in the list using **SelectedIndex()** and **SelectedItem()**.

TextBoxes

TextBoxBase is the base class that provides common functionality for all text controls. The **Windows.Forms** namespace comes with two text controls, **TextBox** and **RichTextBox**, which I'll discuss later in this section.

TextBoxBase has a number of commonly used properties, which are listed in Table 10.8. Many of these properties are self-descriptive, so I'll just make special mention of a few. The **BorderStyle** is the same as that of many other controls

Table 10.8 Commonly used properties of the TextBoxBase class.

Property	Description
AcceptsTab	Determines whether the control uses tab characters instead of causing the focus to move to the next control
AutoSize	Determines whether the size of the control adjusts when the font is changed
BackColor	Represents the background color of the control
BorderStyle	Represents the border style of the control
CanUndo	Indicates whether the user can undo the previous operation
ForeColor	Represents the foreground color of the control
Lines	Gets or sets the lines of text in the control
MaxLength	Represents the maximum number of characters the control will accept
Modified	Gets or sets a value indicating whether the content of the control has been modified
Multiline	Determines whether the control can display more than one line of text
ReadOnly	Determines whether the control is read-only. If true, the control paints with a gray background
SelectedText	Represents the currently selected text in the control
SelectionLength	Gets or sets the number of characters selected in the control
SelectionStart	Gets or sets the starting position of the selection
Text	Represents the text in the control
TextLength	Gets the length of the text in the control
WordWrap	Indicates a multiline control

and has as its value one of the members of the **Windows.Forms.BorderStyle** enumeration. Possible border styles are None (for no border), FixedSingle (for a flat look), and Fixed3D (for a 3D look; also the default style).

The **Lines** property takes the form of an array of strings, which contain the text for the control. If the **Multiline** property is set to **True**, any newline characters in the array of strings passed to **Lines** will cause a new line to be added.

If you pass more than one string into a single-line TextBox, the text is displayed in one long line with nonprintable characters representing the line breaks. You can see the difference between a single-line and multiline edit control in Figure 10.9.

The **MaxLength** property limits the number of characters that can be entered into the control. The default value for this property is zero, which means that there is no limit.

Users can select text in a TextBox using the mouse or keyboard, and there are several properties that can be used to get or set the selection. **SelectionStart** represents the zero-based character at the start of the selection, **SelectionLength** gives the length, and **SelectedText** is a string representing the selected text. All of these properties can be used to set the selected text as well as retrieve it, and so can be used to edit the text in the control.

Table 10.9 lists commonly used methods of **TextBoxBase**.

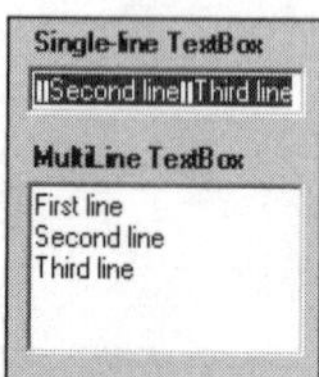

Figure 10.9 Displaying text in single-line and multiline TextBoxes.

Table 10.9 Commonly used methods of the TextBoxBase class.

Method	Description
AppendText	Adds some text to the control
Clear	Clears the text from the control
ClearUndo	Clears information about the most recent Undo operation so it can't be undone
Copy	Copies the selection to the clipboard
Cut	Cuts the selection to the clipboard
Paste	Pastes the clipboard content to the control
ScrollToCaret	Ensures that the caret is visible in the control, scrolling it if necessary

(continued)

Table 10.9 Commonly used methods of the TextBoxBase class *(continued)*.

Method	Description
Select	Selects a range of text in the TextBox
SelectAll	Selects all the text in the TextBox
Undo	Undoes the last clipboard or text change operation

The **Select()** method can be used as an alternative to the **SelectionStart** and **SelectionLength** properties when setting a selection. **Undo()** will undo the previous operation if the **CanUndo** property is set to true:

```
' One button on the form cuts part of the text
Protected Sub ChangeBtn_Click(ByVal sender As System.Object, _
       ByVal e As System.EventArgs) Handles ChangeBtn.Click
  ' Cut part of the text to the clipboard. This will
  ' set the CanUndo property because cutting is undoable
  TextBox1.SelectionStart = 6
  TextBox1.SelectionLength = 6
  TextBox1.Cut()
End Sub

' An 'undo' button on the form undoes the change
Protected Sub UndoBtn_Click(ByVal sender As System.Object, _
     ByVal e As System.EventArgs) Handles ChangeBtn.Click
  If TextBox1.CanUndo = True Then
    TextBox1.Undo()
    TextBox1.ClearUndo()
  Else
    MsgBox("Can't undo")
  End If
End Sub
```

TextBoxBase has an event from **Control**, **TextChanged**, which is fired whenever the content of the control is changed.

The TextBox Class

TextBoxBase has two controls derived from it: **TextBox** and **RichTextBox**. A **TextBox** wraps the functionality of a Windows edit control, but with a few extra features. Table 10.10 lists the extra properties that **TextBox** adds over and above **TextBoxBase**.

TextBox adds one event to **TextBoxBase—TextAlignChanged**, which is called when the text alignment is changed.

Table 10.10 Properties that the TextBox class adds to TextBoxBase.

Property	Description
AcceptsReturn	If true, the Enter key puts a new line in the TextBox; if false, it activates the form's default button. The default value is true.
CharacterCasing	Determines whether the control modifies the case of characters as they are entered.
PasswordChar	Represents the mask character used when passwords are entered.
ScrollBars	Determines which scrollbars should appear in a TextBox.
TextAlign	Represents the text alignment in the control.

The RichTextBox Class

The **RichTextBox** class extends **TextBoxBase** by supporting text formatting, which makes it a "word processor in a control," and it supports a number of extra properties, methods, and events in order to support this functionality. Like the underlying Windows Rich Edit control, the **RichTextBox** supports drag and drop and can contain embedded OLE objects.

NOTE: *If you haven't met rich text controls before, take a look at the Wordpad accessory application. Notepad is essentially a single TextBox in a frame, whereas Wordpad is a RichTextBox in a frame and provides a good overview of what can be done with one of these controls.*

There are more than 40 new properties for this class; Table 10.11 lists some of the most commonly used properties.

Table 10.11 Commonly used properties that the RichTextBox class adds to TextBoxBase.

Property	Description
AutoWordSelection	Determines whether mouse selection snaps to whole words.
BulletIndent	Represents the indentation for bullet points.
DetectUrls	Determines whether the control will automatically highlight URLs. This is true by default.
RTF	A string representing all the text in the control including RTF control codes.
SelectedRTF	Gets or sets the selected RTF text in the control.
SelectedText	Gets or sets the selected text in the control.
SelectionBullet	Determines if a paragraph in the control is bulleted.
SelectionColor	Represents the color of selected text.
SelectionFont	The font of the currently selected text. Returns Nothing (null) if the selection has more than one font.

(continued)

Table 10.11 Commonly used properties that the RichTextBox class adds to TextBoxBase *(continued).*

Property	Description
SelectionLength	Represents the number of characters selected in the control.
SelectionIndent	The distance in pixels between the left edge of the text and the left edge of the control.
SelectionRightIndent	The distance in pixels between the right edge of the text and the right edge of the control.
SelectionTabs	An array of integers representing the pixel positions of tabs within the control.
SelectionType	The type of the selection, as one of the members of the **RichTextBoxSelectionTypes** enumeration (e.g., **Text**, **Object**, **Empty**).
ZoomFactor	Represents the current zoom level for the control. The value can be between 1/64 and 64, with the default value of 1.0 indicating no zoom.

*TIP: **RichTextBox** makes heavy use of fonts, and you may want to refer to Chapter 11 for more details on fonts.*

The class also adds a number of methods to those it inherits from **TextBoxBase** in order to support its extra functionality, as shown in Table 10.12.

DataGrid

DataGrid is an extremely useful and sophisticated control that displays ADO.NET data in a scrollable grid. An example of a DataGrid is shown in Figure 10.10.

Table 10.12 Commonly used methods that the RichTextBox class adds to TextBoxBase.

Method	Description
CanPaste	Tells you whether the control can paste what's currently on the clipboard
Find	A group of overloaded methods that search the control for characters and strings
GetCharFromPosition	Gets the character nearest to the given point
GetCharIndexFromPosition	Gets the index of the character nearest to the given point
GetLineFromCharIndex	Gets the line containing a given character
GetPositionFromCharIndex	Returns the position of a given character
LoadFile	A group of overloaded methods to load text and RTF files into a control
Paste	Pastes the contents of the clipboard
Redo	Redoes an undone operation
SaveFile	A group of overloaded methods for saving the contents of the control to a file

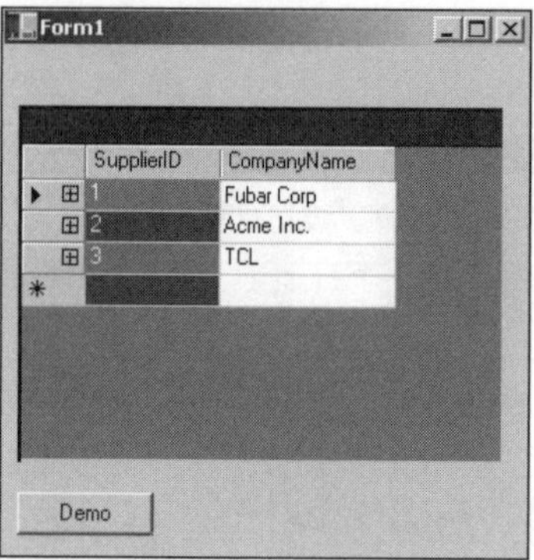

Figure 10.10 A DataGrid displaying sample data.

The control is designed to display data from ADO.NET, but you don't have to be connected to a database in order to use it. The DataGrid displays data sources, which include:

- ADO.NET DataTables
- ADO.NET DataViews
- ADO.NET DataSets
- ADO.NET DataSetViews
- Single dimension arrays
- Any component that implements the IList or IListSource interfaces

This isn't really the place to discuss how the ADO.NET classes work—they are pretty complex, and we are discussing controls rather than databases. For more details about ADO.NET and how to use it, consult Chapter 15.

To give you an idea of how a DataGrid can work with ADO.NET, a DataSet can contain one or more DataTables, and you can use **DataRelation** objects to relate tables by key. A DataGrid is sophisticated enough to be able to display and navigate the relations. The example shown in Figure 10.10 sh1ows + markers in the first column. These indicate that these rows have one or more relations set up, and expanding the row by pressing the + lets you navigate to the related table and back.

There also isn't space here to go into detail on all the features provided by **DataGrid** and how to use them, because it is a very complex and fully featured control. Tables 10.13 and 10.14 detail some of the most useful properties and methods of the **DataGrid** class.

Table 10.13 Important properties of the DataGrid class.

Property	Description
AllowNavigation	Determines whether navigation to child tables is allowed
AlternatingBackColor	Sets alternate rows of the grid to a different color to look like a ledger
BackColor	Gets or sets the background color of the grid
BackgroundColor	Gets or sets the color of the non-row areas of the grid
BorderStyle	The style of the **DataGrid** border, which may be None, FixedSingle, or Fixed3D
CaptionText	The text displayed as the grid's caption
CaptionForeColor, **CaptionBackColor**, **CaptionFont**	Represents the properties of the grid's caption
CurrentCell	Represents the currently selected cell
CurrentRowIndex	Represents the currently selected row
DataSource	Gets or sets the data source that this grid is displaying
FirstVisibleColumn	Gets the index of the first visible column
FlatMode	Determines whether the grid displays in flat or 3D mode
ForeColor, **BackgroundColor**	Represents the colors of the grid
GridLineStyle, **GridLineColor**	Represents the properties of the grid lines
Item	Represents the content of a grid cell
ReadOnly	If true, the grid cannot be edited
TableStyles	Gets the collection of **DataGridTableStyle** objects for this grid
VisibleColumnCount, **VisibleRowCount**	Gets the number of visible rows and columns

Table 10.14 Important methods of the DataGrid class.

Method	Description
BeginEdit, **EndEdit**	Signals the beginning and end of an edit operation
BeginInit, **EndInit**	Signals the beginning and end of initialization, during which the control can't be used
CreateGridColumn	Creates a new column
Collapse, **Expand**	Collapses or expands child relations for a particular row
GetCellBounds	Gets the bounding rectangle of a given cell
HitTest	Gets information about the cell at a given point
NavigateTo, **NavigateBack**	Navigates to and from a table

Figure 10.11 A DateTimePicker with the calendar displayed.

DateTimePicker

The **DateTimePicker** control wraps a standard Windows date-time picker control, an example of which is shown in Figure 10.11. This control lets a user select a date from a drop-down calendar and displays it in one of several formats.

NOTE: *Despite what its name might imply, this control only lets you select a date; the time displayed will always be the current system time.*

The **Format** property lets you choose how the date is to be displayed, using one of the values shown in Table 10.15.

There are a number of useful properties that can be used with **DateTimePicker**, as shown in Table 10.16.

Table 10.15 DateTimePicker formats.

Property	Description
DateTimePickerFormat.Custom	Uses a custom format.
DateTimePickerFormat.Long	Uses the system's long date format. This is the default.
DateTimePickerFormat.Short	Uses the system's short date format.
DateTimePickerFormat.Time	Uses the system's time format.

Table 10.16 Properties of the DateTimePicker class.

Property	Description
CalendarFont, CalendarForeColor	The font and text color for the drop-down calendar.
CalendarTitleBackColor, CalendarTitleForeColor	Colors for the background and foreground of the title.
DropDownAlign	The alignment of the calendar. Default is left-aligned.
Format	The format of the date in the textbox, as detailed in the preceding table.
MinDate, MaxDate	The minimum and maximum dates on the calendar.
ShowCheckBox	If true, a checkbox is shown next to the date.
ShowUpDown	If true, an up-down control is used to adjust date values.

The **ShowCheckBox** property lets you show a CheckBox next to the date. If the checkbox is selected, the date can be changed; if it isn't selected, the date cannot be changed. If **ShowUpDown** is set to true, an up-down control with an increment of one day is used to adjust the date instead of using the drop-down calendar.

MonthCalendar

Still on the topic of dates and times, the **MonthCalendar** class encapsulates the Windows Calendar control. Figure 10.12 shows that this is the same as the drop-down calendar used by the **DateTimePicker** class.

The **MonthCalendar** has a number of useful properties, as summarized in Table 10.17. Methods are available to set many of these properties, such as the bolded dates.

Table 10.17 Properties of the MonthCalendar class.

Property	Description
AnnuallyBoldedDates, MonthlyBoldedDates, BoldedDates	Collections of **DateTime** objects representing dates that are to be shown in bold on an annual, monthly, or nonrecurring basis.
BackColor, ForeColor, BackgroundImage	Background and foreground colors, and the background image to display (if any).
CalendarDimensions	The number of rows and columns displayed by the calendar.
MinDate, MaxDate	The minimum and maximum dates that will be displayed.
SelectionStart, SelectionEnd, SelectionRange	The start, end, and range of selected items in the calendar.
ShowToday, ShowTodayCircle	Determines whether the current day is shown at the bottom of the calendar and whether it is circled.
SingleMonthSize	The minimum size needed on the screen to display a month (read-only).
TitleBackColor, TitleForeColor	Colors of the title bar.
TodayDate	Represents today's date. By default this is the date when the control was created, but it can be reset by assigning a different **DateTime** to this property.
TodayDateSet	True if the **TodayDate** has been explicitly set by the user.

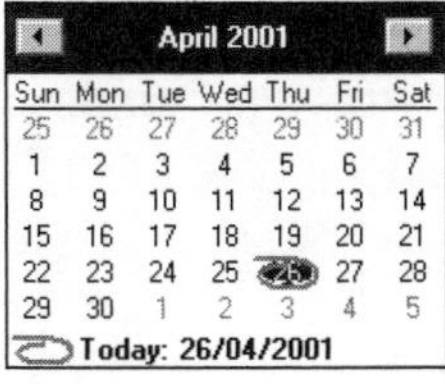

Figure 10.12 A MonthCalendar displayed on a form.

Up-Down Controls

An up-down control consists of a text box plus a small vertical scrollbar, which is used to change the value being displayed.

.NET gives you two up-down classes, **DomainUpDown** and **NumericUpDown**, both of which derive from the **UpDownBase** class.

The **NumericUpDown** class provides an up-down control that displays a numeric value, which is incremented and decremented using scrollbar buttons. Table 10.18 shows the properties of the **NumericUpDown** class. **Value** can be used to get and set the value, and it is validated against the **Maximum** and **Minimum**. If validation fails, an **ArgumentException** will be thrown. A **DomainUpDown** control displays strings from an **Object** collection by clicking the up and down buttons. Table 10.19 shows the properties of this class. **Items** represents the collection of strings held by the control, and you can use the normal collection **Add()**, **Remove()**, and **Clear()** methods to maintain the list.

Table 10.18 Properties of the NumericUpDown class.

Property	Description
DecimalPlaces	The number of decimal places to display. The default is zero.
Hexadecimal	True if values are displayed in hex. The default is false.
Increment	The increment value to use when the up or down button is clicked. The default is 1.
Maximum	The maximum value that can be displayed. The default is 100.
Minimum	The minimum value that can be displayed. The default is 0.
ReadOnly	True if the control is read-only, in which case the user cannot enter text into the textbox.
ThousandsSeparator	True if a thousands separator is to be displayed. The default is false.
Value	The value being displayed in the control.

Table 10.19 Properties of the DomainUpDown class.

Property	Description
Items	The collection of items.
SelectedIndex	Gets or sets the selected item by index.
SelectedItem	Gets or sets the selected item by reference.
Sorted	If true, the list items are maintained in sorted order.
Wrap	If true, the list wraps when the beginning or end is reached.

GroupBox

A GroupBox is a container for other controls that has an optional title, and it is commonly used for two purposes. It can help visibly group controls that belong together, and if used to contain a set of RadioButtons, it will cause them to act together as a group. Figure 10.13 shows a GroupBox containing a group of RadioButtons.

Unlike a Panel, a GroupBox doesn't have any scrolling capability, so you cannot add controls outside the bounds of the box.

You can add controls to a GroupBox in Visual Studio by placing them within the boundary of the box. In order to add or remove children in code, use the **Add()** and **Remove()** methods on the **Controls** property that GroupBox inherits from Control.

Panel

A Panel is a control that can contain other controls. Panels are similar to GroupBoxes, but there are three main differences between them:

- Panels can scroll
- Panels can have a border style
- Panels cannot display a title

Like GroupBoxes, they have virtually no functionality of their own, You use them to group controls for visual emphasis so that you can move them in a group, and so that you can enable or disable a group of controls simultaneously. Figure 10.14 shows a Panel containing four CheckBox controls; in this example, the Panel's **AutoScroll** property has been set to **True** so that scrollbars are automatically provided when controls are positioned outside the visible area of the Panel.

The Panel in Figure 10.14 also shows a 3D border. By default, Panels have no border, but you can choose to set a simple line or 3D border using the **BorderStyle** property.

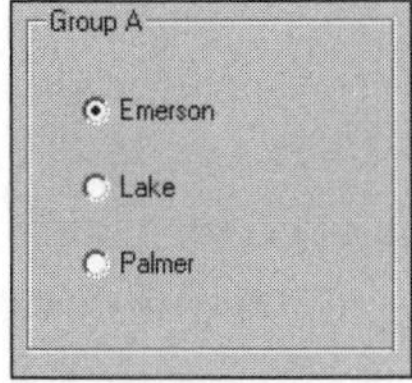

Figure 10.13 A GroupBox containing a group of RadioButtons.

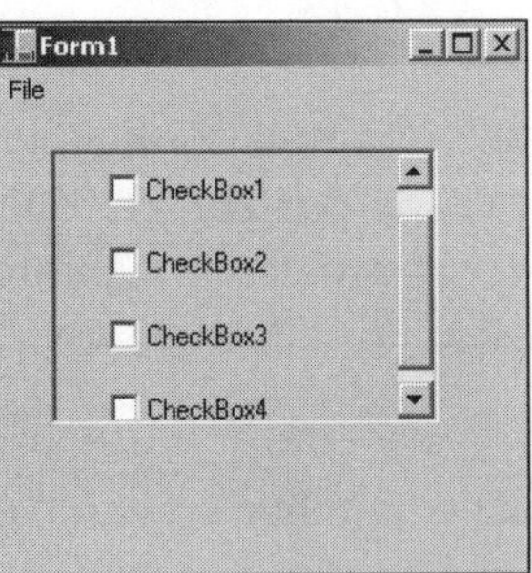

Figure 10.14 A scrollable Panel containing four CheckBox controls.

NOTE: *Adding RadioButtons to a Panel makes them act as a group, so that only one can be selected at a time.*

If you are using Visual Studio .NET, you can add controls to a Panel by placing them onto the Panel in the Designer. If you want to add controls to a Panel in code, use the **Add()** method:

```
panel1.Controls.Add(myButton)
```

As with everything that inherits from the **Control** class, the **Controls** property provides access to the collection of child controls.

Scrollbars and TrackBar

.NET provides four classes that provide a slider capability:

- **ScrollBar**—The base class for scrollbars
- **HScrollBar**—Implements a horizontal scrollbar
- **VScrollBar**—Implements a vertical scrollbar
- **TrackBar**—Implements a slider

The scrollbar classes implement the typical scrollbars seen on the sides of windows, listboxes, and other controls that have a scrolling capability. These are almost always supplied and used by the component that needs them, so you very seldom have anything to do with scrollbars nowadays.

If you need some sort of slider in your UI, use a TrackBar control, which is a scrollbar specially adapted for use as a standalone control. Figure 10.15 shows a TrackBar in place on a form.

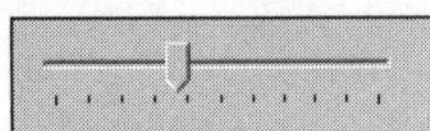

Figure 10.15 A TrackBar control on a form.

As with scrollbars, the slider that you drag along the track is known as the *thumb*, and you can click on the track itself to cause the thumb to jump between tick marks. The **TrackBar** properties in Table 10.20 show how you can configure the look and operation of the object.

A "large change," typically 10 percent of the range, is triggered by clicking on the track or using the PgUp/PgDn keys. A "small change," typically one unit, is triggered by using the arrow keys to move the thumb.

ImageList

An ImageList is a nonvisible control that is used to hold a list of images. It isn't used on its own, but is used to provide lists of images to other controls that need them, such as:

- Images for the buttons on a toolbar
- Large and small icons to be used with a ListView
- Images used in a TreeView

An ImageList maintains a collection of images, and you can use the usual collection methods such as **Add()** and **Remove()** to maintain the list. See the Immediate Solution "Working with Toolbars" for an example of how ImageLists are used in practice.

ListView and TreeView

Everyone is familiar with the Windows Explorer application, which uses a tree control in the left pane and a list control in the right pane. The .NET ListView and

Table 10.20 Properties of the TrackBar class.

Property	Description
AutoSize	Indicates whether the control will autosize to use the minimum amount of space
BackgroundImage	The background image, if any
LargeChange, **SmallChange**	The large and small change increments
Minimum, **Maximum**	The minimum and maximum values (and hence the range) of the TrackBar
Orientation	Indicates whether the TrackBar is horizontal (the default) or vertical
TickFrequency	Indicates how often tick marks appear
TickStyle	Indicates where the tick marks are placed in relation to the track
Value	The current location of the thumb between the minimum and maximum values

TreeView controls wrap the Windows tree and list controls. Because they're often used together in applications in this way, I'll discuss both in this section.

The TreeView Control

A TreeView is a control that displays a hierarchy of items in the form of a tree. The programmer has to load the control with data items representing the nodes, and the control takes care of all the run-time operations including displaying the tree, interacting with the user, and raising events. Each node in the tree has a caption and an optional pair of images, which are used to represent selected and unselected nodes.

The following code fragment shows how a TreeView can be constructed and populated with nodes:

```
Private tv As TreeView

Public Sub New()
   ...
   ' Create and setup a TreeView
   tv = New TreeView()
   tv.Location = New Point(30, 30)
   tv.Size = New Size(120, 150)

   ' Set the ImageList
   tv.ImageList = ImageList1

   ' Add it to the form
   Controls.Add(tv)

   ' Add child nodes
   AddNodes()
End Sub

Private Sub AddNodes()
   ' Create and add a root node
   Dim tn As New TreeNode("Root", 0, 0)
   tv.Nodes.Add(tn)

   ' Add a child node
   Dim tn1 As New TreeNode("Child1", 1, 1)
   tn.Nodes.Add(tn1)
End Sub
```

The code starts by creating a **TreeView** object and setting its size and position. I then associate an ImageList with the control, which contains the images that are going to be used by the nodes, and then add the control to the form. Setting up the child nodes involves creating **TreeNode** objects and adding them to the hierarchy. The **TreeNode** constructor in use takes three arguments: the caption string and the indices of the images in the ImageList that are going to be used when the node is selected and unselected.

TreeNodes have a **Nodes** property that holds references to their children, and so that you can add the first ones to the tree, the TreeView also has a **Nodes** property that refers to the root node(s) in the hierarchy. In the example, the root node is added directly to the TreeView, and the child node is added to the root node. The main problem with building TreeViews is keeping track of where you need to add nodes when you are building the structure.

This code produces the tree shown in Figure 10.16.

Commonly used properties and methods of the **TreeView** class are summarized in Tables 10.21 and 10.22.

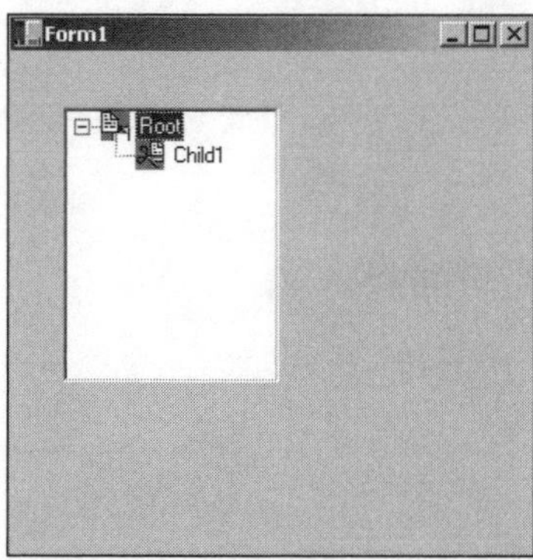

Figure 10.16 A TreeView control with two nodes.

Table 10.21 Commonly used properties of the TreeView class.

Property	Description
BackgroundImage	The background image, if any.
BorderStyle	The style of the control border. Default is a 3D border.
CheckBoxes	True if checkboxes are shown next to the image on each node.
HotTracking	True if the tree nodes are highlighted as the mouse moves over them.
ImageList	The control holding the images for the nodes.
LabelEdit	True if the user can edit the node labels.
Nodes	The collection of TreeNodes managed by this TreeView.
SelectedNode	The currently selected node, or null (Nothing) if no node is selected.

(continued)

Table 10.21 Commonly used properties of the TreeView class *(continued)*.

Property	Description
ShowLines	True if lines are drawn between nodes. Default is true.
ShowPlusMinus	True if the expand button is shown next to a node that has children.
ShowRootLines	True if lines are shown joining nodes to the root.
Sorted	True if nodes in the tree are sorted.
TopNode	The node visible at the top of the TreeView.
VisibleCount	The number of visible nodes.

Table 10.22 Commonly used methods of the TreeView class.

Method	Description
BeginUpdate, **EndUpdate**	Disables and reenables redrawing of the tree. Used when many nodes are to be updated to save multiple redraws.
CollapseAll, **ExpandAll**	Hides or shows all child nodes.
GetNodeAt	Gets the node at a point.
GetNodeCount	Returns the number of nodes in the tree.

The ListView Control

A ListView displays a list of items in one of four formats:

- Using large icons
- Using small icons
- As a list
- As a report

If you're familiar with the ways in which you can display files in Windows Explorer, then you'll have a pretty good idea of what the ListView formats look like. Figure 10.17 shows a ListView displayed in Report format. It also shows the use

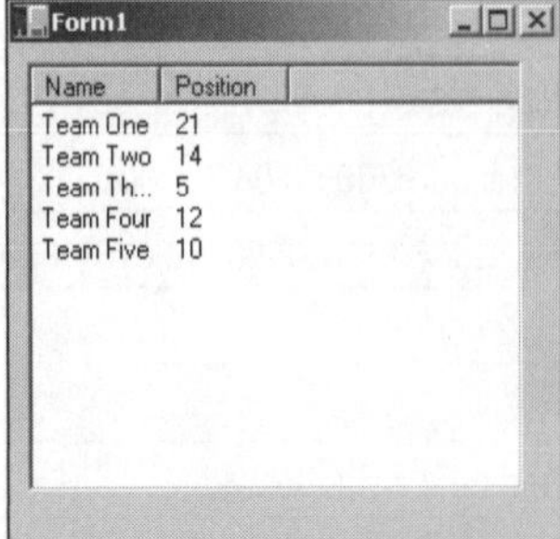

Figure 10.17 A ListView in Report format.

of optional column headers and the way in which text is edited if it is too long to fit into a column.

As with the TreeView, using a ListView involves populating the control with the items it is to display; in this case, the items are **ListItem** objects. The following code fragment shows how a ListView can be constructed and populated with items:

```
Private lv As ListView

Public Sub New()
  ...
  ' Create a ListView, position and size it
  lv = New ListView()
  lv.Location = New Point(8, 8)
  lv.Size = New Size(160, 136)
  lv.ForeColor = SystemColors.WindowText

  ' Set up the ImageList that holds the large icons
  lv.LargeImageList = ImageList1

  Controls.Add(lv)

  ' Add the items
  AddItems()
End Sub

Private Sub AddItems()
  ' Create some list items
  Dim item1 As New ListViewItem("Team one", 0)
  Dim item2 As New ListViewItem ("Team two", 1)
  Dim item3 As New ListViewItem ("Team three", 2)

  ' Add them to the list
  lv.Items.Add(item1)
  lv.Items.Add(item2)
  lv.Items.Add(item3)
End Sub
```

The code first creates a ListView and sets its size, position, and foreground color. Because a ListView can display items using large or small icons, each ListView has two **ImageList** properties. In this example, I'm setting the one that holds the large icons. The **AddItems()** function creates new ListItems, each with a caption and an icon index, and adds them to the list.

This code produces the ListView shown in Figure 10.18.

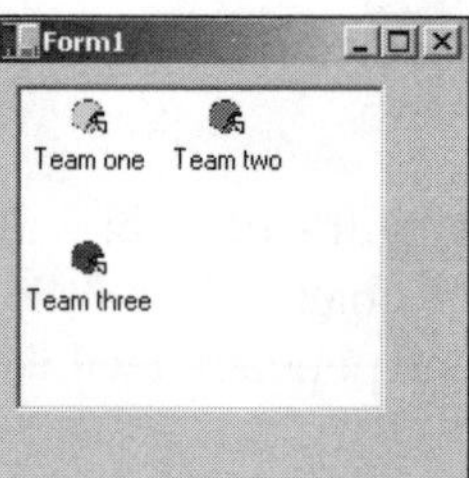

Figure 10.18 A form containing a ListView control.

Commonly used properties and methods of the **ListView** class are summarized in Tables 10.23 and 10.24.

Table 10.23 Commonly used properties of the ListView class.

Property	Description
Activation	Specifies how the user activates the item (single or double-click).
Alignment	The alignment of items in the window.
AllowColumnReorder	If true, users can drag columns to reorder them.
AutoArrange	True if icon views are autoarranged.
BackgroundImage	The background image, if any.
BorderStyle	The style of the control border. Default is a 3D border.
CheckBoxes	If true, every item will display a checkbox.
Columns	The collection of column headers.
FocusedItem	Returns the item that has the focus.
HoverSelection	True if items are selected by hovering over them with the mouse.
Items	The collection of list items.
LargeImageList	The ImageList containing icons for Large Icon view.
MultiSelect	True if multiple selection is allowed.
Scrollable	True if scrollbars are visible.
SelectedItems	The collection of currently selected items.
SmallImageList	The ImageList containing icons for Small Icon view.

Table 10.24 Commonly used methods of the ListView class.

Method	Description
ArrangeIcons	Arranges the icons in a given format.
BeginUpdate, **EndUpdate**	Disables and reenables redrawing of the control. Used when many items are to be updated to save multiple redraws.

(continued)

Table 10.24 Commonly used methods of the ListView class *(continued)*.

Method	Description
Clear	Removes all items from the tree.
EnsureVisible	Ensures that a given item is visible, scrolling it into view if necessary.
GetItemAt	Gets the item at a point.

Menus

Menus are represented by four classes, as listed in Table 10.25.

Menus for an application consist of **MenuItem** objects, which can themselves contain other MenuItems to implement submenus. MenuItems are then stored in a MainMenu, which can be attached to a form or contained in a ContextMenu if it is to be used as a pop-up context menu.

Visual Studio.NET provides a visual menu editor, but it is very simple to manipulate menu items in code. MenuItems within a Menu are accessed through the **MenuItems** property, which returns a **Menu.MenuItemCollection** object representing the collection of MenuItems belonging to that menu. As its name implies, **Menu.MenuItemCollection** is a nested class defined within **Menu** whose sole purpose is to hold a collection of MenuItems. You can use the methods on **MenuItemCollection** to add and remove MenuItems, like this:

```
' References to MenuItems
Private WithEvents item1 As MenuItem
Private WithEvents item2 As MenuItem

' Create a MainMenu
Dim main1 As New MainMenu

' Create a couple of MenuItems
item1 = New MenuItem("foo")
item2 = New MenuItem("bar")

' Add the items
main1.MenuItems.Add(item1)
main1.MenuItems.Add(item2)
```

Note how I've declared the **MenuItem** objects in this code. Because the whole point of a menu item is that someone is going to select it at some time, I declared a **WithEvents** reference to set up event handling, and then created the actual items later on because **WithEvents** and object creation cannot be completed in one step.

Table 10.25 The .NET Menu classes.

Class	Description
Menu	The abstract base class for all menu classes.
MainMenu	Represents the main menu bar for a form
MenuItem	Represents a menu item
ContextMenu	Represents a pop-up menu

TIP: *If you want to add a separator bar, simply use a single dash as the text for the MenuItem.*

The **Add()** method is used to add the MenuItems to the collection, and you can also use the **Remove()** and **Clear()** methods to remove one or all items from the menu. If you know all the menu items you want to add ahead of time, it is more efficient to use the **MenuItems.AddRange()** method to add them in one array:

```
' Create an array
Dim a1(1) As MenuItem
a1(0) = item1
a1(1) = item2

' Add the items
main.MenuItems.AddRange(a1)
```

Because menus are mainly used with forms, two Immediate Solutions dealing with using menus were provided in Chapter 9, "How Do I Work with Menus on Forms?" and "How Do I Associate a Context Menu with a Form?"

PictureBox

A PictureBox is a control that displays graphics from a bitmap, icon, JPEG, GIF, or other image file. It is a very simple class, having few properties and methods.

The **Image** property is used to associate the PictureBox with an image, and the **SizeMode** property is used to control how the image is displayed in the control. Table 10.26 lists the possible values that **SizeMode** can take.

Table 10.26 Possible values for the PictureBox SizeMode property.

Property	Description
PictureBoxSizeMode.Normal	The image is placed in the top-left corner and is clipped to the bounds of the control.
PictureBoxSizeMode.StretchImage	The image is stretched or shrunk to fit the PictureBox.
PictureBoxSizeMode.AutoSize	The PictureBox is resized to fit the image.
PictureBoxSizeMode.CenterImage	The image is centered in the control.

ProgressBar

A ProgressBar, shown in Figure 10.19, lets you show the progress of an operation by displaying a bar proportional in size to the time the operation has taken so far. The ProgressBar control is a wrapper for the underlying Windows control.

A ProgressBar has **Minimum** and **Maximum** properties, which default to 0 and 100 respectively, and a **Value** property that represents the current value. You can assign an integer to **Value** in order to set the position of the control, or alternatively, you can use ProgressBar's two methods: **Increment()** and **PerformStep()**. **Increment()** increments the value by a variable integer amount and wraps back to the minimum if an increment operation takes the value past the maximum. **PerformStep()** increments the value by a fixed amount, the size of which is set through the **Step** property.

StatusBar

A StatusBar, shown in Figure 10.20, is typically displayed at the bottom of a window or form and is used to display graphical or text information to the user. Status bars are normally for display only, and it is unusual for them to interact with the user.

StatusBars often display text, but can also display one or more panels, as shown in Figure 10.20. The following code fragment shows how to create a StatusBar and attach it to a form:

```
Private sb As StatusBar

Public Sub New()
   ...
   ' Create a StatusBar. The constructor takes no arguments
   sb = New StatusBar()

   ' Set its initial text
   sb.Text = "My Status Bar"

   ' Add it to the form
   Controls.Add(sb)
End Sub
```

This code fragment produces a StatusBar like the one in Figure 10.21.

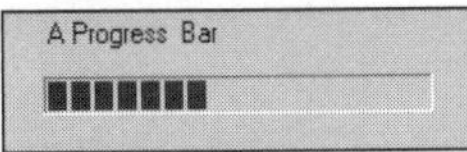

Figure 10.19 A ProgressBar control on a form.

Figure 10.20 A StatusBar control at the bottom of a form, containing two panels and a resize grip.

Figure 10.21 A StatusBar displaying text.

Table 10.27 Default StatusBar properties.

Property	Description	Value
BackgroundImage	Represents a reference to the background image	**null** (**Nothing** in VB)
Dock	Indicates where the bar docks	**DockStyle.Bottom**
Font	Represents the StatusBar font	The container's font
ShowPanels	Determines whether panels should be shown	**False**
SizingGrip	Indicates whether a sizing grip should be displayed	**True**
TabStop	Indicates whether the user can tab to the StatusBar	**False**

To change the text, simply assign a new value to the **Text** property. A StatusBar has a set of default properties, as listed in Table 10.27.

The collection of panels owned by a StatusBar is held in the **Panels** property, and it is empty by default. To add a panel to the bar, you need to create a **StatusBarPanel** object, set its properties, and add it to the collection:

```
Private sb As StatusBar
Private sbp1 As StatusBarPanel

Public Sub New()
  ...
  ' Create a StatusBar. The constructor takes no arguments
  sb = New StatusBar()

  ' Set its initial text
  sb.Text = "My Status Bar"

  ' Add a panel
  sbp1 = New StatusBarPanel()
  sbp1.Text = "Panel1"
  sb.Panels.Add(sbp1)

  ' Make the panel visible
  sb.ShowPanels = True
```

```
    ' Add it to the form
    Controls.Add(sb)
End Sub
```

Like the StatusBar, a **StatusBarPanel** has a set of default properties, which are listed in Table 10.28.

ToolBar

A **ToolBar** is a dockable window that contains a number of buttons; an application can have more than one ToolBar, and they are usually docked at the top of the main window. The **ToolBar** class contains a number of methods and properties that help you create and work with toolbars.

Each **ToolBar** object has a **Buttons** property that represents the collection of **ToolBarButton** objects displayed by the ToolBar. You can use the normal collection methods (**Add()**, **Remove()**, **Clear()**) to manage the buttons or make use of the Editor dialog provided by Visual Studio.

ToolBar buttons can be of three types—normal, toggle, and drop-down—and can display text, an image, or both. A toggle button toggles between its up and down state, whereas a drop-down button displays a menu when an arrow next to the button is pressed.

Table 10.29 lists important properties of the **ToolBar** class.

The images to be displayed on the buttons are held by an **ImageList** object associated with the ToolBar.

Table 10.28 Default StatusBarPanel properties.

Property	Description	Value
Alignment	Represents the alignment of the text in the panel	**HorizontalAlignment.Left**
AutoSize	Determines whether the panel autosizes to text	**StatusBarPanelAutoSize.None**
BorderStyle	The panel border style	**StatusBarPanelBorderStyle.Sunken**
Icon	Represents the icon to display on the panel	**null** (**Nothing** in VB)
MinWidth	Represents the minimum width of the panel in pixels	10
Style	Determines whether the panel style is text or owner-draw	**StatusBarPanelStyle.Text**
Text	The text in the panel	A zero-length string
ToolTipText	The text to be displayed on the tooltip	A zero-length string
Width	Represents the width in pixels	100

Table 10.29 Important properties of the ToolBar class.

Property	Description
Appearance	Determines whether the ToolBar buttons are flat or 3D.
BorderStyle	Determines the ToolBar border. The default is no border.
Buttons	The collection of **ToolBarButton** objects hosted by the ToolBar.
ButtonSize	The size of the buttons on the ToolBar; the default is 22 pixels high by 24 pixels wide.
Divider	True if the ToolBar displays a divider between it and the menu.
DropDownArrows	True if drop-down buttons will display arrows.
ImageList	Represents the collection of images for the ToolBar buttons.
ImageSize	Represents the size of each image in the ImageList.
ShowToolTips	True if tooltips are to be shown for each button.
TextAlign	Represents the alignment of text and images on ToolBar buttons. The default is **ToolBarTextAlign.Underneath**.
Wrappable	True if buttons will wrap to a new line when the ToolBar gets too narrow.

SystemInformation

Although it isn't a control that you can place on a form, the **SystemInformation** class is part of the Windows Forms namespace and is very useful if you need to obtain information about the operating system. The class has a large number of shared (static) properties that can provide information about UI parameters, network availability, operating system settings, and hardware capabilities.

Tables 10.30 and 10.31 list some useful properties of the **SystemInformation** class.

Table 10.30 Common SystemInformation properties relating to the operating system, hardware, and network.

Property	Description
BootMode	Gets a value that specifies how the system was started (e.g., Normal or Safe mode).
ComputerName	Gets a string that holds the computer name.
DBCSEnabled	True if the system can handle double-byte characters.
DebugOS	True if it is a debug version of the operating system.
MidEastEnabled	True if the system is enabled for Hebrew and Arabic languages.
MonitorCount	Returns the number of monitors.

(continued)

Table 10.30 Common SystemInformation properties relating to the operating system, hardware, and network *(continued)*.

Property	Description
MousePresent, MouseWheelPresent	Contains mouse properties.
Network	True if the computer is connected to a network.
Secure	True if the operating system implements security (e.g., Windows NT and Windows 2000).
UserDomainName	Gets the user's domain name.
UserInteractive	True if the current process is running in interactive mode.
UserName	Gets the name of the logged-in user.

Table 10.31 Common SystemInformation properties relating to the UI.

Property	Description
BorderSize	Gets the size of a window border in pixels
CaptionButtonSize	Gets the size of a title bar button in pixels
CaptionHeight	Gets the height of a window title bar in pixels
CursorSize	Gets the size of a cursor in pixels
DoubleClickSize, DoubleClickTime	Gets the limits in space and time for two clicks to be considered a double-click
HorizontalScrollBarHeight	Gets the height of a horizontal scrollbar in pixels
IconSize	Gets the default size of an icon in pixels
MenuHeight	Gets the height of one line of a menu in pixels
SmallIconSize	Gets the default size of a small icon in pixels
WorkingArea	Gets the size of the working area, that is, that part of the screen that can be used by applications

TabControl

A TabControl manages a set of **TabPage** objects, which are used to create the "tabbed dialog" effect seen in many Windows programs. An example is shown in Figure 10.22.

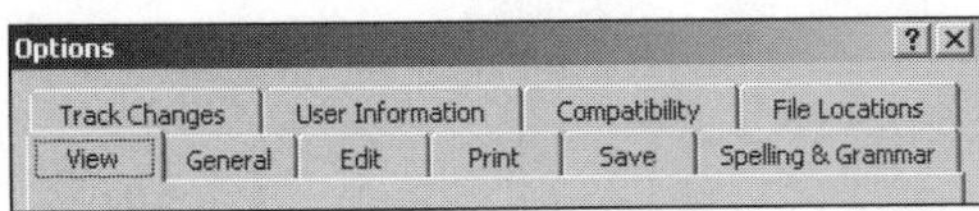

Figure 10.22 A Windows tabbed dialog.

Each page can hold its own set of controls. When the user clicks on a tab, the TabControl causes the requisite set of controls to be displayed. Table 10.32 lists the common properties of the **TabControl** class.

The **Alignment** property lets you position the tabs at the top, bottom, left, or right of the control. This property lets you create tabbed forms that look like notebooks, as shown in Figure 10.23.

Timer

Timer is a nonvisual control that implements a timer that raises an event at user-defined intervals.

The **Interval** property sets the interval in milliseconds at which **Timer** events will be raised, and the **Start()** and **Stop()** methods are used to control the Timer.

Table 10.32 Common properties of the TabControl class.

Property	Description
Alignment	Determines to which side of the control the tabs are displayed.
Appearance	Determines whether the tabs appear as tabs, buttons, or flat buttons.
DisplayRectangle	The area of the control not used by the tabs and borders.
DrawMode	Indicates whether the tabs are owner-draw or not.
HotTrack	Indicates whether the tabs are highlighted when the mouse passes over them.
ImageList	Holds images for tabs that want to display them.
MultiLine	True if there can be more than one row of tabs. If false, navigation arrows will be shown at the ends of the single row.
Padding	The amount of padding around items in tabs.
SelectedIndex	The index of the currently selected tab, or -1 if there isn't a current selection.
SelectedTab	Gets or sets the currently selected tab.
SizeMode	Represents how tabs are sized: large enough for their text, stretched to fill the row, or fixed size.
TabCount	Returns the number of tabs.
TabPages	Returns the collection of tab pages.

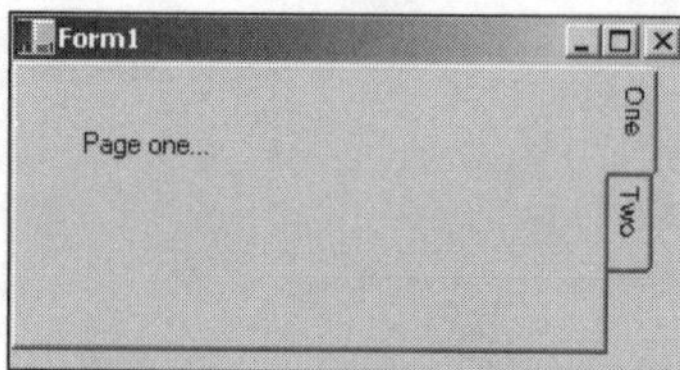

Figure 10.23 A tabbed dialog in notebook format.

If you create a Timer in code, it is important to call the **Dispose()** method when you've finished with it because the Timer uses system resources that otherwise wouldn't be freed up until the Timer is garbage collected or your program exits.

TrayIcon

The TrayIcon control lets you create an entry in the System Tray, the collection of icons that is normally situated at the right end of the taskbar. The control's **Click** event is fired when a user double-clicks on the icon. You can also associate a ContextMenu with the control, which will display when a user right-clicks on the icon, as shown in Figure 10.24.

The Provider Controls

Provider controls consist of a set of three controls that provide new properties for other controls on a form. If you add a HelpProvider control to a form, it adds three new properties to every control on the form, as shown in Figure 10.25.

The new properties include:

- A help string that is displayed if the F1 key is pressed while the control has the focus
- A topic in a help file that can be used to provide context-sensitive help
- A Boolean property indicating whether the HelpProvider control is active for the control

The ToolTip control works in the same way, but only adds one new property to each control. The ToolTip is displayed when the mouse hovers over the control.

Figure 10.24 A TrayIcon control displaying its icon in the System Tray and showing a ContextMenu.

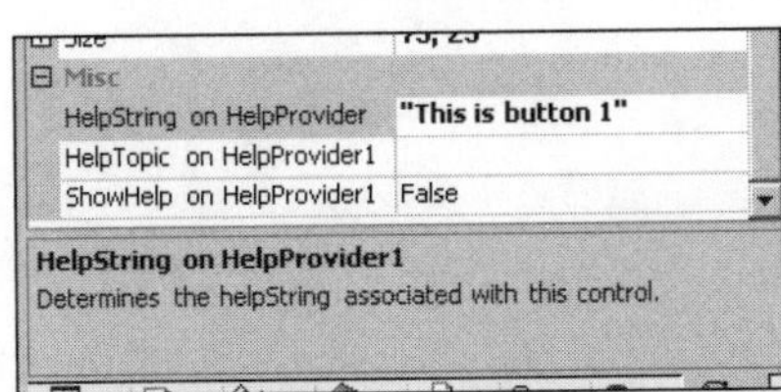

Figure 10.25 The three properties added to controls by a HelpProvider.

The ErrorProvider control provides a simple way to indicate that there is an error associated with a control. It adds a single property called **Error on ErrorProvider1** to each control, and if a string is assigned to this property, an error icon is displayed next to the control. Figure 10.26 shows a TextBox with an error displayed.

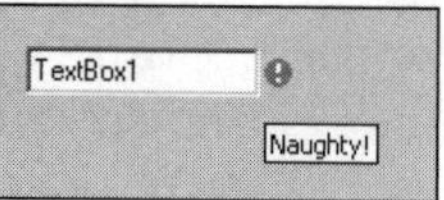

Figure 10.26 An ErrorProvider control associated with a TextBox.

Immediate Solutions

Positioning Controls on Forms

There are four properties that can be used to position and size controls on forms:

- **Location**—Sets the control's X and Y position in pixels
- **Size**—Sets the control's width and height in pixels
- **Anchor**—Affixes the control to one or more borders of the form
- **Dock**—Connects the control to one or more borders of the form

Location takes as its value a **System.Drawing.Point** object, and you can set it in code like this:

```
TextBox1.Location = new System.Drawing.Point(xpos, ypos)
```

The **xpos** and **ypos** values are the X and Y positions in pixels.

Size takes as its value a **System.Drawing.Size** object, and you can set it in very much the same way:

```
TextBox1.Size = new System.Drawing.Size(xval, yval)
```

Once again, **xval** and **yval** give the X and Y dimensions in pixels.

The **Control** class also provides you with two other properties that let you build sophisticated layouts and save you a lot of code while you're doing it. The **Anchor** property lets you "anchor" one or more edges of a control to a form border, so that if the form is resized the control will be as well.

Figures 10.27 and 10.28 show two views of a form containing a TextBox that is anchored to the right and left borders of the form. You can see that the TextBox automatically resizes to fit the width of the form.

The **Anchor** property has as its value one of the members of the **AnchorStyles** enumeration. **None** obviously means the control isn't anchored at all, whereas **All** means that it is anchored on all four borders. **Top**, **Bottom**, **Left**, and **Right** anchor the control to the corresponding border, and the set is completed by a number of combination styles, such as **TopLeft**, **LeftRight**, **TopLeftRight**, and so on.

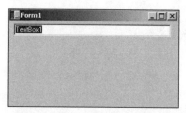

Figure 10.27 Form with anchored control before resizing.

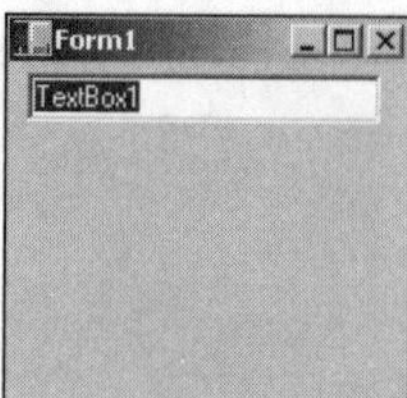

Figure 10.28 Form with anchored control after resizing.

The **Anchor** style can be set in code, and there's also a graphical way of setting the styles in the Property Editor in Visual Studio, as shown in Figure 10.29.

Dropping down the ComboBox for the **Anchor** property displays the graphical chooser, with the gray rectangle in the middle representing the control and the four rectangles to the top, bottom, left, and right representing the anchoring points. Clicking on an anchoring point selects or deselects it. **Anchor** points display in dark gray when selected.

Dock is similar to **Anchor**, but it determines which border of the form a control will dock to. When a control is docked to a form, it adheres to one border and extends the entire width or height of the form.

The value of the **Dock** property is taken from the **DockStyle** enumeration. **None** means that it isn't docked at all; **Bottom**, **Left**, **Right**, and **Top** dock the control

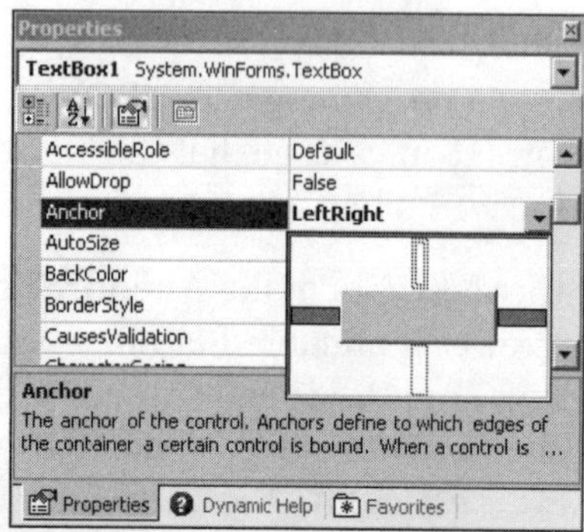

Figure 10.29 Setting the **Anchor** property for a control in Visual Studio.

to the appropriate border, whereas **Fill** docks the control to all borders and adjusts its size accordingly.

***NOTE:** You need to be careful when using **Fill**, as it will cause the control to hide all other controls on the form.*

Related solutions:	*Found on page:*
How Do I Create a Windows Forms Application?	402
How Can I Create a New Form and Display It?	406

Setting the Tab Order of Controls

The Tab key can be used to navigate among the controls on a form. Most controls participate in the tab order, and you can use the Boolean **TabStop** property to include or exclude controls from the tab ordering.

Each control also has a **TabIndex** property, which can be set either from code or Visual Studio. To set the tab order from Visual Studio, select the View | Tab Order menu item. A number appears at the top left of each control, as shown in Figure 10.30. You should click on controls in the order in which you want them to participate in the tab order. When you're done, select View | Tab Order again to exit Tab mode.

To set the tab ordering from code, set the **TabIndex** property of controls to an integer value greater than or equal to zero.

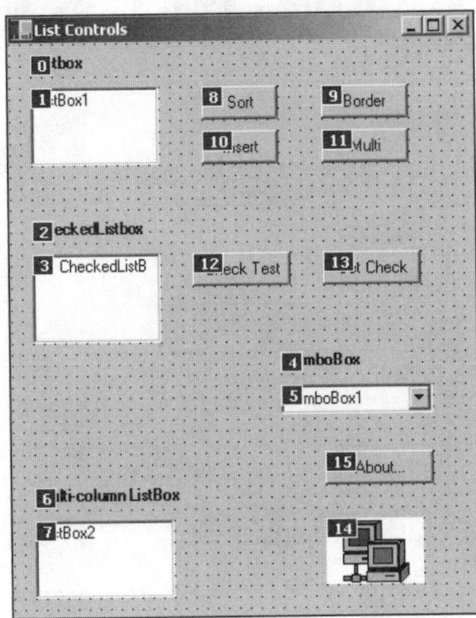

Figure 10.30 Adjusting the tab order for the controls on a form.

Controls within a GroupBox have a decimal **TabIndex** that incorporates the **TabIndex** of the GroupBox. For instance, if a GroupBox has a **TabIndex** of 5, the first control it contains will have a TabIndex of 5.0, the second 5.1, and so on.

Using Labels for Form Navigation

Labels take part in the tab ordering of the form, but don't receive the focus. Instead, the focus passes to the next control in the ordering. This feature can be used to let users navigate around a form using keyboard shortcuts.

The **UseMnemonic** property determines whether "&" characters will be interpreted as marking a keyboard shortcut mnemonic. If this property is set to **True**, pressing Alt plus the mnemonic character selects the next control after the label in the tab ordering.

Simulating Browser Links

You can use a LinkLabel control to display a label that looks like a link in a browser. Select the LinkLabel control in the Toolbox, draw it on a form, and then use the properties listed in Table 10.33 to set its behavior.

The **LinkBehavior** property determines how the link behaves. The default setting is **LinkBehavior.SystemDefault**, but you can also set it to be underlined only when the mouse is over the text (**LinkBehavior.HoverUnderline**) or never to be underlined (**LinkBehavior.NeverUnderline**).

Table 10.33 Properties of the LinkLabel class.

Property	Description
ActiveLinkColor	Represents the color used for active links
DisabledLinkColor	Represents the color used for disabled links
LinkArea	Gets or sets the range of text in the label that is treated as a link
LinkBehavior	Gets or sets the behavior of a link
LinkColor	Represents the color used for normal links
Links	Represents the collection of links contained within the control
LinksVisited	Gets or sets a Boolean value indicating whether a link has been "visited"or not
VisitedLinkColor	Represents the color used for visited links

Any number of links can be represented by the text within the control, and they're held in the **Links** property.

You can set colors using members of the **Color** class. There is a large number of colors predefined as shared (static) members of the **Color** class, or you can use the **FromARGB()** method to define your own colors in terms of red, green, and blue values:

```
LinkLabel1.LinkColor = Color.FromARGB(126,126,0)
```

It isn't necessary for all the text in the LinkLabel to be displayed as a link. You can use the **LinkArea** property to set how much of the text is treated as a link. To do this, create a **Point** object, and assign the start and end character indices to the X and Y values:

```
' Treat characters 13 thru 16 as a link. Remember that the index
' is zero-based
Dim p As New Point()
p.X = 12
p.Y = 15
LinkLabel2.LinkArea = p
```

How Do I Create a Group of RadioButtons?

A group of RadioButtons can be created in two ways. If you're using the Visual Studio Designer, create a GroupBox or a Panel, and then place RadioButton controls inside the box. This will form a group of buttons, and you'll only be able to choose one of them at a time. Figure 10.13 shows RadioButton controls inside a GroupBox.

In code, create a **GroupBox** object, and then use the **Add()** method on its **Controls** property to add the RadioButtons to a group:

```
' Create a GroupBox
Dim gp As New System.Windows.Forms.GroupBox

' Add some RadioButtons to the group...
Dim rb1 As New System.WinForms.RadioButton
Dim rb2 As New System.WinForms.RadioButton

gp.Controls.Add(rb1)
gp.Controls.Add(rb2)
```

Working with TextBoxes

Two varieties of TextBox controls are provided in the .NET Framework. TextBoxes hold unformatted text, which is displayed in a single font, whereas RichTextBoxes can hold fully formatted text.

Both are easily created by selecting the appropriate control from the Toolbox and drawing on a form.

Getting and Setting Content

The **Lines** property is an array of Strings that represent the content of a multiline TextBox. The **Text** property is a single string that also represents the content and is useful when you don't want to consider lines separately. Content can be set by simply assigning an array to the **Lines** property:

```
' Create an array of Strings
Dim myStrings As String() = { "First line", "Second line", "Third line" }

' Add them to the textbox
TextBox1.Lines = myStrings
```

Single- and Multiline TextBoxes

By default, TextBoxes display a single line of text, and any newline characters are displayed as nonprinting characters. The **Multiline** property can be set to true, in which case the TextBox will display multiple lines of text, and newline characters in text will produce line breaks. The **WordWrap** property determines whether a multiline TextBox will word wrap at the end of lines.

Working with Selections

The **SelectionStart**, **SelectionLength**, and **SelectionText** properties represent selected text within a TextBox. The following code shows how they can be used to edit content within a control:

```
Protected Sub ChangeBtn_Click(ByVal sender As Object, _
      ByVal e As System.Event)
  ' Select some text and change it...
  TextBox1.SelectionStart = 6
  TextBox1.SelectionLength = 6
  TextBox1.SelectedText = "foo"
End Sub
```

You can, of course, also use these properties to find out whether any text is currently selected. Note that setting the selection start and length doesn't actually highlight the text. The **Select()** method can be used as an alternative way of selecting text, taking the start and length as parameters:

```
' Select some text...
TextBox1.Select(6, 6)
```

TIP: *By default, selected text will not be highlighted when the TextBox does not have the focus. If you want selected text to be highlighted regardless of what has the focus, set the* ***HideSelection*** *property to* ***False****.*

Changing the Case of Characters

The **CharacterCasing** property lets you change the case of characters as they are entered into a TextBox. The value is one of the members of the **Windows.Forms.CharacterCasing** enumeration and can be Normal (to leave the text as it is), Lower (to convert to lowercase), or Upper (to convert to uppercase).

How Do I Know When the Content of a Text Control Has Changed?

TextBox and RichTextBox controls will fire a **TextChanged** event whenever their content has changed. By handling this event, you'll be able to tell when the user has modified the content of the control.

TIP: *Make sure that you don't modify the content of the TextBox control in the* ***TextChanged*** *event handler, or you may end up with another event being fired while you're in the middle of handling the present one. Likewise, beware of creating two text controls whose* ***TextChanged*** *handlers affect each other's content.*

Entering Masked Passwords into TextBoxes

The **PasswordChar** property of TextBox can be used to create a TextBox that can be used for password entry, and which will mask what the user types:

```
' Set the password character
TextBox1.PasswordChar = "*"
```

How Do I Let the User Pick One of an Array of Strings?

You can use a ListBox or ComboBox to allow a user to pick one of an array of strings, or if space is limited, consider using a DomainUpDown control. This is a control that maintains a list of Strings and displays them one by one in a TextBox in response to the user clicking up and down buttons. Figure 10.31 shows a DomainUpDown control displaying a string.

If you know the strings you want to display in the control, create a String array, and then add the array in one operation:

```
' Create a String array
Dim js() As String = {"one", "two", "three", "four"}

' Add it to the control
DomainUpDown1.Items.AddRange(js)
```

The **Items** property represents the collection of strings managed by the control; you can either use the **AddRange()** method to add an array in one operation, or use the **Add()** method to add strings one by one.

If you want the control to wrap when it gets to the start or end of the items, set the **Wrap** property to true, and set the **Sorted** property to true if you want the items to be maintained in sorted order.

The **SelectedIndex** and **SelectedItem** properties let you get and set the selected item by zero-based index or by reference. An index of -1 or a null reference means that there is nothing selected:

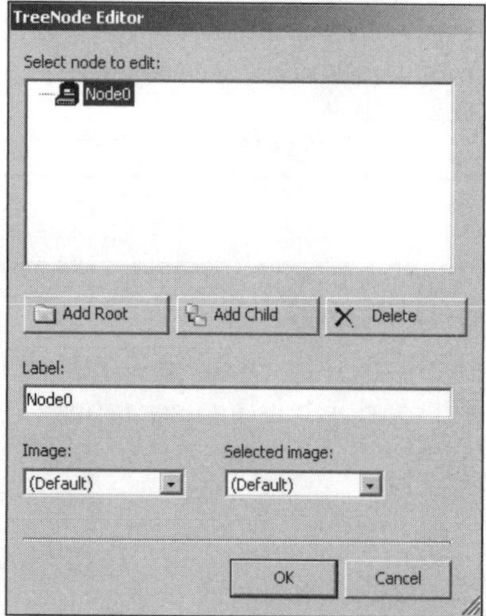

Figure 10.31 A DomainUpDown control.

```
' Set the selection to the first item
DomainUpDown1.SelectedIndex = 0
```

How Can I Show the Value of a TrackBar?

It's very simple to display the current value represented by the position of the TrackBar thumb in an edit control.

Place a TrackBar onto a form, and set its **Minimum** and **Maximum** properties accordingly. Then add a TextBox called TextBox1. Double-clicking on the TrackBar in the Designer will add code for the **Scroll** event, which is triggered whenever the value changes. Simply add the one line of code that sets the TextBox content to the current value of the TrackBar, like this:

```
Protected Sub Trackbar1_Scroll(ByVal sender As Object, _
    ByVal e As System.EventArgs)
  TextBox1.Text = Trackbar1.Value.ToString()
End Sub
```

How Do I Use ListBoxes, CheckedListBoxes, and ComboBoxes?

The three controls—ListBoxes, CheckedListBoxes, and ComboBoxes—can be simply created by selecting the appropriate item in the Toolbox and drawing them onto a form.

Setting Properties

There are several properties that can be applied to ListBoxes. **BorderStyle** determines how the border will be drawn around the ListBox, and it is set to one of the values from the **System.Windows.Forms.BorderStyle** enumeration. The **BorderStyle.None** style will draw the ListBox with no border, **BorderStyle.Single** will give it a simple line border, while **BorderStyle.Fixed3D** will give a beveled 3D look.

The Boolean **Sorted** property governs whether the list of items will be sorted or not. If it is set to true, then all items will be sorted in ascending order when they are added.

The Boolean **IntegralHeight** property determines whether ListBoxes will display partial items or not. If set to true, the ListBox will adjust its height so that it is only displaying whole items.

The **MultiColumn** and **ColumnWidth** properties can be used to create multicolumn ListBoxes. **ColumnWidth** sets the width of each column in pixels, and a value of zero can be used to get a default value. The following code fragment shows how to create the ListBox shown in Figure 10.32:

```
' Set ListBox to multi-column
ListBox2.MultiColumn = True
ListBox2.ColumnWidth = 50

' Add items...
ListBox2.Items.Add(New String("One"))
...
ListBox2.Items.Add(New String("Eight"))
```

The **SelectionMode** property determines how the user is going to be able to select items from the ListBox. The value is taken from the **System.Windows.Forms.SelectionMode** enumeration, which may be None (if nothing can be selected), One (for single selection), MultiSimple (for simple multiple selection), or MultiExtended (for multiple selection that permits the use of the Ctrl and Shift keys to build selections).

Adding Items

ListBoxes have an **Items** property, which is a collection that holds all the items currently displayed by the ListBox. There are two ways to add items to a ListBox:

- Create an array of items to add them all at once
- Add items one at a time

The most efficient way to add items to a ListBox is to create an array—usually of **Strings**—and then add the array using the **Items.AddRange()** method:

```
' Create an array of Strings
Dim listItems As String() = { "One", "Two", "Three" }

' Add them all to the ListBox
ListBox1.Items.AddRange(listItems)
```

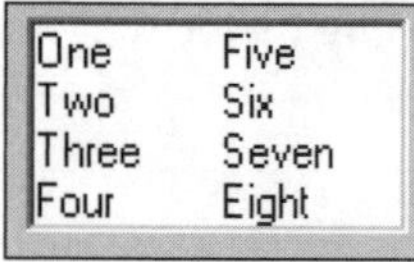

Figure 10.32 A multicolumn ListBox.

If you don't know what you need to add, you can add items one by one:

```
' Add an item to the ListBox
ListBox1.Items.Add(new String("New Item"))
```

If you want to add a lot of items in this way, the ListBox will want to update itself each time you add an item, which can cause the display to flicker. The solution to this is to switch updating off until you've finished adding items using the **BeginUpdate()** and **EndUpdate()** methods:

```
' Turn updating off
ListBox1.BeginUpdate()

' Add items...
ListBox1.Items.Add(New String("One"))
ListBox1.Items.Add(New String("Two"))
ListBox1.Items.Add(New String("Three"))

' Turn updating back on
ListBox1.EndUpdate()
```

Add() will always add an item to the end of the list; you can insert an item into the list by using **Insert()**. The index you provide is the index at which the new item will be inserted:

```
' Insert an item at index 2
ListBox1.Items.Insert(2, New String("New"))
```

NOTE: *If you insert items into a sorted ListBox, the new items will not be sorted correctly because you have specified the position to which they're added.*

Finding Out What Is Selected

It's common to want to find out what is currently selected in a ListBox. The **SelectedIndex** property represents the zero-based index of the item that is currently selected. The value of -1 denotes that nothing is currently selected. **SelectedItem** returns the value of the currently selected item, so you can retrieve the string associated with an item, like this:

```
' Get the selected index
Dim ix As Integer = ListBox1.SelectedIndex

' Display it in a message box
MsgBox("Item selection: index=" + ix.ToString() + _
     ", item=" + ListBox1.SelectedItem.ToString() + "'")
```

Note the use of the **ToString()** method to convert both the index and the item into strings for display. You can also use **SelectedIndex** to set the selected item in case you want to display a ListBox with a particular item selected by default. If you don't select an item, nothing will be selected in the ListBox:

```
' Select the second item
ListBox1.SelectedIndex = 1
```

If you are using a multiple-selection control, you need to use two alternative properties, **SelectedIndices** and **SelectedItems**, which return collections holding information about the currently selected items. These are standard collection objects that implement ICollection and IEnumerable, so they can be manipulated using any of the techniques discussed in Chapter 4. The following example shows how you can find out how many elements are selected by enumerating over the collection:

```
' Get the collection of indices
Dim mbIdx As ListBox.SelectedIndexCollection = ListBox1.SelectedIndices

' How many elements are selected?
MsgBox("Selected " + mbIdx.Count.ToString() + " items")

' Set up an enumerator to iterate over the collection
Dim en As IEnumerator = mbSel.GetEnumerator
While en.MoveNext = True
  Console.WriteLine(en.Current)
End While
```

Handling Item Selection Notification

A ListBox will fire a **SelectedIndexChanged** event when a different item is selected. Double-clicking on a ListBox in the Designer will add a **SelectedIndexChanged** handler to your form class, like this:

```
Protected Sub ListBox1_SelectedIndexChanged(ByVal sender As _
     System.Object, ByVal e As System.EventArgs)
  // Handler code goes here
End Sub
```

As usual, the arguments to the handler function are superfluous and are more useful in C# code than in VB. Once in the handler, you can query the **SelectedIndex** property to find out which index has been selected:

```
Protected Sub ListBox1_SelectedIndexChanged(ByVal sender As Object, _
      ByVal e As System.EventArgs)
```

```
    ' Get the selected index
    Dim ix As Integer = ListBox1.SelectedIndex

    ' Display it in a message box
    MsgBox("Item selection: " + ix.ToString())
End Sub
```

Do not use **SelectedIndex** if you are using a multiselection ListBox because each time you add a new item to the selection, it will report the index of the first item. Use the **SelectedIndices** property to handle multiple selections.

Working with CheckedListBoxes

CheckedListBoxes differ from standard ListBoxes in that they have a checkbox for every item. Additional methods in the **CheckedListBox** class let you manipulate these checkboxes.

It is important to note that CheckedListBoxes usually do not select the item when the item's checkbox is checked or unchecked. You can use the **CheckOnClick** property to determine whether selection and selection of the checkbox state are incorporated into one click.

GetItemChecked() returns a Boolean telling you whether a given item is checked. As usual with ListBoxes, the index is zero-based. **GetItemCheckState()** provides you with more information, returning a value from the **Windows.Forms.CheckState** enumeration. This value may be Checked, Unchecked, or Indeterminate (grayed out).

```
If CheckedListBox1.GetItemCheckState(0) = _
      WinForms.CheckState.Checked Then
  MsgBox("Item 0 is checked")
```

You can use the **SetItemChecked()** and **SetItemCheckState()** methods to set the check state of items from code:

```
CheckedListBox1.SetItemCheckState(0, WinForms.CheckState.Indeterminate)
```

If you want to know which items are checked, you can either loop through the code calling **GetItemCheck()** and **GetItemCheckState()** for each item, or use the **GetCheckedIndices()** method to return a collection of all the checked items.

Working with ComboBoxes

ComboBoxes are created and populated in exactly the same way as ListBoxes. ComboBoxes can be displayed in three ways:

- A ComboBox with the **Simple** style always shows the drop-down list, and the text in the edit control is editable.

- A ComboBox with the **DropDown** style only shows the drop-down list when the button next to the edit control is pressed. The text in the edit control is editable.
- A ComboBox with the **DropDownList** style only shows the drop-down list when the button next to the edit control is pressed. The text in the edit control is *not* editable.

The **DroppedDown** Boolean property indicates whether the list is currently dropped down, and **MaxDropDownItems** indicates the maximum number of items that will be shown in the drop-down list.

SelectedIndex indicates the zero-based index of the currently selected item, with a value of -1 indicating that there's no selection. **SelectedItem** returns the value of the currently selected item, or Nothing (null) if nothing is selected.

If the text in the edit control portion of the ComboBox is editable, you can use **SelectionStart** and **SelectionLength** to find out which portion of the edit control is selected, and then use **SelectionText** to retrieve the selected text. The **Text** property represents the text in the edit control.

Working with StatusBars

It is very common in applications to display a status bar at the bottom of a form, which can be used to pass information to the user. To add a status bar to a form in Visual Studio.NET, select the **StatusBar** control from the Toolbox and drop it onto the form. This produces a nearly invisible default StatusBar with no text and a resizing grip at the bottom right, which is docked to the bottom of the form, as shown in Figure 10.33.

Text and Panels

It is common for a StatusBar to display a text string, and you can set this text string by using the **Text** property. If the StatusBar is going to display a fixed text string, you can use the Property Browser to set the text; if you want to change the text at runtime, simply assign the text you want to display to the **Text** property:

```
StatusBar1.Text = "foo"
```

Figure 10.33 A default StatusBar on a form.

When you update the **Text** property, you'll find that the StatusBar shows the new text immediately. You do not need to tell it to repaint itself. This happens because status bars are repainted automatically during *idle processing* (i.e., when your application has nothing else to do), so the current text will appear on the status bar without intervention on your part.

A StatusBar control can also host one or more panels. To add panels in Visual Studio, find the **Panels** property in the Property Browser, and press the button to the right in order to bring up the StatusBarPanel Collection Editor window (see Figure 10.34).

Each panel is represented by a **StatusBarPanel** object, and this editor window provides you with a simple way of creating new **StatusBarPanel** objects and setting their properties. To create a new panel, click the Add button, and then adjust the properties accordingly.

The **Alignment** property determines how the text will be aligned within the panel; the default is left-aligned. **AutoSize** controls whether the panel will automatically size itself to the text, and **BorderStyle** determines how the text will appear on the StatusBar; the default (and most normal) value is Sunken.

Panels are not displayed by default; if you want to display them, you need to set the **ShowPanels** property to true.

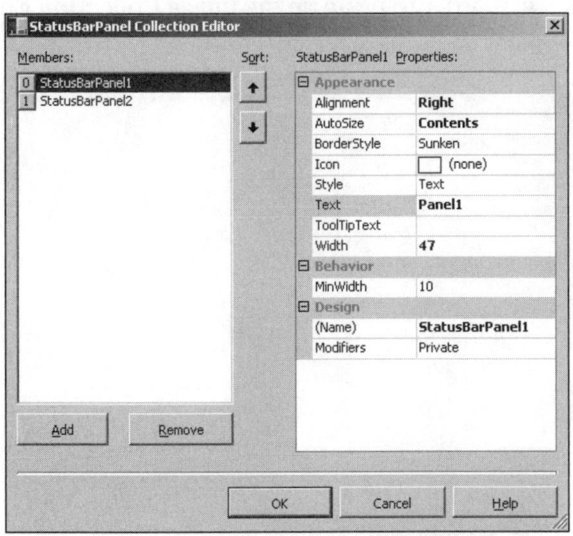

Figure 10.34 The StatusBarPanel Collection Editor.

Working with ToolBars

Just about every application nowadays uses one or more toolbars, which in .NET are represented by the **Windows.Forms.ToolBar** class. A toolbar consists of a window containing a number of buttons, which may display text and/or a bitmap.

Using a ToolBar in an application is a fairly long-winded, although not very complex process:

1. Add a ToolBar control to your form.
2. Add an ImageList to the form, and fill it with images.
3. Associate the ImageList with the ToolBar.
4. Add buttons to the ToolBar and set their images.
5. Add handlers for the buttons.

I'll show you how to use a ToolBar from within Visual Studio.NET, although it is quite possible to do this purely in code without any wizard help.

Setting Up the ToolBar

To set up a ToolBar, start by selecting the ToolBar control from the Toolbox and dropping it onto the form. This produces an empty ToolBar docked at the top of the form. Drag an ImageList onto the form as well, and then click on the button to the right of the **Images** property in order to bring up the Image Collection Editor, as shown in Figure 10.35.

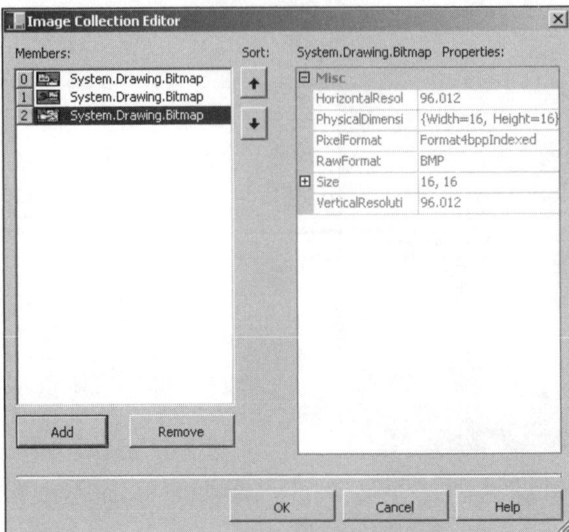

Figure 10.35 The Image Collection Editor dialog.

Use the Add button to browse for images to use on the toolbar buttons; images for use on toolbars are usually bitmap files, 16×16 pixels in size. You can see in Figure 10.35 that I've added three images, which have been given the indices 0, 1, and 2. You can then associate the ImageList with the **ImageList** property of the ToolBar.

The next task is to add the buttons to the toolbar. As you might expect, the **ToolBar** object holds a collection of **ToolBarButton** objects, which is accessible through the **Buttons** property. You can either create **ToolBarButton** objects manually and add them to buttons, or in Visual Studio, you can click on the button to the right of the **Buttons** property to bring up the ToolBarButton Collection Editor, as shown in Figure 10.36.

Use the Add button to add as many buttons as required, and set their **ImageIndex** properties to point to the appropriate bitmap in the ImageList. Once you've done this, you can build and run the application. You should see the toolbar displaying the buttons as shown in Figure 10.37.

Note how the buttons display as 3D. If you want Explorer type buttons that are flat until the mouse moves over them, use the ToolBar's **Appearance** property to change the buttons' appearance to Flat.

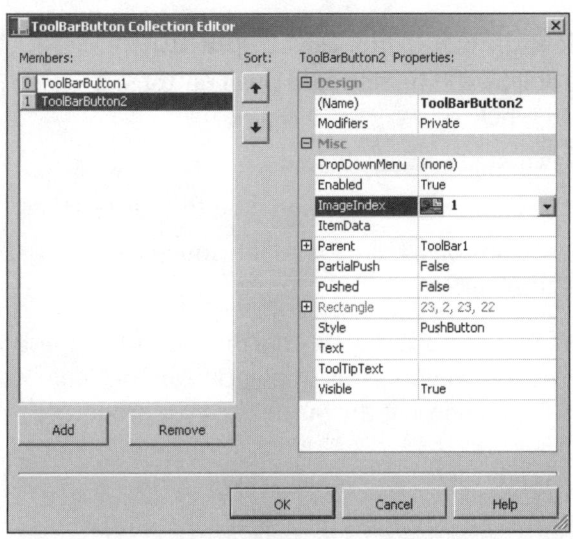

Figure 10.36 The ToolBarButton Collection Editor dialog.

Figure 10.37 A form showing a ToolBar control with two buttons.

Handling Button Events

Toolbar buttons give rise to **Click** events when they are pressed, just like ordinary buttons, so you can add a **Click** handler by double-clicking on one of the toolbar buttons in the Designer. You'll find, though, that no matter how many buttons you have on your toolbar, you only get one event handler. You have to use the button field of the **ToolBarButtonClickEventArgs** object to find out which button was clicked:

```
Protected Sub ToolBar1_ButtonClick(ByVal sender As System.Object, _
     ByVal e As System.WinForms.ToolBarButtonClickEventArgs) _
     Handles ToolBar1.ButtonClick
   ' Check which button was pressed
   If e.button = ToolBarButton1 Then
     MessageBox.Show("Button 1 pressed!")
   ElseIf e.button = ToolBarButton2 Then
     MessageBox.Show("Button 2 pressed!")
   Else
     MessageBox.Show("Whoops...")
   End If
End Sub
```

Using DropDownButtons, ToggleButtons, and Separators

Although most items on the toolbar will be standard push buttons, it is also possible to use three other button types:

- *DropDownButtons*—Display a menu when clicked
- *ToggleButtons*—Toggle between up and down each time they are clicked
- *Separators*—Do not display as buttons, but instead introduce a gap into the sequence of buttons on the toolbar

If you are using Visual Studio, you can use the ToolBarButton Collection Editor to set the style of a button to DropDownButton, ToggleButton, or Separator. If you are creating your toolbar from code, set the button's **Style** property:

```
ToolBarButton3.Style = ToolBarButtonStyle.DropDownButton
```

In order to use a drop-down button, create a ContextMenu and associate it with the **DropDownMenu** property of the button.

Using TreeViews

A **TreeView** control displays a hierarchical collection of items and is very similar in appearance to the left pane of Windows Explorer.

Setting Up the TreeView

To set up a TreeView, start by dragging a TreeView control from the Toolbox onto a form and positioning and sizing it accordingly. Then define the items to be displayed in the tree, which are called *nodes* and are represented by **TreeNode** objects. If you have used Windows Explorer, you'll be familiar with the fact that nodes in a TreeView usually have a small graphic associated with them, and that the graphic changes to show whether a node is selected or not.

The images used for selected and unselected nodes are held in an ImageList, so the next task is to add an **ImageList** object to the form and fill it with images. You can do this by clicking on the button to the right of the **Images** property of the ImageList and choosing graphics files in the Image Collection Editor, as shown in Figure 10.35. Once you've done this, set the **ImageList** property of the TreeView to point to the ImageList you've just created, so that the TreeView knows what images it has to use.

Adding Nodes

Nodes are added to the TreeView by clicking on the button to the right of the **Nodes** property, which brings up the TreeNode Editor shown in Figure 10.38.

When you first display the editor, you'll only be allowed to add a root node. Once you've added the root node, you can select any node in the tree and add children.

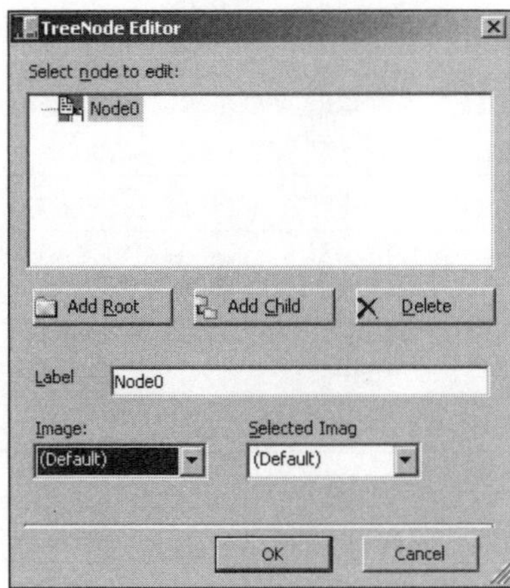

Figure 10.38 The TreeNode Editor dialog.

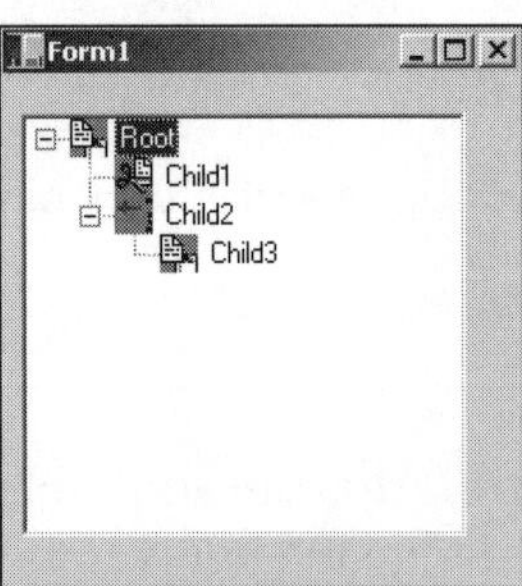

Figure 10.39 A TreeView containing four nodes.

The fields at the bottom of the dialog let you change the text and the two icons that are associated with a node. Figure 10.39 shows the result of adding four nodes to a TreeView.

NOTE: *It is quite acceptable to have more than one root node in a TreeView.*

TreeView Display Options

The TreeView has several properties that let you control the appearance of the node hierarchy. These properties are summarized in Table 10.34.

Handling Events

Once you have loaded the TreeView with nodes, the control will take care of all interactions with the user, but you will usually want to know when an item in the hierarchy has been selected. Double-clicking on the TreeView control in the Designer adds an **AfterSelect** event handler to your form, which is called when a

Table 10.34 Properties affecting the appearance of a TreeView.

Property	Description
BorderStyle	Defines the style of the control border. Default is a 3D border.
CheckBoxes	True if checkboxes are shown next to the image on each node.
HotTracking	True if the tree nodes are highlighted as the mouse moves over them.
Indent	Represents the indentation of child nodes, in pixels.
LabelEdit	If true, node label text can be edited.
Scrollable	If true, the control will show scrollbars when needed.
ShowLines	True if lines are drawn between nodes. Default is true.
ShowPlusMinus	True if the expand button is shown next to nodes that have children.
ShowRootLines	True if lines are shown joining nodes to the root.
Sorted	True if nodes in the tree are sorted.

new item has been selected. This handler takes a **TreeViewEventArgs** object as an argument, which gives you details on what has been selected:

```
Protected Sub TreeView1_AfterSelect(ByVal sender As System.Object, _
    ByVal e As System.WinForms.TreeViewEventArgs) _
    Handles TreeView.AfterSelect
  If e.Node = myNode Then
    ' myNode was selected
  End If
End Sub
```

As you can see from the code fragment, the most important member of the **TreeViewEventArgs** class is the **Node** property, which tells you the node that has been selected.

Using ListViews

A ListView control displays a list of items in a number of different formats and is very similar in appearance to the right pane of Windows Explorer.

Setting Up the ListView

To set up a ListView, start by dragging a ListView control from the Toolbox onto a form and positioning and sizing it. You then need to define the items to be displayed in the list, which are called *items* and are represented by **ListItem** objects. If you've used Windows Explorer, you'll be familiar with the fact that items in a ListView can be displayed as text, or with a large or small icon.

The images used for the large and small icons are held in two ImageLists, so you need to add two **ImageList** objects to the form and fill them with appropriate icons. You can do this by clicking on the button to the right of the **Images** property of the ImageList and choosing graphics files in the Image Collection Editor, as shown in Figure 10.35. Once you've done this, set the **SmallImageList** and **LargeImageList** properties of the ListView to point to the ImageLists you just created.

Adding Items

ListItems are added to the ListView by clicking on the button to the right of the **ListItems** property, which displays the ListItem Collection Editor shown in Figure 10.40.

The important entries are the **Text**, which appears when a ListView is displaying in text mode, and the **ImageIndex**, which governs which images from the

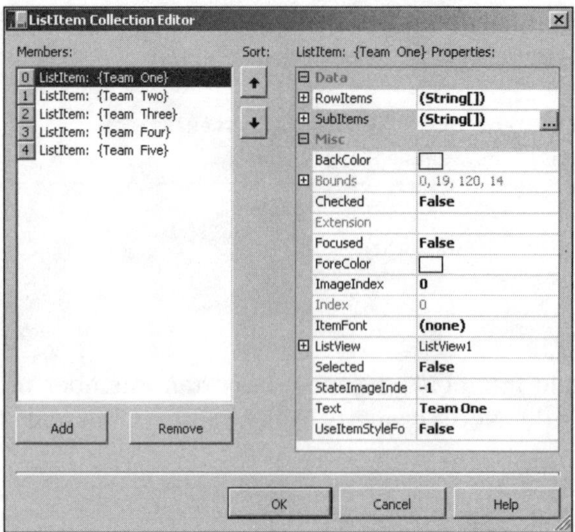

Figure 10.40 The ListItem Collection Editor for adding ListItems to a ListView.

LargeImageList and **SmallImageList** are used to display an item. An item can consist of more than one column, and the **SubItems** collection lets you add extra String items for new columns.

Once you've set up the list items, you can use the **View** property on the ListView to set the initial display mode for the control. There are four possible views:

- LargeIcon
- SmallIcon
- List
- Report

LargeIcon and SmallIcon views display the ListItems as rows of icons with the text underneath each item. List view displays only the text, and Report view displays the text plus any SubItems that have been defined. If you are using Report view, you should also define column headers using the **Columns** property.

There are a number of properties that can be used to affect the appearance of a ListView. These properties are summarized in Table 10.35.

Handling Events

You often want to know when the user has selected an item in the ListView. Double-clicking on the control in the Designer adds a **SelectedIndexChanged** handler, which is called every time an object is selected or deselected. Somewhat unusually, you do not receive any information about which item has been selected, so you have to look at the control's **SelectedItems** collection:

Table 10.35 Properties that affect the appearance of a ListView.

Property	Description
Alignment	Indicates the alignment of icons in the window.
BackgroundImage	Indicates the background image, if any.
BorderStyle	Indicates the style of the control border. Default is a 3D border.
CheckBoxes	If true, every item will display a checkbox.
GridLines	True if grid lines are drawn between items.
HoverSelection	True if items are selected by hovering over them with the mouse.
LabelEdit	True if item labels can be edited.
MultiSelect	True if multiple selection is allowed.

```
Protected Sub ListView1_SelectedIndexChanged(ByVal sender _
    As System.Object, ByVal e As System.EventArgs) _
    Handles ListView1. SelectedIndexChanged
  If ListView1.SelectedItems.Count = 0 Then
    MessageBox.Show("Nothing selected", "ListView" _
     MessageBoxButtons.OK, MessageBoxIcon.Information)
  Else
    MessageBox(ListView1.SelectedItems.Count.ToString() & _
        " items selected", "ListView", _
     MessageBoxButtons.OK, MessageBoxIcon.Information)
  End If
End Sub
```

ListView controls permit multiple selection by default, so the **SelectedItems** collection holds the references to all the currently selected items.

Creating Tabbed Forms

Tabbed forms and dialogs are a very common feature of many Windows applications, and .NET provides the **TabControl** and **TabPage** classes to help you build and manage them. Figure 10.41 shows a form containing a TabControl with two TabPages.

The TabControl occupies the area within the hashed border. It manages two TabPage objects through its **TabPages** collection property. Each of the TabPages has a **Text** property, the value of which is shown on the tab. In order to add TabPages to the TabControl, click on the button to the right of the **TabPages** property in the Property Browser, and the TabPage Collection Editor is displayed, as shown in Figure 10.42.

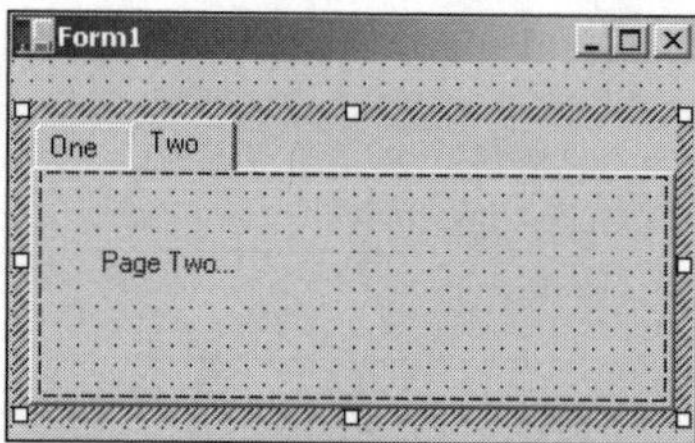

Figure 10.41 A form containing a TabControl with two TabPages.

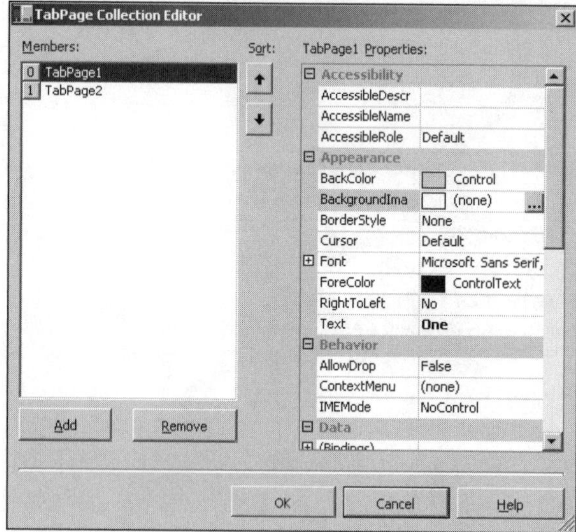

Figure 10.42 The TabPage Collection Editor for maintaining the collection of TabPage objects owned by a TabControl.

Once you've added pages, you can place controls onto the pages just like you place them onto a form; simply click on the tabs to switch to another page.

Using the TabControl's **Appearance** property, you can also display the tabs in two other forms: as buttons (see Figure 10.43) and flat buttons (see Figure 10.44).

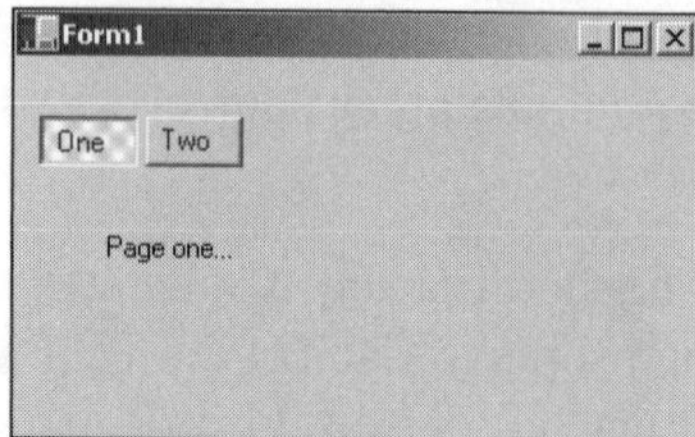

Figure 10.43 A TabControl displaying tabs as buttons.

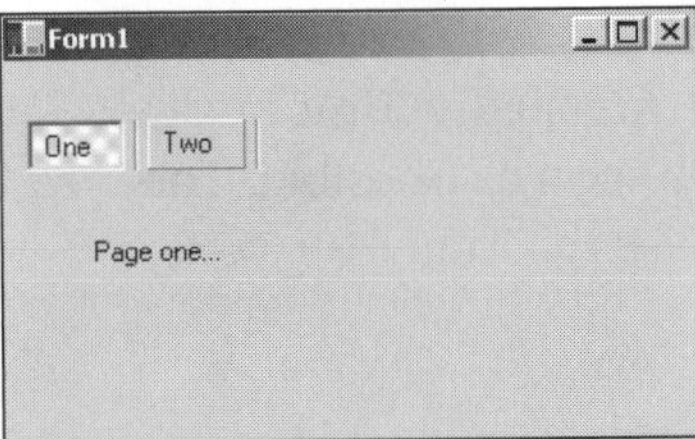

Figure 10.44 A TabControl displaying tabs as flat buttons.

Using Timers

The Timer control fires a **Timer** event at user-defined intervals and provides a simple way to perform an operation for a fixed time or a preset number of times.

To use a Timer, select the control on the Toolbox and drop it onto a form. Because it is a nonvisual control, its icon appears in the panel at the bottom of the Form Designer window. Use the **Interval** property to set the number of milliseconds between **Timer** events. Double-clicking on the Timer icon adds an event handler to the form; this method is called every time the Timer fires its event.

The following code shows how a Timer can be used on a form to update a ProgressBar control:

```
' Counts the number of times the timer has ticked
Private ticks As Integer

' Form constructor
Sub New()
  ticks = 0

  ' Start the timer
  Timer1.Start()
End Sub

Protected Sub Timer1_Tick(ByVal sender As System.Object, _
      ByVal e As System.EventArgs) Handles Timer1.Tick
  ' Increment the tick count
  ticks = ticks + 1

  ' Update the ProgressBar
  Progress1.Value = Progress1.Value + 1
End Sub
```

Note that if you add a Timer in code (rather than using the Form Designer), you must call its **Dispose()** method when you are finished with it because Timers use system resources that should be freed up as soon as possible. The Form Designer inserts code into your project that disposes the Timer for you.

How Do I Host ActiveX Controls on a Windows Form?

It is possible to host existing ActiveX controls on a Windows Form by providing a suitable wrapper. This topic is covered in more detail in Chapter 16.

How Do I Create My Own Controls?

The **UserControl** class is used as the basis for creating your own custom controls. It gives you a blank form on which to draw and provides you with all the infrastructure supplied by the **Control** class hierarchy.

Creating and using a custom control isn't very hard, as you'll see from the following example. Start by creating a Windows Control Library project called VBCustom, which creates a control class that derives from **UserControl**. You should see some code like this in your project:

```
Imports System.ComponentModel
Imports System.Drawing
Imports System.Windows.Forms

Public Class Control1
    Inherits System.Windows.Forms.UserControl
  ...
End Class
```

For simplicity, this control will only have two properties:

- **Integer**, which represents the number of times it has been clicked (read-only)
- **Title string** (read-write)

Initializing the Control

To initialize the control, start by adding the property that represents the number of times the control has been clicked. This is stored as an integer value, and clients get access to it via a read-only property:

```
Private timesClicked As Integer

ReadOnly Property Clicks() As Integer
  Get
    Clicks = timesClicked
  End Get
End Property
```

Don't forget to initialize **timesClicked** to zero in the **Sub New()** or C# constructor.

You can then add the title string and provide access to it via a read-write property:

```
Private ts As String

Property TitleString() As String
  Get
     TitleString= ts
  End Get
  Set
    ts = Value
    Invalidate()
  End Set
End Property
```

Notice the call to **Invalidate()** in the **Set** clause. If someone changes the string, you'll want the control to update itself immediately in order to display the changed string.

Overriding the OnPaint Method

OnPaint is the method where all the drawing of your control's UI is done, so you need to override it in your class:

```
' Override the OnPaint method
Protected Overrides Sub OnPaint(ByVal e As _
       System.Windows.Forms.PaintEventArgs)
  ' Call the base class
  MyBase.OnPaint(e)

  ' Draw a string
  Dim s As String
  s = ts + ": clicked " + timesClicked.ToString + " times"

  ' We need to convert the ClientRectangle (which is an integer
  ' Rectangle) to a floating-point RectangleF. There are
  ' conversion operators, but they can't be used from VB,
  ' hence the rather inelegant construction
```

```
    Dim rct As New System.Drawing.RectangleF(ClientRectangle.Left, _
        ClientRectangle.Top, ClientRectangle.Width, _
        ClientRectangle.Height)
    e.Graphics.DrawString(s, Font, New SolidBrush(ForeColor), rct)
End Sub
```

In this routine, I put together a string consisting of the values of two of the control's properties, so I can get some visual feedback that the control is working and responding to events. **OnPaint()** is passed a **PaintEventArgs** object, one of whose members is a **Graphics** object representing the control's drawing area on the screen. You use the **DrawString()** method of this **Graphics** object to display the string within the bounding rectangle of the control using the default font and color; however, you run into one minor problem.

The **System.Drawing** namespace, which encapsulates all the Windows GDI functionality, contains two classes to represent rectangles: **Rectangle** (which uses integer coordinates) and **RectangleF** (which uses floating point). It turns out that the **ClientRectangle** property that the control inherits from **UserControl** is a **Rectangle**, whereas **DrawString()** requires a **RectangleF**. A rather inelegant but simple way around this problem is to use the coordinates of the **ClientRectangle** to initialize a **RectangleF**, and then use that **RectangleF** in the call to **DrawString()**.

Handling Mouse Events

The control needs to update the click count every time a user clicks the mouse over it and to display the current count. In order to do that, you need to override one of the mouse event-handler methods:

```
' Override the OnMouseDown method
Protected Overrides Sub OnMouseDown(ByVal e As _
      System.Windows.Forms.MouseEventArgs)
  ' Remember to tell the base class
  MyBase.OnMouseDown(e)

  ' Increment the click count
  timesClicked = timesClicked + 1

  ' Invalidate to update the screen
  Invalidate()
End Sub
```

There are two important points to note in this code. First, the base classes do all the clever delegate and event operations, so all you have to do is to override the appropriate handler. It is important that the base class method gets called; otherwise it won't have a chance to notify any clients listening for this event. Second, remember to call **Invalidate()** when the click count has been changed. **Invalidate()** requests a repaint, so **OnPaint()** gets called in order to display the updated count on the screen. If you don't call **Invalidate()**, you can click on the control, but you won't see the text change on the screen until something else forces a repaint.

Testing Out the Control

Once you have defined the basic functionality of the control, you need to test it out in a project. Start by doing a test build of the control; if all is okay, you should find that a new Control1 item has been added to the end of the Windows Forms section of the Toolbox.

To test the control, add a new Windows application project to your solution in Visual Studio by right-clicking on the Solution name in the Solution Explorer and selecting Add | New Project from the context menu.

Before you can use the control, you have to add a reference to the control's assembly to the project. Right-click on the References folder and choose Add Reference from the context menu.

NOTE: *References in .NET serve the same purpose and are used in much the same way as references in earlier versions of VB. They import information that tells the compiler all about components; in the case of .NET, the information that was included in type libraries is made available through metadata.*

You can now select a custom control from the Toolbox and place it on the form, where you should see the text displayed, as in Figure 10.45.

The control properties have attributes attached to them, so you'll be able to modify the **TitleString** using the Property Browser, as shown in Figure 10.46.

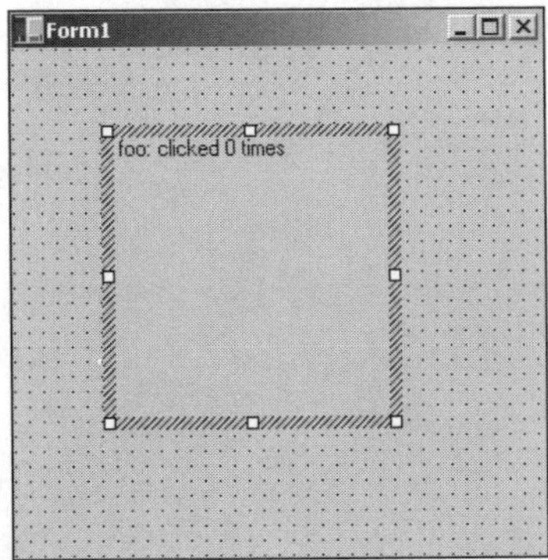

Figure 10.45 A custom control displayed on a form.

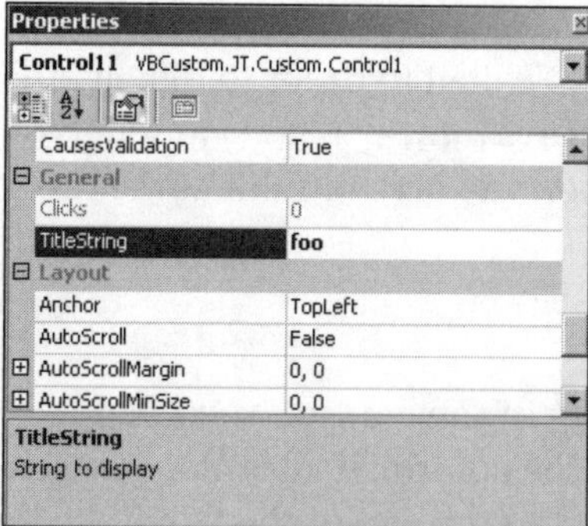

Figure 10.46 Properties of a custom control displayed in the Property Browser.

You can see how the two properties appear in the General category and how the description string appears in the bottom pane of the browser. The **Clicks** property appears in gray because it is read-only; **TitleString** is in black because it is editable.

Chapter 11

The Drawing Namespaces

By Julian Templeman

In Depth

This chapter provides an introduction to the **System.Drawing** namespace that encapsulates .NET's basic graphics functionality, which is known as GDI+.

The name GDI+ comes from the original Windows graphics library, which was called the *Graphical Device Interface*. It is a library of simple 2D graphics designed to draw lines and shapes, draw text, and display bitmaps. There is no 3D functionality in any of GDI+. If you need 3D graphics, you are going to have to consider using Direct3D, the details of which are outside the scope of this book.

System.Drawing contains all the basic functionality, and more advanced drawing features are provided by four other namespaces:

- **System.Drawing.Drawing2D**—Provides advanced 2D and vector graphics
- **System.Drawing.Imaging**—Provides advanced image processing
- **System.Drawing.Text**—Provides typography functionality
- **System.Drawing.Printing**—Provides printing functionality

I am not going to go into the features provided by these four namespaces in any detail, but I'll introduce any functionality they provide that is needed for common tasks.

GDI Drawing Basics

I'll start by describing the basic drawing functionality provided by GDI+ including the use of brushes and pens, the **Graphics** class, how to represent dimensions, and how to work with color.

The Graphics Class

An understanding of the **Graphics** class is fundamental to being able to use GDI+, as it represents the drawing surface on which all output is displayed. GDI+ uses the idea of a graphics object to provide a device-independent way of producing graphical output: You write code to draw on a graphics object, and the GDI+ code fills in the actual pixels on the screen.

The graphics object acts as an intermediary between you and the screen. You send it data to be drawn, and it can provide you with information about the display. I'll discuss the **Graphics** class in more detail once I've covered a few basic points.

***NOTE:** If you've come across device contexts in Windows programming, you are well on your way to understanding the **Graphics** class because a graphics object wraps a device context.*

Basic Data Structures

Drawing operations tend to use points and rectangles a lot, and **System.Drawing** provides a set of classes to represent these data structures.

Point and **PointF** are structures—value types—that both represent a simple (X,Y) point. The difference between them being that **Point** uses integer coordinates, whereas **PointF** uses floats. Tables 11.1, 11.2, and 11.3 summarize the main members of the **Point** classes.

Table 11.1 Members of the Point structure.

Member	Description
IsEmpty	True if both X and Y are zero
X	The X coordinate
Y	The Y coordinate
Equals	True if this point contains the same coordinates as another
Offset	Translates this point by a specified amount
ToString	Returns a string representing the point
+, -	Addition and subtraction operators
==, !=	Equality operators

Table 11.2 Shared methods belonging to the Point structure.

Method	Description
Ceiling	Rounds the coordinates of a **PointF** up to the nearest whole number
Round	Rounds the coordinates of a **PointF** down to the nearest whole number
Truncate	Truncates the coordinates of a **PointF**

Table 11.3 Members of the PointF structure.

Member	Description
IsEmpty	True if both X and Y are zero
X	The X coordinate
Y	The Y coordinate
+, -	Addition and subtraction operators
==, !=	Equality operators

In addition, operators are defined to convert between **Point** and **Size**, **Point** and **PointF**, and **PointF** and **Point**.

The **Rectangle** and **RectangleF** structures are similar in that they are value types representing rectangles, and differ in that **Rectangle** uses integer coordinates, whereas **RectangleF** uses floats.

***NOTE: Rectangles** are always aligned along the X and Y axes. If you want to rotate rectangles, you need to investigate the Drawing2D functionality.*

Tables 11.4, 11.5, and 11.6 summarize the main members of the **Rectangle** classes.

Table 11.4 Members of the Rectangle structure.

Member	Description
IsEmpty	True if both X and Y are zero
X, Y	The X and Y coordinates of the top-left corner
Top, **Left**, **Bottom**, **Right**	The coordinates of the top, left, bottom, and right of the rectangle
Width, **Height**	The width and height of the rectangle
Location	Gets or sets the coordinates of the top-left corner
Size	A Size that represents the height and width of the rectangle
Contains	True if this rectangle contains a given rectangle or point
Equals	True if this point contains the same coordinates as another
FromLTRB	Creates a rectangle from top, left, bottom, and right values
Inflate	Inflates the rectangle
Intersect	Returns a rectangle representing the intersection between two other rectangles
IntersectsWith	True if this rectangle intersects another
Offset	Translates this point by a specified amount
ToString	Returns a string representing the rectangle
Union	Returns a rectangle representing the union of two other rectangles
==, **!=**	Equality operators, operating on the size and location of rectangles

Table 11.5 Shared methods belonging to the Rectangle structure.

Method	Description
Ceiling	Rounds the coordinates of a **RectangleF** up to the nearest whole number
Round	Rounds the coordinates of a **RectangleF** down to the nearest whole number
Truncate	Truncates the coordinates of a **RectangleF**
Union	Returns a rectangle representing the union of two rectangles

Table 11.6 Members of the RectangleF structure.

Member	Description
IsEmpty	True if both X and Y are zero
X, Y	The X and Y coordinates of the top-left corner
Top, **Left**, **Bottom**, **Right**	The coordinates of the top, left, bottom, and right of the rectangle
Width, **Height**	The width and height of the rectangle
Location	Gets or sets the coordinates of the top-left corner
Size	A Size that represents the height and width of the rectangle
Contains	True if this rectangle contains a given rectangle or point
Equals	True if this point contains the same coordinates as another
FromLTRB	Creates a rectangle from top, left, bottom, and right values
Inflate	Inflates the rectangle
Intersect	Returns a rectangle representing the intersection between two other rectangles
IntersectsWith	True if this rectangle intersects another
Offset	Translates this point by a specified amount
ToString	Returns a string representing the rectangle
==, !=	Equality operators, operating on the size and location of rectangles

In addition, operators are defined to convert between **Rectangle** and **RectangleF** in both directions. **RectangleF** has two shared methods—**Truncate()** and **Union()**.

The **Size** and **SizeF** structures represent the size of a rectangular region by a pair of **Width** and **Height** properties. As before, **Size** uses integer coordinates, whereas **SizeF** uses floats.

Tables 11.7, 11.8, and 11.9 summarize the main members of the **Size** classes.

Table 11.7 Members of the Size structure.

Member	Description
Height	The height of a rectangular region
Width	The width of a rectangular region
IsEmpty	True if both height and width are zero
Equals	Tests whether the height and width of two **Sizes** are equal
ToString	Returns a string representing the **Size**
+, -	Addition and subtraction operators
==, !=	Equality operators

Table 11.8 Shared methods belonging to the Size structure.

Method	Description
Ceiling	Rounds the coordinates of a **SizeF** up to the nearest whole number
Round	Rounds the coordinates of a **SizeF** down to the nearest whole number
Truncate	Truncates the coordinates of a **SizeF**

Table 11.9 Members of the SizeF structure.

Member	Description
Height	The height of a rectangular region
Width	The width of a rectangular region
IsEmpty	True if both Height and Width are zero
Equals	Tests whether the height and width of two **Sizes** are equal
ToPointF	Returns a **Point** representing the **SizeF**
ToSize	Returns a **Size** representing the **SizeF**
ToString	Returns a string representing the **SizeF**
+, -	Addition and subtraction operators
==, !=	Equality operators

In addition, conversions are supplied for **Size** to **SizeF**, **SizeF** to **Size**, **Size** to **Point,** and **SizeF** to **PointF**.

Color

Colors are represented in .NET by the **Color** structure. Color values are denoted by four 32-bit integer values—**Alpha**, **Red**, **Green**, and **Blue**—where **Alpha** is the transparency and the other three represent the red, green, and blue components of the color.

.NET provides a large number of standard colors, which are defined as part of the **System.Drawing.KnownColor** enumeration. This is a very large enumeration with well over 100 members, and its values tend to fall into two groups:

- Colors representing items on the screen, such as WindowText, Control, and ActiveCaption. These may be altered if the user uses the Control Panel to change the desktop color scheme.
- Fixed RGB (red, green, blue) values representing named standard colors, such as Azure, Cornflower, LightGray, and MediumPurple.

The **Color** structure also possesses a number of static methods that will return color objects corresponding to the known colors, so that you can easily use them within API calls:

```
' Create a one pixel wide pen having the color Coral
Dim pen2 As New Pen(System.Drawing.Color.Coral, 1)
```

Tables 11.10 and 11.11 list the important properties and methods of the **Color** class.

Note that the **Color** class doesn't have constructors, but instead uses static factory methods to return references to color objects, like this:

```
Dim c2 As Color = Color.FromKnownColor(KnownColor.Chartreuse)
```

The **GetBrightness()**, **GetHue()**, and **GetSaturation()** methods return values that correspond to the color's coordinates in the alternative HSB representation space.

Drawing Implements: Pens and Brushes

The **Pen** and **Brush** classes encapsulate the line thickness, line styles, fill patterns, and colors that you use for drawing on the screen. Pens are used for drawing the outlines of shapes, lines, and curves, and brushes are used for filling areas.

Table 11.10 Properties of the Color class.

Property	Description
A	Gets the "alpha" (transparency) component of the color
R, **G**, **B**	Gets the red, green, and blue components of the color
IsEmpty	True if this color is uninitialized
IsKnownColor	True if this color corresponds to a predefined color
IsNamedColor	True if this color has a name
Name	Returns the name of this color

Table 11.11 Methods of the Color class.

Method	Description
Equals	Tests for equivalence of color objects
FromARGB, **FromKnownColor**, **FromName**	Creates a color object
GetBrightness, **GetHue**, **GetSaturation**	Gets the Hue, Saturation, Brightness (HSB) components of a color
ToARGB	Returns the value of this color as Alpha, Red, Green, and Blue components
ToKnownColor	Returns the **KnownColor** member corresponding to a color
==, **!=**	Tests for equality of colors

Pens

Pens have two basic properties: a width and a fill color or pattern. The pattern is provided by one of the **Brush** classes, so that you can arrange to draw lines with a texture or gradient fill if desired. Table 11.12 lists the most important properties of the **Pen** class.

The alignment describes how the pen is aligned relative to the lines that it draws, and this alignment is represented by a member of the **PenAlignment** enumeration as shown in Table 11.13.

The dash style sets the style of dashed lines drawn with this pen, and the style is represented by a member of the **DashStyle** enumeration as shown in Table 11.14.

NOTE: *Unlike in previous versions of GDI, dashed and dotted lines can be more than one pixel thick.*

Line caps are represented by members of the **LineCap** enumeration and specify how the ends of lines will be drawn. End cap types include round, square, triangular,

Table 11.12 Important properties of the Pen class.

Property	Description
Alignment	Gets or sets the alignment of objects drawn with this pen (see Table 11.13)
Brush	Gets or sets the **Brush** associated with this pen
Color	Gets or sets the color of this pen
DashPattern	Gets or sets the array of custom dashes and spaces used for drawing
DashStyle	Represents the dash style used for this line
LineJoin	Represents the way in which lines join
MiterLimit	Represents the limit of the thickness of the join on a mitered corner
PenType	Specifies the kind of pen
StartCap, EndCap	Represents the start and end caps of the line
Transform	A matrix describing how objects drawn with this pen will be transformed
Width	Gets or sets the width of the pen in pixels

Table 11.13 The PenAlignment enumeration.

Member	Description
Center	The pen is aligned with the center of the line being drawn.
Inset	The pen is aligned with the inside of the line being drawn.
Left	The pen is aligned to the left of the line being drawn.
Outset	The pen is aligned with the outside of the line being drawn.
Right	The pen is aligned to the right of the line being drawn.

Table 11.14 The DashStyle enumeration.

Member	Description
Custom	Specifies a user-defined custom line style
Dash	Specifies a dashed line
DashDot	Specifies a line with a repeating dash-dot pattern
DashDotDot	Specifies a line with a repeating dash-dot-dot
Dot	Specifies a dotted line
Solid	Specifies a solid line (the default value)

and custom. The **PenType** will be one of the members of the **System.Drawing.Drawing2D.PenType** enumeration and can take one of the values shown in Table 11.15. Table 11.16 lists the most important methods of the **Pen** class.

As you'll notice, most of these methods are concerned with the transforms used with this pen. See the Immediate Solutions section "Using Transforms" for more information about transforms and how they work.

Table 11.15 The PenType enumeration.

Member	Description
HatchFill	The pen will be filled with a hatch pattern.
LinearGradient	The pen will be filled with a linear gradient fill.
PathGradient	The pen will be filled with a path gradient fill.
SolidColor	The pen will be filled with a solid color (default).
TextureFill	The pen will be filled with a bitmap texture.

Table 11.16 Methods of the Pen class.

Method	Description
Clone	Creates an exact copy of this pen
Dispose	Releases the Windows resources used for this pen
MultiplyTransform	Multiplies the transform matrix by another matrix
ResetTransform	Resets the transform matrix to identity
RotateTransform	Rotates the local geometric transform
ScaleTransform	Scales the local geometric transform
SetLineCap	Sets the start and end linecaps for this pen
TranslateTransform	Translates the local geometric transform

The **Dispose()** method frees up the underlying system resources used by this pen object. Although these will be freed up for you when the pen object is garbage collected or when the program finishes, it is a good idea to call **Dispose()** once you've finished with the pen object in order to make efficient use of system resources.

Using Standard Pens

If you want to get a pen to represent one of the standard colors, use the **System.Drawing.Pens** class. This class contains static methods for each of the predefined colors in the **Color** class and saves you from having to create a pen and set its color manually:

```
' Methods in Pens return a reference to a new Pen
Dim p As Pen = Pens.AliceBlue
```

If you want a pen to represent one of the standard colors used for UI elements, use the **System.Drawing.SystemPens** class. This class contains static methods for each of the predefined UI colors. Here's an example of how **SystemPens** is used:

```
' Get a pen initialized with the color used for highlighted text
Dim p As Pen = SystemPens.HighlightText
```

Table 11.17 lists all the colors that can be retrieved using the properties of the **SystemPens** class.

Table 11.17 Properties of the SystemPens class.

Property	Description
ActiveCaptionText	The color of text on the title bar of an active window
Control	The color of a button or other control
ControlDark	The colors of the shadowed parts of 3D elements
ControlDarkDark	The colors of the very darkest parts of 3D elements
ControlLight	The color of the highlights of 3D elements
ControlLightLight	The color of the very lightest parts of 3D elements
ControlText	The color of text on controls
GrayText	The color of disabled text
Highlight	The color of a highlighted background
HighlightText	The color of highlighted text

(continued)

Table 11.17 Properties of the SystemPens class *(continued)*.

Property	Description
InactiveCaptionText	The color of text on the title bar of an inactive window
InfoText	The color of text on a tooltip
MenuText	The color of text on a menu
WindowFrame	The color of a window frame
WindowText	The color of a window's text

Brushes

Classes derived from the abstract base class **Brush** are used for filling the interiors of shapes. Two brush classes are defined in **System.Drawing**:

- **SolidBrush**—Defines a brush made up of a single color
- **TextureBrush**—Defines a brush that fills the interior of a shape with an image

The **SolidBrush** class has very few members, and all the significant members are summarized in Table 11.18. **TextureBrush** is slightly more complex, and its properties and methods are described in Tables 11.19 and 11.20. See the Immediate Solutions section "Using Transforms" for more information about transforms and how they work.

Table 11.18 Important members of the SolidBrush class.

Member	Description
SolidBrush	Constructor that takes a color
Clone	Creates an exact copy of this brush
Dispose	Releases the Windows resources used for this brush
Color	Gets or sets the color of this brush
OnSystemColorChanged	Called when a system color changes

Table 11.19 Properties of the TextureBrush class.

Property	Description
TextureBrush	Constructors that take **Image** and **Rectangle** arguments
Image	Gets the image associated with this brush
Transform	Gets or sets the matrix representing the transformation of this brush
WrapMode	Represents the wrapping mode for the image

Table 11.20 Methods of the TextureBrush class.

Method	Description
Clone	Creates an exact copy of this **TextureBrush**
MultiplyTransform	Multiplies the transform matrix by another matrix
ResetTransform	Resets the transform matrix to identity
RotateTransform	Rotates the local geometric transform
ScaleTransform	Scales the local geometric transform
TranslateTransform	Translates the local geometric transform

Using Standard Brushes

If you want a brush to represent one of the standard colors, use the **System.Drawing.Brushes** class. This class contains static methods for each of the predefined colors in the **Color** class:

```
' Create a solid brush initialized with Azure
Dim br As Brush = Brushes.Azure
```

If you want a brush to represent one of the standard colors used for UI elements, use the **System.Drawing.SystemBrushes** class. This class contains static methods for each of the predefined UI colors. Here's an example of how you can use **SystemBrushes**:

```
' Get a brush initialized with the color used for the desktop
Dim br1 As Brush = SystemBrushes.Desktop
```

Table 11.21 lists all the colors that can be retrieved using the properties of the **SystemBrushes** class.

Table 11.21 Properties of the SystemBrushes class.

Property	Description
ActiveBorder	The color of the border of an active window
ActiveCaption	The color of the title bar of an active window
ActiveCaptionText	The color of text on the title bar of an active window
AppWorkspace	The color of text on the title bar of an active window
Control	The surface color of 3D elements
ControlDark	The shadow color of 3D elements
ControlDarkDark	The darkest color of 3D elements
ControlLight	The highlight color of 3D elements

(continued)

Table 11.21 Properties of the SystemBrushes class *(continued)*.

Property	Description
ControlLightLight	The lightest color of 3D elements
ControlText	The color of text on controls
Desktop	The color of the desktop
Highlight	The color of a highlighted background
HighlightText	The color of highlighted text
HotTrack	The color used to represent hot-tracking
InactiveBorder	The color of the border of an inactive window
InactiveCaption	The color of the title bar of an inactive window
Info	The background color of a tooltip
Menu	The background color of menus
ScrollBar	The background color of a scrollbar
Window	The color of a window background
WindowText	The color of text on controls

More Advanced Brushes

The **System.Drawing.Drawing2D** class defines three more advanced brush types:

- **HatchBrush**—Defines a foreground color, a background color, and a hatch pattern. Hatch styles are chosen from the **HatchStyle** enumeration.
- **LinearGradientBrush**—Fills using a gradient between two or more colors. This class can use both standard two-color gradients as well as custom user-defined multicolor gradients.
- **PathGradientBrush**—Shades between the center of a path and the outside boundary. Various properties, such as **Blend**, can be used to affect where the gradient starts and how fast the color changes.

Details of the Graphics Class

As previously mentioned, the **Graphics** class represents a device-independent abstraction of a drawing surface, and it implements a large number of methods that allow you to draw basic shapes.

Note that the **Graphics** class does not have any constructors; instead, you use a form's **CreateGraphics()** method to get a reference to a graphics object. This is because a graphics object is actually a .NET wrapper around a Windows system object, which is called a *device context*. **CreateGraphics()** tells GDI+ to obtain a graphics object for you:

```
' Get a Graphics object
Dim g As Graphics = CreateGraphics()

' Use it
g.DrawLine(pen1, 10, 10, 100, 100)
```


If you call **CreateGraphics()** within a function, the underlying system object will be released when the graphics object is garbage collected. In order to release it earlier, you can call the **Dispose()** method on the graphics object to release its resources. You obviously have to make sure that you don't try to use the graphics object after you have called **Dispose()**.

NOTE: *It is good practice to hold onto Graphics objects for as short a time as possible, because the supply of underlying system objects may be limited on some systems.*

Once you have obtained a graphics object, you can use it to draw on the form. Table 11.22 lists the main methods of the **Graphics** class involved with producing graphical output. Other, nondrawing methods of the **Graphics** class are shown in Table 11.23.

Table 11.22 Drawing methods in the Graphics class.

Method	Description
Clear	Fills the drawing surface with a given color
DrawArc	Draws an arc from an ellipse
DrawBezier, **DrawBeziers**	Draws one or more Bezier curves
DrawCurve, **DrawClosedCurve**	Draws open or closed curves specified by an array of points
DrawEllipse	Draws an ellipse
DrawIcon	Draws an icon
DrawImage	Draws an image
DrawLine, **DrawLines**	Draws one or more lines
DrawPie	Draws a pie chart segment
DrawPolygon	Draws a polygon
DrawRectangle, **DrawRectangles**	Draws one or more rectangles
DrawString	Draws a string
FillClosedCurve	Fills a closed curve specified by an array of points
FillEllipse	Draws a filled ellipse
FillPie	Draws a filled pie chart segment
FillPolygon	Draws a filled polygon
FillRectangle, **FillRectangles**	Draws one or more filled rectangles

Table 11.23 Other methods in the Graphics class.

Method	Description
Dispose	Releases the Windows resources used by this graphics object
Finalize	Called when this graphics object is garbage collected
Flush	Forces immediate execution of all graphics commands in the queue
FromHdc	Creates a graphics object from a Windows HDC handle
FromHwnd	Creates a graphics object from a Windows HWND
FromImage	Creates a graphics object from an image object
GetHdc	Returns the Windows HDC representing this graphics object
GetNearestColor	Gets the color nearest to a given color
IsVisible	Indicates whether a point or rectangle is contained in the clip region for this graphics object
MeasureString	Returns the **Size** of a string drawn in a given font
SetClip, **ResetClip**	Sets or resets the clip region associated with this graphics object
ResetTransform	Resets the graphics transform associated with this graphics object
RotateTransform	Adds a rotation to the graphics transform associated with this graphics object
Save, **Restore**	Saves or restores the state of a graphics object
ScaleTransform	Adds scaling to the graphics transform associated with this graphics object
TransformPoints	Uses the current transform to transform an array of points
TranslateTransform	Adds a translation to the graphics transform associated with this graphics object

The properties of the **Graphics** class provide a link to the capabilities of the actual display device, and you can use them to set and query those capabilities. The most useful properties are listed in Table 11.24.

The **PageUnit** property determines the units to be used for drawing, as it takes one of the values from the **GraphicsUnit** enumeration. If you do not set this property, it will take the default value of **GraphicsUnit.Pixel**, and the drawing will be done in pixels. Table 11.25 lists the other units that you can choose.

Table 11.24 Properties in the Graphics class.

Property	Description
CompositingMode	Determines whether pixels from an image will overwrite (**CompositingMode.SourceCopy**) or are combined with the background pixels (**CompositingMode.SourceOver**)
CompositingQuality	Represents the quality level used for compositing
DpiX	The horizontal resolution in pixels supported by the graphics object

(continued)

Table 11.24 Properties in the Graphics class *(continued)*.

Property	Description
DpiY	The vertical resolution in pixels supported by the graphics object
InterpolationMode	Specifies how data is interpolated between points
PageScale	The scale between world units and page units
PageUnit	The unit of measure used for page coordinates
SmoothingMode	The rendering quality (default, antialiased, high speed, high quality)
Transform	The current graphics transform

Table 11.25 Members of the GraphicsUnit enumeration.

Member	Unit of Measurement
Display	1/75 of an inch
Document	Document units (1/300 inch)
Inch	Inches
Millimeter	Millimeters
Pixel	Pixels
Point	Printers points (1/72 inch)
World	User-defined world coordinates

Here's how you would draw lines using millimeters as the units:

```
' Create a Graphics object
Dim gr As Graphics = CreateGraphics()

' Set the units to millimeters
gr.PageUnit = GraphicsUnit.Millimeters

' Draw a line using a black pen
gr.DrawLine(Pens.Black, 10, 10, 20, 20)

' Dispose of the Graphics object
gr.Dispose()
```

The advantage of using units in this way is that the graphics you draw will come out the same size—within device limitations—on whatever screen or printer is used. If you use pixels, your graphics will come out a very different size on a 72 dots-per-inch screen than on a 600 dots-per-inch printer.

Graphics Objects and Painting

You have seen how to obtain a graphics object and create graphical output, but you will find that it is very easy to "lose" the graphics that you have drawn on the form. Whenever anything causes your form window to need updating—such as minimizing it to the taskbar and then restoring it or placing another window on top of it and then removing it—you will find that .NET restores the "system" parts of the window, such as the caption, scrollbars, and controls, but you are responsible for redrawing your graphics.

In order to handle the redrawing, forms get sent a paint event when it is necessary for them to repaint their content, and it is in the **OnPaint()** function that you should redraw the content of your form:

```
Protected Overrides Sub OnPaint(ByVal e As _
      System.Windows.Forms.PaintEventArgs) Handles MyBase.Paint
  ' Get the repaint graphics object
  Dim gr As Graphics = e.Graphics

  ' Handle repainting here
End Sub
```

This function gets passed a **PaintEventArgs** object that contains two useful properties. The first is **ClipRectangle**, which tells you the area of the form that needs repainting, and the second is **Graphics**, which returns a reference to the graphics object you should use for painting.

Once you have a **Graphics** reference, you can use it to redraw your graphics on the screen; this does, of course, presuppose that you have saved the details that you have to redraw! Note that you should not call **Dispose()** in this graphics object. You did not create it, so it is not up to you to dispose of it!

Fonts

Text fonts in .NET are represented by two classes in the **System.Drawing** namespace, **Font** and **FontFamily**. A font object defines a set of characteristics for text display including the font face (the font name), text size, and style attributes. A **FontFamily** object represents a group of type faces that are similar but may differ in style. The style attributes for fonts are defined in the **FontStyle** enumeration (see Table 11.26) and will be familiar to anyone who has used a word processor.

Table 11.26 The members of the FontStyle enumeration.

Member	Description
Bold	Represents bold text
Italic	Represents italic text
Regular	Represents regular text
Strikeout	Represents text with a line through it
Underline	Represents underlined text

Table 11.27 lists all the properties of the **Font** class; note that they are read-only because a font object cannot have its characteristics changed once it has been created. Table 11.28 lists the important methods of this class. Note that there are several that let you convert between Windows API font structures and GDI+ fonts.

Table 11.27 Properties of the Font class.

Property	Description
Bold	True if this font is bold (read-only)
FontFamily	Returns the **FontFamily** for this font (read-only)
Height	Returns the height of this font (read-only)
Italic	True if this font is italic (read-only)
Name	Returns the name of this font (read-only)
Size	Returns the size of this font (read-only)
SizeInPoints	Returns the size of this font in points (read-only)
Strikeout	True if this font is struck-out (read-only)
Style	Returns a **FontStyle** object describing the style of this font (read-only)
Underline	True if this font is underlined (read-only)
Unit	Returns the graphics units used for this font (read-only)

Table 11.28 Important methods of the Font class.

Method	Description
Clone	Creates an exact copy of this font object
Dispose	Releases Windows resources for this font
FromHdc	Creates a font from a Windows HDC
GetHeight	Gets the height of a font in a specified Graphics context
ToHfont, **FromHfont**	Converts to or from a Windows HFONT
ToLogFont, **FromLogFont**	Converts to or from a Windows LOGFONT structure

Handling Images

The **System.Drawing.Image** class is an abstract base class that has two derived classes: **Bitmap** and **Metafile**. The first of these will be familiar to all GUI programmers, so I'll describe it in more detail later in this section.

The second class, **Metafile**, represents a Windows metafile, which provides a way of storing the commands used to create an image rather than the pixel and color information. This means that although you "display" a bitmap, you speak of "replaying" a metafile to regenerate the image, and it makes metafiles very suitable for use where you may need to display an image on different devices or use different aspect ratios or color depths. Because metafiles are rather specialized, I won't discuss them any further.

The Image Class

The base for all the image classes is **Image**, which provides a number of useful methods and properties. Because this is an abstract class, you cannot create an image object, but you can use **Image** references to refer to objects of derived types. Table 11.29 lists some of the most important properties of the **Image** class. The pixel format describes how pixels are formatted—such as 8 or 24 color bits per pixel—and these formats are described by the **PixelFormat** enumeration.

Image formats are described by the **ImageFormat** class, which has its members listed in Table 11.30. Table 11.31 lists the most important methods of the **Image** class.

Table 11.29 Important properties of the Image class.

Property	Description
Height	The height of the image
HorizontalResolution	The horizontal resolution of the image
Palette	Gets or sets the palette used for this image
PhysicalDimension	Gets a **SizeF** object describing the dimensions of this image
PixelFormat	The pixel format
RawFormat	Gets the format of this image
Size	Returns a **Size** object describing the dimensions of the image
VerticalResolution	The vertical resolution of the image
Width	The width of the image

Table 11.30 Important members of the ImageFormat class.

Member	Description
BMP	Specifies Windows bitmap format
EMF	Specifies the Enhanced Windows Metafile format
GIF	Specifies the GIF image format
Icon	Specifies the WIndows icon image format
JPEG	Specifies the JPEG image format
PNG	Specifies the W3C PNG image format
TIFF	Specifies the TIFF file format
WMF	Specifies the Windows Metafile format

Table 11.31 Important methods of the Image class.

Method	Description
FromFile	Creates an image from data in a file
FromHBITMAP	Creates an image from a Windows HBITMAP
FromStream	Creates an image from a stream
GetBounds	Returns the bounds of the image
GetThumbnailImage	Returns a thumbnail of this image
Save	Save the image to a file

The **FromFile()** and **Save()** methods will read and write images in a variety of formats as defined by the **ImageFormat** enumeration described earlier. The following line of code shows how to save a bitmap as a JEPG file:

```
myImage.Save("thisdir/thisfile.jpeg", PixelFormat.JPEG);
```

The Bitmap Class

Bitmap objects are used to represent images. They can be initialized with data from a file or created in memory and built up manually.

The **Bitmap** class contains a dozen constructors that let you create and initialize bitmaps in a variety of ways:

- From an existing image object
- From a stream or a file
- From a resource
- As a blank bitmap of a specified size

The following code fragment shows how to create a Bitmap from an image in a JPEG file:

```
Dim bm As New Bitmap("c:\temp\image.jpg")
```

The **Bitmap** class has no properties except those it inherits from **Image**. Table 11.32 lists the important methods of the **Bitmap** class.

The Icon Class

The **Icon** class is used to represent icons, which are small bitmaps used by the system to represent objects and can be thought of as bitmaps with a transparent background.

Icon objects can be created in a number of ways, such as:

- From a stream
- From a Win32 icon handle (an HICON)
- From a file
- From a resource
- From another icon object

Icons can be converted to bitmaps using the **ToBitmap()** method.

The **SystemIcons** class represents a set of icons that are provided by the system and can be used in any application. These icons are provided as a set of properties as listed in Table 11.33. Many of these properties will be familiar from their use in message boxes and other system dialogs.

Table 11.32 Important methods of the Bitmap class.

Method	Description
Clone	Creates an exact copy of a Bitmap
FromHicon	Creates a Bitmap from a copy of a Windows HICON
FromResource	Creates a Bitmap from a resource
GetHbitmap	Returns a Windows HBITMAP representing this object
GetHicon	Returns a Windows HICON representing this object
GetPixel, **SetPixel**	Gets or sets a pixel in the Bitmap
MakeTransparent	Makes a color transparent for this Bitmap
SetResolution	Sets the resolution for the Bitmap

Table 11.33 Properties of the SystemIcons class.

Property	Description
Application	The default application icon
Asterisk	The system asterisk icon
Error	The system error icon
Exclamation	The system exclamation icon
Hand	The system hand icon
Information	The system information icon
Question	The system question icon
Warning	The system warning icon
WinLogo	The Windows logo

Printing

The **System.Drawing.Printing** namespace provides the printing functionality for GDI+. In this section, I'll provide an overview of how the printing process operates and the main classes involved. In the Immediate Solutions, I'll show how you can get a document to a printer in a practical way.

Table 11.34 lists the main classes involved in the printing process.

The PrintDocument Class

PrintDocument is the main class involved in printing, and a **PrintDocument** object represents a reusable object that sends output to a printer. The following outline describes the sequence of events involved in using a PrintDocument:

1. Create the **PrintDocument** object.
2. Set its parameters, including the printer to be used and page and printer settings, but *not* the document details.

Table 11.34 The main classes involved in the printing process.

Class	Description
PrintDocument	Sends output to a printer, making use of a **PrintController** to control the process
PageSettings	Represents a set of page settings, such as paper size
PrinterSettings	Represents a set of printer settings, such as the printer name and duplex capability
PrintController	An object responsible for outputting individual pages, which calls a **PrintPage** event handler
PrintPageEventArgs	An object passed to a **PrintPage** event handler that passes information to and from a **PrintController**

3. Register a callback function to be called for each page.
4. Call the **Print()** function to start printing.

This object is reusable in that you do not associate the details of what is to be printed with the **PrintDocument** object; therefore, you can call **Print()** more than once in order to print more than one document.

The **PrintDocument** class has four properties as summarized in Table 11.35.

The Settings Classes

The printer settings—such as color options and available paper sizes—are represented by a **PrinterSettings** object. The page parameters—such as paper size and orientation—are represented by a **PageSettings** object. The **PageSettings** object is based on the printer settings because it is only reasonable to, for instance, offer landscape orientation or color printing if the printer supports it.

These classes have many properties and few commonly used methods. Tables 11.36 and 11.37 list the most useful properties of each class. Note especially the **InstalledPrinter** property, which returns a list of all installed printers.

Table 11.35 The four properties of the PrintDocument class.

Property	Description
DefaultPageSettings	Gets or sets a **PageSettings** object that represents the default page settings, such as paper size and orientation
DocumentName	Gets or sets a string representing the document name
PrintController	Gets or sets a **PrintController** object that controls the printing process
PrinterSettings	Gets or sets a **PrinterSettings** object that controls how and where the document is printed

Table 11.36 Important properties of the PrinterSettings class.

Property	Description
CanDuplex	True if the printer can do double-sided printing
Collate	True if the document is to be collated
Copies	Gets or sets the number of copies to print
DefaultPageSettings	Gets the default **PageSettings** object for this printer
Duplex	True if the printer is set for duplex printing
FromPage, ToPage	Indicates the first and last pages to print

(continued)

Table 11.36 Important properties of the PrinterSettings class *(continued)*.

Property	Description
InstalledPrinters	Returns a list of the names of all installed printers
IsDefaultPrinter	True if the **PrinterName** property matches the default printer
IsValid	True if the **PrinterName** property matches an installed printer
MaximumCopies	Get the maximum number of copies supported by the printer
PaperSizes	Returns the collection of paper sizes supported by the printer
PaperSources	Returns the collection of paper source trays available on the printer
PrinterName	Represents the printer name
PrinterResolutions	Represents the range of resolutions supported by the printer
PrintToFile	True if the output is being sent to a file
SupportsColor	True if the printer supports color printing

Table 11.37 Important properties of the PageSettings class.

Property	Description
Bounds	Returns a rectangle representing the bounds of the page.
Color	True if the page is printing in color.
Landscape	A Boolean value representing the landscape setting.
Margins	The margins for this page in hundredths of an inch. The default margin is one inch on all sides.
PaperSize	The current paper size as a **PaperSize** object.
PaperSource	The current paper source, for example, **PaperSourceKind.Upper** for the upper bin.
PrinterResolution	The X and Y resolution of the printer.
PrinterSettings	The **PrinterSettings** object associated with this **PageSettings** object.

The PrintController Class

PrintDocument uses a **PrintController** object to perform the printing process. **PrintController** is an abstract class that defines the standard methods needed for printing documents, and it is extended by three classes in **System.Drawing.Printing**:

- **StandardPrintController**—Used for normal printer output
- **PreviewPrintController**—Used for print preview
- **PrintControllerWithStatusDialog**—Has a status dialog to show how the printing job is progressing

There are only four methods that these classes need to implement, which are listed in Table 11.38.

Table 11.38 Methods of the PrintController class.

Method	Description
OnStartPrint	Called at the start of the print process
OnStartPage	Called at the start of each page
OnEndPage	Called at the end of each page
OnEndPrint	Called at the end of the print process

Printing Events

Every time a page is printed, the **PrintDocument** will raise a **PrintPage** event, and you need to provide a handler to do the actual printing. The number of **PrintPage** events that are raised will depend on how the **PrintDocument** has been set up; there are two main configurations.

One configuration uses the **FromPage** and **ToPage** properties of the **PrinterSettings** object to specify the range of pages to be printed. This determines how many times **PrintPage** events are raised. This works well if you know in advance how many pages need to be printed, but often you don't. In this case, it is up to the handler to indicate whether printing is to continue or not; how it does this is covered later in this section.

A print handler function looks like this:

```
Private Sub myPagePrintFunction(ByVal sender As Object, _
        ByVal ev As PrintPageEventArgs)
   ' Print the page
End Sub
```

The first argument is common to all the event handlers and tells you who originated the event. In the case of printing, this information is not usually of interest. The second argument is more interesting because it lets you communicate with the **PrintController** object in charge of the printing process. Properties of the **PrintPageEventArgs** object let the **PrintController** pass information to you, and you can also use properties to tell the **PrintController** how to proceed after a particular page has printed.

As an example, if you are printing from page to page, you use the **HasMorePages** property of the **PrintPageEventArgs** object to tell the **PrintController** whether to continue:

```
Private Sub myPagePrintFunction(ByVal sender As Object, _
        ByVal ev As PrintPageEventArgs)
   ' Print the page
```

```
  ev.HasMorePages = true  ' if more to print, or false if we're done
End Sub
```

Table 11.39 lists the properties of the **PrintPageEventArgs** class.

Table 11.39 Properties of the PrintPageEventArgs class.

Property	Description
Cancel	Set to true if the job should be cancelled.
Graphics	Gets the graphics object associated with this page. Use this for output.
HasMorePages	Set to true if another page should be printed.
MarginBounds	Returns the rectangle of the page inside the margin.
PageBounds	Indicates the rectangle enclosing the entire page.
PageSettings	Retrieves the **PageSettings** object for the current page.

Immediate Solutions

How Do I Draw on a Form?

In order to perform any drawing on a form, you need to use the **CreateGraphics()** member of the **Form** class to get a graphics object:

```
' Get a Graphics object
Dim g As Graphics = CreateGraphics()
```

CreateGraphics() obtains a graphics object from the system and returns a reference to it. Using a method rather than a constructor to obtain graphics objects hides the precise way in which these objects are obtained, cached, and/or recycled.

In earlier versions of Windows, there was a limited supply of the underlying system device context objects. Therefore, it was very important that you did not hold on to these any longer than absolutely necessary, or else you could severely impact system performance. These limitations do not exist in later versions of Windows, but you are still strongly advised to hold on to graphics objects for the shortest possible time.

If you create a graphics object using **GetGraphics()**, it will release its resources when it gets garbage collected or when the application finishes. In order to make good use of resources, call the object's **Dispose()** method to release the underlying device context object when you are finished with it.

Using Members of the **Graphics** Class

Once you have obtained a graphics object, you can use the members of the class to draw on the form. The **Graphics** class has a number of methods that allow you to perform simple 2D output, including:

- Lines
- Rectangles
- Polygons
- Arcs, ellipses, and pie chart segments
- Bézier curves
- Open and closed curves

- Strings
- Icons and images

A summary of the drawing functions is provided in Table 11.22. The following code example shows how these functions are used:

```
' Draw a line from (10,10) to (100,100)
g.DrawLine(pen1, 10, 10, 100, 100)

' Draw a filled rectangle, size 50 by 50, at (200,200)
g.FillRectangle(brush1, 200, 200, 50, 50)
```

There are several important points to note from these lines of code. All drawing takes place through the graphics object, so that all drawing methods are part of the **Graphics** class. Pens and brushes are used to define the drawing properties for the current operation: Pens are used where outlines are being drawn, and brushes are used when shapes are being filled. See the Immediate Solution section "Working with Pens and Brushes" for details on how to set up and use these objects.

NOTE: *Unlike in earlier versions of Windows, the pen or brush is included in every function call rather than being selected into a device context.*

Coordinates are specified in pixels, with the origin at the top left of the form. You can choose from a number of coordinate systems by setting the **PageUnit** property of the graphics object to one of the values in the **GraphicsUnit** enumeration, as shown in Table 11.25.

Here's an example showing how to set the units so that coordinates are specified in millimeters:

```
Dim g As Graphics = GetGraphics()
' Set up to draw in millimeters
g.PageUnit = GraphicsUnit.Millimeter

' Draw a line from (10,10) to (100,100)
g.DrawLine(pen1, 10, 10, 100, 100)
```

If you want to use another custom coordinate system, you'll have to use transforms, which are described in the Immediate Solution "Using Transforms." You'll also need to use transforms if you want to draw ellipses, rectangles, or other shapes that are not aligned along the X and Y axes.

Related solutions:	Found on page:
How Do I Create a Windows Forms Application?	402
How Can I Create a New Form and Display It?	406

Working with Colors

Colors are represented by the **System.Drawing.Color** structure, and a color is defined by four components. The "Alpha" component represents the transparency, whereas the actual color itself is represented by red, green, and blue values. All these components are represented by integers in the range 0–255.

A large number of predefined colors—more than 120—are provided as properties of the **Color** class, and you can use these directly in API calls and when creating pens and brushes. The following code shows how you can use a standard color and find its components:

```
' Define a Color as RosyBrown
Dim myColor As Color = Color.RosyBrown

' Print out its components
Console.WriteLine("R={0}, G={1}, B={2}, A={3}", _
   myColor.R, myColor.G, myColor.B, myColor.A)
```

Executing this code gives the following output:

```
R=188, G=143, B=143, A=255
```

An Alpha value of zero means complete transparency, and 255 means no transparency, so this color is as "solid" as possible.

The "known colors" are also provided as members of an enumeration, **KnownColor**, which is used in several API calls. As well as named colors, this enumeration also contains entries for system colors, such as the colors of buttons and window text.

Note that you cannot modify the color components using the **R**, **G**, **B**, and **A** properties. Once created, colors are effectively read-only, and you can only modify color values by creating a new one. The various overrides of the **FromARGB()** method let you create a color from a set of components. So, I could create a new color based on RosyBrown, like this:

```
' Define a Color as RosyBrown
Dim myColor As Color = Color.RosyBrown
```

```
' Create a new color based on RosyBrown, with alpha=255
Dim myNewColor As Color = Color.FromARGB(255, myColor.R+10, _
   myColor.G-20, myColor.B+40)
```

You can also create colors by using a reference to the **KnownColor** enumeration:


```
' Create a color representing the color of title bars on
' active windows
Dim myKnownColor As Color = _
    Color.FromKnownColor(KnownColor.ActiveCaption)
```

The alpha components of colors provide you with some interesting graphic effects. In Figure 11.1, all three lines have full Alpha values of 255, so there is no transparency. In Figure 11.2, the horizontal line is the last one drawn, and its Alpha value has been set to 125, so it has a significant degree of transparency.

Here's the code for drawing the transparent line:

```
' Create a color based on Plum, with Alpha=125
Dim ctr As Color = Color.FromARGB(125, Color.Plum)

' Create a 10-pixel wide pen and draw the line
Dim pen6 As New Pen(ctr, 10)
g.DrawLine(pen6, 75, 125, 225, 125)
```

Converting Colors

The **ColorTranslator** class provides several methods for converting to and from other color types used in Windows programs, such as:

- Win32 colors represented as integers
- HTML colors represented as strings
- OLE colors represented as integers

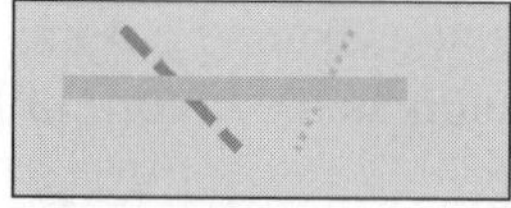

Figure 11.1 Lines with **Alpha=255.**

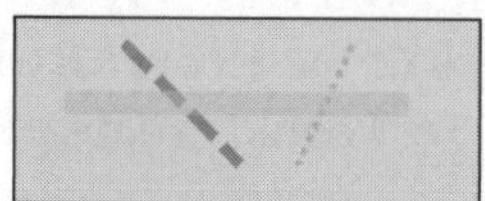

Figure 11.2 The horizontal line has an Alpha component of 125.

Working with Pens and Brushes

The **Pen** class lets you create objects that are used to draw lines and outlines, and have properties such as colors, thickness, and line styles. A **Pen** reference is passed as a parameter to all drawing functions that involve drawing lines. The **Brush** class performs the same function for those drawing functions that involve filling shapes.

Creating and Using Pens

Pens have three fundamental properties—color, width, and line style. Four constructors are provided to let you create pens in a variety of ways:

- From a color with a default width of 1.0
- From a color and a width
- From a brush with a default width of 1.0
- From a brush and a width

Initializing a pen from a brush means copying the color attribute from the brush. The following code shows how to create pens of various types:

```
' A black pen, default width of one pixel
Dim pen1 As New Pen(Color.Black)

' A red pen, width of two pixels
Dim pen2 As New Pen(Color.Red, 2)

' A pen initialized from a brush, width of ten pixels
Dim pen3 As New Pen(myBrush, 10)
```

It is also possible to create pens representing standard system colors using the **Drawing.Pens** class, which has one property for each of the standard colors:

```
' Create a one-pixel wide lime green pen
Dim spen As Pen = Pens.LimeGreen
```

Pens also have a **Color** property that lets you get or set the color of the pen. Line styles are set using the **DashStyle** property, which in turn uses members of the **DashStyle** enumeration. Consult Table 11.14 for all the possible members of this enumeration. Figure 11.3 shows two lines drawn with **Dash** and **Dot** styles.

Here's the code that produces those lines:

```
' Create a dashed pen 5 pixels wide, and draw a line
Dim pen4 As New Pen(c2, 5)
```

```
pen4.DashStyle = Drawing.Drawing2D.DashStyle.Dash
g.DrawLine(pen4, 100, 100, 150, 150)

' Create a dotted pen 3 pixels wide, and draw a line
Dim pen5 As New Pen(Color.Goldenrod, 3)
pen5.DashStyle = Drawing.Drawing2D.DashStyle.Dot
g.DrawLine(pen5, 200, 100, 175, 150)
```


The **DashPattern** property lets you define custom line styles by providing an array that gives the sizes of each dash and space. Here's an example:

```
' Create an array of sizes
Dim patt(5) As Single
patt(0) = 0.5
patt(1) = 1
patt(2) = 1.5
patt(3) = 2
patt(4) = 2.5

' Create a 4-pixel wide pen and set its DashPattern
Dim pattPen As New Pen(Color.Blue, 4)
pattPen.DashPattern = patt

g.DrawLine(pattPen, 75, 125, 225, 125)
```

Note that the sizes of the dashes and spaces are relative to the width of the pen. Figure 11.4 shows the output from this code.

Before moving on to brushes, let me briefly mention end caps, which determine what lines look like at their start and end. For very narrow lines, end caps normally don't matter, but as lines get thicker the style of the end points becomes more noticeable, and you may not want the default straight-cut termination. The **Pen** class defines the **StartCap** and **EndCap** properties, which let you select values from the **LineCap** enumeration that determines how the line ends are drawn. Figure 11.5 shows a line with a round start cap and a triangular end cap.

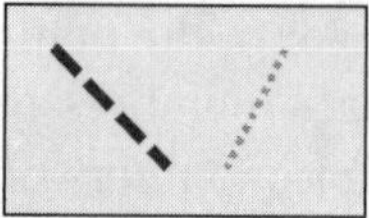

Figure 11.3 Pens showing the **Dash** and **Dot DashStyle** properties.

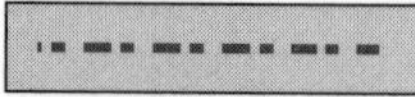

Figure 11.4 A custom dashed pen.

Figure 11.5 A pen with a round start cap and triangular end cap.

Here's the code to set up and use that pen:

```
' Create a medium purple pen
Dim c2 As Color = Color.FromKnownColor(KnownColor.MediumPurple)
Dim pen3 As New Pen(c2, 10)

' Set the end caps
pen3.StartCap = Drawing.Drawing2D.LineCap.Round
pen3.EndCap = Drawing.Drawing2D.LineCap.Triangle

' Draw a line
g.DrawLine(pen3, 140, 20, 180, 60)
```

Creating and Using Brushes

The **System.Drawing** namespace defines an abstract base class called **Brush**, together with two concrete brush classes, **SolidBrush** and **TextureBrush**. As you might expect, a **SolidBrush** paints using a solid color, whereas **TextureBrush** paints using a texture supplied as an image.

SolidBrush is a very simple class: It uses a simple constructor that takes a color as an argument and a **Color** property, which lets you get or set the color of the brush:

```
Dim br1 As New Brush(Color.DarkGoldenRod)
g.FillRectangle(br1, 100, 10, 100, 100)
```

TextureBrush is slightly more complex because you need to set up the Image that is going to be used for the texture and control how it is going to be used. Here's an example showing how to set up and use the small bitmap shown in Figure 11.6 in a **TextureBrush**.

data

Figure 11.6 A bitmap for use in a TextureBrush.

You can use this bitmap as follows:

```
' Create the Graphics object
Dim g As Graphics = CreateGraphics()

Try
  ' Open the bitmap - edit the path for your own
  ' filename!
  Dim bm As Bitmap = Bitmap.FromFile("c:\dev\data.bmp")

  ' Create the TextureBrush
  Dim tbr As New TextureBrush(bm)

  ' Use it to fill a rectangle
  g.FillRectangle(tbr, 50, 50, 100, 100)
Catch ex As Exception
  MessageBox.Show(ex.ToString, "Error", MessageBoxButtons.OK, _
         MessageBoxIcon.Exclamation)
End Try
```

Note how I've enclosed the code—especially the creation of the bitmap—in a **Try** block, as this provides a chance to trap errors, such as a bad file name. Figure 11.7 shows the result of running this code.

More Advanced Brushes

The **System.Drawing.Drawing2D** namespace defines three extra brush classes:

- **HatchBrush**—Fills using one of a fixed set of hatch patterns
- **LinearGradientBrush**—Fills with a gradient fill
- **PathGradientBrush**—Can interpolate along a path

I'll briefly discuss the use of the first two brush classes in the list. A **HatchBrush** is constructed from a hatch pattern, a foreground color, and a background color. You can construct a **HatchBrush** like this:

```
Dim hbr1 As New HatchBrush(HatchStyle.Vertical, _
   Color.ForestGreen, Color.Honeydew)
```

Figure 11.7 A rectangle filled with a TextureBrush.

You can see the results of using all six possible hatch patterns (Vertical, Horizontal, ForwardDiagonal, BackwardDiagonal, Cross, and DiagonalCross) in Figure 11.8.

To construct a **LinearGradientBrush**, you specify two points and two colors, and the color at each point is interpolated. Here's an example showing how to create a **LinearGradientBrush**:

```
Dim lbr As New LinearGradientBrush(New PointF(50, 50), _
  New PointF(200, 200), Color.Black, Color.White)
```

The reference points are given as (50,50) for black and (200,200) for white; all points in between will have their values interpolated. Figure 11.9 shows the result of running this code.

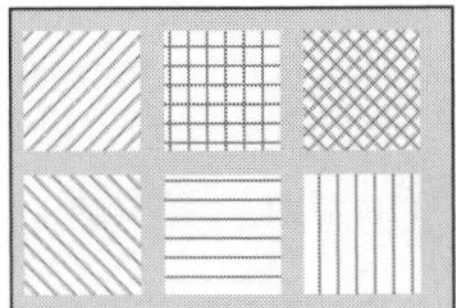

Figure 11.8 **The six hatch patterns used by HatchBrush.**

Figure 11.9 **A LinearGradientBrush filling a rectangle.**

Using Transforms

Transforms are a powerful feature of GDI+ that enable you to get some impressive effects. In fact, transforms form the basis of many 2D and 3D graphics packages. An understanding of how they work and what they do is essential if you want to produce professional graphics. In GDI+, transforms can be applied to graphics objects, to pens, and to brushes.

This isn't the place for a full tutorial in graphics transforms, but I'll present enough information to get you started. The basic idea is that you take coordinates and transform them before display, using combinations of scaling, rotation, and translation. As a simple example, suppose you take the point (10,10) and apply a translation of (10,20) to it; this means that you add 10 to the X coordinate and 20 to the

Y coordinate, giving an output of (20,30). The same transform could be applied to a rectangle and would have the effect of shifting all four corners of the rectangle by 10 in X and 20 in Y.

The following code example shows transforms in use. I create a **TextureBrush** and use transforms to show how they affect the way the texture is painted onto the screen. I start with some simple code for creating a **TextureBrush** from an image and use it to paint a rectangle:

```
Dim bm As Bitmap = Bitmap.FromFile("c:\dev\data.bmp")

' Create the TextureBrush
Dim tbr As New TextureBrush(bm)

' Use it to fill a rectangle
g.FillRectangle(tbr, 50, 50, 100, 100)
```

The image produced by this code is shown in Figure 11.7 (in the previous solution). I then add a transform to rotate the brush by 45 degrees:

```
' Create the TextureBrush and rotate it
Dim tbr As New TextureBrush(bm)
tbr.RotateTransform(45)

' Use it to fill a rectangle
g.FillRectangle(tbr, 50, 50, 100, 100)
```

The output is shown in Figure 11.10. You can see that the fill pattern has been rotated by 45 degrees.

You can do exactly the same thing to introduce scaling and translation. If you want to apply more than one transformation you can, but you need to be aware that the order in which you apply the transforms matters. A minute's thought will enable you to figure out that rotating something about the origin by 45 degrees and then translating it by 20 units in X is not the same as translating it by 20 units and then rotating by 45 degrees about the origin!

Figure 11.10 Using a transform to rotate a brush.

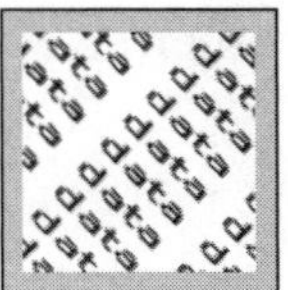

Figure 11.11 Applying rotation and then scaling to a brush.

Figure 11.12 Applying scaling and then rotation to a brush.

You can see this difference quite clearly in Figures 11.11 and 11.12, which apply a 45-degree rotation before and after a 2x scaling in X.

Representing Transforms

This section provides an introduction to the math involved in transforms.

Homogeneous transforms in 2D are represented by an equation like this:

```
P' = P M
```

where P is the original point, P' is the transformed point, and M is a 3-by-3 transformation matrix. The elements in the transformation matrix govern the amount of translation, scaling, and/or rotation that will be applied to the point. As an example, translation fills in two of the elements in the matrix:

$$\begin{bmatrix} 1 & 0 & 0 \\ 0 & 1 & 0 \\ T_x & T_y & 1 \end{bmatrix}$$

T_x and T_y are the amounts of translation required in the X and Y directions, respectively.

In order to make the matrix multiplication work correctly, points are represented by homogeneous coordinates, which are vectors of the form:

$$\begin{bmatrix} x \\ y \\ 1 \end{bmatrix}$$

Multiplying the transformation matrix and the point matrix together gives you the resulting vector:

$$\begin{bmatrix} x + T_x \\ y + T_y \\ 1 \end{bmatrix}$$

For completeness, scaling fills in two diagonal elements of the matrix:

$$\begin{bmatrix} S_x & 0 & 0 \\ 0 & S_y & 0 \\ 1 & 0 & 1 \end{bmatrix}$$

S_x and S_y are the scaling factors required in the X and Y directions, respectively.

The rotation matrix looks like this:

$$\begin{bmatrix} \cos\theta & \sin\theta & 0 \\ -\sin\theta & \cos\theta & 0 \\ 0 & 0 & 1 \end{bmatrix}$$

where θ is the angle of rotation in radians.

How Do I Handle Repainting?

Whenever a form needs repainting, it gets sent a paint event. These paint events may arise because .NET has determined that part or all of your form needs repainting, or it may arise from a call to **Invalidate()**, which can be used to cause a form to repaint from within code.

Paint events are handled by the **OnPaint()** function, which you should override in the form class:

```
Protected Overrides Sub OnPaint(ByVal e _
        As System.Windows.Forms.PaintEventArgs)
   ' Handle repainting here
End Sub
```

You get passed a **PaintEventArgs** object, which has two properties of interest:

- **ClipRectangle**—Defines the area of the form that needs repainting. You can use this if you have a complex form and don't want to waste your time updating areas that don't need it.

- **Graphics**—Provides a reference to a graphics object that you must use for painting to the screen. It is important that you don't create your own **Graphics** reference for painting, and that you don't try to call **Dispose()** on the one you are given.

The following code example shows how to display a string on the screen that will get redrawn every time the form needs to be updated:

```
Protected Overrides Sub OnPaint(ByVal e _
        As System.Window.Forms.PaintEventArgs)
  ' Get the Graphics object for repainting
  Dim gr As Graphics = e.Graphics

  ' Strings need a font and a brush, so create a gradient
  ' brush and a suitable font
  Dim lb As New LinearGradientBrush(New Point(10, 20), _
        New Point(200, 20), Color.Blue, Color.Red)
  Dim fnt As New Font("Verdana", 45, FontStyle.Regular)

  gr.DrawString("My String", fnt, lb, 10, 10)
End Sub
```

Figure 11.13 shows the result of running this code.

Figure 11.13 A string being displayed on a form using the **OnPaint()** handler.

Working with Fonts

A basic knowledge of fonts is essential if you are going to output any text using GDI+. In this section, I cover the basic information you need to know in order to start working with fonts on forms.

There are two classes that represent fonts in GDI+. **Font** represents an individual font and consists of a font face name, a size, and style attributes. An example of a font would be Times Roman, 12 point bold. **FontFamily** represents families of related fonts, which have similar characteristics but differ in details. An example of a **FontFamily** would be the Franklin Gothic collection of fonts, which includes Franklin Gothic Book, Franklin Gothic Medium, Franklin Gothic Heavy, and several others.

Creating Fonts

Creating fonts is simple, but there are no fewer than nine constructors that let you build fonts by specifying combinations of the following attributes:

- Font family, either by name or by providing a **FontFamily** object
- Font size
- Style attributes
- Another existing font

Here's an example showing how to create a font:

```
' Create a font from a family name, a size and a style
Dim fnt As New Font("Verdana", 25, FontStyle.Regular)
```

The font styles will be familiar to anyone who has used a word processor. They are all members of the **FontStyle** enumeration and are listed in Table 11.26. By default, the size is in printer's points (1/72 in.), but several constructor overloads take a final parameter that lets you specify the units in which you are specifying the size:

```
' Create a font with a size in millimeters
Dim fnt As New Font("Verdana", 25, FontStyle.Regular, _
       GraphicsUnit.Millimeters)
```

The members of the **GraphicsUnit** enumeration are listed in Table 11.25. The **Size** property tells you the size of the font in the current units, and the **SizeInPoints** property tells you the size in points if you are using different units.

Drawing Text

The GDI+ **DrawString()** function is used to draw text on a form. There are several overloads for this function, but they all require four elements:

- The string to be drawn.
- The font object to be used.
- The brush to be used for filling the font.

- The place at which the text should be drawn, which may be given as X and Y coordinates, as a point, or as a bounding rectangle.

Fonts are drawn as outlines filled by a brush, which you specify. You must provide a brush to fill the font, or you will receive a runtime error. Here's a simple example showing how to create and use a font to draw a string:


```
' Create a solid black brush
Dim br As SolidBrush = Brushes.Blue

' Create a 25 point font
Dim fnt As New Font("Tahoma", 25, FontStyle.Regular)

' Draw the string at 50,50
gr.DrawString("Another", fnt, br, 50, 50)
```

The result is shown in Figure 11.14. Although it may not be easy to see from the black and white illustration, strings drawn in this way are only filled and do not have an outline.

Another

Figure 11.14 Displaying a string filled with a SolidBrush.

Drawing String Outlines

In order to draw outlines around characters, you have to use a *graphics path*. The **GraphicsPath** class is one of the basic building blocks of GDI+ and simply holds a list of points and their connections. They are used to draw the outlines of shapes, fill the interiors of shapes, and create clipping regions. All the standard drawing functions, such as **DrawRectangle()**, create paths, and you can also create your own. I will not go into detail about paths, but if you are interested, refer to the documentation for the **System.Drawing.Drawing2D.GraphicsPath** class.

In order to display the outline of a string, you need to create a **GraphicsPath**, and then add the string to it, which has the effect of adding the points and connections that represent the letters to the path. Once you have added the string to the path, you can use the **DrawPath()** and **FillPath()** methods to either draw the outline or fill the interior of the path. Here's an example showing how to add a string to a path and then draw its outline:

```
' Create a GraphicsPath
Dim gp As New GraphicsPath(FillMode.Winding)
```

```
' Add a string to the path
gp.AddString("Path", New FontFamily("Impact"), FontStyle.Regular, _
        40, New PointF(30, 70), New StringFormat())

' Draw the path using a black pen
graphicsObject.DrawPath(Pens.Black, gp)
```


The argument to the **GraphicsPath** constructor determines the way in which shapes will be filled. Because I am not concerned with filling shapes, it doesn't matter which value I select. The **AddString()** method has a number of parameters: the string to be displayed, followed by the **FontFamily** to be used, the style, the size, and the position. The final parameter is a **StringFormat** object, which can be used to hold special formatting information, such as "right to left rendering." No special **StringFormat** is needed here, so I simply create a default object. Figure 11.15 shows the result.

Drawing Rotated Text

If you want to draw rotated text—or any other shape, for that matter—you need to set the transform of the graphics object you are using before drawing. If you are unfamiliar with graphics transforms, read the Immediate Solution section "Using Transforms" before continuing.

Drawing rotated text is simply a matter of setting a rotation before drawing. The following example displays a string as an outline and draws it rotated by 45 degrees:

```
' Create a GraphicsPath
Dim gp As New GraphicsPath(FillMode.Winding)

' Add a string to the path
gp.AddString("Path", New FontFamily("Impact"), FontStyle.Regular, _
        40, New PointF(120, 70), New StringFormat())

' Rotate by 45 degrees
gr.RotateTransform(45)

' Draw the path
gr.DrawPath(Pens.Black, gp)

' Reset the transform
gr.ResetTransform()
```

Figure 11.15 A string displayed as an outline using a path.

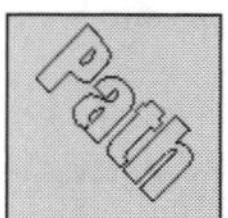

Figure 11.16 A string displayed as an outline and rotated.

The result of this code is shown in Figure 11.16. Note that rotations are cumulative, so calling **RotateTransform(15)** and then **RotateTransform(30)** will rotate by 45 degrees. The **ResetTransform()** method clears the current transform.

Enumerating Fonts

If you want to find out which fonts are available to you, use the **InstalledFontCollection** class from the **System.Drawing.Text** namespace. The following code fragment shows how to create an **InstalledFontCollection** object and use its **Families** property to enumerate all the available fonts:

```
Imports System.Drawing
Imports System.Drawing.Text

Module Module1

  Sub Main()
    ' Create the InstalledFontCollection
    Dim ifc As New InstalledFontCollection()

    Dim ff As FontFamily

    ' Enumerate over each member of the collection
    For Each ff in ifc.Families
       Console.WriteLine(ff)
    Next
  End Sub
End Module
```

The following are the first few lines of output displayed on my system:

```
[FontFamily: name=Century Gothic]
[FontFamily: name=Comic Sans MS]
[FontFamily: name=Courier New]
[FontFamily: name=Garamond]
[FontFamily: name=Georgia]
```

***NOTE:** The **InstalledFontCollection** class appears to return only True Type and Open Type fonts.*

How Do I Display Images on a Form?

Images can be displayed using the **DrawImage()** member of the **Graphics** class. This function has 30 overrides, which provide you with a lot of ways to specify how you want the image to be drawn. All of them, however, require the same basic information:

- The image to be drawn
- The position at which it is to be drawn
- The space in which the image is to be drawn

Here's how to display a JPEG file on a form in response to a button click:

```
Protected Sub Button1_Click(ByVal sender As Object, _
          ByVal e As System.EventArgs)
  ' Create a Graphics object to draw on
  Dim g As Graphics = CreateGraphics()

  Try
    ' Create the bitmap
    Dim bm As New Bitmap("c:\dev\animals09.jpg")

    ' Draw it on the form
    g.DrawImage(bm, 10, 10)
  Catch ex As Exception
    MessageBox.Show(ex.ToString(), "Error", _
            MessageBoxButtons.OK, MessageBoxIcon.IconHand)
  End Try
End Sub
```

The first task is to create a graphics object to draw on. Once that has been done, I create a new bitmap object, passing over the name of the file as the only parameter. It is a good idea to enclose this operation in a **Try** block in case there is anything wrong with the file name or the file itself. I then use **DrawImage()** to draw the entire image on the screen at position (10,10) and implement a **Catch** handler that will display a **MessageBox** if anything goes wrong with opening or displaying the file. Figure 11.17 shows the result of running this code.

You can, of course, apply transforms to images when you plot them. If I add the following few lines of code, I can change the image to the one shown in Figure 11.18:

```
Try
    ' Create the bitmap
    Dim bm As New Bitmap("c:\dev\animals09.jpg")
    ' Draw image half the size, so calculate the new
    ' height and width
```

```
    Dim ht As Integer = bm.Height * 0.5
    Dim wd As Integer = bm.Width * 0.5

    ' Translate by 100 pixels in X
    g.TranslateTransform(100, 0)

    ' Rotate by 90 degrees
    g.RotateTransform(90)

    ' Draw it half size
    g.DrawImage(bm, 10, 10, wd, ht)

    ' Reset the transform again
    g.ResetTransform()
  Catch ex As Exception
    MessageBox.Show(ex.ToString(), "Error", _
            MessageBoxButtons.OK, MessageBoxIcon.IconHand)
  End Try
```

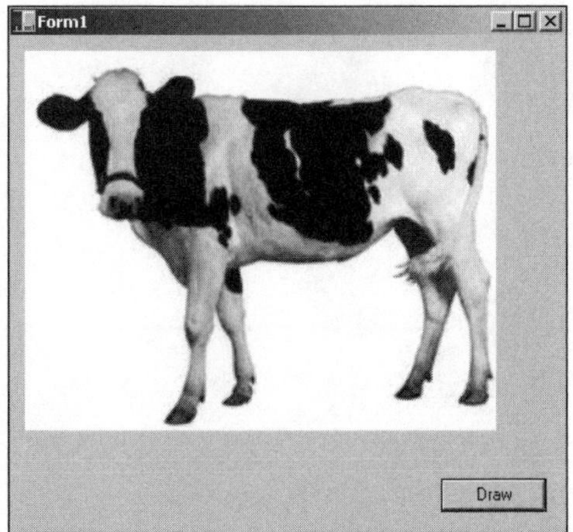

Figure 11.17 Displaying an image on a form.

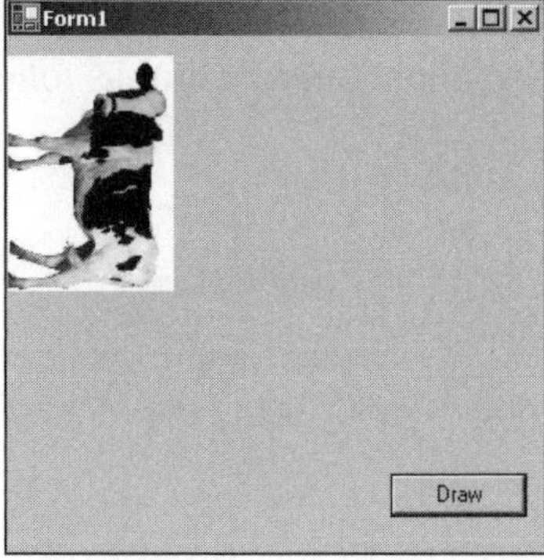

Figure 11.18 Displaying a transformed image on a form.

How Do I Print?

Printing in GDI+ makes use of the classes, structures, and enumerations defined in the **System.Drawing.Printing** namespace. The main classes you need to know about are listed in Table 11.34. Remember that you'll have to import the **System.Drawing.Printing** namespace before you can do any printing.

Finding and Choosing a Printer

The **InstalledPrinters** property of the **PrinterSettings** class returns a list of strings containing the names of all installed printers. The following code fragment shows how to use this property to print out a list of all the printers installed on the system:

```
Imports System.Drawing.Printing

Module Module1

Sub Main()
  ' Create a PrinterSettings object
  Dim ps As New PrinterSettings()

  ' Get the list of installed printers
  Dim en As IEnumerator = ps.InstalledPrinters.GetEnumerator

  ' Print out all the printer names
  While en.MoveNext = True
    Console.WriteLine(en.Current)
  End While
End Sub
End Module
```

The **InstalledPrinters** property returns a collection of strings containing all the printer names, so you can use an enumerator to iterate over the collection in the normal way.

You can also use the **PrinterSettings** object to find out about a printer as follows:

```
' Choose the first printer in the list
ps.PrinterName = ps.InstalledPrinters.Item(0)
Console.WriteLine("Set printer to {0}", ps.InstalledPrinters.Item(0))

' See what it can do...
If ps.IsDefaultPrinter = True Then
  Console.Write("  default")
```

```
Else
  Console.Write("  not default")
End If

If ps.SupportsColor = True Then
  Console.Write(", supports color")
Else
  Console.Write(", monochrome")
End If

If ps.CanDuplex = True Then
  Console.Write(", double-sided")
Else
  Console.Write(", single-sided")
End If

Console.WriteLine()
```

This code selects the first printer from the list of installed printers and sets it as the **PrinterName** property of the **PrinterSettings** object. This means that any reference to printer properties will now refer to the named printer. Once the name has been set, the **IsDefaultPrinter**, **SupportsColor,** and **CanDuplex** properties are used to determine what the printer can do.

Setting Up a Print Document

All printing is done through **PrintDocument** objects, so the first task you need to undertake is to create a **PrintDocument** and connect it to a printer:

```
' Create the PrintDocument object
Dim pd As New PrintDocument()

' Set its properties, especially the printer name
pd.PrinterSettings.PrinterName = "LaserJet"
```

Once you have created the **PrintDocument**, you can set its properties. There are four properties that you might want to use:

- **DefaultPageSettings**—Gives you access to the page settings
- **DocumentName**—Represents the name of this document and may be used in printer progress or cancel dialogs, or in spooler messages
- **PrintController**—Represents the controller object responsible for actually doing the printing
- **PrinterSettings**—Represents the printer settings this **PrintDocument** is using

You can see an example of the **PrinterSettings** in use in the preceding code. Note that you do not associate the document to be printed with the **PrintDocument** object: The idea is that once you have set up a **PrintDocument** object, you can use it to print more than one document.

The **DefaultPageSettings** and **PrinterSettings** objects give you access to objects that let you control the output. You can find details of the properties of these classes in Tables 11.36 and 11.37.

Creating a Print Handler

The actual printing process is carried out on behalf of the **PrintDocument** by a **PrintController** object. If you don't create another **PrintController** yourself, the **PrintDocument** will work with a **StandardPrintController** that is suitable for default output to most printers. If you want to manually specify print preview, you can create a **PreviewPrintController** object that handles printing to print preview windows.

PrintController classes have four methods:

- **StartPrint**—Called at the start of the job
- **StartPage**—Called at the start of each page
- **EndPage**—Called at the end of each page
- **EndPrint**—Called at the end of the job

You don't have to worry about what these methods do unless you want to customize the printing process by deriving your own **PrintController** class.

You interact with the printing process by responding to the four events that are fired by the **PrintController**:

- **BeginPrint**—Raised at the start of the job before the first page prints
- **EndPage**—Raised after the last page has been printed
- **PrintPage**—Raised in order to print each page
- **QueryPageSettings**—Raised immediately before each **PrintPage** event in case you want to change the page settings

Immediately after each call to **StartPage()** the **PrintController** raises a **PrintPage** event, and you need to provide a handler for this event in order to do the printing for the current page. The following code shows how you would define a handler routine and attach it to the **PrintController**:

```
' Create the PrintDocument object
Dim pd As New PrintDocument()
```

```
' Add the page callback method
AddHandler pd.PrintPage, AddressOf myPagePrintFunction

' Set its properties, especially the printer name
pd.PrinterSettings.PrinterName = "LaserJet"

' Print
pd.Print()

...
' Define the handler function
Private Sub myPagePrintFunction(ByVal sender As Object, _
        ByVal ev As PrintPageEventArgs)
  ' Print the page
End Sub
```


I then add the event handler for the **PrintPage** event using the **AddHandler** statement. Once that is done, **Print()** tells the **PrintController** to start the print process, and it will call **myPrintPageFunction()** every time a page needs to be printed.

The **PrintPageEventArgs** object passed to the handler provides information about the page to be printed and can also be used to communicate back to the **PrintController**. The most important properties that are passed via the **PrintPageEventArgs** object are:

- **Graphics**—Gives you a reference to the Graphics you should use for all output. This Graphics object is mapped onto the printer.
- **MarginBounds**—Tells you the portion of the current page that is inside the margins.
- **PageBounds**—Tells you the size of the current page.
- **PageSettings**—Gives you access to the page settings.

You can also communicate back to the **PrintController** using two properties:

- **Cancel**—Set to true if the job should be cancelled
- **HasMorePages**—Set to true if the job still has more pages to print

The **HasMorePages** property is useful when you don't know exactly how many pages you need to print. If there is another page, set it to true before returning, and the **PrintController** will raise the **PrintPage** event once more.

Printing Multipage Documents

If you are printing a form and everything fits on one sheet of paper, the task is simple. You only need one call to the page print handler, and you simply draw everything to the **PagePrintEventArgs.Graphics** object as you would to the screen.

If your output does not fit on one sheet of paper, you'll have to calculate what is to be printed in each call to the handler. Just how you do this depends on the form of your document. The following complete example shows how to print the contents of a text file:

```
Imports System.IO
Imports System.Drawing
Imports System.Drawing.Printing

Module Module1
  Public Class PrintFile
    ' Font to use for printing
    Private fnt As Font
    Private str As StreamReader
    ' Page counter
    Private pageCount As Integer

    ' Handler function
    Private Sub myPagePrintFunction(ByVal sender As Object, _
            ByVal ev As PrintPageEventArgs)
      pageCount = pageCount + 1
      Console.WriteLine(«Page: {0}», pageCount)

      Dim s As String
      Dim linesPerPage As Single = 0
      Dim yPosition As Single = 0
      Dim count As Integer = 0

      Dim leftMargin As Single = ev.MarginBounds.Left
      Dim topMargin As Single = ev.MarginBounds.Top

      ' Calculate the lines per page based on the page height and the
      ' font size
      linesPerPage = ev.MarginBounds.Height / _
          fnt.GetHeight(ev.Graphics)
      Console.WriteLine("  lines/page: {0}", linesPerPage)

      ' Read the file, printing each line
      While True
        ' Have we filled the page?
        If count >= linesPerPage Then
          Console.WriteLine("Going to end of page")
          Goto endOfPage
        End If
```

```
        ' Get a line
        s = str.ReadLine
        Console.WriteLine("Line {0} <{1}>", count, s)
        ' If ReadLine returns null, we're done
        If s Is Nothing Then
          Console.WriteLine("Going to end of file")
          Goto endOfFile
        End If

        ' Output the line
        yPosition = topMargin + (count * fnt.GetHeight(ev.Graphics))
        ev.Graphics.DrawString(s, fnt, Brushes.Black, leftMargin, _
             yPosition, New StringFormat())
        count = count + 1
      End While
endOfPage:
      ev.HasMorePages = True
      Return
endOfFile:
      ev.HasMorePages = False
      Return
    End Sub

    ' Function to do the printing
    Public Sub DoPrint(ByVal s As String)
      Console.WriteLine("Printing...")
      Try
        str = New StreamReader(s)
        Try
          ' Create a font to use
          fnt = New Font("Arial", 10)
          ' Create the PrintDocument
          Dim pd As New PrintDocument()
          ' Assume we're using the default printer
          ' Add the handler
          AddHandler pd.PrintPage, AddressOf _
                Me.myPagePrintFunction
          ' And print
          pd.Print()
        Finally
          str.Close()
        End Try
      Catch e As Exception
        Console.WriteLine(e.ToString())
      End Try
    End Sub
  End Class
```

```
    Sub Main()
      ' Create an object and do the printing
      Dim pd As New PrintFile()

      pd.DoPrint("c:\temp\value.txt")
    End Sub

End Module
```

The program starts by importing the three namespaces needed by the example—**System.Drawing** for the GDI+ functionality, **System.Drawing.Printing** for the printing, and **System.IO** for the file I/O.

The printing process is encapsulated in the **PrintFile** class, which has several members:

- **fnt**—A font object that represents the font to be used for printing. This is created at the start of the job and used each time a page is printed.
- **str**—A **StreamReader** object that handles reading the text file.
- **pageCount**—An integer that holds the current page number.
- **DoPrint()**—Opens the file, creates a **PrintDocument** object, and starts the printing process.
- **myPrintPageFunction()**—Handles the **PrintPage** event and does the printing for each page.

The **Main()** function simply creates a **PrintFile** object and calls **DoPrint()** with a suitable file name. **DoPrint()** creates a **StreamReader** to read the file, and then creates a font for printing. Finally, a **PrintDocument** object is created, and my event handler, **myPrintPageFunction()**, is added to its list of event handlers using **AddHandler**.

NOTE: *If you are not familiar with **AddHandler** or the notion of events, consult Chapter 2.*

Notice how the code uses nested exceptions and a **Finally** block. The outer **Try...Catch** block catches all exceptions and prints an error message to the console. The inner **Try** uses a **Finally** clause to ensure that the **StreamReader** will be closed if an exception occurs during the printing process. Because I have not provided a **Catch** clause in the inner **Try**, any exceptions will automatically be propagated back to the outer block for processing.

Most of the work is done in the event handler, **myPrintPageFunction()**, which starts by printing the current page number to the console. I then extract the left and top margin information from the **PrintPageEventArgs** argument and calculate the number of lines per page by dividing the height of the printable area by the height of the current font.

***TIP:** In production code, assuming that the font isn't going to change partway through the printing process, the number of lines per page could be calculated once at the start of the job.*

The output of each page is done by a **While** loop, which first checks to see if enough lines have been printed. If they haven't, another line is obtained from the **StreamReader** using its **ReadLine()** function. When the **StreamReader** gets to the end of the input stream, **ReadLine()** will return a **null** reference (**Nothing** in VB). I use this reference to tell the **PrintDocument** that there is nothing more to print.

The **PrintDocument** object will keep calling the event handler as long as the **HasMorePages** member of the **PrintPageEventArgs** object is set to true. By setting it to false, I ensure that no more pages will be printed.

If I get a string back from the **StreamReader**, it gets printed with **DrawString()** using properties from the **Font** and **PrintPageEventArgs** objects to ensure that it is printed in the correct place. The loop continues to print pages until the maximum is reached, and then the function exits, setting **HasMorePages** to true in order to tell the **PrintDocument** that there is more to print.

Chapter 12

Other Namespaces

By Julian Templeman

In Depth

The Other .NET Namespaces

This chapter introduces a number of namespaces that don't naturally fit into any of the other chapters, but which are nevertheless useful in their own right. I will introduce you to six:

- **System.Threading**—Used to write multithreaded code
- **System.Globalization**—Used to provide culture-specific information
- **System.SystemProcess**—Used for writing Windows service applications
- **System.Diagnostics**—Used to monitor application execution and write to the Event log
- **System.Text**—Contains (among other things) classes to represent character encodings and classes for converting characters to and from bytes
- **System.Text.RegularExpression**—Used to access the .NET regular expression engine in order to use regular expressions in code

Threading

The **System.Threading** namespace provides you with classes and interfaces for writing multithreaded code. Threading is a very complex topic and writing good multithreaded code is not a trivial task, so this section does not intend to teach you how to design and write multithreaded code, but only provides an overview of how threading works and how you might use it.

What Are Threads?

Every programmer is used to the idea of multitasking, where two or more programs execute simultaneously. Unless you're running on a multiprocessor machine, these programs aren't really running simultaneously. Instead, the processor is giving each program a *time-slice* of a few milliseconds and is switching between running programs to give the illusion of simultaneity. Modern operating systems, such as Windows 2000, schedule program execution intelligently, so that if one program is blocked waiting for input, other programs get more chances to execute.

The same idea of parallel execution can be applied within programs as well as between them, and at its simplest, a *thread* can be thought of as a function that is executing at the same time as the rest of the program. Function calls are normally synchronous, so that the calling function blocks until the call returns. When you start a thread, the call returns immediately, and the *thread function* is then running in parallel with the calling code, using the same time-slicing mechanism that the operating system uses for multitasking programs.

Every process consists of at least one thread that the main function runs on, and if it doesn't create any more, it is a *single-threaded* program. If the process creates more threads, it becomes *multithreaded*, and there are then several issues that you need to think about, which I'll cover in the following sections.

Every thread within a process has data associated with it, including its own program stack and set of register contents, known as the thread's *context*. When the operating system wants to switch between threads, it needs to save the context of the current thread and load into memory the context of the thread it is going to run next. This process is called a *context switch* and takes a small (but measurable) amount of time.

When Are Threads Useful?

Threads can be useful in several circumstances, and I'll describe several of the most common.

First, there's the *background task*. Imagine that you want to put a spinning logo in the top left corner of a form. You have a sequence of images, so you want to display each of them for a short amount of time. How are you going to integrate this into the rest of the application? It would be great if you could somehow set up a loop that displays the images while the rest of the program runs. Running the image display code in a separate thread will let you do this. Another example is background printing: If your application wants to print, you don't want the user to have to wait while the data is sent to the printer and the call to **Print()** returns. If you do the printing in a separate thread, it can execute in the background and not impact the rest of the application.

Second, there's performing a task more than once. Suppose you have an image-processing program that takes an image and performs some operation on it. You could split the image into four parts and run four copies of the image-processing routine, each of which processes a quarter of the image. This can result in great time savings on multiprocessor machines, but is unlikely to be very useful on single-processor machines because of the overhead of context switching between the threads.

Third, there are those cases where using threads is a natural way to structure a program. Consider the case of a Web or mail server, which sits on a port waiting for clients to connect. The server can handle more than one client, so how it is going to handle the first client while still waiting for the second one to call? This is made difficult by the fact that waiting on a port is a blocking operation, so the server can't easily go off and do something else. The answer is to use a separate thread to handle each client. When a client connects, the server starts a thread to handle the session with the client, and then loops around and waits for the next client. In this model, the main server thread spends most of its time blocked waiting for clients to call in, and each client is running the same code in a different thread. In addition, talking to six clients is no more complex than talking to one, because you simply have to start six identical threads.

Thread Synchronization

You may need to synchronize threads for two reasons: use of shared resources and timing.

Each thread has its own stack and set of registers, which means that each thread function has its own set of local variables because local variables are declared on the stack. So local variables in different threads cannot interfere with one another because they are created on different stacks.

Global variables are a different matter because they belong to the process as a whole. Therefore, they are accessible by all threads in the process. This immediately gives rise to potential problems because its possible for two threads to access the same global variable, resulting in data corruption. You can see how this works in Figure 12.1.

Thread A sets the value of the global variable **globalX** to 3. At this point, a context switch occurs and Thread B gets to execute; it sets the value of **globalX** to 4. When Thread A gets another turn; it uses the value of **globalX**, unaware that it has been changed by Thread B. These errors can be very hard to fix because they

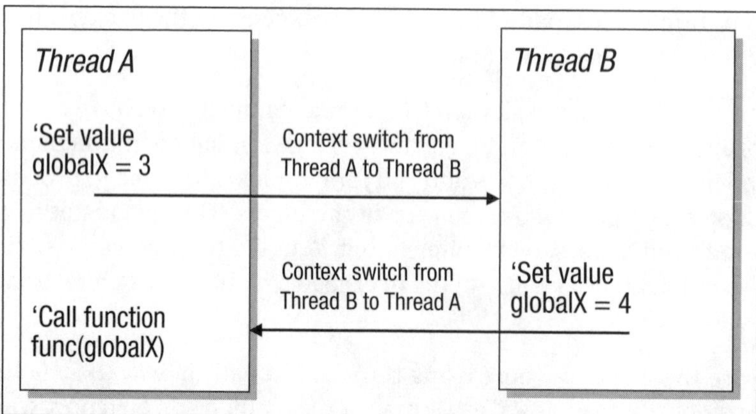

Figure 12.1 Two threads using the same global variable.

often depend on timing. If, the next time you run the program, swapping between Threads A and B doesn't happen at exactly the same points, the same errors may not occur.

This problem of shared resources isn't restricted to global variables, but can occur with any resource that is shared between threads, including files and database tables. Operating systems that support multithreaded programs provide mechanisms that allow a thread to claim exclusive usage of a resource for a period of time—a lock, if you like. **System.Threading** provides the **Mutex** class, and objects can use mutexes to get exclusive use of a resource.

Sometimes you might want other threads to have read access to a resource provided that only one thread can write to it. The **ReaderWriterLock** class provides this functionality for .NET classes.

NOTE: *Code that is written so that it executes correctly when accessed concurrently by multiple threads is called thread-safe code.*

The second need for thread synchronization concerns timing. If it is important for one thread to wait until another has reached some point in its operation—for example, suppose the second thread has to prepare some data for the first thread to use—*events* can be used as signals between the threads. An event is simply a flag that is set or unset and can be shared between threads. One thread acquires the event, and one or more of the others wait for the event to be set.

The Thread Class

The **System.Threading.Thread** class represents an operating system thread. Some of the most commonly used properties and methods of this class are listed in Tables 12.1 and 12.2.

Table 12.1 Commonly used properties of the Thread class.

Property	Description
CurrentPrincipal	Gets or sets the thread's current security principal
CurrentThread	Gets a reference to the currently running thread
IsAlive	Returns **True** if the thread has been started and is not dead
IsBackground	If true, this thread is a background thread
Name	Gets or sets the name for this thread
Priority	Gets or sets the priority for this thread
ThreadState	Gets the state of this thread

Table 12.2 Commonly used methods of the Thread class.

Method	Description
Abort	Kills the thread
Interrupt	Interrupts a thread that is in the **WaitSleepJoin** state
Join	Waits for a thread to terminate
Resume	Resumes a suspended thread
Sleep	Sends a thread to sleep for a period
Start	Starts a thread
Suspend	Suspends a thread

Controlling Threads

Once a **Thread** object has been created and has been passed the address of a function to execute, you call its **Start()** method to begin execution. The thread function executes, and when it returns, the thread has finished executing. The underlying operating system thread is then dead, even though the **Thread** object still exists. You can check the thread's state using the **IsAlive** property to see if it has died.

If you want to terminate a thread, you can call the **Abort()** method. You need to be careful when calling this method, though, because it simply stops the thread dead in its tracks. In some cases—for example, a thread that is spinning a logo at the top of a form—this won't matter, but in other cases, it can lead to serious problems. Because **Abort()** simply stops the thread, the thread function has no chance to tidy up. If it was in the middle of updating a database or writing a file, this could result in corrupted data.

In these cases, it is better to use some kind of flag, which the thread function checks from time to time and can be set to indicate that it ought to exit. The "abort flag" can be a simple Boolean variable, and when it is set, the thread function can tidy up before exiting.

The **Suspend()** and **Resume()** methods can be used to temporarily stop a thread from executing, and then restart it again. These methods suffer from the same problem as **Abort()** because the thread is suspended from outside without having any opportunity to make sure that it has finished its current operation. Once again, if this is going to be a problem, it is better to use a flag-driven method to request a suspension rather than simply calling **Suspend()**.

Sleep() is used to put a thread to sleep for a period of time—normally specified as a number of milliseconds. This is a very useful method because a sleeping thread does not use processor time. A sleeping thread may be interrupted—for instance, by program termination or machine shutdown—in which case a **ThreadInterruptedException** will be thrown.

NOTE: *See the Immediate Solution "Creating Windows Service Applications" for an example of how to create and use threads in a Windows application.*

Thread State and Priority

The **ThreadState** enumeration, listed in Table 12.3, describes the possible states a thread can occupy.

Before the **Start()** method is called, a thread is **Unstarted**, and it then moves to a **Running** state. The **Pause()** method puts the thread into a **Suspended** state, and a subsequent call to **Resume()** puts it back into the **Running** state. The **IsAlive** property returns true if the thread has been started and is not yet dead; that is, if it is in the **Running**, **Background**, **Suspended**, **SuspendRequested**, or **WaitSleepJoin** states.

A *foreground thread* runs indefinitely, whereas a *background thread* terminates once the last foreground thread has stopped. It is often useful to make threads started by your application background threads, because they will automatically shut down when the program terminates. You can use the **IsBackground** property to change the foreground or background state of a thread.

Every thread has a priority relative to other threads in the process. By default, threads are created with an average priority, and you can adjust the thread priority by assigning a new value to the **Thread** object's **Priority** property. This takes a member of the **ThreadPriority** enumeration, whose values are listed in Table 12.4.

Table 12.3 Members of the ThreadState enumeration.

Member	Description
Aborted	The thread has been aborted and is now dead.
AbortRequested	The thread is being requested to abort.
Background	The thread is being executed as a background thread.
Running	The thread is running.
Stopped	The thread is stopped (this value is for internal use only).
StopRequested	The thread is being asked to stop (this value is for internal use only).
Suspended	The thread has been suspended.
SuspendRequested	The thread has been asked to suspend.
Unstarted	The thread has not yet been started.
WaitSleepJoin	The thread is blocked on a call to **Wait()**, **Sleep()**, or **Join()**.

Table 12.4 Members of the ThreadPriority enumeration.

Member	Description
Highest	The thread has the highest priority.
AboveNormal	The thread has a higher than normal priority.
Normal	The thread has an average priority.
BelowNormal	The thread has a lower than normal priority.
Lowest	The thread has the lowest priority.

All threads are initially created with a **Normal** priority. Beware of playing with thread priorities too much. The operating system uses thread priorities to decide when to run threads, and the algorithms used can be complex. This means that adjusting thread priorities may not always return the results you want.

The Synchronization Classes

The **System.Threading** namespace contains several classes that help with thread synchronization. The **Interlocked** class contains four shared thread-safe methods for operating on variables. All four of these methods are atomic, so that they won't be interrupted by thread context switches:

- **Increment**—Increments a variable
- **Decrement**—Decrements a variable
- **Exchange**—Sets a variable to a value and returns the original value
- **CompareExchange**—Compares two values for equality and replaces the destination value if they are equal

The Mutex Class

Mutex provides a simple synchronization mechanism that allows one thread to get exclusive access to a shared resource. Threads attempt to *acquire* a mutex; one will achieve it, and the others will block until the owning thread has finished and *releases* it.

The following skeleton code shows how a mutex might be used:

```
' Importing this namespace makes using classes easier
Imports System.Threading

' This Mutex is used to synchronize two threads
Dim mtx As New Mutex()

' The AcquireData method is running on one thread
Public Sub AcquireData()
```

```
    ' Try to get the Mutex
    mtx.WaitOne()

    ' Acquire the data...

    ' Release the mutex
    mtx.ReleaseMutex()
End Sub

' The UseData method is running on a second thread
Public Sub UseData()
    ' Try to get the Mutex
    mtx.WaitOne()

    ' Use the data...

    ' Release the mutex
    mtx.ReleaseMutex()
End Sub
```


Code in the first thread calls **AcquireData()**, which attempts to acquire the mutex object via a call to **WaitOne()**. If the mutex is available, this call returns immediately, and the calling thread then "owns" the mutex. The function then acquires its data. If during this time the second thread calls **UseData()**, it will block at the call to **WaitOne()** because the mutex isn't available. At some point **AcquireData()** finishes its task and releases the mutex by calling **ReleaseMutex()**. This causes the call to **WaitOne()** in **UseData()** to return, so that it can use the data.

This process may sound simple, but there are a lot of subtle problems that can arise when synchronizing threads in this way. What if **UseData()** has opened a file or used some other resource that **AcquireData()** needs? It's possible that **UseData()** will block waiting for **AcquireData()** to release the mutex, but **UseData()** needs the resource that **AcquireData()** has before it can complete its task and release the mutex. The result is *deadlock*, with both threads blocked and unable to move forward. Designing applications so that deadlock cannot occur can be difficult.

The SyncLock Statement in Visual Basic

The Visual Basic **SyncLock** statement provides an alternative to using mutexes in many cases. It allows the programmer to synchronize a block of code on some type of object, and only one block synchronized on a given object can execute at any given time.

***NOTE: SyncLock** is part of the Visual Basic language. Programmers working in other .NET languages, such as C# and Visual C++, need to use the **Monitor** class, described in the next section.*

As an example, consider the idea of a multithreaded program that is using a single **ArrayList** object to store a set of program-wide data values. Functions are available to add data to the list, remove a value from the list, search the list for a value, and print the list. The problem is that these functions can be called from different threads, so how can the search and print functions be sure that the add or remove functions aren't modifying the list at the same time?

One approach is to use **SyncLock** to synchronize blocks of code on the **ArrayList** object, as shown in the following code fragments:

```
' The Add method can run on any thread...
Public Sub Add(ByVal o As Object)
  ' Lock on the list
  SyncLock myArrayList
    myArrayList.Add(o)
  End SyncLock
End Sub

' The Print method can run on any thread as well
Public Sub Print()
  ' Lock on the list
  SyncLock myArrayList
    ' Print the list
    Dim ie As IEnumerator = myArrayList.GetEnumerator()
    While ie.MoveNext()
      Console.WriteLine(o.ToString())
    End While
  End SyncLock
End Sub
```

The **SyncLock** statements enclose blocks of code, and only one block of code can be executed at one time. So, if the **Print()** function is executing, **Add()** will block at the start of the **SyncLock** until the print has finished. In this way, **Print()** can be sure that other functions aren't modifying the list while it is being printed.

One drawback with **SyncLock** is that you have to be sure that you have protected every use of the **ArrayList**. If you have a piece of code that manipulates the **ArrayList** without putting it in a **SyncLock** block, you may end up with data corruption.

The Monitor Class

SyncLock is specific to Visual Basic, but the **Monitor** class provides a general mechanism that can be used from any .NET language to synchronize access to objects using locks.

Every object in .NET has a lock that can be acquired by a thread. Once this lock has been acquired—once the monitor has been entered—no other thread can acquire it until the owning thread lets it go, or exits from the monitor. It is easy to rewrite the **Add()** function from the previous example to use **Monitor** directly:

```
' The Add method can run on any thread...
Public Sub Add(ByVal o As Object)
  ' Lock on the list
  Monitor.Enter(myArrayList)

  ' Use the list
  myArrayList.Add(o)

  ' Release the monitor
  Monitor.Exit(myArrayList)
End Sub
```

As a general principle, you should only synchronize on private or internal objects. Using public objects can lead to deadlocks because some object might decide to lock the object for reasons of its own.

Monitor also includes a wait/notify mechanism that allows one thread to wait until it is told to continue via a notification from another thread, using the **Wait()**, **Pulse()**, and **PulseAll()** methods. When it is in a synchronized block, a thread can call **Wait()**, which effectively puts the thread to sleep. It will wait in this state until it is woken up by another thread calling **Pulse()** or **PulseAll()**.

Globalization

The **System.Globalization** namespace contains a number of classes that define culture-related information, such as:

- Language
- Country or region
- Calendars in use
- Formats for dates, currencies, and numbers
- Sorting order for strings

Culture Information

The **CultureInfo** class provides culture-specific information and operations, such as printing dates and sorting strings. You create a **CultureInfo** object by specifying one of the many predefined culture identifiers as an argument, for example:

```
' Create a CultureInfo object for the "English-United Kingdom" culture
Dim ci As New CultureInfo("en-GB")

' Create a CultureInfo object for the «Italian-Italy» culture
Dim ci As New CultureInfo("it-IT")
```

The culture identifiers—of which there are more than 200—are specified either as hexadecimal values or as strings consisting of the language as a two-letter lowercase identifier plus an optional country/region as an uppercase two-digit identifier. This format lets you distinguish, for instance, between UK English (**"en-GB"**) and US English (**"en-US"**).

Once you've obtained a **CultureInfo** object, you can use its properties and methods to find out about the culture. Some commonly used properties of the **CultureInfo** class are summarized in Table 12.5.

Calendar Information

Calendar information is provided by the abstract **Calendar** class and its derived classes. The methods of the **Calendar** classes are listed in Table 12.6.

A calendar takes an instant in time—such as a value provided by the **DateTime** class—and converts it into measures, such as days and years. A number of different world calendars are supported:

- The **GregorianCalendar** used by most of the western world
- The **HebrewCalendar**
- The Muslim **HijriCalendar**

Table 12.5 Common properties of the CultureInfo class.

Property	Description
Calendar	Gets the default calendar used by the culture.
CompareInfo	Gets a **CompareInfo** object that defines how to compare and sort strings.
DateTimeFormat	Gets a **DateTimeFormat** object that defines how to format dates and times.
DisplayName	Gets the culture name in the form "language (country/region)"; for example, "English (United Kingdom)".
EnglishName	Gets the same result as **DisplayName**.
NativeName	Gets the culture name in the culture's own language. May not display correctly on English systems.
NumberFormat	Gets a **NumberFormatInfo** object that defines how to format numbers, including currencies.
TextInfo	Gets a **TextInfo** object that defines how to format text.

- The **JapaneseCalendar**, based on the reigns of Japanese emperors
- The **JulianCalendar**
- The **KoreanCalendar**
- The **TaiwanCalendar**
- The **ThaiBuddhistCalendar**

Calendar and its subclasses only have two properties: **Eras** and **TwoDigitYearMax**. The **Eras** property returns an array of integers representing the numbers used to represent eras in a calendar. A calendar can have one or more eras: for the Gregorian calendar, there are two: BC and AD. The Japanese calendar has several because year numbering starts again when a new emperor ascends to the throne. **TwoDigitYearMax** represents the last year in a 100-year range that can be represented by two digits. For example, if the value of **TwoDigitYearMax** is 1977, the 100-year range is 1878 to 1977. This means that for this calendar object, a two-digit year of "10" is interpreted as 1910, whereas a value of "88" means 1888.

Table 12.6 Methods of the Calendar class.

Method	Description
AddYears, AddMonths, AddWeeks, AddDays	Adds time values to the calendar object
AddHours, AddMinutes, AddSeconds, AddMilliseconds	Adds time values to the calendar object
GetDayOfMonth	Gets the day of the month as an integer
GetDayOfWeek	Gets the day of the week
GetDayOfYear	Gets the day of the year as an integer
GetDaysInMonth	Gets the number of days in the specified month
GetDaysInYear	Gets the number of days in the specified year
GetEra	Gets the current era as an integer
GetHour, GetMinute, GetSecond, GetMillisecond	Gets time values for the current calendar object
GetMonthsInYear	Gets the number of months in the specified year
GetWeekOfYear	Gets the number of the week in the year
IsLeapDay, IsLeapMonth, IsLeapYear	True if the calendar object represents a leap day, month, or year
ToDateTime	Converts a calendar object to a **DateTime**
ToFourDigitYear	Converts a two-digit year to a four-digit year using the **TwoDigitYearMax** property

Format Information

System.Globalization defines several classes that help with locale-specific formatting tasks, such as:

- **NumberFormatInfo**—Defines how numbers are formatted and displayed
- **DateTimeFormatInfo**—Defines how dates are formatted and displayed
- **TextInfo**—Defines properties and behaviors specific to a writing system, in particular, methods for converting to uppercase and lowercase

NumberFormatInfo is used to specify culture-dependent number formatting information, such as currency symbols, decimal and group separators, how negative values are displayed, and so on. Table 12.7 contains a selection of the 28 properties supported by this class, so that you can get a feel for how it is used.

Table 12.7 Properties of the NumberFormatInfo class.

Property	Description
CurrencyDecimalDigits	The number of decimal places to use for currencies. The default is 2.
CurrencyDecimalSeparator	The string to use as the decimal point for currencies. The default is ".".
CurrencyGroupSeparator	The string to use as the group separator for currencies. The default is ",".
CurrencyGroupSizes	The number of digits in each group of numerals to the left of the decimal point. The default is 3.
CurrencySymbol	The string to use as the currency symbol. The default is "$".
NegativeSign	The string to use as the negative symbol. The default is "-".
NumberDecimalDigits	The number of decimal places to use for numbers. The default is 2.
NumberDecimalSeparator	The string to use as the decimal point for numbers. The default is ".".
NumberGroupSeparator	The string to use as the group separator for numbers. The default is ",".
NumberGroupSizes	The number of digits in each group of numerals to the left of the decimal point. The default is 3.
PercentDecimalDigits	The number of decimal places to use for percentages. The default is 2.
PercentDecimalSeparator	The string to use as the decimal point for percentages. The default is ".".
PercentGroupSeparator	The string to use as the group separator for percentages. The default is ",".
PercentGroupSizes	The number of digits in each group of numerals to the left of the decimal point. The default is 3.
PercentSymbol	The string to use as the percent symbol. The default is "%".
PositiveInfinitySymbol	The string that represents positive infinity. The default is "Infinity".
PositiveSign	The string to use as the positive symbol. The default is "+".

NumberFormatInfo also has a number of properties that specify patterns, such as **NumberNegativePattern** and **CurrencyPositivePattern**. These properties are writable, so that you can choose from a number of alternatives provided for each pattern. As an example, Table 12.8 lists the pattern values for **NumberNegativePattern**.

NumberFormatInfo objects are often used with the **ToString()** method to let you print numbers in custom formats, for example:

```
Dim d As Double = -200

' Create a NumberFormatInfo and set its negative number format
Dim nf As New NumberFormatInfo()
nf.NumberNegativePattern = 0

' Print out the value
Console.WriteLine(d.ToString("N", nf)
```

The first argument to **ToString()** is a format specifier: "N" means "number," so it uses the **NumberXxx** properties of the **NumberFormatInfo** object passed to it to decide how to print the value. A list of the format characters (which may be specified in upper- or lowercase) is given in Table 12.9.

NOTE: *See Chapter 3 for more details on how to produce formatted output.*

Table 12.8 Values of the NumberNegativePattern property.

Value	Pattern
0	(n)
1	-n
2	- n
3	n-
4	n -

Table 12.9 Format characters associated with the NumberFormatInfo class.

Format Character	Meaning
C	Currency format. Uses the **CurrencyXxx** properties.
D	Decimal format.
E	Scientific exponent format.
F	Fixed-point format.

(continued)

Table 12.9 Format characters associated with the NumberFormatInfo class *(continued)*.

Format Character	Meaning
G	General format.
N	Number format. Uses the **NumberXxx** properties.
R	Roundtrip format, which ensures that numbers can be converted to strings and back, returning the same number.
X	Hexadecimal format.

Windows Services

The special class of applications that were known as NT Services under Windows NT are now known as *Microsoft Windows Services*.

A *service* is a special kind of program that runs in the background and rarely has a user interface. Services can run regardless of who is logged on—or even if anyone is logged on at all—and they can run under their own account rather than the account of whoever is logged in to the machine. They can be started manually or automatically when the computer boots, and it is possible to start, stop, pause, and resume them either from a program, by using the Services Control Panel applet, or by using the **net** command from a console window.

Services are ideal for system-level background tasks, which simply sit in the background working away without interfering with what the logged in user is doing. Good examples of services include print spoolers, logging services, FTP and Web servers, the process that notices new hardware, and so on.

Interacting with Services

Services are run by the Service Control Manager (SCM). You can interact with the SCM in several ways, including through the Control Panel, as shown in Figure 12.2, and by using routines in the Services API from programs. The .NET Framework exposes this API through classes in the **System.ServiceProcess** namespace, which allows you to write and control classes. I'll discuss this namespace later in this section.

The SCM keeps a list of the services it controls in the Registry, together with their properties. To obtain more details about a service, double-click one of the entries in the right pane, and a property dialog like the one in Figure 12.3 is displayed.

The Service Properties dialog lets you customize some properties of services, such as the name, description, and startup type. Services may have one of three startup types:

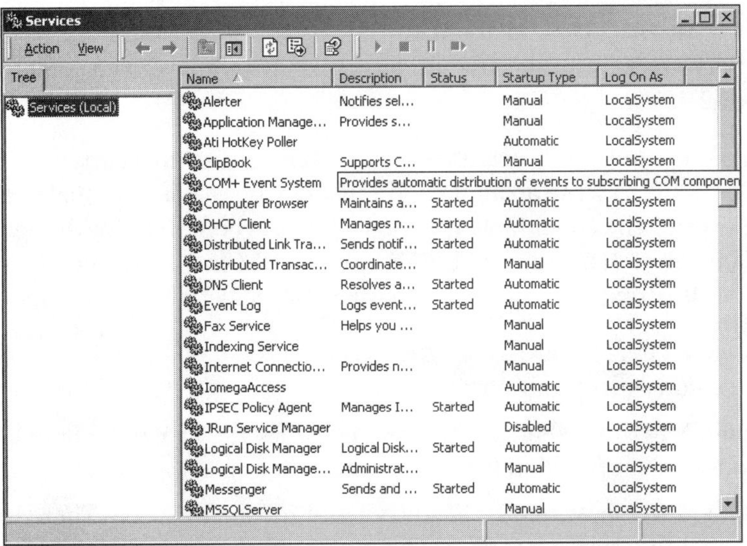

Figure 12.2 The Services Control Panel applet.

- **Automatic**—The service is started automatically at boot time.
- **Manual**—The service is not started at boot time and can be started later by a user or an application.
- **Disabled**—The service cannot be started by a user or an application.

All services have to interact with the SCM, so it is possible to start, stop, pause, and resume them from the Control Panel applet or from code.

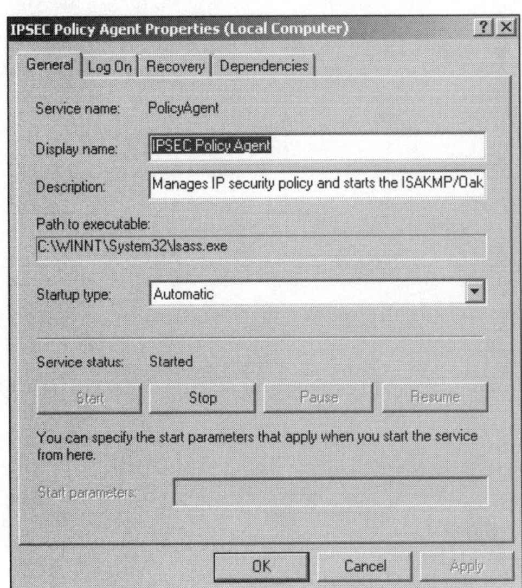

Figure 12.3 The Service Properties dialog.

Service Process Architecture

All Windows Services share the same architecture, which is shown in diagram form in Figure 12.4.

A service process is a normal executable, which is structured in a particular way, and it is quite possible to write an application that can be run as a normal executable and as a service. The executable is actually just the container for the service code in the same way that a dynamic link library (DLL) is used to contain an ActiveX control. It is quite possible for a service process to contain more than one logical service.

A logical service consists of four parts:

- A process main function, which is the entry point for the process. There is only one process main function for the service process.
- A service main function, which is the entry point for the function. There is one service main function for each logical service in the process; when this function returns, the service is considered to have terminated.

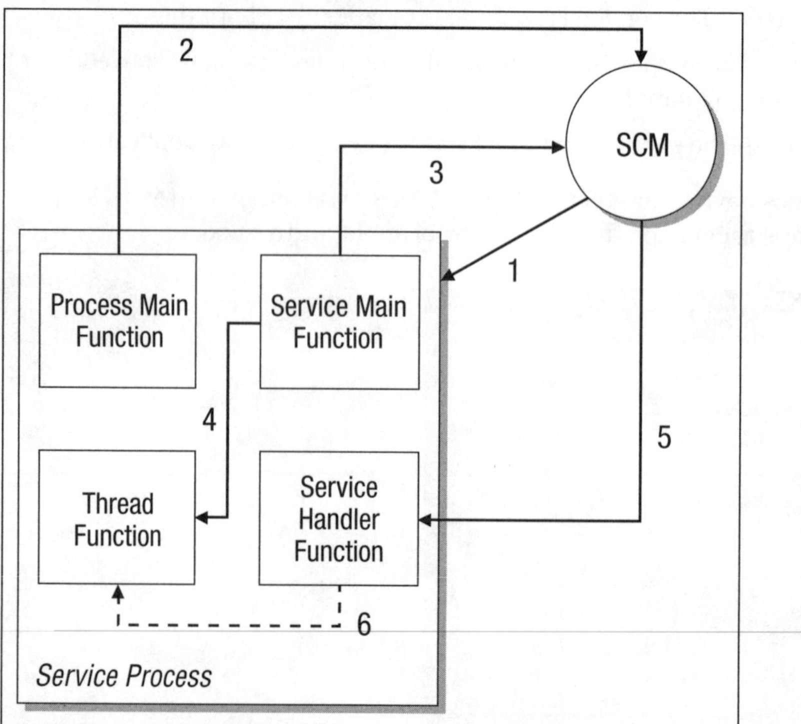

Figure 12.4 The architecture of a Windows Service.

- A service handler function, which the SCM calls in order to control the service. Again, there is one service handler function for each logical service in the process.
- The work that the service is going to perform. This is usually implemented by starting a separate thread to run the service; using a separate thread makes it easy for the SCM to pause, continue, and stop the service.

Figure 12.4 shows how the SCM interacts with a service. The numbers in the diagram denote the sequence in which events occur:

1. The SCM loads the service process, either at boot time or on demand.
2. The process main function then has a limited time to register the service main function of each logical service with the SCM. If the process does not register the services with the SCM within this time, the SCM aborts the startup.
3. In the same way, the service main function of each logical service has a limited time to register its handler function; otherwise, the SCM assumes that the service isn't going to load.
4. Once the handler functions are registered with the SCM, the service main function can then start the real work of the service. This is usually done by starting a separate thread; the service main function blocks until the thread has finished running.
5. The SCM uses the handler function to pass commands to the service, and the handler function returns status information to the SCM. The service code needs to ensure that it keeps the SCM up-to-date with status information, or the SCM may decide that the service has hung and terminate it.
6. The handler function can pause and resume or stop the thread on demand.

The System.ServiceProcess Namespace

All service executables tend to be based on the same skeleton code, and writing a service in traditional C++ or C using the Windows API involves a lot of copying and pasting of boilerplate code. The .NET Framework simplifies this greatly by providing the classes in the **System.ServiceProcess** namespace, which gives you an object-oriented (OO) skeleton that you can use to create and manipulate services.

The namespace contains four major classes:

- **ServiceBase**—Used for creating custom services
- **ServiceController**—Used to connect to a running or stopped service, controls it, and gets information about it
- **ServiceInstaller** and **SystemProcessInstaller**—Used to install services

The ServiceBase Class

As its name implies, **ServiceBase** is the class from which all services derive. It provides all the basic interaction with the SCM. In order to create a service, you derive a class from **ServiceBase** and override its standard methods.

Table 12.10 lists the properties of the **ServiceBase** class. Many of these properties are self-explanatory. Some services may not let users or other applications control them once they have been started. The SCM can use the **CanPauseAndContinue** and **CanStop** properties to check the control a service will allow. Some services may want to be notified when the system is being shut down so that they can tidy up. The **CanShutdown** property tells the SCM whether it should notify the service of shutdowns.

Services don't usually interact with the screen at all, and if they have anything to report, they write entries in the system Event log. The **AutoLog** property controls whether the four standard commands (**Start**, **Stop**, **Pause**, and **Continue**) are going to be logged automatically, and the **EventLog** property gets an object you can use to write to the Event log.

***NOTE:** See the Immediate Solution "Using the Event Log" for details on how to use the system Event log.*

Table 12.11 contains details of the methods of the **ServiceBase** class. Almost all of the methods of **ServiceBase** are "On" methods, called in response to one or another of the commands that the SCM sends to the service. The shared **Run()** method is used to load a service into memory and create the process, although the service will not start accepting commands until the SCM has sent it a **Start** command.

The ServiceInstaller Class

ServiceInstaller is a utility class that is used to install and uninstall services that have been derived from **ServiceBase**. Its main task is to write or remove the

Table 12.10 Properties of the ServiceBase class.

Property	Description
AutoLog	If true, reports **Start**, **Stop**, **Pause**, and **Continue** events in the Event log.
CanHandlePowerEvent	If true, the service can handle power status change reports.
CanPauseAndContinue	If true, the service can handle **Pause** and **Continue** commands.
CanShutdown	If true, the service should be notified when the system is shutting down.
CanStop	If true, the service can be stopped once it is started.
EventLog	Gets an **EventLog** object that you can use to write notifications to the Application Log.
ServiceName	Gets or sets the service name.

Table 12.11 Methods of the ServiceBase class.

Method	Description
OnContinue	Called when a **Continue** command is passed to the service. Services are expected to override **OnPause** when the **CanPauseAndContinue** property returns **True**.
OnCustomCommand	Called when a custom command is passed to the service.
OnPause	Called when a **Pause** command is passed to the service. Services are expected to override **OnPause** when the **CanPauseAndContinue** property returns **True**.
OnPowerEvent	Called when a **PowerEvent** command is passed to the service. Services are expected to override **OnPowerEvent** when the **CanHandlePowerEvent** property returns **True**.
OnShutdown	Called when a **Shutdown** command is passed to the service. Services are expected to override **OnShutdown** when the **CanShutdown** property returns **True**.
OnStart	Called when a **Start** command is sent to the service.
OnStop	Called when a **Stop** command is sent to the service. Services are expected to override **OnStop** when the **CanStop** property returns **True**.
Run	Provides the main entry point for a service.

Registry keys that are needed by the SCM, and the **Install()** and **Uninstall()** methods can be used to install and uninstall services.

***NOTE:** See the Immediate Solutions section "Creating Windows Service Applications" for details on how to install a service.*

The ServiceController Class

The **ServiceController** class is effectively a link to the SCM in that it lets you connect to a running or stopped service, manipulate it, or get information about it. As well as letting you send all the standard commands to a service, **ServiceController** also lets you send custom commands to services, a feature that isn't available with the Control Panel applet. Table 12.12 contains details of the properties of the **ServiceController** class.

It is quite common for services to depend on one another, so that one service starts another and makes use of its features. The **DependentServices** and **ServicesDependedOn** properties provide you with information on these dependency relationships.

The **ServiceType** may be one or more of the values shown in Table 12.13. If you want to use more than one, the **OR** operator is used to combine them.

Table 12.12 Properties of the ServiceController class.

Property	Description
CanPauseAndContinue	If true, the service can handle **Pause** and **Continue** commands
CanShutdown	If true, the service should be notified when the system is shutting down
CanStop	If true, the service can be stopped once it is started
DependentServices	Gets an array of **ServiceController** objects representing services that depend on this one
DisplayName	Gets or sets the service that this **ServiceController** binds to
MachineName	Gets or sets the name of the machine on which this service is running
ServiceName	Gets or sets the service that this **ServiceController** binds to
ServicesDependedOn	Returns an array of **ServiceController** objects representing the services that the current service depends on
ServiceType	Returns the type of service as a member of the **ServiceType** enumeration
Status	Returns the status of the service as one of the values in the **ServiceControllerStatus** enumeration

***NOTE:** Windows device drivers are also considered to be services, and they have slightly different rules than user-written services. The services I'm discussing in this section will always be **Win32OwnProcess** or **Win32ShareProcess** types, and I won't discuss device driver services in any detail.*

The service status is represented by one of the members of the **Service ControllerStatus** enumeration listed in Table 12.14. These status codes are used by services to report their status to the SCM. The SCM insists that every service keep it regularly informed about its status, so services send status updates to the SCM every few seconds. If too much time elapses without getting a status update, the SCM may assume that the service has hung and terminate it.

This fact makes it hard to debug a running service because stopping a service in the debugger means that it won't be sending updates to the SCM. For this reason,

Table 12.13 The members of the ServiceType enumeration.

Member	Description
Adapter	A service for a hardware device that requires its own device driver
FileSystemDriver	A file system driver
InteractiveProcess	A service that can communicate with the desktop
KernelDriver	A kernel device driver, such as a disk driver
RecognizerDriver	A type of file system driver
Win32OwnProcess	A Win32 program containing one logical service
Win32ShareProcess	A Win32 program containing more than one logical service

Table 12.14 The members of the ServiceControllerStatus enumeration.

Member	Description
ContinuePending	The service is starting up after a **Continue** request.
Paused	The service is paused.
PausePending	The service is preparing to pause after a **Pause** request.
Running	The service is running.
StartPending	The service is starting up.
Stopped	The service has stopped.
StopPending	The service is preparing to stop in response to a **Stop** request.

Table 12.15 Methods of the ServiceController class.

Method	Description
Close	Disconnects the **ServiceController** from the service and frees resources
Continue	Sends a **Continue** command to a paused service
ExecuteCommand	Sends a custom command to a service
GetDevices	Gets a list of the device driver services available on the local machine
GetServices	Gets a list of the nondriver services on the local machine
Pause	Sends a **Pause** command to a running service
Refresh	Refreshes all the property values
Start	Sends a **Start** command to a service
Stop	Sends a **Stop** command to a running service
WaitForStatus	Waits for a service to reach a specified status

it is common to run the service as a normal executable until you're sure that the basic functionality works, and then switch to running it as a service.

Table 12.15 contains details of the methods of the **ServiceController** class. The **Continue()**, **Pause()**, **Start()**, and **Stop()** commands are used to send the appropriate commands to the service via the SCM. **ExecuteCommand()** can be used to send a custom command to a service, and **WaitForStatus()** can be used to wait until a service sends back a specified status value.

System.Diagnostics

As its name implies, the **System.Diagnostics** namespace contains classes that help you debug and monitor applications. As well as specialized tasks such as talking to debuggers, the namespace contains classes to help you with several particularly useful tasks:

- Verifying correct program operation
- Tracing program execution
- Writing to the Event log

Using Assertions to Verify Correct Operation

Assertions have been used by C and C++ programmers for many years and are now available in all .NET languages. An assertion takes the form of a logical expression, which is usually coupled with an error message. The expression is evaluated at runtime: If it is **True**, no action is taken, but if it is **False**, an assertion dialog is displayed, like the one shown in Figure 12.5, which displays the error message and stack trace information to show you where the problem occurred.

The idea behind assertions is this: As you're developing a program, you get to know what ought to be happening at various points in the code—if we're *here* in the code, then *this* ought to be true. For example, you may perform a database query at some point, which always returns at least one record. You could put an assertion in the code to check this:

```
Trace.Assert(numberOfRecords > 0, "Number of records is not positive")
```

If at any point in the future something changes and zero records are returned by the search, the assertion will fail and you'll get an error message. You can see that the first parameter to the **Assert()** function is an expression that evaluates to a Boolean value; it can be as complex as you like, but it must eventually evaluate to **True** or **False**. The second parameter is the error message that is displayed if the assertion fails.

The .NET assertion dialog gives you a choice of aborting the program, running the debugger, or continuing.

NOTE: *You may wonder why the buttons in the assertion dialog in Figure 12.5 are labeled Abort, Retry, and Ignore rather than Quit, Debug, and Continue. The reason for this is that message boxes come with a preset selection of button combinations: You can choose OK, or OK and Cancel, or any of a number of common combinations; you see one of these combinations in Figure 12.5. You cannot specify your own text for the buttons.*

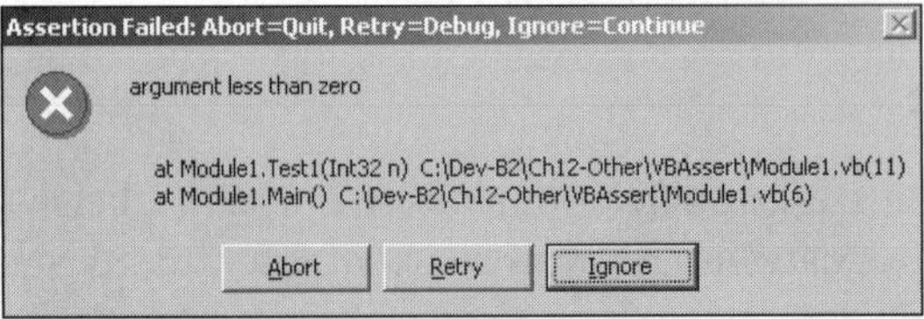

Figure 12.5 The dialog displayed when an assertion fails.

The Trace and Debug Classes

The **Assert()** function mentioned in the previous section is actually a member of two classes, **Trace** and **Debug**. Rather unusually, these two classes have exactly the same properties and methods, which are listed in Tables 12.16 and 12.17.

What is the difference between these two classes? If you use the methods in the **Debug** class, they are disabled when you create a release build, but the methods in the **Trace** class are always active, so they work in both debug and release builds of your programs.

Tracing Program Operation

The four **Write** methods listed in Table 12.17 are used to write trace text output, but it isn't quite as straightforward to use them as you might think.

The **Trace** and **Debug** classes each have a **Listeners** property, which is a collection of objects to which trace output is sent. You can create listeners that output to the console, to files, or to other places, and you can have more than one listener logging trace information at one time. See the Immediate Solution "Tracing Program Execution" for details on how to create and use listeners with the **Write** methods.

Table 12.16 Properties of the Debug and Trace classes.

Property	Description
AutoFlush	If true, causes output buffers to be flushed after each write
IndentLevel	Represents the current indentation level for output
IndentSize	Represents the number of spaces in an indent
Listeners	Gets the collection of listeners monitoring debug output

Table 12.17 Methods of the Debug and Trace classes.

Method	Description
Assert	Checks a condition and displays a message if the expression evaluates to **False**
Close	Flushes the output buffer and closes the listeners
Fail	Displays a failure message box
Flush	Flushes output buffers
Indent	Increases the current indent level by one
Unindent	Decreases the current indent level by one
Write	Writes a string to the listeners
WriteIf	Writes a string to the listeners if a condition is met
WriteLine	Writes a line to the listeners
WriteLineIf	Writes a string to the listeners if a condition is met

In order to make tracing output more readable, the **Indent()** and **Unindent()** methods can be used to increase and decrease the indentation applied when writing output. The number of spaces used for each indentation is determined by the **IndentSize** property.

Controlling Tracing

It is useful to be able to control how much trace output is produced by your applications and be able to change it without having to recompile the code. For this reason, trace output is under the control of a **TraceSwitch** object, which is used to set the level of tracing that will be logged. This can be done within code, but what makes it very useful is that the trace levels can be set in an external configuration file, so you can reconfigure what will be output without having to rebuild the application. This has obvious benefits when trying to resolve problems with release builds.

The Event Log

The Windows Event log mechanism provides a way in which system processes and applications can write error and status information to a central, systemwide point on Windows 2000 and NT systems. This information can be read by humans and accessed by programs, and it is a useful, standard way of storing log information.

The Event log is particularly useful for services, as it provides a central place for them to log status and error information when they don't have access to the Windows desktop. It is also possible to connect to the Event log on a remote machine if you have sufficient access; this can be very helpful when trying to diagnose problems with remote services.

You can access the Event log using the Event Viewer application, which on Windows 2000 lives in the Administrative Tools folder in the Control Panel. If you start the Event Viewer, you'll see a user interface similar to the one in Figure 12.6. Obviously the events you see logged will be specific to your machine.

As you can see from the figure, Windows 2000 has three default Event logs:

- *Application Log*—Is the default location for logging events generated by applications.
- *Security Log*—Logs security and audit information. The Security log is read-only from applications.
- *System Log*—Logs events from system processes.

Other applications and services can add their own specialized logs to the three default logs.

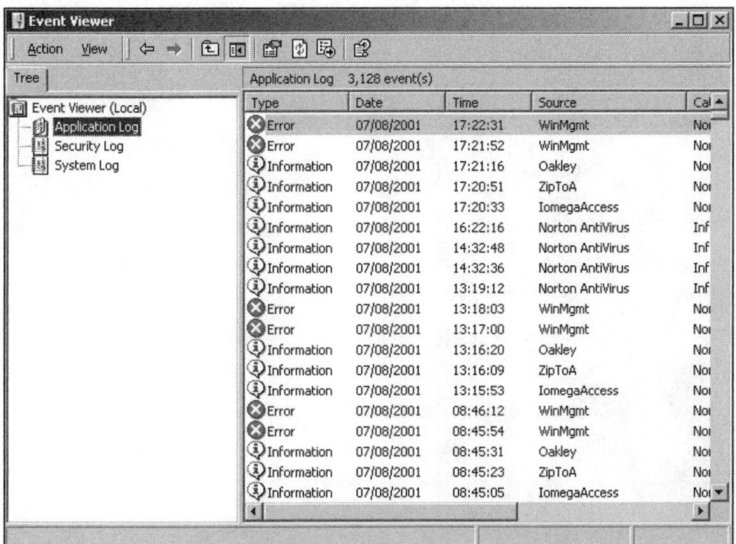

Figure 12.6 The Event Viewer application in Windows 2000.

A log contains three types of events, each identified by their own icon:

- *Information events*—Log events such as services starting up and shutting down
- *Warning events*—Report noncritical problems
- *Error events*—Report serious problems

Each line in the right pane of the Event Viewer represents the summary of an event, detailing when it was logged and who originated it, among other details. If you want more information, you can double-click one of the lines, and the full properties of the event will be displayed in a dialog, as shown in Figure 12.7.

As well as the information displayed in the summary, this dialog displays a description message in the middle pane, which can be as long as you want. It is also possible to log binary information as well, which if present will be displayed in the bottom pane.

Using the Event Log from .NET

The **EventLog** class lets you write to or customize Windows 2000 Event logs. You can:

- Read from existing logs
- Create new logs
- Write to new or existing logs
- Create or delete event sources

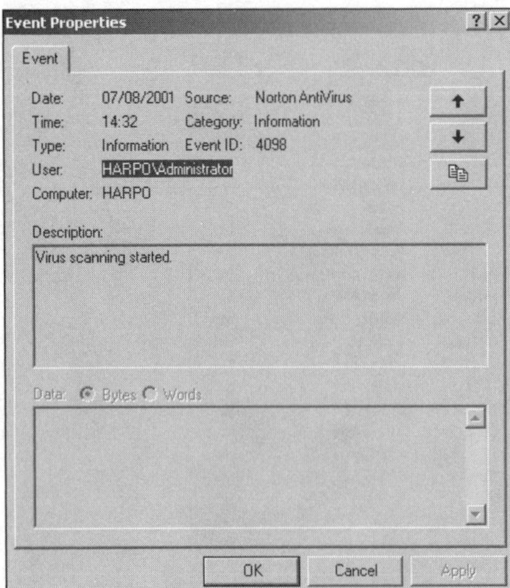

Figure 12.7 Event information being displayed in Windows 2000.

- Delete logs
- Respond to log entries

See the Immediate Solutions section "Using the Event Log" for examples of using the **EventLog** class.

The Text Namespaces

The **System.Text** and **System.Text.RegularExpression** namespaces contain a number of useful classes, including:

- Classes representing the ASCII, Unicode, UTF-7, and UTF-8 character encodings
- Classes for converting blocks of characters to and from blocks of bytes
- A class for building **String** objects
- Classes that provide access to the .NET Framework regular expression engine

The Encoding Classes

A *character encoding* is a way of representing characters as a set of bits in memory. For instance, there are several ways in which you can represent the character "A". For years, the most common was American Standard Code for Information Interchange (ASCII), which represents each character as a 7-bit number. This meant that there were 127 possible characters, and "A" was number 65. Obviously, 127 characters isn't going to go very far if you want to include the character sets of languages such as Japanese or Greek, so more recently, Unicode has become popular. This represents each character by 16 bits, which allows for 65,536 possible characters. In Unicode, "A" is hex 0041. ASCII and Unicode represent two different character encodings: You can represent the letter "A" in both, but they use different bit patterns to do so.

The **Encoding** class is the base class for the four character-encoding classes provided by **System.Text**:

- **ASCIIEncoding**—Encodes Unicode characters as single 7-bit ASCII characters
- **UnicodeEncoding**—Encodes Unicode characters as two consecutive bytes
- **UTF7Encoding**—Encodes Unicode characters using the UTF-7 encoding
- **UTF8Encoding**—Encodes Unicode characters using the UTF-8 encoding

The StringBuilder Class

If you look at the documentation for the **String** class, you'll see that **String** "represents an immutable string of characters." In other words, once a **String** has been created, its content cannot be changed. The **String** class contains several methods that appear to change the content of a **String**—such as **Insert()**, **Replace()**, and **ToLower()**—but on closer observation, you'll find that they all return a new **String** on which the appropriate changes have been made.

Why are **String**s immutable? One reason is that some operations can be implemented more efficiently if you know that the content is not going to change. A more important reason is that constant strings don't have to be thread safe: If the content of the string can't change, it doesn't matter how many threads are using the object at once. This means that although you can make changes to **String**s, it is at the expense of continually creating new **String** objects. The alternative is to use the **StringBuilder** class, which operates on a character buffer in situ and doesn't keep creating new instances.

The properties and methods supported by **StringBuilder** are listed in Tables 12.18 and 12.19. See the Immediate Solution "Using **StringBuilder**" for an example of its use.

Table 12.18 Properties of the StringBuilder class.

Property	Description
Capacity	Gets or sets the number of characters the **StringBuilder** is capable of holding.
Chars	Gets or sets the character at a given index.
Length	Gets or sets the length of the **StringBuilder**. If it is set to less than the current length, the **StringBuilder** is truncated.
MaxCapacity	Gets the maximum capacity of a **StringBuilder**, which defaults to hex 7FFFFFFF.

Table 12.19 Methods of the StringBuilder class.

Method	Description
Append	Appends characters to the **StringBuilder**
AppendFormat	Appends formatted characters to the **StringBuilder**
EnsureCapacity	Ensures that the capacity of the **StringBuilder** is at least a specified value
Insert	Inserts characters into the **StringBuilder**
Remove	Removes characters from the **StringBuilder**
Replace	Replaces characters in the **StringBuilder**
ToString	Converts a **StringBuilder** to a **String**

Regular Expressions

Regular expressions first became popular in text editors on the Unix operating system and have become widely used elsewhere as a way of specifying text patterns. They are supported in many programming editors, such as Vi and Emacs, and .NET provides the **System.Text.RegularExpressions.Regex** class to let you use them in code to match patterns in strings.

Tables 12.20 and 12.21 list the most common elements that you use to make up regular expressions.

Here are some examples showing the elements in Table 12.20 in use:

- **a..c**—Matches "abbc", "aZZc", "a09c", and so on
- **$a..c**—Matches "abbc", "aZZc", "a09c", and so on, provided it occurs at the end of a line

Table 12.20 Regular expression syntax elements for character matching.

Symbol	Name	Description
.	Wildcard single character	Matches any character except a line break.
[]	Set of characters	Matches any one of the characters in the square brackets. To specify a range, separate the staring and ending characters with a dash, for example, [0-9].
[^]	Exclusive set	Matches any character not in the set.
^	Beginning	Anchors the match to the beginning of a line.
$	End	Anchors the match to the end of a line.
()	Group	Groups a subexpression.
|	Or	Used for alternates. Normally used with groups.
\	Escape	Matches the character following the backslash, so that you can match special characters such as **$** and **|**.

Table 12.21 Regular expression syntax elements for controlling repetition.

Symbol	Name	Description
*	Zero or more	Matches zero or more occurrences of the preceding expression
+	One or more	Matches one or more occurrences of the preceding expression
?	Zero or one	Matches zero or one occurrences of the preceding expression
@	Zero or more	Matches zero or one occurrences of the preceding expression, matching as few characters as possible
#	One or more	Matches one or more occurrences of the preceding expression, matching as few characters as possible
^n	Repeat	Matches *n* occurrences of the preceding expression

- **[Bbw]ill**—Matches "Bill", "bill", or "will"
- **0[^23456]a**—Matches "01a", "07a", and "0ba", but not "02a" or "05a"
- **(good|bad) day**—Matches "good day" and "bad day"
- **a\(b\)**—Matches the string "a(b)", the backslash meaning that the parentheses aren't interpreted as group delimiters

Here are some examples showing the elements in Table 12.21 in use:

- **a+b**—Matches one or more a's followed by one b; for example, "ab", "aab", "aaab".
- **[0-9]^4**—Matches any four-digit sequence.
- **\([0-9]^3\)-[0-9]^3-[0-9]^4**—Matches a phone number of the form "(666)-666-6666".
- **^.*$**—Matches an entire line because **.*** matches zero or more of any character, and **^** and **$** anchor the match to both the start and end of the line.

.NET contains a regular expression engine that will take a string and a regular expression, and match the expression against the string. Access to this engine from any .NET language is via the **Regex** class. The Immediate Solutions section "Using Regular Expressions to Match Patterns in Text" shows you an example of how to use **Regex** to implement regular expression text searching in your programs.

Immediate Solutions

Writing Multithreaded Code

Using threads in code is not simple to master, and there are many pitfalls for the unwary. This Immediate Solution is intended to introduce you to the world of multithreaded coding by showing you how to write a simple application that uses threads, but it isn't a comprehensive introduction to writing threaded code.

NOTE: *If you are not familiar with the concept of threading, refer to the In Depth section "Threading" for details.*

Creating the Basic Application

This simple application draws lines on a form on the screen, with the drawing of each line controlled by a separate thread.

Create a Windows application project, and place a panel and three buttons on the form, as shown in Figure 12.8. The Add button will be used to create extra drawing threads, whereas the Pause and Resume buttons will be used to control the threads.

Add four **Imports** statements to the top of the project:

```
Imports System.Threading
Imports System.Windows.Forms
Imports System.Drawing
Imports System.Collections
```

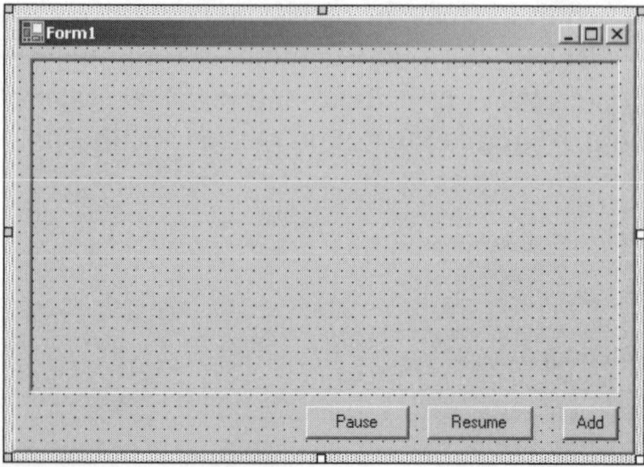

Figure 12.8 The basic form for the multithreaded application.

You need **System.Threading** for the threading-related classes, **Forms** and **Drawing** for the GUI, and **Collections** because you'll use an **ArrayList** to store the threads as they are created.

Now add some member variables to the top of the class definition:

```
' The original drawing thread
Dim thrd As Thread

' A graphics object to use for painting
Dim grp As Graphics
' The form size
Dim sz As Size

' An ArrayList to hold references to the active threads
Dim threadList As New ArrayList()
```

The application will have one thread drawing lines when it starts up, and you can add more threads by pressing the Add button. All threads share the same **Graphics** object when drawing, so the code contains a reference to this object and another to the form's size.

Setting Up

Expand the "Windows Form Designer generated code" region so that you can see the constructor, and add the following highlighted lines:

```
Public Sub New()
  MyBase.New()

  'This call is required by the Windows Form Designer.
  InitializeComponent()

  'Add any initialization after the InitializeComponent() call
  ' Create the Graphics object for the threads to use
  grp = Panel1.CreateGraphics()
  ' Set the panel's background to white
  Panel1.BackColor = Color.White

  ' create the initial thread
  thrd = New Thread(AddressOf ThreadFunc)
  thrd.IsBackground = True
  thrd.Start()
  threadList.Add(thrd)
End Sub
```

The first two code lines you've added create a **Graphics** object to let you draw on the panel—because that's where the lines are going to be displayed—and set the background of the panel to white, which will make it easier to see the lines.

You can then create the first drawing thread by creating a new **Thread** object. Because a thread executes a function in parallel with the rest of the application, you need to pass the **Thread** object the address of the function it is going to use, using the **AddressOf** operator. As you can guess from the code, the function the thread is going to run is called **ThreadFunc**. You'll see how this is coded in the next section.

The thread's **IsBackground** property is set to **True**; this makes the thread into a *background thread*, which means that it will automatically die when the program exits. The thread function doesn't start running until the **Thread** object's **Start()** function is called, so it is necessary to call this in order to start the drawing process. Finally, a reference to the thread is added to the **ArrayList**, so that it can be used later on.

The Thread Function

The class that holds the application code contains a single function, **ThreadFunc**, which draws a single line on the panel. The line starts at a random point and draws in a random color at 45 degrees, reflecting when it meets a boundary. Figure 12.9 shows what this looks like in action, with only one drawing thread running.

Add a new member function to the class, and start by choosing a random color for this thread to use for drawing:

```
Protected Sub ThreadFunc()
  ' random number for color choosing
  Dim rnd As New Random()

  ' choose a color
  Dim col As Color = Color.FromArgb(rnd.Next(0, 255), _
        rnd.Next(0, 255), rnd.Next(0, 255))
```

The **System.Random** class is used for generating random numbers. You use it by creating a **Random** object, and then calling the **Next()** function to generate a pseudo-random integer in a given range, which in this case is 0 through 255. Three random numbers are used to select red, green, and blue values for the **Color** object that is going to be used for drawing.

NOTE: *See Chapter 3 for more details on the **Random** class and Chapter 11 for details on using the **Color** class.*

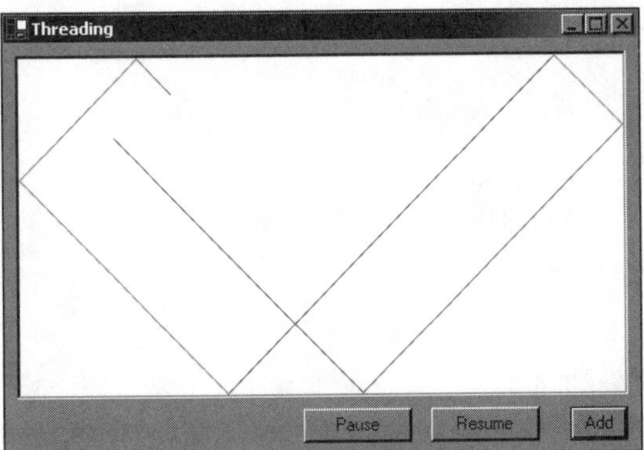

Figure 12.9 One thread drawing a line in the threading solution.

The next task is to choose a starting point for the line, which involves using **Random** once more:

```
' pick a starting point
sz = Panel1.Size
Dim x As Integer = sz.Width * rnd.NextDouble()
Dim y As Integer = sz.Height * rnd.NextDouble()
```

The size of the panel is stored in the **sz** member, and a random starting point is calculated from the width and height. You then need to set up four variables to be used in the drawing calculations:

```
' The increment for each drawing operation
Dim dx As Integer = 1
Dim dy As Integer = 1

' The previous position
Dim oldx As Integer
Dim oldy As Integer
```

The **dx** and **dy** variables hold the increments to be applied each time around the drawing loop. By making them both one pixel, the lines will be drawn at 45 degrees. The **oldx** and **oldy** variables are used to hold the previous endpoint of the line each time around the loop.

The following code draws the loop:

```
' The drawing loop
While True
   ' Save the last point
   oldx = x
   oldy = y
```

```
    ' Calculate the next one
    x = x + dx
    y = y + dy

    ' Check for hitting the side of the panel.
    ' If it has hit, reverse the drawing direction
    If x >= sz.Width - 5 Or x <= 0 Then
      dx = -dx
    End If
    If y >= sz.Height - 5 Or y <= 0 Then
      dy = -dy
    End If

    ' Create a pen for the line
    Dim pn As New Pen(col, 1)
    ' Draw the line
    grp.DrawLine(pn, oldx, oldy, x, y)

    ' Sleep for a few milliseconds so it doesn't go too fast
    Thread.Sleep(20)
  End While
```

The loop starts by saving the last point and calculating the new one by adding the **dx** and **dy** offsets. You could experiment with varying the values of **dx** and **dy** if you want to create more interesting looking lines. If the line has hit any of the four sides of the panel, the increments are reversed in sign in order to reflect the line back into the interior of the panel.

NOTE: *The* ***-5*** *used in the width and height checks is a correction needed because the width reported for the panel doesn't seem to match the actual size on the screen in the Beta 2 release of .NET. Try removing it and see how the lines reflect from the panel boundaries.*

The next step is to draw the line. Create a pen of the appropriate color and use it in a call to **DrawLine()**. The thread sleeps for a few milliseconds so that the animation doesn't go too fast and to give other threads a chance to execute. Try commenting out the call to **Sleep()** and see what difference it makes to the way the program runs.

Related solution:	Found on page:
How Do I Generate Random Values?	150
Working with Colors	521

Adding More Threads

Add a handler for the **Add** button. In the handler, add some code to create and start a new thread in exactly the same way as the original was created and started:

```
Private Sub AddBtn_Click(ByVal sender As System.Object, _
        ByVal e As System.EventArgs) Handles AddBtn.Click
  ' Create a new thread each time the button is clicked
  Dim t1 As New Thread(AddressOf ThreadFunc)
  t1.IsBackground = True

  ' Start the thread
  t1.Start()
  ' Add it to the list
  threadList.Add(t1)
End Sub
```

Every time you click the **Add** button a new thread will be created, which runs another copy of **ThreadFunc**, so you'll see another line being drawn on the screen.

Controlling the Threads

Add two handlers for the **Pause** and **Resume** buttons:

```
Private Sub PauseBtn_Click(ByVal sender As System.Object, _
        ByVal e As System.EventArgs) Handles PauseBtn.Click
  Dim ie As IEnumerator = threadList.GetEnumerator
  While ie.MoveNext
    Dim t As Thread = CType(ie.Current, Thread)
    t.Suspend()
  End While
End Sub

Private Sub ResumeBtn_Click(ByVal sender As System.Object, _
        ByVal e As System.EventArgs) Handles ResumeBtn.Click
  Dim ie As IEnumerator = threadList.GetEnumerator
  While ie.MoveNext
    Dim t As Thread = CType(ie.Current, Thread)
    t.Resume()
  End While
End Sub
```

These handlers are almost identical with the exception that one calls **Suspend()** to pause the running threads, whereas the other calls **Resume()** to start them again. In each handler, you obtain an enumerator so you can iterate over the elements in the **ArrayList**, and then use the **While** loop to access each element in turn. Because **Current** property on the enumerator returns generic **Object** references, it is necessary to use **CType** to cast them to **Thread** references before they can be used to call **Suspend()** or **Resume()** on the thread. The effect of these handlers is to pause all the running threads when the Pause button is pressed, so the drawing stops immediately, and to restart them all when the Resume button is pressed.

Creating Windows Service Applications

A service is a special kind of program that runs in the background and rarely has a user interface. See the In Depth section "Windows Services" for details on how services work and how they are implemented in the .NET Framework.

In this solution, I'll show you how to write a simple service, how to install it, run it, and control it when it is running.

Creating the Framework Service

The application that I'm going to write implements a service called "Beeper," whose sole purpose is to beep every two seconds. This is a good example of a simple service because it is easy to write, it is very easy to tell whether it is running or not (unless you have the PC speaker turned off!), and it is easy to demonstrate controlling a service by sending it requests.

Start Visual Studio .NET, and use Ctrl+Shift+N or select File|New to display the New Project dialog. Make sure that Visual Basic Projects is selected as the project type, and select Windows Service as the project type, using Beeper as the project name.

A Windows Service project contains a class that inherits from **System.ServiceProcess.ServiceBase**, which overrides two functions, as shown in the following code:

```
Imports System.ServiceProcess

Public Class Service1
    Inherits System.ServiceProcess.ServiceBase

' Component Designer generated code

    Protected Overrides Sub OnStart(ByVal args() As String)
      ' Add code here to start your service. This method should set
      ' things in motion so your service can do its work
    End Sub
```

```
    Protected Overrides Sub OnStop()
        ' Add code here to perform any tear-down necessary to
        ' stop your service.
    End Sub
End Class
```

The **ServiceBase** class implements all the basic structure needed by a service, leaving you free to concentrate on providing the functionality you need.

Services are controlled by the SCM, either via the Services applet on the Control Panel or by other applications using the Services API. The SCM sends your service requests in order to control it. The most common of these requests are:

- **Start**—Sent when a service is being started. A service can respond to this request in order to initialize itself.
- **Stop**—Sent to a service when it is going to be stopped. A service can respond to this request if it needs to tidy up when it is being shut down.
- **Pause**—Sent to a service to tell it to pause operation.
- **Continue**—Sent to a paused service to tell it to continue operation.

Other commands can be sent by the SCM to tell a service about changes in power status (such as suspending) and about machine shutdown. The default service created for you by the wizard overrides the **OnStart()** and **OnStop()** functions to respond to **Start** and **Stop** requests, so that you can provide custom startup and termination code.

If you look at the **Main** method for the service class, you can see how a service is started:

```
' The main entry point for the process
Shared Sub Main()
  Dim ServicesToRun() As System.ServiceProcess.ServiceBase

  ' More than one NT Service may run within the same process. To add
  ' another service to this process, change the following line to
  ' create a second service object. For example,
  '
  '   ServicesToRun = New System.ServiceProcess.ServiceBase () _
  '        {New Service1, New MySecondUserService}
  '
  ServicesToRun = New System.ServiceProcess.ServiceBase () {New Service1}

  System.ServiceProcess.ServiceBase.Run(ServicesToRun)
End Sub
```

As the comment remarks, one process can host more than one service. The **ServicesToRun** member is an array of **ServiceBase** objects that represent the services to be run, so if you want to have more than one service hosted in your process, add more entries to the **ServicesToRun** array.

The services are started by calling the shared **Run()** method in the **ServiceBase** class and passing it the array of service objects. If you write a service process manually—or in another language—you'll have to ensure that **Run()** is called from the program's main function.

In order to make sure that the service can be paused and stopped, I need to add some entries to the constructor for the service object. You need to expand the "Component Designer generated code" section in order to view Sub **New()**. Add the following highlighted lines:

```
Public Sub New()
  MyBase.New()

  ' This call is required by the Component Designer
  InitializeComponent()

  ' Set properties for the service object
  Me.CanPauseAndContinue = True
  Me.CanStop = True
  Me.AutoLog = True
End Sub
```

Setting the **CanPauseAndContinue** and **CanStop** properties to **True** means that the service will accept **Pause**, **Continue**, and **Stop** commands. Setting **AutoLog** to **True** means that **Start**, **Stop**, **Pause**, and **Continue** commands will automatically be logged to the Event log.

Adding Service Functionality

The work of a service is typically done in a separate thread, using the thread function to do whatever the service is designed to do.

NOTE: *See the solution "Writing Multithreaded Code" for details on how to use threads.*

When you create a thread, you nominate a function that is going to be run by the thread, and schedule it so that it runs in parallel with the rest of your application. The thread function that I'm going to use follows. Add it as a member of the class:

```
Sub DoBeep()
  ' This is the function that does the work of the service.
  ' It runs in a thread, and simply beeps every two seconds
  While bContinue = True
    Beep()
    Thread.Sleep(2000)
  End While
End Sub
```

This is a very simple function. When this is run by a thread, the **While** loop will run, emitting a beep and then sleeping for two seconds, as long as the Boolean flag **bContinue** is set to **True**.

Creating and Starting the Thread

I first create the thread object and the Boolean flag by adding the highlighted lines to the project:

```
Imports System.ServiceProcess
Imports System.Threading

Public Class Service1
    Inherits System.ServiceProcess.ServiceBase

    ' Create a thread
    Dim workThread As New Thread(AddressOf DoBeep)
    ' Create a flag
    Dim bContinue As Boolean
```

The **Imports** statement makes it easier to refer to classes in the **System.Threading** namespace. The **workThread** variable is the thread that will do the work of the service; when I create it, I pass the address of the function that the thread is going to run, which in this case is **DoBeep()**.

The thread object has been created, but the thread is not running yet. I add a call to the thread's **Start()** function in the service class **OnStart()** method so that the thread will start running as soon as the service is started:

```
Protected Overrides Sub OnStart(ByVal args() As String)
        ' Start the thread going...
        workThread.Start()
    End Sub
```

Controlling the Thread

This service can be paused and resumed from the Control Panel or by other applications, so I add overrides of the superclass **OnPause()** and **OnContinue()** methods:

```
Protected Overrides Sub OnPause()
  ' This will pause the work thread, so the beeping ought to stop!
  workThread.Suspend()
End Sub

Protected Overrides Sub OnContinue()
  ' This resumes the work thread, so beeping ought to resume
  workThread.Resume()
End Sub
```

The **Suspend()** and **Resume()** methods do just what they say: **Suspend()** pauses a thread, and **Resume()** sets it running again. Suspending and resuming threads is done by the operating system and does not require any action on the part of the thread itself. This makes threads a very useful way to implement services that need to be pausable.

***NOTE:** See the In Depth section "The **Thread** Class" for a discussion of the possible dangers of using **Suspend()** and **Resume()** with threads.*

In order to stop the thread function from running, modify the **OnStop()** function to set the flag **bContinue** to **False**:

```
Protected Overrides Sub OnStop()
  ' Add code here to perform any tear-down necessary to
  ' stop your service.
  bContinue = False
End Sub
```

It is also possible to call the **Abort()** method on the thread object, but it's not generally recommended because the thread function has no chance to tidy up. It doesn't matter in this case, but the technique of setting a flag and exiting the thread function when it is set to **False** gives the function a chance to tidy up before exiting.

You can now build the project to make sure that there are no errors. However, there is another step that has to be completed before you can run your service.

Creating Installation Components for the Service

Services need to be properly registered with the SCM, so you need to provide installer components for a service project. I'll show you how to do this using Visual Studio .NET, but it isn't very much harder to do it manually.

Open the Design view for the service project, and look at the Properties tab. At the bottom of the Properties window you'll see a link called Add Installer, as shown in Figure 12.10.

Click the link, and a new class called **ProjectInstaller** is added to your project. This class contains two installation components:

- **ServiceProcessInstaller1**—Deals with the installation of the service process itself.
- **ServiceInstaller1**—Deals with the installation of a service within the service process. If you have more than one service hosted in a process, you'll need to add an extra **ServiceInstaller** component for each service.

Click **ServiceInstaller1** in the Design view for ProjectInstaller.vb, and verify that the **ServiceName** property specifies the name of the service, which in this case should be **Service1**. The **StartType** property determines how the service will be started and can be one of three values:

- If it is **Automatic**, the service will be started at boot time.
- If it is **Manual**, the service will be started on demand, either through the Control Panel or by another application. This is the default start type.
- If it is **Disabled**, the service cannot be started.

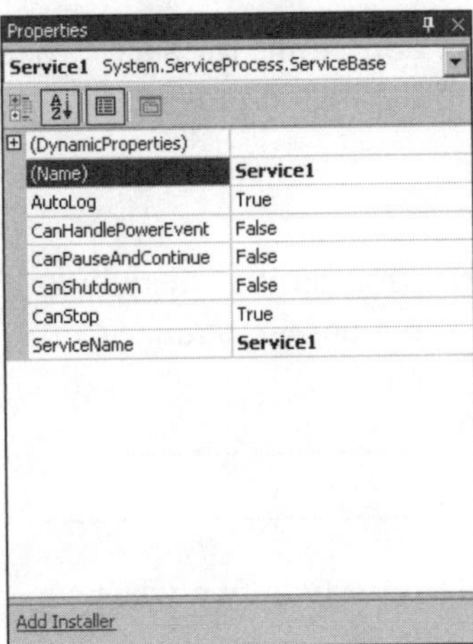

Figure 12.10 The Properties window for a service project, showing the Add Installer link.

Make sure the **StartType** is **Manual**. You can enter a word or name as the **DisplayName** if you want the service to be called something other than **Service1** in the Control Panel applet.

Now look at the properties for the **ServiceProcessInstaller1** component. The only property that you need to modify is **Account**, which specifies the user account under which the service will run. The default is **User**, which will run the service under a specified user ID. If you choose this default option, you'll have to provide the ID and password either in the Properties dialog or when the service is installed.

Most services run under the **LocalSystem** account, which gives them a high level of access to system resources. This is a good default account to run under, so change the **Account** property to **LocalSystem**.

Now build the project, and you're ready to install the service.

Installing the Service

The easiest way to install and uninstall services is to use the installutil.exe utility from the command line. This utility doesn't live in the Visual Studio directory tree, but instead lives in the .NET Framework directories. In Beta 2, you can find it in \Winnt\Microsoft.NET\Framework\v1.0.2914, although this may well be different in the final release.

The best way to run this utility is to use (from Start|Programs) Microsoft Visual Studio .NET 7.0|Visual Studio .NET Tools|Visual Studio .NET Command Prompt. This brings up a command shell with all the environment variables set correctly to run all the .NET Framework and Visual Studio .NET tools from the command line.

Open a command shell and change to the directory containing the service executable, which is called beeper.exe. Then, type the following command:

```
installutil beeper.exe
```

The utility displays several lines of status information as it is installing. If the installation completes successfully, you should see a screen similar to the one shown in Figure 12.11.

NOTE: *You can uninstall a service by running installutil.exe with the **/u** flag.*

You can verify that the service has been installed properly in two ways:

- Using the Control Panel's Services applet
- Using Visual Studio's Server Explorer

```
Select Visual Studio.NET Command Prompt
exe assembly's progress.
The file is located at C:\Dev-B2\Ch12-Other\Beeper\bin\beeper.InstallLog.
Call Installing. on the C:\Dev-B2\Ch12-Other\Beeper\bin\beeper.exe assembly.
Affected parameters are:
   assemblypath = C:\Dev-B2\Ch12-Other\Beeper\bin\beeper.exe
   logfile = C:\Dev-B2\Ch12-Other\Beeper\bin\beeper.InstallLog
Installing service Service1...
Service Service1 has been successfully installed.
Creating EventLog source Service1 in log Application...

The Install phase completed successfully, and the Commit phase is beginning.
See the contents of the log file for the C:\Dev-B2\Ch12-Other\Beeper\bin\beeper.
exe assembly's progress.
The file is located at C:\Dev-B2\Ch12-Other\Beeper\bin\beeper.InstallLog.
Call Committing. on the C:\Dev-B2\Ch12-Other\Beeper\bin\beeper.exe assembly.
Affected parameters are:
   assemblypath = C:\Dev-B2\Ch12-Other\Beeper\bin\beeper.exe
   logfile = C:\Dev-B2\Ch12-Other\Beeper\bin\beeper.InstallLog

The Commit phase completed successfully.

The transacted install has completed.

C:\Dev-B2\Ch12-Other\Beeper\bin>
```

Figure 12.11 Installutil.exe installing a service process.

In order to use the Server Explorer, open the Server Explorer window. This is usually a pop-up window docked to the left of the main Visual Studio pane. If it isn't displayed, you can show it by selecting View|Server Explorer or by pressing Ctrl+Alt+S. The Server Explorer window for my machine is shown in Figure 12.12.

You'll always have one entry in the Servers list, which represents the local machine. Expand the Services tab, and browse down for the Service1 entry. If the service name is displayed, the service has been installed. Clicking the Service1 entry displays the properties of the service, as shown in Figure 12.13. You can see that the service is running in its own process, and that it is currently stopped.

You can start the service in two ways: right-click the entry in the Server Explorer window and choose Start, or use the Control Panel applet. Whichever way you choose to start the service, you should hear a regular beeping sound as soon as

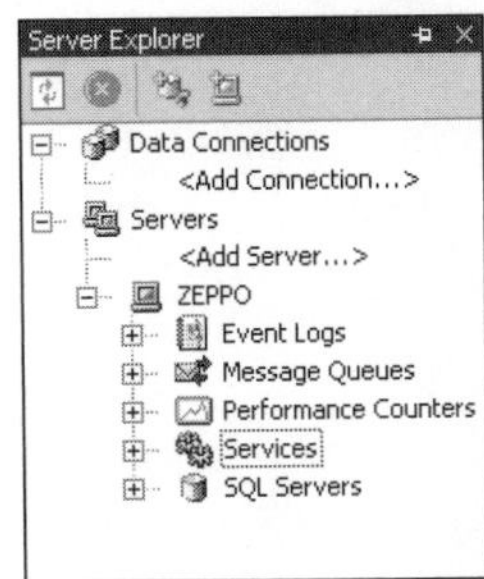

Figure 12.12 The Server Explorer window.

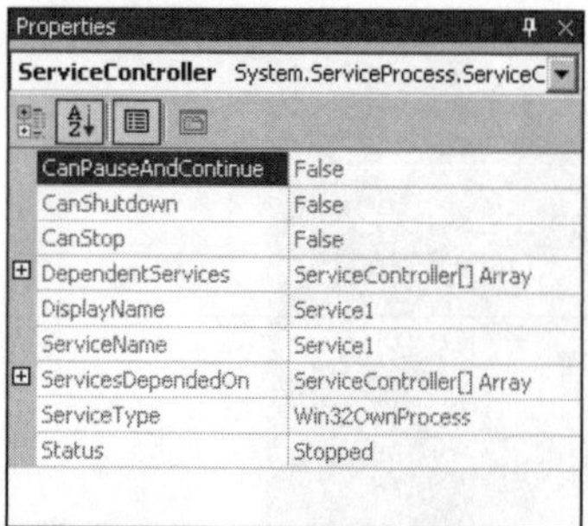

Figure 12.13 The properties of a service displayed from the Server Explorer.

the service starts. Experiment with the Stop and Pause/Continue functionality to make sure that it works.

Using Assertions

Assertions let you check whether an application is behaving as you expect at a particular point. The following example shows you how to use an assertion in your code:

```
' Assertions need the System.Diagnostics namespace
Imports System.Diagnostics

Module Module1

  Sub Main()
    ' Call the function
    Test(-1)
  End Sub

  ' A test function
  Public Sub Test(ByVal n As Integer)
    Trace.Assert(n > 0, "Argument is not positive")
    ' more code...
  End Sub
End Module
```

The program starts by importing the **System.Diagnostics** namespace: The assertion facility is part of this namespace, so you'll save yourself a lot of typing by importing the namespace at the beginning of your program.

The function **Test()** takes an integer as an argument, and it should probably never be called with an argument that is less than or equal to zero. If I'm sure of this, I put a call to **Trace.Assert()** in to check the value of the argument.

***NOTE: Assert()** takes two arguments: The first is an expression that evaluates to **True** or **False**, whereas the second is a message that is printed in the event of failure. **Assert()** checks the condition: If it is **True**—in this case, if n is greater than zero—no action is taken. If it is **False**, an error dialog is displayed, which is similar to the one shown in Figure 12.5.*

***NOTE:** There are two other overloads of **Assert()**: the first, with one argument, simply checks a condition and prints a standard message. The second takes three arguments—the condition, a brief message, and a detailed message.*

The idea is that you scatter assertions throughout your code as you write it, and these assertions mark invariant conditions—that is, conditions that must be **True** all the time. If at some point something happens to change the behavior of the program (such as changes in the code or data) and it causes an assertion to fail, you'll find out about it.

There are two versions of **Assert()**, both are shared methods. The version belonging to the **Debug** class is only active in debug builds and is disabled in release builds, whereas the version in the **Trace** class is active in all builds. Which one you choose depends on whether you want your assertions to be active all the time or not.

There is also a shared **Fail()** method, which is similar to **Assert()** but doesn't have an expression to evaluate. Whenever **Fail()** is executed, it displays the assertion dialog with an error message, so you use it to mark places in the code that should never be reached.

Tracing Program Execution

Sometimes it is useful to be able to write trace information to a log file in order to see just what a program is or has been doing. Sometimes, if a program fails or is behaving incorrectly, the debugger isn't very useful because all it tells you is where you are, and you need to know *how* you got there. In those cases, a log file is very useful, and the **Write** methods provided by the **Trace** and **Debug** classes will help you construct one.

There are four methods that can be used to generate output: **Write()**, **WriteIf()**, **WriteLine()**, and **WriteLineIf()**. If you think these look familiar you're correct. They parallel the **Console** methods you use for writing to the screen. The

WriteLine() and **Write()** methods write output with and without a new line respectively, and the "if" versions only write if a condition is met.

The following short example shows how to use the tracing features of **System.Diagnostics**:

```
' Tracing needs the System.Diagnostics namespace
Imports System.Diagnostics

Module Module1
  Sub Main()
    ' Add a listener
    Trace.Listeners.Add(New TextWriterTraceListener(Console.out))

    ' Call the function
    Trace.WriteLine("Main: calling Test")
    Test(1)
    Trace.WriteLine("Main: back from call")
  End Sub

  ' A test function
  Public Sub Test(ByVal n As Integer)
    Trace.Indent
    Trace.WriteLine("Test: entry")

    // more code...
    Trace.WriteLine("Test: exit")
    Trace.Unindent
  End Sub
End Module
```

The program starts by importing the **System.Diagnostics** namespace, so you don't have to use fully qualified names for all the tracing functions.

In order to log any output, you need to create one or more listeners and hook them up to the **Trace** class. A listener is simply an object that represents a destination for output, and there are three types of listener objects, which are listed in Table 12.22. You can also derive your own listener classes from the **TraceListener** base class if necessary.

TextWriterTraceListener is perhaps the most useful class, because it will let you log output to the console or to a text file. In this example, I've set up a **TextWriterTraceListener** to log output to the console and added it to the **Trace** class's **Listeners** collection. You can add as many listeners as you like at one time and can also remove those you don't need, so that you could, for instance,

Table 12.22 The TraceListener classes.

Class	Description
DefaultTraceListener	Writes output to the usual debug destination
EventLogTraceListener	Writes output to the Event log
TextWriterTraceListener	Writes output to the console or a file

log output to the screen for most of a program, but arrange to have trace output logged to a file as well in one particular function.

Once a listener is set up, I use the **WriteLine()** method to output trace information and the **Indent()** and **Unindent()** methods to adjust the indentation of the output. The default indentation increment is four spaces, but you can change it using the **Trace.IndentSize** property.

NOTE: *The indentation only affects the trace output, not any normal output generated by calls to* ***Console.WriteLine()****.*

Controlling Tracing

You can control how much output is generated by using a switch object, which enables you to place a lot of detailed tracing code in your program and determine at runtime how much is going to be logged. There are two standard switch classes provided in **System.Diagnostics**, **TraceSwitch** and **BooleanSwitch**. You can derive your own from the **Switch** base class if necessary.

Switch objects are especially useful in that they can read their settings from an external text file, so it is easy to tailor the amount of trace output you're going to get without having to recompile the code. You can also use switch objects to control which output is sent to listeners, so you could arrange for a subset of the trace information to be logged to the screen and have much more information saved to a file.

Using the Event Log

The Windows Event log provides a place where applications—especially services—can log status and error information. See the In Depth section "The Event Log" for details on what the Event log is and how you can view it.

Access to the Event log is through the **System.Diagnostics.EventLog** class. In this solution, I'll show you how to write entries to and retrieve entries from the log.

Writing to the Event Log

The following sample program shows you how to write events to the Event log. An explanation follows the code:

```
' You need System.Diagnostics for the EventLog class
Imports System.Diagnostics

Module Module1
  Sub Main()
    ' Create an EventLog object
    Dim el As New EventLog()

    ' Create an event source
    If Not EventLog.SourceExists("VBEventLog") Then
      EventLog.CreateEventSource("VBEventLog", "Application")
      Console.WriteLine("Event source created")
    End If

    ' Associate the object with the source.
    el.Source = "VBEventLog"

    ' See what we're writing to...
    Console.WriteLine("Writing to: " + el.Log)

    ' Now write something
    el.WriteEntry("Hello, mum!")

  End Sub
End Module
```

The first task is to create an **EventLog** object. I've used the default constructor, but there are several others that will let you connect to logs on other computers, provided you have the access rights to do so.

Every entry in the Event log needs to have an associated *event source*. This may represent a whole application or just a part of a complex application, and you can create as many event sources as you want. Once an event source has been created and registered, it is remembered by the Event log, and you'll get an error if you try to create the same source again. You can see how in the code I use **EventLog.SourceExists()** to check whether the source VBEventLog exists, and if it doesn't, I create it using **EventLog.CreateEventSource()**. If necessary, you can unregister an event source by calling **EventLog.DeleteEventSource()**.

When you create an event source, you specify the name of the source, the name of the log to use, and optionally a machine name. In this case, I'm not specifying a machine name, so the local Event log will be used. The name of the source can be one of the predefined logs, such as Application, and a custom log will be created if any other name is provided.

Once the event source is created (or I've verified that it already exists), I associate the source with the **EventLog** object using its **Source** property. If you don't associate a source with the **EventLog** before trying to write an event, you'll get an **ArgumentException**.

At this point, I'm ready to write something to the log using the **WriteEntry()** method. I've used the simplest overload, which simply takes a message string and writes an information entry, but there are several others that let you specify other details, such as the entry type, an event identifier, a category, and binary data.

Compile and run the program, and then open the Event Viewer, which you'll find in the Administrative Tools folder in the Control Panel. Once the main window appears, click the Application log entry in the left pane; you should see an event at the top of the right pane with VBEventLog as the source, as shown in Figure 12.14. If you double-click the entry, the Event Properties dialog is displayed, which should look like Figure 12.15.

This event does not have all the information that many other events have—for instance, there's no category or user, and the Event ID is zero—but you can clearly see the source, the time it was logged, the machine it was logged on, and the message.

Reading from the Event Log

Reading from the Event log is no more difficult than writing to it. The following program shows how to read events from the Application log:

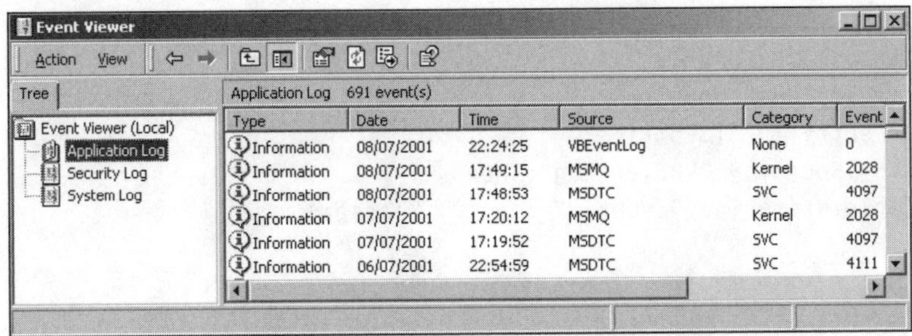

Figure 12.14 The Application log, showing the event that has been written by the VBEventLog program.

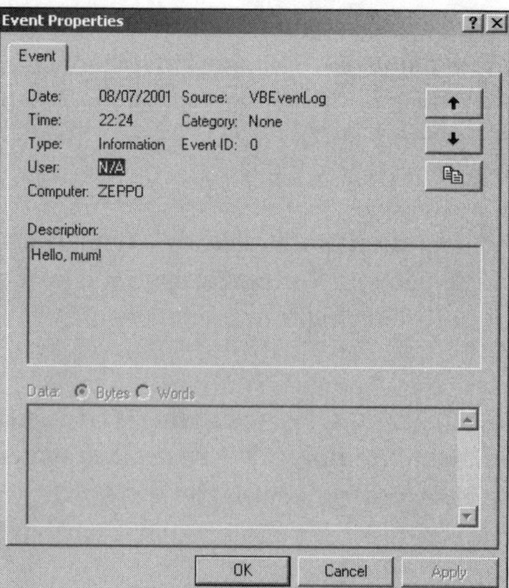

Figure 12.15 The Event Properties dialog for the event you've just added to the Application log.

```
' You need System.Diagnostics for the EventLog class
Imports System.Diagnostics

Module Module1
  Sub Main()
    ' Create an EventLog object
    Dim el As New EventLog()

    ' Set it to use the Application log
    el.Log = "Application"

    ' See how many entries there are...
    Console.WriteLine("Entries in log: " + el.Entries.Count.ToString())

    ' Process all the entries
    Dim entry As EventLogEntry
    For Each entry In el.Entries
      If entry.Source = "VBEventLog" Then
        Console.WriteLine("Event: " + entry.Message)
      End If
    Next
  End Sub
End Module
```

The purpose of this program is to scan the Application log for events that were written to it by the VBEventLog source, which is the source used in the previous application. If you built and ran that program, you should have one such event in the log.

As before, I need to create an **EventLog** object in order to access the event log, and I need to set its **Log** property in order to tell it which log to use. Note that when you read from the Event log, you don't have to specify a source, as they are only used for writing.

The collection of entries in the log are represented by the **Entries** property of the **EventLog** object. The **Count** property of **Entries** tells you how many entries there are in the log you're looking at. If you haven't cleared out the log for some time, there may be a lot.

The **Entries** property is a collection of **EventLogEntry** objects, each of which represents one entry in the log, so by using a **For Each** loop I can examine each entry in turn. **EventLog** has a number of properties, which are listed in Table 12.23, that let you examine the various pieces of data associated with an Event log entry.

The event type is represented by one of the members of the **EventLogEntryType**, as listed in Table 12.24. As you might expect, the **SuccessAudit** and **FailureAudit** entries will only occur in the Security log. Because there are only three types of log entries—**Information**, **Warning,** and **Error**—it is possible for an application to

Table 12.23 Properties of the EventLogEntry class.

Property	Description
Category	Gets the text associated with the event category
CategoryNumber	Gets the category number for this event
Data	Gets the binary data associated with this event as a byte array
EntryType	Gets the event type as an **EventLogEntryType**
EventID	Gets the application-specific ID associated with this event
Index	Gets the index of this entry in the Event log
MachineName	Gets the name of the machine on which the event was logged
Message	Gets the message associated with the entry
ReplacementStrings	Gets any replacement strings associated with this entry
Source	Gets the source that logged the entry
TimeGenerated	Gets a **DateTime** object representing the time the event was generated, in local time
TimeWritten	Gets a **DateTime** object representing the time the event was written to the log, in local time
UserName	Gets the name of the user responsible for this event

Table 12.24 Members of the EventLogEntryType enumeration.

Member	Description
Information	Represents a significant successful event
Warning	Represents a problem that is not immediately significant, but may cause more problems later
Error	Represents a significant problem, usually involving a loss of functionality or data
SuccessAudit	Represents a successful security audit event, such as a successful logon
FailureAudit	Represents a failed security audit event, such as a failed attempt to access a file

provide its own "event categories" in order to further subdivide them. An application can also associate an ID with an event for later tracking.

Using **StringBuilder**

As its name implies, the **System.Text.StringBuilder** class provides you with a way to interactively build and modify strings. This happens on a single copy of the data in situ, in contrast to the methods provided by the **System.String** class, which always create new **String** objects whenever any modification is required.

The following sample program shows you how to create and use **StringBuilder** objects:

```
Imports System.Text

Module Module1
  Sub Main()
    ' Create an empty StringBuilder
    Dim sb As New StringBuilder()

    ' Append some data...
    sb.Append("Can it be ")      ' Append text
    Dim b As Boolean = True
    sb.Append(b)                 ' Append boolean
    sb.Append("?"c, 2)           ' Append two question marks

    ' Write it out
    Console.WriteLine(sb.ToString())

    ' Remove everything
    sb.Remove(0, sb.Length)
```

```
    ' Format up a short and add it
    Dim s As Short = 101
    sb.AppendFormat("{0} dalmatians", s)

    Console.WriteLine(sb.ToString())

    ' Empty it again
    sb.Remove(0, sb.Length)

    ' Format up a double and add it
    Dim pie As Double = 22 / 7
    sb.AppendFormat("Would you like a piece of {0,-6:F3}?", pie)

    Console.WriteLine(sb.ToString())

  End Sub
End Module
```


If you build and run the program, you'll get the following output:

```
Can it be True?
101 dalmatians
Would you like a piece of 3.143 ?
```

The **StringBuilder** class contains several constructors that enable you to initialize **StringBuilder** objects by specifying a number of parameters:

- All or part of an existing **String**. If not specified, the **StringBuilder** is created empty.
- An initial capacity. If not specified, the default capacity is 16 characters.
- A maximum capacity.

You can manipulate the content of the **StringBuilder** using the **Append()**, **AppendFormat()**, **Insert()**, **Remove()**, and **Replace()** methods. **Append()** has no fewer than 19 overloads, allowing you to add a wide variety of basic data types to the content. Examples of some of these methods are shown in the previous code.

A **StringBuilder** can be converted to a **String** using the **ToString()** method, and a new **String** object is only created when you call **ToString()**.

AppendFormat() lets you format character data before appending it, using the same curly-bracket format specifiers that are used in **Console.WriteLine()**. The first specifier, **{0}**, simply inserts the first object in the list in place of the marker, giving it default formatting. If there were two objects in the list, they would be marked by **{0}** and **{1}** in the format string.

The second specifier is slightly more complicated. Let's assume I want to print out a floating-point value to three places of decimals, left-justified in a field six characters wide. The format **{0,-6:F3}** can be broken down as follows:

- **0** denotes the first object in the list.
- **-6** denotes the field width, with the - signifying left justification.
- The **F3** after the colon denotes the formatting I want. **F** is fixed-point format, and **3** is the number of decimal places.

You can see from the output that the field is indeed six characters wide because there is a space after the number and before the question mark.

NOTE: *Using format specifiers is discussed in more detail in Chapter 3.*

The other methods provided by **StringBuilder** are quite simple to use. For example, the **Replace()** method can be used to replace all occurrences of a substring by another substring:

```
sb.Replace("a piece", "two pieces")
```


Related solution:	Found on page:
How Do I Produce Formatted Output?	147

Using Regular Expressions to Match Patterns in Text

Regular expressions provide a concise way to describe patterns in text, and the **Regex** class in the **System.Text.RegularExpressions** namespace provides a way to match patterns against text strings.

A few samples of simple regular expressions are provided in the following list. More of the syntax is described in the In Depth section "Regular Expressions".

- **^Dav(e|id)**—Matches "Dave" or "David" where it occurs at the start of a line. The **^** anchors the pattern to the start of the line, the **()** delimits a group, and the **|** provides alternatives.
- **ab+**—Matches an "a" followed by one or more "b" characters, so it matches "ab", "abb", "abbb", and so on.
- **(ab)+**—Matches one or more occurrences of "ab", so it matches "ab", "abab", "ababab", and so on.

The following sample program shows the basic steps involved in using regular expressions:

```
Imports System.Text.RegularExpressions

Module Module1
  Sub Main()
    ' Create a Regex object
    Dim rx As New Regex("[Bbw]ill")

    Dim s As String = "My friend Bill will pay the bill"

    ' Look for the first match
    Dim m As Match = rx.Match(s)

    If m.Success = True Then
      Console.WriteLine("Match was successful")
    Else
      Console.WriteLine("Match failed")
    End If

    ' Look for all matches
    Dim mc As MatchCollection = rx.Matches(s)
    Console.WriteLine("There were {0} matches in all", mc.Count)

  End Sub
End Module
```

Importing the **System.Text.RegularExpressions** namespace makes it much easier to use **Regex** later in the program, as the fully qualified names get rather long!

The first step in using the .NET regular expression engine is to create a **Regex** object. There are several constructors for **Regex**, but in the preceding code I'm using the constructor that creates a **Regex** to work with a particular expression. Specifying the expression in the constructor means that it can be precompiled by the **Regex** object, which makes pattern matching quicker later on.

***NOTE: Regex** objects are immutable, so the expression they use cannot be changed. The same **Regex** object can, however, be used for as many searches as you like.*

The expression I'm using is **[Bbw]ill**. The square brackets enclose a set of characters, any one of which can be used in a match. This means that the pattern will match the strings "Bill", "bill", and "will". You can see that the test string I'm going to use contains all of those strings, so I ought to get three matches.

The basic **Regex** operation is **Match()**, which examines an input string for the first match. The overload I'm using starts matching at the beginning of the string, but other versions let you start from an arbitrary character position. **Match()** returns a **Match** object that represents the results of the match process, so you can examine its properties to see where the match was and exactly what was matched. Table 12.25 lists some useful properties of the **Match** class.

If you simply want to check for the occurrence of a match but don't want any information about it, the **IsMatch()** function simply returns a Boolean value indicating whether any matches are found in the string.

Given the properties of the **Match** class, it would be easy to modify the code to list every match in the test string, like this:

```
' Look for all the matches
Dim m As Match = rx.Match(s)

While m.Success = True
  Console.WriteLine("Match '{0}' found at {1}", m.Value, m.Index)
  m = rx.Match(s, m.Index + m.Length)
End While
```

The **While** loop keeps asking for matches until **Success** is set to **False**, in which case there aren't any more matches. In order that I don't search from the beginning of the string every time—which would result in an infinite loop, of course—I use an overload of **Match()**, which specifies the start position of the next **Match()** to be just past the end of the previous matched string. If you run the preceding code, you'll see the following output:

```
Match 'Bill' found at 10
Match 'will' found at 15
Match 'bill' found at 28
```

You don't have to loop through the matches manually, though, because **Regex**'s **Matches()** function automatically finds all the matches for the expression and

Table 12.25 Useful properties of the Match class.

Property	Description
Index	The position in the string where the match was found
Length	The length of the matched string
Success	**True** if the match was successful
Value	The actual string that was matched

returns them to you as a **MatchCollection**. You can see how this function is used in the program to verify that there are, indeed, three matches for the expression in the string.

A More Advanced Example

The **Regex** class can provide far more advanced pattern matching than the previous simple example. The following is a more complex example that touches on more advanced features. The idea behind this example is that you want to process a hospital telephone list, extracting names and extensions, and print them out. So every entry looks like this:

```
Dr. David Jones, Ophthalmology, x2441
```

You want to extract the surname and the extension, and print them out so that they look like this:

```
2441, Jones
```

In the real world, you would be getting your data from a file or a database query, but in this example I'll provide a few sample entries as an array of strings. Here's the code that will reformat the entries:

```
Dim sa(4) As String

sa(0) = "Dr. David Jones, Ophthalmology, x2441"
sa(1) = "Ms. Cindy Harriman, Registry, x6231"
sa(2) = "Mr. Chester Addams, Mortuary, x1667"
sa(3) = "Dr. Hawkeye Pierce, Surgery, x0986"

Dim rx1 As New Regex(_
   "^[ \.a-zA-z]+ (?<name>\w+), [a-zA-z]+, x(?<ext>\d+)$")

Dim i As Integer
For i = 0 To 3
  Dim mm As Match = rx1.Match(sa(i))
  Console.WriteLine(mm.Result("${ext}, ${name}"))
Next
```

The idea is the same as before: Create a **Regex** object, initialize it with an expression, and then get it to match on each string in the array by calling **Match()**. In this case, the expression is much more complex than you've seen before:

```
^[ \.a-zA-z]+ (?<name>\w+), [a-zA-z]+, x(?<ext>\d+)$
```

Let's break it down to see how it works:

- **^** matches the start of the string.
- **[\.a-zA-Z]** will match any one of space, dot (escaped by a backslash because dot is special character in expressions), uppercase, or lowercase letters.
- The **+** after the set means "match one or more". This pattern will match the title and first name up to the space between the first and surnames.
- The space after the **+** matches the space between the first and surnames.
- **(?<name>\w+)** defines a special kind of group. The **?<name>** tags the matched string with the tag **name**, and you can use this later to refer to the matched text. **\w** means the same as **[a-zA-Z_0-9]** and is a useful abbreviation. So this part of the pattern matches the next word, which consists of one or more letters, numbers, or underscores and saves it with the tag **name**.
- The next section, **[a-zA-z]+**, matches the punctuation and the word defining the department. This isn't tagged because you're not going to use it again.
- The extension number occurs after an "**x**", and the pattern that matches the extension is **(?<ext>\d+)**, which captures a sequence of digits and saves it with the tag **ext**.
- The final **$** means that the extension pattern has to occur at the end of the line.

When the **Match()** is run, the resulting **Match** object has two tagged items, **name** and **ext**, representing the name and extension. The **Result()** method lets you take a **Match()** and generate a string as output, substituting in the matched strings. In the example, I've referred to the **name** and **ext** tags by enclosing them in **${}**.

Chapter 13

.NET Remoting

By David Vitter

If you need an immediate solution to:	*See page:*

In Depth

Remoting is a new name for an old familiar concept, and it is the .NET world's successor to Microsoft's Distributed COM (DCOM) technology. This chapter examines how Remoting works from both a client and a server's perspective. You will gain an understanding of how Remoting compares to DCOM as well as another new .NET technology, XML Web services. If you already have some experience developing distributed applications with DCOM, you will find many exciting new improvements made in Remoting, although it is still a complicated technology that takes some patience and time to understand and use.

Remoting Basics

Distributed applications separate themselves into individual components that can be housed or hosted on individual machines. Dividing an application into distributed components is known as *scaling out*, which means you are spreading your application out among many different machines to better handle an increase in workload. If all of your components were located on one single-processor machine, your application would slow down in response to an increased number of users because that one processor would be overwhelmed with operations to perform. If you move one or more components to a separate server, you can offload some of the processing to that new server, thereby improving your application's response time.

I will begin by discussing the different technologies used throughout the years to enable object-to-object calls, and then discuss some of the major Remoting concepts that you should be familiar with.

Remoting Technologies

Application scaling is an easy concept to understand, but the task of actually making a component on one machine talk to another component on a completely different machine is quite complicated. Microsoft's COM was initially designed to make object-to-object calls simple, provided they were both on the same machine. This made object calls easier to code, but COM by itself did not make distributed applications possible. To enable developers to distribute their COM objects, Microsoft next released DCOM. This allowed one COM object to call another COM object on a different machine using a proprietary Microsoft communications protocol to send that request across the network.

DCOM opened the door for Microsoft developers to create truly distributed applications. Unfortunately, to utilize DCOM you had to accomplish a long list of administrative tasks to configure both the client and the server objects to work properly. DCOM even had its own administration tool, Dcomcnfg, which developers had to master in order to use DCOM in their applications. In addition, because objects using DCOM to communicate used a proprietary protocol, you could not use DCOM to talk to objects written in other development environments, such as Java. Java has its own distributed communications protocol to work with, and development teams could not connect Java to COM and DCOM without the use of a third-party communications bridge. Figure 13.1 shows a COM, DCOM, Java, and .NET object all in the same environment and also shows the communication limitations that these individual objects face.

.NET improves upon its DCOM predecessor through a new technology called Remoting. Within the .NET Framework, you will find Remoting and its subclasses under the **System.Runtime.Remoting** namespace. Remoting is the technology of choice for .NET developers wanting to make remote object calls from their .NET assemblies. What exactly is a remote object call? A Remoting call is a request sent to an out-of-process object's interface. This remote object could be on the same machine or on a separate machine. When the object you are calling is not hosted in the same process as the object that is calling it, the data that is exchanged between these two objects must go through a special marshaling or packaging process to transfer back and forth across processes. Your interface calls will not use Remoting when the object being called is within the same process or application domain as the caller. Think of Remoting calls as having to go through a long-distance phone carrier and making in-process calls as using a local phone carrier. It's those long distance calls that can really run up the phone bill!

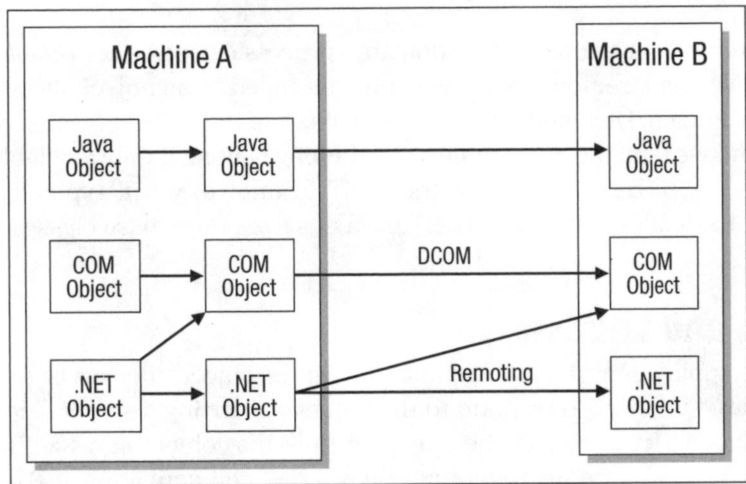

Figure 13.1 Distributed object technologies in the application environment.

Developers with DCOM experience should find Remoting a bit easier to work with, although those developers that are new to distributed object communications might still find Remoting to be complicated and intimidating. Probably the best news of all when talking about Remoting is that it embraces open source technologies such as Simple Object Access Protocol (SOAP) and HTTP to make object-to-object calls. This change of protocol not only tears down the wall that previously separated Visual Studio application components from non-Microsoft components, but also extends the reach of your object calls far beyond its previous boundaries. You'll read more about these improvements in the "Remoting Communications" section later in this chapter. In the next section, I'll discuss some high-level concepts that Remoting is based on.

Remoting Clients and Servers

When one object calls out to another object, the object that makes the initial call is known as a *client object*. The object that responds to that call and provides some function or data in return is known as a *server object*. The connection that is formed between these two objects is called a *channel*; I will further examine these object communication pipes in the "Channels" section. Before I dive into the details of how these objects communicate, it is important to establish the roles an object can take on, which is either client or server.

During a single call, only one object can be the client and the other object can only be a server. This is a simple, yet critical, concept to understand when you are developing your objects for use with Remoting. It is possible to create an object that will act as both a server to other objects and as a client that calls out to another server object. To keep the examples found in this chapter simple and understandable, I focus in on objects that are designed to perform only one of the two roles, client or server.

An object hosted within an application domain's process can be either *remotable* or *nonremotable*. A nonremotable object cannot be called by an object outside of its application domain. Depending on the design goals of the object you are creating, you can choose to make it nonremotable, thereby making it only available to a single application. Base classes in the .NET Framework will typically be nonremotable by default, but you can derive classes from these base classes that are remotable.

Activation and Lifetime

When a client application object calls out to a server object, the server object must be activated in order to respond to the requests. Starting a server-side object is known as *activation*, and the length of time that object stays active is called the object's *lifetime*. In Remoting, there are three activation methods, each with their own lifetimes. In this section you will learn about the three activation types:

- Single call
- Singleton
- Client activated objects (CAO)

Single Call

An object is said to have *single call* activation when one copy of that object is activated for each client request. If four client objects simultaneously make the same request for the same server-side object, four instances of that object will be created to handle those four calls. One single call from a client results in a new, matching server-side object being created. The single call object's lifetime is only long enough to satisfy the client object's single call.

If the client makes a second call to the server object, an entirely new instance of the server-side object will be created to handle the call. With the garbage collector deciding when to remove object instances from memory in .NET, it is possible for a single call object to still be in the server's memory when the second call from the same client object comes through. Despite the fact that the previous server object instance is still alive in memory, a single call object will create a brand new instance to respond to the new client request.

Singleton

When a server object uses *singleton* activation, only one instance of that object will be active on the server. If those same four client objects I used as an example in the "Single Call" section make a call to a singleton server-side object, one and only one object will be created to service all four requesting client objects. On the first client call, the server will create a single instance of the singleton server object. As long as the one singleton object is loaded into memory, all additional object calls will be connected to this active object.

A singleton object has a limited lifetime, and when it expires, the current instance of the object is destroyed, requiring that the server create a new instance for the next client call. For this reason, your client object might make multiple server object calls that use the same instance of the singleton object, and then make yet another call and suddenly encounter a brand new instance of the object.

If the life of a singleton object seems random and impersonal, brace yourself because it gets sadder. Each singleton object gets a lifetime lease that dictates what that object's life span will be. Some singletons can live longer, whereas others may have very short life spans, but when their lifetime lease is up, they're gone. In fact, this lease on life is so strict that even if a client object is using that poor singleton object at the moment its lease runs out, it is still destroyed (and replaced with a younger version of itself). Despite the cruel fate of a singleton object, using it is a very efficient way of making your server object available because it avoids draining server resources with multiple object instances. You will find more information on setting up singleton object lifetime leases in the Immediate Solutions section.

Client Activated Objects

The activation, lifetime, and deactivation of both the single call and singleton objects are controlled by the server that hosts these objects. Working with single call and singleton objects requires a little more thought than dealing with local objects that your application directly activates and deactivates. With *client activated objects* (CAO), your client objects can have the same direct influence on your Remoting objects as you have on your local objects. Like single call objects, the server creates a brand new instance of the server object for each client calling it through CAO. Each instance of the server object created holds a direct reference to the calling client, and its lifetime is controlled by that client object.

When you look at a CAO's lifetime, you will find a lifetime lease similar to the singleton object's. The big difference with the CAO's lifetime lease is that the client defines and controls this lease, not the server object. In the "Creating a Client Activated Object and Determining Its Lifetime" Immediate Solution, you will find an example of how a client can use CAO to create an instance of a server object and control that object's life span.

Stateless versus Stateful Objects

A stateless object does not maintain state from one call to the next. Every time you call out to a stateless object, it is like talking to a stranger who does not remember you or anything about your last call. Because the single call activation method connects the client object to a brand new instance of the server object every time, this is a stateless form of Remoting. The singleton activation method continues to connect client calls to the same instance of a server object until that object's lifetime expires. This means that the singleton object can remember pieces of information from one call to the next. The CAO is also a stateful communications method because the same instance of the server object stays active until the client object decides to release it.

Comparing Remoting to DCOM

As your development teams begin to develop their distributed application projects using Visual Studio .NET, they will have to decide whether to continue to use DCOM or step up to the new Remoting model. Remoting offers numerous improvements over DCOM that should be considered when making this decision:

- Remoting can communicate using the open source technologies of SOAP and HTTP instead of DCOM's proprietary protocol.

- .NET objects using Remoting can call and be called by objects created in non-Visual Studio development tools.
- Remoting calls made via HTTP can pass through most corporate firewalls that would normally block DCOM calls.
- Remoting, although still somewhat complicated, is arguably easier to configure and use when compared to DCOM.

For developing managed objects that communicate with each other remotely, using .NET's Remoting technology is the clear choice. But what can you do to remotely communicate with unmanaged COM objects from your .NET assemblies? You still have the option of using DCOM within the .NET environment, which you will read more about in the "Using DCOM in .NET" section.

***TIP:** Because .NET supports COM objects, you can still use DCOM from your .NET assemblies to remotely access COM objects. If you are making remote calls from one .NET assembly to another, you should use .NET's Remoting and not DCOM to do so.*

Comparing Remoting to XML Web Services

As you read about how Remoting uses open source protocols and allows you to call out to objects distributed beyond the traditional reach of the corporate intranet, you might think that Remoting sounds a lot like the new .NET XML Web services project type. Both can use HTTP and SOAP to communicate globally using the Internet as their communications medium of choice. But there are a couple key differences between these two technologies that will influence whether you develop an object as a Remoting object or as an XML Web service.

An XML Web service must be hosted by a Web server, whereas a Remoting object does not require a special server to host it, only that the common language runtime (CLR) is installed on the hosting server. XML Web services operate in the connectionless and stateless world of the Internet. Each request made to an XML Web service creates a new instance of that service on the Web server. Data cannot be shared among multiple visitors to a single XML Web service without the use of a back-end database or some form of data persistence to pass the data around. A Remoting object, on the other hand, can be made to service multiple clients and can share data between callers without any additional back-end infrastructure. To learn more about creating and using XML Web services, see Chapter 8.

Remoting and Tiered Application Designs

The ability to remotely call server objects allows you to really spread out your application's components. You can place a datacentric server object directly on the machine hosting your database and call it from a separate Web or application server. The data services tier is an excellent candidate for Remoting server objects. Any time your application accesses a remote resource, such as a file system or a nontraditional data store, consider using a Remoting server object to make this available. Moving your resource access codes to their own servers helps offload some of the processing from an application server or from the client's machine.

There is a price to be paid when using any form of Remoting. Whenever the network becomes involved in an application's communication functions, the remote object's response time will not be as quick as if that object were on the same machine as the calling object. For this reason, distributing application objects should only enter into the plan if the performance gains realized by the additional machine's processing power outweigh the network slow downs experienced by your objects. Objects that perform the bulk of your application's work should be co-located on one server to minimize Remoting calls across the network.

Channels

When a client and a server object connect, they create a communications channel between them. DCOM also creates a channel between objects and uses a proprietary protocol to exchange messages between the two objects. .NET Remoting has the ability to create and use two different channel types for your client and server objects: the Tcp channel and the Http channel. The Tcp channel is very similar to Remoting's proprietary DCOM predecessor. The Http channel fits in with .NET's open source recurring theme. Which channel you use depends on what your communication goal is. Let's review the two most common .NET Remoting channel types and discuss when you should use a particular type of channel.

The Tcp Channel

Similar to DCOM's proprietary transmission method, Remoting's Tcp channel sends the data back and forth between the client and server objects using a proprietary binary format. The objects on both ends of a Tcp channel must be able to understand this binary formatted message, which means you should only plan to use the Tcp channel to communicate from one .NET object to another.

The Tcp channel is a two-way street, which means your objects can send and receive data through this channel. Unfortunately, aside from the fact that the messages being exchanged through a Tcp channel are binary encoded, you cannot encrypt your Tcp channel communications. Despite this limitation, when compared to the Http channel, the Tcp channel is the quickest and most efficient Remoting channel you can use.

The Http Channel

SOAP is a tool that allows applications to send their object-to-object calls across the Internet using the HTTP transmission protocol. HTTP calls traditionally go through the computer's port 80, which is the same port used for standard Web browser requests and responses. Because SOAP allows you to send your object requests through this universally acceptable port, your calls are able to pass through most firewalls unhindered. This ability to pass through firewalls gives the Http channel a longer reach than the more restrictive Tcp channel and the older DCOM method. Like the Tcp channel, the Http channel allows message traffic to move in both directions.

SOAP is based on the XML technology, which means the message and its enclosing envelope are self-describing and can be read and created by any application. Because of this openness, client and server objects involved in a Remoting scenario using the Http channel do not both have to be created in .NET. As you read in the Tcp channel description, you do not have this kind of freedom when connecting objects through the Tcp channel because an object using this channel must be able to understand its proprietary binary message format. Because of the Http channel's XML text formatting and the fact that it uses the popular and sometimes busy port 80, the Http channel is a little less efficient than its Tcp channel cousin.

Sinks

A communications *sink chain* is the entry and exit point that messages use when entering and leaving a particular application domain. Within the sink chain are multiple sinks, each with their own function. One sink handles the formatting of the message to prepare it for transmission, whereas another sink handles the task of transmitting that formatted message across the network. On the receiving end, another sink receives the message from the network and passes that message to yet another sink that decodes the message's format and hands the original message to the receiving application domain. This process might sound very familiar to anyone with an understanding of the seven network layers and how they work to format and transmit application data across a network.

Figure 13.2 shows a client and a server object, each enclosed in their own application domain. The client object in this example sends a request to a function encased in the server object. You can see by looking at this figure how the original message is passed from one sink to another in the client's application domain until the message reaches the network. On the server's end of the network, the message goes through a similar process in reverse until the original message is presented to the server object.

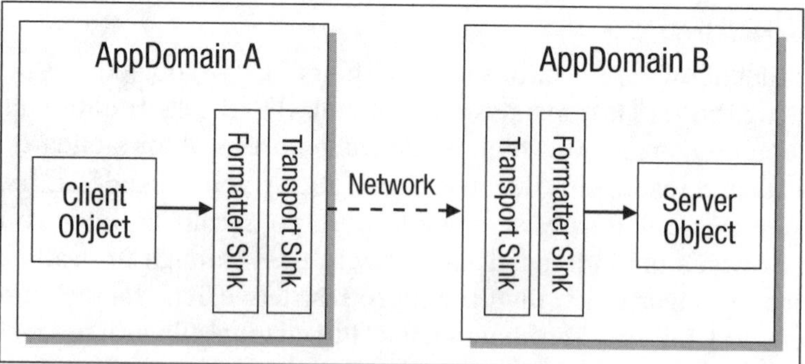

Figure 13.2 Remoting and communication sinks.

Ports

Communications passing into and out of a computer go through a port. When your Web browser requests a Web page from a remote Web server, this call normally goes through port 80, and the Web server listens for your request on its port 80. Other Internet utilities such as Telnet and FTP use their own ports to send data out to the world. DCOM uses many different ports to communicate, and which port it uses is out of your control. You have to rely on DCOM to decide which port to choose. The downside of this is that most firewalls block the ports that DCOM uses to communicate.

In .NET Remoting, you have the ability to define which port your channel will use to communicate. By default, the Http channel uses port 80 to send out your requests mixed in with the Web traffic, which almost ensures that your calls will not be blocked by any firewalls lying between your client and server objects. You can opt to use another port to send your calls through, although you will need to examine the network layout between your client and server objects to ensure that this port is not blocked along the way, which will cause your object calls to fail. You can even change ports with the Http channel, which enables you to send messages using the HTTP protocol and SOAP message across any port in the same way you would use port 80.

When choosing a port to use, be careful not to use a port that is already in use. You should not use a customized port number under 1000 because most of these numbers are reserved for server-specific uses. One example of defining a new port is a machine that houses more than one instance of a Web server. The first Web server will use the standard port 80, whereas other instances of the Web server will define other ports to listen to. Port 8088 is a popular port on which to set up a new Web server instance.

If you are using a Windows NT/2000/XP system, you can view your machine's port configuration by using the Notepad program to look at the Services file located in

C:\Windows\System32\Drivers\Etc. This file lists the ports your computer has defined as being in use and which communication protocol is using them. You should find the HTTP protocol pointing to port 80 in this configuration file.

Registering a Channel

Before a client and server object can communicate across a channel, that channel must first be configured and registered with the server. The client object will register a channel on the calling machine, and the server object will have a channel registered to listen for client requests on. Because a server object can have multiple listening channels configured, the developer of the client object must know what type of channel is being used in order to configure and register the client's channel appropriately.

Channels can either be created on the fly within your application's code, or you can use a predefined channel using a *channel template* or configuration files. Channel templates are external configuration files that can be loaded into an application at startup and save you a great deal of coding effort. You will see examples of both of these methods in the Immediate Solutions section. You'll learn how to create client and server objects that register their own channels directly from their source code. You'll also see an example of how you can create a channel registration template and use it from your application's code.

Remoting Communications

Now that you have an understanding of how Remoting uses channels to send messages back and forth between the client and the server objects, it is time to take an in-depth look at the messages themselves. I'll examine how your client's call is formatted and how the parameters that are passed over to the server object are marshaled. You will learn about the role that the formatter sink plays in the Remoting process and how your client-side objects work with proxy versions of the server-side object.

Remoting Messages

Data is sent back and forth across the communications channel inside of a Remoting message. During its trip, this message can be transformed and modified in many ways. The initial message is generated by a routine that calls out to the remote server object. This remote procedure call can include parameters to pass along information needed by the server object to perform its duties. The message passes through both the client's and the server's sink chain, and the format of the message is altered to prepare it for transmission on the client's end, which extracts the original message on the server's end. Additional information can be added to the message during transmission through the message's **CallContext**.

Messages created in .NET Remoting implement the IMessage interface, which in essence is a dictionary object containing the data and properties of that message. You will find the IMessage interface in the .NET Framework under the **System.Runtime.Remoting.Messaging** namespace. Remember that the message is the client's request and its associated parameters. This message is sent from one object to another across a channel, and the message's format is modified by one or more sinks. Next, let's take a look at how parameters are marshaled in a Remoting call.

Marshaling Data in Remoting

When making method calls to local objects, you have the choice of passing your data **ByRef** (by reference) or **ByVal** (by value). The **ByRef** option keeps a copy of the data at the source location and only passes a reference pointer to the receiving procedure to tell it where the data it needs is located. The **ByVal** option makes a copy of the data and passes that copy over to the receiving object. **ByVal** gives the receiving object its own copy of data, so if any changes are made to it, the original data is not affected. Although **ByVal** does provide protection for your original data values, there is a performance cost to be paid for passing actual data values back and forth between objects as opposed to the slim and efficient pointers passed in the **ByRef** method.

In Remoting, the server object resides in a separate application domain, often on a separate machine. Any **ByRef** pointers passed would not be understood because the data would remain back in its native application domain, out of reach from the server object. A class's default method is to serialize itself, which means an exact copy of your data is sent to the server object for processing. For Remoting purposes, objects that serialize themselves cannot be used in Remoting and are said to be nonremotable. In order to properly exchange data between Remoting objects, you need a **ByRef** marshaling method that can travel between two different application domains.

You can bypass the class's natural tendency to serialize itself through the use of inheritance. The **System.MarshalByRefObject** base class does not serialize itself, but instead maintains the copy of the object within that object's own application domain. The following example shows a class that inherits from the **System.MarshalByRefObject** base class to use this functionality:

```
Public Class Utilities
    Inherits System.MarshalByRefObject
    'Class source code goes here
End Class
```

Like the **ByRef** data marshaling method, the object that is inherited from the **MarshalByRefObject** base class will maintain a copy of the data within the object's application domain and pass a simple reference to that copy to the remote object. The .NET Framework and the CLR will recognize a **MarshalByRefObject** situation and use that reference pointer to make calls back to the client's application domain to examine and access the marshaled object.

You may see marshaling by reference abbreviated as MBR, as in "I am using an MBR object in my Remoting application." Using a **MarshalByRefObject** can greatly decrease the network traffic that occurs between your client and server objects. Because only a simple pointer to the original object instance is passed in lieu of the entire object itself, **MarshalByRefObject** is without a doubt the most efficient way to marshal data in Remoting.

TIP: *When designing your application's base classes for use in inheritance, if the base class you design inherits from the* ***System.MarshalByRefObject*** *base class, any classes derived from your base class will also use* ***MarshalByRefObject****.*

Formatters

The formatter sink is responsible for serializing your client object's message and applying any channel-specific formatting to that message. If you are using the Tcp channel, the formatting sink turns your message into a binary file. The formatter sink for the Http channel places your message into a SOAP envelope to prepare it for transmission. The formatter is only responsible for transforming your message to a format suitable for transmission.

Thanks to formatter sinks, your code does not have to deal with the complexity of serializing and formatting messages to comply with specific channel formats. The formatter sink uses one of two classes to do its work. If your objects are using a Tcp channel to communicate with, the formatter uses the **Binary.BinaryFormatter** class of the **System.Runtime.Serialization.Formatters** namespace. If you are using the Http channel with your objects, the formatter is derived from the **Soap.SoapFormatter** class.

NOTE: *You will need to add a reference to the* ***System.Runtime.Serialization.Formatters.Soap*** *base class to reference the* ***Soap.SoapFormatter*** *in your source code.*

Proxies in Remoting

When your .NET routines call out to a remote function, they do so through the use of a local version of that function, which is known as a *proxy*. A proxy is a hollow ghost image of the object located on the remote server, which appears locally to the calling function. It is the proxy's job to reroute that function call to the remote object, and then receive that object's response and present the results to the caller. Chapter 8 covers proxies within the discussion of XML Web services.

In Remoting, there are two levels of proxies. The top-level proxy that the calling client object deals with is known as a **TransparentProxy**. As the name implies, this is a very thin, see-through proxy class that acts as the intermediary to **RealProxy** class. It should come as no surprise that all of the real proxy work is done in the **RealProxy** class. The **TransparentProxy** handles all of the client object interaction and basic data packaging, whereas the **RealProxy** class handles the bulk of the work, including communications with the server object. You can see where the **TransparentProxy** and **RealProxy** fit in the communications between the client and server objects by looking at Figure 13.3. Developers wanting to enhance the role of the Remoting proxy object can extend and customize the **TransparentProxy** class.

Call Context

The *call context* is a package of information that is sent along with your object's message. Your application can make configuration settings that are stored in the call context and read by communication sinks along the way. Those sinks can also make entries into the call context to pass informational data along with the message. Remoting creates an object named **CallContext** to give your code access to this data. This object's two main methods are **SetData** and **GetData**, which provide write-to and read-from access to the data stored within the **CallContext**. You will see a couple of examples of the **CallContext** object's use scattered throughout the Immediate Solutions section of this chapter. Here is an example of some code that writes an informational message to the **CallContext** object, and then immediately reads it back out again:

```
Dim MyObject As New Object()
CallContext.SetData("UserObject", MyObject)
```

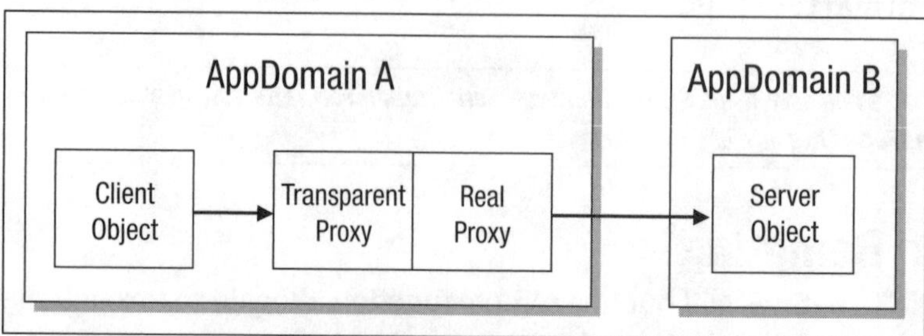

Figure 13.3 Proxy classes in a Remoting client-server session.

The **CallContext** object can be found in the **System.Runtime.Remoting.Messaging** namespace. You can use its **SetData** method to attach an object to the message traveling across the channel between the client and the server. This message can be added at any level of the communications chain and can be added to both the incoming and outgoing messages. The first parameter of the **SetData** method is the name you reference your stored object by. The second parameter must be an object. To read data added to a message using the **SetData** method, you use the **GetData** method like this:

```
Dim ReadObject As New Object()
ReadObject = CallContext.GetData ("UserObject")
```

The **GetData** method takes only the reference name as its single parameter and provides as its output the object stored under that reference tag. Use the **CallContext** object to attach special notes and handling instructions to your Remoting messages. These attachments can include additional parameters or client information. Obviously, attaching a **CallContext** that either the client or the server object is not aware of is futile, so you might only elect to use the **CallContext** when your development team is working on both objects involved in the Remoting session.

SOAP in Remoting

With SOAP, you can wrap a message or object call in an XML-based envelope that enables you to send this message using the HTTP protocol. You will learn a great deal more about SOAP in Chapter 14. SOAP is the technology that makes XML Web services possible, and it also plays a crucial role in .NET Remoting as well. A primary advantage of using SOAP messaging across the Internet using the HTTP protocol is that you use a widely understandable and universally accepted network protocol and message format. SOAP, XML, and HTTP are not Microsoft controlled technologies, and any developer, no matter which tool they prefer working with, is free to use these technologies in their applications.

Another advantage of using SOAP messaging in Remoting is that SOAP makes it possible for anyone to read your messages, which is not true of the DCOM and Tcp channel methods of Remoting. SOAP is self-describing, so the receiver of your message does not have to have preexisting knowledge of that message's format, nor do they have to perform any secret handshakes or use a proprietary communications protocol to receive those messages. SOAP opens up a whole new world of possibilities in the subject of remote procedural calls. In the next few years, SOAP over HTTP will probably become the universal standard for all development languages to follow.

Remoting Servers

When discussing client and server Remoting objects, it makes sense to start by describing the server object because without a server object, the client object cannot participate in any Remoting activities. Server objects are also a little bit harder to create than their partner client objects, so once you get the gist of how the server object is created, the rest of Remoting comes easy.

A server object is not part of the client object's application, even though the client object calls out to the server object for help. The server object lives in its own application domain, typically on a different machine than the client object. Your development team might have a hand in developing the server object, or your application might be calling on a server object from an outside source (also known as "black boxes" because you have no idea what's going on inside of these objects). In many circumstances, the server object will not be running when the client object makes its call to it, so the object will need to be initialized and connected to the Remoting channel. Because server objects can be very complicated, a great deal of planning needs to go into their development and configuration. This section discusses how you should design and configure the server objects you create.

Developing Remoting Servers

Developing a Remoting server requires that you address many different issues in addition to your normal object development planning issues. You have to consider your server object's use of resources and estimate the number of concurrent client objects that will use your server object. A server object can present a significant drain on a machine's resources, so careful planning of that object's activation and lifetime settings is critical. The following questions should be answered when you are planning a Remoting server object:

- Should my server object be available to the outside world or is it a nonremotable object?
- What type of activation should I use with my server object?
- Will my server object be stateless or stateful?
- What is the life span of my object?
- Should I use the Http or Tcp channel?
- What type of formatter should I use?
- Is my object's configuration reusable, and if so, should I place it in an external configuration file?
- How should I manage the versioning of my server object?

Next, you will learn about configuring your server objects and implement the answers to the preceding questions in the actual design and development of your server objects. Following the configuration section, you will learn about how server objects are versioned.

Host Applications

A server object must actively listen for requests from client objects. Server objects will typically be created within class Library projects, which by themselves are not capable of staying active and listening to a port on the host machine. In Microsoft Transaction Server (MTS) and COM+, you had the ability to register your class Libraries inside an MTS package that would handle the listening chores for you. For a .NET server object, you need to create an application that acts as the listener and agent for your server object. This application will be loaded on the host server and will remain active to monitor the registered channels. If the server object's hosting application closes, the server object will not be accessible to its clients.

You could host a server object from many different types of applications, including Windows Services or a Console project. You could even host a service from a Windows Application project as long as that hosting application stays loaded to do its job. In most cases, making your hosting application a Windows Service that loads when the server boots up is the best solution. Windows Services are closely tied to the operating system; they can automatically start at server boot, and they can operate behind the scenes without any forms or windows being opened on the desktop.

When the host application starts, it registers the channel and the server object with the .NET Framework. Once the server object is initialized, the host application listens for client requests on the registered channel. When a request is received, the host application loads the server object into its application domain and passes the client's call to the service. In Figure 13.4, you see a host applica-

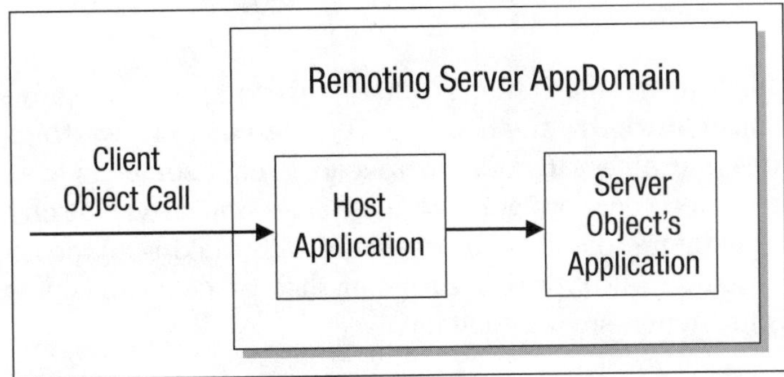

Figure 13.4 The host and the server object applications.

tion and a class Library project containing a server object. Both applications run in the same application process.

Remember, it is the host application that registers the channel and configures the Remoting environment, either programmatically or through the use of an external configuration file. The class Library containing the actual server object can remain dormant and quiet until called upon by a client. If the class containing the server object is not contained within the host application, that application will need a reference to the class so it can load it when needed. When the server object is called upon, it will be loaded into the host application's application domain and processed.

Remoting Server Configuration

As you might have guessed from reading about all the details involved in setting up a Remoting object (types of channels, registering channels, sinks, etc.), configuring your Remoting objects will take a little bit of time and knowledge. Luckily, once you have one object configured correctly, future object configuration tasks will seem pretty simple. In fact, one proven Remoting configuration file can be reused again and again, either through the reuse of a single configuration file or through the tried and trusted method of copying and pasting. In this section, I discuss how you can load a server object configuration file and how to create that configuration file.

Loading a Configuration

You can store your server object's configuration settings in a text-based file and read those settings into the server when the object is initialized. Within the **System.Runtime.Remoting** namespace is a class named **RemotingConfiguration**. You can use this class's **Configure** method to read in the text configuration file and initialize your class. Here is an example of a **Sub New()** that does this:

```
Public Sub New()
    RemotingConfiguration.Configure("remoteserver.cfg")
End Sub
```

Because reading a file from the file system is inherently error prone, I highly suggest you surround this **Configure** method in a **Try**, **Catch**, **Finally** structure. This will allow your server object to continue to load, even if someone has mistakenly deleted or renamed your configuration file. Server objects can be created without the aid of a configuration file by programmatically making all the necessary settings. Next, you'll see the type of information that can go into a configuration file and why using them is such a good idea.

The Configuration File

If you choose to configure your Remoting object through the use of an external configuration file, you will use a set XML schema to create this file and make your settings. The advantage of using an external configuration file is that this one file can be reused by more than one channel-creating function and even by multiple projects. The little bit of time spent configuring a channel through an external file will save you a lot of time later on—time you would otherwise spend typing out code to configure your channels programmatically.

Visual Studio .NET Remoting understands a specific schema of XML tags to configure your objects. Table 13.1 lists these tags and provides a description of their usage. The following example shows what a configuration file might look like for a Remoting server object:

```
<configuration>
   <system.runtime.remoting>
      <application>
         <service>
            <wellknown mode="SingleCall" objectUri="MyServer"_
              type="Class1, Class1"/>
         </service>
         <channels>
            <channel ref="http"/>
         </channels>
      </application>
   </system.runtime.remoting>
</configuration>
```

In this configuration file, you see that the server object is configured to be a “wellknown” object using single call activation. The server object’s name is **MyServer**, which is the name that the client objects will use to reference it. The **MyServer** object creates an Http channel that uses binary formatting to prepare its messages.

Table 13.1 Remoting configuration file schema tags.

Tag Name	Description
<configuration>	The open tag for the configuration file.
<system.runtime.remoting>	The namespace under which Remoting falls.
<application>	Entries contained within this tag all belong to a single application.
<service>	Contains the server object configuration tags.
<channels>	The parent tag of the channel configuration section.

(continued)

Table 13.1 Remoting configuration file schema tags *(continued)*.

Tag Name	Description
<channel>	Specific information to configure the channel, such as an Http or Tcp channel type.
<clientProviders>	Parent tag for the client object's channel sink configuration information; client only.
<serverProviders>	Configures the server object's channel sink; server only.
<client>	Encloses the client channel configuration tags.
<formatter>	Configures the formatter the channel uses to format its messages.
<wellknown>	Declares the server object instance that this client object will use.
<lifetime>	Can be used to configure the object's activation lifetime.
<activated>	Used to configure client activated objects (CAO); client only.

Programmatic Configuration

Using the **RemotingConfiguration** class in the **System.Runtime.Remoting** namespace, you can configure your client or server object and register it directly from your source code without calling out to an external configuration file. The first step in configuring an object for Remoting is to establish a channel, either Tcp or Http. You create a new instance of the **TcpChannel** or **HttpChannel** class and assign a port number to it. The next step is to register this channel instance with the .NET Framework. Once the channel is established, you can register your object to use this channel. In the following example, I establish a channel and register a server object named **MyServer** to respond to Tcp calls coming in on port 8881:

```
'Configure the channel
Dim MyChannel As New TcpChannel(8881)

'Register the channel
ChannelServices.RegisterChannel(MyChannel)

'Register your service as a WellKnownServiceType
RemotingConfiguration.RegisterWellKnownServiceType(Type.GetType(_
    "MyClass"), "MyServer", WellKnownObjectMode.SingleCall)
```

The process of registering your server object occurs during the application's startup phase. The application is started on the host machine, and the configuration code sets up the communication channel and registers the server object with the host, making it available to the outside world. In my example, the object I am making available is a class called **MyClass**. The URI that the outside world will use to reference this object is **MyServer**. During registration, you declare what type of activation you will be using. In my configuration example, the **MyServer** object is registered to use single call activation.

Registering a Server Object

When you register a server object with the .NET Framework, you are making that object available to client objects through Remoting and you are declaring that object's URI and activation type. You use the **RegisterWellKnownServiceType** method of the **RemotingConfiguration** class to register a server object for use. This method accepts the following parameters:

- The type of object you are registering
- The URI that clients will use to identify that object
- The activation mode the server will use to activate the object

In my programmatic configuration example, the object I am making available is a class called **MyClass**, which is available inside the same application domain as my registering code. The URI that the outside world will use to reference this object is **MyServer**. During registration, you declare what type of activation you will be using. In my configuration example, the **MyServer** object is registered to use single call activation.

Versioning

Yet another advantage that Remoting holds over DCOM and other methods of making remote object calls is that Remoting takes advantage of .NET's assembly-versioning feature. Before, with DCOM, your client objects would be built to call upon a single instance of a server object on a remote server. If that server object's creator developed an upgraded version of that component that changed something about that object's interface, there was a good possibility that your client object would encounter an exception when calling the upgraded server object. This problem is one of many symptoms of a common problem known as "DLL Hell." COM developers could also cause problems for client objects by recompiling DLLs and generating a new Globally Unique Identifier (GUID), which is the unique identifying ID number that a COM object uses to call out to another COM object.

With non-Remoting objects in .NET, every time you recompile an assembly, a brand new instance of that assembly is created. Your machine can have many instances of the same assembly, each with its own unique address. When a client object is compiled with a reference to another object, it references that object's exact version ID, so even though a developer changes and recompiles that object, the version that the client object references remains unchanged, and the client object continues to work.

In Remoting, clients can reference server objects by their unique ID, which is also known as a *strong name*. If the client controls the activation of the server object, as in a CAO activation, the client's configuration settings will decide which version of the server object is used. If the server object is activated by the server, as in single call and singleton objects, the server object's configuration setting decides the version that will be used. Specifying a version number for a server object is not required, and if no version number is given, the server object uses the latest version of the assembly to create its object. The configuration settings used in a client and server configuration setting file was covered in the previous section "The Configuration File."

Remoting Clients

The client object is the customer in a client-server transaction. A client does not have any control over how a server object works or how it does its job. It only has the ability to ask for something and hopefully get the results it expects. In order to use a server object, the client object must have an understanding of the server object's interfaces and how the server object communicates with the outside world. Obtaining either the server object's source code or a detailed description of its interfaces and channel configuration is a crucial first step to using that object. Of course, if your development team created the server object, this information is easy to obtain. But if you are working with a third-party object, a little more work may be involved.

When a client object needs to work with a server object, that client object needs to configure a communication channel for use in its call. If the server object is using singleton or single call activation, the client object does not have to control that server object's lifespan. If the server object allows for CAO, the client will have some additional configuration to make in order to control the lifetime of the server object. In this section, I cover client object configuration issues and discuss how to make calls to server objects.

Calling a Remoting Server

From the client object's perspective, there are two ways of calling a server object: using remote server-side activation and using client-side activation. There is no difference between singleton and single call server objects from the client object's point of view. In the next two sections, I discuss the two ways that client objects can call on remote server objects and explain how this can work using both external client object configuration files and programmatic configuration commands.

Remote Server Object Activation

If the server object only allows server-side activation, as in singleton and single call objects, the client object's job is quite easy. The server object is referred to as a "wellknown" object because on the server object's host machine, that service has been registered and therefore is known publicly. In a client object using an external configuration file, you will see a **<wellknown>** tag that sets up the reference to the server object. Here is an example of a **<wellknown>** tag pointing to a server named **RemoteServer** listening on port 8881. The server object's URI name is **MyServer**. The **MyServer** object is said to be of type **Class1** in this example:

```
<wellknown url="tcp://remoteserver:8881/MyServer" type="Class1,_
      Class1" />
```

After this configuration file has been loaded using the **RemotingConfiguration. Configure** method, the client object's code will be able to create a local proxy class instance of the **MyServer** object through its type, **Class1**. To programmatically register a server object that uses server-side activation, use the **RegisterWellKnownClientType** like this:

```
RemotingConfiguration.RegisterWellKnownClientType(GetType(RemotingServer._
     Class1), "tcp://remoteserver:8881/MyServer")
```

This line of source code registers the **Class1** object hosted on the remote server machine. The server object uses a Tcp channel listening at port 8881. The server object was registered with its host server using the URI name of **MyServer**.

Client Activated Objects

If the client object needs to control the server object's activation and lifetime, it can do so through CAO if the server object allows it. When the server object configures itself, it can specify that CAO is allowed. Take a look at the following configuration file:

```
<configuration>
   <system.runtime.remoting>
      <application>
         <lifetime
            leaseTime="5S" sponsorshipTimeout="5S" renewOnCallTime="25S"_
               leaseManagerPollTime="30S" />
         <service>
            <wellknown type="MyServerType, RemoteType" objectUri=_
               "MyServer" mode="Singleton" />
            <activated type="MyClientType, RemoteType" />
         </service>
         <channels>
            <channel port="8881" ref="http" />
         </channels>
      </application>
   </system.runtime.remoting>
</configuration>
```

The server object configured by this file listens to the Http channel defined at port 8881 using the **<wellknown>** tag. The server object also allows client objects to activate and control it through CAO. The **<activated>** tag lets the hosting machine know that this server object allows client-side activation.

If a client opts to use client-side activation instead of the provided server-side activation channel, the client object will modify its configuration settings. If your client object uses an external configuration file, use the **<activated>** tag to configure this. Here is an example of a CAO client object configuration file:

```
<configuration>
   <system.runtime.remoting>
      <application>
         <client url="http://remoteserver:8883">
            <activated type="MyClientType, RemoteType" />
         </client>
         <channels>
            <channel ref="http" port="0" />
         </channels>
      </application>
   </system.runtime.remoting>
</configuration>
```

In the **<client>** tag, you see a URL pointing to port 8883 on the remote server. The **<activated>** tag names the URI defined for CAO activation by the server object, **MyClientType** (seen previously in the **<activated>** tag in the server object's configuration file). To programmatically configure a client object to activate and control a server object, you use the **Activator** object.

The Activator

The **Activator** is a class found directly under the **System** namespace that you could use to create instances of both local and remote objects. Table 13.2 lists the four methods found within the **Activator** class. Because this chapter is only concerned with Remoting, I will focus on the **GetObject** method.

Table 13.2 Methods of the Activator class.

Method	Description
CreateComInstanceFrom	Allows you to create a COM object instance from an assembly instance
CreateInstance	Creates an instance of an assembly
CreateInstanceFrom	Creates a new assembly instance from an already running instance of that assembly
GetObject	Used to create proxy classes that represent remote objects and XML Web services

Client objects use the **Activator.GetObject** method to create a local proxy instance of the remotely located server object. Here is an example of using the **GetObject** method to set up a local instance of the object named **MyObject**:

```
'Declare a new Http channel for the client
Dim MyChannel As Http.HttpChannel
MyChannel = New Http.HttpChannel(8881)

'Register the Http channel
ChannelServices.RegisterChannel(MyChannel)

'Dim a variable for the remote server object
Dim MyObject As MyClientType

'Use Activator to get a local proxy instance of this object
MyObject = CType(Activator.GetObject(Type.GetType("MyClientType, object"),_
      "http://remoteserver:8883/MyServer"), MyClientType)
```

The server object's URI is **MyServer**; it is hosted on a machine named remoteserver listening to port 8883. The server object's type is **MyClientType**. I start out by declaring an Http channel for the client object and registering this with the machine. Next, I **Dim** an object to be of type **MyClientType**. In addition, I use the **Activator.GetObject** to get a local proxy instance of the remote server object specified.

Client Configuration Files

Like server objects, a client object can be configured programmatically through its source code or through the use of an external configuration file. You will again use the **RemotingConfiguration.Configure** method to load the XML configuration file into your client object. The **Configure** method reads in the file settings and use those settings to configure your client object's channels and formatters for use with the remote server object. Here is an example of a client object's external configuration file:

```
<configuration>
   <system.runtime.remoting>
      <application>
         <channels>
            <channel ref="http">
               <clientProviders>
                  <formatter ref="binary" />
               </clientProviders>
            </channel>
         </channels>
```

```
      <client>
         <wellknown url="http://remoteserver:8881/MyServer"_
            type=" Class1, Class1" />
      </client>
    </application>
  </system.runtime.remoting>
</configuration>
```

This configuration file sets up an Http channel using a binary formatter. The client calls out to a **<wellknown>** server object located on remoteserver, which is accessible through port 8881. The client in this example relies on the server to activate the object, using either single call or singleton activation.

Remoting Security

Making an object available to other objects outside of its parent application domain can raise a lot of security issues during the server object's design phase. You might not want everyone to have access to your server object, or you might be concerned about exchanging messages that can be intercepted and read by a third-party not involved in the client-to-server object transaction. The two main areas of security you need to be concerned about with Remoting are object-level security and communications security.

Communications Security

As messages travel back and forth between the client and the server object, there is a possibility that these messages can be intercepted and read, even without your application being aware of it. If your client and server objects are inside a corporate firewall, the threat of exposure to unauthorized personnel is pretty slim, but if your object communicates over a great distance or uses the Internet to exchange messages, that threat is very real. The Tcp channel, although more efficient than Http, does not have any built-in methods of encrypting and protecting its messages. For this reason, you should only opt to use Tcp when your application resides within a secure corporate networking environment.

If your client and server objects use the Internet to communicate, you should strongly consider using an Http channel to connect them. If you host your server objects on an Internet Information Server (IIS) and use Http as its channel, you can take advantage of IIS's encryption and authentication technologies to protect your messages. Secure Socket Layers (SSL) allows a server and a client to authenticate each other through the use of certificates, and then creates a secure pipeline between them that uses encryption to protect the exchanged data from being read. The IIS Web server is also capable of authenticating requests from a client against NT login accounts using NT LAN Manager (NTLM). If the requester does not provide a username and password that the Web server recognizes, the request is denied.

Object Security

The objects you create in .NET can use code access security to control who can use your objects and what actions those objects can perform on behalf of that user. You can perform code access checks within any .NET object, including your Remoting server objects. Using the new security features in the .NET Framework, you can permit or deny certain actions within your code. This explicit control on an object's powers helps prevent malicious use by unauthorized client objects. You can read more about .NET's security features in Chapter 7.

Immediate Solutions

Creating a Remoting Server

It is the Remoting server object's job to wait for calls from client objects, and then service those calls as needed. Creating a server object involves creating the object itself and creating a host to administer and execute your object on the client's behalf. You must configure the host application with all of the necessary Remoting information, such as channel type and port number, and the host application will then use this setup whenever it is run. When the host application closes down, so too does the listening channel; therefore, it is important to create a host application that remains running. Console applications and Windows Services are good choices for server object host applications.

To create a host application and a server object, follow these steps:

1. Add a reference to the **System.Runtime.Remoting** namespace.
2. Add **Imports System.Runtime.Remoting** to the top of your host application's class file.
3. In the host application's startup function (the **Main()** or **New()** subroutine), configure your Remoting server object programmatically or by using an external configuration file.
4. Inherit your server object's class from the **MarshalByReferenceObject** base class.

In the following example, I create a Console application project to act as the host for my server object. Next, I create a class Library project named Utilities, inherit this class from the **MarshalByRefObject** base class, and give it one method named **CalcSalesTax**. This portion of my server object is self-explanatory, and creating classes and methods can be understood by any object-oriented developer. The hosting application will be started on the server to register and configure the Remoting channel the server object will respond to.

1. Create a new Visual Basic .NET Console Application project, and call it RemotingServerHost.
2. In the Solution Explorer window, right-click the RemotingServerHost project title, and select Add Reference. On the .NET tab of the Add Reference window, double-click **System.Runtime.Remoting** to add it to the list

at the bottom of this window. Click OK at the bottom of the window to finalize the addition of this reference.

3. Select File|Add Project|New Project.
4. Select the Visual Basic .NET Class Library project, name it RemotingServer, and click Open to add it to your solution.
5. Within the **Class1** class in the file Class1.vb, enter the following source code:

```
Public Class Class1
    Inherits System.MarshalByRefObject

    Public Function CalcSalesTax(ByVal SalesPrice As Double) As Double
        Dim TaxRate As Double = 0.05
        CalcSalesTax = SalesPrice * TaxRate
    End Function
End Class
```

6. In the Solution Explorer window, right-click the host application project, RemotingServerHost, and select Add Reference. Click the Projects tab of the Add Reference window. You should see the RemotingServer project available in the top listbox. Double-click this item, and then click OK to add a reference to this project.
7. In the Solution Explorer window, double-click the Module1.vb item found underneath the RemotingServerHost project. Edit this module to add the following source code:

```
Imports System.Runtime.Remoting
Imports System.Runtime.Remoting.Channels
Imports RemotingServer

Module Module1

    Sub Main()
        'Register and configure the server object and its channel
        RemotingConfiguration.Configure ("C:\RemotingCfg\Server.cfg")

        'Add a delay here to keep the Console Application running
        Console.WriteLine("Press any key to close the
RemotingServerHost")
        Console.ReadLine()
    End Sub

End Module
```

8. Save your Solution by selecting File|Save All.

9. Open a text-editing tool such as Microsoft Window's Notepad. Enter the following server configuration information into the text file:

```
<configuration>
   <system.runtime.remoting>
      <application>
         <service>
            <wellknown mode="SingleCall" objectUri="TaxServer"_
               type="Class1, Class1"/>
         </service>
         <channels>
            <channel ref="tcp"/>
         </channels>
      </application>
   </system.runtime.remoting>
</configuration>
```


10. Select File|Save As. Save this file to c:\RemotingCfg\Server.cfg (you can use the Create New Folder icon on the Save As window to create the RemotingCfg folder). If you choose to save this configuration file elsewhere, be sure to update the **RemotingConfiguration.Configure**'s path to this file in the **Module1** Main subroutine.
11. In Visual Studio .NET, start your application by pressing F5. A console window opens, and after a brief pause, displays the message: "Press any key to close the RemotingServerHost." As long as this window is open, your server object is available to service client requests.
12. Press Enter to end your Console application and terminate your server object.
13. Click the RemotingServer project in the Solution Explorer window, and then select Build|Build Solution. A DLL is created named RemotingServer.dll.
14. Click the RemotingServerHost project in the Solution Explorer, and then build it by selecting Build|Build Solution. An executable file named RemotingServerHost.exe is created in your project's Bin directory.

The host application uses a configuration file loaded during the Console application's **Main()** subroutine to configure the server object's communication channel and register the server object with the .NET Framework. Notice that it is the Console application that loads this configuration file and establishes the Tcp channel to listen on. During your test run, the RemotingServer project is never called and loaded into the application domain. You then need to create a client object to call upon this server object. You will create this client object in the "Creating a Remoting Client Using the Tcp Channel" Immediate Solution.

Let's look at the class Library project that contains the **CalcSalesTax** function that the server object exposes. This class looks like any other class you might create, with no signs of the Remoting namespace. It is the host application that acts as the Remoting agent for the class Library project that performs all of the difficult work. The host application holds a reference to the RemotingServer project as well as the **System.Runtime.Remoting** namespace, whereas the RemotingServer project does not have any such references added to it.

Save this project because you will use this sample project in numerous other Immediate Solutions, such as "Creating a Remoting Client Using the Tcp Channel." Remember that your host application must be running in order to allow your server objects to respond to client object requests.

Programmatically Configuring a Remoting Server

In the "Creating a Remoting Server" Immediate Solution, you created a host application that configures the Remoting server through the use of a text file containing the configuration settings. You can also configure your server programmatically inside your source code. This is useful for specialized, highly customized server configurations; the configuration you create in your Remoting server host will not be reusable.

Instead of loading a configuration file in the host application's **Main()** or **New()** subroutine, you can configure your channel and register your server object like this:

```
Sub Main()
    'Register channel
    Dim MyChannel As New Tcp.TcpChannel(8881)

    'Register MyChannel with server
    ChannelServices.RegisterChannel(MyChannel)

    'Register server object
     RemotingConfiguration.RegisterWellKnownServiceType(GetType_
       (RemotingServer.Class1), "TaxServer", _
       WellKnownObjectMode.SingleCall)

End Sub
```

In this **Sub Main()** routine, a new instance of a **TcpChannel** is created and assigned to port 881. This channel instance is then registered with the server. Then, the routine uses the **RegisterWellKnownServiceType** method to register the server object. The host application project holds a reference to the RemotingServer project, which contains a class named **Class1**. The class is the first parameter in the **RegisterWellKnownServiceType** method. The second parameter is the URI for that service that clients will use to reference it. In my example, I call my server object **TaxServer**. The last parameter tells the server object what type of activation the server will use, which is **SingleCall** in my example. This could also be **Singleton** if the situation calls for this activation method.

Creating a Remoting Client Application

The way a client object uses a remote server object is very similar to how any class instance uses any other class. The big difference in Remoting is that the client object must first configure a Remoting channel to talk to the remote object, and then register that object for the client code to use.

In a non-Remoting scenario, when one class talks to another, the two classes talk directly to each other without any special assistance. In Remoting, the client class talks to a proxy class that forms a local representation of the remotely located server object. This gives the client object the sense that it is talking to a locally located class, even though the proxy class and the Remoting framework are repackaging and communicating the client object's calls to a far off location. Unless you want to extend the proxy class's functionality, its existence and role will virtually go unnoticed when creating a Remoting client application.

Use the following steps when connecting a client object to a server object:

1. Add a reference to the **System.Runtime.Remoting** namespace within your client application.
2. Add a reference to the server object's assembly.
3. Add **Imports System.Runtime.Remoting** to the top of your client object's class.
4. In your client object's startup function (the **Main()** or **New()** subroutine), configure your client object by either loading an external configuration file or through source code configuration.

To show how a client object works, I will create a Windows application that accepts a dollar value as its input and calls out to a remote server object to get the sales tax for that dollar value. The output of the Windows application will be a message telling the user what the total price of the item is, including the sales tax provided by my remote server object.

***NOTE:** This example requires the RemotingServer example created in the "Creating a Remoting Server" Immediate Solution. If you have not completed the server object, please return to that section and do so; then return to this example.*

---

1. Create a Windows Application project in Visual Basic .NET and call it RemotingClient.
2. Add a TextBox control to the upper-left of the surface of **Form1**. Add a Button control directly beneath the TextBox and a Label control below the Button control.
3. Set the Button's Text property to read "Calculate Sales Price". Set the TextBox's and Label's Text properties to be blank. Figure 13.5 illustrates what your Windows Form should look like.
4. Double-click the Button control to access the code behind.
5. In the Solution Explorer window, right-click the project name, RemotingClient, and select Add Reference. Click the Projects tab at the top of the Add Reference window. Click Browse and locate the project directory for the RemotingServerHost application created earlier. Once located, double-click the Bin subdirectory. Double-click the RemotingServer.dll file to add it to the lower listbox, and then click OK to finish adding this reference.
6. Add the following code to the top of the **Form1**'s source code:

```
Imports System.Runtime.Remoting
Imports System.Runtime.Remoting.Channels
Imports System.Runtime.Remoting.Channels.Tcp
```

7. In the **Form1**'s **New** event, add the following source code below the **InitializeComponent()** line:

```
'Configure the Remoting environment
RemotingConfiguration.Configure("c:\RemotingCfg\Client.cfg")
```

8. Locate the **Button1_Click** event, which was exposed when you double-clicked the Button in step 4, and add the following code to this event:

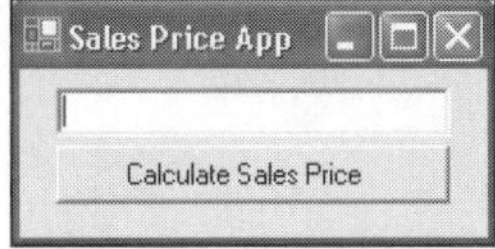

Figure 13.5 The Sales Price application Windows Form.

```
Private Sub Button1_Click(ByVal sender As System.Object, ByVal e As_
      System.EventArgs) Handles Button1.Click
    Dim FinalPrice As String
    Dim TotalPrice, SalesTax As Double

    'Make sure there is a number in the textbox and if not, error out
    If Not (IsNumeric(TextBox1.Text)) Then
        MsgBox("Please enter a number in the TextBox!",_
           MsgBoxStyle.Exclamation)
        Exit Sub
    End If

    'Create an instance of the server object
    Dim MyUtil As New RemotingServer.Class1()

    'Place the code using the remote server in a Try/Catch/Finally
    'structure to catch any access errors that might occur when you
    'use that object
    Try
        SalesTax = MyUtil.CalcSalesTax(CDbl(TextBox1.Text))
    Catch MyErr As Exception
        'If remoting session had trouble, report it here
        MsgBox(MyErr.Message)
        Exit Sub
    End Try

    'Figure final price (returned SalesTax plus the entered value)
    TotalPrice = SalesTax + CDbl(TextBox1.Text)
    FinalPrice = Format(TotalPrice, "###,##0.00")
    Label1.Text = "Final Price = $" & FinalPrice
End Sub
```

9. Save your RemotingClient project by selecting File|Save All.
10. Open a text editing tool such as Window's Notepad. Enter the following configuration file:

```
<configuration>
   <system.runtime.remoting>
      <application>
         <channels>
            <channel ref="tcp">
               <clientProviders>
                  <formatter ref="binary" />
               </clientProviders>
```

```
            </channel>
         </channels>
         <client>
            <wellknown url="http://localhost:8881/TaxServer"
type="Class1,_
               Class1" />
         </client>
      </application>
   </system.runtime.remoting>
</configuration>
```

11. Select File|Save As and save this file as c:\RemotingCfg\Client.cfg. Close the text editing tool.
12. Using the Window's Explorer tool, locate the RemotingServerHost application created in the "Creating a Remoting Server" Immediate Solution. This should be located in your Visual Studio Projects folder under RemotingServerHost/Bin. Execute and run the file named RemotingServerHost.exe to start the Console application. When the console window starts, you should see the message "Press any key to close the RemotingServerHost." Do not press any keys; simply leave this host window active for the next step.
13. Return to your RemotingClient project in Visual Studio .NET and run it by pressing F5.
14. Type a dollar amount (example: **44.68**) into the TextBox, and click the Button. The Label control displays the price of the item with the sales tax figured in.

In the RemotingClient application, I placed the client configuration code in the **Form1 New** event. This ensures that the configuration is executed as soon as the form is created, but never re-executed during the form's lifetime. If you placed the configuration inside the **Button1 Click** event, the function would work the first time, but on the second time around, it would error out because that channel and remote server object has already been configured. Even though the **Click** event ends, the configuration stays active within the application.

Because dealing with remote objects can be dangerous, it is a good idea to surround your remote procedure calls in exception-handling structures, such as a **Try**, **Catch**, **Finally**. Your code should be able to recover from a situation where the remote server object becomes unavailable.

Programmatically Configuring a Remoting Client

In the Sales Price application, I used an external configuration file to set up my client object for Remoting. I could also configure my channel and connect to the server object through my source code without accessing the file system. Using programmatic configuration can make your object more customized, but for most cases, I would recommend using an external configuration file that you can reuse in multiple projects. Having to type in your configuration calls for each and every server and client object involved in a Remoting transaction can be time-consuming and error prone, and I am a big fan of saving time and avoiding errors.

Now that I have preached the virtues of code reuse and external configuration files, I'll show you how to configure your objects programmatically (also known as the hard way). Take a look at the following example:


```
Dim cliChannel As TcpChannel
cliChannel = New TcpChannel(8882)
ChannelServices.RegisterChannel(cliChannel)
Dim MyUtil As RemotingServer.Class1
MyUtil = CType(Activator.GetObject(GetType(RemotingServer.Class1),_
      "tcp://remoteserver:8881/TaxServer"), RemotingServer.Class1)
```

As with the server object, my first step with the client object is to configure a communications channel. I create a new instance of a **TcpChannel**, assign it to port 8882, and then register this channel with the machine. Next, I create a new instance of the **RemotingServer.Class1** class. Your project must be holding a reference to this class before you can create an instance of it. Then, I use the **Activator** object's **GetObject** method to call out to the RemotingServer object. Notice that the first parameter figures out the data type of the **RemotingServer.Class1** object. The second parameter looks like an Internet URL except the protocol used is "tcp" instead of the familiar "http" before the **://**. Because the **TaxServer** server object is listening to port 8881, I append this port to the end of the server name. The final parameter is the **RemotingServer.Class1** object itself.

Using the programmatic configuration method is a bit more complicated because you need to remember which items need to be configured and the exact syntax to perform this task. With the external configuration file, you only need to know the tagging schema and which data elements and their matching values you need to pass in. The **RemotingConfiguration**'s **Configure** method handles the rest of the job, matching up your elements and values with the proper configuration commands.

Using the Http Channel to Call Remote Objects

So far in my examples I have used the Tcp channel to create a client and a server object. You can opt to use the Http channel in place of the Tcp channel. Although not as efficient as Tcp, the Http channel uses SOAP to wrap its Remoting messages, which makes your messages universally understandable. Http can also pass through common Internet ports, such as port 80, which allows this protocol to pass through most firewalls unabated.

As mentioned earlier, there are two ways to configure your object: programmatically or by loading an external configuration file. Here is an example of a configuration file setting up a client object to use an Http channel:

```
<configuration>
   <system.runtime.remoting>
      <application>
         <client>
            <wellknown type="RemoteType, RemoteAssembly"_
               url="http://remoteserver:8883/MyHttpServer" />
         </client>
         <channels>
            <channel type="System.Runtime.Remoting.Channels.Http._
                HttpChannel,System.Runtime.Remoting" port="8884" />
         </channels>
      </application>
   </system.runtime.remoting>
</configuration>
```

The Remoting server called in this configuration is named MyHttpServer, and it listens to port 8883. The remote server object is registered for the client object in the **<wellknown>** tag. The client object sets up its own communication channel within the **<channels>** tags, declaring port 8884 to be its own.

You can perform the exact same configuration within your object's startup code like this:

```
'Declare a new instance of the HttpChannel
Dim MyHttp As Http.HttpChannel
MyHttp = New Http.HttpChannel(8884)

'Register the HttpChannel with the machine
ChannelServices.RegisterChannel(MyHttp)

'Declare the remote server object
Dim MyService As RemotingServer.Class1
```

```
MyService = CType(Activator.GetObject(GetType(RemotingServer.Class1),_
      "http://remoteserver:8884/MyHttpServer"), RemotingServer.Class1)
```

The programmatic version creates the exact same client object configuration as the external file schema example.

Setting Up a Lifetime Lease

Both server controlled singleton and client controlled CAO objects can have lifetime leases defined for them. These leases decide how long the object will live before its instance is destroyed, requiring the creation of new instances to handle additional object calls. Lifetime leases do not apply to the server-controlled single call object because the object's instance is destroyed at the end of every call, never to be reused again.

In contrast to the single call object, a single instance of the singleton object can live beyond the call that created it, and this one object will be used to service all client calls received before its lifetime lease runs out. The CAO method lets the client object control the server object's lifetime. The client can keep the server object active for multiple calls or deactivate that object at will. You will see an example of using lifetime leases with CAO objects in the next solution.

The lifetime lease for a server controlled singleton object can be defined either in its configuration file or through the source code that configures your server object. Here is an example of a configuration file that defines a lifetime lease for a singleton object:

```
<configuration>
   <system.runtime.remoting>
      <application>
         <lifetime leaseTime="1M" sponsorshipTimeout="0S"_
            renewOnCallTime="1M" leaseManagerPollTime="30S" />
         <service>
            <wellknown type="ServerActivatedType, RemoteType"_
               objectUri="MyServer" mode="Singleton" />
         </service>
         <channels>
            <channel port="8881" ref="http" />
         </channels>
      </application>
   </system.runtime.remoting>
</configuration>
```

Look at the contents of the **<lease>** tag because this is where the lifetime lease of the object is defined. This tag has four attributes, each with a time value assigned to it. Values that end in M are in minutes, S in seconds, H for hours, and MS for milliseconds. If an attribute has a time value of zero, that attribute's lifetime is set to be indefinite.

The first attribute, **leaseTime**, declares the standard lifetime an object will have. When the lease expires, the server sends a notice to the object that has sponsored or created that object. The **sponsorshipTimeout** setting declares how long the object waits to hear back from its sponsor before completely destroying itself. Every time a client object calls this server object, the server object's lifetime is extended by the amount of time declared in the **renewOnCallTime** parameter. This helps keep the server object busy and alive for the next call. The **leaseManagerPollTime** parameter decides the time interval that the lease manager uses to recheck this object. In my example, I set the lease manager to 30 seconds, which means every 30 seconds the lease manager examines this object to see if it has expired.

An object can monitor its own lifetime lease through the ILease interface. The object can use the **CurrentLeaseTime** property to find out exactly how much time it has left to live (don't we all wish we could find this out!). Even better, the object calls the ILease's **Renew** method to reset its lifetime lease to a new duration. The four attributes in the **<lease>** tag can also be read and set programmatically through the ILease interface.

Creating a Client Activated Object and Determining Its Lifetime

CAO objects give the power of activation and lifetime lease control to the client. The server object must explicitly declare that it is allowing CAO activation before a client can use this power. This is a defensive measure on the server object's part because if client objects are allowed to control the server object's lifetime, it is possible that server object lifetimes can be set to some fairly high numbers, thereby keeping those server objects in memory for far longer than they might be needed. As more and more clients activate your server object through CAO, the more server resources will be drained. It's probably best to only use CAO within a single application and avoid allowing outside developers to decide the lifetime your server objects will use.

To use CAO, you need to make special configuration settings for both your server and your client objects. The server object's configuration file must specify that it will allow CAO calls. You can support more than one type of activation type, just as an object can support more than one channel or port. In the following configuration file, the server object, which uses an Http channel listening on port 8881, defines a lifetime lease, and in the **<wellknown>** tag, states that it uses singleton activation. In the **<activated>** tag, the server object declares that it will allow CAO:

```
<configuration>
   <system.runtime.remoting>
      <application>
         <lifetime
            leaseTime="30S" sponsorshipTimeout="10S" renewOnCallTime="15S"_
               leaseManagerPollTime="25S" />
         <service>
            <wellknown type="ServerTypeName, RemoteType"_
               objectUri="MyServer" mode="Singleton" />
            <activated type="ClientTypeName, RemoteType" />
         </service>
         <channels>
            <channel port="8881" ref="http" />
         </channels>
      </application>
   </system.runtime.remoting>
</configuration>
```

A client object can call this server object without using a CAO configuration, and the server object will work using its singleton configuration settings. But, if the client object wants to control the server object's activation and lifetime, the client object will change its Remoting configuration to use CAO. Here is the configuration file a client would use to take advantage of CAO in its server object calls:

```
<configuration>
   <system.runtime.remoting>
      <application>
         <client url="http://remoteserver:8881">
            <activated type="ClientTypeName, RemoteType" />
         </client>
         <channels>
            <channel ref="http" port="0" />
         </channels>
      </application>
   </system.runtime.remoting>
</configuration>
```

Instead of using the **<wellknown>** tag to register the server object, the CAO client object configuration file uses the **<activated>** tag. The URL and port number in the **<client>** tag matches the remote server object's listening port (shown inside the **<channels>** tag of the previous configuration file). The **<activated>** tag calls the server object's **<activated type>**, which was named **ClientTypeName** in this example.

Encrypting Your Remoting Object's Messages

The Tcp channel uses a binary message format, which can provide your Remoting messages with some degree of security, but it is not capable of encrypting your messages with strong encryption algorithms. If your application design calls for remote object communications across an unsecured environment (i.e., the Internet), you should forgo the Tcp channel and select the Http channel. Because the Http channel can work in concert with the Microsoft's IIS Web server, you can encrypt your Remoting messages the same way you can your Web page request and response calls.

The IIS Web server uses SSL to encrypt the communication between the server and the remote Web browsers. The Web server administrator must first install the SSL package into IIS before you can use it to secure your Remoting messages. Once installed, using SSL is simply a matter of adding a single letter to your object reference URLs. Without SSL, you would reference your Http objects like this:

```
http://remoteserver:8881/MyServerObject
```

To enable SSL in your Remoting calls, simply add an "s" after the "http". This tells the server to use the secure channel, which is on a different port than the normal unsecure Http channel. If a Web server normally uses port 80 to listen for unencrypted Web page requests, it might use port 8080 to listen to the "https" version of those requests. Here is the same URL using SSL:

```
https://remoteserver:8080/MyServerObject
```

You need to make this change wherever the "http://" appears in your configuration files or in your programmatic configuration section. You will also want to change the port you are using to match up with the Web server's SSL port number. To find out which port your Web server is using for SSL, use the Internet Services Manager application found under the Start|Program Files|Administrative Applications menu.

Chapter 14

SOAP and XML

By David Vitter

In Depth

In this chapter, I revisit XML and discuss some of its associated features, such as XML schemas, transformations, and how ADO.NET uses XML. Next I will cover Simple Object Access Protocol (SOAP), which plays a vital role in Microsoft's XML Web services and Remoting technologies. Visual Studio .NET was built on top of an XML framework, which is really amazing considering the fact that XML is an open source technology not under Microsoft's control. You will see how XML and SOAP can be used to level the playing field in the development world and make cross-platform applications a reality. Imagine a world where Java-based applications and Windows applications can interact and exchange data. This is the brave new world that open source messaging formats are making possible today.

Advanced XML

It is pretty hard to create a Visual Studio .NET project and not work with XML. It's in your XML Web services, it helps you make remote calls to objects located on another machine, and XML forms the backbone of the ADO.NET data access technology. In this section I will talk about XML's role in ADO.NET, how XML can be used to persist your application data, and how XPath can help you search through large files of XML data. You will also be introduced to the **XmlConvert** class, which will help you convert data types from .NET to native XML and back again.

XML and ADO.NET

As you will read about in Chapter 15, ADO.NET is a complete reworking of Microsoft's Active Data Objects (ADO) data access component. This latest version was designed to natively use XML to describe and communicate data where past versions were only able to translate their contents to XML or vice versa. The ADO.NET DataSet, which is the main object you will work with when manipulating your data, is capable of reading and writing not only XML, but XML schemas as well. Table 14.1 lists the DataSet methods you can use to work with XML using ADO.NET. In Chapter 5, you learned about the many tools found within the **System.Xml** namespace to work with XML messages, but you should be aware that ADO.NET DataSets provide another powerful way to work with your data.

ADO.NET also uses XML to serialize the contents of a DataSet and transmit that data from one point to another. Past versions of ADO used COM interfaces to

Table 14.1 ADO.NET DataSet methods for working with XML.

Method	Function
ReadXml	Fills a DataSet with the contents of an XML message
WriteXml	Dumps the contents of a DataSet to an XML file
ReadXmlSchema	Reads a schema file into the DataSet and uses that schema to define that DataSet's structure
WriteXmlSchema	Creates a schema file that describes the DataSet's structure

serialize data, which worked well until that data ran into a firewall that did not permit COM to pass through. XML is text-based and can be passed through a firewall using SOAP messaging via the same port that HTML Web pages are allowed to pass through. This gives ADO.NET developers the ability to move their DataSets beyond the firewall and the corporate network.

Data Persistence with XML

XML can be used for more than simply exchanging data between applications or moving DataSets from one point to another. XML is capable of describing and storing data in such a sophisticated fashion that a file of data in XML format is almost like a miniature database. This feature of XML allows you to create temporary storage files to remember bits of information. Web applications often use XML to persist data on a Web server, so pieces of information about a user's visit to a particular Web site can be remembered from one page request to the next.

Picture a Web surfer visiting an online widget store. When he spots a widget he cannot live without, he can add it to his shopping cart with the click of a button and then continue shopping for more items. Back on the Web server, the store's application creates a temporary XML file on the server with some unique data to identify that shopper (such as a **SessionID**) and appends the requested widget to that file. Web servers are inherently connectionless and stateless, which means that without a little help, the Web server cannot remember information about a visitor once a requested page has been delivered. As the user selects more and more items, the temporary file grows, allowing the Web server to remember these shopping selections. When the visitor finally purchases the items and leaves the Web site, the server can erase this temporary mini-database, making room on the hard drive for more files. You can also use XML to persist data such as user settings, preferences, personal information such as age or interests, and much more.

XPath

When dealing with very large XML messages, it can often be difficult to find the exact item you are looking for. XPath was created as a supporting technology for

XML that allows users to search through an XML message and locate particular items. You will find XPath in the .NET Framework located prominently within the **System.Xml.XPath** namespace.

XPath parses your XML message into tag elements and their values, which allows you to perform searches such as "FirstName is equal to Dave" or "EmpID is greater than 50". Because XPath knows which parts of the message are the data element names and which parts are their corresponding elements, it can step through your message and locate the items that match your search criteria.

XmlConvert

Because schemas were designed to be universally understood, the data types you will find inside an XML schema file do not directly match up with your .NET data types. Where .NET uses an **Integer** data type, the XML schema uses an **int** data type. A **String** in .NET is also a **string** in XML, but that is about as close as these two get to agreeing on a data name. In order to deal with their differences, .NET provides a class named **XmlConvert** to help you convert between the common language runtime (CLR) compliant data types and those that the XML schema uses.

The **XmlConvert** class does all of its work through exposed methods, which act as conversion tools. When writing **String** values from your .NET code to an XML document, you can use methods such as **ToBoolean**, **ToInt32**, and **ToDouble** to convert your **Strings** to an XML schema format. Schemas have to be more restrictive because the receivers of your message might not know they need to convert a **String** value to an **Integer** to use it in an equation, so you must be careful to use the most restrictive data type when writing your XML schemas and messages. The following code example reads in a node from an XML message and converts that value to an **Integer** for storage in a .NET data type:

```
Dim Converter As New Xml.XmlConvert()
Dim MyReader As New Xml.XmlTextReader("c:\XmlDocs\Employees.xml")
Dim MyInt As Integer
MyInt = Converter.ToInt32(MyReader.Read)
```

An XML message's structure closely resembles that of the ADO.NET DataSet, which comes as no surprise when you consider that the new DataSet was built with XML in mind. In Chapter 15, you'll learn all about the DataSet and its relationship to XML. The **XmlConvert** class provides two methods that allow you to translate XML message structures into DataSet structures and vice versa. The **DecodeName** method converts an XML object name into a DataSet object name, and the **EncodeLocalName** converts your DataSet objects back into XML object names. These DataSet object names include the **DataTable** and **DataColumn**, which are not XML-compliant object types.

XML Schemas

A schema provides an outline for your document to follow and provides critical data rules to control the values entered into your document. In the movies, when the bad guys come up with a scheme, they plan out their evil deeds in great detail. Of course, it's that one little detail that they fail to plan for that thwarts their evil doings. When you create a schema for your XML messages, you plan the exact format and data types that your message will be required to use. If you apply a schema to a message that violates any of the rules you defined, bad things can happen!

Your schemas will be written using the XML Schema Definition (XSD) language, which defines the tagging formats that you use to define your messaging formats. If you worked with or read about XML prior to Visual Studio .NET's release, you may have heard of Document Type Definitions (DTDs). XSD schemas have evolved from DTDs and offer many improvements over their predecessor, such as reusable and inheritable data types. All of the pieces and functions associated with an XML schema are found within the **System.Xml.Schema** namespace.

Examining an XML Schema

Pull out your scalpels, because it's time to dissect another message. This time you are going to look at an XSD schema file, which closely resembles the XML files you have already looked at. Despite the resemblance, you will not see any actual data surrounded by tags within the schema document. Take a look at the following example:

```
<xsd:schema id="NewDataSet" targetNamespace="" xmlns="" xmlns:xsd=_
    "http://www.w3.org/2001/XMLSchema" xmlns:msdata=_
    "urn:schemas-microsoft-com:xml-msdata">
  <xsd:element name="NewDataSet" msdata:IsDataSet="true">
    <xsd:complexType>
      <xsd:choice maxOccurs="unbounded">
        <xsd:element name="Employees">
          <xsd:complexType>
            <xsd:sequence>
              <xsd:element name="EmpID" type="xsd:int" minOccurs="0" />
              <xsd:element name="EmpName" type="xsd:string"  _
                 minOccurs="0" />
              <xsd:element name="HireDate" type="xsd:string"_
                 minOccurs="0" />
              <xsd:element name="OfficeID" type="xsd:int" _
                 minOccurs="0" />
            </xsd:sequence>
```

```
            </xsd:complexType>
          </xsd:element>
        </xsd:choice>
      </xsd:complexType>
    </xsd:element>
</xsd:schema>
```

Once again, this example is presented in a neat and organized fashion that uses spaces and carriage returns to neatly separate data elements. Indentations mean nothing to the procedure that is reading in this schema, but the order in which these tags appear means everything. Notice that many of the tags in this schema are self-terminating, meaning that there is a / at the end of the tag's description, and you do not see a closing version of the tag such as you did with the **<Employee>** and **</Employee>** tags in the XML example.

The tags that do have a matching closing tag do not enclose data, only other elements of the schema. In fact, nowhere in this schema will you find any actual data, only tags that describe what format a message using this schema will adhere too. The following sections list the individual schema pieces, some of which are shown in the preceding example, whereas others are not. Understanding what these items are and how they fit in to the scheme of things will help you create your own schemas.

Simple Types

In an XML schema, a **simple** type is like a single property or attribute that you can define and customize. For instance, every XML message you author may have a single standalone data element named **CompanyURL** to let the receiving party know the URL to your company's Web site. If you defined this data element using a **simple** type, it would look like this:

```
<xsd:simpleType name="CompanyURL">
    <xsd:restriction base="xsd:string" />
</xsd:simpleType>
```

The only tag that is included with your **simple** type is a **<xsd:restriction>** that defines the acceptable data type for this field, which is the XML **string** type. **Simple** types do not have a subelement, nor do they allow you to define attributes. You can add more restrictions and rules for your **simple** data type by including facets within your **simple** type's tag set, which I will cover in the "Facets" section.

Complex Types

A schema **complex** type is an element that contains separate attributes and other elements below it. In the object-oriented world, your objects are **complex** types because they have properties and methods that describe them. Here is an example of a **Car complex** type in XML schema format:

```
<xsd:element name="Car">
    <xsd:complexType>
        <xsd:sequence>
            <xsd:element name="CarMake" type="xsd:string" />
            <xsd:element name="CarModel" type="xsd:string" />
        </xsd:sequence>
        <xsd:attribute name="NumDoors" type="xsd:string" />
    </xsd:complexType>
</xsd:element>
```

The **Car** is an element that has two string type elements below it, **CarMake** and **CarModel**, and one string attribute named **NumDoors**. Notice that the subelements below **Car** are placed within a **<xsd:sequence>** set of tags to separate these elements from their parent element, the **Car**. A **complex** type can closely resemble a database table, and you can even assign a key to one of the elements or attributes of your **complex** type, just as you would define a primary key in a database table. You will use a key element to do this, which I will discuss in the "Key" section.

Elements

The *element* is the basic unit in a schema. Elements were all over the schema example I provided earlier. **EmpName**, **EmpID**, and **HireDate** are all elements of the schema. An element tag can contain other element tags, as the **Employees** element tag does in the sample schema file. At a minimum, the element tag defines both the name of this element and the data type this element must use. Here is an element tag from the previous example:

```
<xsd:element name="EmpID" type="xsd:int" minOccurs="0" />
```

This element's name is **EmpID**, which in the actual XML message will be enclosed by **<EmpID>** and **</EmpID>** tags. The data type for **EmpID** is an **Integer**, which in XSD translates to **xsd:int**. The **minOccurs** parameter is an optional attribute of the **EmpID** tag. Setting the **minOccurs** or minimum occurrences to zero means that this parameter is not mandatory. If the **minOccurs** attribute is not a part of an element tag, then this element is mandatory and must be represented in the message.

Attributes

An attribute can be added to a **complex** type to help describe that type in some way, just like you would add attributes to your objects when creating a class in your source code. Examples of attributes include **FirstName**, **LastName**, **Age**, and **OfficeID**. An attribute cannot have attributes or elements below it in the schema hierarchy. Attributes can only use predefined data types, such as the XML **string** or **int** data types. Because the **simple** type is a way to create your own customized data type in XML, you can assign your attribute to use a **simple** type that has already been defined within the schema.

In the following example, a **complex** type named **MyStore** uses one attribute that uses the basic XML **string** data type to define **MyStore**'s address and a second attribute called **Name** that uses a customized **simple** type named **StoreName** to define this new data type:

```
<xsd:element name="MyStore">
    <xsd:complexType>
        <xsd:attribute name="Address" type="xsd:string" />
        <xsd:attribute name="Name" type="xsd:StoreName" />
    </xsd:complexType>
</xsd:element>
```


Groups

Using a group in your XML schema allows you to define the exact order that a set of elements or attributes must appear in. Picture a schema that defines attributes named **CarMake**, **CarModel**, and **CarPrice**. Without a group, these tags could appear in any order within the XML message. Here is what these tags would look like within a group tag:

```
<xsd:attributeGroup name="CarInfo">
    <xsd:attribute name="CarMake" type="xsd:string" />
    <xsd:attribute name="CarModel" type="xsd:string" />
    <xsd:attribute name="CarPrice" type="xsd:string" />
</xsd:attributeGroup>
```

In an XML message adhering to a schema that includes this group, all three attribute tags would have to appear in order for that message to be considered valid. If the **CarPrice** tag comes before the **CarMake** tag, the message will not be valid.

Element groups come in three different forms: *all*, *sequence*, and *choice*. The all version of the element group requires that all elements listed inside of that group appear within your XML message, but they can appear in any order. The sequence group also requires that all of the elements be present, and they must be listed in the exact same order defined within the XML schema. The choice version allows the message's author to choose one, and only one, of the elements listed within the group. For example, you could have a choice group named **FuelType**, and the elements could be **Leaded**, **Unleaded**, and **Diesel**. In an XML message that uses the **FuelType** group, the author would choose only one **FuelType** element and use that in his message, ignoring the other element choices.

Keys

Complex types in your XML schema can have keys, just like a database table. A primary key is the main identifying item for that **complex** type, and it must always be present and always be a unique (no duplicates) value. If you created a **complex** type to define your **Employees**, every employee in that table would be assigned a unique **EmpID** to identify them. Within your XML schema, you would add a key directly below your **complex** type that defines which element within the **Employees complex** type is a key. This is what the schema tags would look like to define the **EmpID** element as a unique primary key for the **Employees complex** type:

```
<xsd:key name="EmpPriKey" msdata:PrimaryKey="true">
  <xsd:selector xpath=".//Employees"/>
  <xsd:field xpath="EmpID"/>
</xsd:unique>
```

A primary key is the identifying field for a **complex** type and therefore can never be blank or null. You can define keys for **complex** types that are not the primary key and are allowed to be null. These are known as *unique* keys, and the schema tags to define such a key would look like this:

```
<xsd:unique name="UserIDKey">
  <xsd:selector xpath=".//Employees"/>
  <xsd:field xpath="UserID"/>
</xsd:unique>
```

In the unique example, an element of the **Employees complex** type named **UserID** is defined to be a unique key, but not the primary key for this **complex** type. This means that each record can have a blank **UserID** field, but it cannot have a value in the **UserID** field that duplicates a value entered in another record.

Facets

A facet is a way to place a constraint or a data rule on a **simple** type. The facet tags appear nested within a **simple** type's tag set, and the settings defined within the facet place a limit on the data type defined for that **simple** type. The facet tags do not explicitly say "facet" in them, but instead are named after the type of data limit that is being defined. Here is an example:

```
<xsd:simpleType name="StoreName">
    <xsd:restriction base="xsd:string">
        <xsd:maxLength value="20" />
        <xsd:minLength value="4" />
```

```
    </xsd:restriction>
</xsd:simpleType>
```

The **simple** type, **StoreName**, accepts a **string** data type. There are two facets applied to this **simple** type, which declare that any value entered in the **StoreName** tag must be greater than or equal to four characters and less than or equal to 20 characters. There are six facets that you can define for a **simple** type: **enumeration**, **length**, **maxLength**, **minLength**, **whiteSpace**, and **pattern**.

Relations

A schema relationship item defines a relationship between two elements within that schema. Just as two tables in a database can have a parent-child relationship, so can two elements in an XML schema. Going back to the **Employees** and **Offices** tables example; these two tables have a relationship through a shared **OfficeID**, which is the primary key of the **Offices** table and a foreign key in the **Employees** table. The following XML schema defines the structure of both of these tables:

```
<xsd:element name="Employees">
    <xsd:complexType>
        <xsd:sequence>
            <xsd:element name="EmpID" type="xsd:string" />
            <xsd:element name="EmpName" type="xsd:string" />
            <xsd:element name="HireDate" type="xsd:string" />
            <xsd:element name="OfficeID" type="xsd:string" />
        </xsd:sequence>
    </xsd:complexType>
    <xsd:key name="EmployeesKey1" msdata:PrimaryKey="true">
        <xsd:selector xpath="." />
        <xsd:field xpath="EmpID" />
    </xsd:key>
    <xsd:keyref name="OfficesEmployees" refer="OfficesKey1">
        <xsd:selector xpath="." />
        <xsd:field xpath="OfficeID" />
    </xsd:keyref>
</xsd:element>
<xsd:element name="Offices">
    <xsd:complexType>
        <xsd:sequence>
            <xsd:element name="OfficeID" type="xsd:string" />
            <xsd:element name="OfficeName" type="xsd:string" />
            <xsd:element name="OfficeSym" type="xsd:string" />
        </xsd:sequence>
    </xsd:complexType>
    <xsd:key name="OfficesKey1" msdata:PrimaryKey="true">
        <xsd:selector xpath="." />
        <xsd:field xpath="OfficeID" />
```

```
    </xsd:key>
</xsd:element>
```

After the **Employees complex** type is defined, you see a **<xsd:key>** and a **<xsd:keyref>** section highlighted. The key tag defines the primary key within the **Employees complex** type as being the **EmpID** element. The **keyref** tags define the foreign key relationship pointing the **OfficeID** element to the matching element in the **Offices** table. Below the **Office complex** type definition tags, you see another set of highlighted tags that define the **OfficeID** key for this table. Because the relationship points from the **Employees** table to the **Offices** table, there is only one **keyref** set of tags in this message. If you were viewing this XML schema in Visual Studio .NET's schema designer window, it would look like Figure 14.1.

Internal Schemas

Some XML messages come complete with their own built-in schemas. When provided, you will always find an internal schema at the top of the XML message because it is critical to first communicate the rules and structure that your data will follow before you actually communicate the data values. The plus side to using internal schemas is that you only have to transmit one file to exchange the XML and schema with another party. The downside to using internal schemas is that they are not reusable like external schemas.

To use an internal schema in a message, you first write your schema to your output file, and then add the XML message below the schema. The schema tags will indicate to the processor that schema elements are being read in until the processing application encounters the **</xsd:schema>** tag, which indicates the end of the schema portion.

External Schemas

An external schema is a separate file from the XML message that is referenced at the top of that message. To use external schemas, both the schema and the XML message that references it need to be sent to the receiver unless of course that receiver already has a copy of the schema that can be used. If you create an external schema for your messages, you only have to write the schema once, and then make a simple reference to that file from each message. If you opt to use an

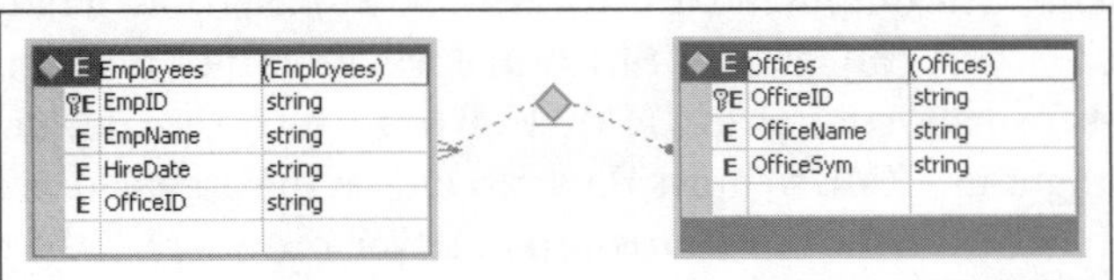

Figure 14.1 Two related elements in the XML schema designer window.

internal schema, the schema must be written every time you send a message, which can slow down your messaging time. To reference an external schema file, you can add a parameter to your top-level tag inside your XML message, which will look like this:

```
<Company xmlns="http://www.myserver.com/MySchema.xsd">
```

In this sample reference to an external schema file, the schema is stored in a file named MySchema.xsd on a Web server named www.myserver.com. This schema defines the structure and data rules for a **Company** message, so all tags in between this **<Company>** tag and its ending **</Company>** tag must adhere to the schema rules.

One way to simplify the storage and availability of your external schemas is to make them available on the Internet or your company's intranet. You would simply make your reference tag point to a URL that tells where the schema is located and let the network take care of the rest. If you are using industry-wide schemas or multicompany messaging systems, placing your schemas in a common location allows everyone to access and use those schemas, ensuring that all parties involved will be using the exact same schema every time.

XML Transformations

If you are developing an application that must exchange XML messages with an application that was developed by someone else, odds are that your messaging schemas and the other person's messaging schemas are not an exact match. Even within the same industry, different companies have different terms for their data elements and often focus on different pieces of data, which can cause one person's version of an XML message to look nothing at all like another person's version of the same message. In cases like these, you need a tool that will translate one message schema into a schema that your application can understand and work with. That tool is eXtensible Stylesheet Language Transformations (XSLT), which is sometimes simply called transformations.

An XSLT transformation document is a standalone file that is based on the XML technology. Using tags and logic statements, the XSLT file can act as a conversion tool that can read in a file of XML, translate its contents to a different schema, and write out this newly formatted file. The output file will always be text-based, but it may not always be an XML message. You can create XSLT transformation files that convert XML messages into other formats, such as an HTML Web page. If you are developing a Web application, you might use XML to move data around on the application servers, but when it comes time to send the results to the user's Web browsers, XML alone will not work. However, you can perform a transformation of your XML data into HTML and provide the browser with a neatly formatted page for display.

XslTransform

The **XslTransform** class in the **System.Xml.Xsl** namespace provides you with the means to take an XML message and an XSLT transformation file and create a new version of the original XML message. There are two main methods in the **XslTransform** class that you will deal with: **Load** and **Transform**. The **Load** method pulls in the XSLT file that you want to use to perform your transformations. This file could be a part of your application or an available XSLT file located somewhere on the Internet.

The **Transform** method takes in an XML file, applies the loaded XSLT file to it, and creates an output file that is the result of your transformation. To use the **XslTransform** class, you would create a new instance of this class, **Load** the XSLT file, and then **Transform** your source XML document like this:

```
Dim MyXslt As Xml.Xsl.XslTransform = New Xml.Xsl.XslTransform()
MyXslt.Load(CType("http://myserver/MyXslt.xsl", String))
MyXslt.Transform(InputFile, OutputFile)
```

In this example, the **MyXslt** object is loaded with an XSLT file located on the myserver Web server. You can add XSLT files to your Visual Studio .NET solution, or you can create these files manually using any text editor, such as Windows Notepad. You will learn how to create your own customized transformation file in the Immediate Solutions section of this chapter.

Introduction to SOAP

SOAP was designed to be a simple, lightweight (in other words, efficient) way to move XML and other message types back and forth across the Internet. Before XML became the preferred way to format data messages, Web browsers and servers used methods called **GET** and **POST** to transport data to each other in a request/response pattern. If you want to read more about how **GET** and **POST** work, you can find their descriptions in Chapter 8. The **GET** and **POST** methods were well suited for the simple form data you often encounter inside a Web page, but these two methods were not robust enough to handle a complex data structure such as an XML message. As a result, a new Internet-ready protocol was needed to support the growing XML developer's movement.

SOAP is a messaging protocol that serializes a message for transport by wrapping an XML message in what is known as an envelope and sending this package across the Internet using HTTP, which is the primary transport protocol of the Web. It is possible to send SOAP encapsulated messages using other protocols such as the file transfer protocol (FTP), but in the majority of cases you will see the HTTP protocol employed. Figure 14.2 shows a step-by-step example of how an XML

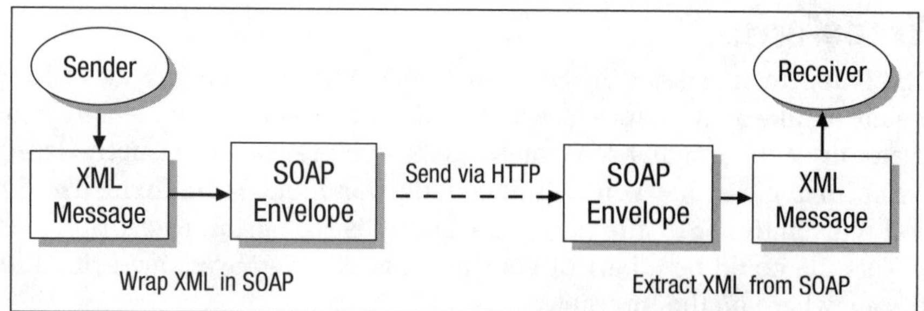

Figure 14.2 Sending XML messages across the Internet using SOAP and HTTP.

message is packaged using SOAP, transported across the Internet to the receiver, and then unpackaged for processing.

The SOAP Envelope

If you printed out all of the data in your database and wanted to send it to another company for its review, you couldn't just place that printout into the mailbox and expect it to reach its destination. The mail service prefers that you place items inside an envelope that includes a to and from address along with proper postage. XML messages by themselves are not capable of journeying into the world without first being placed within an envelope. The SOAP protocol provides this encapsulating envelope, which contains all of the necessary information to get your data from point A to point B. Because SOAP is based on the XML technology, the tags within a SOAP envelope look a lot like any other XML message. Take a look at this example of a SOAP envelope:

```
POST /Customers HTTP/1.1
User-Agent: Windows2000
Host: 255.255.255.255
Content-Type: text/xml; charset=utf-8
Content-length: 999
SOAPAction: "/Company"

<?xml version="1.0"?>
<SOAP-ENV:Envelope xmlns:SOAP-ENV="http://schemas._
  xmlsoap.org/soap/envelope/" SOAP-ENV:encodingStyle="http://schemas._
  xmlsoap.org/soap/encoding/"/>
  <SOAP:Header>
    <v:From SOAP:mustUnderstand='1'>dotnet@exploringvb.net</v:From>
  </SOAP:Header>
  <SOAP:Body>

      <Company>
         <Employees>
```

```
            <EmpID>11</EmpID>
            <EmpName>James Moffet</EmpName>
            <OfficeID>1</OfficeID>
            <HireDate>09/10/01</HireDate>
        </Employees>
    </Company>

  </SOAP:Body>
</SOAP-ENV:Envelope>
```

You can see the XML message contained within the SOAP envelope beginning with the **<Company>** tag and ending at the **</Company>** tag. The actual XML data of a SOAP message is called the *Body* of that message and is surrounded by a **<SOAP:Body>** set of tags. The rest of this message was added by SOAP to prepare this DataSet for transmission. The top six lines are a **POST** header added to the SOAP message that describes the transmission file's format (text using utf-8 characters), the total size of the message, and the IP address of the machine that sent the message. The first tag of the SOAP portion of the message lets the receiver know which version of XML this message is based on. Next, the **<SOAP-ENV>** tag defines the location of the formatting and encoding schemas used to build the SOAP tags.

The **<SOAP:Header>** section is where developers can create customized tags to send information concerning this SOAP transmission to the receiver. It's important that the application that receives your SOAP message can understand those customized tags; otherwise, that data will be ignored. In my example, I have a tag named **<v:From>**, which communicates the developer's Web address within the SOAP header. There is a **mustUnderstand** attribute within this tag that is currently set to 1, which equates to the Boolean value of **True**. This means that the receiving application must be able to understand this SOAP header tag, and if it cannot, it will return an error to the sender. If you do not include a **mustUnderstand** attribute in your customized tag, you allow the receiver to process your message even if it is unable to understand your header tag.

SOAP and XML Web Services

XML Web services promise to be the next big thing in enterprise development, and it is XML and SOAP that give XML Web services their power and flexibility. An XML Web service is really just a component hosted on a Web site that other components can send requests to and receive back information from. You format your requests to an XML Web service using XML, and that service's response will be returned in XML format as well. This makes it possible for any application or development tool that can use XML and the Internet to take advantage of XML Web services.

SOAP's role in XML Web services is the packaging and transporting of XML messages back and forth between the XML Web service and the caller. XML by itself is not capable of traveling across the Internet, but if you wrap XML messages inside a SOAP envelope, you have the ability to make a remote procedure call to any XML Web service located anywhere in the world. SOAP can even carry those requests and responses through corporate firewalls, which in the past were barriers that prevented application-to-application communications. To allow for maximum flexibility, .NET XML Web services can also support the **GET** and **POST** messaging protocols to send and receive data, although SOAP is certainly the preferred protocol for XML Web services.

SOAP in Visual Studio .NET

You can find SOAP in the .NET Framework under the **System.Xml.Serialization** namespace. If you want to work with SOAP programmatically, you should explore this namespace, particularly the **XmlSerializer** class, which is directly responsible for serializing messages for transmission and deserializing received messages for processing. For the majority of .NET developers, this is deeper into the framework than you will want to venture because Visual Studio .NET does a terrific job of handling your XML serialization chores for you.

In Chapter 8, I discussed how applications can make calls to XML Web services, and you learned how Visual Studio .NET creates a proxy class that is a local version of the remote XML Web service sans any actual code (in other words, interfaces only). When a function in your application makes a call to this remote service, the proxy class handles the chores of translating your .NET data types and requests to an XML message, wrapping this message in a SOAP envelope, and then sending it to the waiting service. When the response is received from that XML Web service, the proxy class works in reverse, extracting the XML message from the SOAP envelope, and then translating the XML data elements back into .NET data types that your function will understand. Visual Studio .NET uses XML and SOAP behind the scenes, hiding all of the complexity of Internet messaging and making your life so much easier.

Messaging Using DCOM versus Using XML

Distributed COM (DCOM) is an enhanced version of COM that allows components to call other components located on remote machines. Prior to DCOM, you could create a COM component that made a procedural call to another COM component, but only if both components resided on the same machine. With the introduction of DCOM, your components could communicate across the enterprise's network to make remote procedural calls. This ability greatly improved your application's scalability because you could locate a single application's components on multiple machines. If a particular component on a server-based application was being heavily used, it could be moved to another server to balance some of that application's workload.

The communications that go between one COM object and another are in a Microsoft proprietary format. Any components that do not understand COM are not able to make calls to these COM components. For the same reasons, COM developers are not able to make procedural calls to CORBA objects created in Java. This places a large wall between Java and Microsoft developers, making cross-development tool projects almost impossible. In addition to these DCOM limitations, most firewalls do not allow DCOM calls to pass through them, limiting the reach of your procedural calls to the enterprise's network and locking out the rest of the known world.

XML and SOAP can be used to package your remote procedure calls and the response from those remote components in a way that all development languages and tools can comprehend. It does not take any special proprietary knowledge or technology to read and write messages in XML, so your Visual Studio applications can make calls to XML and SOAP-enabled Java components, and those objects can make calls to your .NET code. Because SOAP transports XML messages using the same communications medium that Web servers and Web browsers use to communicate, those corporate firewalls will normally allow these remote procedural calls to pass, making around-the-globe procedure calls a distinct possibility.

Immediate Solutions

Creating an XML Message in Visual Studio .NET

There are a couple of different ways to create an XML message. Most developers use a simple text editing tool, such as Windows Notepad, to create their first XML message. This is fine if your message is short and sweet and you do not mind typing out your tags, but the longer your message is, the more painful it is to create it using a text editor. Adding to the pain in your fingers is the additional pain of ensuring that all of your tags are valid and that no mistakes were made during input. A second method to create XML messages is to dynamically write these messages from your source code.

Obviously, an automated tool that handles tag creation and validation for you would really come in handy, and there are already some third-party tools available that can do just that for you. In Visual Studio .NET, you have access to an XML editing tool directly inside of your native development environment. This XML designer allows you to add a new item called an XML File to your .NET solutions, and then edit this file in either a textual mode or a designer mode, which provides you with tables in which to enter your data elements. The following steps show you how to add an XML File to your solution, and then create a simple XML message using both the text and data views:

1. Create a new Windows Application project using any .NET language you desire.
2. In the Solution Explorer window, right-click the project name, and select Add|Add New Item.
3. From the Add New Item window, look under the folder named Data, and select the XML File item. In the Name textbox, call this file SimpleMessage.xml, and then click the Open button to add this item to your solution.
4. The XML File opens in text-editing mode. At the bottom of the main viewing area, you will see two buttons: XML and Data. The XML view of your XML File shows the raw text included in your message, whereas the Data view allows you to enter your data elements using a table control. Click the Data button, and you will see a message telling you that your XML document is not well formed. This is because the document has not had a schema defined, so the Data view does not know which data elements your document requires.

5. Click the XML button to return to the text editing view of your document. Notice the **targetSchema** property in the Properties window. If you are creating an XML message based on a predefined XML schema, you should bind your message to that schema using this Properties window box. Adding a schema to a message will avoid having to create your message's structure. This will also enable the Data view because the schema will provide all of the necessary information to outline the document's data elements. For this example, I will not use a predefined schema for my XML message.
6. In the XML view of your message, notice that there is one tag already added for you:

```
<?xml version="1.0" encoding="utf-8" ?>
```

   This first tag tells the receiver which version of the XML specification you will be using (version 1.0) and which character set the text is based on (utf-8).
7. On the line below this tag, type this tag: **<Employees>**
8. When you type the final > of the **<Employees>** tag, you will notice that the editor automatically adds a matching closing tag. Press Enter twice to move the **</Employees>** tag down two lines.
9. In between the two **<Employee>** tags, type the following lines:

```
<EmpID></EmpID>
<EmpName></EmpName>
<HireDate></HireDate>
<OfficeID></OfficeID>
```

10. Again, all of the ending tags will be added for you automatically. You now have a simple document schema planned but no data elements filled in. You could enter some data between these tags, and then retype each set of tags for every employee you want to place in this message, or you could do it the easy way. I prefer the easy way, so click the Data button at the bottom of your XML message.
11. You will see two panes in your Data view. The left pane lists all tables defined within the messages schema, which for this short message is just the **Employees** table. In the right pane, there is a table much like a DataGrid control that lists the columns within this table. You will see four columns corresponding to the four tags you entered inside the **Employees** table.
12. In the DataGrid, enter data in all four columns for three separate employees. Use the Tab key to move from field to field. When you tab out of the fourth column, a new row will be added to your table.
13. Click the XML button at the bottom of this window.

14. Notice that there are now a lot more tags in your XML message. Your multiple employee records are surrounded by a new pair of tags named **<NewDataSet>**. This groups all of your employee records into a single DataSet, just like the one you would find in ADO.NET.

The Visual Studio .NET XML designer tool is really helpful when you want to create static and unchanging XML messages. But how often do you need to send a static message with the same old data elements to someone? To create dynamic messages at runtime, use either the **XmlTextWriter** class to write out your message in code or the ADO.NET DataSet's **WriteXml** method to extract your DataSet in XML format for transmission.

Related solutions:	*Found on page:*
Writing an XML Document Using **XmlTextWriter**	223
Parsing an XML Document Using **XmlTextReader**	214
Using **XPath**	238
Using DataSets to Generate XML Messages	718
Filling a DataSet from an XML Message	720

Using the Document Outline Tool to View XML Message Structures

XML messages can contain a great deal of hierarchical data, so much that it can be hard to locate specific items in a message. If the message is not formatted using indentations and carriage returns to separate data elements, it can also be difficult to visually comprehend a message hierarchy. Fortunately, Visual Studio .NET provides a tool to simplify your message layout into a familiar and easy to navigate outline view. When you are looking at an XML message in Visual Studio .NET, you can open this window by selecting View|Other Windows|Document Outline.

The Document Outline window provides a tree view look at your XML message's elements. Child elements are located beneath their parent elements in expandable and collapsible trees, just like Windows Explorer uses to show directories and files. When you click an item in the Document Outline window, the matching element's definition tag is highlighted in the XML design window. The link between these two windows only works when the XML message is being shown in XML mode not in graphical Data mode. Figure 14.3 shows a screenshot of the Document Outline window and the corresponding XML message. In the Document Outline window, one of the **HireDate** elements is highlighted, and the matching

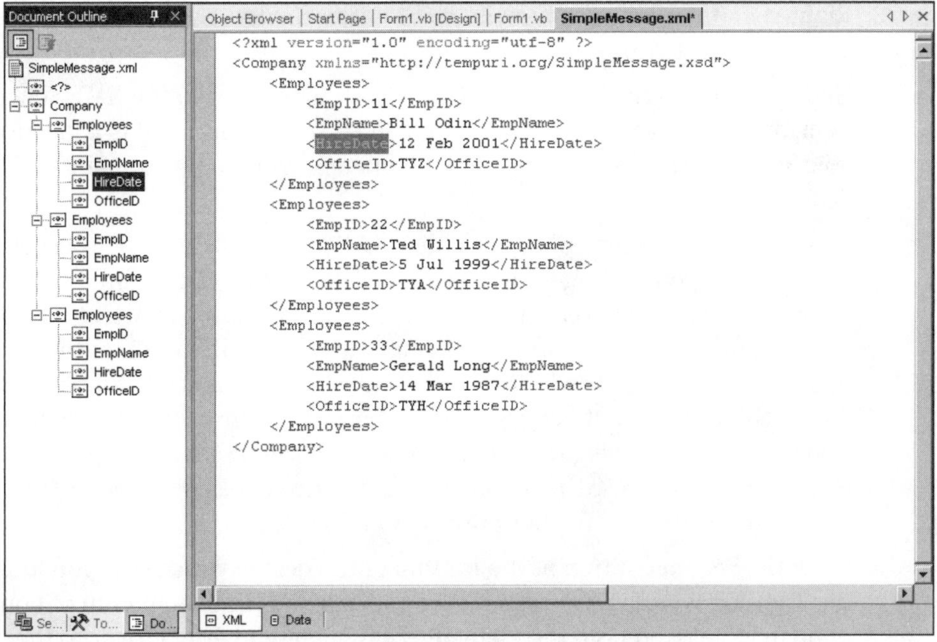

Figure 14.3 The Document Outline window and an XML message.

HireDate tag is highlighted in the text of the XML message. You can use the Document Outline window with other text-based files, such as HTML Web pages.

Creating an XSD Schema in Visual Studio .NET

A schema is a file that defines the structure and a set of data rules that an XML document will adhere to. You can create your schemas the hard way using a text editing tool such as Windows Notepad, or you could opt to use the Visual Studio .NET schema designer tool, which allows you to visually create your schema using familiar drag-and-drop techniques.

Defining a schema for your messages to follow avoids a lot of unnecessary trouble and confusion between the sending and receiving applications. Because schemas do not contain the actual data elements, they are highly reusable. You can add a single schema to your .NET solution and reuse that file to send XML messages and also validate those you receive from outside sources. Here is an example of how to add an XML schema to your project and then define its structure and rules using the GUI designer tool:

1. Create a Windows Application project using any development language.

2. Right-click the project's name in the Solution Explorer window, and select Add|Add New Item.
3. Under the Data folder in the Add New Item window, select the XML Schema item, and then click Open. An item named XMLSchema1.xsd is added to your project. This item should now be open in your coding area in designer mode.
4. The schema designer tool has two modes: Schema and XML. The Schema mode allows you to drag-and-drop items from the ToolBox window over to your design view, whereas the XML mode shows you the raw text-based tags that make up your defined schema. Click the XML button at the bottom of the designer window to see the basic schema definition tags that are added to the top of every schema. These tags define the XML specification version being used, the character set, and the target namespace that owns this schema. A URL link is provided to the W3C's definition of the XSD specification for further information.
5. Click the Schema button at the bottom of the design window. If you look at the ToolBox window, you will see a pane called XML Schema full of components. Click and hold the element component and drag it over to the surface of your schema.
6. This element component appears as a miniature DataGrid that you can enter data into. The top line contains the name of the element, so enter the word **Employees** in the top-left box, and then press the Tab key three times. Your cursor should now be in the box directly below the **Employees** name you typed in. The schema you will be creating will match the one shown in Figure 14.1, so you can reference this figure at any time to see if your schema values are correct.
7. In the current box, enter the word **EmpID**, and then press Tab three times. Repeat this step to enter the words **EmpName**, **HireDate**, and **OfficeID** on the next three lines.
8. Click the XML button at the bottom of the schema designer window. Note that your **Employees** element is a **complex** type, and the four values you entered below it are elements of the **Employees complex** type.
9. Click the Schema button to return to the designer view. From the ToolBox window, drag a key component over to your **Employees** box and drop it. A window pops up asking you to define this key. Because the **EmpID** element is the first in the list, it appears at the top of the Fields list window. This will be the **complex** type's primary key, so leave **EmpID** selected in the Fields list window and click the checkbox next to the DataSet primary key item. Click OK, and you will see a small key to the left of the **EmpID** element.

10. From the Toolbox, drag another element component and drop it to the right of the **Employees** element. Name this element **Offices**, and then add the following three elements to it: **OfficeID**, **OfficeName**, **OfficeSym**.
11. Drag a key from the ToolBox to the **Offices** box. The **OfficeID** element should be selected in the Fields list window, and the DataSet primary key item should be selected. Click OK to add this primary key to the **Offices** element.
12. Next, you want to add a relationship between your two elements. Drag a relation component from the ToolBox over to the **Employees** element and drop it. Set the parent element drop-down list to **Offices**. The child element box should already display **Employees**. In the Fields list window, the key fields value on the left should already display **OfficeID**. Set the Foreign key field value on the right side to **OfficeID** as well. This means that the **OfficeID** value in the **Employees** table will be a foreign key pointing to the **Offices** table's **OfficeID** value.
13. Click OK, and you will see a line added to the schema design view connecting the two tables. At the **Offices** end of this line, you will see a single dot connecting the line to the element. On the **Employees** end, this line fans out into three lines touching the **Employees** element. This represents a one-to-many relationship between the **Offices** and **Employees** elements (as in, one office can have many employees assigned to it). Your final schema should look like the one shown in Figure 14.1.
14. Click the XML button at the bottom of the design view and look at the schema tags you created. You will see **<xsd:key>** tags that define the primary and foreign keys as well as the relationship defined between your two elements.

You can add multiple XML schemas to your .NET solutions, and you can use these to write new XML messages and validate existing messages for proper format. Creating standalone schema files allows for maximum code reusability. Within your project directory, your schema files will end in a .xsd extension, which is a standard naming convention for XML schemas in XSD format.

Creating an XSD Schema from an Existing XML Message

You may be presented with an XML message that was supplied without the benefit of an XML schema. Because schemas are the preferred way to define a message's format, it would be beneficial to your application to possess a schema for this message so it can be used to validate future messages. One word of caution: before you create a schema from a raw XML message, be sure that all parties agree on that message's format before you begin coding to its schema. If the message's format changes after you code your application or if the message you generated your schema from was missing some elements, your application code will have problems when presented with other XML messages.

If you are certain that the sample XML message you possess does follow an agreed upon standard, you can use Visual Studio .NET to generate a schema based on that message. To illustrate how to do this, I will use the simple XML message created in the "Creating an XML Message in Visual Studio .NET" solution. If you have already tried this exercise and have saved your steps, you can open that project now and skip to step 2.

1. Create a new Windows Application project, and add an XML File item named SimpleMessage.xml to that project. Enter the following tags into the XML File's XML view:

```
<?xml version="1.0" encoding="utf-8" ?>
<Company>
    <Employees>
        <EmpID>11</EmpID>
        <EmpName>Bill Odin</EmpName>
        <HireDate>12 Feb 2001</HireDate>
        <OfficeID>TYZ</OfficeID>
    </Employees>
    <Employees>
        <EmpID>22</EmpID>
        <EmpName>Ted Willis</EmpName>
        <HireDate>5 Jul 1999</HireDate>
        <OfficeID>TYA</OfficeID>
    </Employees>
    <Employees>
        <EmpID>33</EmpID>
        <EmpName>Gerald Long</EmpName>
        <HireDate>14 Mar 1987</HireDate>
        <OfficeID>TYH</OfficeID>
    </Employees>
</Company>
```

2. Right-click the surface of your XML message, and click Create Schema.
3. A new item named SimpleMessage1.xsd is added to your project. Double-click this item to open it. You will see the **Employees complex** type defined in the graphical Schema view.
4. Click the Data button at the bottom of your schema's design view to see the raw schema tags. Notice that the data types for your data elements have been set to **xsd:string**.

5. At the top of the code view window, click the SimpleMessage.xml tab to go back to the XML message. You will then see a link to your schema in the **<Company>** tag near the top of this message.

You can also add existing XML messages to your .NET solutions if you need to generate a schema from a message not created in Visual Studio .NET. Any future messages your application receives can be validated using the schema you just created to verify that the latest XML message follows the same rules that the original message did. The more restrictive a schema is, the better, so you might want to edit a generated schema to add data rules (called facets) to further restrict the message's data elements.

Validating an XML Message Using an XSD Schema

If you are working with a stored bank of message schemas and an outside application sends you a message to work with, you may want to first validate that message against one of your schemas. This will ensure that your code does not encounter an incorrect or ill-formed node in the message when it comes time to process its contents. To validate an XML message, you can use the **XmlValidatingReader** object, which uses an **XmlTextReader** object to pull in the XML message combined with a schema that provides a reference with which to compare the source document.

The following source code uses a function named **ValidateXml**. I developed this function to be reusable by accepting an XML file name, an XML schema file, and the unified resource name (urn) for that schema. The urn is the schema's name, which is contained within the opening schema tag inside the schema file. When adding a schema, you must use the correct urn name for the file name that you specify. Take a look at this example:

```
Private Function ValidateXml(ByVal CheckFile As String, ByVal _
      CheckSchema As String, ByVal CheckUrn As String) As Boolean
    'Create a XmlTextReader and point it to the XML message
    Dim txtReader As Xml.XmlTextReader = New Xml.XmlTextReader(CheckFile)
    'Create a XmlValidationReader and point it to the XmlTextReader
    Dim valReader As Xml.XmlValidatingReader = New_
       Xml.XmlValidatingReader(txtReader)

    'Add the XML Schemas to the XmlValidationReader
    valReader.Schemas.Add(CheckUrn, CheckSchema) 'XSD schema
```

```
    'Define an event handler to respond to Validation errors
    AddHandler valReader.ValidationEventHandler, AddressOf _
        ValidationHandler

    'Loop through XML message to compare to schema
    Do While (valReader.Read())
    Loop

    'Close valReader and show the results of ValidateXml
    valReader.Close()
    Console.WriteLine("ValidateXml found " & ErrorsFound & " errors")
    If ErrorsFound > 0 Then ValidateXml = False Else ValidateXml = True
End Function

Public Sub ValidationHandler(ByVal sender As Object, ByVal args As_
      xml.Schema.ValidationEventArgs)
    Dim ErrMsg As String = "Validation Error = " & args.Message
    Console.WriteLine(ErrMsg)
    ErrorsFound = ErrorsFound + 1
End Sub
```


To use the **ValidateXml** function, you would set up your parameters and call out to this function like this:

```
Dim CheckFile As String = "c:\XmlDocs\Employees.xml"
Dim CheckSchema As String = "c:\XmlDocs\Company.xsd"
Dim CheckUrn As String = "urn:employee-schema"
Dim Results As Boolean
Results = ValidateXml(CheckFile, CheckSchema, CheckUrn)
```

The **ValidateXml** function first creates an **XmlTextReader** that handles the duties of reading in the XML message. Next, an **XmlValidatingReader** is created and pointed to the **XmlTextReader**. A schema is added to the **XmlValidateReader**'s **Schema** collection and is used during the **Read** method to compare the XML message. You do not have to do anything with the data that the **Read** method scans, but you do have to run your **XmlValidatingReader** through the document once to run a full comparison. This is why you see an empty **Do While** loop in this function.

The **XmlValidatingReader** raises an event whenever it encounters a validation problem. To catch this event, you need to add an **EventHandler** to your function, and then a subroutine to deal with the event. The **ValidationHandler** subroutine is executed whenever the **XmlValidatingReader** raises an event, which in my example increments the **ErrorsFound** variable by one and writes the validation error message (provided by args.message) to the console window. The code that calls the **ValidateXml** function can check the Boolean output for **True** if the validation succeeded or **False** if it has failed.

Designing an XSLT Transformation File

Just like its XML and XSD relatives, you can create XSLT transformation files by using either a simple text editor or by using the Visual Studio .NET editor. Unlike XML and XSD files, you will not be able to graphically create your transformation file. This is due to the fact that XSLT files are more like source code than they are schemas or datasets. Still, using the Visual Studio .NET environment has many distinct advantages over the dull and dreary text editors. These advantages include color coded tags and parameters, and automatic creation of ending tags for every tag you type in.

Here is an example of an XSLT file that you can add to one of your .NET solutions:

1. Start a new Windows Application project using any development language.
2. Right-click the project name in the Solution Explorer window, and select Add|Add New Item.
3. In the Add New Item window, select the XSLT file under the Data folder, and click Open.
4. The XSLT file opens in the code view area and shows you a few default tags that have been created for you. Enter the following lines above the **</stylesheet>** tag and below the opening **<stylesheet>** tag:

```
<xsl:template match="/">
  <HTML>
    <HEAD>
      <TITLE>Employee Records List</TITLE>
    </HEAD>
    <BODY>
      <CENTER>
      <H2>Employee Records</H2>
      <TABLE BORDER="2">
        <TR>
          <TD BGCOLOR="#00FFFF">EmpID</TD>
          <TD BGCOLOR="#00FFFF">EmpName</TD>
          <TD BGCOLOR="#00FFFF">HireDate</TD>
          <TD BGCOLOR="#00FFFF">OfficeID</TD>
        </TR>
        <xsl:for-each select="/Company/Employees">
```

```
            <TR>
              <TD><xsl:value-of select="EmpID" /></TD>
              <TD><xsl:value-of select="EmpName" /></TD>
              <TD><xsl:value-of select="HireDate" /></TD>
              <TD><xsl:value-of select="OfficeID" /></TD>
            </TR>
            </xsl:for-each>
          </TABLE>
          </CENTER>
        </BODY>
      </HTML>
    </xsl:template>
```

5. To view your XSLT file's outline, select View|Other Windows|Document Outline. The Document Outline window opens and displays the elements in your transformation file along with their relationships.
6. Save your Solution by selecting File|Save All. You will use this XSLT file in the next Immediate Solution when you learn how to apply transformation files to XML messages.

The XSLT file in this example uses HTML tags with embedded **<xsl>** tags that insert values from the XML message being processed into the resulting HTML page. If you have ever created Active Server Pages (ASP) Web pages with VBScript embedded in them, this will feel like familiar territory to you. The **<xsl:for-each select="/Company/Employees">** tag acts as a **For** loop to iterate through all of the **Employees** records in the source message. The **<xsl:value>** tags print out the value of the corresponding elements that belong to the **Employees** record currently being processed. If there are four employees in the XML message, this **<xsl:for-each>** loop is processed four times, resulting in four rows being added to the HTML table. For a complete list of **<xsl>** tags you can use in your XSLT transformation documents, consult the Visual Studio .NET MSDN Library.

Transforming an XML Message to a New Schema

Once you have created an XSLT transformation file, it is reasonably easy to put this file to work in your source code. A transformation requires two items: the XSLT transformation file and the incoming XML message. The output of the transformation process will be a new file, which could be another XML message or maybe a different format such as HTML.

The following source code example was written in Visual Basic .NET and uses the XSLT file created in the previous Immediate Solution to convert an XML message named SimpleMessage.xml, which I created in the "Creating an XSD Schema from an Existing XML Message" solution. The output of this transformation is an HTML file on the hard drive named NewDoc.htm, which displays a table of all employee records found in the XML message using HTML tags that any browser can understand.

***NOTE:** Copy the XSLTFile1.xslt and the SimpleMessage.xml files from previous Immediate Solutions to a directory named c:\XmlDocs. This is where this code example will be looking for these files.*

```
Private Sub TransformXml()
    'Load XML
    Dim SourceDoc As New Xml.XPath.XPathDocument("C:\XmlDocs\_
      SimpleMessage.xml")
    Dim NewDoc As New Xml.XmlTextWriter("c:\XmlDocs\NewDoc.htm", System._
      Text.Encoding.UTF8)
    'Transform XML file here
    Dim Transformer As New Xml.Xsl.XslTransform()
    'Load the XSLT file into the Transformer
    Transformer.Load("C:\XmlDocs\XSLTFile1.xslt")
    'Pass the SourceDoc into the Transformer and set the output to NewDoc
    Transformer.Transform(SourceDoc, Nothing, NewDoc)
End Sub
```

To see a picture of the resulting Web page, take a look at Figure 14.4. In the preceding code example, I stored my XSLT and XML files in a directory named XmlDocs to keep things simple and the file paths short. When you are working with XML and XSLT files that you have added directly to your .NET solution, you

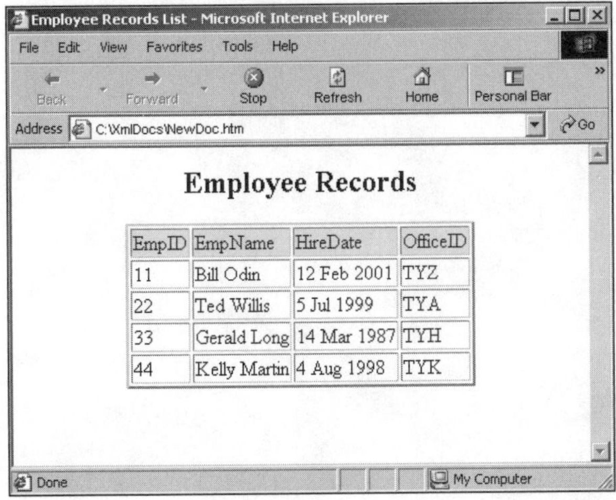

Figure 14.4 The HTML version of the transformed **Employees** XML message.

need to reference these in your code by the path to the file's actual location on the hard drive. One quick and easy way to do this is to drag the XML or XSLT item from the Solution Explorer window to your code view and drop it where you want the file's path to appear. This can save a lot of typing, but be sure to enclose the path in quotation marks!

The XmlTransform's **Transform** method takes in three parameters: the name of the incoming source document, an XSLT argument parameter, and an output document in which to write the newly created message. To keep my example simple, I am not using any XSLT arguments for this transformation. My source XML document is first loaded into an **XpathDocument** object, which is later passed into the **Transform** method. For the transformed document, I created an **XmlTextWriter** object to handle the transformation's output. You could also pass this output to an **XmlTextReader** to facilitate working with the transformation's results.

Chapter 15

ADO.NET

By David Vitter

If you need an immediate solution to:	*See page:*

In Depth

Information is the lifeblood of the business world, and business application developers have been reading and writing these bits of information for decades. Data can be found in many different forms, from the traditional tables in a relational database to a file system full of textual documents. Some bits of data are easier to access than others, and often the methods used to access different data sources are as diverse as the sources themselves. In the last few years, ActiveX Data Objects (ADO) has become a popular way for Visual Studio developers to access these numerous data stores from their applications. In this chapter, I introduce you to the latest version of ADO, appropriately named ADO.NET. As you will learn, ADO.NET is not so much an upgraded version of ADO as it is a redesigned tool that takes a whole new approach to accessing data from .NET applications.

Introduction to ADO.NET

Throughout the years, there have been many database access methods made available to the developer community. Most of these technologies have been more closely related to the database they access than to the development tools they can be used in. Open DataBase Connectivity (ODBC), for example, was developed by database vendors to provide access to multiple database types. The major drawbacks of using ODBC are that the API is complex and difficult to work with, and its interfaces are not COM-based.

Microsoft worked hard to make data access easier by developing numerous technologies built on top of ODBC. Data Access Object (DAO) was one of the first such efforts developed specifically for use in Microsoft's Access product. Remote Data Object (RDO) was developed next to bring data access to the Visual Basic community. Like its predecessor DAO, RDO was designed to use ODBC database connections but make it easier for the developer to work with. RDO quickly evolved into ADO, which was aimed at the entire community of Microsoft developers. Although ADO could still use ODBC to connect to databases, Microsoft built ADO to use a new database provider named Object Linking and Embedding DataBase (OLE DB), which was designed to be a COM-based follow-up to the ODBC provider. In the next section, you will see how ADO and OLE DB work together to provide access to your database.

When Microsoft created ADO, it wanted to provide developers with an interface to its data sources that fit naturally within its COM-based development projects.

The API exposed by ADO felt very comfortable to COM developers, and they could work with their ADO connections in an object-oriented fashion. ADO also used COM to marshal its Recordsets of data from one point to another. For new developers, ADO was by far the easiest data access method to learn, and it even offered access to nontraditional data stores such as email servers. ADO went through a couple of different revisions, each one adding new additional features while leaving the basic structure and format of ADO unchanged. The last few versions of ADO added support for reading in and writing out XML data from your Recordsets, even though the ADO Recordset itself was not based on XML.

Comparing ADO to ADO.NET

ADO.NET is far more than an upgraded version of its predecessor, but before you can use this new version, you need to fully comprehend the differences. Some of the most important changes are:

- The ADO Recordset is now called the ADO.NET DataSet.
- DataSets can contain multiple tables.
- Tables within a DataSet can have relationships.
- ADO.NET uses XML to communicate DataSets from point to point.
- DataSets are a disconnected form of data access.
- Developers do not need to concern themselves with database cursors and locks when using DataSets.

At the top of the list of changes is the old ADO Recordset. Formerly, the Recordset was the main data-containing object you worked with in ADO. The information held within a Recordset equated to a single table of data. When one of your code-based objects transferred a Recordset to another object, it used COM as the communication medium to do so.

In ADO.NET, the Recordset is gone and the DataSet is at the center of this new universe. Not only has the name changed, but its structure has as well. A DataSet is capable of holding many tables of data, and it can remember relationships between these multiple tables. For example, you could create a DataSet that contains an **Employees** and an **Offices** table and identify within that DataSet that the **Employees** table is related to the **Offices** table through its **OfficeID** attribute. This makes a DataSet far more powerful than a Recordset and gives you the ability to create a mini-database.

Because ADO.NET was built on top of an XML framework, ADO.NET uses XML to move its DataSets around. This means that your DataSets can now pass through firewalls that would normally block Recordsets that use COM to move about. You can pass DataSets between application components that are separated by a firewall. Let's examine a few more differences between ADO and ADO.NET.

Disconnected versus Connected Database Access

Prior to ADO.NET, database access was typically handled in a connected fashion. Say, for example, that you want to edit an employee's record in the database. To program this, you would establish a connection to the database, locate the record by moving the database cursor, make your changes to that record, and then disconnect from the database. The data you were working with stayed on the database server, and your code manipulated this data using the established open connection. Databases do not have an infinite number of available connections, so only a few clients can connect to a database at any single moment. From the point where your code establishes its connection until the moment when that connection is released, one of those valuable database connections is being used, possibly delaying or preventing other accesses. Freeing up these connections is the database developer's number-one concern.

ADO.NET works with data in a disconnected mode. Communication with the database server is short and to the point, allowing .NET to quickly release the connection for someone else. If you wanted to modify an employee's record using ADO.NET, the process would work like this: ADO.NET would establish a connection to the database, and then the data you want to work with would be extracted from the database to the local machine. Having this copy of the data allows ADO.NET to release its connection to the database. Your code could then modify, manipulate, and mangle that data for as long as you wanted without tying up a database connection. When you are ready to save your changed data, ADO.NET would again connect to the database and update the record. Because ADO.NET only stays connected to the database for short periods of time, this data access method offers the least drain on your database's resources.

Database Cursors

If you have worked with past versions of ADO, you are familiar with database *cursors*. Before you could establish your ADO connection to your database, you had to decide on whether to use a client-side or server-side cursor. If you selected the server-side cursor route, you had a few more cursor types to choose from, such as the Forward-only and the Static cursors, each with its own advantages and drawbacks. Connecting to a database took a great deal of thought and planning, and still some functions would neglect to release their connections when finished, thereby hogging those resources needlessly. Because ADO.NET disconnects from the database when performing changes to your data, cursors are no longer needed. The one exception to this rule is the ADO.NET **DataReader** object, which uses a server-side cursor similar to the ADO Forward-only cursor. You will read more about the DataReader later in the In Depth section.

Data Locking

Yet another decision you had to make when using ADO was your choice of locking mechanism. A lock is used by the database server to protect the row of data you are manipulating from being changed by another client. Common lock types included *ReadOnly*, *Optimistic*, and *Pessimistic*. Because ADO.NET disconnects from the database when you are manipulating the retrieved data, it would be impractical for the database server to hold a lock on the withdrawn data elements. If the ADO.NET DataSet never calls back to the database server with an update, any instances of locked data would remain locked and prevent future calls from changing their values. Instead of placing locks on rows of data on the server, ADO.NET can detect changed data rows during its update phase and decide which version of the data should be saved. You will learn more about how ADO.NET does this in the "Working with ADO.NET DataSets" section.

Using Past Versions of ADO in .NET Projects

For the vast majority of your new Visual Studio .NET projects, you will want to use ADO.NET to connect to your databases and work with your data while disconnected. Because ADO.NET does not support connected database transactions, if you need to work with your data in a connected fashion, you will have to use an older version of ADO to do so. Simply add a COM reference to a past version of ADO, such as version 2.6, and you will be able to code your data access routines in the older ADO style. You can even use ADO.NET and ADO in the same project if need be, but because these two data access methods are extremely different, they will not be able to interact or exchange sets of data. The following list contains situations that may warrant the use of a prior version of ADO:

- You need to migrate an existing project to .NET that already uses ADO.
- You need to work with a large set of data that is too large to pull back to the client and load into a DataSet, so you will need to use a server-side cursor.
- Your code relies on server-side data cursors or data locking mechanisms.

Migrating older ADO code to ADO.NET will take a great deal of work, but the benefits far outweigh the amount of work required. If you must use an older version of ADO, I highly recommend you choose ADO version 2.5 or later due to the added XML support features introduced by these versions. This functionality will come in handy if you need to exchange some data between an ADO Recordset and an ADO.NET DataSet because you can do so through the use of an XML dump file.

Data Access Layers in ADO.NET

When you are developing an application that uses ADO.NET to access a database, your code will be using multiple technologies to get at the data. In Figure 15.1, the top of the figure shows your code, and the bottom of the figure shows your database. In between these two end-points you will see multiple layers, which include data access providers and drivers or interfaces. ADO.NET is the layer closest to your code that provides the API that your code will use to control the database

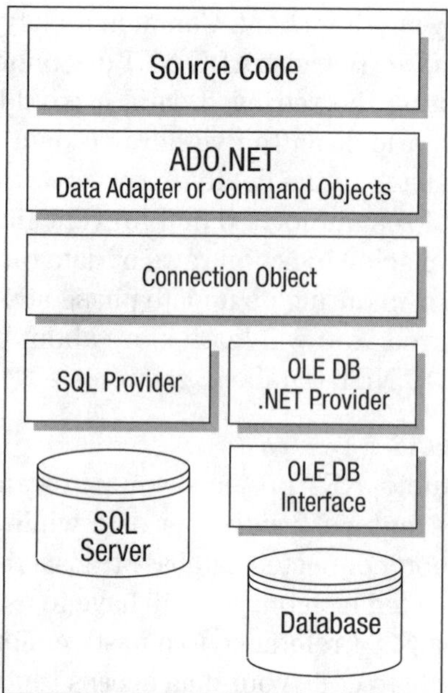

Figure 15.1 The data access layers.

transaction. ADO.NET does not have the ability to deal directly with databases. Because there are many different types of data stores in existence, ADO.NET relies on specialized providers to act as interpreters for the ADO.NET calls. ADO.NET can use one of two different providers: the OLE DB .NET data provider and SQL Server .NET data provider. Microsoft will be releasing a .NET version of the ODBC .NET data provider shortly after the release of Visual Studio .NET.

The OLE DB Provider

ADO.NET's OLE DB provider is built on top of Microsoft's OLE DB interfaces, which are a COM-based replacement for the ODBC data access interfaces. Having an OLE DB layer on top of another OLE DB layer is pretty confusing, but remember that the OLE DB interfaces were developed back in the days of COM to replace ODBC, and the OLE DB provider is new with ADO.NET and sits on top of the OLE DB interfaces (see Figure 15.1 for further clarification). The OLE DB interfaces are at the database system level, and although you can use OLE DB to access data stores without the added provider layer, most developers will find that the time they save using the OLE DB provider outweighs the slight performance gained by going directly through OLE DB to your data.

The OLE DB provider is known as a *managed* provider because it communicates with OLE DB, which is COM-based, by using a wrapper to disguise this COM object as a .NET assembly. You will find the OLE DB provider in the

System.Data.OleDbClient namespace. The OLE DB provider can access any database for which an OLE DB connection exists, such as the Oracle and Jet OLE DB connections. You can also access a SQL Server database using OLE DB, but if you are using version 7 or later of this database, it is highly recommended that you use the SQL Server provider that I discuss in the next section.

The SQL Server Provider

Because Microsoft developed the SQL Server database, it was also able to create a specialized .NET data provider that offers a significant performance boost over the more generalized OLE DB provider. This provider does not use ODBC or OLE DB to connect with the database, which removes an entire layer between your code and the data, resulting in faster data connections. The SQL Server provider is located in the **System.Data.SqlClient** namespace. If you look in the Data panel of the Toolbox window, you will see a separate selection of SQL Server-specific data components.

Choosing between the OLE DB and SQL Server Providers

In most cases, the choice between using the OLE DB provider and using the SQL Server provider will be pretty obvious. If you are developing an application that works exclusively with a SQL Server 7 or later database, choosing to use the SQL Server-specific provider is a wise choice. If you are using any other database type, or you are using a version of SQL Server prior to 7, you have no choice but to use the OLE DB provider. The ADO.NET layer lies between your code and the provider, so you work with both providers in exactly same way. If you develop a function that uses the SQL Server provider, you can simply modify the provider declaration lines to quickly switch this function over to the OLE DB provider without having to change any other lines of code.

The DataSet

A relational database is made up of one or more tables, each containing one or more rows of data. Tables in a relational database can either stand alone or they can have a relationship with another table in that database. Structurally, an ADO.NET DataSet closely resembles a database structure. Data is contained within tables and displayed in rows and columns. These tables can stand alone or be related to other tables within the DataSet. Figure 15.2 illustrates the parts of a DataSet. You will find the **DataSet**, **DataTable**, **DataRow**, **DataColumn**, and **DataRelation** classes directly under the **System.Data** namespace. Let's examine each piece of a DataSet separately.

The DataTable

A DataSet contains a collection of DataTables, which allows you to add more than one table to a DataSet. Like a table in a database, the DataTable is made up

DataSet - Company

DataTable - Employees

DataColumn

EmpID	EmpName	OfficeID	HireDate
11	James Foster	1	5/12/01
21	Tanya Pope	2	2/28/96
41	Winston Anders	3	10/3/00
31	Hank Miller	4	6/14/97

DataTable - Offices

OfficeID	OfficeName	OfficeSym
1	Finance	FDV
2	Budgets	BDV
3	Travel	TDV
4	HR	HDV
5	Credit Union	CDV

< DataRow

Figure 15.2 The DataSet structure.

of rows and columns, which represent elements and attributes respectively. The names of the individual tables within the DataTable's collection are case sensitive, so you can have both a **Customers** and a **customers** table in the same DataSet. Be sure that you use the correct case-sensitive table name when typing in your source code.

In order to work with a DataTable, you should be familiar with its many properties, methods, and events. In your code you can react to events that occur within a DataTable, such as the changing of a value within a row or the deletion of a row. You can also accept or reject all changes made to a DataTable. Use Table 15.1 to quickly become familiar with the most useful parts of the DataTable.

The DataRow

Every DataTable has a collection of DataRows. You add, delete, and modify data within a table by using DataRows. Each row is the equivalent of a single record, such as a single customer in a **Customers** table. You add a brand new row to a table by using the DataTable's **NewRow** method. Once the row exists within the table, you can use the DataRow's interfaces to modify it. The majority of your editing and data modifications are done using the **DataRow** object to manipulate your tables on a record-by-record basis. Table 15.2 lists the most commonly used properties and methods for the **DataRow** object.

Table 15.1 DataTable properties, methods, and events.

Property	Purpose
CaseSensitive	String value comparisons within the table can either be case sensitive (**True**) or not (**False**)
HasErrors	Indicates that one or more data elements within this table has an error
PrimaryKey	Sets the primary key for the table
TableName	The identifying name of the table
DefaultView	Identifies a customized view of the table, if desired
DataSet	The name of the DataSet this table belongs to
Method	**Purpose**
AcceptChanges	Accepts and commits all changes made within the table
NewRow	Adds a new DataRow to the DataTable
RejectChanges	Rejects and rolls back all changes made within the table
GetChanges	Produces a version of the DataTable containing items that have been changed since the last commit or data load
Clone	Creates a copy of the DataTable's format, including the loaded schema and constraints
Copy	Creates a copy of both the DataTable's format and the data currently contained in the DataTable
Clear	Removes all data from the DataTable
ImportDataRow	Loads a DataRow from an external source into your DataTable
GetErrors	Creates an array of rows that currently contain errors
Select	Allows you to create an array of rows that match a certain criteria, similar to executing a SQL **SELECT** statement against your DataTable
Event	**Purpose**
RowChanged	Raised when data within a row is changed
ColumnChanged	Triggered by changes being applied to a column
RowDeleted	Fires when a row of data has been deleted

The DataColumn

A single DataTable also contains a collection of DataColumns. Whereas rows represent records in a table, the columns represent the attributes of the table. If a **Customers** table has a **FirstName** attribute, a **FirstName** column within the table will represent this attribute. Every column has a data type associated with it. The **FirstName** attribute uses a **String** data type to store the customer's name. A DataTable's column names and their data types can be summarized to form a schema, which is a record describing the format and rules of a table.

Column values can also have constraints placed on them. Table 15.3 lists some of the properties and methods for the **DataColumn** object.

Table 15.2 DataRow properties and methods.

Property	Purpose
HasErrors	Boolean value that indicates this row has an error
Item	Provides access to column values based on the column name you provide it
RowError	Allows you to check or modify the error message for this row
RowState	Provides you with the row's current state
Table	Returns the name of the table containing this DataRow
Method	**Purpose**
AcceptChanges	Commits any changes made to this row
ClearErrors	Clears all errors raised for the DataRow
Delete	Removes this row from the table
ToString	Converts the value of the indicated column to a **String** data type
RejectChanges	Rejects and rolls back any uncommitted changes to the row
GetType	Returns the data type of the indicated column
GetColumnError	Provides a description for the chosen column

Table 15.3 DataColumn properties and methods.

Property	Purpose
AllowDBNull	Indicates if null values are allowed in this column.
AutoIncrement	The value of this column is automatically set when a new row is added to the table. Often used for attributes that provide unique numbers, such as a CustomerID.
Caption	Sets the column name displayed at the top of a data displaying control.
ColumnName	Sets the official name of the column used in queries.
DataType	Indicates the data type allowed in this column.
DefaultValue	Provides a default value for this column if needed.
MaxLength	Sets the maximum length a column value can be.
ReadOnly	Indicates that a column value cannot be changed.
Table	The name of the table containing this column.
Unique	Indicates that every value in this column must be a unique value within the column, no duplicates.
Method	**Purpose**
Equals	Allows you to compare the column's value to another column's value.
GetType	Returns the data type of the column.
ToString	Converts the column's value to a **String** data type.

DataSet Relationships

An example of a table-to-table relationship is a database that contains a **Products** and a **Suppliers** table. To find out where a particular product in the **Products** table can be purchased, you would locate that product's **SuppliersID** attribute, which would correspond to one of the companies listed in the **Suppliers** table. Each supplier has a unique **SuppliersID** attribute assigned to it, which is known as a primary key. When the **Products** table uses the **SuppliersID** key to point to some information in another table, this is known as a *foreign key relationship*. A DataSet keeps track of the relationships between its tables using the DataSet's **Relations** collection.

Typed and Untyped DataSets

DataSets are said to be in either a typed or an untyped format. The difference between these two formats is the presence of a preexisting data schema. If you first define a data schema for your DataSet prior to loading it with data, your DataSet is said to be typed. If you load a DataSet that has not been given a data schema, the DataSet is untyped. Creating a typed DataSet takes a little extra planning as you need to create a schema that lays out all of the rules and formats that your DataSet will adhere to. Choosing to create an untyped DataSet is quicker and easier, but you will be giving up many additional features and tools that are only available with typed DataSets.

One of the big differences between using typed and untyped DataSets is how you reference the data elements within those two different sets. Because a typed DataSet has a predefined structure, Visual Studio .NET automatically knows the table and column names within that DataSet, even before it has been populated. This enables you to reference these elements by name like so:

```
dsCompany.Employees(6).FirstName = "Matt"
```

This line of code directly references the table name, **Employees**, and the column name, **FirstName**. The row being edited in this example is located at index position six, which follows the table's name. With a predefined schema loaded into your DataSet, Visual Studio's IntelliSense is able to tell you which tables and columns are available, making your coding job faster and easier.

In an untyped DataSet, the IDE does not have enough knowledge about the data's structure to allow you to call tables and columns by name, so to make the exact same change to an untyped DataSet, you would have to reference these items more explicitly like this:

```
dsCompany.Tables("Employees").Rows(6)("FirstName") = "Matt"
```

You would have to type this line out without the benefit of IntelliSense filling in the table and column name, which means you would have to have a firm understanding of the table's structure to create this line. Try editing both a typed and an untyped table, and I think you will immediately see the advantage of working with typed DataSets with predefined schemas applied.

Constraints

Each table has a collection of constraints that define the rules placed on the column values within that table. For example, one column could be restricted to allow only unique values, which would prevent a value from being entered in a column twice. You could also define one of the columns within a table as being the primary key for that table, which is also a data constraint very similar to the unique constraint. Anyone that has ever created a table in a database is already familiar with defining constraints to restrict and control the data elements within that table. When you fill a DataSet from a data source of an XML file, all of the constraints from that source will be duplicated within the tables created in your DataSet.

Any relationships defined within your DataSet through its **Relations** collection will be a constraint placed on your data because the value in one table's column must be a pointer to a unique value in another table's columns. Each DataSet has a property named **EnforceConstraints**, which by default is set to **True**. Developers have the option of disabling all constraints within a DataSet by setting this property to **False**. This prevents exceptions from being raised whenever defined constraints are violated by data changes within a table. Disabling constraints can be useful for temporary changes that you think may cause exceptions, but you should always try to repair any constraint violations and reenable those checks as soon as possible.

Connecting to Data Sources

The most common use for ADO has traditionally been to connect to a database such as SQL Server, Oracle, or Access to work with the data contained within that database. With all of the new XML functionality and the improvements made to the DataSet, developers will begin to use ADO.NET in many situations that do not directly involve a database. Of course, database access will remain ADO.NET's bread and butter, so let's discuss how these connections are made and controlled. In the following section you are introduced to another new object named the **DataAdapter**, which makes connecting your DataSets to a database easier than ever. You will also learn about the **Command** and **Connection** objects, which both appeared in previous versions of ADO. In addition, you will learn about the new **DataReader** object, which provides a quick way to extract read-only data from your database.

Table 15.4 OLE DB and SQL versions of ADO.NET objects.

Object	OLE DB Provider	SQL Provider
DataAdapter	System.Data.OleDb.OleDbDataAdapter	System.Data.SqlClient.SqlDataAdapter
Connection	System.Data.OleDb.OleDbConnection	System.Data.SqlClient.SqlConnection
Command	System.Data.OleDb.OleDbCommand	System.Data.SqlClient.SqlCommand
DataReader	System.Data.OleDb.OleDbDataReader	System.Data.SqlClient.SqlDataReader

For each of these three objects, there are two versions: one for the OLE DB providers and the other for the SQL providers. Table 15.4 lists the different versions of these objects and their associated namespaces.

The DataAdapter

Developers use the ADO.NET **DataAdapter** object to connect their DataSets to their chosen data sources. Think of your database as a large tank of fuel at the local gas station, and your DataSet as your car's gas tank, which is a mini-version of the bigger fuel tank. The gas pump is the **Connection** object and the hose that connects the pump to your car is the DataAdapter. Once your car is full, you disconnect that hose so other cars can pull up and get gas. Of course, with ADO.NET data access, the DataAdapter and connection are not permanently attached to either your DataSet or the database, and the **Connection** object can work both ways to provide and return data. If you are creating a DataSet programmatically or filling it up from an XML message, you do not need a DataAdapter in your code.

The two primary interfaces of the DataAdapter that you will be working with are the **Fill** and **Update** methods. The **Fill** method activates your database connection, sends your request for data across the network, and then pumps the returned results into your DataSet. The **Update** method works in the reverse direction. When called upon, the **Update** method examines the changes you made to the data within your DataSet and communicates only those items that have changed back to the original data source. These changes include inserted rows, deleted rows, and rows that have had column values changed. There is no need to formulate SQL commands to handle these changes because the **Update** command uses a **CommandBuilder** object to generate these SQL strings for you and act as a translator between your DataSet and the database.

The Connection Object

The ADO.NET **Connection** object is responsible for establishing and controlling the connection between your code and the database. Both the **Command** and **DataAdapter** objects enlist the help of a **Connection** object to reach out to your data store. When you are configuring the provider type and connection string within Visual Studio .NET, you are actually configuring the **Connection** object.

Because the **Connection** object represents the actual link between your code and the database, this is the object that you open and close during your database communications. If you use a DataAdapter to manage your connection, the opening and closing of your connection is handled automatically. If you use the **Command** object to work with your database, you need to manually call the **Connection** object's **Open** and **Close** methods in your code. As with past versions of ADO, when controlling the **Connection** object manually, you need to always remember to **Close** your connection at the earliest possible time to free up that valuable database connection for other callers to use.

The Command Object

If you need to issue SQL commands directly against the database and do not want to work with a DataSet, use the **Command** object to do so. Using the **Command** object to make changes to your database can be more efficient than working with a DataSet because only your SQL command is sent across the network. These commands include the SQL **INSERT**, **DELETE**, and **UPDATE** statements. You assign your SQL command to the **Command** object's **CommandText** property, and then set the **CommandType** property to **Text**. Your **Command** object uses a **Connection** object to communicate this command directly to the database. You can also work with stored procedures using the **Command** object; I will show you an example of this in the Immediate Solutions section.

The DataReader

A DataSet is designed to hold data in order to facilitate client-side editing. Sometimes you will need to access a data store in order to fill in a data-bound control. If you first brought the data over and filled up a DataSet before pouring the data into your control, you would be adding an unnecessary layer between your control and the data, which would only slow down your application. Previously, ADO used a Forward-only server-side cursor commonly referred to as the "fire hose" cursor to quickly move through a database and draw all of the required data back to the application. This server-side cursor sacrifices flexibility in favor of speed because you will not be able to edit data when using it, nor will you be able to move backwards through the table.

ADO.NET introduces the **DataReader** object to provide you with an easy method to quickly pull an uneditable chunk of data out of your database. Unlike the DataAdapter's connection to your database, the DataReader utilizes a server-side cursor. The way that the DataReader connects to a database and deals with your data request differs greatly from the DataSet's usage. To connect to the database, the DataReader does not use the **DataAdapter** object. You also do not use a DataSet in your code to store the retrieved data in. The DataReader uses a **Connection** object to talk to the database and a **Command** object to execute the query that pulls back the needed data. The DataReader's **Read** method allows you to step forward through the database's table one record at a time.

***TIP:** Use the DataReader to fill in form controls with data. DataReader is the fastest way to pull uneditable data out of your database.*

Working with ADO.NET DataSets

The ADO.NET DataSet is the main object you interface with when working with your data. In past versions of ADO, the main data-containing object was called the Recordset. Not only has the name changed, but all of the functionality has changed as well. DataSets are far more complex than their Recordset ancestors, and they have the ability to act as a miniature standalone database. In this section, I discuss how a DataSet works, and how you interface with its data elements to make changes and then update your data store with these changes.

Filling DataSets with Data

The DataSet is the container within which you place the data you need to work with. You can build a DataSet from scratch by programmatically adding tables and rows, and then populating these with data. You can also fill a DataSet using the data elements found in an XML message, a method I discuss further in the "XML in ADO.NET" section. The final method of filling a DataSet involves using a **DataAdapter** object to connect it to a data store. Remember that a DataSet can contain multiple tables, and those tables can have relationships with each other. In the Immediate Solutions section, you will find examples of all three methods of filling a DataSet.

The Three Copies of Your Data

Within your DataSet, there are three copies of each data element. When your DataSet is first populated with data, a copy of this data is stored as the *original version*. Whenever you make changes to your data, these changes become part of a copy known as the *proposed changes version*. Proposed changes do not become official until you execute the **AcceptChanges** method, which moves all proposed changes over to a third version known as the *current copy*. Changes never affect your original copy because this version of your data is compared to the current version of your data by the DataAdapter's **Update** method to decide which data elements have actually been changed and need to be communicated back to the data store. Figure 15.3 illustrates these three levels of data.

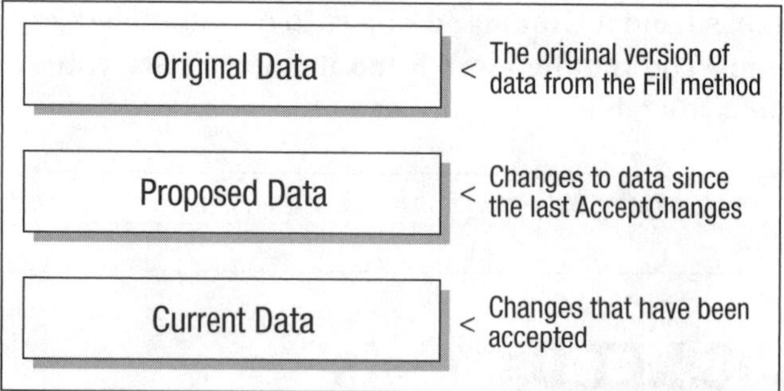

Figure 15.3 The three levels of data within the DataSet.

Changing Data in a DataSet

A single DataSet can contain multiple tables. Each table contains multiple columns and multiple rows. Figure 15.3 shows how these tables, rows, and columns fit into the overall DataSet structure. When you want to make changes to the data contained within a DataSet, you have to be specific about where your changes will take place. You need to specify which table, which row within that table, and which column within that row will be affected by the change. Tables can have new rows added to them, and they can have rows deleted from them as well. As you edit the rows within your DataSet's tables, each row states changes to indicate the type of operations that have been performed on it. These changes are noted, so when it comes time to update the data store with your changes, only those items that have been changed are sent back to the data store.

Examining RowState

Every row has a **RowState** property that can tell you what has been done to the data within that row. A **RowState** can be one of five values: **Added**, **Deleted**, **Detached**, **Modified**, and **Unchanged**. The **Detached** row state is given to a row that has been created using the table's **NewRow** method but has not officially been added to that table using the **Rows** collection's **Add** method. This row exists in the table in a detached state until you add it to the table, at which time the **RowState** is changed to **Added**. As you edit the rows in your DataSet, those rows **RowState** values change accordingly. Once you execute an **AcceptChange** that commits the changes made to your rows, their **RowStates** are reset to their default value, **Unchanged**.

Accepting and Rejecting Changes

You can accept or reject changes at the DataSet level, table level, or on a row-by-row basis. When you accept your changes, you are moving the proposed copy of your data to the current copy of the data. If you only **AcceptChanges** to a row, only that row in the current copy is affected. In contrast, if you decide to **RejectChanges** made to your data, the proposed copy of it is replaced with the values in the current copy, in effect rolling back your data to the last acceptable state.

XML in ADO.NET

XML plays a very large role in ADO.NET. Not only is ADO.NET capable of reading and writing its contents in XML format, which past versions of ADO could do on a limited scale, but also the entire ADO.NET Framework was built using the open source XML technology. ADO.NET natively speaks in XML and even uses XML to serialize its DataSets for communication. Because XML is a nonproprietary messaging format, supporting XML gives ADO.NET the ability to interface with non-Microsoft technologies. You can also pass ADO.NET DataSets through network firewalls due to their XML messaging format, which means you can literally pass your DataSets around the world without worrying about being blocked by servers that might not understand your format.

Writing XML

ADO.NET DataSets have the ability to create XML files based on their contents. Using XML, you can create a message that both provides data and describes the data elements, which makes your message readable by any software that can read XML. Previously, ADO Recordsets had the ability to stream their contents into an XML message, but because the contents of the Recordset were somewhat one dimensional, the resulting XML messages were also watered down due to the lack of a robust data schema. DataSets can hold multiple tables, and the DataSet can remember the relationships between these tables. These information elements can be communicated through an XML message to give the message's receiver a detailed picture of your data.

Reading XML

You can use an XML data file to populate your DataSet using the **ReadXml** method. With this ability, not only can you build DataSets from scratch and load them from DataAdapters pointing to data stores, but you can also create a DataSet using XML messages received from external applications. If your business application has to work with a set of data provided by another application, as long as that data is formatted using XML, all you need to do is to read the XML message into your DataSet and you will be able to work with it the same way you would any other DataSet. The DataSet dynamically creates its framework and schema based on the XML description of your data, and then populates the tables with the actual data elements.

This method of pulling data into a DataSet that did not originate from another DataSet can also help you connect past versions of ADO to ADO.NET. In ADO version 2.5 and later, the **Recordset** object has the ability to write its contents in XML format, even though the Recordset itself does not use XML natively. Once you drop the Recordset's contents into an XML file, you can then build an ADO.NET DataSet from this message.

XML Schemas

A schema defines the content and structure of an object. It also helps enforce data rules by defining the data types for each element. In XML messaging, the messages schema can be defined within the message itself or through a link to an external file. Developing a separate schema file is a smart way to reuse that schema from one message to another. DataSets also use schemas to define their structure. If you create a DataSet and immediately fill it with data through a DataAdapter, the DataSet dynamically creates a schema that mirrors the source you pulled your data from.

An alternative to this approach is to first load a schema into your DataSet prior to filling it with data. This approach ensures that your data rules and restrictions (also known as constraints) are already in place and being enforced when the data is poured in. You use the DataSet's **ReadXmlSchema** method to load a schema. There is also a **WriteXmlSchema** method that enables you to extract a DataSet's schema for later use. If you need to ensure that the schema of one DataSet exactly matches another, you can first use the **Fill** method to build the first DataSet and its schema, and then extract its schema and load that file into a second DataSet.

Using Visual Studio .NET Data Tools

Visual Studio .NET comes with an arsenal of powerful database development tools all aimed at making your job easier and faster. You can now create DataSets and connections to your data sources using the same drag-and-drop techniques you used to design your interface forms. Using the Server Explorer and Toolbox windows can save you a tremendous amount of time as they create the necessary code for you. You can modify and administer your databases from within Visual Studio .NET, and you can generate database queries by just using your mouse. Becoming familiar with these many timesaving tools is a must if you want to get the most out of the .NET development environment.

Using Visual Studio .NET Data Components

In Visual Studio .NET, you have the ability to create database connections and objects using the same drag-and-drop techniques that you used to create Windows Form interfaces. When you are looking at a Windows or Web Form in Design mode, you will notice that your Toolbox window has a Data panel on it. On this data panel is a set of data components that you can drag over to your form. Unlike the control components you will find in the Toolbox window, these data components do not directly affect the interface you are designing. Instead of adding a visible control to the form's surface, dropping a data component onto a form adds that component to a small window below the form's designer area.

Figure 15.4 shows the Visual Studio .NET IDE with a Windows Form in the design area. Below this form, you see two boxes in a small window. These are two data components that were dragged over from the Toolbox's Data panel, which you also see to the left of the Windows Form. Although adding a data component to your form does not directly affect the visual appearance of your form, it does affect the code that goes behind your form. If you switch over to a code view of a form with data components added, you will find the declaration and configuration statements for these components located in the Windows Form Designer code area.

The advantage of using data components is that they create a great deal of code for you and allow you to work with your data objects visually, just as you would a Windows control. You can click on a data object added to a form and modify its properties via the Properties window. Next, you will learn about the Server Explorer window, which helps you add preconfigured data components to your Windows Form, saving you even more development time and effort.

Accessing Data with the Visual Studio .NET Server Explorer

The Visual Studio .NET IDE includes a window called the Server Explorer window that allows developers to quickly identify resources on a machine within

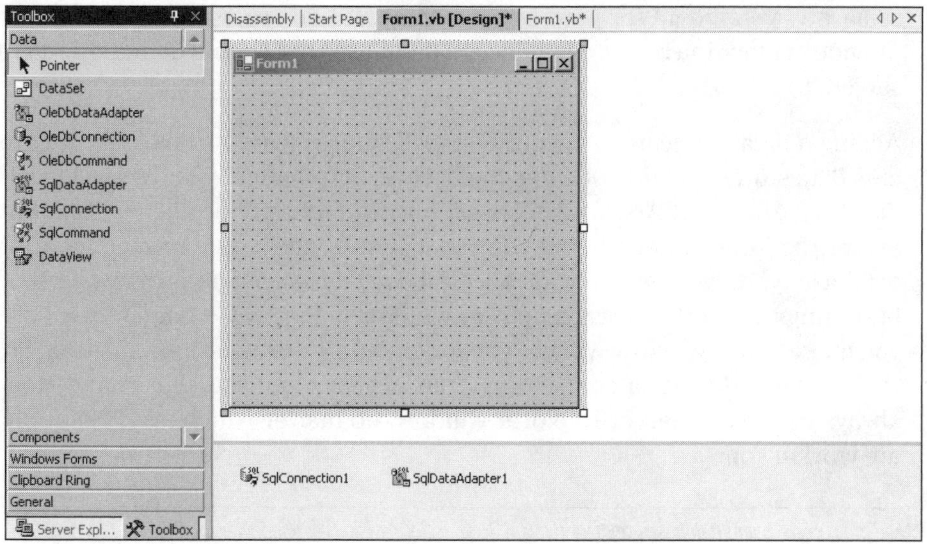

Figure 15.4 Data components in Visual Studio .NET.

their code. These resources can include log files, counters, and databases. Not only can you see which resources a machine has, but you can also drag these resources from the Server Explorer window over to your project to quickly create the necessary connections and configurations to use these resources. Because this chapter focuses on ADO.NET and data access, I will discuss the Server Explorer window from a database developer's point of view.

The first step to incorporating the Server Explorer window into your development session is to configure this window to display all of the databases you may need access to. By default, when you first open this window, the resources for your local machine are displayed. You will find your machine's name listed under the Server's tree view item in this window. If you expand your machine's tree, you will see groupings of resources underneath it such as Event Logs, Message Queues, Performance Counters, and Services. If your local machine has an instance of a SQL Server database running on it, you will be able to locate the databases hosted by this server under a SQL Server's item. This means that you will automatically have access to available SQL Server database items without having to make any changes to your Server Explorer window. There are two main items you may want to add to the Server Explorer window to give you access to even more resources:

- Other servers on your network that you have access to
- Data connections to non-Microsoft databases such as Access and Oracle

You can add another machine to the Server Explorer window by right-clicking on the Server's tree view item and selecting Add Server. Your user account must have permission to use the remote machine that you are adding to this window. Once added, you will be able to access resources on that remote machine the same way you would for your own machine. If you are using remote servers to provide application resources such as a database, you should definitely add those servers to your list.

Adding a data connection to your Server Explorer window is a great way to access data stores that do not make themselves automatically known to Visual Studio .NET. Microsoft Access databases, for instance, will not be displayed in the Server Explorer by default, but you can manually add a data connection to these database types to speed up your Access-based development projects. One of the best things about the Server Explorer window is that any configuration changes you make to this window will be remembered for future sessions by Visual Studio .NET. If you add a data connection to an Access database, that connection will always be in your Server Explorer window, no matter which .NET Solution you are working on.

***TIP:** Add other servers and databases on your network to your Server Explorer window so you can quickly locate and use their resources in your .NET projects.*

Database Projects and the Query Designer Tool

One of the many project types available for creation in Visual Studio .NET is the Database Project. When you are creating a new project, you will find this project type under the Other Projects|Database Projects folders. Instead of enabling you to create an application, the Database Project allows you to work with a database directly from within Visual Studio .NET. When creating a Database Project, you must first define the connection to the database you want to work with. Once this project has been created, you will be able to edit the target database, or create files within your project to work with this database, such as scripts, stored procedures, and queries. The scripts that you add to your project will already have much of the code completed for you. You can also create SQL queries from scratch using the powerful SQL query designer, which you will learn how to use in the Immediate Solutions section.

The Data Form Wizard

You can add an item to your Visual Studio .NET projects called the Data Form Wizard. This item uses a wizard interface to step you through creating a DataSet that you will then use to create a data-driven Windows Form. Using this wizard to create your form can save you a lot of time because it creates the data-bound controls for you. If you have previously worked with Microsoft Access, using wizards to create interactive data forms will be familiar to you.

You will find the Data Form Wizard item by right-clicking on the project's name in the Solution Explorer window and selecting Add New Item. The Data Form Wizard item is located within the Data folder of the Add New Item window. When you first add this item, a wizard window opens to help you configure your Windows Form. The first step in setting up your data-centric form is to declare the DataSet you plan to attach this form to. You can either use an existing DataSet, or you can create a brand new DataSet while you are using the Data Form's wizard. Only DataSet items that appear within the Solution Explorer window can be used as preexisting DataSets. You cannot use DataSets added to other forms using data components or code-based creation.

If you opt to create a new DataSet for your Data Form, you will be walked through the various steps necessary to create a database connection with which to fill your new DataSet. Once the Data Form has a DataSet identified or created, you will then be asked to select which tables and columns you want to create items for on your form. You will also have the choice of whether to use a DataGrid control to group all of your displayed values in an easy-to-use table or use separate controls for each data element. When you complete setting up your Data Form, either a DataGrid or a collection of controls representing your data elements will be added to your Windows form along with a Load button. When you run this form and click the Load button, the associated DataSet is filled with data and then bound to the form's controls. All of the necessary code is created for you, although you may want to customize these functions to give your form that personal touch.

Advanced ADO.NET Topics

Once you are familiar with the basic operations and features of ADO.NET, you can begin to work with the more advanced portions, such as events, errors, and stored procedures. Events are how objects communicate important pieces of information back to you, and if you choose to not create code for these events, you could be missing out on some important alerts. Because data is so important, making sure your DataSets contain valid data before trying to update your data stores is an important step in avoiding exceptions being raised or data from being corrupted. ADO.NET's error properties and methods let you check for problems in your data so that you can avoid any kind of trouble. In addition, stored procedures are a great way to implement some of your business logic within the database and speed up your database calls.

ADO.NET Events

Events in ADO.NET allow you, the developer, to create some customized code that will react to changes in your data or database connection. ADO.NET raises these events wherever a significant change has occurred, and if your application includes some source code to handle this event, your code will automatically be executed. You do not have to create code to handle every event, only those you want to react to.

In ADO.NET, you can work with events raised by the **Connection**, **DataAdapter**, **DataTable**, **DataRow**, **DataColumn**, and **DataSet** objects. The **Connection** object events raise a warning flag for you whenever the status of your connection changes or the **Connection** object has a message to relay to you. Often, these **Connection** events are not a sign of trouble, but there may be times when you need to know about these changes, such as when you want to write some code to run as soon as the **Connection** object is closed.

The DataAdapter's **FillError** event, for example, is triggered when the **Fill** method encounters a problem. If you are working with typed DataSets, you should include some code in the **FillError** event to check for data mismatches encountered during DataSet **Fills**. An example of this would be a DataSet with a **NumDependants** column set to an **Integer** data type. If the DataAdapter's **Fill** method tries to pour a data type into this column that is not of the **Integer** data type, the **FillError** event is triggered. You can create some code in the **FillError's** event to check for such a mismatch and correct the problem so your DataSet can continue filling.

The DataSet and its components provide many useful events to let you know that the data within has been modified in some way. Whenever data within a DataSet is changed or deleted, an event is fired to notify you of this change or deletion. You might use this event to check the DataSet's **HasErrors** property to see if the latest change has corrupted your DataSet in any way. Many of these "change" events come in two versions, which I call "ed" and "ing". For the deletion events, you will be able to react to both the **RowDeleted** event and the **RowDeleting** event. The same holds true for change events with the **RowChanged** and **RowChanging** versions. The difference between these two versions is that the "ing" event occurs before the action is committed, whereas the "ed" event is triggered when the action is complete. If you want to check a value and prevent some changes or deletions from happening, you should place code in the "ing" events. If you only want to deal with the changes after they have been made, use the "ed" versions.

ADO.NET Errors

Working with data is a delicate operation, and many problems can occur that you need to be aware of to prevent further problems. Sometimes the connection to the data store will result in an error, not because of your code, but it may be due to a network or hardware problem. The **DataAdapter** object provides a **FillError** event to let you know that something went wrong during the DataAdapter's call to your data store. Adding some code to this event to recover or retry your **Fill** attempt is a great idea if you cannot be 100 percent sure your data store will be available 100 percent of the time.

Your DataSet and the object contained within it also raise error events and provide you with ways to discover these errors so that you can fix them and move on. The **DataSet**, **DataTable**, and **DataRow** objects all have a **HasErrors** property, which is set to **True** if an error is present at that object's level. These properties cascade up the DataSet's hierarchy, so if you have an error in a row within one of your tables, that **DataRow** will have **HasErrors** set to **True** along with the **DataTable** containing that row and the DataSet containing that erroneous table. Once you know an error exists, you can use one of many different methods within the DataRow to locate and correct the error. Whenever you make changes to a DataSet, be sure to check its **HasErrors** property, and only move on to the next function when its value is **False**.

Working with Stored Procedures in ADO.NET

A stored procedure is a piece of code that is stored within the database itself. Applications running outside of this database can trigger a stored procedure using only a minimal amount of code and network communications. For example, you could create a stored procedure that would delete an employee's record in the **Employees** table. All this stored procedure would need to perform this feat is the employee's ID number. Without stored procedures, you would have to execute a SQL **DELETE** command, which would require that even more information be sent across the network.

Besides limiting network communications, stored procedures also execute more efficiently than SQL commands. This is because a SQL statement sent to the database server needs to be compiled before it can be executed, whereas a stored procedure is stored in a compiled state, ready to act at a moment's notice. The larger and more complex your database actions, the more benefit you will gain from using stored procedures. If you need to generate queries dynamically, you should probably use SQL statements, but if your statements are fairly static or only contain a few changing parameters, you should strongly consider moving these to stored procedures, which can accept parameters to customize their actions.

Some stored procedures do not provide any output, such as deleting an employee's record. Other stored procedures can return data to the caller. You can also create stored procedures that generate reports from your database. Typically, report formats and the databases these reports are pulled from do not change, making them an ideal candidate for stored procedures. Once again, you can customize these reports by providing the stored procedure with a few dynamic parameters, such as starting and ending dates to base your report on. Developing stored procedures is often a task left to the database gurus, but you can create and edit these from within Visual Studio .NET. I discuss this technique in the Immediate Solutions.

Immediate Solutions

Creating a DataSet Programmatically

Typically, you will fill a DataSet using an external data source, such as a database or an XML file. But DataSets are such a powerful way to group and organize data that you will often find yourself in programming situations where creating a DataSet programmatically in your code and using it to store relational data elements is the perfect answer. Creating a DataSet from scratch is also the perfect way to gain a firm understanding of how the different parts of a DataSet fit together. Using Visual Studio .NET's drag-and-drop data is a fast and powerful way to create DataSets, but by design, they hide a lot of the details and complexity that goes on behind the scenes. Therefore, I highly recommend that your first introduction to a DataSet be made programmatically without the benefit of Rapid Application Development (RAD) tools.

The following code example shows you how to create a DataSet named **dsCompany**, which contains a single **DataTable** named **dtEmployees**, which in turn contains several **DataRows** that represent individual employee records. The individual steps that this block of code follows to programmatically create this DataSet are numbered and explained via code-based comments:


```
'Visual Basic .NET example of how to build a DataSet programmatically
'1. Declare the individual parts of the DataSet, create new instances of _
   a DataSet and a DataTable
Dim dsCompany As New DataSet("Company")
Dim dtEmployees As New DataTable("Employees")
Dim drEmpRecord As DataRow

'2. Define the table's column names and their data types
dtEmployees.Columns.Add("EmpID", Type.GetType("System.Int32"))
dtEmployees.Columns.Add("EmpName", Type.GetType("System.String"))
dtEmployees.Columns.Add("OfficeSym", Type.GetType("System.String"))
dtEmployees.Columns.Add("HireDate", Type.GetType("System.String"))

'3. Create the first record/DataRow
drEmpRecord = dtEmployees.NewRow
drEmpRecord("EmpID") = 11
drEmpRecord("EmpName") = "James Moffet"
```

```
drEmpRecord("OfficeSym") = "DTR"
drEmpRecord("HireDate") = "09/10/01"

'4. Add this new DataRow to the DataTable
dtEmployees.Rows.Add(drEmpRecord)

'5. Create the first record/DataRow
drEmpRecord = dtEmployees.NewRow
drEmpRecord("EmpID") = 22
drEmpRecord("EmpName") = "Paul Foster"
drEmpRecord("OfficeSym") = "BHI"
drEmpRecord("HireDate") = "03/22/98"

'6. Add this new DataRow to the DataTable
dtEmployees.Rows.Add(drEmpRecord)

'7. Add the DataTable to the DataSet
dsCompany.Tables.Add(dtEmployees)
```

When you first declare the **Company** DataSet and the **Employees** DataTable, these two objects have no relationship. In Step 2, you define the columns that make up your table by adding a column to the table, giving it a name, and defining this column's data type. You only have to define the columns within a single table once. In Step 3, you see that you must first declare a **NewRow** to the DataTable before you can start defining the data elements that go into that row. Once you are finished filling in that row, you complete it by using the DataTable's **Add** method to attach it to the **Employees** table. In Steps 5 and 6, you create a second employee record and add that to the DataTable as well. The last step of this example takes the table you built, along with its two employee records, and adds this package to the **Company** DataSet.

You could continue to add to this DataSet in many different ways. You could add more rows to the **Employees** table, or you could create a new table and add that to the **Company** DataSet along with the **Employees** table. If your DataSet has more than one table in it, you could define some relationships that link different tables together, just like you would with a relational database.

Adding a DataSet Relationship

If you have a DataSet that contains two or more tables, you can define a relationship that can connect your tables together. These relationships can be used to connect two tables together in a way that they share data elements. In a relationship between two tables, one table is said to be the parent, whereas the other is known as the child. Each DataSet contains a property called **DataRelationCollection** which is a collection of **Relations** objects. Any relationships you define for the tables contained in the DataSet are held within the **DataRelationCollection** collection.

To picture how a relationship between two DataTables within a single DataSet works, consider the following example. You have a DataSet named **Company** that contains two DataTables named **Employees** and **Offices**. A single office within the company can contain many employees. When creating an employee record, you want to indicate which office an employee belongs to, but you do not want to include all of that office's information in the employee's record. This would result in a great deal of data duplication in the **Employees** table. Instead, you want to create a second table (**Offices**) that lists unique offices within the company, and then link an employee's record in the **Employees** table to that employee's associated office in the **Offices** table. Figure 15.5 shows a database entity relationship drawing of the **Employees** and **Offices** tables.

From looking at the two tables in Figure 15.5, you can see a line connecting these tables, which represents the relationship they have. This line connects the two

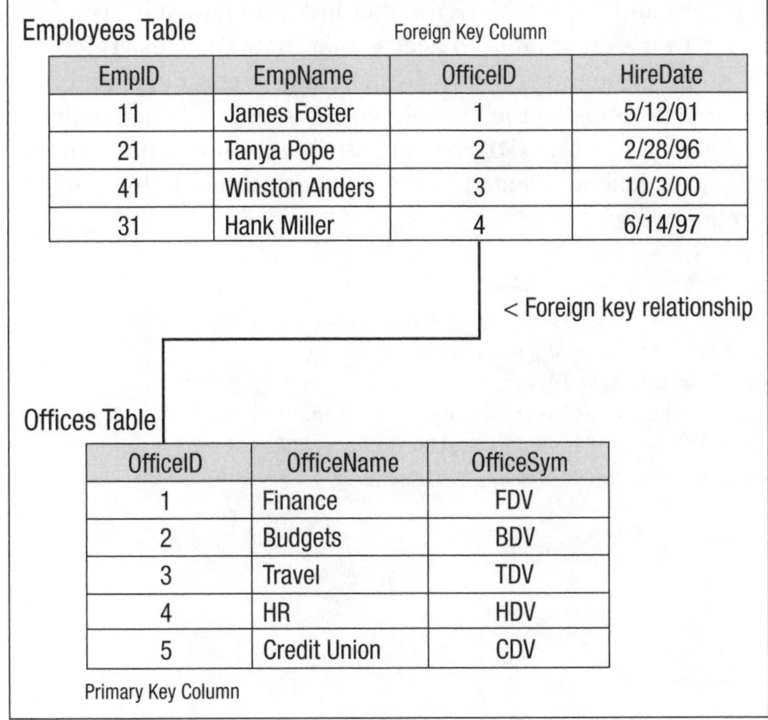

EmpID	EmpName	OfficeID	HireDate
11	James Foster	1	5/12/01
21	Tanya Pope	2	2/28/96
41	Winston Anders	3	10/3/00
31	Hank Miller	4	6/14/97

OfficeID	OfficeName	OfficeSym
1	Finance	FDV
2	Budgets	BDV
3	Travel	TDV
4	HR	HDV
5	Credit Union	CDV

Figure 15.5 The **Employees** and **Offices** tables and their relationship.

tables at their **OfficeID** attributes. In the **Offices** table, the **OfficeID** attribute is a unique value; each office must have a unique **OfficeID** assigned to it. In the **Offices** table, the **OfficeID** attribute would be the primary key in database terms. The **Employees** table also has an **OfficeID** attribute. Because many employees belong to the same office, this is not a unique field, so there are duplicate **OfficeID** values in the **Employees** table. In the **Employees** table, the **OfficeID** is said to be a foreign key because it links the **Employees** table to an outside table, **Offices**. The **Employees** table is said to be the parent because this table points to the **Offices** table, but the **Offices** table does not contain any pointers back to the **Employees** table.

If you have a DataSet that contains both an **Employees** and **Offices** table, you can establish a relationship between these two tables as follows:

```
dsCompany.Relations.Add("EmpOffice", dsCompany.Tables("Employees")._
     Columns("OfficeID"), dsCompany.Tables("Offices").Columns("OfficeID"))
```

This line of code adds an item to the DataSet's **Relations** collection. Notice that the first parameter declares a name for this relationship (**EmpOffice**), the second names a column in the parent table, and the third parameter names the child table's column. The relationship is made between the two declared columns contained in the parent and child tables. You can programmatically step from the parent table over to the child table to access that table's values. The following code example steps through every row in the **Employees** table, and for each employee, writes a message to the console output window listing which office that employee belongs too. The **OfficeName** attribute is not actually in the **Employees** table, but is instead located in the **Offices** table—a child table in the **EmpOffices** relationship:


```
Dim ParentRow, ChildRow As DataRow
Dim PCRelation As DataRelation = dsCompany.Relations("EmpOffice")
'Step through each row in the Employees table
For Each ParentRow In dtEmployees.Rows
    'Step through the relationship to get to the Offices table's data
    For Each ChildRow In ParentRow.GetChildRows(PCRelation)
        Console.WriteLine(ChildRow("OfficeName"))
    Next
Next
```

Adding a Data Connection to the Server Explorer Window

SQL Server databases are automatically displayed for any servers listed in your Server Explorer window. In order to access other database types from this powerful window, you need to create a data connection to tell the Server Explorer how to connect to this data store. These are the steps you would take to add a Microsoft Access database to your Server Explorer window:

1. Open the Server Explorer window in Visual Studio .NET.
2. You will see two top-level items in the Server Explorer's tree view: Data Connections and Servers. Right-click on the Data Connections item, and select Add Connection.
3. A Data Link Properties window opens. If you have previously used Visual Studio version 6 or 7 to configure a database connection, this window will look very familiar to you. When the window first opens, you will see the Connection tab. Make a mental note of the options currently available on this tab. Click on the Provider tab at the top of this window.
4. In the list of available OLE DB providers, notice that the SQL Server OLE DB provider is currently selected. Highlight the Microsoft Jet 4.0 OLE DB provider.
5. Click on the Connection tab at the top. Some different configuration properties appear on this tab. Item 1 asks for the file system path to your database file. Click on the button to the right of this text box and browse for an Access database file (any Access database ending in .mdb will do for this exercise). When you locate the database file, double-click on it to select it.
6. If your database requires a special user account and password to access it, fill in this information in the Connection tab. By default, Access databases do not restrict user access to them, so you can leave the Blank Password option checked.
7. Click Test Connection to verify that this connection works as expected. If you receive a "Test connection succeeded" message, you can click OK on this message, and then click OK at the bottom of the Data Link Properties window to finish adding this new data connection.
8. In the Server Explorer window, you should now have a database entry below the Data Connection tree. If you expand this entry, you will be able to access the individual tables within that database as well as other important items, such as defined stored procedures.

Different database types use different OLE DB providers. For an Access database, you would use the latest Jet provider, whereas for an Oracle database, you would use the OLE DB Oracle provider. SQL Server also has its own OLE DB provider, and you should see a general-purpose ODBC provider in the providers list as well. Generally, it is best to choose the provider that explicitly names your database's vendor instead of using the ODBC connection.

Each provider has different configuration options on the Connection tab you used in Step 5. For instance, the SQL Server and Oracle providers ask you to provide the name of the machine that is housing this database. The Jet provider I used to add the Access database only looks at your computer's file system to locate a database, so if you are trying to add an Access database on a remote machine, you need to map a drive in Windows Explorer to a remote shared drive where this database can be found.

Using Data Components to Quickly Access Data Sources

The Visual Studio .NET Toolbox and Server Explorer windows both provide the developer with the ability to quickly create database connections by dragging components found in these windows over to a project. When you drop a data component onto your project, a great deal of coding is automatically completed for you. Let's take a look at how you can use the data components found in the Toolbox and Server Explorer windows, and also take a look at the code that these components create for you behind the scenes.

Using Data Components from the Toolbox Window

In the Toolbox window, there is a panel named Data that contains a collection of data components. The Data panel is only available when you are working on a Windows or Web Form, which means you cannot use data components in a class Library file. On the Data panel, you will find the following components: DataSet, DataView, and both OLE DB and SQL versions of the **DataAdapter**, **Connection**, and **Command** components. Let's take a look at how you can use these components to generate database code in your project:

1. Start a new Windows Application project using Visual Basic .NET.
2. Click on the Data panel in the Toolbox to view the available data components.
3. Click and hold on an OleDbConnection component and drag it over to your Windows Form, dropping it on the form's surface. You will now see an **OleDbConnection** object in the component window below your Windows Form.
4. Click once on the OleDbConnection component to highlight it. Look in the Properties window, and click in the ConnectionString property box. Using the drop-down list, select <New Connection>.

5. A Data Link Properties window opens. Click on the Providers tab at the top of this window. Double-click on the Microsoft Jet 4.0 OLE DB Provider item in the providers list.
6. Click the button to the right of the database name text box, and browse for a Microsoft Access database (ending in .mdb). When you locate a database file, double-click on it.
7. Click Test Connection to verify that this data connection works. If your database requires a special user account to access it, be sure to enter that data below the text box containing the database's path. When your connection tests successfully, click OK at the bottom of the window.
8. From the Data panel in the Toolbox window, drag an OleDbDataAdapter component over to your Windows Form and drop it. When the Data Adapter Configuration Wizard opens, click Next.
9. The window that appears should list the path to your Access database as defined within the OleDbConnection component. If the text box is blank, click the drop-down arrow to the right, and select the Access database from the list. Click Next at the bottom of this window.
10. The third window asks if you want to use a SQL statement or a stored procedure when accessing this database. Select the SQL statement option and click Next.
11. You will then see a window asking you to enter a SQL query. For this example, just enter a simple **SELECT** query against one of the tables in the Access database you selected. If you are not sure about the database's structure, click Query Builder at the bottom of this window and build a query using populated tables lists and attribute lists. The following simple SQL query pulls all of the records out of the **Employees** table:

```
SELECT * FROM Employees
```

12. The final DataAdapter configuration screen should report that the configuration was successful. Click Finish at the bottom of this window. You will then see an OleDbDataAdapter component next to your OleDbConnection component.
13. Once again, go to the Data panel of the Toolbox window, and drag a DataSet component over to your form. A window opens asking if you want this DataSet to be typed or untyped. Select the untyped item and click OK.
14. Right-click on the surface of the form, and select View Code. Click inside the form's **New** event, which is located inside the Windows Form Designer code area, and enter the following line of code:

```
OleDbDataAdapter1.Fill(DataSet1)
```

When you run this Windows Form, your DataSet will be filled through the DataAdapter using the SQL query you designed. In addition, you could add data controls, such as the DataGrid control, to your form and set its **DataSource** property equal to **DataSet1** to see this data. You could also programmatically manipulate the data within your DataSet. Using data components from the Toolbox requires a little bit of configuration. In the next section, I discuss the Server Explorer window and show you how you can drag and drop preconfigured components over to your form.

Server Explorer Data Components

The database objects you drag from your Server Explorer window over to your project work just like their Toolbox cousins, but with one significant difference. When you drag objects over from the Server Explorer, the data objects that are added to your code will already be configured with all of the necessary settings. The following exercise shows you how to use the Server Explorer to drag a database table over to your project:

1. Create a new Windows Application project.
2. From the Windows Form panel of the Toolbox, select a Label control, and drag it to the center of your Windows Form.
3. In the Server Explorer window, select a database (either under Data Connections or under a server's name), and expand it until you see a list of tables within this database.
4. Click and hold on one of the tables, drag it over to the surface of your Windows Form, and drop it. In the component area located below your Windows Form, you will see both an **OleDbDataAdapter** and an **OleDbConnection** object added to your form. Both of these objects are already fully configured to point to the selected database and table.
5. From the Toolbox window's Data panel, drag a DataSet component over to your form, and drop it.
6. Right-click on the Windows Form's surface, and select View Code. In the form's **New** event, add the following lines of code:

```
OleDbDataAdapter1.Fill(DataSet1)
Label1.Text = DataSet1.Tables.Count
```

7. Save and run your project. When the form loads, your label displays the number 1, meaning that there is one table loaded into **DataSet1**. You could continue to drag tables from the Server Explorer window over to your form, and then add lines of code to add these tables to **DataSet1**.
8. To see the code that was automatically generated by these data components, take a look at the code behind your Windows Form. If you expand

the section of code that reads Windows Form Designer generated code, you will see where the data components are declared and configured in your code.

Filling a DataSet from a Database

There are many different ways to place data inside your DataSet. You can create the DataSet's contents from scratch in your code, you can read a file of XML into your DataSet, or you can use a **DataAdapter** object to connect your DataSet to a database and fill it from the database. Because your DataSet is not directly connected to the database you are pulling your data from, you first need to configure a **DataAdapter** and a **Connection** object before you can pull the data you need. The following code creates a **DataSet**, **DataAdapter**, and **Connection** object, configures that connection, and then uses it to fill the DataSet with the desired data:

```
'Declare a DataSet, DataAdapter, the query and the connection string
Dim dsMyData As New DataSet()
Dim daAdapter As OleDb.OleDbDataAdapter
Dim strSql As String = "SELECT * FROM Employees"
Dim strConn As String = "Provider=Microsoft.Jet.OLEDB.4.0;Data Source=_
      C:\Databases\Company.mdb"

'Initialize the DataAdapter with a connection and query
daAdapter = New OleDb.OleDbDataAdapter(strSql, strConn)

'Use the DataAdapter to fill up the DataSet
daAdapter.Fill(dsMyData)
```


The key to getting the data out of the database and into your DataSet is the DataAdapter's **Fill** method. Once you have configured the DataAdapter with a connection (**strConn** in the example) and a query to run on the database (**strSql** in the example), all you need to do is to execute the **Fill** method and point it to your awaiting DataSet. The **Fill** method is responsible for opening the specified connection, executing your command, and then closing the connection to the database. In past versions of Visual Studio, each of these steps would require its own line of code, but the **Fill** method greatly simplifies data access by handling the opening, querying, and closing steps for you.

***NOTE:** If the connection being used by the **Fill** method is already open when the **Fill** method is executed, it remains open after the **Fill** method is complete. In most cases, it's best to let the DataAdapter handle the opening and closing of database connections for you.*

Modifying Data in a DataSet

When working with a DataSet filled with data, you must think in three dimensions: tables, rows, and columns. With the old ADO Recordsets, you only had to worry about rows and columns, but now you have to be more specific when locating the DataSet's cursor to edit a row. The following code line shows how you would change the value of a single column located in a single row within a specific table:

```
dsCompany.Tables("Customers").Rows(0)("FirstName") = "Dave"
```

To make this change, this line of code needs to specify the exact table name, the exact row index, and the column's name in order to locate the data element that is being changed. The column's name in my example is **FirstName**, but you could substitute an **Integer** for the name of the column if you prefer to reference columns in this way. If you try to assign a value that violates the constraint placed on a particular row, an exception will be raised. You can temporarily disable a row's constraint checks by using the row's **BeginEdit** method. Here is an example of using **BeginEdit** to do this:

```
dsCompany.Tables("Customers").Rows(0).BeginEdit()
dsCompany.Tables("Customers").Rows(0)("FirstName") = 100
'No exception raised on the previous line
dsCompany.Tables("Customers").Rows(0).EndEdit()
'EndEdit re-enables constraints, and an exception is raised
```

If you want to make multiple row changes at one time without the trouble of having constraints get in the way, you can use the **BeginEdit** to do so. Calling the **EndEdit** method reenables the constraint checks, and any constraint violations still remaining from your editing session will result in exceptions being raised. Calling the **AcceptChanges** method automatically triggers the **EndEdits** for any **BeginEdits** you called but left disabled.

Adding and Deleting Rows

Earlier, when you created a DataSet programmatically, you also learned how to add a new row to a table by using the DataTable's **NewRow** method to first create that row, and then by using the **Add** method of the DataTable's **Rows** collection to add the completed row to the table. The following code shows how you would use the **NewRow** and **Add** methods to attach a new employee record to the **dtEmployees** table:

```
drEmpRecord = dtEmployees.NewRow
drEmpRecord("EmpID") = 33
```

```
drEmpRecord("EmpName") = "Oliver Westin"
drEmpRecord("OfficeSym") = "DTJ"
drEmpRecord("HireDate") = "03/22/95"
dtEmployees.Rows.Add(drEmpRecord)
```

To delete a row from a table, you just need to know the index number of that row so that you can call the row's **Delete** method like this:

```
dsCompany.Tables("Employees").Rows(7).Delete()
```

Locating Data in a DataTable

If you have a large number of records loaded into a DataTable, it could be very time-consuming to step through each and every record looking for a particular column value. You could always create a new DataSet and table from the data source using a more specific query, but that too takes time and resources to perform. Instead of all this work, you can use the DataTable's **Select** method to run a mini-query against your table and locate the desired items. Take a look at this code example:

```
Dim Results() As DataRow
Dim MyTable As DataTable
Dim strSelect As String = "EmpName = 'James Moffet'"
Dim strSort As String
Dim strRowState As DataViewRowState
'Decides how to sort the resulting rows
strSort = "EmpID DESC"
'Filter rows searched by their current status
strRowState = DataViewRowState.CurrentRows

'Pick the table to search
MyTable = dsCompany.Tables("Employees")
'Load the results of the Select into an array
Results = MyTable.Select(strSelect, strSort, strRowState)
'Print out the first returned record, first column (EmpID)
MsgBox(CStr(Results(0)(0)))
```

The **strSelect** variable in this example contains the search criteria you want to use on your table. **String** values should be enclosed within single quotes when declaring your **strSelect** statement in this way. It is also critical that the column name you search against, **EmpName** in this example, exists in the DataTable. The sort parameter of the **Select** method allows you to sort the results by any column for easier handling. The **DataViewRowState** parameter acts as a filter that you can use to only look at certain versions of the rows in the table, such as **Added**, **Deleted**, **Current**, or **Original**. The output of the **Select** method should be saved in an array of DataRows. You now have a much smaller set of rows to look through, and if your search criteria is detailed enough, you may even have that one single row you've been looking for.

Accepting and Rejecting Changes

When you accept a series of changes made to your DataSet, you move all of these recently updated or proposed values over to what is called the current copy of your data. Accepting changes is like committing data at the DataSet level. Until you execute the DataAdapter's **Update** method, you will not be committing these changes to the actual database. Remember, you can accept changes at the DataSet, DataTable, and DataRow levels. The following three lines of code show you how the **AcceptChanges** method works for the DataSet, DataTable, and DataRow:

```
DataSet1.AcceptChanges()
DataSet1.Tables("Customers").AcceptChanges()
DataSet1.Tables("Customers").Rows(9).AcceptChanges()
```

Be careful when using the **AcceptChanges** method. Once you accept all of your changes, those values are committed to the current copy of your data and cannot be rolled back unless you use the DataSet's **Reset** method to replace all of the data in the current and proposed copies with the data from the original copy. You can also execute a **RejectChanges** at all three levels. The following example shows the **RejectChanges** method used at the DataSet, DataTable, and DataRow levels:

```
DataSet1.RejectChanges()
DataSet1.Tables("Customers").RejectChanges()
DataSet1.Tables("Customers").Rows(3).RejectChanges()
```

You need to be aware of the level at which you are performing your **RejectChanges** because all changed data elements at that level will be affected. For example, if you execute a **RejectChanges** at the DataSet level, all changes within every table and every row of that DataSet will be rolled back to their original value.

Saving Changes to a DataSet Back to a Database

If you use a DataAdapter to fill your DataSet with elements from a data store, you will also use a **DataAdapter** object to update your data stores with any changes made within your DataSet. The **Update** method of the DataAdapter makes this a simple process, just as easy as it was to use the **Fill** command. Here is an example of the **Update** method being called:

```
OleDbDataAdapter1.Update(DataSet1)
```

This one simple little method performs a whole slew of functions on your behalf to efficiently merge the changes in your DataSet with the original data source. The **Update** method first examines your DataSet to see which items have been changed since the DataSet was last filled. As you already learned, the DataSet maintains three copies of the data contained within it. By comparing the current values in the DataSet to the original values that were in the DataSet after the last **Fill** was done, the **Update** method can determine which records need updating. By fully concentrating on communicating back to the data store only those records that have changed, the **Update** method prevents a great deal of unnecessary data from being sent across the network.

In order to communicate these changes to the data store, the **Update** command translates these changed values into SQL commands, such as the **INPUT**, **DELETE**, and **UPDATE** commands. The DataAdapter by itself is not able to create these SQL statements, so it must rely on an object called the **CommandBuilder** to do this job. In a procedure that uses the DataAdapter's **Update** method, you need to declare an instance of a **CommandBuilder** object at the top of your procedure, preferably right after you declare the **DataAdapter** object. This is how you would declare both of these objects:

```
Dim daAdapter As OleDb.OleDbDataAdapter
Dim SQLBuilder As OleDb.OleDbCommandBuilder = New _
      OleDb.OleDbCommandBuilder(daAdapter)
```

Notice that the **CommandBuilder**'s declaration points to the **DataAdapter** object it will be working with. If you try to use the DataAdapter's **Update** method without first assigning that DataAdapter a **CommandBuilder**, your **Update** method will fail to affect the data source.

Creating a Typed DataSet

Creating a typed DataSet is like creating a database. First, you define the tables within your database; second, you add attributes to those tables, restricting which data types each attribute can be; and third, you define the relationships that exist between your tables. Using schemas with DataSets does take a little extra time and more than a little extra thought, but all this work is done in the name of preventing data corruption. You could create a database that uses **Varchar2**s (the database equivalent of the **String** data type) everywhere, but this would open your database and allow any value to be added anywhere. You would not be able to prevent someone from entering a name in an **Age** attribute or an age in the **FirstName** attribute. Defining a set of rules to restrict the data elements contained within your database or DataSet prevents mistakes and errors from occurring. These schemas act like a security guard, checking all values that are trying to enter your DataSet and validating them against an approved list of data types.

Developing a schema to rule over your database or DataSet takes a great deal of forethought and planning, so step one of creating any type of schema is to sketch out your planned data structure. Decide on meaningful names for your elements, and be sure to select the best data type for each attribute. In the following sections, I discuss how to create the actual schema to define your DataSet, show you how to load the schema into your DataSet, and then discuss the effects this schema will have on your data interactions.

Creating the DataSet's Schema

Although there are many ways to create a DataSet schema, there are two smart ways I want to show you to help you get the job done quickly. The first method involves using an already loaded DataSet. If you have a DataSet loaded with the proper data elements and relationships, all you need to do to create a schema to "lock-in" this DataSet's format is to use the **WriteXmlSchema** method like this:

```
Dim XMLOut As IO.FileStream = New IO.FileStream("c:\XMLSchema.xsd", _
      IO.FileMode.OpenOrCreate, IO.FileAccess.Write)
dsCompany.WriteXmlSchema(XMLOut)
```


This code creates a schema on your hard drive that you can then load into future DataSets to enforce the format you worked so hard to develop the first time around. Notice that the output file I am creating ends in a .xsd extension, which represents an XML schema definition. For a DataSet containing an **Employees** and **Offices** table, the schema contained in this file would look like this:

```
<xsd:schema id="Company" targetNamespace="" xmlns="" xmlns:xsd=_
   "http://www.w3.org/2001/XMLSchema" xmlns:msdata="urn:schemas-microsoft-_
    com: xml-msdata">
  <xsd:element name="Company" msdata:IsDataSet="true">
    <xsd:complexType>
      <xsd:choice maxOccurs="unbounded">
        <xsd:element name="Employees">
          <xsd:complexType>
            <xsd:sequence>
              <xsd:element name="EmpID" type="xsd:int" minOccurs="0" />
              <xsd:element name="EmpName" type="xsd:string" minOccurs="0" />
              <xsd:element name="OfficeID" type="xsd:int" minOccurs="0" />
              <xsd:element name="HireDate" type="xsd:string" _
                    minOccurs="0" />
```

```
          </xsd:sequence>
        </xsd:complexType>
      </xsd:element>
      <xsd:element name="Offices">
        <xsd:complexType>
          <xsd:sequence>
            <xsd:element name="OfficeID" type="xsd:int" minOccurs="0" />
            <xsd:element name="OfficeName" type="xsd:string" _
                 minOccurs="0" />
            <xsd:element name="OfficeSym" type="xsd:string" _
                 minOccurs="0" />
          </xsd:sequence>
        </xsd:complexType>
      </xsd:element>
    </xsd:choice>
  </xsd:complexType>
  <xsd:unique name="Constraint1">
    <xsd:selector xpath=".//Employees" />
    <xsd:field xpath="OfficeID" />
  </xsd:unique>
  <xsd:keyref name="EmpOffice" refer="Constraint1">
    <xsd:selector xpath=".//Offices" />
    <xsd:field xpath="OfficeID" />
  </xsd:keyref>
 </xsd:element>
</xsd:schema>
```


The second method for creating data schemas should be used when you do not have a perfected DataSet available to dump a schema from. Database developers will like this second method because they get to use a nifty graphical tool to plan and design the schema, much like creating a database schema in SQL Server. Visual Studio .NET allows you to add an item named the XML Schema item to your projects. You can edit this item in one of two modes: Designer and XML. The Designer mode allows you to drag and drop items from the XML Schema panel of the Toolbox over to your schema's surface, and then configure these items in a graphical way. The XML editing mode allows you to manipulate the actual text behind the schema, which is a pretty complicated way to work with XML.

Within the XML Schema panel, you will see designer components that you can use to add elements, attributes, complex and simple types, keys, and relationships. Looking back to the schema example generated from the **Employees** and **Offices** tables, you can see that the **Employees** and **Offices** tables translate into two different complex types. The attributes to these tables are elements within the schema, listed within their associated tables/complex types. A simple type can be used to create a customized data type, such as one you call **Age**. After naming a simple type, you can define characteristics about it, such as its length and ability to support white spaces. Using the XML Designer tool requires a certain degree of knowledge of XML tagging and its supported data types, so if you are new to the world of XML, you might want to review Chapters 5 and 14 before trying out this tool.

Add the Schema to the DataSet and Fill the DataSet

You must create the schema before you can create any DataSets using that schema. Once the schema is finished, you can use it to initialize the DataSet's structure prior to loading any data into that DataSet. Schemas that you generate using the **WriteXmlSchema** method and those created using the Visual Studio .NET schema designer can both be loaded by referencing their file locations on the hard drive. Here is an example of how you would load an XSD file on your hard drive into a DataSet created programmatically:

```
Dim dsWithSchema As New DataSet()
Dim SchemaIn As IO.FileStream = New IO.FileStream("c:\XMLSchema.xsd", _
      IO.FileMode.OpenOrCreate, IO.FileAccess.Read)
dsWithSchema.ReadXmlSchema(SchemaIn)
DataGrid1.DataSource = dsWithSchema
```

If you were to view this DataSet using the DataGrid control, you would see that despite the lack of data elements, this DataSet has a predefined set of columns. If you were to load the schema created for the **Employees** and **Offices** tables, the relationship between these two tables would be part of your new DataSet as discovered through the loaded schema. Any attempts to add data to a table that does not meet the schema's data type definition will result in an exception being raised in your code. This includes data added both programmatically using the DataTable's **NewRow** method, and data that is loaded from a data source using the **Fill** method.

TIP: *Because adding a schema to a DataSet greatly restricts the type of data you can add to the tables within, you should make generous use of exception-handling routines around any code that attempts to add or modify this DataSet.*

Using DataSets to Generate XML Messages

To show you how a DataSet can write its contents to an XML message, I will use a DataSet named **DataSet1** that contains both an **Employees** and an **Offices** table. These two tables have a relationship based on their **OfficeID** attribute with the **Employees** table being the parent and the **Offices** table being the child. To extract these tables out of **DataSet1** and into an XML file, you would use the

DataSet's **WriteXml** method. The **WriteXml** method needs a **Stream** object from the **System.IO** namespace to perform the actual writing of data to the file system:

```
'Create a FileStream object to write to your file system
Dim XMLOut As IO.FileStream = New IO.FileStream("c:\XMLOUT.xml", _
      IO.FileMode.OpenOrCreate, IO.FileAccess.Write)
'Use the WriteXml method and connect it to your FileStream object
DataSet1.WriteXml(XMLOut)
```

I first declare a new instance of the **FileStream** object and set up its parameters to write to my XMLOUT.xml file. Then I simply execute the DataSet's **WriteXml** method, providing it with my established **FileStream** object as a means of writing the data. After executing these lines of code, a file named XMLADO.xml is found on my the hard drive. If I double-click on this file, it opens in my XML file viewer of choice, which is Internet Explorer unless there is a third-party utility installed. I then see an XML representation of the contents of **DataSet1**. Here is an example of an XML message that lists two employees and two offices:

```
<Company>
  <Employees>
    <EmpID>11</EmpID>
    <EmpName>James Moffet</EmpName>
    <OfficeID>1</OfficeID>
    <HireDate>09/10/01</HireDate>
  </Employees>
  <Employees>
    <EmpID>22</EmpID>
    <EmpName>Paul Foster</EmpName>
    <OfficeID>2</OfficeID>
    <HireDate>03/22/98</HireDate>
  </Employees>
  <Offices>
    <OfficeID>1</OfficeID>
    <OfficeName>Finance</OfficeName>
    <OfficeSym>ZZZ</OfficeSym>
  </Offices>
  <Offices>
    <OfficeID>2</OfficeID>
    <OfficeName>HR</OfficeName>
    <OfficeSym>WWW</OfficeSym>
  </Offices>
</Company>
```

DataSets communicate their contents using XML, so if you could view the stream of communication moving from a DataSet on one server to a DataSet on another server, it would look exactly like the XML message I just generated. Moving data via XML overcomes a major problem with older versions of ADO. In the past, ADO used COM to transfer Recordsets, which worked great inside a company's network, but usually failed if users tried to pass their COM-based Recordset through a firewall. Although most firewalls will block COM calls, they do not block XML messaging. You can use this ability of DataSets and XML to your advantage if you need to transfer data to a server that lies behind a firewall.

Filling a DataSet from an XML Message

The ADO.NET DataSet is a powerful way to contain and manipulate data. You learned how to create a DataSet within your code and how to fill a DataSet using a database connection. In this section, you will learn how to fill a DataSet using an XML message. XML is a great way to exchange messages between applications because XML can describe complex data structures such as table relationships. You can also persist data by writing it to an XML file and then reading that file back into a DataSet when you again need its contents. Using XML files to persist data is commonly used on Web servers.

The following piece of code creates a DataSet and then fills it using an XML message located on the local machine's file system. In order to access a file on your hard drive, you need to use the **FileStream** object found under the **System.IO** namespace. If you have completed the "Using DataSets to Generate XML Messages" Immediate Solution, you can easily use the XML message created by that solution to fill a new DataSet.

```
'Create a brand new DataSet
Dim NewDataSet As New DataSet()
'Create a new instance of the FileStream to read in your XML message
Dim XMLIn As IO.FileStream = New IO.FileStream("c:\XMLOUT.xml", _
      IO.FileMode.Open, IO.FileAccess.Read)
'Use the ReadXml method and connect it to your FileStream object
NewDataSet.ReadXml(XMLIn)
```

One terrific way to examine a DataSet's contents when you are first learning about ADO.NET is to use the DataGrid control. I like to perform my experiments using a Windows Application project because I can drop a DataGrid control onto **Form1**, and then point it to my newly created DataSet like this:

```
DataGrid1.DataSource = DataSet1
```

Not only is the DataGrid a great control you can use to allow your application's users to view and manipulate data, but it is also a great tool for the developer to perform spot checks on a DataSet's contents. The DataGrid can also display DataSets that contain multiple tables by offering you a clickable list of available tables to view.

Using the DataReader to Access Data

If you need a block of data, but you have no need to edit and return that data back to its source, you should avoid using a DataSet and instead opt to use the DataReader to pull your data. The DataReader uses a quick server-side cursor to connect to your database and pull out the data you need. This server-side cursor only moves forward through the database, and the DataReader's connection will not allow you to write data to the database, only extract it. This makes the DataReader ideal for filling in controls on your interfaces with data from a table. You can also use the DataReader if you need to do a quick value lookup in your code.

The following code example creates a **DataReader** object and connects it to an Access database containing a table named **Jobs**. After the DataReader's connection is established, I use the DataReader to fill in a ComboBox with the job titles returned from the database:

```
Dim strConn As String = "Provider=Microsoft.Jet.OLEDB.4.0;Data Source=_
     C:\Databases\Company.mdb"
Dim strSql As String = "SELECT JobTitle FROM Jobs"
Dim MyReader As OleDb.OleDbDataReader
'setup the connection with the connection string
Dim MyConn As New OleDb.OleDbConnection(strConn)
'setup the command with the SQL query and my connection
Dim MyCommand As New OleDb.OleDbCommand(strSql, MyConn)

'open the connection object
MyConn.Open()

'tell the DataReader to execute the command object
MyReader = MyCommand.ExecuteReader

'as each item is read, add it to the combobox
While (MyReader.Read)
    ComboBox1.Items.Add(MyReader("JobTitle"))
End While
```

```
'close the connection
MyConn.Close()
```

This code example starts by creating instances of **DataReader**, **Connection**, and **Command** objects. The **Connection** object is first told how to connect to the database, and then the **Command** object is told what query it will be running (**strSql**) and the name of the **Connection** object it will be using. The DataReader is then pointed to the **Command** object, and the query is executed. The *While* loop steps through the **Jobs** table one record at a time, and the DataReader pulls back that record's **JobTitle** attribute and adds it to the ComboBox control. Because you are not using a DataAdapter to connect to the database, you need to explicitly open and close your connection at the proper times.

TIP: *Be sure to close your connection when you are finished using your DataReader.*

Issuing Direct Database Commands

If you need to execute a SQL command against a database that will not extract some data into a DataSet, you can forego the unnecessary **DataSet** object and simply use the **Command** object. You can use this method when executing SQL **INSERT**, **DELETE**, and **UPDATE** commands directly against the database. Executing these SQL commands through a **Command** object is far more efficient than using a DataAdapter to pull all of the data across the network into your DataSet, modify those records, and then send the updated items back across the network. With the **Command** object, only the SQL command is sent across the network, and all processing of that command occurs on the database server. The following code uses the SQL **DELETE** statement to delete all records from the **Customers** table where the company's name is equal to WidgetSpot:

```
Dim MyConn As SqlClient.SqlConnection = New SqlClient.SqlConnection("Data _
      Source=localhost;Integrated Security=SSPI;Initial Catalog=NorthWind")
Dim MyCmd As SqlClient.SqlCommand = New SqlClient.SqlCommand("DELETE FROM _
      Customers WHERE (CompanyName = N'WidgetSpot')", MyConn)
MyConn.Open()
MyCmd.ExecuteNonQuery()
MyConn.Close()
```

Using this code example, you could easily replace the **DELETE** statement inside the **SqlCommand** declaration line with either an **INSERT** or **DELETE** statement. When executing SQL statements directly against the database, the results you are hoping for are that no exceptions will be raised. There will not be any feedback from a **Command** object's **ExecuteNonQuery** if the operation was successful. Of course, how often does that happen? Just to be safe, it is better to surround your execute direct functions with plenty of exception-handling code to trap all of those unexpected conditions that could crash your code.

Using Stored Procedures in ADO.NET

You can execute a database's stored procedure using the ADO.NET **Command** object. Some stored procedures will execute on their own without any input from the caller. Other procedures require that some data be provided to it in the form of **Command** object parameters.

In this first example, I am using the SQL providers to access the Northwind database on a SQL Server 2000 machine. This piece of code triggers the Ten Most Expensive Products stored procedures, which requires no parameters to execute. The output of this stored procedure is read in to my code using a **DataReader** object. Notice that I must establish a connection to the database and manually open and close that connection in order to use my **Command** object. After pulling the stored procedure's results back into my code, I step through the DataReader and add the top 10 most expensive products to a ListBox control on my Windows Form.

```
Dim MyConn As SqlClient.SqlConnection = New SqlClient.SqlConnection("Data _
      Source=localhost;Integrated Security=SSPI;Initial Catalog=NorthWind")
Dim MyCmd As SqlClient.SqlCommand = New SqlClient.SqlCommand("Ten Most _
      Expensive Products", MyConn)
MyCmd.CommandType = CommandType.StoredProcedure

'Open the connection before executing the stored procedure
MyConn.Open()

'Use a DataReader object to accept the stored procedures output
Dim Results As SqlClient.SqlDataReader = MyCmd.ExecuteReader()

'Write the contents of the Results object to the ListBox
Do While Results.Read()
    ListBox1.Items.Add(Results.GetString(0))
Loop

'Close the Results and connection objects
Results.Close()
MyConn.Close()
```

If you are working with a stored procedure that requires parameters in order to do its job, you need to configure these parameters and assign them values within the **Command** object prior to opening your connection and executing your command. The following code executes the "Northwind's Sales by Year" stored procedure. This procedure requires two input parameters, one for the starting date and one for the ending date. It returns a table of data, listing the sales that occurred during the requested time frame including the sales dates and purchase totals. In this piece of code, I set up these two parameters prior to executing my stored procedure, and then I add the sales totals to my ListBox control:

```
Dim MyConn As SqlClient.SqlConnection = New SqlClient.SqlConnection("Data _
     Source=localhost;Integrated Security=SSPI;Initial Catalog=NorthWind")

Dim MyCmd As SqlClient.SqlCommand = New SqlClient.SqlCommand("Sales by _
     Year", MyConn)
MyCmd.CommandType = CommandType.StoredProcedure

Dim StartDate As SqlClient.SqlParameter = MyCmd.Parameters.Add_
     ("@Beginning_Date", SqlDbType.DateTime)
StartDate.Value = "01/01/1996"
Dim EndDate As SqlClient.SqlParameter = _
     MyCmd.Parameters.Add("@Ending_Date", SqlDbType.DateTime)
EndDate.Value = "12/31/1996"

MyConn.Open()

Dim Results As SqlClient.SqlDataReader = MyCmd.ExecuteReader()

Dim TotalSale As String
Do While Results.Read()
    TotalSale = Results.Item(2)
    ListBox1.Items.Add(TotalSale)
Loop

Results.Close()
MyConn.Close()
```

If you look at the highlighted portion of code, you will see that I have to configure these parameters within the **Command** object. To configure these correctly so that the stored procedure does not reject your parameters, you must know the exact parameter names and required data types. If you use a wrong parameter name or mismatched data type, the stored procedure will fail when you try to execute it. One way to discover these parameters is to use the Server Explorer window. Locate the stored procedure under its associated database, right-click on it, and select Edit Stored Procedure. This shows the raw text behind the procedure, including the expected parameters and their data types that you can mirror in your code.

Working with ADO.NET Events

ADO.NET events allow your code to react to changes that occur during your data manipulation actions. Events, by nature, are meant to inform or notify you that something significant has happened. Even if you choose to ignore an object's events, that object will still fire off these events. Your event code will decide what happens when these events are triggered, and it is up to you to decide if it is important to react to a certain event or not. To show you how you can work with ADO.NET, I will examine the two **Connection** object events. The **Connection** object provides two handy events called **StateChange** and **InfoMessage**. The **StateChange** event fires whenever the **Connection**'s **State** property changes, such as from **Open** to **Close**. The following example uses some event code to check and see which state the **Connection** has changed to:

```
Private Sub OleDbConnection1_StateChange(ByVal sender As Object, _
      ByVal e As System.Data.StateChangeEventArgs) Handles _
      OleDbConnection1.StateChange
    If e.CurrentState = ConnectionState.Closed Then
        'The connection just closed, add some code here to react to that
    ElseIf e.OriginalState = ConnectionState.Open Then
        'The connection was previously Open, but is not currently closed
    End If
End Sub
```

The **Connection**'s **State** property can be **Open**, **Closed**, **Broken**, **Executing**, **Connecting**, or **Fetching**. Knowing when a particular state has been entered (using the **CurrentState** property of the **StateChangeEventArgs** parameter) or the state's last value before the current change (**OriginalState**) can help you detect exactly where a problem has occurred.

The **Connection**'s **InfoMessage** event is used to relay messages from the .NET data provider back to the caller. The arguments that are passed into your **InfoMessage** event-handling code will tell you the name of the object that sent the message (**Source**), the **Message** itself, and an **Errors** collection containing all of the errors reported by the data source. Here is an example of the **InfoMessage** event checking for the existence of errors within the **Errors** collection:

```
Private Sub OleDbConnection1_InfoMessage(ByVal sender As Object, _
      ByVal e As System.Data.OleDb.OleDbInfoMessageEventArgs) Handles _
```

```
        OleDbConnection1.InfoMessage
    If e.Errors.Count > 0 Then
        'Some errors were reported by the data source
    End If
End Sub
```

Examining Errors in ADO.NET

In ADO.NET, errors can exist within the DataSet, and errors can occur during data operations, such as the DataAdapter's **Fill** method. In this section, you learn how to check your DataSets for errors, locate these errors, and then fix them so that you can save your data safely. Take a look at the following code example:

```
Dim BadRows() As DataRow
Dim CheckCol As DataColumn
Dim z As Integer
Dim TotalErrors As Integer
If DataSet1.HasErrors = True Then
    'There is an error somewhere in this dataset
    If DataSet1.Tables("Customers").HasErrors = True Then
        'The error is in the Customers table!
        BadRows = DataSet1.Tables("Customers").GetErrors
        TotalErrors = BadRows.GetUpperBound(0)
        'step through each row that has an error
        For z = 0 To TotalErrors
            'check which column has the problem
            Console.WriteLine(BadRows(z).GetColumnError(CheckCol))
            'fix the problem then clear the error flag
            BadRows(z).ClearErrors()
        Next
    End If
End If
'If no errors found in the DataSet, then Update the data source
DataAdapter1.Update(DataSet1)
```

You can check your DataSet for errors by starting at the highest level, the DataSet itself. If the **HasErrors** property is **True**, you know there is an error somewhere, and the next step is to figure out which table contains that error. If the DataSet does not contain any errors, the code skips over all of this error checking and proceeds directly to the **Update** call. Once you locate the table that contains the error, you can examine an array containing all of the rows with errors within the table. Each row that has an error points you to that error using the **GetColumnError** property. Once you have located and resolved the problem, you should turn off the row's error flag by using the DataRow's **ClearErrors** method. It's a good idea to rerun the **HasErrors** checks before you finally try to execute an **Update** with a DataSet, just to be on the safe side.

When working with DataAdapters, any errors encountered during your code's connection to the database will be reflected in either an **OleDbError** class or a **SqlError** class, depending on which .NET data provider you are using. The DataAdapter will create a collection of these errors whenever a connection problem is encountered. You will be able to examine the error's **Message** (the .NET data provider's interpretation of the problem), **Source**, **NativeError** (the database's version of the problem), and **SQLState** of the database. To trap DataAdapter errors, enclose your adapters in a **Try**, **Catch**, **Finally** structure and **Catch** either **OleDbExceptions** or **SqlExceptions**, depending on which .NET data provider you are using.

Generating SQL Queries Using the Query Designer

Unless you are a SQL guru who enjoys thinking about inner and outer joins, you will certainly appreciate Visual Studio .NET's abilities to make creating SQL statements as easy as point-and-click. Lets face it, if you want to talk to a database, whether to ask for some data or to make some changes to existing data, you have to know how to talk SQL. Fortunately, using the .NET query design tools can generate this complex language for you. To see how easy it is to generate a query, try the following example:

1. Open any project in Visual Studio .NET and look at the Server Explorer window. Expand one of the database entries found within this window. You can use either a data connection you have created or a SQL Server database located under the Servers tree. Expand the Tables tree located under the selected database.
2. Right-click on one of the tables that you want to create a query for, and select Retrieve Data From Table. In the Design area, you will see a grid displaying all of the returned data values from this table.

WARNING! Be very careful not to accidentally change a table value displayed in the DataGrid during a query design session. These changes are communicated directly to the database through the Server Explorer, which is helpful if you need a quick way to edit the actual database, but not very helpful if you did not intend to make any changes.

3. Display the Query toolbar by selecting View|Toolbars|Query.
4. Click the three leftmost buttons on the Query toolbar, which show you the Diagram Pane, Grid Pane, and SQL Pane. The grid listing the contents of this table is the Results Pane, which is the fourth button on this toolbar.

Figure 15.6 shows the Query toolbar. Within the query designer window, the top pane is the Diagram Pane, the next one down the Grid Pane, followed by the SQL Pane, and the Results Pane at the bottom. You can see the query designer's layout in Figure 15.7.

5. The SQL Pane displays the actual SQL language query that you are generating. You can manually enter queries in this pane, but if you enjoy typing SQL statements, you probably do not need this tool in the first place. The Grid Pane displays items that have been selected in the Diagram Pane and allows you to set criteria and parameters for these items. The Grid Pane displays all of the currently selected tables, each in its own separate box. Within each box is a list of that table's attributes with a checkbox next to each attribute.
6. To add a table, right-click inside the Diagram Pane, and select Add Table. You are shown a list of tables available in the current database connection. Select one of the tables, and click Add. You can add multiple tables this way. Click Close when you are finished. You can also add tables to the Diagram Pane by dragging them to this pane from the database's tree, which is shown in the Server Explorer window. To remove a table, right-click its title bar within the Diagram Pane and select Remove.
7. To create a table relationship: If you add two tables to the Diagram Pane that have a declared relationship, you will see a line connecting these tables. Each end of the line points to the attribute from which this relation is made. You can remove a relation by right-clicking on this line and selecting Remove. You can add a new relation to the Diagram Pane by clicking and holding on an attribute in one table, and then dragging your mouse over to an attribute in another table and letting go. This added relation will not affect the actual database, only your query. Relationships shown in the Diagram Pane affect the JOIN syntax of your SQL statement.
8. To edit the queries criteria: For each attribute checked within a table shown in the Diagram Pane, an item will be added to the Grid Pane. You can enter an Alias for this attribute, which renames the column's header value during the query. If you want to sort the returned values by a particular column, you can set its Sort Type setting to either **Ascending** or **Descending**. You can also define which particular items will be returned or affected by setting some Criteria for a particular attribute. For example, for a **UsersAge** attribute, you could set a Criteria value to say ">17" to only affect records where the age is 18 or higher.
9. To validate your SQL statement, right-click within the SQL Pane, and select Validate SQL Syntax. A message box lets you know if the text of your query is in fact a valid statement that can be used or an invalid statement that requires some fixing before it can be run.

Figure 15.6 The Query toolbar.

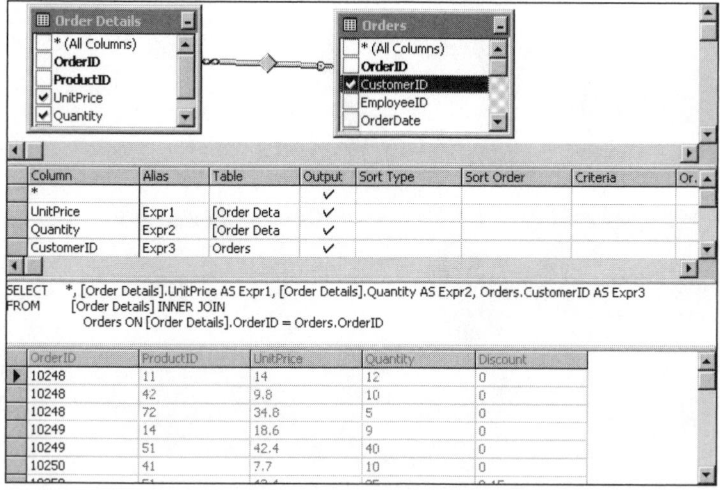

Figure 15.7 The query designer interface.

10. To change the query type, click Change Type on the Query toolbar. A list of SQL statement types that you can create in the query designer appears. Changing a query type changes the syntax used in the SQL Pane.
11. To run your query, right-click within any of the four panes, and select Run. If your query is a valid **SELECT** query, the returned results are displayed in the Results Pane. If you are executing an **UPDATE** or **DELETE** query, you will receive a message box letting you know if the action succeeded or not. Be careful when running queries that change data because you are actually affecting the live database!

Chapter 16

Working with COM and the Win32 API

By Julian Templeman

In Depth

The .NET Framework is very much the "new kid on the block" in the Windows world, and .NET applications are going to have to be able to interact with existing Windows technologies for some time to come. This is especially true in two areas: the Component Object Model (COM) and the Windows Application Programming Interface (API).

COM was Microsoft's original technology for building language-independent software components. It is heavily used at system level and is often seen in applications because it forms the basis of the many ActiveX controls that are widely used in Visual Basic and C++ projects. As you'll see shortly, .NET provides a way to interoperate seamlessly between .NET and COM objects, which is known as *COM Interop*.

The Windows API is the collection of functions used by Windows programmers to write Windows applications. The .NET Framework provides an OO layer on top of the Windows API, but there are times when you may need to use an API call that isn't accessible through .NET. In those cases, you can use the .NET *Platform Invoke (P/Invoke or PInvoke)* mechanism to call C or C++ functions from .NET. Because the Windows API functions live in DLLs, P/Invoke provides a general mechanism for calling C or C++ functions in DLLs from within .NET code.

Although there is a brief explanation of COM in the sections that follow, this chapter does assume some knowledge of what COM is and how it works as well as a passing knowledge of the Win32 API.

Working with COM

This section describes how COM and .NET objects can interoperate. It covers two scenarios:

- How .NET code can use COM objects
- How .NET objects can be used as COM objects

In the early days of .NET, the first scenario is going to be by far the most common, because there are a lot of "legacy" COM objects in existence—especially ActiveX controls—that will have to be used by .NET code.

The second scenario will be less common, but may occur from time to time. For example, you may want to write a new .NET class that has to be used as part of an existing COM-based application.

Does .NET render COM obsolete? I think that the answer has to be in many cases, no. There are some types of COM objects, such as ActiveX controls, that will be superceded by their .NET equivalents, but there are many cases where low-level COM programming in C++ is the most efficient delivery mechanism, and where only COM gives access to specialized low-level functionality. Indeed, in Visual Studio .NET the Active Template Library (ATL), the C++ library for writing COM objects, has been upgraded to support writing efficient server-side components.

What Is COM?

If you already know what COM is, you can proceed directly to the next section, where you'll see how to use COM objects in .NET code.

COM is a specification for writing software components that is designed to be language and platform independent. The specification is a set of rules that developers must follow if their objects are to work as COM objects. If your code follows the rules, it is a COM object and will be able to work with other COM objects.

The basis of COM is the *interface*, which is simply a collection of addresses of some functions inside an object; if a client can get hold of this collection of pointers, it can use the addresses to call the functions. Interfaces simply take the form of an array of pointers in memory, and mechanisms exist to help client code find the interfaces exposed by an object.

Interfaces have two identifiers: a name that begins with *I* by convention, such as IDispatch and IErrorInfo, and a numeric ID called an *interface ID*. Interface IDs are one particular use of Globally Unique Identifiers (GUIDs), which are unique 128-bit identifiers used to identify items in COM, and they are never duplicated. They are used to identify COM object types (or "co-classes"), interfaces, and anything else that needs to be uniquely identified. You'll often see references to these GUIDs. They are most often written as a string of hex digits, like this:


```
{EEC6FCC4-1973-495A-9BB6-910F0A49175C}
```

All the information about COM objects and their interfaces is stored in the Windows Registry using these GUIDs to identify them. If you are interested and know how to use the Registry, you can see all the COM object information by using RegEdit or RegEdt32 to browse the HKEY_CLASSES_ROOT Registry hive.

One of the problems with COM is that the information about objects—where they live and what they can do—is held external to the object in the Registry. If the link is broken somehow—maybe by the Registry entries becoming corrupted or by the object being moved somewhere else without updating its registration—the COM object can become orphaned and clients will not be able to use it. .NET uses metadata stored with the objects themselves in assemblies, so that there is no need for Registry entries, as objects are self-describing.

Because COM was introduced after all the common Windows programming languages had been developed, the COM specification had to define a set of types that could be used to communicate between languages, together with rules and mechanisms to ensure that cross-language function calls worked correctly. This meant that COM programming could be tricky, especially from C++ where you had to do literally everything yourself.

COM programming wasn't quite so hard in Visual Basic, because the designers of VB went to great lengths to hide the complexities of COM from the VB programmer. The drawback with this approach was that it was difficult—and sometimes impossible—to do some COM programming in VB, because the VB runtime hid some of the COM functionality programmers needed to use.

Type Libraries and IDL

One of the foundational principles of COM is that clients should be able to find out what a COM object can do. In other words, clients can find out what interfaces a COM object supports and what functions make up the interfaces. This means that a COM object has to have an equivalent of .NET metadata: a way of describing what a COM object can do in terms of what interfaces it supports. This is done in the COM world using the Interface Definition Language (IDL) and type information.

IDL is a notation for describing COM objects and their interfaces, and COM programmers in the C++ world are used to using IDL. At compile time, a tool called MIDL compiles the IDL into binary information known as a *type library*. The type library may be part of the COM object code attached to the DLL or EXE, or it may be held in a separate file.

.NET lets you find out about COM object capabilities in two ways. First, it allows you to read the type library when you're constructing the code, so that the compiler knows what your COM object can do and can perform compile-time checks, such as checking parameter types. This is known as *early binding* to a COM object, because it happens at compile time. You perform early binding by adding a reference to the COM object to the .NET project.

.NET also allows you to create a COM object dynamically at runtime and find out what it can do. COM has a mechanism that lets you ask COM objects whether they support a particular interface. This mechanism lets you use *late binding* to

COM objects, so called because deciding which object to talk to and how to talk to it happens at runtime. .NET provides a mechanism to access COM objects using late binding.

Dispatch Interfaces and Automation

Before moving on, it is worth mentioning dispatch interfaces. Many Windows programmers will have come across *Automation* (previously called "OLE Automation"), but many developers really don't know what it means.

Early versions of Visual Basic, and some current scripting languages, cannot use type libraries. This means that they cannot find out what COM objects can do before using them, which makes life difficult. In addition, early versions of VB were designed so that the programmer had no idea that COM even existed. COM designers didn't want VB programmers to have to know anything about interfaces at all.

COM designers therefore decreed that any COM object that was to work with VB had to support one particular interface called IDispatch, and all other functions could be invoked through this interface. This was called Automation, and it provided a very late-bound way of using COM objects where you could ask a COM object whether it supported a particular method or not.

Using COM Objects from .NET Code

COM objects can be used very simply from .NET code by using a *runtime-callable wrapper (RCW)*, a proxy class that makes the COM object look exactly like a native .NET object as far as .NET is concerned. The RCW exposes all the methods and properties of the COM object and handles all the work involved in creating the COM object at runtime and using its interfaces.

RCWs can be created in one of two ways. If you are using the Visual Studio .NET IDE, you can simply add a reference to the COM object to the project. This will cause Visual Studio to read the object's type library and create a wrapper based on what it finds. The alternative is to use the command-line utility TlbImp.exe (Type Library Importer), which produces a DLL containing a wrapper assembly. In the Immediate Solutions I'll show you how to use both methods of creating RCWs.

Using ActiveX Controls in .NET Code

ActiveX controls are widely used in VB, Visual C++, and other Windows programming languages. Although the job an ActiveX control does may be simple, the underlying COM structure is more complex for ActiveX controls than for almost any other COM object. There are a number of interfaces that need to be implemented by the control and several others that have to be implemented by the control container.

In order to use an ActiveX control from .NET, it is just as necessary to provide an RCW as for any other COM object. However, because ActiveX controls are so complicated, a predefined class called **System.Windows.Forms.AxHost** is provided to simplify the process of writing the RCW for ActiveX controls. This class also handles the interaction of the control with the development environment, such as displaying the control in the toolbox.

When you want to host an ActiveX control in a .NET project, you need to derive a new class from **AxHost** for each control that you want to host. The derived class will expose all the methods and properties of the underlying COM object and handle all the COM work necessary to create and communicate with the object.

If you are using Visual Studio .NET, you can simply add a reference to the ActiveX control to your project, and this will create the RCW classes automatically. If you are working from the command line, the .NET Framework SDK contains a command-line tool, Aximp.exe, which produces the wrapper classes for an ActiveX control.

Using .NET Objects as COM Objects

As well as using COM objects in .NET projects, it is also possible to use .NET objects as COM objects. This scenario will be much less common, but you might have a situation where you need to add .NET code into an existing COM project.

The same model is used: A wrapper sits between the .NET object and COM, providing all the COM-specific behavior that .NET objects don't support. In this case, you use a *COM-callable wrapper (CCW)*.

You need to follow some rules if you want to use a .NET class from COM. The rules are summarized here, and are discussed in more detail immediately following:

- The class must contain a default constructor—one that takes no arguments.
- The assembly in which the class lives must be signed with a strong name.
- The assembly must live somewhere where it can be easily found by the Common Language Runtime (CLR).

COM doesn't pass over any initialization information when it creates objects, so any class you want to use as a COM object must support a default constructor.

A *strong name* is a way of uniquely identifying assemblies. Normally, an assembly can be identified by its text name, version number, and optional culture information, but there's nothing to stop two developers from creating assemblies with the same name. If you want to avoid the possibility of clashes, you can generate a strong name for an assembly that consists of the text name, version number, and culture information along with a public key and digital signature. Because the last two items are generated using the contents of the assembly, they will be unique, and assemblies with the same strong name are expected to be identical in all respects. COM requires components to be uniquely identified, and a strong name is the way you do this in .NET.

Assemblies that are referenced in .NET code typically live in one of two places: in a subdirectory somewhere under the client executable directory or in the Global Assembly Cache (GAC). Private assemblies—ones that are only going to be used by a single client—can be placed in any directory under the one that contains the client executable, and .NET will search this directory tree at runtime. .NET also provides the GAC to hold shared assemblies, which can be accessed from any client, and tools are provided to place assemblies into the GAC. A .NET assembly that contains a component that will be used from COM must live in one of these two locations, because the CLR will look for it at runtime in order to instantiate the object.

The other requirement that must be satisfied before you can use a .NET object from COM is that the correct Registry entries must be created. COM uses the system Registry to locate COM objects, so appropriate entries must be made for the .NET object, including generating a class ID.

Working with the Win32 API

It may sometimes be necessary to call a function that exists in a DLL outside of .NET. This may be a Win32 API function that doesn't have a .NET equivalent, or it may be a third-party DLL that hasn't been—or maybe can't be—updated to use .NET. Whatever the reason, the .NET Framework provides the P/Invoke mechanism to let you call functions in DLLs from within .NET code.

When P/Invoke calls an unmanaged function in a DLL, it performs the following steps:

1. It locates the DLL containing the function.
2. It loads the DLL into memory.
3. It finds the address of the function to be called and pushes any arguments onto the stack.
4. It calls the function.

In order to call a function in a DLL, you first have to know the name of the function or its ordinal number and the name of the DLL that contains it.

***NOTE:** Although functions are most often called by name, it is possible to assign a unique integer to a function within a DLL and to call the function by an ordinal number rather than by name.*

Win32 API functions are held in three system DLLs; you'll need to find out which of the three hosts the function you want to call. GDI32.dll contains graphics functionality, including drawing, printing, and font management. Kernel32.dll contains lower-level operating system functions for tasks such as memory management and resource handling. User32.dll contains the window-management functionality, including message handling, timers, menus, and communications.

To use a function in a DLL, you need to create a prototype in the code that tells the compiler the name of the function, its arguments, and which DLL hosts it. How this prototype is constructed will be language dependent. The following example shows how to declare the prototype for calling the Win32 **MessageBox** function in VB, C#, and C++:

```
' The VB Prototype
Declare Auto Function MessageBox Lib "user32.dll" (hwnd As Integer, _
        text As String, caption As String, type As Integer) As Integer

// The C# Prototype
[DllImport("user32.dll", CharSet=CharSet.Auto)]
public static extern int MessageBox(int hwnd, String text,
            String caption, uint type);

// The C++ Prototype
[DllImport("user32.dll", CharSet=CharSet::Auto)]
extern "C" int MessageBox(HWND hwnd, String* text,
            String* caption, unsigned int type);
```

The **Declare** statement has been used in VB for some time to declare references to external DLLs, and .NET augments it with some extra keywords. C# and C++ declare the function as external and use the **DllImport** attribute to specify the DLL and any other parameters that may be needed.

Visual Basic programmers can also use attribute notation to declare DLL imports instead of using the **Declare** statement, as shown in the following declaration:

```
' The VB Prototype using attributes
<DllImport ("user32.dll")>
Public Shared Auto Function MessageBox Lib (hwnd As Integer, _
        text As String, caption As String, type As Integer) As Integer
```

You need to use this form in VB if you want to specify some of the more obscure options that are available when declaring prototypes.

Choosing Character Sets

The **Auto**, **CharSet.Auto**, and **CharSet::Auto** keywords are used to specify automatic character-set selection. The Win32 API has two versions for any function that takes character or string arguments: A version with an "A" suffix is used with 8-bit ANSI characters, whereas the version with a "W" suffix uses 16-bit Unicode characters. Using **Auto** ensures that the correct version will be chosen without having to explicitly provide prototypes for the **MessageBoxA** and **MessageBoxW** functions.

Renaming DLL Functions

You may want to call a DLL function by a different name in your code for several reasons:

- You may have a naming convention that you want to follow in your .NET code.
- You may want to create multiple versions of the same DLL function for functions that can take different data types.
- You may want to simplify using ANSI and Unicode versions of Win32 functions.

In VB, you use the **Alias** keyword in the **Declare** statement to define an alias for a function name:

```
' Call the function RealName using MyName as an alias
Declare Auto Function MyName Lib "user32.dll" _
      Alias RealName () As Integer
```

C# and C++ both specify the alias in the **DllImport** attribute, using the **EntryPoint** keyword:

```
// C# example
[DllImport("user32.dll", EntryPoint="RealName")]
public static extern int MyName();
```

Immediate Solutions

Using a COM Object in a .NET Project

This solution shows you how to use a COM object from a .NET program, using .NET's COM Interop facility.

For this solution, I've created a very simple COM object called "Simple" using C++ and the ATL library. This object exposes two methods called **square()** and **cube()**, and it's not hard to guess what these two methods do: Given a number, they return the square and the cube of that number.

If you want to try this solution using the **Simple** COM object, you'll have to copy the project files from the CD and build the project in Visual Studio .NET. Simply open the project and build it; this is all that is necessary to install and register the COM object. If you want to use another COM object instead of **Simple**, you should be able to get the same results without any trouble.

1. Start by creating a console application called VBUseCom. I'm using a console application because the COM object I'm going to use isn't a graphical object.
2. Right-click on the project name in the Solution Explorer, and select Add Reference from the context menu, as shown in Figure 16.1.
3. This will display the Add Reference dialog, as shown in Figure 16.2. Select the COM tab, and scroll down the list of component names until you find the entry for the Simple 1.0 Type Library. Click Select to add it to the list of selected components, and then click OK to close the dialog.

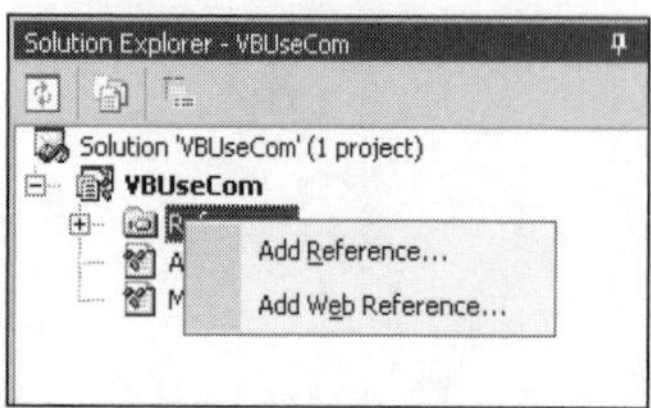

Figure 16.1 Adding a reference to a project.

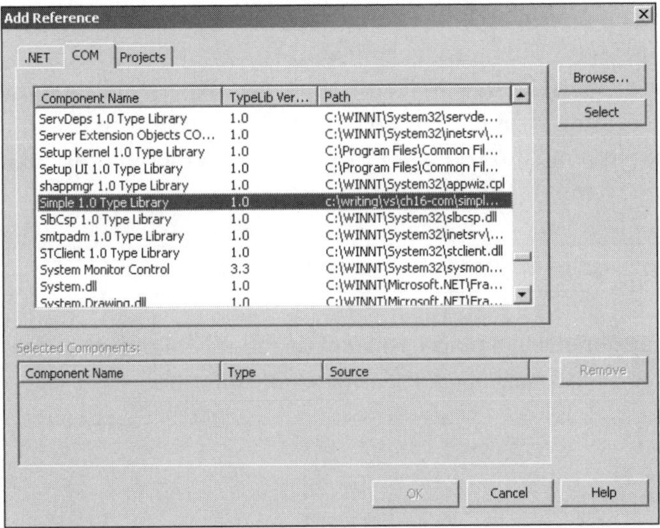

Figure 16.2 The Add Reference dialog.

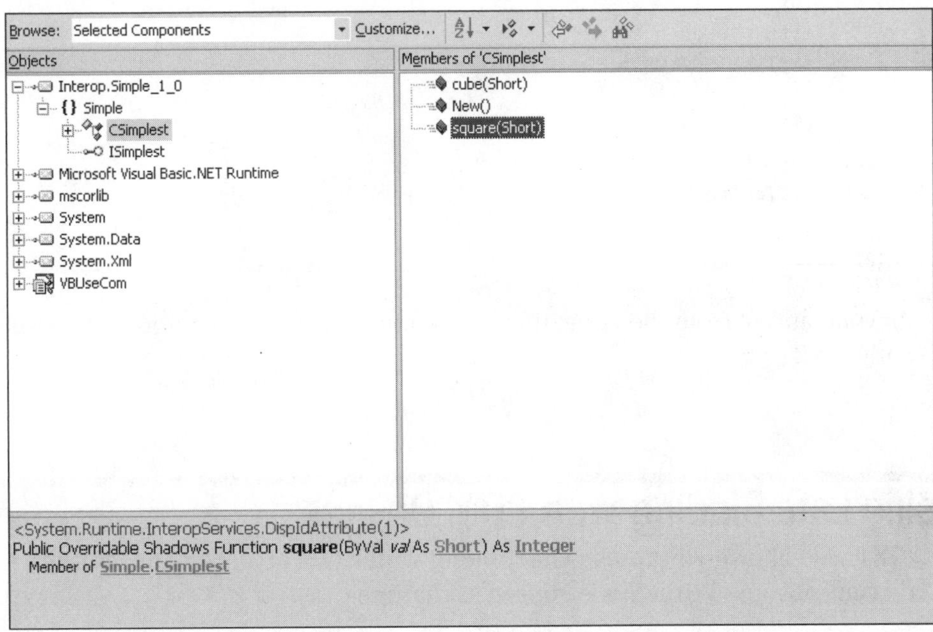

Figure 16.3 The Object Browser displaying one of the methods for the COM wrapper of the **Simple** COM object.

Once the wrapper has been created, you'll find that a new reference called **Simple** has been added to the project. Figure 16.3 shows the new reference in the Object Browser. You can see how the wrapper class exposes the **square()** and **cube()** methods as standard VB .NET methods.

Note how the actual name of the object is **CSimplest** because that's the name of the class in the ATL project. This isn't very useful to client programmers, but because you don't use COM GUIDs in .NET, the tools use the type library and co-class names when generating wrapper classes. If you have access to the original COM IDL files, you can rename the co-class or use a user-defined IDL attribute to change the name given to the wrapper class.

NOTE: *See the documentation on the TblImp.exe utility for details of how to use user-defined IDL attributes.*

Once you have the wrapper class in place, you can use the COM object just as you would if it was a native .NET class, as in the following example:

```
' Import the namespace to make naming easier
Imports Simple

Module Module1

  Sub Main()
    ' Create the object
    Dim obj1 As New CSimplest()

    ' Call a method
    Dim res As Integer = obj1.Square(3)
    Console.WriteLine("Result is {0}", res)
  End Sub
End Module
```

As you can see from the code, there's nothing to tell you that you're not using a native .NET object.

Using Late Binding with COM Objects

.NET also allows you to use late binding with COM objects, using IDispatch to dynamically invoke methods chosen at runtime.

NOTE: *This solution is included for existing COM programmers. If you are not familiar with IDispatch, Automation, and late binding, you probably won't want to complete this solution.*

When you add a reference to a COM object to a .NET project, the IDE reads the type library and uses it to create an RCW class that lets you use the COM object as if it were a .NET object.

If you want to use a COM object that implements IDispatch and you need to invoke methods and use properties dynamically at runtime, the procedure is more complex and makes use of the **System.Type** and **System.Activator** classes.

The following example shows how to dynamically invoke a method on an object. I'm using the same simple COM object as in the previous solution, which was created with a dual interface, so that it can be used early or late bound:

```
Module Module1

  Sub Main()
    ' Get a Type object representing the COM object
    Dim aType As Type = Type.GetTypeFromProgID("Simple.Simplest")
    If aType Is Nothing Then
      Console.WriteLine("GetTypeFromProgID failed")
      Return
    End If

    ' Use an Activator to create an object
    Dim obj As Object = Activator.CreateInstance(aType)

    ' Make up the parameter list
    Dim params() As Object = {2}

    ' Call the method
    Dim o As Object

    Try
      o = aType.InvokeMember("square", _
          Reflection.BindingFlags.InvokeMethod, _
          Nothing, obj, params)
    Catch e As Exception
      Console.WriteLine("Exception from InvokeMember: " + e.ToString())
    End Try

    ' Convert and print the result
    Dim res As Long = Convert.ToInt32(o)

    Console.WriteLine("Result is {0}", res)
  End Sub
End Module
```

COM objects can be identified in two ways: Every COM object type has an associated *class ID* (CLSID)—a 128-bit GUID that uniquely identifies the type, but isn't very readable. The second, optional identifier is the *programmatic ID* (ProgID), which provides a more readable name for the COM object.

In .NET, objects of the **System.Type** class are used to represent the types, and **Type** has many methods that let you find out about a type and manipulate it. In this example, I'm creating a **Type** object to represent the COM object by using the **GetTypeFromProgID()** shared method. This method uses the COM ProgID to create a type, and there is a corresponding **GetTypeFromCLSID()** method that creates a **Type** object from a COM CLSID. In both cases, the method looks up the details of the COM object in the Registry; if this lookup fails, the call returns a **null** reference, so it is good idea to check the return value.

The **System.Activator** class can be used to create local or remote instances of types using its **CreateInstance()** method. Once the object has been created, I can use the **Type** object's **InvokeMember()** method to execute a method. You can see that **InvokeMember()** has a number of parameters:

- The name of the function to be executed or the property to get or set.
- A member of the **BindingFlags** enumeration that determines what is going to be done by this call. In this example, a method is going to be invoked.
- A reference to a **Binder** object, which isn't being used in this example.
- A reference to the object on which the method is going to be invoked.
- An array of **Object** references containing any parameters needed by the call.

The parameters are provided as an array of objects, although in this case, there is just one integer to be passed to the **square()** method.

There are many exceptions that can be thrown by **InvokeMember()**—the documentation lists seven—so it is a good idea to use a **Try** block in case any of them get thrown.

The final stage is to convert and print out the result. **InvokeMember()** is a general function, so it returns an object reference, which you need to convert into the appropriate type. I've used the **System.Convert** class to convert the object to the Int32 I expect from **square()**, and then print it out.

NOTE: *If you've ever done any COM programming and have tried using the* ***Invoke()*** *method on the IDispatch interface, the way it is done in .NET will probably look very familiar!*

Using COM Objects from Managed C++

Programmers using Managed C++ have to take a slightly different route in order to use COM objects in .NET projects.

The .NET Framework SDK contains a tool called TlbImp.exe, which reads a COM type library and creates an RCW for use in Managed C++ code. This solution shows you how to use TlbImp.exe to create a wrapper, and then how to use the wrapper class in a .NET project.

Start by finding the COM object you want to use. You need the type library, which may be part of the object itself or may be in a separate file with a .tlb extension. TlbImp.exe is a console application. The easiest way to run it is to open a Visual Studio .NET command prompt window by selecting Start|Programs|Microsoft Visual Studio .NET 7.0|Visual Studio .NET Tools|Visual Studio .NET Command Prompt. This creates a console with the path set up to include all the Visual Studio and .NET Framework SDK directories, so that you can run tools directly from the command line. Figure 16.4 shows TlbImp being run on Simple.dll, which contains a single COM object. The output is directed to SimpleObject.dll, which results in the creation of an assembly called SimpleObject.

Once you've created the wrapper, you can use it in code. Here's a simple program that uses the COM object in Managed C++ code:

```
#include "stdafx.h"

#using <mscorlib.dll>
#include <tchar.h>
// Import the Simple RCW
#using "SimpleObject.dll"

using namespace System;
using namespace SimpleObject;

// This is the entry point for this application
#ifdef _UNICODE
```

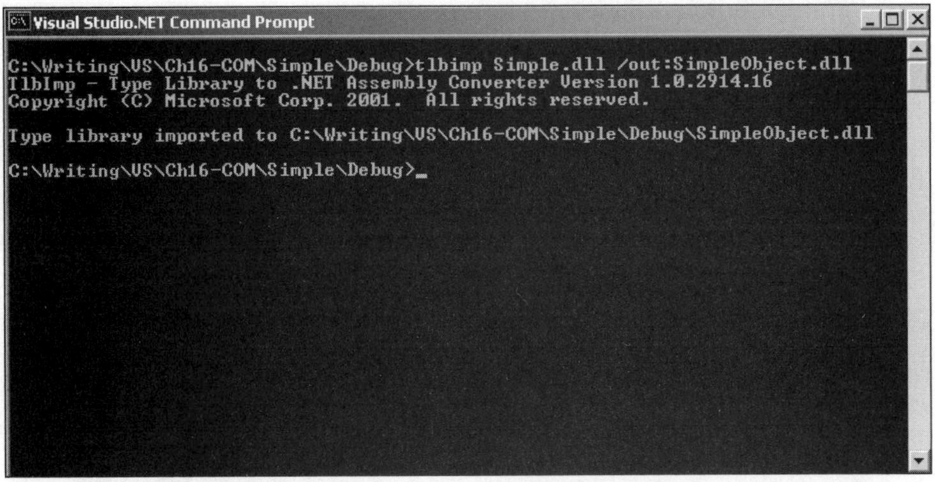

```
Visual Studio.NET Command Prompt

C:\Writing\VS\Ch16-COM\Simple\Debug>tlbimp Simple.dll /out:SimpleObject.dll
TlbImp - Type Library to .NET Assembly Converter Version 1.0.2914.16
Copyright (C) Microsoft Corp. 2001.  All rights reserved.

Type library imported to C:\Writing\VS\Ch16-COM\Simple\Debug\SimpleObject.dll

C:\Writing\VS\Ch16-COM\Simple\Debug>_
```

Figure 16.4 Using TlbImp.exe to create an RCW for a COM object.

16. Working with COM and the Win32 API

```
int wmain(void)
#else
int _tmain(void)
#endif
{
    CSimplest* ps = new CSimplest();
    long l = ps->square(3);

    Console::WriteLine("Square of 3 is {0}", __box(l));
    return 0;
}
```

The lines I've added to a standard Managed C++ application project are highlighted. The **#using** directive loads the DLL at runtime and reads the metadata for the type. So that I don't have to qualify every name with "SimpleObject," I use a using directive to import all the names in the namespace. Note how you can choose the name for the assembly when you run TlbImp.exe.

Once that's been done, I can use the type as if it was a normal .NET object, using **new** to create an object, and then calling methods on it. It is not obvious at all that I'm using a COM object and not a native .NET object.

Using an ActiveX Control in a .NET Project

It is very likely that in the early days of .NET, developers are going to need to use existing ActiveX controls in .NET projects. In this solution, I'll show you how it can be done.

The problem is that .NET knows nothing about ActiveX controls, only about .NET controls, so you need to generate a .NET wrapper class for the ActiveX control:

1. Create a new Visual Basic Windows Forms application. Once the application has been created and the form has appeared on the screen, bring up the toolbox, and right-click anywhere on it. Select Customize Toolbox from the context menu, as shown in Figure 16.5.
2. This displays the Customize Toolbox dialog, which is shown in Figure 16.6.
3. As you can see, the Customize Toolbox dialog lets you add both .NET and COM components to the toolbox; make sure the COM tab is selected for this exercise. I've chosen to add the Calendar control that comes with Microsoft Office—you can select this control or use any other that you choose from the list. Click the checkbox to the left of the control name in order to select it, and then click OK.

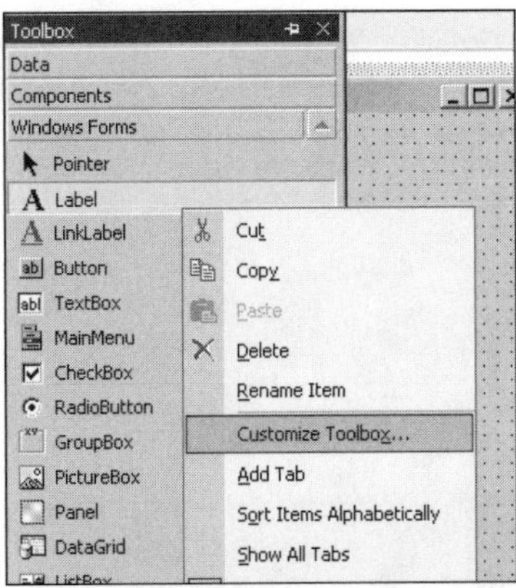

Figure 16.5 The Customize Toolbox context menu item.

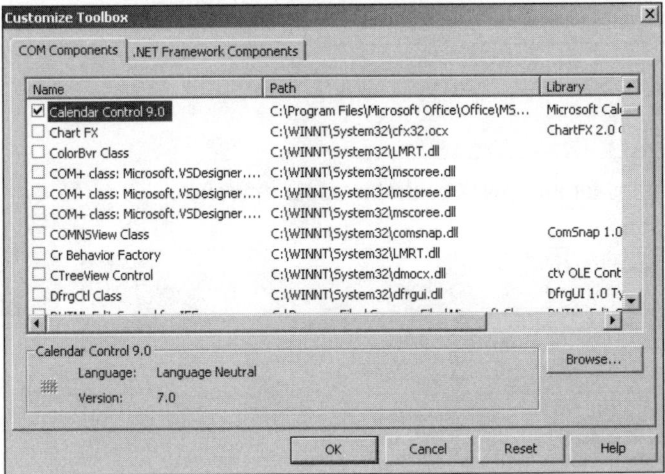

Figure 16.6 The Customize Toolbox dialog for customizing the Visual Studio .NET toolbox.

4. Scroll down to the end of the list of components in the toolbox, and you'll find that a new entry has been added, which represents the ActiveX control, as shown in Figure 16.7.

If you look at the project references in the Solution Explorer, you'll find that several new references have been added to the project. In the case of the Calendar control, I get three new references: **AxMSACAL**, **MSACAL**, and **stdole**. The first two references are to the wrapper class that's been generated to let you talk to the ActiveX control. If you right-click the one whose name starts with "Ax" and choose Properties from the context menu, you'll see the properties for the reference displayed in the property browser. They'll look similar to the properties shown in Figure 16.8. Of special interest is the path, which points to AxInterop.MSACAL_7_0.dll. This is the .NET wrapper that's been created to work with the Calendar control.

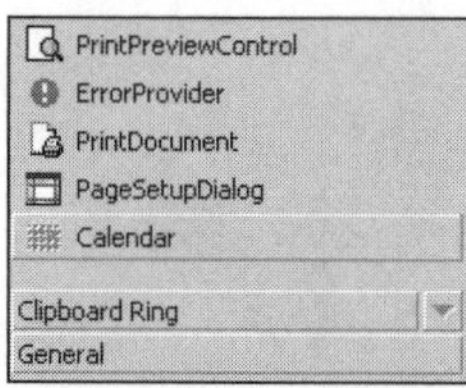

Figure 16.7 An ActiveX control added to the toolbox.

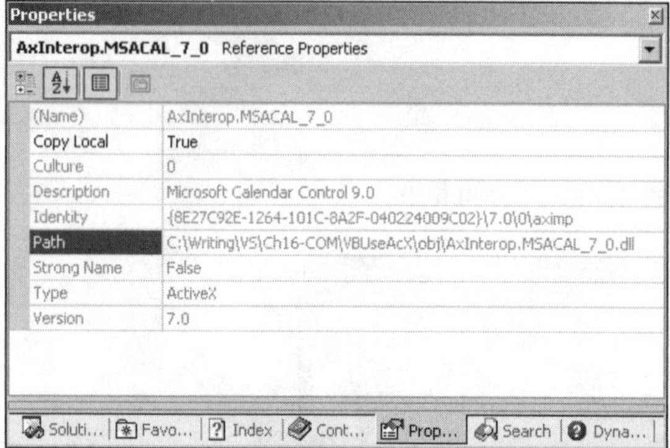

Figure 16.8 The properties for an ActiveX control wrapper reference.

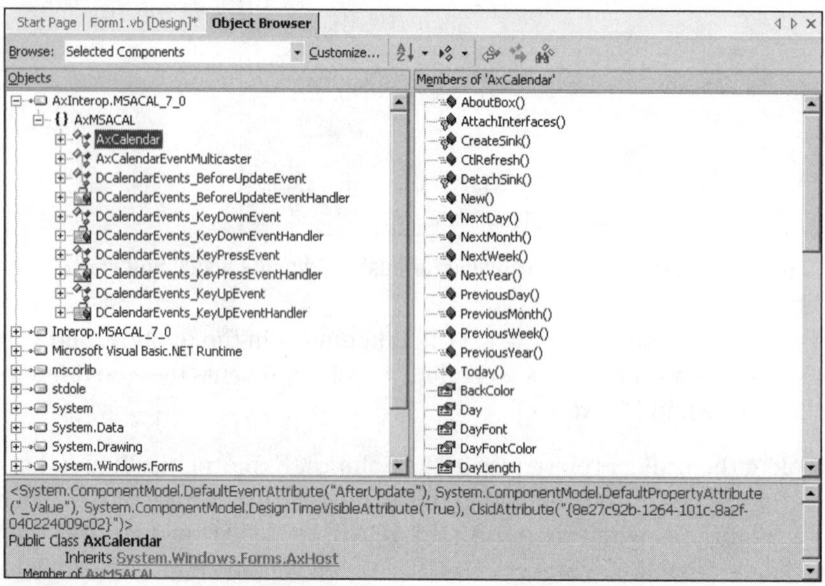

Figure 16.9 The Object Browser showing an ActiveX control wrapper.

If you display the Object Browser—shown in Figure 16.9—by pressing Ctrl+Alt+J or selecting View|Other Windows|Object Browser, you can see just how complex the underlying ActiveX control is. You can also see in the right-hand pane how the wrapper exposes all the methods and properties of the original control. Just like the original Visual Basic Object Browser, you can click on any method or property and its details will be shown in the bottom pane.

You can then select the control and drop it onto a .NET form exactly as you would a native .NET control. It will appear on the form, as shown in Figure 16.10, and you can manipulate its properties and use it in code just as you would any other .NET component.

Figure 16.10 An ActiveX control on a Windows Form.

Calling an Unmanaged Function in a DLL Using Platform Invoke

The following example shows how to call an unmanaged function in a DLL from within .NET code. I'll use the **MessageBox()** function from the Win32 API, as it provides a simple example, and it is easy to check that the call has worked correctly.

A Visual Basic Example

Here's an example using Visual Basic:

1. Start by creating a simple Visual Basic Windows Forms project. On the form, place a textbox and a button, as shown in Figure 16.11.
2. When the button is clicked, a Win32 MessageBox is displayed, which contains the string entered into the textbox. Add an **Imports** statement to the top of the project code:

```
Imports System.Runtime.InteropServices
```

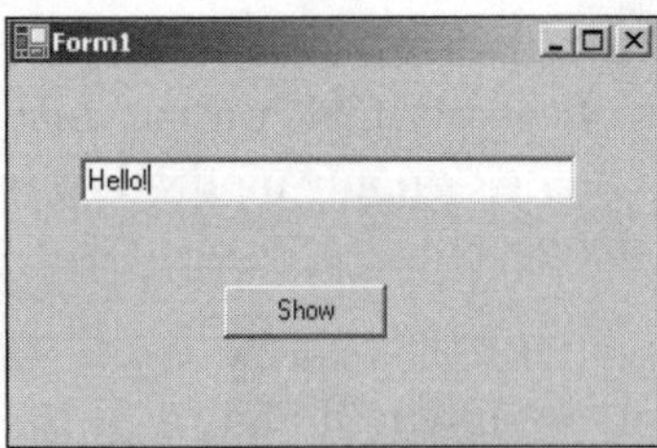

Figure 16.11 A simple form for displaying a Windows MessageBox.

3. This namespace contains the classes that perform the interoperation. Next, add a **Declare** statement to the top of the class to define the prototype for the **MessageBox** function and to specify which DLL it lives in:

```
Public Class Form1
    Inherits System.Windows.Forms.Form

    Declare Auto Function MessageBox Lib "user32.dll" _
          (ByVal hwnd As Integer, ByVal text As String, _
           ByVal caption As String, ByVal type As Integer) _
           As Integer
```

Declare may be familiar to you if you've used previous versions of Visual Basic. You use it to declare the prototype for a function that you want to use in a DLL. It tells the compiler the name of the function, the name of the DLL that has to be loaded, and the arguments and return type of the function.

The **Auto** keyword tells the compiler to automatically choose the correct version of the **MessageBox** function because there are two: **MessageBoxA()**, which uses 8-bit ANSI characters, and **MessageBoxW()**, which uses 16-bit Unicode characters. This is usually the option you want, but if you need to specially call one or the other, you can use the **Ansi** or **Unicode** keywords instead.

4. Add a handler for the button, and use it to call the function in exactly the same way as you would any other .NET function:

```
Private Sub Button1_Click(ByVal sender As System.Object, _
      ByVal e As System.EventArgs) Handles Button1.Click
  ' When the button is clicked, show a message box
  Dim s As String = TextBox1.Text
  MessageBox(0, s, "MessageBox Example", 0)
End Sub
```

The Win32 API function takes four arguments. The first is the handle of the window that is the parent of the MessageBox; by making it zero, I'm specifying that the desktop is the parent. You probably wouldn't do this in real code, but then in real code you'd be using the .NET **MessageBox** class instead of calling the API function.

The second and third arguments are the text to be displayed in the MessageBox and its caption. The fourth parameter determines the type of the MessageBox. It is an integer value that determines the combination of buttons and icons that will be displayed, and a value of zero gives you the simplest possible version with a single OK button and no icon.

A C# Example

The way that you declare a reference to an external DLL function is very different in C# and C++ than how you do it in VB, so I'll provide a C# example to round out the examples:

1. Create a C# Windows application, and place a textbox and a button on the form, as shown in Figure 16.11. Add a reference to **System.Runtime. InteropServices** to the list at the start of the code, as this defines the **DllImport** attribute that you'll be using later:

```
using System.Runtime.InteropServices;
```

2. Next, add the prototype for the **MessageBox** function to the class:

```
// The C# Prototype
[DllImport("user32.dll", CharSet=CharSet.Auto)]
public static extern int MessageBox(int hwnd, String text,
        String caption, uint type);
```

Note the attributes in square brackets. **DllImport** tells the compiler that this is the declaration of a function that's been imported from a DLL, and the first argument tells it the DLL that has to be loaded at runtime. The second argument specifies automatic character-set selection, so that the Unicode version of **MessageBox()** will be called automatically.

Index

B

C

E

F

H

I

J

K

L

M

N

O

P

R

S

T

U

V

W

X

Z

What's on the CD-ROM

The *Visual Studio .NET: The .NET Framework Black Book* companion CD-ROM contains elements specifically selected to enhance the usefulness of this book, including:

- *The .NET SDK*—The SDK features:
    - The complete CLR class library
    - The most current version of the command-line C# compiler
    - Complete debugging libraries and symbol files
    - Documentation for the .NET class libraries
    - Complete example applications ready to compile and run
    - Up-to-date documentation for the .NET system

Note: This program was reproduced by The Coriolis Group under a special arrangement with Microsoft Corporation. For this reason, The Coriolis Group is responsible for the product warranty and for support. If your diskette is defective, please return it to The Coriolis Group, which will arrange for its replacement. PLEASE DO NOT RETURN IT TO MICROSOFT CORPORATION. Any product support will be provided, if at all, by The Coriolis Group. PLEASE DO NOT CONTACT MICROSOFT CORPORATION FOR PRODUCT SUPPORT. End users of this Microsoft program shall not be considered "registered owners" of a Microsoft product and therefore shall not be eligible for upgrades, promotions or other benefits available to "registered owners" of Microsoft products.

Please note that Coriolis is providing the .NET SDK under license from Microsoft Corporation. While we are happy to assist you with defective, damaged or unusable CDs, we are unable to address any technical or product support issues associated with the Microsoft SDK.

- *Source code for the book's projects, arranged by chapter*

Note: The following software (not included on this CD-ROM) is required to complete the projects in this book:

- Visual Studio .NET (Visual Studio 7.0)

System Requirements

Software Requirements

- Your operating system must be Windows ME, Windows NT 4, Windows 2000, or Windows XP.
- You must have Internet Explorer 5.5 or higher to view some of the newer documentation.

Hardware

- An Intel (or equivalent) Pentium 300MHz processor is the minimum platform required; an Intel (or equivalent) Pentium 500MHz processor is recommended.
- 64MB of RAM is the minimum requirement. 128MB is the minimum amount you should consider.
- The .NET CLR requires approximately 200MB of disk storage space.
- A color monitor (256 colors) is recommended.